To:
Kristi
Merry Christmas.
.We love you
Wayne
+
Paula

Dec '88

THE
WINE BOOK

THE WINE BOOK

OZ CLARKE

Portland House
New York

Editor	Sandy Carr
Art Editor	Ruth Prentice
Deputy Editor	Catherine Dell
Deputy Art Editor	Alison Shackleton
Picture Researcher	Sharon Hutton
Editorial Assistant	Mary Pickles
Wine Consultant	Jane Hunt (Master of Wine)
Food and Wine Consultant	Kathryn McWhirter
Indexer	Naomi Good

First published in the UK in 1987 by
Webster's Wine Price Guide, 5 Praed Street,
London W2 1NJ

This 1987 edition published by Portland
House, distributed by Crown Publishers, Inc.,
225 Park Avenue South, New York, New York 10003.
Printed in Italy
ISBN 0-517-64162-3

h g f e d c b a

·CONTENTS·

·3·

THE WORLD OF WINE

· INTRODUCTION ·

This book is about the wines of the world as they are *today*. This book is about the wine world as I expect it to be *tomorrow*. It is *not* about the tarnished long-gone glories of a bygone age, because, much as I love to drink those time-worn classics when I get the chance, there have been too many wine books which seem more concerned with giving the reader a history lesson rather than enthusing him or her with the excitements and adventures of *now*.

Some of those classics *are* relevant today: the startlingly good wines of Bordeaux's best properties, enjoying at present a seemingly endless string of good vintages; the stunning wines of Hermitage in the Rhône valley which in the nineteenth century were France's most sought-after wines and are now at last again making wine great enough for us to see why; the glories of vintage port and fully matured madeiras – wines such as these excite me. And such wines form the models upon which many of the best of the world's new wines have based themselves. But there are other so-called classics which I believe are revered, bowed and scraped to, way over and above their true worth. The taste of the wine always matters more than the fanciness of the label.

Instead, I want to show you what a glittering showcase of wines the world contains today, some of the greatest coming from vineyards which didn't exist when the fame of Hermitage was at its peak, and made in ways which are unrecognizable from the hit and miss methods that were employed as little as 20 years ago.

And the results are there for *all* of us to try. It's no longer necessary to be rich, or well-connected, or well-travelled to catch a glimpse of the glorious flavours wine is capable of. You don't have to be a connoisseur to taste the ebullient fruit of a Napa Valley Cabernet

The wine world is no longer confined to the traditional areas of excellence established over the centuries, principally in France, but also in Spain, Portugal, Italy and Germany. And the wine is more likely to be made in a vast, faceless but highly efficient co-operative rather than a turretted château – although Château Monbazillac (*left*) is in fact the headquarters of a very up-to-date co-operative. However, more and more wines come from what we would call the New World and, in particular, New Zealand, Australia and California (*right*) where high-tech knowhow and heavy investment are producing a new range of classics to challenge the old.

Sauvignon, a Sonoma Chardonnay, an Oregon Pinot Noir, an Australian Hunter Valley Sémillon, a New Zealand Sauvignon Blanc or a barrel-aged Sangioveto from the Tuscan hills where Chianti once held sway. These wines are not only available nationwide, but, as the fame-flattered classics raise their prices blindly through the roof of common sense, they are also offering us great flavours – yes, *classic* flavours – at prices we can well afford.

And it's all happened in the last 20 years. The world of wine has undergone a revolution which has seen as much progress in the last 20 years as in the 20 centuries which went before. From being a haphazard affair fraught with mystique and mistakes, wine-making is now a process which is understood and controlled by brilliant technicians around the world. The result has been a flood of affordable, enjoyable wine on to our markets often from areas previously considered incapable of producing even a half-decent bottle of jug wine, so much so that there has *never* been such a variety of good wine to try, and it has never been cheaper in real terms. The result is that wine is now seen as a drink, as a social experience, as an accompaniment to food, and as far more interesting, far more satisfying, and far better value for money than any other beverage.

This good fortune can also bring problems in its wake. With all these different names cropping up all over the place – many of them totally unfamiliar, since every month sees more previously unheard-of wines start to jostle for our attention – how can we possibly tell which wines we'll like and which we won't? Will I like a Sauvignon better than a Soave, or a Californian Cabernet Sauvignon better than a Chianti? Can I take wine seriously if it's grown in North Africa or New Zealand – or England, for goodness sake? Is there really a difference between Bordeaux and burgundy or is it just wine-buffs' chit-chat? Why does everyone make such a fuss about champagne – isn't any old sparkling wine just as good? Why is one bottle of German wine only $4 a bottle, yet another one more like $4 a sip? Why? How? What?

· A WINE-MAKING REVOLUTION ·

The freeing of wine from the shackles of generations of wine-making tradition – primarily through the dramatic advances in technique worked out by the Californians in the 1960s and 1970s – has brought the production of good wine within the grasp of thousands of winemakers in areas previously thought unfit for anything other than plonk.

Instead of the Spanish 'burgundy' of old, we can now choose between a dozen proper regional styles in Spain, Jumilla, Valdepeñas, Penedés, Rioja . . . which would previously have been blended together casually and forgotten. Instead of some anonymous French 'red', we now have a bewildering array of named country wines – *vins de pays* – as well as *appellation contrôlée* names like Costières du Gard, Côtes de Roussillon, Fitou and so forth, which would previously never have seen the light of day under their own colours. But what do they taste like? Where are they made? What grapes are used? Should they be drunk young or old? That's why this book is here – to sort out the multiplicity of options in order to offer you the best possible chance of choosing a wine you'll like, and that is right for your purpose.

And what about these New World tyros? Should we take them seriously? We most certainly should. As the prices of the classic wines from Bordeaux to Burgundy have moved ever upwards, we have been in danger of losing touch with the thrilling flavours of top-class wine made by masters and matured in expensive small oak barrels. That was until the Californians, the Australians, the New Zealanders, the Up-State New Yorkers and some equally forward looking Spaniards and Italians arrived. They filled the vacuum. They provided the new classics which bring those flavours back once more within our grasp. But who is who? And which regions make which types of wine?

· THE SHAPE OF THE BOOK ·

The book gets immediately to the heart of things. After an outline of the history of wine, we go straight to the most fundamental thing affecting the flavour of wine, the different grape varieties, how and where they are grown. This is followed by a look at the processes of turning these grapes into the numerous different styles of wine which exist. And then we devote a feature to the way the modern winemaker can influence the wine-making procedures, and 'style' the wine according to his or her ideals and the market's needs.

By this time, I hope you'll have a good grasp of what makes the wines taste the way they do, so now we have to find those flavours as easily and accurately as possible on the shelves. The next sections show you how to do just that, and also explain how to care for your wine to ensure drinking it at its best, as well as giving some idea as to the kind of food and wine combinations which seem to work best and why. In particular, we have a feature called 'Finding the Wine You Want'. This works through the main classic wines and lists alternatives in the same style. It means that if you like, say, the crisp sharply fruity taste of a Sauvignon wine like Sancerre or Sauvignon de Touraine, you only need look up this section to find alternatives that will give you a similar taste experience. It works both ways of course, if you don't like a particular style (or grape variety) it will tell you what wines to avoid. After this you're plunged into the nitty gritty of who makes what, where, and how! But don't worry, this isn't going to be an academic discussion of the minutiae of fermentation, temperatures or

subspecies of obscure vines. It's more like a journey through the world of wine I've come to know and love in the last 10 years or so, to visit the places I think the most exciting, tell about the wines I think are most delicious, from the producers I think are most talented. For quick reference, at the beginning of the chapters on the major wine-producing countries there are checklists of the most important wines; and at the end of the book there's a comprehensive 'A–Z of Wines and Wine Terms'. But, above all, I want to enthuse you, to persuade you to be adventurous, to make the best of this golden age of wine in which we now live, when there has never been more good wine more easily available at such affordable prices.

Wine is the produce of millions of men and women in every corner of the world, using a thousand different grape varieties in a hundred different ways, influenced by dozens of age-old cultures as well as the tidal wave of new ideas and philosophies sweeping away prejudice and inefficiency and mediocrity and replacing it with bright, thrilling flavours which make the best use of the best grapes the land can grow. If we decide to find out a little more about these men and women, where they live and work, why they employ the grapes and the techniques that they do, what their wines are called – and, above all, how they taste, then our enjoyment of wine can be immeasurably enhanced. This book sets out to show all these things, and I hope that, whether you just dip into it or devour it cover to cover, it will inspire you to be adventurous, to be both critical and appreciative – in fact, to make the best of the wonderful world of wine which we are lucky enough to inhabit.

The face of experience in two different hemispheres. A cellar worker at Château Mouton-Rothschild in Bordeaux (*left*) gazes lugubriously at his glass to check the colour against a candle. Max Schubert (*right*), the great winemaker at Penfolds in South Australia takes a good sniff to check on the development of his wines.

·1·
ABOUT
WINE

· THE STORY OF WINE ·

Far left **Tomb painting with grape decoration. In Ancient Egypt many vineyards were planted as formal gardens: the vines, trained high, provided grapes – both for eating and wine-making. The Roman mosaic (*left*) shows picking and treading. In Roman Italy, the vintage happened late, when grapes were overripe, as the Romans liked their wine sweet.**

Wine is as old as civilization – probably older – while the vine itself is rooted deeply in pre-history. There was at least one species, *vitis sezannesis*, growing in Tertiary time – just a mere 60 million years ago. I don't expect that *sezannesis* ever turned into wine – not on purpose, anyway, but aeons later its descendant *vitis silvestris* surely did (and still does in Herzegovina, Yugoslavia where it is called the Iosnica) and by the Quaternary era – around 8000BC – the European vine, *vitis vinifera* (from which nearly all the world's wines are now made) had come on the scene.

The metamorphosis of grape into wine was almost certainly a happy accident. Imagine Stone Age people storing their hedgerow harvest of wild grapes, *vitis silvestris*, in a rocky hollow . . . some of the grapes squash, juice oozes out and, in a flush of autumn sunshine, begins to ferment. The result – however unpalatable to today's tutored taste – must have cheered the chill of cave-dwelling and provided a few much-needed laughs at the onset of pre-central heating winter. Similarly, in the houses of ancient Persia, Mesopotamia, Armenia, Babylon . . . the occasional jars of raisined grapes, ready for winter eating, would surely have begun unexpectedly to bubble and froth and magic themselves into a sweet, heady drink. From such haphazard beginnings, wine evolved into an adjunct of civilization: ancient paintings and sculptures show that

both Egypt and China were making and drinking it around 3000BC, but it was really the Greeks who first developed viticulture on a commercial scale and turned vinification into a craft. Their wines tended to be so richly concentrated that they were normally drunk diluted: two parts wine to five of water. And they were syrupy sweet – yet with a sting of salt or a reek of resin, cadged from casks washed out in sea-water or from amphoras lined with pitch-pine. Through their trading travels, the Greeks spread their vine-and-wine knowledge round the Mediterranean and were particularly influential in Italy – to the benefit of the world's wine-drinkers ever since.

· THE ROMANS ·

By the middle of the first century BC, vineyards criss-crossed the Italian landscape from southernmost Sicily to the Alpine foothills and wine was both an everyday beverage and major export. More importantly, as the Empire gained ground, so did the grape: in all their newly-won territories, the Romans established vineyards – climate permitting (and even if it didn't look too promising they persevered, as in the Mosel, where they used straw fires, between the vines, to combat autumn frosts). Today, Europe's traditional wine regions – Bordeaux and Burgundy, Rioja and Rhine, Loire and Languedoc . . . can all claim to have had Roman foundations.

Most of Rome's wine – whether made at

home or in the provinces – was somewhat plebeian tipple: tart and tough, for quaffing young before it turned to vinegar. Often its taste was softened by the addition of honey, herbs or spices – which also acted a preservatives. But not the top-notch wines. These, we must suppose, were noble creations, aged for a decade or more: the legendary Falernian – according to Pliny, so fiery it would catch light from a spark – reached its prime at 20 years yet would happily survive 100. The Romans' ability to age wine – in wooden casks and then in earthenware or glass amphoras (sealed with pitch or plaster) – represented a significant development in wine-making. But it was short-lived, doomed to disappear with the Empire.

Since the art of amphora-making was lost and wine could no longer be matured in 'bottle', quality suffered. But that aside, the Dark Ages were not as murky, in wine terms, as they might have been. In fact, the thrusting barbarians – ever thirsty – not only maintained existing vineyards but also extended them, as in Burgundy where Germanic settlers cleared the forests and replanted with vines. But throughout medieval times, the guardian of Western culture and civilization – Rome's legacy – was the Church; so, for 1,000 years, Europe's wine heritage was largely nurtured by the monasteries. They were expert agriculturalists able to study and develop vine and wine sciences; they were also powerful landowners whose expansionist policies often involved acquiring established vineyards or planting new ones. The monks produced wine for sacramental purposes, for their own use – fairly frugal in most orders – but primarily for sale; along with other farm produce, it was a major source of income. In the absence of storage know-how, the wines themselves were mostly light and fresh – ripe for quick consumption. At that time, burgundy was prized for drinking within the year and Bordeaux considered the better for being younger – the exact opposite of today.

· CORKS AND BOTTLES ·

The role of the Church declined with the Reformation – at least in northern Europe – but this did not convulse the wine world half as much as the discovery of the usefulness of corks a century later. For the first time since the Roman era, wine could now be stored and aged in bottle. Throughout the Middle Ages it had been kept in cask which presented a dual handicap: first, too long in wood could rob a wine of all its fruit; second, once the cask was broached the wine inevitably deteriorated unless drunk within a few days. The bottle, with its much smaller capacity, solved the former problem by providing a neutral, non-porous material which allowed wine to age in a different, subtler way and removed the latter problem by providing sealed containers of a manageable size for a single session's drinking.

However, the cork-and-bottle revolution wasn't an instant success: bottles were then so bulbous they would only stand upright which meant the corks eventually dried out and let in air. But, by the mid-1700s, longer, flat-sided bottles were designed which would lie down, their corks kept moist by contact with the wine. Wine-making now took on a dimension. It became worthwhile for a winemaker to try to excel, wines from distinct plots of land could be compared for their qualities, and the most exciting could be classified and separated from run-of-the-mill plot wines. Today's great names of Bordeaux, Burgundy and the Rhine first began to be noticed.

In the early nineteenth century, Europe seemed one massive vineyard. In Italy eight out of ten people were earning their living from wine and in France there were vast plantings rolling southwards from Paris. And *vitis vinifera* had emigrated – thanks to explorers, colonists and missionaries. It went to Latin America with the Spaniards, to South Africa with French Huguenots and to Australia with the English. . .Could anything halt its triumphal progress?

Yes, phylloxera could, and it did. Phylloxera is an aphid, which feeds on and destroys *vinifera* roots. It came from America in the 1860s and, by the turn of the century, had destroyed all Europe's vineyards and most of the rest of the world's as well. The solution, grafting *vinifera* on to American rootstocks – the phylloxera-resistant *vitis riparia* – was exhausting and expensive. The most immediate effect in Europe was that only the best sites were replanted and the total area under vines shrank dramatically. Elsewhere the havoc was comparable; vineyard acreage is only now expanding to old original sites destroyed almost a century ago.

The present century has brought further change as science and technology revolutionized viticulture and vinification. But despite the chemical formulae and computerized wineries, the grape retains its magic and, in the Psalmist's words, 'maketh glad the heart of man'.

Above **A vintage scene from a medieval French manuscript; the conical-style basket is still used in some vineyards. The Cruikshank engraving (*below*), shows an 18th century wine-tasting at London Docks; the tapers are for judging the wine's clarity.**

· GROWING THE GRAPES ·

Left In northern Italy vines are often trained high to give cooler ripening conditions and a big, healthy crop.

Anyone planting grapes to make wine must ask him or herself two questions. What will the natural conditions (geography, geology, soil, climate) of my vineyard *allow* me to achieve? What do I, as a winemaker, *want* to achieve? Winemakers in the world's classic vineyard areas have developed their wine styles over the centuries by endlessly asking and answering these questions. Today the world of wine is turbulent with change as old vineyards are altered and new ones planted; yet these two questions are as important as ever.

A grape variety is chosen primarily for its ripening qualities: its ability to ripen at all in cooler areas, like Germany, or its ability to resist overripening in hot areas, like the Mediterranean. The interaction of grape variety and climate produces a staggering spectrum of results. The Greeks pick Liatiko grapes in July while the Germans fill in time between Christmas and New Year bringing in their late, late Riesling.

Given that, genetically, the 5,000 or so grape varieties so far identified as remotely connected with wine production are all different and react differently to soil and climate,

let's look at these two basics and how they affect the siting of the vineyards before we go into detail about the grape varieties and the flavours they produce.

· SOIL ·

Many traditional producers consider soil the most important factor in the creation of great wine. Christian Moueix, who makes the world's most expensive red wine at Château Pétrus in Bordeaux, reckons soil contributes 80 per cent of the quality; others dismiss this view, particularly in places such as California, Australia and New Zealand, where the link between soil and personality is not as yet proven by generations of experience. The truth is generally somewhere in between. There is no doubt that in certain remarkable vineyards – like Château Pétrus – the soil is unique and capable of shaping a wine's flavour. However, these 'chemical' and 'mineral' component parts defy analysis: in the Burgundy Grands Crus, for instance, great efforts have been made to explain palpable variations in flavour from vines in different parts of the same vineyard – with no success whatsoever.

On the other hand, the physical attributes of soil are more easily defined and are, in general, more significant. Most important of these is drainage. Well-drained soil – slate or gravel or chalk – pushes the vine roots down and down to find moisture. Furthermore, porous soils are generally poor – another reason for roots thrusting deep, this time in search of nourishment. The result is a stable environment way below the surface, which makes the vine itself less vulnerable to stress from drought and flood. Riesling likes slate, Cabernet likes gravel, Chardonnay likes limestone or chalk – all of them drain well.

A dry soil is also a warmer soil. This is absolutely crucial in cool climate regions where the stones which break up the soil and boost porosity also retain vital heat. Gravel in the Médoc and slate on the Mosel aid drainage and store heat for the chilly autumn evenings. It is very noticeable in Bordeaux that the late-ripening Cabernet Sauvignon – which thrives on the Médoc gravel – cannot ripen on the heavy cold clay of St-Emilion and Pomerol, where the quick-ripening Merlot rules supreme. However, for this reason, clay's coolness is useful in hot areas: Chardonnay,

Far left A vineyard in northern Europe. The vines, sited on a south-facing slope, run north-south to gain maximum sunshine. They are planted densely to trap heat within the rows and trained low to benefit overnight from warmth retained in the ground – but not too low as this increases vulnerability to frost. The hillside setting aids both insulation and drainage, while a slate or stone soil will reflect back heat during the day. On the crown of the hill, a tree belt provides shelter against prevailing winds. In southern Europe (**left**) a vineyard lay-out changes in response to a hotter, drier climate. Vines run across the slope to maximize shade and are often trained high with thick foliage. Rows are more widely planted, thus allowing air to circulate freely and reducing pressure on limited water supplies. A clay soil, with good moisture retention, is ideal.

· ORGANIC WINE ·

Current preoccupation with 'natural' products has encouraged a small, but increasing, number of producers to go organic. The back-to-nature process begins in the vineyard with a ban on artificial fertilizers. Manure is the most common option (or a flock of grazing sheep in winter) but some growers also plant a nitrogen-rich crop, such as clover, between the rows. Of all the fungicides and pesticides in general use, only the traditional Bordeaux mixture, against mildew, is allowed (its copper sulphate ingredient does, after all, occur naturally). Weeds are either pulled up or discouraged under plastic sheeting, but not sprayed with herbicides. Wine-making itself is kept as natural as possible: no artificial yeasts, no additives – except for the lowest concentrations of sulphur dioxide (around 10–20 per cent of legal maximums), and only traditional clarifying agents. So far, there is no standard label for organic wine and you have to scan the small print for indications such as 'vino biologico', 'méthode agrobiologique' and 'farm verified organic'.

which grows well in Burgundy only on limestone, can grow very well on clay in hotter areas. Light-coloured soils, such as chalk and limestone, will reflect back heat – another plus point in cooler regions.

· CLIMATE ·

The second major influence on grape-growing is climate: water and warmth. Since wine, at its most basic, is rain-water sucked up and transformed by the vine (picking up a bit of flavour from the soil on the way), too little water means not enough juice. Either you irrigate to provide this moisture – a common practice in America and the southern hemisphere (but largely forbidden in Europe to alleviate the wine lake crisis) – or you choose a favourable site, somewhere with a reliable rainfall, a porous top soil, and water-retentive subsoil underneath. Since such geological balance is rare and the weather generally unreliable, this perfect combination is seldom achieved. Too much water, however, is far worse than too little, because all you can do then is watch as your grapes swell and swell with excessive liquid. Just before vintage time, especially, rainstorms, which dilute the character of the juice by swelling the grapes, can have a serious effect on wine quality – and a dramatic effect on quantity.

Obviously heat is essential to ripen grapes. But different varieties need different amounts, and though lack of sun is the chief problem in the traditional 'classic' regions of Europe, in most new areas, such as the United States , Australia and South Africa, a surfeit of sun makes the grapes ripen too fast, before they have picked up enough character and flavour from the soil, and before a good balance of grape sugar and acidity has been achieved.

· SITING THE VINEYARD ·

In cool areas, you want to maximize warmth. Consequently rows are ideally planted on a north-south axis to catch the midday sun. The best slopes may incline south-eastwards, as in Burgundy, for the morning sun to warm the vineyard; or south-westwards as in Germany's Rheingau, where morning mists shroud the vines and so late afternoon sun becomes all important. To conserve heat the vines are planted close together and trained low; they are also aligned *across* the prevailing wind, so that precious warmth doesn't get blown out of

the rows. Hot climates demand the opposite. Vineyards frequently face away from the sun, are trained high with lots of foliage to shade the grapes; they are also spaced further apart so that heat can disperse and what little water there is will not be divided among too many plants. (Interestingly, inspired winemakers like Torres in Spain are beginning to reverse the low-density rule, saying that best results come from vines which *do* have to struggle, and that excessive evaporation from wide-spacing is just as damaging as over-heating.) The norm in 'new' areas is about 1,000 vines to the hectare; in Burgundy it is 10,000 to the hectare! Somewhere between 3,000 and 5,000 is probably about right in most places.

· A YEAR IN THE VINEYARD ·

Whether or not your vineyard – planted with the right grapes in the right place – actually produces great wine depends on your year-long efforts and your luck with the endless vagaries of the weather. So let's look at a typical vineyard year in a temperate European area like Bordeaux. The year starts straight after the grape harvest, in November: that's what growers call the beginning of winter.

· *WINTER* ·

After the exhilaration and hyperactivity of the vintage, there's a hiatus. Wine-making becomes the priority. The vines relax, exhausted, as the temperature drops. At below 52°F (11°C), the vine gradually becomes dormant and will be quite safe in this state down to a minimum of -18°F (-28°C).

Now is the time for lopping off the long branches (they make ideal fuel for grilling meat and fish next spring); for manuring; for ploughing – especially in cold areas where earth is heaped up around the vine base as protection against frost; and, on steep slopes, for redistributing soil washed down by heavy rains. In some vineyards, December sees the start of pruning. If you prune severely, you'll get far less fruit, but far higher quality. So do you go for quantity or quality? It's a major decision. Old or weak vines may require more lenient treatment, but the experienced pruner – with next year's vintage in mind – will assess each vine's capacity and cut accordingly.

January comes. The bone-chilling job of pruning back the vines continues. Indoors, fires burn bright, bottles are drunk and, as February shuffles in, thoughts of springtime and the world alive again begin to get the better of the fierce damp winds.

The last job of winter is to take cuttings for grafting on to rootstocks. In Europe especially, grafting is the only effective way of propagating *vitis vinifera* – the vine species used for all serious wine-making. You have to do this because of a vine aphid the *phylloxera vastatrix* (wonderful name) which came from America in the 1860s and proceeded to eat its way through all of Europe's vineyards, and most of the rest of the world's as well. The sole remedy was – and still is – to graft European *vinifera* cuttings on to rootstocks of American varieties which, since phylloxera has transatlantic origins, can tolerate the nasty little beast. Without this grafting system, there would be no fine wine made in Europe today!

· *SPRING* ·

March is when the vine wakes up: sap rises and the pruned shoots drip with 'tears'. Pruning can be finished without coat and scarf, and the soil can at last be worked again to give it a good airing and to uncover the base of the vines. Frosts in March aren't too much of a threat but in April – when buds burst and shoots begin to emerge – they're far more menacing. Even so, there will be late-bursting buds to fall back on if frosts do harm the new growth. You'll also have to start spraying against insects and disease, because the vine isn't the only thing to wake up with the spring: its predators are on the move again – spiders, bugs and beetles are out looking for food.

May brings hopes and fears in equal proportion. The shoots lengthen by the hour,

Right Winter sees the start of pruning, here being done in Yakima Valley, Washington, USA. Pruning controls the quantity of fruit produced and so, ultimately, wine quality. Methods vary from region to region and according to grape variety. In spring, as soon as shoots appear, spraying begins – shown here (*far right*) at Epernay in Champagne.

leaves and tendrils sprout and the first signs of the flower buds appear. Yet you must temper optimism with prudence. You must begin to spray against the two fungi, downy and powdery mildew (peronospera and oidium). From now on you'll be spraying against one threat or another right through to autumn. The weeds will be enjoying the spring sunshine and you'll have to deal with those, too. And you'll be on the phone to the local weather office. Is there a risk of frost? The vine shoots can be killed outright by a late May frost and the harvest will be devastated. In areas like Chablis in Burgundy, the Rhine in Germany, and the Napa Valley in California, they use stoves, flame guns, torches and great propellers to stop the frozen air sliding into the hollows and murdering the young vines. In some places they continually spray the vines with water, which freezes into ice and so keeps the temperature at zero. Uncomfortable for us, but just about OK for a young vine.

· SUMMER ·

Then it's summer. You want sun right through June because this is when the vine flowers. If it pours during this crucial 10–14 day period, the flowers will not be fertilized: the bunches of grapes – and consequently the vintage – will be drastically reduced. Once flowering is over you thin the shoots, keeping only the best, and tie them to wires to shape their growth. Throughout the long 100-day haul from flowering to within striking distance of the harvest, spraying continues.

In July, you till the land again, and also trim back excessive growth and vegetation so that you don't get too many grapes which will dilute quality – unless you don't care, in which case you go on holiday.

Some *vignerons* never seem to go on holiday at all, but August is the most usual month to take time off. However, someone should be there, spraying and thinning the bunches. The grapes are changing colour, softening and gaining sugar. Yet hail can sweep up and ravage your vines without warning, while wet, warm weather can cause the onset of rot.

· AUTUMN ·

Vintage looms! It may be September, it may be October. Indoors everyone is feverishly preparing equipment. Outdoors the temptation is to sit in the sun, chew the grapes and dream of great things. But you must keep at it. Greatness *is* within your grasp: make a last spray against rot, check daily for insect invasion, and keep the birds off – by nets, by scarecrows, by shotguns – but keep them off! It's your livelihood they're eating.

Then at last – the great day. Vintage starts. Out go the tractors, the troops of pickers, or maybe the giant harvesting machine, to pluck the results of another year's labour. Hand-pickers cut the bunches off, then place them in boxes or baskets for collection. Depending on the height of the vines, the work is either back-breaking or knee-creasing and, depending on the time of day, cripplingly cold in the morning mist but happily hot in the afternoon sun. Mechanical harvesters, straddling the rows, knock the grapes off with fibreglass rods; stalks remain on the vine while a blower separates out stray leaves and twigs from the fruit.

Whatever the method, as the grapes pile up you are looking at your due reward or just deserts – nature's bounty or nature's revenge.

Far left **Throughout the world's vineyards, birds can create havoc – especially in summer when the grapes, almost ripe, are lusciously tempting. Protective measures range from nets, like these in Germany, to sprays and scarers. The climax of the growing year is the vintage which, in Europe, can be early September or late November, according to climate and grape variety. In Rioja, Spain (*left*), the grape harvest traditionally begins on 10 October and is still done by hand.**

· GRAPE VARIETIES ·

My glass is filled with a dark purple fluid whose savage scent of smoke and plums and spices rages in my nostrils. It is wine. My glass is filled with pale, sharp liquid, thin as misery and puckering to my tongue. That's also wine. And my glass is filled with something honeyed, gently golden, succulent and soothing. . .or perhaps pale brick-red, seeming slight yet redolent of mint and blackcurrant and eucalyptus trees in bloom. These, too, are wine. All made only from grapes, but different varieties of grapes, each imprinting the wine with its own character. Yet, if we pulled them off the vine and chewed them, they would taste much like any other black or white grape – though not as good. For these grapes come from a single species among many – the *vitis vinifera*, whose character is only properly expressed through the conversion of its juice, by yeast action on its sugars, into wine.

· VITIS VINIFERA ·

The *vitis vinifera* makes *all* the decent wine in the world (though Canada and the US East Coast have developed a certain liking for their native *vitis labrusca* wines – so far not shared by anyone else). Basically it is a European species, with some influence from ancient oriental vine types. The berries are generally smaller than those of non-*vinifera* types and certainly wouldn't fetch much of a price at the greengrocers for eating. Also it has developed into a hermaphrodite, bearing fruit every year, unlike its 'wild' forebears whose female vines alone bore fruit. This hermaphroditic style of propagation has another effect – mutation. At least 5,000 varieties of *vitis vinifera*, all genetically different, have been identified as well as countless 'mini-mutations' inside each variety. Yet within this vast number, there are only about 100 important wine grape varieties, and far fewer, perhaps 20 or 30, with more than local relevance. But just as grapes like the Sauvignon Blanc and the Gamay were little regarded in France a few generations ago and are now fêted and imitated, so there are sure to be others lurking in the background, full of personality, awaiting their turn.

It is the grape variety, above all else, which gives distinctive flavour to a wine. The winemaker can *manipulate* the flavour but the fundamental taste remains, and the fundamental balance of sugars, acid and tannin is particular to each grape.

Different varieties ripen at different times, need different soils and different climatic conditions. In Europe the most suitable variety for each region has evolved over centuries, so much so that the grape name is rarely used on the label: if it is a white wine from a village in Burgundy, for instance, it has to be from the Chardonnay grape. In the newer wine regions, the grape variety is all-important and virtually all labels, except for 'jug wine', prominently feature the grape name, or names, as a means of identifying the probable style and flavour of the wine.

· CLASSIC VARIETIES ·

The description 'classic' is a controversial one, because European winemakers are notoriously parochial and chauvinistic about their local vines. The vines I have placed in the first division are vines which not only produce fine wine in their own region, but have also significantly influenced winemaking elsewhere. There is only one exception – Nebbiolo – which I include as the leader of the totally idiosyncratic group of great Italian varieties that, so far, have completely failed to spread their influence outside their own hills and valleys. Among the reds, I've defined the 'classics' as Cabernet Sauvignon, Pinot Noir, Syrah, Merlot and Nebbiolo; and among the whites, Chardonnay, Riesling, Muscat, Chenin Blanc, Sauvignon Blanc, Sémillon and Gewürztraminer.

· CABERNET SAUVIGNON ·

This *has* to be the greatest of the red wine grapes. Small, tough and late-ripening, Cabernet has the most identifiable of flavours – managing to taste of blackcurrants and cedar wherever it is grown – which is almost anywhere with enough sunshine and reasonably warm soil; in the Bordeaux region of France and certain parts of California and Australia, it produces a remarkably high proportion of the world's greatest red wines. It is now apparent that in southern France, northern Spain and Tuscany in Italy, as well as in Chile, South Africa and Eastern Europe, great Cabernet wines are also possible, each subtly different, but each triumphantly recognizable. In Bordeaux, Cabernet is usually blended with the Merlot grape, which both softens and enhances the flavours.

· PINOT NOIR ·

If I were judging purely by quantity of great wine produced, Pinot Noir certainly wouldn't make the first division: no other grape so regularly disappoints, and no other grape so bemuses yet captivates the world's winemakers. It is a softer, earlier-ripening variety than Cabernet, much more prone to spring frosts and autumn rot; it is also the most degenerate of all the great vines, mutating at the drop of a hat. Yet in Burgundy, and in Burgundy alone, these qualities of animal passion, soft red-fruit ripeness, and perfumes as fragrant as a warm oriental night, *can* all come together – just often enough for me to forgive its more usual mediocrity. Occasionally, in Western Australia and New South Wales, in the southern tip of South Africa and isolated pockets of California and Oregon, we can also see signs of greatness. Elsewhere, the Pinot is surprisingly widely planted – in Italy, Germany, Switzerland, even England! In France, apart from Burgundy, it is planted in Alsace, the Loire, Jura and Savoie, where it produces light, perfumed reds, but it is more important as a component of champagne.

Cabernet Sauvignon

Pinot Noir

· SYRAH ·

Syrah is a marvellous grape, but has never achieved the popularity of Pinot Noir or Cabernet Sauvignon. Its reputation is for producing dark, tannic wines – black as hell's mouth when young, and almost as fierce to taste. Yet, on top of its high tannin content and deep colour, it is the positive cornucopia of rich fruit flavours which is Syrah's greatest achievement. Syrah can cover the whole spectrum of black- and red-fruit flavours, overlay them with smoky, gamy textures, and finish off with creamy, spicy softness. Such is its genius in the dizzy vineyards of the northern Rhône. In the southern Rhône and the Midi it is usually blended, but still produces delicious wines on its own. However, Syrah does need warm conditions to blossom – it can be peppery and rather rooty in cool conditions – so it isn't surprising to find that Australia is the only other major producer. Here the Shiraz – as Syrah becomes in Strine – is the most widely planted red grape but, despite producing wonderful plummy, chocolaty reds in good hands, it is mostly overcropped and underappreciated. There is a little promising Syrah in California.

· MERLOT ·

Without doubt, this is a great classic – Château Pétrus, the world's most expensive wine and Merlot to the core is there to prove the point – yet it is strangely underestimated. This is because, except in St-Emilion and Pomerol,

Merlot is the subordinate Bordeaux red grape, used as a blender and softener for the Cabernet Sauvignon. In fact, there is nearly twice as much Merlot as Cabernet Sauvignon in Bordeaux, because it ripens earlier and produces a delicious, almost grapy, gentle red, adding mint and honey flavours to the harsher Cabernet. (Outside the Médoc it is often Cabernet Sauvignon which acts as the blender for predominantly Merlot wine!) Merlot is, however, less adaptable than Cabernet Sauvignon: although it is used in the south of France and extensively in northern Italy, it tends to overcrop and produce light, ultra-soft wines of no great style. However it is highly successful in Bulgaria and Romania, and is beginning to be recognized, both as a blender and in its own right, in Australia and California with increasingly impressive results.

Merlot

· NEBBIOLO ·

Nebbiolo is *not* one of my favourite red grapes. But I can see its enormous potential for exciting, deep-textured flavours and that is why it is included as a first-rank grape. At present, Nebbiolo is virtually exclusive to north-west Italy – though Switzerland, California and Australia each have a tiny bit. It is a desperately tannic grape, ripening very late, if at all, and only on the best slopes. The wine is intensely coloured and positively chewy with tarry, pruny tastes. In Piedmont, particularly

in Barolo and Barbaresco, it is aged for years in big old wooden barrels on the assumption that this would soften it; but the effect is normally of a haggard, fleshless mammoth dragging itself from the barrel towards the table. However, times are changing, and an increasing number of modern winemakers are finding less brutal ways to bring out the weird tobacco, chocolate, prune and hung-game wonders which lie in this grape.

· CHARDONNAY ·

In terms of popularity, Chardonnay must surely rank Number One in the world with consumers – ahead, even, of Cabernet Sauvignon. Yet it doesn't even feature in the top 20 most-planted grape varieties! In fact, there is a serious shortage of good Chardonnay because it has suddenly become the most sought-after white-wine name, so that winemakers and winegrowers cannot secure supplies of it fast enough. Its home is Burgundy and Champagne in eastern France, and the relatively recent vogue for white Burgundy – especially from American consumers – has catapulted demand way ahead of supply. Chardonnay is still at its greatest in Burgundy, from the lean, austere wines of Chablis, to the wonderfully complex wines of the Côte de Beaune, to the fat, yeasty delights of the Mâconnais. It grows so easily that its only problems are a tendency to be hit by spring frosts in Chablis and a tendency to overripen

Nebbiolo

Chardonnay

further south. Both California and Australia have opted for the Côte d'Or approach, relying on ripe fruit and ageing in small oak barrels; so, to some extent, have the Pacific North-West of the US, New York State and New Zealand. Italy and the rest of France, where it is increasingly planted to cash in on the magic name 'Chardonnay', are more inclined to follow the Mâconnais line of stainless steel wine-making for fresh, fruity flavours. Chardonnay is also grown in places as far apart as England, Germany, Bulgaria, Chile, Argentina – and even India! Truly, the most international of varieties.

· RIESLING ·

There is a very good argument for claiming that Riesling is a more remarkable white grape than Chardonnay in terms of its enormous range of wine styles. Right now, however, it is strangely, inexplicably unfashionable. Possibly this is because – in a very France-orientated wine world – the Riesling is hardly allowed to grow on French soil. Where it does, in Alsace on the French-German border, the mixture of a steely edge with honey and musky fruit is memorable. However, the Riesling is primarily seen as a German variety, and it does produce all the greatest German wines, from bone dry to intensely sweet. It has been planted worldwide with varying success: Australia, in particular, makes remarkable lime-juice-and-

honey flavoured wines from it, while California is producing some exciting 'noble-rot' sweet wines. Italy, Luxembourg, Austria and even Catalonia in Spain produce good to great dry Rieslings. Outside Germany and France it must carry prefixes such as Rhine-, White-, Johannisberg-, because 'Riesling' as a name has been adopted by numerous other grape varieties, usually inferior and in no way related.

· MUSCAT ·

There are numerous Muscat varieties, but the indisputably great one is *Muscat blanc à petits grains* (the small-berry Muscat). The reason people dismiss Muscat is because its wines taste of grapes and therefore can't be serious! This is plain daft – as anyone who has tasted a crunchy-green dry Muscat from Alsace, a luscious but ultra-fresh Italian Moscato Naturale or a deep sticky Browns Liqueur Muscat from Australia well knows. That grapiness is one of the most delicious flavours known to man; it's only because it is so *easy* to appreciate that we think there must be something cheap about it. Muscat is a low yielder and doesn't ripen easily – consequently it is often replaced by lesser versions. But the true Muscat is unique – and it's also worth remembering that some experts say all *vitis vinifera* grape varieties are initially descended from Muscat!

· CHENIN BLANC ·

The majority of Chenin Blanc wine made in the Loire valley is tart, raw, and scarcely

Riesling

digestible, the acidity being so high and the fruit so little in evidence. Yet Chenin from the Loire valley is the grape variety for some of France's greatest whites. The trouble is that Chenin is a very late-ripening, high-yielding vine, which only gives decent wines when it is planted on special sites and is vigorously pruned to restrict production. Then, as a dry wine in Savennières or Vouvray, or a sweet one at Vouvray or Quarts-de-Chaume it can be sublime. The high acidity makes ageing imperative and sweet wines will happily last 50 years. Outside France, Chenin is grown in California and South Africa where its character is completely different – fresh and forward, ideal quaffing wine; and Australia and New Zealand are getting to grips with it. So far, though, Chenin is used too much as a work-horse grape, and not enough as a superstar.

Sauvignon Blanc

· SAUVIGNON BLANC ·

Sauvignon Blanc wines from the Upper Loire villages of Sancerre and Pouilly epitomize the slightly sharp, grassy-green flavours which became so popular in the 1970s as the world changed its drinking habits from red to white. Now Sauvignon is grown worldwide, in imitation of Sancerre, as well as reasserting itself in Touraine, Anjou and Bordeaux. It is this chilly, almost aggressive, acidity backed up by a lot of fruit – which might be raw and green but is still *fruit* – which has created its cult status. In California, New York State, and Oregon it produces delicious tangy wine, frequently called Fumé Blanc – or smoky white (after the French Pouilly Blanc Fumé) – and often softened by a little oak ageing. Oak is also sometimes used in New Zealand, Australia and South Africa, but Italy, the other chief European producer, makes it green and fresh. Sauvignon's less obvious, but equally important, claim to fame is its susceptibility to 'noble rot' which makes it a crucial ingredient of the great sweet wines of Bordeaux.

· SEMILLON ·

Sémillon shines at opposite ends of the wine world in completely different ways. In Bordeaux it is extensively planted, so much so that it rates as France's second most-planted

Sémillon

white variety, after the undistinguished Ugni Blanc. Much of this plantation is for dull dry whites, although it can excel in the Graves. However, in Sauternes and Barsac, this thin-skinned, fairly early-ripening variety gets affected by 'noble rot' and produces a deep golden, smooth, syrup-sweet wine of supreme quality. It is hardly found elsewhere in Europe, but is common in Chile and present in South Africa and the US West Coast. However, Sémillon resurfaces far, far south as one of Australia's greatest varieties. In Western

Gewürztraminer

Australia and Victoria it can sometimes outperform Chardonnay, and in the Hunter Valley, near Sydney, intense, painfully solid dry whites are produced, needing a dozen years or more to mature.

· GEWURZTRAMINER ·

Gewürztraminer, like Muscat, is often dismissed by pundits as an inferior variety because it is so easily recognizable and patently enjoyable. Gewürz means 'spice' in German and Tramin is a village in Italy's northernmost Alto Adige region – so Gewürztraminer translates as 'the spicy grape of Tramin'. It certainly is spicy, and the scents of fresh-ground pepper, tropical fruits and positively boudoir perfumes often burst out of the glass. However, in Alto Adige this slightly pink grape produces dry, balanced, softly perfumed wines, while in the Alsace region of France they can be at once mouth-fillingly rich and totally dry. Germany produces both dry and sweet Gewürztraminers, as does the West Coast of the US; but many of the most exciting wines – splendidly dry, yet exotically perfumed – have come from Australia and New Zealand.

· OTHER VARIETIES ·

If you've ever drunk a cheap Spanish white or a cheap Spanish or French red, you'll have drunk the two most widely planted wine grapes in the world – but the names are not likely to be on the label. Airén, a pretty basic Spanish white, is the world's most widely planted grape, while the red Garnacha (or Grenache)

is Number Two. Grapes like these along with the Russian Rkatsiteli, a dull soft white, Trebbiano (alias Ugni Blanc), the *extremely* ordinary Mediterranean white, and Carignan, the beefy Mediterranean red-wine work-horse dominate the vineyards of the world. The reason is that in warm areas, wine is made and consumed as a staple of life – just like bread or local vegetables – and the most productive and disease-free varieties will always be preferred to something more capricious yet more delicious. In Germany, for instance, the Riesling has always been thought of as the foremost grape, but it is the Müller-Thurgau – only 'invented' a century ago – which now occupies the majority of vineyard land simply because it ripens earlier and yields more. Sad, because the wine is definitely not in the same league. However, there are other grapes, which, if they don't hit the headlines, are either crucial to famous wines or so identified with a single wine that we forget what grape variety is behind it all.

Sangiovese is the tough, turbulent red grape which gives Chianti its unique personality, and is widely grown throughout the rest of Italy.
Gamay, the *only* grape allowed for red Beaujolais, is generally not highly regarded. But Beaujolais is a classic wine-style – all juicy, slaphappy fruit and fun – and only the Gamay grape can produce that effect.
Cabernet Franc on its own produces a grassy, blackcurranty red wine in the Loire valley and northern Italy; it is also an important part of the 'Bordeaux mixture' of red grapes.
Tempranillo is the red grape which gives the soft, slightly strawberryish fruit to Rioja.
Palomino stays pretty dull *until* it is subjected to the sherry-making process – when it springs splendidly to life.
Pinot Blanc, Chardonnay's look- and taste-alike, shines in Alsace and Italy's Alto Adige.
Viognier, the brilliant white grape which creates Condrieu, a startling pear-skin and apricot-flavoured wine in the northern Rhône valley, has just been rescued from extinction by the development of virus-free plants.

Of course, there are many, many others, and the most important of these are covered when I discuss the wines with which they are most closely associated.

· FROM GRAPES TO WINE ·

· MAKING RED WINE ·

After fermentation the new wine is drained off, leaving a residue which is pressed to extract more wine. Old wooden hand presses have largely been replaced by horizontal rotating machine presses.

Wine for everyday drinking is stored in glass-lined cement, epoxy-resin or stainless steel tanks and soon bottled; quality wine is often still aged in oak casks, as it has been for centuries. Use of new wood, slightly porous and full of flavour, can, if not overdone, greatly improve the wine.

Traditionally the red wine cycle began with treading the grapes, but today most winemakers use a machine which crushes and destems. The end product is called must.

The must is emptied into vats or tanks; modern tanks have pressure and temperature controls. During fermentation, the skins form a thick surface layer. To keep this moist, must is regularly pumped over it, or, traditionally, it is pushed down with poles.

W ine would 'happen' whether we wanted it to or not. All it takes is a bunch of ripe grapes, a few degrees of heat and some hungry yeasts. You only need a skin-nick in some of those grapes, or a reasonably warm autumn day, and the yeasts – occurring naturally around the vineyard – will be straight in, gorging themselves on their favourite food: grape sugar.

There is a formula which shows that, in the course of their feast, these yeasts will turn 100 parts of sugar into 47·86–48·12 parts of ethyl alcohol and 47·02–47·86 parts of carbon dioxide. Well, that's what it *says*! But I'll put it more simply: yeasts feed on the grape sugar and thereby transform it into alcohol and carbon

dioxide, creating a fair amount of energy – that is, heat – in the process. That's why fermentation is such a frothy, bubbly – and steamy – affair. If someone in the long distant past hadn't happened to discover that juice which underwent this transformation not only tasted rather good but also made them feel ever so slightly frisky – then this accident of nature might have been dismissed as a mere nuisance, mucking up a perfectly decent bunch of dessert grapes.

Having discovered fermented grape juice, man readily adopted the wine habit. Right now, we're living in an age which has learnt more about wine-making during the last two decades than in the last two millenia. But we have

reached the stage when some winemakers freely admit that they have more science at their fingertips than they know what to do with – and the 'soul' of wine is in jeopardy as modernists zealously pursue their vision of 'the perfect wine'. Bordeaux's greatest experts say that the art of winemaking is to know when to do nothing – and I'll drink to that. So let's look at the basic procedures by which a wine 'makes itself' – with just a little help from the winemaker. There are four main stages: preparation, fermentation, maturation and bottling.

· MAKING RED WINE ·

When black grapes arrive at the winery they are tipped into a crushing machine which lightly

Above The marc, the grapy mass of skins, pips, and sometimes stalks, left after pressing, can either be distilled into a kind of brandy or used as a fertilizer on the vineyard.

During ageing wine is racked – drawn from its sediment or lees and put into fresh containers. It is also fined – cleansed with a coagulant, like beaten egg-white, that carries all impurities to the bottom.

The whole process of bottling, capsuling and labelling is now mostly automated although some small producers still bottle straight from the cask and apply capsules and labels by hand.

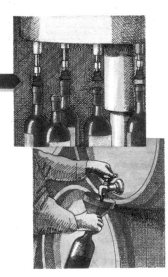

Left This diagram shows the main stages in making red wine, featuring both old and new techniques. For some processes, modern technology is ousting tradition, but for others time-tested methods still predominate – because they're best. Procedures vary slightly according to wine style and according to the region – New World wineries, for example, are usually more hi-tech than their European counterparts, but also prepared to invest in tradition by using new oak barrels. However, the basics remain the same: grapes must be picked, prepared and fermented; and the wine matured and bottled (or bagged or canned) – and drunk!

Similarly, skins contain most of the flavouring matter. This is partly tannin, which is bitter-tasting but which provides the skeleton for fruit flavours in the ageing process, and it is partly all the nuances of perfume and individuality which the grape possesses by virtue of its particular variety, or which it has absorbed from the soil.

If fermentation takes place at a low temperature, say 20°C, the result is a light, simple wine. If it takes place at between 25°C and 30°C far more colour and taste are extracted from the grapes. At over 30°C there is a risk that fermentation will get out of control, causing a hot-vinegar taste to develop in the wine.

During fermentation, the grape skins – and any other solids such as stalks and pips – rise like a 'cap' to the top of the vat on a bubbling swirl of carbon dioxide. This 'cap' must be mixed back continually, first because it contains the colouring and flavouring matter, and second because if exposed to air, it dries, attracts bacteria and gives the wine a bruised, acetic taste. Traditionally, the 'cap' was pressed down with poles but is nowadays more usually submerged with a spray of fermenting juice pumped up from the vat.

When fermentation is over, the juice is run off: called *vin de goutte* or free-run wine, it usually comprises 80 per cent of the total. The remaining mush of skins is then pressed, producing *vin de presse* or press wine. Dark and tannic, this is added to the free-run wine in varying quantities, depending on how firm and

squeezes them, breaking their skins and releasing the juice. Normally, the crusher also pulls off the stalks, which have a tough tannic taste, but in some cases these are left on to produce a firmer wine. The resulting mush of flesh, skins and juice (called the 'must') is then pumped into a fermentation vat.

Fermentation takes place in large vats, traditionally made of wood, but nowadays often of glass-lined cement or stainless steel. The prime object is to convert grape sugars into alcohol. With most yeasts this happens spontaneously at 18°C or above (although some begin to work at much lower temperatures). However, the juice may be heated to start things off, and cultured yeasts can be added

instead of relying on the more haphazard habits of natural yeasts. Left to themselves, yeasts will ferment the juice to dryness – converting all the sugar to alcohol – at which point the process ceases. With quick-drinking reds, fermentation may only take a few days. For classic reds up to two weeks are normally required – perhaps even three or four weeks in some cases.

The second objective is to acquire colour and flavour. The colouring matter is in the grape skins and is best extracted at a fermentation temperature of around 25–29°C. For a light red wine, the juice and skins may be separated after a day or two; more usually, the skins stay with the juice until fermentation is over.

tough the winemaker intends the final product.

The wine is now 'made' in that the sugar has been converted into alcohol. It is unlikely to taste good yet – which is where maturation comes in, beginning with the secondary, or malolactic, fermentation. During this process, vital for most red wines, bacteria convert the sharp malic (green-apple) acid – naturally present in the grape – into mild lactic (milk) acid. The wine, losing much of its harshness, becomes softer and rounder and few reds would be drinkable without it. Traditionally, this secondary fermentation used to take place in the warmer weather of the following spring, but it can now be induced by warming the cellar or by inoculating the wine with malolactic bacteria.

Wines for drinking young are stored in large containers of concrete or stainless steel before bottling. Ideally, wines for maturing are put into wooden barrels of about 50 gallons (225 litres) for anything from nine months to $2\frac{1}{2}$ years; if the barrels are fairly new the wines will extract tannin and vanillin flavourings from the oak cask, becoming both richer and firmer. But, in the simplest terms, with the malolactic fermentation over, we could simply bottle the wine and drink it – which in most parts of the world is exactly what happens.

· MAKING WHITE WINE ·

When the grapes – which can be white or black because the *flesh* of all decent wine grapes is colourless – arrive at the winery, they are destemmed as well as crushed. Mechanically harvested grapes will have been destemmed as they are picked. In some cases the skins will 'macerate' in the juice for a few hours to increase aroma. Then the pulp of broken flesh and skins is pressed. The juice is left to settle, since there will be a fair amount of solids in suspension. Sometimes the solids are allowed to drop naturally. Otherwise they are filtered or centrifuged, collecting all the solids round the sides of the tank, and leaving the clear juice to drain out the bottom. When the solids have been separated the juice is pumped into vats for fermentation.

Fermentation is usually much cooler than for reds, since no colour extraction is required and freshness and fruit are frequently the most

important characteristics to be preserved. In cold countries this may take place naturally at between 15–20°C, but in warm countries the vat surface is cooled with cold water or with a 'jacket' full of cooling agents.

Alternatively, the fermenting juice can be pumped through a refrigerated coil to keep it cool. Increasingly, specially cultured 'cold temperature' yeasts are used for white wines. At very low temperatures, 15°C or less, fermentation may take a month or more. Occasionally, as in some Burgundy estates, the wine is fermented in small oak barrels for shorter periods and at a higher temperature.

The malolactic fermentation, so crucial in reds, is frequently prevented in whites to preserve a sharper, more tangy acidity. This is achieved either through the addition of sulphur dioxide or through clarification – separating the wine from its 'lees' or solid matter followed by sterile filtering. Most white wine is stored briefly in a neutral container before bottling for early drinking. Some top Chardonnays, Sémillons, Sauvignons and Rieslings are matured in barrels to enhance their flavour.

· OTHER WINES ·

Rosé is red wine which has not been allowed to extract much colour from the skins. The

Left Filling a press with white wine grapes. There are two common types of press: one contains a bag which, when inflated, pushes the must against the perforated sides; the other squeezes the must between two end plates which are drawn together by a screw.

Below Checking fermentation inside a stainless steel vat at a Californian winery.

grapes are crushed, destemmed and fermented on their skins for a day or less. The juice is then drawn off and continues to ferment in a separate vat, generally at low temperatures. Some of the best wines are made when juice is 'bled' off a normally fermenting red, thereby

Above **Oak vats are used in many traditionally minded wineries as here in Cahors.**

Above **Removal of yeast deposits is necessary in the making of all bottle-fermented wines.**

increasing the concentration of the red and giving a fuller flavoured rosé.

Sweet whites occur naturally when the sugar in the grape is not fully transformed into alcohol but partially retained for its sweetness. To produce genuinely sweet wine, the grapes must be very overripe, and, usually, infected with

'noble rot' (*botrytis cinerea*) which dehydrates the grapes and concentrates the sugar levels, often to a potential alcohol level of 20–30°. Yeasts will in any case stop fermenting at about 15° alcohol, but usually the winemaker will add sulphur dioxide to stop fermentation before this level is reached. In the great sweet wines of Sauternes, the Loire and Tokay, this is likely to be at 12–13° alcohol producing a luscious glyceriny wine. In Germany, Australia and California it is more likely to be stopped at 8° or 9°, producing a wine of intensely fruity sweetness. The grapes for such wines are pressed very gently, perhaps two or three times, and then fermented slowly for maybe one or two months – or until the winemaker decides to stop the fermentation according to the type of wine he wishes to make.

Alternatively, sweet wines can be artificially made. Even when the grapes are not overripe, you can still stop the fermentation while some sugar remains, either by adding sulphur dioxide, by removing the yeasts through fine filtration or centrifuge, or by cooling the wine to 0°C and precipitating the yeasts. Another method involves fermenting the wine to dryness then

adding some sterilized grape juice to capture a certain sweetness. Both these methods, 'stop-fermentation' and 'back-blending', are more successful for creating medium sweet, rather than very sweet, wines.

Sparkling wine results from a second fermentation, induced by the addition of yeast and sugar to the wine while it is under pressure. The 'champagne' method, which produces all the great sparkling wines, creates this fermentation inside the bottle from which the wine will be drunk. It is difficult (requiring expert removal of yeast deposits), expensive, and incomparably delicious.

In the 'transfer' method, much used in the United States and Australia, the second fermentation takes place inside *a* bottle, but the wine is then filtered and 'transferred' under pressure to another bottle. This avoids the tricky problem of yeast deposits, and the results aren't bad. The third method is the *cuve close*, 'closed vat', procedure where everything happens under pressure in a sealed tank. With the exception of Asti Spumante and a few German Deutscher Sekts, the results are usually pretty poor, but are preferable to the 'bicycle pump' method where they just pump in some gas and hope for the best!

Fortified wines are created by the addition of brandy or neutral spirit to the grape juice about halfway through the first fermentation. This raises the alcohol level – thereby killing the yeasts – and also preserves the sugar in the unfinished wine. The result, as in port and the best madeira, is usually a strong, sweetish wine – with fairly rough tannins and spirits – which needs considerable maturation in barrel or bottle to soften up. Some madeiras are fermented right out, fortified and sweetened to the desired level with *surdo*, a sweet blend of grape juice and high-strength spirit.

Sherry types are made differently. The wine, completely fermented out, is then left in a barrel four-fifths full. If allowed, it will then develop a creamy yeast growth called *flor* which gives a most remarkable taste. However, the sherrymaker usually encourages this growth only on the most delicate wines. Fuller wines have their *flor* growth arrested by being fortified, then sweetened according to the style required.

· THE MODERN WINEMAKER ·

The fermentation of grape juice into alcohol is a completely natural process which can take place without any help from human hand. The creation of 'wine', however, the individual flavours and styles we find attractive, is much more complex – the result of local growing conditions, traditional skills and, increasingly, science.

Human intervention in the wine-making process proper – leaving aside earlier stages such as genetic engineering of grape varieties, vineyard maintenance and climate control – begins at harvest-time. During the preceding weeks, as he walks through the vineyard, the winemaker has been testing the grapes for ripeness: at first by feeling them between thumb and forefinger, later by tasting at random, then ultimately with a refractometer – an instrument for measuring sugar content. From daily readings, he estimates the optimum moment for picking, when rising sugar and falling acid levels are correctly balanced. Obviously the weather might upset his calculations, but if storms are forecast or the acid level suddenly plummets, the winemaker can counteract by initiating the harvest within hours. In modern vineyards this picking is increasingly mechanized; a large machine can harvest as many grapes as 70 to 80 hand-pickers and can operate day and night. In hot climates where grapes rapidly overripen or in temperate regions where a break in the weather threatens a perfect crop, use of mechanical harvesters can make or break a vintage.

· IN THE WINERY ·

Having crushed, destemmed and pressed the grapes according to the kind of wine he's after, the winemaker moves on to fermentation – a process where his continuing intervention is all important. His first decision concerns yeast types. In traditional areas, especially Europe, the grapes' own yeasts have always been left to start fermentation unaided. However, many modern winemakers – particularly in the New World – don't want to risk unexpected (and possibly unpleasant) flavours. They therefore inhibit wild yeast growth with sulphur dioxide and then initiate fermentation with a pure yeast culture. This use of cultured yeasts is often necessary – especially in new vineyard areas which have a limited natural yeast population – but it can result in too many wines tasting too similar.

Temperature is also a major control in fermentation. It can range from less than 15°C to as high as 30°C and, by means of refrigeration and heating devices, can be altered from day to day – according to the amount of flavour, colour or tannin the winemaker wishes to extract.

There are two fundamental processes which may be necessary during fermentation: chaptalization and adjustment of acid levels. Chaptalization – allowed, for instance, in most of northern Europe but not in the warmer south – involves adding extra sugar during fermentation to increase the degree of alcohol: by up to 2° in Bordeaux or Burgundy or 4·5° (almost doubling the natural level) in cooler England and Germany. Wine needs a certain alcoholic strength to be stable but in temperate regions grapes do not always reach a sufficient ripeness to guarantee this, so sugar – normally beet sugar but sometimes grape concentrate – is added to the fermenting must. Chaptalization does not sweeten the wine, since yeasts convert the sugar into alcohol, and if properly done is a necessary 'manipulation' in any area where grapes do not easily ripen.

Adjustment of acid levels is also necessary and desirable. Hot countries like Australia, Spain and Italy, find it difficult to preserve attractive levels of acid in their grapes. Since acid is crucial for a wine's stable development – as well as for its taste – tartaric acid, naturally present in grapes, can be added at the beginning of fermentation. Non-European winemakers often add the less subtle – but cheaper and easier to handle – citric acid at a later stage. In contrast, cold country grapes often have too high an acid level. This is reduced by adding chalk or a rather more ruthless substance called Acidex. All these processes – chaptalization, acidification and

Below **Harvesters save on labour and time but are best for robust varieties, like Cabernet Sauvignon, which bruise less easily than thin-skinned grapes such as Merlot and Pinot Noir. This harvester is at work in Bordeaux.**

de-acidification are perfectly acceptable when required to make a balanced wine.

Throughout fermentation, especially with white wines, care is taken to prevent the must from oxidizing. Traditionally, this was achieved by adding sulphur dioxide in large doses but, increasingly, modern winemakers are reducing their use of sulphur: it does stay in the wine, can affect the taste and *can* cause an allergic reaction. Instead, more and more wine is made under a protective blanket of carbon dioxide held in the head of the vat. This not only keeps away oxygen but may also give the wine a faint, refreshing prickle.

· MATURATION ·

Once fermentation is over, the winemaker has various options. He can bottle early to preserve a crisp, young taste – in which case he will first filter the wine and perhaps, through cooling, precipitate any tartrate crystals which, though harmless and tasteless, don't look so good.

He may store the wine in a neutral tank of glass-lined cement or stainless steel. Reds and whites can exist for years like this – especially if kept under a layer of nitrogen or carbon dioxide to prevent oxidation – but they will not improve or change to any appreciable extent. He may use large wooden barrels or vats. In cool areas like Germany, a gradual interaction generally produces more flavour and complexity. In the warm south, although a brief big-barrel treatment may soften the wine, a long spell thins it out, oxidizes it and, in a word, wrecks it.

The most interesting – and demanding – option is the use of small oak barrels. Oak contains a galaxy of aromatic sensations: herby-spicy fragrances of which the most precious is vanillin – the honeyed taste characteristic of so many classic reds and whites. All these flavours – along with wood tannins – leach into the wine to enhance and enrich it.

Below Coopering is a traditional craft linked with wine-making. These staves are being coaxed into shape by the flame, which also chars the wood imparting special flavours to the wine.

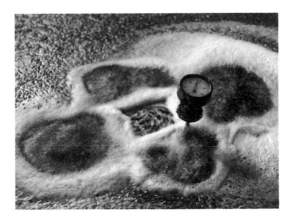

Above Monitoring temperature in a fermentation vat. White wines and light reds are fermented in cool conditions, under 20°C, but rich full reds require temperatures nearer 30°C.

Below During racking the wine is constantly checked for clarity. When a trace of sediment appears in the glass this shows that the lees at the cask bottom have been reached and no more wine is drawn off.

A winemaker in Valencia, Spain. Even in the most traditional areas quality levels are being raised dramatically by the use of up-to-date equipment.

the top of the cask. The wine is also periodically 'racked' – drawn off its sediment and transferred to a clean barrel. This is particularly important for red wines which deposit tannins, colouring matter, dead yeast cells, and acid during maturation.

The last stage before bottling is 'fining' – removing small particles held in suspension by means of a clarifying agent. This is added to the surface and, like a porous membrane, it sinks through the wine, dragging all impurities with it. Some of wine's most dubious-sounding ingredients are, in fact, fining agents: substances like dried ox blood, sturgeon's air bladders and potassium ferrocyanide. But, by definition, a clarifying agent leaves nothing of itself in the wine so there is no need to be apprehensive. In fact, the most traditional of all fining agents is utterly reassuring: beaten egg white.

For white wines, many modern winemakers prefer advanced filtration techniques to racking and fining (some even do both); but although finely filtered wine is crystal-clear it often lacks personality – snatched away with the debris.

Most wines – including fine wines – are the result of blending different components. Often the selection process starts in the vineyard: from experience the winemaker knows that a few rows of vines on a certain slope or field produce grapes with distinctive characteristics such as extra acidity or tannin. He tends to ferment different batches of grapes in separate vats – so that he knows what he is dealing with when, eventually, he makes his blend for barrel or bottle. In some cases, blending simply consists of matching different vats (all filled with wine from the same grape variety) for taste and quality. In others – as happens with fine château-bottled Bordeaux – the blend is of different grape varieties, traditionally put together to create a harmonious whole.

At the end of the wine-making cycle, choosing the right moment for bottling is as crucial as it was for picking. Bottling a bold wine too early kills its potential; bottling a light wine too late wastes its fruity youth.

Ideally bottling should be cold and sterile – with hoses, bottling lines, corks and bottles all

These 'Potter' self-drainers, in a New Zealand winery, are used to recover free-run juice from the crushed white grapes before pressing.

sterilized. The bottles, injected with nitrogen or carbon dioxide, are filled with cool wine; a gas lock forms between wine and cork to prevent oxidation. Unfortunately, many cheaper wines are subjected either to pasteurization or to 'hot' bottling – where the wine is heated at the moment of bottling. Pasteurized wines lose their fresh colour rather quickly while hot-bottled ones can have a stale sweet smell and (since liquids expand when heated) a great gap between wine and cork, which can't be good for the wine.

With many wines, ageing continues in the bottle – the finest go on improving for 30 years or more: flavours drawn from the wood marry with the fruit, tannin and acidity, soften, and create, over time, each wine's individual, incomparable personality.

At the same time, air seeps through the cask's pores and further fosters the ageing process.

The newer the oak the more forceful its impact. New barrels are suitable for a big-bodied wine but often overwhelming for a light one; older barrels work on wine less hurriedly, while the amount of charring inflicted on the staves during cooperage also has an effect. Although ageing in oak can be overdone, all the greatest reds – plus the best Chardonnay dry whites and some 'noble rot' sweet whites – are matured for between six months and two years in small 50-gallon (225-litre) oak barrels.

Since wine breathes through barrels, a certain amount of evaporation inevitably occurs. To prevent oxidation, regular topping-up takes place through a bung hole at

·2·
MAKING
THE MOST OF
WINE

· FINDING THE WINE YOU WANT ·

It used to be a simple enough job to tick off the names of the world's great wines: claret, burgundy, hock, sherry, port and one or two others. No one would argue, and any young whippersnapper who meekly raised his hand and said, 'But, but. . .what about Italy, Australia, California and the rest – don't they ever make great wine?' would be slapped down pretty sharply.

Well, times have changed, and we can now confidently assert, with no fear of a bashing from wine snobs, 'Great wines are bursting out all over the place'. You may not recognize the names; the flavours may startle you; but there's never been more good and great wine available than now, and at prices we can all afford. Certainly, in some cases, the names *may* be unfamiliar, but that should not stop us stepping out bravely and grabbing our share, experimenting to find the flavours that suit our palates at the prices that suit our pockets.

So here is a description of ten of the world's great classic wine styles, each one accompanied by a list of alternatives that bear a close resemblance to it (even though they may not be made from the same kind of grapes). They won't taste exactly the same, of course, but they *will* be tending in the same general direction; and in many cases they're cheaper. Not that you should think of them as just the poor man's claret, or port, or whatever: many of them have indeed been modelled on one of the classics, but have quickly developed exciting flavours of their own. Some, like Rioja, began as imitators, but are now considered great wines in their own right. It took Rioja about a hundred years, but things move faster nowadays. Many of these 'understudies' will be household names in less than a decade, if they aren't already, so let's be the first ones to discover these exciting alternatives, before we all get trampled in the rush.

· CLASSED GROWTH RED BORDEAUX (CLARET) ·

Of all the red wines, this is held up as the supreme achievement, and the world's winemakers have been falling over themselves in attempts to approximate its remarkable flavours. Luckily, it is based on the Cabernet Sauvignon grape, with a little help from Cabernet Franc and Merlot, and these three are some of wine's most adaptable grapes. Great claret is a firm, dry wine, one of the driest. The unique magic enters in as, with time, the raw, dark, new wine reacts with the small, new oak barrels in which it is matured. Over the years, this produces a mixture of blackcurranty richness and cedary, or even cigar-box, spiciness and fragrance which twists and twines in an endlessly fascinating combination of flavours, and yet stays totally, deliciously dry.

· GOOD ALTERNATIVES ·

France Cahors (Tannat and Auxerrois grapes) – a full dry red from the South-West with a plums and tobacco spice; Cabernet Sauvignon from Coteaux d'Aix-en-Provence – light, slightly herby, southern French red; Cabernet and Cabernet/Syrah blends from Coteaux des Baux-en-Provence – delicious, juicy cassis-flavoured reds; Côtes de Buzet from the Lot-et-Garonne *département* – earthy, but full of flavour when aged in small barrels; the Loire reds, Chinon and Bourgueil, delicious, dry Cabernet Franc wines in ripe years (1985, 1983, 1982).

Italy Cabernet or Sangiovese/Cabernet blends from Tuscany – such as Sassicaia and Tignanello. These are some of the most exciting classic reds to emerge in the last decade.

Spain Cabernets from Raimat and Penedés, Catalonia. These are marked by the purity of Raimat's fruit and the weight, ripeness and tannin of Penedés.

USA Cabernet Sauvignon or Cabernet/Merlot from California can achieve the weight and flavour of the great Bordeaux classed growths, if not always the complexity.

Australia Cabernet Sauvignon, Cabernet-Shiraz and Cabernet-Merlot wines – marked by a deep, strong blackcurrant and mint fruit and good tannic structure.

Chile Cabernet Sauvignon wines – a remarkable mix of smoke and blackcurrant.

· RED BURGUNDY ·

The key to great burgundy is not – as some maintain – power, or richness, but fragrance and a gentle strawberry or cherry fruit. The Pinot Noir is a thoroughly difficult grape, unused to doing what it's told even in its own backyard of the Côte d'Or in Burgundy. But because the mixture of almost 'sweet' fruitiness and exotic scent produced by a few Burgundian alchemists is so exciting, there is a queue of would-be conquerors of the Pinot Noir in California, Australia, Italy and elsewhere. Maybe if they behaved more like suitors, and less like warriors, in their efforts to evoke the magic of fine red burgundy, the Pinot Noir might be more generous with its favours.

· GOOD ALTERNATIVES ·

France Côte Chalonnaise – this is part of Burgundy, but is frequently overlooked, despite producing good, light-weight reds especially in Givry and Mercurey.
Italy Pinot Noir from Alto Adige can have a delicious, soft cherry flavour much like the real thing, but without oak-barrel influence.
Spain Rioja Reserva (from the Tempranillo grape) at seven to ten years old develops a scented strawberry softness.
USA Pinot Noir from Oregon is light but true to type. Pinot Noir from Carneros at the bottom of the Napa and Sonoma valleys is fuller and more exciting.
Australia Pinot Noir occasionally comes up trumps in Western Australia, Victoria and in the Hunter Valley, New South Wales.
New Zealand The Pinot Noirs from the South Island may prove to be some of the most exciting New World efforts.

· BEAUJOLAIS ·

Twenty years ago Beaujolais was just a local jug wine way down in the heart of France made from the Gamay grape. Today it is a symbol of red wines that are purple-fresh and bright-eyed, to be knocked back for the pleasure of that rush of simple fruit and their complete lack of stuffy 'seriousness'. Made by a slightly unorthodox method of fermentation, akin to carbonic maceration – where the grapes are not crushed before fermentation – the wines are soft and full of colour and easy fruit flavours. They should usually be drunk as young as possible. These are the 'now' red wines, and in France, Italy and elsewhere, an increasing amount of inexpensive red wine is made like this – thank goodness.

· GOOD ALTERNATIVES ·

France Gamay de Touraine, Gamay de l'Ardèche; 'modern' Côtes du Rhône, Ventoux, Luberon, Roussillon and southern *vins de pays*. These are fresh, fruity wines usually made by carbonic maceration to be drunk young.
Italy Casteller from Trentino, Santa Maddalena and Kalterersee from Alto Adige are extremely light and gentle wines – hardly red at all. Dolcetto from Piedmont is a riot of flavours but should be wonderfully soft and gulpable.
USA Young Zinfandel from California can be fresh, very fruity and taste of pepper and blackberries in about equal proportions.
Australia Some modern Shiraz is being produced to drink young and fruity.
South Africa Young Pinotage can be like a smoky version of Beaujolais.

· WHITE BURGUNDY ·

The Chardonnay grape makes great white burgundy in a mere handful of villages lying between Chablis in the north and Pouilly Fuissé in the south, but it is the central Côte d'Or villages of Meursault, Puligny-Montrachet and Chassagne-Montrachet which are the inspiration for makers of white wine around the world. Perfect soils, perfect slopes and the judicious use of new and nearly-new charred oak barrels to mature the wine can produce something so full, so honeyed – almost luscious, yet drawn back to dryness by a savoury nuttiness – that it often seems the perfect dry white wine. The world is full of winemakers who would agree, and who are hell-bent on proving that if you can't beat 'em, at least you can try to join 'em.

· GOOD ALTERNATIVES ·

France Côte Chalonnaise makes good light burgundy. Classed growth Graves, from Sémillon and Sauvignon grapes and aged in new oak, can be brilliantly nutty and honeyed and very like top burgundy.
Italy Chardonnay from top estates in Trentino and Alto Adige, with oak barrel ageing, can produce good full wine. Chardonnays from Piedmont, Tuscany and Umbria (for example Gaja, Villa Banfi, Lungarotti) are often very exciting although still only *vino da tavola*.
Spain Old style white Rioja Reserva can be very like a solid, richly oaked burgundy. New Chardonnays from Catalonia are delicious and much closer to the 'real thing'.
USA Some Chardonnays from New York State, and especially Long Island, are very Burgundian and delicious. North-West Pacific Chardonnays can be similiar though not quite so fine. California has some marvellous Chardonnays either full and heavily-oaked, or lighter and fresher though always ripe.
Australia Many Chardonnays balance oak and fruit beautifully, though few have yet shown the same ability to age. Some oaked Sémillons are like fat burgundies and *do* age.
New Zealand These Chardonnays are lighter and less ripe, but can be good.

· SANCERRE ·

This too was an unknown country wine 20 years ago and is now a superstar. The Sauvignon Blanc is the grape responsible; it gives a tangy, dry wine, as fresh and sharp as any. It is packed with fruit, which *can* be almost green in its sting, but can also be as ripe as late summer gooseberries and blackcurrants. Freshness, however, is the key, and all over the world the Sauvignons of Sancerre have become the model for 'modern', quick-drinking, dry white wines. The alternatives are from a variety of grapes.

· GOOD ALTERNATIVES ·

France Sauvignon *vins de pays* from the Loire and Haut-Poitou; Colombard from Gascogne; Sauvignon from Côtes de Duras, Bergerac, St-Bris near Chablis; single estates in Bordeaux – all cool-fermented wines with a good green zing, to be drunk as young as possible.
Italy Pinot Bianco from Alto Adige is creamier but can be similarly fresh. Some Sauvignon wines are also made here, and in Friuli, but the results are patchy. Arneis and Cortese from Piedmont, and new-style Tuscan whites are more likely to deliver the goods.
Spain New-style white Rioja is one of the sharpest, greenest wines going. There are also some new-style whites in Penedés and Rueda.
Portugal Good quality *vinho verde*, sometimes from a single estate, can be tangy and dry.
USA Sauvignon is at its best in the Pacific North-West and New York State. Some Mendocino, Sonoma and Monterey Sauvignon is grassy and fresh, but most Napa wine is too rich, and is often sold, slightly oaked, as Fumé Blanc.
Australia Sauvignon can be highly successful in Tasmania and Victoria and occasionally in Western Australia, but cold-fermented, unoaked Sémillon is often better.
New Zealand The South Island makes some of the greatest Sauvignon in the world, though the intensely gooseberry and grassy taste can sometimes be a bit overpowering.

· GERMAN RIESLING ·

With the present flood of Liebfraumilch, we're in danger of losing sight of Germany's greatest wine achievements: Rhine and Mosel wines from the Riesling grape. These wines can be sweet or dry, but always keep at their heart a shining steely acidity and a fruity fragrance that may evoke anything from the muskiest melons and mangoes – in a wine from the southern Rhine – to the crunchy green freshness of a just-picked English Cox's apple – in a northern Mosel. To this, a suggestion of honey adds softness, producing wine which, at its best, is as close as wine ever gets to the essence of the grape itself. To be honest, the Riesling is such an individual grape that it produces different flavours almost everywhere it is grown, and outside Germany rarely achieves that remarkable blend between fruit, acidity and relatively low alcohol. Even so, here are the nearest approximations to its classic dry-to-medium style.

· GOOD ALTERNATIVES ·

France Alsace Riesling is fuller and drier than German Riesling, but as it ages it gets the same petrolly slate flavour.

Italy Pinot Grigio, Riesling Renano and Müller-Thurgau from Alto Adige, Friuli and Trentino. Although not the same, these fresh, aromatic grapes achieve the same kinds of easy-drinking effect.

USA The Pacific North-West and New York State *can* produce beautifully fragrant, slightly grapy, slightly honeyed wine, delicious when young. Californian dry Rieslings are usually a little flat.

Australia The Rhine Riesling, or 'Rhine' as it is known, makes marvellous slaty, dry wine, as well as a certain amount of 'thinking man's Liebfraumilch' when necessary.

UK Dry UK wines resemble German Trocken Rieslings. The sweeter styles can be a little more like superior Liebfraumilch.

Austria Some of Austria's best wines are the dry Rieslings and Müller-Thurgaus of the Donau valley.

· SAUTERNES ·

Sauternes is the greatest of natural sweet table wines, by which I mean that nothing is added to the wine to sweeten it: the richness is simply the product of intensely concentrated overripe grapes which have had their sugar virtually turned into syrup by the action of a fungus colourfully entitled 'noble rot'. For some reason this fungus prefers to suck the water out of the grapes, leaving the sugar inside ever thicker and stronger. When the wine is made, a lot of this concentrated sugar will remain after fermentation has stopped, and this causes the wine to be rich in an intense, slightly oily way, and full of a honeyed sweetness which is quite stunning, even if you swear that you don't like sweet wines. Only top properties produce wine of this class: bottles labelled simply 'Sauternes' are unlikely to inspire much purple prose. Even so, there are some wonderful sweet wines available at prices that won't entail a visit to your bank manager. Sauternes is made from Sémillon and Sauvignon grapes but the following alternatives are based on various grape types.

· GOOD ALTERNATIVES ·

France Some single-estate Monbazillac is luscious and honeyed; Graves Supérieures is an unfashionable *appellation* which just occasionally hides a lovely sweet wine; Muscat de Beaumes de Venise is different to Sauternes in its fresh table-grapy perfume, but should be similarly sweet.

Germany Beerenauslese, Trockenbeerenauslese and Eiswein from the Riesling may be unfamiliar words and unpronounceable too, but these wines can be even sweeter than Sauternes and have even more fruit.

Italy Moscato Naturale from Piedmont is grapy nectar. It isn't made like Sauternes but it's wonderfully fresh, wonderfully sweet, even slightly fizzy, and absolutely irresistible. Few other Italian sweet wines are exciting, though the Verduzzo and the Picolit grapes can produce a few in the north-east.

Australia/USA Wines marked 'botrytis-affected' or Beerenauslese from the Rhine Riesling, Sémillon or Chardonnay can be tremendously rich and luscious.

Austria The Beerenauslese and Trockenbeerenauslese of the Burgenland are some of Europe's sweetest wines.

Hungary Tokay 5 *puttonyos*, a deep raisiny slightly maderized wine style, resembles an old rather than young Sauternes.

· CHAMPAGNE ·

It is no insult to the other sparkling wines of the world to say that there is not one of them which can equal the quality of the best champagne. True champagne can come only from the province of Champagne, in northern France. The soil there is poor and mostly chalk, and the weather is gusty, damp, and frequently sunless. But this unlikely combination provides the perfect territory for the Chardonnay, Pinot Noir and Pinot Meunier grapes, which struggle through the chilly autumn to reach a hard-won ripeness. The wine they produce is raw and sharp, but when it undergoes the champagne method of creating bubbles (see page 109), it is transformed into a light, fragrant, exhilarating, golden sparkling wine which has no rivals. Even so, there are good sparkling wines made, from a variety of grapes, in a variety of places, and usually at a lower price. Not champagne, but good nonetheless.

· GOOD ALTERNATIVES ·

France Good Crémant de Bourgogne made from 100 per cent Chardonnay grapes is the best champagne alternative. Crémant d'Alsace, Saumur and Blanquette de Limoux can also be good, though with a sharper fruit since they contain little or no Chardonnay.

Italy Dry *spumante* from Lombardy, Piedmont and Trentino-Alto Adige can be like a light, dry, young champagne.

Spain Cava is not like champagne but is a good, slightly peppery sparkling wine. New wines like Raimat sparkling wine from Chardonnay are much closer to champagne in style.

USA The best champagne alternatives are from the coolest parts of the Sonoma, Mendocino and Anderson valleys, though some excellent, fuller, riper styles are also made in the Napa.

Australia Australian champagne-method wines are good though can have a little too much flavour.

UK First signs are that England can make good, though expensive, ultra-dry champagne-method wines.

· PORT ·

Port's greatest feature is its richness. No wonder its reputation was created in the chilly taverns and dining rooms of northern Europe, for no other wine has the remarkable mixture of peppery 'attack' and rich sugar-sweetness which can keep the cold out in any climate. Port can come only from the Douro region of Portugal, and the greatest are full-blooded and red, and can sting your mouth with their power. Others, gentler and lighter, lose all their scarlet fury after years of ageing in wooden casks, and become a glinting russet gold, soothingly sweet to sip and linger over, whatever the weather. There are other good, sweet fortified wines, but only madeira and some Australian wines offer similar excitement.

· GOOD ALTERNATIVES ·

Spain Málaga is sweet and raisiny and fairly strong and satisfying.

Portugal Madeira (Verdelho, Bual, Malmsey) – entirely different smoky, tangy flavours, but equally fine quality.

Australia Australia has two high quality substitutes. Her 'vintage ports' are even richer and sweeter, incredibly plummy and big. Her Liqueur Muscats from North-East Victoria are startling, intense, perfumed and exotic, the richest, grapiest Muscats in the world.

Cyprus Commandaría is a big, raisiny wine of historical importance now making a comeback.

· SHERRY ·

Spanish sherry is the best – and strictly speaking, the only true sherry; Australian and South African sherries get pretty close to it. Good sherry, whether sweet, medium or dry, has a sharp bite to it, and a slightly woody tang. Indeed, dry sherries absolutely must have this 'attack', which is caused by the action of the 'flor' yeast on the young wines; otherwise they will be bland and dull.

· GOOD ALTERNATIVES ·

France France has no equivalent to dry sherry, though the herby dry vermouths may fill the same 'aperitif' role. *Vin Doux Naturel* is a slightly solid sweet equivalent.

Spain Montilla wines are a little softer and lighter than sherry, but make a good value alternative.

Italy Virgin Marsala can be reasonably dry and appetizing. Lungarotti make a remarkable dry alternative called Solleone.

Portugal Sercial madeira has the tang of dry sherry.

Australia The best dry and sweet 'sherry look-alikes' are from Australia, where the quality of the top wines can equal Spain's.

South Africa Good medium and sweet styles, adequate dry styles.

· LAYING DOWN WINES ·

The most common reason for laying down wine is because you have bought the wine before it is ready to drink. In the distant days of zero inflation, a wine merchant could afford to finance and stock a wide range of mature wine. Nowadays, however, it is the consumer's responsibility to provide any extra ageing. The objective is different for each category of wine.

Champagne Many people like their champagne fresh and frothy. If you like it with a less aggressive bubble, with a full golden colour, and a toasty, honeyed flavour, then you should expect to lay down a non-vintage champagne for at least 12–18 months, and not drink a vintage until it is about eight years old.

Port Young port can have a fiery, peppery attack and a broad sweep of intense sugary richness. Many people like it like this, but if you want it to become smoother and milder, further maturity is a must. Vintage ports from great years need to be at least 15 years old, and 'single quinta' wines should certainly be 10 years old. Crusted port should be ready to drink about four years after bottling. Even basic Ruby port will improve for a year or two, but Tawnies, and Late Bottled Vintage wines rarely improve much.

White wines Chardonnay wines, especially from Burgundy's Côte d'Or, Australia or California, can gain a deeper nutty, buttery flavour if stored until four or five years old. German wines of Spätlese quality and upwards lose sweetness if stored but gain in character for several years. Sweet wines from Sauternes in particular, but also Graves Supérieures and the Loire get a nuttier, spicier taste when stored for anything from one year (for Graves Supérieures) to ten (for good Sauternes).

Red wines Many red wines have a surfeit of harsh tannin and rasping acidity when young. This applies in particular to wines from Cabernet Sauvignon, Syrah or Nebbiolo grapes. Though modern reds are often made to mature early, even an 'ultra-modern' wine like Beaujolais Nouveau tastes better for a few weeks' rest. 'Cru' Beaujolais are usually best at 1½–2 years old, though they will last much longer. Red burgundy is drinkable young, though often gets richer and more exciting after 3–5 years. Northern Rhône reds need a couple of years and wines like Hermitage often improve for 10–15 years. Red Bordeaux *can* be drunk young but from a single property in the Médoc, Graves or St-Emilion can improve for 3-20 years!

· IDENTIFYING WINES ·

Not long ago the shape and colour of the bottle would tell you with a fair degree of accuracy what kind of wine it contained. But now the world is awash with wines all copying someone else's bottle shape and hue. Even so, there are some rules which still generally hold true. (See below for the classic bottle shapes.)

The Bordeaux bottle

1 Dark green glass for red wine (such as claret).

2 Light green glass for dry white wine (such as Sauvignon).

3 Clear glass for medium to sweet white wine (such as Sauternes).

4 Light green and clear are both used for dry Graves – clear implies oak ageing.

5 Outside France the dark green bottle (or the same shape in brown) implies dry red – mostly from Cabernet and Merlot. Clear bottles are used for dry, white, oaky Rioja and California Sauvignon. Clear bottles are used in Italy for dry white wines.

The Burgundy bottle

It is usually in a pale olive green glass and is used throughout the Burgundy region, from Chablis to Beaujolais, for all colours of wine, as well as in the Rhône valley and much of the south of France.

1 For red wines it implies a bigger, softer style than the Bordeaux bottle.

2 World-wide, however, the shape is most widely used for white wines from the Chardonnay grape world-wide – these are generally the softest and mellowest of dry white wines.

3 The Loire valley wines, especially those of Sancerre and Pouilly Blanc Fumé use similar bottles, though the glass is a brighter green.

4 Anjou bottles (for red and white) are similar but usually have longer necks.

5 Outside France it is used for red wine in northern Spain, especially Catalonia; in Australia for some of the heavier Shiraz types and in America for Pinot Noir and some Zinfandel. Dry wines from such grapes as Sémillon and Pinot Gris and some Sauvignons may also use this shape.

The Rhine bottle

is tall and brown. When used outside Germany it indicates either a vaguely Germanic wine, as in the Laski Rieslings of Eastern Europe, the Johannisberg Rieslings and Gewürztraminers of the United States, and the Rhine Rieslings and Müller-Thurgaus of Australia and New Zealand, or a very sweet wine, as in the noble-rot-affected wines of Australia and the United States. Many English wines use this bottle.

The Mosel bottle

is tall and green; a slightly taller, thinner version is also typical of Alsace. This shape and colour is commonly used to denote light, fresh fruity wines in Italy, Spain, England, Luxembourg and Eastern Europe. Portugal often uses it for Vinho Verde as does Australia for many of its freshest Rhine Rieslings. The Loire often uses a clear glass version for rosé.

The champagne bottle

This looks similar to the burgundy bottle, but is made of heavier glass to resist the pressure; the punt is usually heavier and the glass a darker green. Although self-styled 'de luxe' champagnes come in a variety of weird bottles, this is the generally accepted shape not only for champagne but for the world's other sparkling wines (the bottles for pink champagne are the same shape but usually in clear glass).

The port bottle

This is of very dark glass with a slight bulge in the neck to catch the particularly heavy sediment of a vintage port, but only the very best ports (including the top examples from California and Australia) and a few madeiras use this shape.

The Chianti flask

Not much used, even in Chianti, these days, largely because it is expensive to make and has become associated with a cheap and cheerful image which Chianti growers wish to upgrade. Still, it is now making a comeback. Some Orvietos use a similar bottle.

Other bottles

The use of brown glass for red table wine is a typically Italian or Australian habit. The shapes are usually Bordeaux – for Chianti and many other reds in Italy, and for many Australian reds; and Burgundy – for Piedmont reds and various other full-bodied Italian styles.

These are the main bottle styles. Others include the squat Bocksbeutel flask for German Franconian wine, Mateus Rosé and some Vinho Verde, the amphora-shaped Verdicchio bottle and the 'dancing girl' bottles used for Provence rosé.

· BOTTLE SIZES ·

These can vary quite a lot. The general size for cheap wines is 70cl – though the EEC is intending to make 75cl the standard 'bottle' size – and this contains six reasonably-sized glasses of wine. However, most classier wines already come in 75cl bottles which give you

Some bottle shapes are only used for particular wines from particular regions, but there are a number of bottles which are used fairly generally round the world: *left to middle* the Bordeaux red and dry white; Bordeaux sweet; the burgundy red or white; the champagne and other sparkling wines; the hock bottle for German Rhine and other Riesling styles; the Mosel or Alsace bottle.

six rather *more* reasonably-sized glasses of wine! Half-bottles are 35cl or 37·5cl, and there are a very few 50cl bottles (Hungary's Tokay uses one). One-litre bottles are common, usually for cheaper wines, and this is the normal 'drinking wine' size in Europe. A magnum is 1·5 litres; this is generally regarded as the ideal size for maturing wine over a long period – and it also looks tremendous on a table. It will yield 12–13 glasses of wine, so is excellent for a dinner party.

There are bigger sizes – two litres which is only used for basic wines, usually Italian, and a variety of giant bottles usually with Biblical names like Jeroboam, Rehoboam, Methuselah, Salmanazar, Balthazar and Nebuchadnezzar – (these are names of the four, six, eight, twelve, sixteen and twenty bottle sizes respectively for champagne). Bordeaux also has some very big bottles – the double magnum (four bottles), the *marie-jeanne* (six bottles) and the *impériale* (eight bottles).

The half-bottle is a useful size but is not likely to be good value for money since it is almost as expensive to make, fill and transport as a bigger size. Although the one- and two-litre sizes are supposed to save you money, they don't necessarily, so do your sums before buying a bottle which may be bigger than you want. Also check the label to see if a bottle is 70cl or 75cl – you may be missing out on an extra seven per cent of wine.

· ALTERNATIVE PACKAGING ·

There are now a number of alternative packagings. None of these is aesthetically as pleasing as glass but they can be useful.

Bag-in-boxes are the most common. These are usually three litres in size and people tend to think they save you money. They are also supposed to be ultra-convenient, fitting easily into your fridge and allowing you to draw off a glass at a time. Well, they are not always cheaper – it is almost always less expensive to buy by the bottle. They may be convenient but the standard of the wine in them, though better than it used to be, is rarely exciting enough for me to want to have a constant supply on tap.

Tetrabricks those little cardboard blocks, looking like milk cartons, are a much better packaging idea, since the wine can be kept completely free of oxygen until opened. For cheap wines like Liebfraumilch and full-bodied Spanish reds, they can be extremely good; the only problem is you may squirt yourself when you open them – and you have to finish them at one sitting. Is that a problem?

Cans work well for basic wines, and 'spritzer' and wine cooler mixes.

· ANATOMY OF A BOTTLE ·

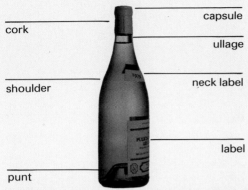

The cork Cork is from the bark of cork trees chiefly found in Portugal and around the edges of the Mediterranean. It is the most efficient form of closure for wines requiring ageing and the minute interchange of air which develops character, although modern plastic tops can provide a complete seal more efficiently.

Capsule Traditionally, and most people think ideally, made of lead, but often of tin-foil or plastic, it is to keep the cork clean, stop insects like cork weevil eating it, and help maintain moisture, stopping the cork drying out.

Ullage This is the gap between the closure and the wine. You want as small a gap as possible, because a large gap will show that the wine has begun to seep through the cork; since it will be replaced by air at a faster rate, decay will set in. Older wines have naturally more 'ullage' because the cork will eventually shrink. In general, try to choose a wine with little ullage.

Neck label Not all wines have this and it usually merely shows the vintage date and maybe the shipper's name.

Shoulder This is a typical high-shouldered Bordeaux shape. It is the easiest of all to store, since the straight sides lie tightly on top of each other. Burgundy bottles have sloping shoulders.

Label This should tell you all the necessary information concerning the wine. It varies with the type of wine and from country to country (numerous examples are shown on the next four pages). There may also be a back label with additional information.

Punt This indentation in the bottom of the bottle is to catch sediment. Since few cheap wines have sediment, many of them are in bottles without punts.

Middle to right
The Chianti flask; the Verdicchio amphora; the sherry bottle; the vintage port bottle; Franconian Bocksbeutel and Portuguese flask.

· READING THE LABEL ·

Château Léoville Barton (France)

a The vintage – 1982 was a classic in Bordeaux.
b The wine-producing property. 'Château', means castle but in Bordeaux applies to any vineyard with some buildings attached.
c The classification of this château. The top properties of the Médoc, Graves and Sauternes were classified in 1855. Léoville Barton is a Deuxième Cru Classé (Second Classed Growth).
d St-Julien is a leading Haut-Médoc commune.
e *Appellation contrôlée* – the French method of guaranteeing the origin of the wine.
f The name of the company owning this château.
g Meaning 'bottled at the château'. Obligatory for Cru Classé wines in the Haut-Médoc.
h The contents.

Beaune Clos des Mouches (France)

a The producer's name, in this case a leading merchant house.
b The village name. Beaune is the largest wine-producing commune in Burgundy's Côte d'Or.
c The *appellation contrôlée*.
d The vineyard name. 'Clos' means that the vineyard is enclosed by a wall. Clos des Mouches is a Premier Cru but, although allowed to, Drouhin does not use the title on the label.
e Meaning the crop of a single estate.
f The bottler.
g The contents.

Bollinger Brut 1976 (France)

a The wine type – champagne does not need to include *appellation d'origine contrôlée* on the label, though some companies do.
b The producer's name.
c The wine style. Brut is the second driest of the generally available styles. There are a few speciality ultra-dry champagnes called 'Brut Zéro' and so on.
d The vintage. Wine from a single year. Most champagne is a non-vintage blend.
e The village name. Ay is a small, high-quality village near Epernay.
f The code number indicating the status of the producer. 'N.M.' means *négociant-manipulant* – a merchant who has also created the wine by the champagne method in his own cellars.

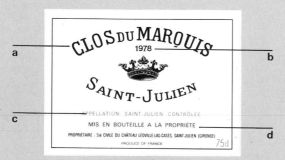

Clos du Marquis (France)

a A 'created' name for the 'second wine' of Château Léoville-Las-Cases in Bordeaux. A second wine is a wine from the same vineyard as the château itself but excluded from the *grand vin* for a variety of technical reasons.
b The vintage.
c *Appellation contrôlée*. St-Julien.
d Since Clos du Marquis is not technically a château, the wine is described as bottled 'at the property'.

Sauvignon du Haut Poitou (France)

a The wine region.
b *Vins délimités de qualité supérieure*, 'delimited wines of superior quality', often abbreviated as VDQS – the middle rank of quality for French wines.
c Bottled at the property, in this case the local co-op. Use of the word 'propriété' instead of 'domaine' or 'château', often implies that a wine is bottled at the local co-operative.
d The grape variety, Sauvignon.
e The contents.
f The official stamp of the VDQS showing the wine has been tasted and officially approved.
g The address. 'C.C.' stands for *cave-co-opérative*, a co-operative cellar, 'H.P.' for Haut Poitou.

Clos des Goisses (France)

a The vineyard name. Very few champagnes are from a single vineyard but Clos des Goisses is just such a rarity – a high-quality walled vineyard bottled unblended with other wine.
b The wine name.
c The name of the company which owns Clos des Goisses and makes the wine.
d The address of the company. Mareuil-sur-Ay is a small village just to the east of the better known village of Ay.
e The code number which indicates that this is a *négociant-manipulant*, a merchant who has also created the finished product in his own cellars.
f The contents.
This is a vintage wine, but the date is shown on a neck label.

Vin de Pays du Gard (France)

a The name of the property.
b The wine name – 'Country Wine from the Gard'. *Vin de pays* (country wine) is the third level of quality control in France.
c Table wine, the bottom category, here superseded by *vin de pays*. *Vins de pays* may show both categories on the label, but the quality level will be the superior one of *vin de pays*.
d The producer's name. This 'domaine' is a member of the local co-op.
e The bottler. The wine is bottled by a merchant at Sorgues in the Rhône valley.

Kreuznacher Narrenkappe (Germany)

a The crest and name of the producer.
b The region. Nahe, a tributary of the Rhine, is one of the 11 wine regions in Germany.
c The vintage.
d Kreuznach is a leading Nahe village.
e The vineyard name – Narrenkappe.
f The grape variety. Riesling is the best German grape. If the wine is a blend of varieties, the grape names will often be omitted.
g The quality rating. This is the top rank, meaning 'quality wine with special attributes' often abbreviated as QmP.
h QmP wines are rated according to ripeness. Spätlese means 'late-picked'. The grapes are therefore fully ripe.

Barbera d'Alba (Italy)

a A pleasantly long-winded way of giving both the vintage and the winemaker's name and address.
b The winemaker's name.
c The wine name, a red from the Barbera grape in North-West Italy.
d The Italian appellation of origin.
e The site of the vineyard, in this case the Bussia vineyard just inside the Barolo area near Monforte.
f Meaning 'bottled in the zone of production'.
g This form of labelling is specifically designed for the US market. It is not necessary to specify 'red table wine' or the volume in fluid ounces for other markets.

Niersteiner Gutes Domtal (Germany)

a The village name. Nierstein in Rheinhessen (Niers*teiner* means 'from Nierstein').
b The vineyard site. This always follows the village name except in the rare occurrences where no village name is needed. Gutes Domtal is a 'Grosslage', or grouping of vineyards.
c The vintage.
d The quality rating. *Qualitätswein bestimmte Anbaugebiete*, often abbreviated as QbA – the medium quality level in Germany.
e A.P. the quality number necessary for all quality wines – showing who made it, who bottled it, who tested it and so forth.
f The region, Rheinhessen.
g The contents. 70cl is now less common than 75cl.

Alto Adige Rhein-Riesling (Italy)

a The crest and name of the producer.
b The region. A peculiarity of the Alto Adige is that labels may be in Italian, or German, or both, since the region was part of Austria.
c DOC – the abbreviation for the Italian controlled appellation of origin, *Denominazione di Origine Controlata*.
d The grape variety, in German. There is an increasing move in Italy towards labelling wines according to grape variety.

Chianti Classico (Italy)

a The name of the property.
b The type of wine – Chianti from the central and best Classico region.
c The quality level. Riserva denotes superior wine aged before release.
d Denominazione di Origine Controllata, the Italian controlled appellation of origin. Since 1984 Chiantis have been elevated to DOCG, Denominazione di Origine Controllata e Garantita.
e *Imbottigliato all' Origine da di Napoli, Rampolla*, 'bottled at the Rampolla property by the di Napoli family'.

Rioja Royal (Spain)

a The brand name.
b The bottler.
c The wine name.
d The seal showing the number of the bottler. In Rioja usually the same as the producer, so in the case of a subsidiary label being used, it allows the producer to be identified.
e The official seal of the Rioja *denominación*.
f The quality designation. Reserva shows that this is a special selection aged for a minimum of three years in barrel and bottle before release.

Sherry (Spain)

a The producing company.
b Bottled *in* and imported *from* Spain.
c The brand name.
d The wine style, a dry *oloroso*; Jerez is the Spanish name for sherry, derived from the name of the main sherry-producing town, Jerez de la Frontera.
e Produced and bottled by Pedro Domecq.

Dão (Portugal)

a The brand name. This is one of the best reds in Portugal.
b The type of wine – Dão (although the vintage is not shown here, it will be marked on a neck label).
c *Região Demarcada.* The Portuguese controlled appellation of origin.
d The wine style – red wine.
e Meaning 'bottled by'.
f The name and address of the bottler. São João is one of Portugal's finest. Anadia is in fact in neighbouring Bairrada.

Graham's Vintage Port 1980 (Portugal)

a The shipper's name. Most port is made for sale on the export market by a group of shippers with offices at Oporto and Vila Nova de Gaia. Graham's is one of the oldest houses.
b Vintage port is the product of a single year of special quality which will normally be 'declared' as such by the shipper.
c The bottling date. Vintage port must be bottled after between 22 and 31 months cask ageing. Most is bottled at around two years old.
d The shipper's trade mark.
e The contents. The 'e' means that the maker has conformed with EEC regulations regarding volume.

Taylor's 10-years-old Tawny (Portugal)

a The producer's name.
b The wine style – a tawny, matured in wood for at least ten years.
c A short description of the shipper.
d The date of bottling, important to know to gauge the wine's maturity, but frequently omitted.
e Further confirmation that the wine is matured in wood. Some less good brands will be largely matured in concrete.
f The contents.
g The alcohol level by degrees.
h Oporto, the leading town of the north of Portugal from which port takes its name.

Great Western (USA)

a Wine from a single estate, a relatively new phenomenon in New York.
b Special selection. Top of the line selection.
c The name of the producing winery and its seal.
d The vintage.
e The vineyard in which the grapes were grown.
f The geographical designation.
g The grape variety, a French-American hybrid.
h Grapes harvested late for extra ripeness.
i Description of wine. American labels usually give more description than European ones.
j Alcohol level. Eight per cent is low. Since the grapes were late-harvested ripe, this means some of the ripeness is still in the wine as unconverted residual sugar.

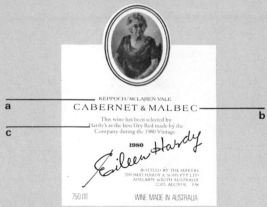

Phelps Johannisberg Riesling (USA)
a The ripeness category. 'Special Select Late Harvest' means overripe grapes, possibly affected by 'noble rot'.
b The name of the winery.
c The leading wine region of California.
d The grape variety, classic German Riesling.
e The alcohol level. This is low. Because we know that the grapes were overripe (see a), and residual sugar has been retained.

Hardy's Cabernet/Malbec (Australia)
a The two regions the grapes come from. Blending between quite distant regions for quality wines is not uncommon in Australia.
b The grape varieties. Australia also blends grapes a good deal. Cabernet is the world's leading red grape, Malbec a lesser variety particularly suited to Australia.
c Explanation of the 'top of the line' status of this wine. Australian wineries usually have a number of different selections, or 'bins' in any one vintage.

Breaky Bottom (UK)
a The vineyard name.
b The wine description - the lack of a more specific indication shows that this is probably a blend of several grape varieties. Dry means very dry normally in the UK, and in Breaky Bottom's case, very, very dry.
c The name and address of the grower and bottler.
d Country of origin.
e The contents. English wine can be in 70cl or 75cl bottles.

Opus One (USA)
a The brand name. This is the result of a historic collaboration between Robert Mondavi, a leading Napa Valley winemaker, and Baron Philippe de Rothschild, a leading Bordeaux grower and owner of Mouton-Rothschild.
b The Opus One logo showing the Mondavi profile back to back with the Rothschild profile.
c The vintage. 1979 was the first vintage.

Nobilo's Pinotage (New Zealand)
a The winemaker. Nobilo is one of the most respected producers in the north of New Zealand.
b The wine region.
c Estate-bottled.
d The grape variety – a cross between Pinot Noir and Cinsaut.
e Self-styled description of the wine.
f Vinted! I love it. A rather pretentious way of saying 'wine made by'. It is in the dictionary, but I've not seen it on any other label.

Cabernet Sauvignon (Bulgaria)
a The country. Being a fairly new wine country, the nationality is announced in bold terms.
b The grape variety. Bulgaria can be very successful with Cabernet Sauvignon.
c The vintage. Bulgarian wines are often released later than their Western counterparts.
d The producer's description of the wine – in this case fairly accurate.
e The wine region. Suhindol is particularly good for Cabernet Sauvignon.

· ENJOYING WINE ·

Enjoying a glass or two of the local red in the Basque country of the Pyrenees. Every time I see a picture like this, I long to pull up a chair with them, order another carafe and while away an hour or two far from the pressured mainstream of life.

which is which? Sure, you can. If I ask you to shut your eyes and then give you a plate of beef and a chunk of Cheddar cheese, will you have any trouble saying which is which? Or a tomato, a peach and a plum? Of course not, it's a snip! You can taste the difference between all those. Well, the flavour differences in wine are just as marked – and you *can* tell them apart if you just set your mind to it.

Are you still not convinced that you can really taste the difference between wines and make use of that knowledge to pick out the wines *you* like off a shelf? Well, let's go even further. Remember the slogan: 'Think While You Drink'. Now, you do this automatically every time you say, 'Wow, this coffee's good today', or 'Ugh, the tea's been stewed for too long'. If I said, 'Tell me *why* the coffee is better than usual', you might not be able to put it into words, but you've drunk enough coffee to recognize the difference between good and bad, even if you can't quite verbalize it.

Coffee and tea are an everyday experience for most of us. Wine may not be. Consequently we haven't built up the memory bank of good, bad and indifferent which we take for granted with our basic food and drink. But it can be built up – in two ways. First, by following the simple procedures of wine-tasting which I'll outline in just a moment. And second, by being honest with yourself. Be confident to say the first thing – *whatever* it is – which comes to mind. Only use words which mean something to you as an individual and never get involved with the high-falutin' language of wine snobbery. Root out images from familiar smells and flavours – the smells of street, office, autumn and spring, of last year's holiday and this year's garden – and from the tastes of everyday food and drink. Many of the strongest tastes in wine are very common – apples, blackcurrants, strawberries, peaches, lemons; others are more surprising and maybe more fanciful – guavas and lychees, yoghurt, coal smoke, nettles and petrol. You'll find all these words in the book and they're there because wine has no valid language of its own. Its vocabulary is borrowed from what our senses of sight, feel, smell and taste have already experienced elsewhere in life. If I get a little

Everything I believe and write about wine is passionately motivated by one thing and that alone – the conviction that wine exists solely for our enjoyment. From the cheapest bottle to the most expensive, from the rarest to the household name, there is no point in *ever* buying a bottle of wine unless your intention is to enjoy it. It is for this reason that wine snobbery and its attendant evils of over-pricing and over-acclaimed mediocrity, should always be challenged head-on; and I would have no place as a writer on wine unless what I told you was honest, constructive, and likely to lead you – and me, for goodness sake

– to flavours that we enjoy and to sensations that are fun . . . at prices that are fair.

· FLAVOUR ·

We can all taste wine and there's only one slogan to remember: 'Think While You Drink'. Being a wine expert takes practice, but so long as you can walk along a street and say, 'Ah, don't the roses in that garden smell nice, isn't the stench of garbage from that house disgusting, and that creosote!' – then you can smell the differences between different wines. Let's take it a stage further. If I give you a cup of tea and a cup of coffee, can you tell me high-flown, it's because something tells me: be true to yourself; that's what you feel – that's what you must say. So I do. I hope you will too.

· COLOUR ·

Let's *look* at the wine first. Sight is the least important element, but there is pleasure to be gained from the splashy pink red of a new Beaujolais, the cascade of bubbles and froth in a glass of champagne, or the burnished sunset gold of an old Sauternes. It is also the first test as to whether a wine is healthy. Unless it is an old wine which has thrown a sediment, it shouldn't be hazy, murky or milky. If you want, you can simply admire the colour and move on. But if you are interested – here's the best way to test colour. Only part fill your glass then tilt it above a white surface – a napkin, table-cloth, your host's laundered shirt – and peer through the wine to the white background. White wines show whether they are light and young – they have almost no colour although maybe the slightest green tinge; whether they are maturing – usually the wine deepens in colour and is something between a very light gold (for a Chablis) and a full rich gold for a hot country New World Chardonnay; or whether they are tiring – old, dry wines go deep gold and ultimately a light stale brown, though sweet wines can get very dark indeed and still be good.

Red wines also tell you quite a bit. Very young wines have a pink to purple spectrum in their 'red'. Mature wines have a gradually encroaching orange from the edge – the meniscus – of the wine, and the red itself will be lightening. Old wines which may *still* be good are considerably lighter and fading to something between orange and brown. But some wines, like Rioja, which have spent a long time in oak barrels will naturally be this colour.

· SMELL ·

The trouble with the sense of smell is that it tires quickly. But just think what life would be like if it didn't. If you don't want to see something, you shut your eyes. If you don't want to hear something, you cover your ears. So if you don't want to smell something – what

do you do? Hold your nose? So how do you breathe? If the smell sense didn't quickly tire, there would be no alternative but to endure all the smells around you *all* the time. How could people who work in abbatoirs or tanneries or chemical plants cope? They couldn't. The reason these people say, 'Oh, after a day you don't notice the stench', is that their sense of smell stops reacting to it.

This is where 'Think While You Drink' becomes important. Most of the time the sense of smell is dormant and unresponsive to all except particularly arresting smells – unless it is told to jump into action. You have to *want* to smell things for your sense of smell to perk up and transmit the astonishingly accurate signals that allow you to say: 'This smells of peach and that smells of new mown hay'. So when you get a glass of wine, just say to yourself: 'I *want* to find an aroma here. I *want* to establish some memory trace so that I understand better why I do or don't like it'. Soon it'll be second nature, but you have to start like that.

So take your glass, and swirl the wine very

Left to right **The bright red of a young Beaujolais; the browner more mature colour of a 5-year-old Chianti; rosé should be fresh pink, perhaps slightly tinged with salmon, but not orange or brown; Mosel wines are very light and slightly green in hue; champagne should have a good persistent bubble, and be pale gold to full straw gold, depending on age; sweet wines are a full luscious gold, going darker as they age; port is very dark and purple red when young, and gradually lightens through brick red to russet to tawny; sherry is very pale when dry and goes towards a deep dark brown colour as it gets sweeter.**

gently in a circular motion so that it laps about the bowl. If you're worried about spilling it all over the carpet remember, gently does it; you're not trying to imitate the whirlpool effect in a jacuzzi, only to disturb the wine so that the volatile aroma elements get agitated and rise up from the surface. It's just the same principle as, say, rubbing some herbs or flower petals between your hands to smell them better. Smells are volatile and escape into the atmosphere. You want to catch them in the

TASTING WINE

1 Look at the wine against a white background to check the colour, its intensity and its tone.

2 Swirl the wine in the glass to release the volatile aromas which constitute a wine's smell.

3 After swirling, the wine's smell will collect in the narrow mouth of the glass – that's why the best glasses do taper at the top.

4 Take a good long sniff so that you can get a really good idea of what the wine smells like – and register the first impressions.

5 At last you get the wine into your mouth! Take a reasonable mouthful (but not so much that you can't roll it around your mouth).

6 Roll it around your mouth and breath out through your nose since all the sensitive taste buds are in the nasal cavity.

The first taste of the new wine! This is an exciting moment in the wine calendar – but don't expect the wine to be at its best yet. This young Chardonnay wine is golden and cloudy because it has hardly finished fermenting and hasn't been treated and filtered. It won't be a sophisticated experience, but I wouldn't pass it up for anything, even if I do have to taste it out of a tooth glass.

top of your glass as they escape.

Now put your nose into the mouth of the glass and take a good healthy, steady sniff – don't snort as though you're in the critical stages of a catarrh bout, but don't be too dainty either. And, as aroma rises up into your nasal cavity, register the first thoughts that come into your head. Anything goes – after all it's your nose, so anything *you* smell is valid. It may be a simple smell like apples. It may be something rich like honey or rough like tar. But it may also be a memory – of a childhood beach, of the moonlit evening you first held hands with your heart's desire, perhaps a memory of panic, or pain, of celebration or sadness. Somewhere in your memory all your experiences are stored, and the most evocative sense is that of smell. Many wines remind me of people and places rather than tastes and flavours. If a wine brings back a memory, happy or sad, don't be afraid; be grateful and enjoy it. But whatever you smell, just think on it for a moment, just register it, and soon you'll be building up a new memory bank which will enable you to recognize wines, and to compare bottles long since drunk with the one you have in front of you, and that's good fun. One more thing. Some wines really don't smell of anything much. So, register that too, and buy something else next time. And now. Shall we taste? After

7 Take a few seconds to make up your mind as to what the wine tastes of – and whether you like it!

8 Yes, spit! Obviously, you're not going to do this at a party, but it's the way to stay sober when you have to taste dozens of wines.

all, that is the whole point, although we've been rather a long time getting to it!

· TASTING WINE ·

Right – up with that glass and take a good mouthful, and concentrate very hard for a moment. You *can* taste the wine, can't you. But where is the 'taste' occurring? The wine is in your mouth, sure, rolling around your tongue, but the real tasting is happening not on your tongue but in your nasal cavity again. Now you know what the wine tastes like swallow that mouthful, and try this: hold your nose – I mean it! – hold your nose and take another mouthful of wine. Now, can you taste anything at all? The flavours which were obvious a moment ago, can you find them now? I rather suspect not. So release your nose – and breathe out through it – and you *should* get a flood of flavour.

What happened is that all the aromas of the wine have been breathed out through your nasal cavity – and *that* is where we taste, not in our mouths. The tongue simply registers saltiness, sweetness, bitterness and acidity. Everything else – the difference between a plum and a peach, between chicken and cheese – is registered by those 'volatile aroma elements' rising up into the nasal cavity. So that is where we must concentrate to find flavours. Take the wine in your mouth, chew

it slightly, roll it around, all the while breathing out through your nose – and you're really smelling it in reverse. So do the same thing – any thoughts you have, any memory traces or flavours that strike you – latch on to them. This is where it pays to keep a little notebook if you're really interested so that you can note down – Médoc 1982, tastes of blackcurrants – or something like that.

Where the mouth is important is for checking out acidity and toughness. All wines must have acidity, it's getting it in balance that matters. Fruit without acidity is *very* boring: think of the difference between a cool-climate Cox's Orange Pippin and a hot-country Golden Delicious – the Cox's delicious character comes from the acidity balancing the sugar, whereas the Golden Delicious tastes like cotton wool because it hasn't enough acidity. In wines, sweet or dry, there must be acidity, and your mouth will tell you when it's just right, or when it's too sharp from under-ripe wines, or too flabby from overripe grapes.

All *red* wines must have some element of toughness too. This comes from tannic acid in the grape skins and stalks. Tannin is the same bitter element you get in tea which is too strong and which furs your gums and tongue. But without it *no* decent red wine could age more than a couple of months or develop any of the deep exciting flavours that make it special. Too little tannin and the wine seems flat and feeble, too much and it strikes you as harsh and raw. Your tongue and gums will tell you which it is. Young wines which need more age will probably have too much acid and tannin, and be difficult to taste.

The final element is the aftertaste. If you are 'tasting' rather than drinking the wine, you'll spit your mouthful out then ponder the flavour a moment to see what develops. But let's assume you're drinking it at table – a moment's pause to concentrate on what flavour remains is simply the last stage of 'Think While You Drink'. Good wines have a lovely lingering flavour which often seems to get better after the wine has been spat out or swallowed. Unready young wines – which *will* be good – also have this delicious 'finish' or aftertaste to make up for being tough in the mouth.

· THE TASTE OF THE GRAPE ·

The taste of the wine is intimately bound up with the grape variety. Here are some of the classic flavours, as well as some of the more bizarre nuances we may think we detect in more fanciful moments.

Red

Cabernet Franc Medium, blackcurrant, grassy.

Cabernet Sauvignon Dark, tannic, blackcurrant, cedar, mint.

Gamay Light to medium, strawberry, peach, pepper, going to farmyard earthiness, and Pinot-like strawberry jam.

Merlot Full, soft, blackcurrant, honey, raisins, mint, plum.

Nebbiolo Dark, very tannic and difficult to appreciate, prunes, raisins, tobacco, tar, hung game, chocolate.

Pinot Noir Middleweight, fragrant, often delicate, strawberry, cherry, plum.

Sangiovese Medium to full, tobacco, cherry stone, herbs, sometimes vegetal, raisins.

Syrah Dark, tannic, savage sometimes, raspberry, blackcurrant, plum, herbs, pepper, smoke.

Tempranillo Light to medium, strawberry, vanilla, sometimes blackcurrant, pepper.

White

Chardonnay Dry white, from light, appley and acid to full yeast, butter, cream, toast, sometimes slightly grapy.

Chenin Very dry to sweet, green apples, lemon, nuts, chalk, to apricots, peach, honey.

Gewürztraminer Fairly dry to sweet, above all spice, then tropical fruit, cosmetic perfume, freshly ground pepper.

Muscat Dry to very sweet, above all grapes, peppery yeast, eating apples to deep orange peel, treacle, raisins and toffee.

Palomino Sherry grape, very dry to sweet, from sharp, almost sour, herbs, to raisin, treacle, toffee, moist brown sugar.

Pinot Blanc Dry, apples, yeasty, cream, spice.

Riesling Very dry to very sweet, steely, slate, apple to lime, petrol, raisins, even honey and tropical fruits.

Sauvignon Blanc Very dry to sweet, green flavours, grass, nettles, gooseberry, asparagus, elderflower, going to raisin and honey though still with an acid edge.

Sémillon Dry to very sweet, green apple, lemon, lanolin, herbs, to cream, honey, nuts, peaches.

Viognier Full dry, apricot, may blossom.

· SERVING AND STORING WINE ·

It is easy to be flip about serving wine and say, 'Oh, it doesn't matter what the temperature is, what the glasses are like, so long as I can get the cork out'. That's fair enough if you're the kind of person who always buys the cheapest bottle, regardless of taste. Well, you're obviously *not* that kind of person, otherwise you wouldn't have bought this book, so since you've taken the trouble actually to *choose* a wine, it's worth giving it the best possible chance to shine.

On the other hand, don't take it all *too* seriously. Young wines can undergo a fair amount of battering and still come up smiling. You *can* serve a red wine too cold, or a white wine too warm, and still enjoy it. You can drink your Muscadet out of a toothmug and, if it makes you happy, no wine snob has *any* right to jeer. So, having got that off my chest, let's try to look at a few factors which *can* make the wine more fun and the flavours more delicious.

· STORAGE ·

Perhaps you're not into buying wine for long-term consumption, but you do want to put a few bottles aside for a special occasion or those unexpected guests; and even cheap wines – ready for on-the-spot drinking – benefit from a few days' rest when you get them home, to recover their balance. If you've got a cellar to keep them in – marvellous. If not, look around for a suitable nook – like an understair cupboard or disused fireplace – that is relatively dark, quiet, vibration-free and cool. So avoid the kitchen and radiator pipes or boilers. Some reasonable constancy of temperature is also crucial, so the loft and the garage – freezing in winter, boiling in summer – are not recommended.

Store the wine on its side to keep the corks moist: if it dries out it will shrink and let air in. Either buy a wine rack or use an old cardboard box – ideally one used for spirits with the bottle divisions still inside because the card used for these is stronger.

· TEMPERATURE ·

If you've stored the wine cool, you may need to do no more than open and pour it. But if you're not sure, here are some guidelines. Cheap white wines can often spend days in the fridge and may even taste nicer for it, while cheap fizz is all the better for being close to freezing point. But most whites prefer just a couple of hours in the fridge – ideally, upright in the door. To chill a white wine quickly, fill a bucket with a mixture of ice cubes and water – you *must* have water – put the bottle in, and it will cool down far more rapidly than in a fridge.

Red wines *can* be chilled – especially Beaujolais, Loire reds, and some of the fresh, light styles from southern France. Even so, one hour is enough. Otherwise red wines, ports, madeiras and medium to sweet sherries are best served at 'room temperature' – a term from the last century before central heating! So don't overdo it; just stand the bottle for a few hours in the dining room before you eat. In a hurry, you can always warm red wine by cupping the glass in your hand; whatever you do, don't heat it artificially on the cooker or in front of a fire because the alcohol starts to separate from the body of the wine and sabotages the flavour.

In hot weather, all wines – red or white – will taste more refreshing slightly cooler. And especially in high summer or on a picnic, you *can* even add ice cubes to a wine – so long as it's not anything special.

· GLASSES ·

Glasses should be big enough – that's the crucial thing – and thoroughly rinsed, since it is amazing how a residue of washing-up liquid hangs around and wrecks a wine's flavour. If you pour out some champagne and it doesn't bubble in the glass, the reason is probably washing-up liquid left on the surface. Champagne really shouldn't be served in those silly wide-brimmed glasses – you waste all the bubbles. Fizz is best in glasses as tall and thin as you can muster.

Although received opinion says that white wine should be served in smaller glasses than red, there's no need to take this as gospel. Good whites with lots of perfume and flavour benefit from large glasses just as much as red wines. But it is the *shape* of the glass which is most important: it must have a reasonable stem for holding it by, and a 'generous' bowl curving in towards the top. This shape has two advan-

tages; when you swirl the glass round, all the smell gets concentrated in the top – and you don't spill the wine over everything. And for both these reasons, don't fill the glass too full.

· OPENING THE BOTTLE ·

To get the cork out, cut off the capsule, wipe the bottle rim clean, and insert the corkscrew in the middle of the cork. Twist it gently down till the tip has just reached the bottom of the cork. If you're using an old-fashioned twist and pull variety, then gingerly place the bottle between your knees and pull as smoothly as possible. If you are using the 'Waiter's Friend' type with a metal clasp to provide leverage against the bottle mouth – again – apply pressure carefully: you don't want a broken cork or a chipped bottle. Ideally, buy a 'Screwpull' – a single action corkscrew: just continue turning to draw out the cork gradually and delicately. Don't use one of those 'pump-action' air-pressure devices you sometimes see around– bottles have been known to explode.

Old bottles may have crumbly corks, so need particularly careful treatment. However a little bit of cork in the wine will *not* affect the taste. 'Corked' wine is something completely different, caused by the use of an infected

cork, and you should easily recognize this foul mouldy stench. There is an implement called a 'Butler's Friend' (all these friends!) – comprising three metal prongs which can be inserted, either to remove pieces of cork, or even the whole cork if this has been inadvertently pushed into the bottle. Some very young sparkling wines or cheap table wines – particularly from Italy – have corks that won't budge. Try warming the neck of the bottle under a hot tap: this will expand the glass and soften any wax the cork may be coated in.

With champagne, the golden rule is – keep your hand over the cork as you twist it to loosen it, because it can shoot out at a hell of a rate and cause serious damage to someone standing in the way. As you feel the pressure on your hand, control it so that the cork eases out. This way you'll minimize the chances of the wine frothing all over the floor.

Many red wines do benefit from being opened for a few hours before drinking – especially young ones, because contact with the air softens them and allows their bouquet to develop. There is a school of thought which says the big Italian brutes like Barolo and Barbaresco can even benefit by being opened the day before! Hmmm. Old wines, however, are much more fragile and too much air contact may send them into a fairly rapid decline. With these, open and pour, and any 'aeration' they need will happen in the glass.

· DECANTING ·

Decanting can be good fun, but it *isn't* strictly necessary. With young wines, decanting speeds up the aeration process and looks classy. With old wines, its chief job is to separate off any sediment. To decant a wine of this type, make sure the bottle has been standing up for a couple of days, thus allowing the sediment to settle. Then place a lit candle or torch on a convenient surface and pour the wine very gently in *one single* motion with the light source under the neck of the bottle. As you near the end of the bottle, you'll see an arrowhead of sediment creeping up. Keep pouring until the arrowhead reaches the mouth of the bottle, then stop. If you've done it carefully there should only be about half a glass of wine left, but if the sediment appears with half the bottle remaining, keep pouring. Sediment isn't harmful, it just doesn't look nice. The wines most likely to *need* decanting because of sediment are mature red Bordeaux, red burgundy, northern Rhônes and vintage or crusted ports.

A variety of shapes from which you can drink your wine: *Left to right* Two different champagne flutes; a classic tasting glass; a traditional Alsace glass; a highly ornate German glass with the brown glass stem of the Rhine; a *Römer*, the traditional German *Weinstube* glass, with a green base for Mosel wine; a large burgundy glass; an excellent all-purpose shape for red or white; another all-rounder, usually associated with red Bordeaux; the Paris goblet, probably the most common of all wine glasses – OK if big enough; a port glass; a sherry *copita*, tall and tapering to capture the remarkable bouquet of a good *fino* or *oloroso*.

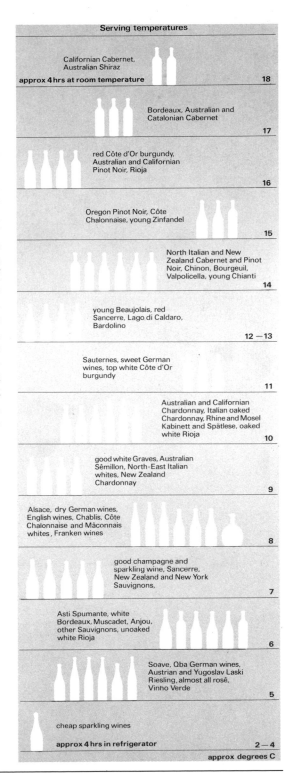

Serving temperatures	
Californian Cabernet, Australian Shiraz	
approx 4 hrs at room temperature	18
Bordeaux, Australian and Catalonian Cabernet	17
red Côte d'Or burgundy, Australian and Californian Pinot Noir, Rioja	16
Oregon Pinot Noir, Côte Chalonnaise, young Zinfandel	15
North Italian and New Zealand Cabernet and Pinot Noir, Chinon, Bourgeuil, Valpolicella, young Chianti	14
young Beaujolais, red Sancerre, Lago di Caldaro, Bardolino	12 –13
Sauternes, sweet German wines, top white Côte d'Or burgundy	11
Australian and Californian Chardonnay, Italian oaked Chardonnay, Rhine and Mosel Kabinett and Spätlese, oaked white Rioja	10
good white Graves, Australian Sémillon, North-East Italian whites, New Zealand Chardonnay	9
Alsace, dry German wines, English wines, Chablis, Côte Chalonnaise and Mâconnais whites, Franken wines	8
good champagne and sparkling wine, Sancerre, New Zealand and New York Sauvignons,	7
Asti Spumante, white Bordeaux, Muscadet, Anjou, other Sauvignons, unoaked white Rioja	6
Soave, Qba German wines, Austrian and Yugoslav Laski Riesling, almost all rosé, Vinho Verde	5
cheap sparkling wines	
approx 4 hrs in refrigerator	2 –4
	approx degrees C

· WINE AND FOOD ·

Even if you were the greatest gastronomic snob you wouldn't laugh at the sight of your grandmother, or the entire Chinese race, drinking tea with fish, or a teetotaller knocking back orange juice with cheese, would you? But tea, just like red wine, tastes of tannin (that mouth-furring, harsh taste that's particularly noticeable in strong tea) and every wine snob knows that tannic red wines don't 'go' with fish. And orange juice? It's sweet! No one who knows anything about wine would drink sweet wines with savoury foods.

Wrong. A lot of wine lore about what to drink with what has been handed down from book to mouth without anyone ever really bothering to taste the effects or try out alternatives. If *you* think red wine tastes good with Dover sole, then drink red wine. It's nobody's business but yours. Drinking and eating should be fun, and fun is doing what *you* enjoy.

But it is worth thinking as you eat *and* drink about how the flavours are blending together. Think of wine as a sort of super-sauce, and take as much care in matching it to the food as you would a sauce from the kitchen. You might say that any old sauce on a piece of dry pork is better than none, and there are plenty of possibilities. But a few sauces, especially fruity ones such as apple or prune, go especially well, while the thought of serving roast pork with custard is downright disgusting. It's just the same with wine.

Why do certain wines 'go' while others clash? It depends on all sorts of properties of the wine: fullness, fruitiness, acidity, tannin and sweetness, as well as specific flavours the wine may have from the grape variety or perhaps from the wooden barrels in which it has been fermented or matured.

Body The relative weights of the wine and food are among the first things to consider. A big, heavy wine (red or white) will swamp a delicately flavoured grilled trout, and a hefty stew will overpower a feeble Liebfraumilch. Wines from hotter regions are likely to be heavier than those from cooler climates.

Acidity is just as important, especially if the food itself, or its sauce, contains some acidity such as lemon juice, wine or vinegar. Many foods and sauces – fruits, taramasalata, salad dressings, apple sauce, mint sauce, tomatoes – contain acidity, and will make a wine with low acidity taste dull and flat. A fresh, acidic wine also makes an effective *contrast* to rich foods made with butter, oil or cream. The sharpness cuts through and counteracts fat just as vinegar makes fried fish taste less greasy.

It's not as easy as it used to be to predict which wines will have good acidity. Cooler places make naturally sharper wines, but most modern hot-country winemakers – the Australians and Californians, for instance – *add* acidity quite effectively (and legally) to give a sharper, fresher taste. Even so, you can count on finding *really* good acidity in all but the hottest years from England, Germany, Chablis, Champagne, Alsace, the Loire and the *vinho verde* region of Portugal.

Tannin has a similar cutting effect on oily dishes, especially in conjunction with acidity. It can taste very bitter, often very hard, especially in dark, young red wines. But wines that taste tooth-rottingly hard on their own without food taste remarkably softer drunk with fairly strongly flavoured food. Big, astringent central Italian reds like Chianti are a good example. Many may taste unappetizing alone, but they can be delicious with the oily, strongly flavoured local food. Milder foods are

completely overwhelmed by tannic wine, hence the traditional prohibition of red wine with fish. But not all reds are aggressively tannic. Light red wines – Beaujolais and Bardolino, for example – especially those you can drink cool, can be very good with fish.

Tannin is extracted from red grape skins, and sometimes also from the pips and stalks, as the grapes are crushed and fermented. There's rarely a tastable amount of tannin in white wines, since the juice is usually run straight off the presses, leaving the skins behind. The skins of some grape varieties contain more tannin than others – Cabernet Sauvignon, Syrah and Nebbiolo have a lot, Cabernet Franc and Gamay less, for instance. But the same grape variety will produce different amounts of tannin in different climates – more in hot countries, where the skins are baked thicker and harder by the sun and the stalks are young and soft, easily releasing their tannin if allowed into the press. Cooler places produce thinner-skinned grapes, and the stalks, too, release less tannin because they've

had time, in the long, slow ripening season, to become hard, woody and less penetrable. With time, tannin's hard effect fades, so look for an older wine, or a wine from a cooler climate if you need a soft red. Reds made by carbonic maceration (see page 100) are also low in tannin because the tannin is in the outer part of the skins, and in carbonic maceration the fermentation takes place inside the grape, with little juice outside to soak the tannins out.

Fruit Carbonic maceration wines (often Beaujolais or light Côtes du Rhône) are also a good source of reds that have plenty of fruit. All wines need fruit to taste good, and any well-made, well-stored wine that has not been kept past its peak will be fruity. Fruit becomes less vibrant as it matures, so if you want something really fruity, young wines are best. Fruitiness in an accompanying wine is especially important for savoury dishes that contain fruit in their sauce, duck with orange or cherry sauce, roast pork with apple sauce, lamb stuffed with apricots and so on. It's also important with savoury dishes sweetened in some other way,

perhaps with honey, sweet cider or sweet wine. Mature wines with subdued fruit will simply taste dull with these dishes, and dull wines will taste even duller.

Sweetness is more difficult to match with really sweet dishes, puddings and desserts. You have to match the level of sweetness fairly accurately; if the wine is sweeter the pudding will taste as if it was made for a weight-watcher; if the pudding is sweeter, the wine will taste dry and dull or tart. A German or Austrian Spätlese or Auslese, though sweet, is rarely sweet enough for the sweet course. A Beerenauslese or Trockenbeerenauslese, a sweet Loire wine such as Quarts-de-Chaume or Bonnezeaux from a good year, or a Sauternes, or a fortified Muscat such as Muscat de Beaumes-de-Venise, is more likely to get it right.

Surprisingly, sweet wines also go very well with the contrasting salty-tangy flavours of a lot of cheeses, especially Sauternes' traditional partner, the sharp, salty, blue-veined Roquefort, but try it and see how good it is with traditional English cheeses – Cheshire, Lancashire or Cheddar.

· MATCHING THE FLAVOURS ·

So much for how the wine's basic components influence its matchability with food. Its flavour is very likely to be a deciding factor, too. Most winewriters receive letters now and then from scornful readers to the effect that 'wines smell and taste of grapes, so what's all this twaddle about asparagus, gooseberries, blackcurrants and herbs?' But some wines genuinely *do*

remind people of other food smells and flavours: blackcurrant, green peppers and herbs for Cabernet, gooseberries or asparagus for Sauvignon Blanc, for instance, (see 'The Taste of the Grape' on page 46 for other examples) and matching closely associated flavours of this sort can work really well. Other, less directly associated flavours also seem to reflect and bring out the best in each other: lamb tastes wonderful with Cabernet Sauvignon, as does game with the 'rotty' flavours of a good Pinot Noir (like old burgundy). Herbs such as dill, thyme and rosemary need a highly aromatic wine to stand up to them. A 'petrolly' maturing Alsace Riesling tastes good with dill sauces, which taste awful with most other wines.

Another hard-to-match category is smoked food. The aromatic tang of smoked food makes a good match for oaky white wines – expensive burgundies, old-style white Riojas, or oaky Californian or Australian wines, for instance. It can sometimes taste good with the more aromatic grape varieties, such as Gewürztraminer or even with a good cru Beaujolais. And

surprisingly, sweet wines blend wonderfully with smoky flavours – Sauternes makes an absolutely delicious combination with smoked Austrian cheese, and a slightly sweet German Kabinett from Rheinhessen or Rheinpfalz is an excellent match for smoked eel.

Just a few foods fairly consistently clash with wines, and give rise to finger-wagging in the wine books: never drink wine, they say, with chocolate, especially the bitter, darker types, never with dressed salad, citrus fruits, ice cream or curries. It's true that such very strong or mouth-numbing flavours would overpower most wines, and it would certainly be a shame to choose an expensive wine and then taste nothing but chocolate or vinegar. But it's perfectly possible to find cheap or modestly-priced wines to make a pleasant combination.

Chocolate dishes taste scrumptious with wines made from the Muscat grape (Samos Muscat, Muscat de Beaumes-de-Venise, Asti Spumante and Australian sweet Muscats for instance), wines with high acidity (such as the slightly sweeter styles of English wines) can cope with dishes containing vinegar and citrus

fruits. Ice-cream literally numbs your taste buds, but a strongly flavoured wine, especially a fortified one like madeira, can pierce the cold – and is all the better if you eat slowly enough for your tongue to warm up a little between mouthfuls. Match the wine's flavour and acidity to the ice-cream as closely as possible. Curries *are* more problematic with their longer-term numbing and burning effects. Water and beer make less intoxicating fire-extinguishers – milk or *lassi*, a thin yogurt, are also antidotes to chillies and spice. Or this may be the moment to drink up bad buys, or old lay-about bottles, while your senses are dulled.

Less powerful foods can be spoilt by poor wines, however. (Disappointing bottles come expensive as well as cheap.) With very fine wines, the traditional advice is to eat good but very plain food – such as rare roast beef or plain roasted chicken. That's perhaps the best advice for really old, mature wines, whose flavours are often subtle and disappear fast. But if the wine isn't so frail, there's no reason why you shouldn't use a more complicated dish to show off a fine wine if you really match the food and wine well.

· COOKING WITH WINE ·

Wine is almost as exciting an addition to the kitchen as it is to the glass on the dining table. It can be used in all sorts of ways.

● Marinading raw meat (covering it with wine, a little olive oil and herbs and perhaps onion and garlic, and leaving it to soak for about six hours or overnight) leaves it tender and infused with flavour, and you can cook the meat in the marinade liquid.

● 'Deglazing' makes a delicious and impressive 'instant' sauce or gravy: simply splash in a little wine to the pan or roasting tin in which the meat has been cooked, and boil it vigorously as you scrape off the solid bits with a wooden spoon. (You may need to pour off any fat before serving.)

● Used as a cooking liquid, perhaps mixed with water or stock, wine can be cooked briefly so that the food and sauce retain the wine's distinctive flavour, or simmered with the food for ages to make a rich, full-bodied sauce.

● Wine might not need cooking at all – it can

be poured neat over fruits, ices or sorbets, or frozen into the sorbets themselves.

You can enjoy most wine-cooked dishes even if you're strictly off the booze, since the alcohol quickly boils off in the cooking. Any subtly aromatic qualities in the wine will also be off and away on the kitchen air with few minutes' heating. So if you're after a specific wine flavour, short cooking is essential, unless you've a big bruiser of a wine like Madeira or a good *oloroso* sherry, and even they will lose a lot of their flavour with really long boiling.

Most of the wine's other constituents simply become concentrated as the water evaporates. (Between 80 and 90 per cent of any wine is water.) The acidity concentrates along with the rest, so beware of acidic wines in dishes where the volume of wine will be greatly reduced during the cooking. A whole bottle's worth of refreshing acidity can taste mouth-puckeringly sour in a few spoonfuls of sauce.

Wine merchants' 'cooking wine' can be a cook's ruin for just this reason. More often than not, the merchant has demoted it because it has turned vinegary. Or because it has developed a faulty or unclean flavour. Who wants a filthy or vinegary sauce? If it's just a bit tired and fruitless, fine. It will do for recipes that call for long boiling, and need no fruit or aroma from the wine.

Your own wine dregs, kept in a nearly empty bottle, will soon turn to vinegar, too. Most wines will keep well enough like this for a week or more, but they'll keep longer if you tip them into a smaller bottle, and indefinitely if you boil out the alcohol and freeze them. (Wine won't freeze properly with the alcohol left in because alcohol has a low freezing point.) Freeze it in the ice cube tray, then transfer the wine cubes to a freezer bag or box. That way, you can use a little at a time, in perfect condition.

· PLANNING A MEAL ·

There's no need to serve a different wine with every course. Changing glasses or urging slow drinkers to drain their dregs before a wine change can be tiresome, and you may end up with expensive left-overs. It simplifies matters to use one wine to bridge two or more courses.

As with the successive dishes in a menu, it's generally best to progress from light to heavy flavours in the wines you serve. A fine white burgundy is likely to taste weedy after a full-flavoured Australian Chardonnay, even if it happens to be a better wine. The bitter effect of tannin can linger as you drink subsequent wines, and sweetness is nearly as difficult. Really sweet wines can make the wine and food that follow taste dull. This means that the logical order is usually white or rosé before red, light red before heavier reds, dry before sweet. But rich, flavoursome whites can easily follow many lighter, barely tannic reds. However, acidity in a wine drunk at a meal rarely lasts more than a few mouthfuls into a later course.

Aperitifs The French custom of serving sweet aperitifs such as port is a strange one, although a *little* sweetness with pre-eats does no harm. A splash of a fruit liqueur (*crème de cassis, framboise* or *mûre*) in still or sparkling white wine is a delicious way to disguise an unexciting wine, and tastes really refreshing if the wine has good acidity. Alsace and German wines make good aperitifs, too, especially Kabinetts – and they go remarkably well with cheesy or smoked nibbles. Any dry or dryish white, rosé, light red or dry sherry is refreshing as an aperitif, especially chilled.

Starters The advantage of a light, dry wine before the meal is that it can carry through to the starter if you choose. Or you might change to something else fairly light and fruity.

Most fishy starters go well with any light white wine with good acidity, and fried fish starters such as whitebait or scampi are in special need of acidity to counteract their greasiness, as is a prawn cocktail, since its sauce contains oily mayonnaise as well as sharp tomato paste and lemon juice. Crab, with its rich meat, tastes good with a fuller, richer white such as white burgundy or Australian or Californian Chardonnay. Some difficult fishy starters to match are smoked salmon, which goes well with oaked Chardonnay or champagne; *gravad lax* (sweet-salty salmon with the strongly flavoured herb dill and a sweet, dill and mustard-flavoured mayonnaise), whose sweetness and sharp pungent flavour is a good match for a Vouvray demi-sec; and caviar,

salty in flavour and oily in consistency: many wines would clash, but champagne seems to stand up to the strong, fishy-salty flavours. (Even so, chilled vodka is best.)

Most pâtés and terrines need a wine with good acidity, as do pasta dishes, which are usually prepared with olive oil. Fruity reds with good acidity (such as Beaujolais, a light Zinfandel or Dolcetto) may be a good choice. Chardonnays go well with the flavour of mushroom dishes, Sauvignons with onion flavours, and a cheaper Sauvignon, perhaps Sauvignon de Touraine or Sauvignon du Haut-Poitou, can cope with some problematic vegetable flavours – artichokes, avocados and asparagus – which mix unattractively with many wines.

Fish Most fish has a delicate flavour, and can be overpowered as easily by a big, fat wine as by an over-flavoured sauce. A few fishes – herrings, mackerel, sardines – have an oily flesh, and they, as well as fried non-oily fish, can take a light or a fuller wine, preferably with good acidity to counteract the oiliness.

You'll need to take the flavour and richness of any sauce into account, too. There's nothing to stop you serving gently chilled light red wines with fish, but the tannin in medium bodied or full reds is usually overpowering.

Meat The fullness of the wine you choose depends very much on the intensity of flavour of the meat and its sauce. For a casserole or sauced dish, look at the ingredients, and check especially for acidity (from cooking wine, tomato or fruit) or sweetness (from wine, cider, fruit, honey or whatever). You'll need to match acidity in the dish with an appropriately sharp wine, while a sweet or fruity dish will need a young wine bursting with fruit. *Coq au vin*, for instance, with wine acidity in the sauce, needs an accompanying wine with good acidity, perhaps a red burgundy or a Cabernet from Anjou. Pork with prunes would need a very fruity yet acid wine such as a cru Beaujolais to match the prunes and counteract the fattiness of the pork. With a really gooey dish like oxtail, firm tannin helps the wine's acidity

to clear the palate: a well-made Chianti or Vino Nobile would cope.

A few meaty flavours are a perfect match for certain grape varieties. Lamb with Cabernet Sauvignon from Bordeaux or elsewhere; well-hung game with red burgundies; duck and chicken with Chardonnay – choose one with good acidity for fatty duck or fried chicken.

Vegetables and vegetarians Unless you are feeding vegetarians, you will probably serve the vegetables along with the meat and prefer to match the wine to the meat, but bear in mind any acidity or fattiness in the vegetable dishes. If catering for a vegetarian among carnivores, choose a dish that will go with the meat-eaters' wine. If the dish contains cheese, you might match the wine to that (see below). Egg dishes go well with light, fruity reds or medium-full to full whites.

Cheese Matching cheese to wine is not as easy as you think. In fact, some of the traditional pairings taste horrible: Cheddar and claret simply clash, while Stilton can make some less

than vintage quality ports taste spirity and flat. Claret and other Cabernets with their grassy, herby flavours actually clash with most cheeses, though they taste reasonable with some – Chaume, Roquefort and goat's cheese, for instance. Mature red burgundy, because of its acidic and savoury overtones, is more successful with cheeses, from Brie to Cheddar to goat to Reblochon; but mature red burgundy is expensive, and since the cheese will flatten out the wine's flavour you might prefer to keep them separate. It can be a good though pricy choice if you are serving a wide selection of cheeses, and it is especially good with Brie and Camembert, which are difficult flavours with most wines.

But, interestingly, although many people automatically associate cheese with red wines, *white* wines are often a better match, especially if they have a bit of sweetness. Sweetness is a good foil for the saltiness. Chardonnays and Gewürztraminers, for example, actually match more cheeses than

Chianti, claret or Châteauneuf-du-Pape. Perhaps the best matches are the really sweet wines with added pungency of noble rot. Sauternes tastes wonderful not only with its traditional match of Roquefort, but with smoked cheeses, too; it's pretty good with Cheshire and Cheddar, and goes quite well with a range of other cheeses. Madeira is also an excellent cheese match, and especially wonderful with strong veined cheeses like Blue Cheshire and Shropshire.

Puddings and desserts An important guideline for sweet wines is that they should be slightly sweeter than the food they are to accompany. Most fruity or citrus puddings need wines with acidity – a sweet Loire or a German wine will guarantee good acidity. The flavours of peaches, pears or *crème brûlée* go beautifully with Sauternes. Almond and chocolate dishes are delicious with wines from the Muscat grape, and sparkling Moscato d'Asti Spumante will give them an extra refreshing lift at the end of a long meal.

· CHECKLIST ·

STARTERS
Soups fino sherry; dry madeira
Mixed hors d'oeuvres dry white; champagne; good sparkling white
Fruit sweet port, madeira or sherry
Egg dishes dry, medium-full white; fruity red
Dressed salads dry, astringent white
Pâté/terrine fruity red with good acidity; medium-full white
Foie gras vintage champagne; sweet white
Smoked fish oaky or aromatic white; dry sparkling white; chilled fruity young red
Shellfish light, high-acid white
Pasta vigorous, young red or light, astringent white, according to sauce
FISH
Plain fish dry white; chilled fruity young red
Fried fish dry, astringent white
Sauced fish dry white, match body to sauce
Seafood dishes dry, medium-full white
MEAT
Roasts fine, full red
Grills young red with body
Poultry dry, medium-bodied white with good acidity; fruity, bright young red
Game aromatic, flavourful red
Spicy dishes full, astringent, tannic red; soft spicy oaked red
Rich casseroles full-bodied red, fruity or acidic according to sauce flavour (richer sauces need a fruitier wine)
Cold meats full, aromatic white; young, light red; dry rosé
CHEESES
Soft/cream/fresh medium-full red or white
Blue-veined sweet dessert wine; sweet *oloroso* sherry; ruby port
Semi-hard full, acidic red
Hard dry, full-bodied white; for strong, matured cheeses, sweet dessert wine; port; *oloroso* sherry
Smoked sweet dessert wine; aromatic full-bodied white
Matured goat dry, medium-full white; sweet dessert wine; madeira
DESSERTS
Fruit dishes sweet white with good acidity
Chocolate strong, sweet dessert wine; fortified wines, preferably grapy
Ice-cream sweet sherry or madeira; sparkling Muscat white
Rich puddings demi-sec champagne; sweet sparkling white
Pancakes sweet sparkling white

· VINTAGES ·

A 'vintage' is the term for the year in which the grapes used in a wine were harvested. Vintage guides are only relevant to wines which have personality and individuality – to the top five or ten per cent of any country's produce. The majority of the wine we drink is made in ultra-modern 'factory-wineries' where ordinary grapes are expertly processed into a consistent product, designed for quick consumption with the minimum of fuss and the maximum of pleasure.

Even so, let's try a few basic guidelines. Since the winemaker requires ripe healthy grapes, there must be sunlight and warmth; consequently the warmer parts of the world – Southern Europe, California, South America and mainland Australia – have more consistent vintages. But often their most applauded vintages are when they got *less* sun than usual, and consequently the grapes didn't overripen on the vine. The cooler parts of the wine world – New Zealand, Tasmania, New York State, and Europe from around Bordeaux and Burgundy northwards – are the exact opposite: in many years, a desperate shortage of sun prevents the grapes from ripening at all.

And yet within this overview there are always little microclimates and other variables – like soil – which make it difficult to give a general assessment of a vintage's quality. If I say 'Bordeaux 1982 is outstanding' all I mean is that the weather patterns were highly favorable in that year and the potential for great wine was particularly marked. But the best vineyard sites will always make far better wine than the less privileged sites; a conscientious vineyard manager will deliver better grapes to the winery than a lazy one; a talented winemaker will make better wine than a careless one. And so it goes on.

However, the good thing is that although *I* am forced to rate a vintage and risk the brickbats from anyone who disagrees with me, *you* can have it both ways. If you agree with me – splendid, it's always nice to have one's opinions confirmed. And if you *don't* agree with me – then you have the perfect excuse to try all kinds of bottles and argue and discuss at length. I'm only providing the broadest of guidelines, to steer you away from the bad bottles and towards the good.

· READING THE TABLES ·

The 1–10 rating indicates the quality of any given vintage: '1' would be unspeakably feeble, '10' wonderfully memorable and long-lasting. Today, modern viticulture ensures that no vintage is ever a complete disaster, making '4' about the lowest mark normally scored; and there are always some good wines in a 4/5-rated vintage – though they may be a little light. In 6/7-rated vintages, there are many lovely wines but falling just short of the highest class. Vintages rated 8/9 have a high concentration of exciting wines.

Not ready (NR) reds are still likely to be rather tough and fierce, because their tannins and acidities take time to soften.

Just ready (JR) good examples are already delicious to drink, but should get even better in a year or two.

At peak (AP) the wine realizes all its potential and gives you the greatest possible pleasure.

Past best (PB) in general, losing fruit and personality from now on (but some wines will still be good).

· BORDEAUX ·

Red Bordeaux holds a position of such overriding importance in wine-lovers' minds that frequently a vintage is judged *worldwide* on how it did in the Médoc, Graves and St-Emilion. Burgundy, in particular, is frequently tarred with the Bordeaux brush. This is clearly absurd and can be most unfair to other wine areas in years like 1980, when red Bordeaux was initially – and wrongly – written off as a washout, while Sauternes was fairly good, red burgundy and vintage port did well, and both Australia and California registered superb vintages. Conversely, 1982 was outstanding for red Bordeaux and so Sauternes, Burgundy, the Loire, Germany and Portugal all received undue reverence.

The basic wines of Bordeaux are less subject to meaningful vintage variation than the major wines; so the following marks, and the suggested readiness of the wine, are most useful when applied to the leading wines of each area. By this I mean the Classed Growths and main 'Bourgeois' Growths in the Haut-Médoc, Graves and Sauternes, and the top 50 or so properties in Pomerol and St-Emilion. Remember, these *are* generalizations. Lesser wines will mature correspondingly faster and fade faster too. Some properties always excel in poor years, some blow it in excellent years.

RED	86	85	84	83	82	81	80	79	78	77	76
Northern Haut-Médoc esp. Pauillac, St-Estephe, St-Julien	8NR	8NR	6NR	8NR	10NR	7NR	6JR	7JR	9JR	4AP	6AP
Southern Haut-Médoc esp. Margaux	7NR	8NR	5NR	9NR	8NR	7NR	5AP	7AP	8JR	4PB	5AP
Graves	7NR	8NR	6NR	9NR	9NR	8NR	6AP	7AP	8JR	4AP	6AP
St-Emilion/Pomerol	9NR	10NR	3NR	8NR	10NR	6JR	5AP	7AP	7AP	4PB	7AP
WHITE	**86**	**85**	**84**	**83**	**82**	**81**	**80**	**79**	**78**	**77**	**76**
Graves (dry)	6NR	7JR	7JR	8AP	6AP	7AP	4PB	8PB	7PB		
Sauternes	9NR	6NR	4JR	10NR	5AP	6JR	6AP	5AP	4AP	8AP	

· BURGUNDY ·

Burgundy is more difficult to generalize about than almost any other region. Unlike Bordeaux where most single properties are substantial, the units of production here are so tiny and fragmented that a grower may often own half-an-acre or less in numerous different villages. If he is good, then all his wines may be good. His neighbour can possess the same ragbag of plots but be a ne'er-do-well, so his wines will be duff. When we go into a shop, how are we to tell which is which on the shelf?

There is another complication: the *négociants*, or merchants, who control much of the production. In a good vintage they'll simply buy wherever they can find wine, often regardless of quality. Their objective has always been to provide a consistent product in reasonable quantities, which means that with all but the best of them, the shading of different producers' talents, and different villages' personalities, has been blurred in the name of expedience. Burgundy is a minefield. There is much fine white burgundy about although it is wildly overpriced. There is desperately little great red burgundy, since the Pinot Noir grape needs cosseting, and only a committed minority of winemakers are prepared to wear themselves out on the challenge.

RED	86	85	84	83	82	81	80	79	78	77	76
Côte de Nuits	6NR	10NR	6JR	7NR	**6AP**	3AP	**6AP**	5AP	8AP	2PB	**7AP**
Côte de Beaune	5NR	9NR	5JR	7NR	**6AP**	3PB	**6AP**	6AP	8AP	2PB	**6AP**
Beaujolais Crus	6JR	10JR	**5AP**	**8AP**	5PB	**7AP**	4PB	7PB	**9AP**	3PB	9PB
WHITE	86	85	84	83	82	81	80	79	78	77	76
Chablis	8NR	7JR	6JR	**8AP**	**6AP**	**8AP**	4AP	5PB	**8AP**	3PB	6PB
Meursault, Montrachet Puligny-Montrachet	9NR	8NR	6JR	7JR	**7AP**	5AP	4AP	**7AP**	8AP	3PB	6PB
Pouilly-Fuissé	9NR	8JR	**5AP**	**8AP**	6PB	7PB	4PB	6PB	8PB	2PB	5PB

· CHAMPAGNE ·

Most champagne is non-vintage. This used to mean it was a blend of several years created to achieve a consistent 'house' style. Nowadays the blend is normally based on the lighter wines from a single vintage with, if you're lucky, a splash or two of something more mature to add interest. Champagnes are mostly released very young and will always benefit if you keep them for at least a few more months.

Vintage champagne is 'declared' in the best years. It is fuller in style, more exciting and more balanced. Most years will improve by ageing for up to eight years or more, though fresh, bright years, like 1982, can reach their peak at five years. Blanc de Blancs wines do reach their peak more quickly than wines based on black grapes, but still age extremely well.

	86	85	84	83	82	81	80	79	78	77	76
Champagne	7NR	9NR	2NR	8NR	7JR	7JR	4JR	**8AP**	**7AP**	4PB	**6AP**

· LOIRE ·

Most modern Loire wine is for drinking within a year or so of the vintage. Almost no Muscadet, and few Sauvignon-based wines will improve beyond that. However the Chenin grape – in various Anjou appellations and Vouvray – can make wine which positively demands ageing since it is so tart to start with. The great sweet wines rarely show their true colours before a decade has passed. The red wines from the Pinot Noir at Sancerre are quickly ready, and rarely last; but the Anjou and Touraine wines based on Cabernet Franc, although drinkable young, can age for 10–20 years in the best vintages.

WHITE	86	85	84	83	82	81	80	79	78	77	76
Muscadet	9JR	**9AP**	**7AP**	6PB	6PB	7PB	5PB				
Sancerre	8JR	**6AP**	**7AP**	6PB	5PB	8PB	4PB	5PB	9PB		
Sweet Anjou and Vouvray	6NR	10NR	4NR	9NR	7NR	5NR	4JR	6JR	**5AP**	2PB	**8AP**
RED	86	85	84	83	82	81	80	79	78	77	76
Cabernet (Bourgeuil, Chinon)	9NR	4NR	8NR	7JR	**6AP**	3PB	5PB	8AP		2PB	**10AP**
Sancerre	9JR	**5AP**	**8AP**	**7AP**	6PB	3PB	5PB	8PB		3P	8PB

· RHONE ·

There is a major divide between the northern and southern Rhône. The north is primarily a red wine country, using the Syrah to make long-lasting, impressive, but often difficult wines which frequently need 10 years of ageing; even at the lower levels of Crozes-Hermitage and St-Joseph, they benefit from 3–5 years. White Hermitage *can* last even better than red, although the Viognier-based Condrieu should always be drunk young. The southern Rhône is a vast grape-basket, mostly employing quick maturing red grape types like Grenache and Cinsaut; only the occasional Châteauneuf-du-Pape, Gigondas or exceptional Côte du Rhône-Villages, with Syrah and Mourvèdre blended in, will benefit from more than 2–3 years' ageing.

RED	86	85	84	83	82	81	80	79	78	77	76
Hermitage	7NR	9NR	5NR	10NR	7JR	4JR	**7AP**	**6AP**	10JR	3PB	**7AP**
Côte Rôtie	7NR	9NR	4NR	9NR	7JR	4JR	**6AP**	**6AP**	9JR	3PB	**6AP**
Châteauneuf-du-Pape	7NR	8NR	6NR	7JR	**5AP**	4AP	**6AP**	6PB	**8AP**	5PB	7PB
WHITE	86	85	84	83	82	81	80	79	78	77	76
Hermitage	7NR	8NR	6JR	9JR	8NR	6JR	6JR	7JR	9JR	**4AP**	7PB

· ALSACE ·

Alsace wines are delicious young but can age surprisingly well. There is now an increasing trend to allow 'noble rot' to develop on the grapes and make special 'late-harvest' selections. These are frequently not at their best for at least five years and may peak at 10–15. You will notice two marks of 10. 1983 is famous for its high-priced 'late-harvest' wines. 1985 is quite different – the 10 rating is given because the pure fresh beauty of Alsace fruit is unparalleled in 1985 – and it's affordable too.

	86	85	84	83	82	81	80	79	78	77	76
Alsace	8NR	10JR	5JR	**10AP**	5PB	**7AP**	4PB	7PB	5PB	3PB	9PB

· GERMANY ·

The vast majority of German wine doesn't benefit from any ageing at all and wines like Liebfraumilch and Niersteiner Gutes Domtal should be drunk just about as fast as you can get them open. However, there are a few wines at the top-quality level of Qualitätswein mit Prädikat which do age. Kabinetts will mature most quickly, often at 2–3 years old, followed by Spätlese, at 3–5 years, Auslese at 3–7, Beerenauslese at 5–15 and Trockenbeerenauslese at 7–20. Whatever quality level you possess, a little ageing of these wines will almost always make them more enjoyable.

	86	85	84	83	82	81	80	79	78	77	76
Mosel-Saar-Ruwer	6NR	8JR	**4AP**	9JR	**4AP**	5AP	3PB	5PB	4PB	3PB	8PB
Rheingau	5NR	7JR	**3AP**	10JR	**5AP**	6AP	3PB	5PB	4PB	3PB	**10AP**
Rheinhessen	6NR	7JR	**4AP**	9AP	**6AP**	6AP	4PB	6PB	5PB	4PB	**10AP**

· ITALY ·

If you are surprised that only four wines figure in a vintage chart for Italy, the world's largest producer, it is simply because the vast majority of Italian wines don't benefit from ageing, are made in the climatically consistent centre and south of the country, or are made in such small quantities that we never see them on the export market. Even in the four groups below, there is as yet little consistency of production standards: some Chianti Classico is made to be drunk within the year, while other wines valiantly strive to age for 10. In general don't overage Chianti, don't underage Barolo – and don't overpay for Brunello.

	86	85	84	83	82	81	80	79	78	77	76
Barolo	9NR	9NR	3NR	8NR	9NR	4NR	6JR	7JR	8JR	3PB	**6AP**
Brunello	8NR	9NR	3NR	9NR	8NR	6NR	5NR	6NR	8NR	8JR	3PB
Chianti Classico	9NR	9NR	4JR	8NR	8JR	**5AP**	4PB	6PB	7PB	6PB	2PB
Amarone	7NR	10NR	4JR	8NR	5JR	**AP**	**7AP**	8JR	9JR	**8AP**	4PB

· SPAIN ·

Spain has very few wine areas which are as yet sufficiently uniform or quality-orientated to make ageing a fruitful exercise. Most vineyards are in hot areas, controlled either by agricultural co-operatives or big blending merchants. Rioja Reserva is generally released ready to drink, and, though it may well last a number of years it rarely improves all that much. Penedés is potentially an exciting quality area which may produce a wide range of highly individual wines. This chart applies to the top wines only.

	86	85	84	83	82	81	80	79	78	77	76
Rioja Reserva	7NR	8NR	3NR	7JR	8JR	**6AP**	**5AP**	**6AP**	**7AP**	3PB	**7AP**
Penedés Red	6NR	8NR	5NR	6JR	8NR	8JR	9JR	**7AP**	**9AP**	**6AP**	**7AP**
Penedés White	**7AP**	**6AP**	**9AP**	6PB	8PB	9PB	7PB	6PB	8PB	6PB	7PB

· PORTUGAL ·

For Portuguese table wine, the general rule is that you should drink the whites as young as possible, whereas the reds, so long as you like their strong, assertively dry style, can age well for some time. Vintage port is more dependable. A house will 'declare' a vintage and set aside its best wines to bottle as such. Lesser years can produce delicious Single Quinta wines – lighter, but still with much of the smouldering brilliance of true vintage port – and it is often at its peak at only 10 years old. There is no vintage chart for madeira since it is almost always sold as a blend – and they don't even decide which years to declare a vintage till the wines are over 20 years old!

	86	85	84	83	82	81	80	79	78	77	76
Red Dão	4NR	8NR	6NR	9NR	4JR	4JR	7JR	**5AP**	**6AP**	**5AP**	**8AP**
Vintage port	6NR	7NR	4NR	9NR	7NR	4NR	8NR	5JR	6JR	10NR	**5AP**

· ENGLAND ·

Vintage matters a great deal in England, because the vineyards are so far north that the grapes may not ripen at all. However, the last few years, against all the odds, have been good. There are two distinct styles of wine: the 'Germanic' style wines – with a 'Süssreserve' of unfermented grape juice blended into the wine to provide fruit and some sweetness – are usually ready to drink in 1–2 years; the 'new English' style ones, dry and unashamed, usually need 3–5 years ageing to soften, and may well improve for as much as 10.

	86	85	84	83	82
Kent-Sussex whites	6NR	7JR	**8AP**	**7AP**	**6AP**

· AUSTRALIA ·

Australia's reputation is for relentless sunshine. New vineyards, however, are increasingly planted in cool, high-altitude areas or in the far south where sea influences and lower temperatures can mirror the conditions of Burgundy and Bordeaux in France. However, many of these trend-setting vineyards are still too young to have an established track-record, and so two traditional areas are featured here.

	86	85	84	83	82	81	80	79	78	77	76
Coonawarra Cabernet Sauvignon	8NR	9NR	10NR	**4AP**	8JR	**5AP**	**10AP**	**8AP**	**7AP**	6PB	**9AP**
Hunter Valley Sémillon	10NR	8NR	7JR	8NR	7JR	5JR	7JR	**8AP**	**5AP**	4PB	**7AP**

· CALIFORNIA ·

The weather conditions in California are *not* all the same. Sunny California 'where it never rains' used to be the clichéd description of this multi-faceted vineyard land, and 'they're like Coca-Cola – they all taste the same' used to be the absurd judgement on the wines. Well, an apology is long overdue to Californian winemakers, and climate conditions, which range from cool temperate to exhausting desert. In years to come, California may be as sub-divided as France is for vintage differences, because they are indeed dramatic, even though the general quality level is far higher than in Europe. For now, the following generalizations concern the most famous areas and the most sought-after wines. Other areas – and other wine styles – have every right to feel miffed. It won't always be so.

	86	85	84	83	82	81	80	79	78	77	76
Napa Cabernet Sauvignon	8NR	10NR	9NR	8NR	7JR	**6AP**	8JR	**8AP**	**7AP**	**9AP**	**8AP**
Napa Chardonnay	9NR	10NR	10JR	**7AP**	**8AP**	**9AP**	**7AP**	**7AP**	6PB	8PB	6PB
Sonoma Cabernet Sauvignon	8NR	10NR	9NR	9JR	7JR	**7AP**	**9AP**	**8AP**	**8AP**	**9AP**	**8AP**
Sonoma Chardonnay	9NR	10NR	10JR	8JR	**8AP**	**9AP**	**8AP**	**8AP**	6PB	8PB	6PB

·3·
THE WORLD OF WINE

· FRANCE ·

I suppose it is possible that other countries like the USA, Australia, Italy or Spain may eventually be able to come up with the perfect match between climate, geology, choice of grapes and style of wine. It may take them some time, of course, because the country which *has* achieved such a balance is France, and it has been testing, abandoning, re-discovering and finally settling on the magic formula, for the best part of 2,000 years. And while legislators and pundits are only now beginning to attempt classifications of the good, the bad and the ugly in most other countries, France has been cataloguing and classifying the best vineyards in minute detail for nearly 200 years.

Of course, France's geographical position does give it a head start. Between Champagne in the north and the Pyrenees in the south, France has virtually every grape-growing condition you could ask for, from the chilly and desperate, to the torrid and broiling. As different grape varieties do ripen at different times, a millenia-long process of natural selection has narrowed down the choice of the local varieties which ripen best in each area.

France is only the second biggest wine producer in Europe, behind Italy, but virtually all the classic wine styles the rest of the world tries to copy have been created here. Along with red Bordeaux and champagne there is red burgundy, regarded as the pinnacle of Pinot Noir performance. There is white burgundy, leading the way with what is at present the world's most fashionable grape – Chardonnay. Sauternes is regarded as the text-book sweet white wine. The Hermitage wines from the Syrah, the quick maturing fruity styles of the Gamay grape of Beaujolais and the snappy, ultrafresh light white Sauvignon wines of Sancerre are also picked out as prototypes and copied throughout the world. There is of course, a lot of bad wine made in France as well, but our concern is with the good which we might actually want to drink.

· THE CLASSIFICATION SYSTEM ·

This pre-eminence does bring one major headache with it – fraud. If everyone is envious of a wine's reputation, and, consequently, of the price it can charge, imitators spring up, fraudulent labels multiply, and pretty soon a wine's reputation can become totally debased. For this reason the French have worked out a system of guaranteeing the origin of a wine which is *also* copied throughout the world by people trying to authenticate their own local wines.

Appellation d'Origine Contrôlée (AC) – Appellation of Controlled Origin is awarded to the top wines, now nearly a quarter of French production. Note that it is the *origin* which is controlled, because you can't actually control what a winemaker does, you can only control the material he does it with. To qualify for an AC, a wine must have been made under specific conditions laid down in seven different categories.
1 The land itself. Since flavour *does* come from the soil, and ripeness is affected very much by the lie of the land, suitable vineyard land is precisely defined. Anything outside it doesn't get the *appellation*.
2 Choice of grape. The permitted grape variety or varieties are defined.

This may be a single grape, as in, say, Sancerre with the Sauvignon, or it may be several, as in Châteauneuf-du-Pape. You plant the wrong grapes, you don't get the *appellation*.
3 Degree of alcohol. All wines must guarantee a minimum alcohol level, and some, like Muscadet, also have a maximum. This is because unless you have reasonably ripe grapes, you don't get the flavour. In the more northern parts of France you are allowed to 'chaptalize' (add sugar at fermentation time) to increase alcohol.
4 Yield. There is a maximum yield set for the vines. It is expressed in hectolitres of juice per hectare (an acre is just under half a hectare) of vines. Although there is a move to raise many of these maximums, and they can be adjusted on a local basis for each vintage, overproduction dilutes character. So – you produce too much, you don't get the *appellation*.
5 Methods of grape-growing. The number of vines per hectare and the way the vines are pruned can dramatically affect the quality of the wine. Maximum density and acceptable pruning methods are laid down. If you don't do it right – you don't get the *appellation*.
6 Ways of wine-making. Sugar, acidifying, de-acidifying, things you can and can't add. Each area has its own rules. Obey them, or you lose the *appellation*.
7 Analysis and tasting. Since 1979 all wines wanting the *appellation* have to pass a tasting panel. You are allowed one failure, but if it doesn't taste good – it doesn't get the *appellation* – which is really what the whole thing is all about.

Vin Délimité de Qualité Supérieure is the second rung. This is a shrinking category, because wines get promoted up to AC when they've earned the spurs, but the rules are basically the same as for AC.

Vin de Pays is the third category, representing about 14 per cent of total production. This is a relatively recent initiative (1968 was when they were first started, 1973 was when they really began to appear on the shelf) and the objective is to give regional definition to wines that would previously have gone straight to the blending vats. The rules follow the same guidelines as for AC, but are laxer, with more grape varieties allowed, higher yields and lower minimum alcohol. Which goes without saying, really. If they were faithful to the same quality levels as for AC, they'd *be* AC, wouldn't they?

Vin de table Table wine. This is for the rest – the wines that don't make the effort or haven't got the right grapes in the right places. There is an enormous volume of *vin de table* particularly in the south, and the 'wine lake' consists of these wines. They are actually sold purely on alcoholic strength, not on pleasantness of taste, and their prices are quoted daily in the newspapers, just like industrial shares. They are subjected to simple health regulations so that consumers don't actually get sick, but otherwise it is up to the merchant to find the good vats which do exist amid the concrete jungle of bad.

Even so, what it all adds up to is that France has made more effort than any other country to guarantee the quality of its wines, to the consumer. But enough of this technical talk – let's get on to the wines.

Far left South of Reims virtually every *département*, except those of Normandy, will boast vines. These vines produce burgundy at Aluze in the Côte Chalonnaise.

Left One of the joys of France is that even the tiniest town will have its *charcuterie*, bursting with savoury goodies of every kind. This one is at Tain l'Hermitage in the Rhône.

Above Every autumn all hands flock to bring in the year's grape harvest. These pickers toil in the sun at Bergheim in Alsace.

Left A timeless café scene in France; tobacco smoke clouding the air – and litres of red *vin ordinaire* on every table.

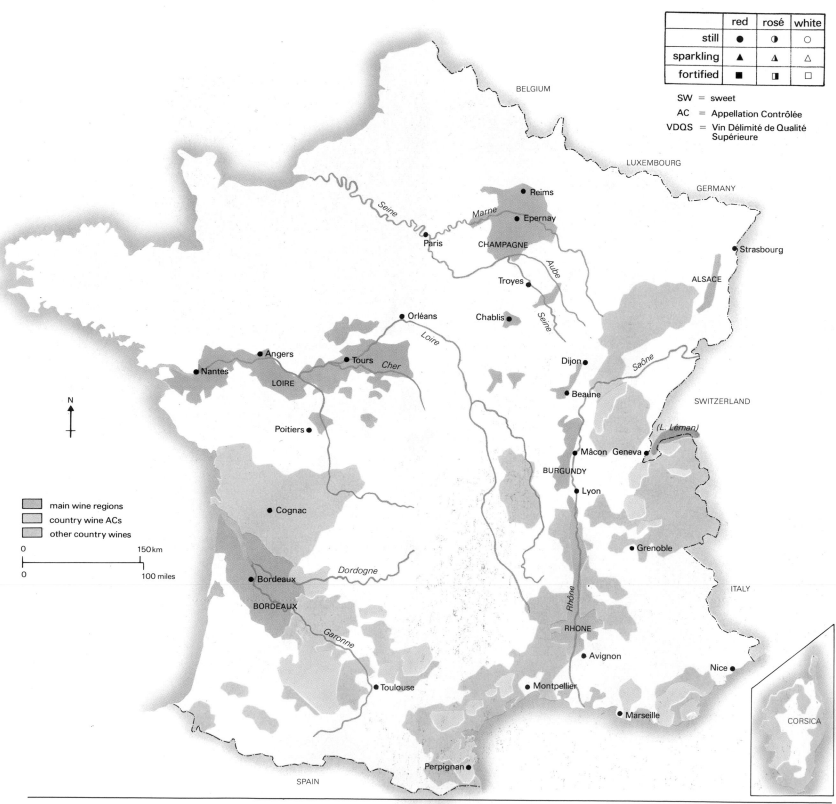

	red	rosé	white
still	●	◐	○
sparkling	▲	◮	△
fortified	■	◧	□

SW = sweet
AC = Appellation Contrôlée
VDQS = Vin Délimité de Qualité Supérieure

BELGIUM

LUXEMBOURG

GERMANY

● Reims

Seine

Marne

● Epernay

● Paris

CHAMPAGNE

● Strasbourg

Aube

ALSACE

● Troyes

Seine

● Orléans

Chablis ●

Loire

Dijon ●

Saône

● Angers

● Tours

Cher

LOIRE

● Beaune

● Nantes

SWITZERLAND

(L. Léman)

N

● Poitiers

● Mâcon Geneva ●

BURGUNDY

● Lyon

main wine regions
country wine ACs
other country wines

● Cognac

● Grenoble

0   150km

0   100 miles

Dordogne

Rhône

ITALY

● Bordeaux

BORDEAUX

Garonne

RHONE

● Avignon

● Nice

● Toulouse

● Montpellier

● Marseille

CORSICA

Perpignan ●

SPAIN

• SELECTED WINES •

All wines are AC unless otherwise indicated.

• BORDEAUX •

○ Barsac SW
○ – Ch. Brousset SW
○ – Ch. Climens SW
○ – Ch. Coutet SW
○ – Ch. Doisy-Daëne SW
○ – Ch. Doisy-Védrines SW
○ – Ch. Nairac SW
●◐○ Bordeaux
▲▲△ Bordeaux
●◐ Bordeaux Clairet
●◐○ Bordeaux Supérieur
○ Cadillac SW
● Canon-Fronsac
● – Ch. Canon-de-Brem
○ Cérons SW
● ○ Côtes de Bourg
● ○ Côtes de Francs
○ Entre-Deux-Mers
● Fronsac
● – Ch. de la Dauphine
● – Ch. la Rivière
● ○ Graves
● ○ – Ch. Carbonnieux
● ○ – Domaine de Chevalier
● ○ – Ch. de Fieuzal
● – Ch. Haut-Bailly
○ – Ch. Haut-Brion
● ○ – Ch. Malartic-Lagravière
● – Ch. La Mission-Haut-
       Brion
● ○ – Ch. Pape-Clément
● ○ – Ch. Rahoul
● ○ – Ch. Smith-Haut-Lafitte
● ○ – Ch. Tour-Martillac
● ○ – Ch. Tourteau-Chollet
○ Graves-Léognan
○ Graves Supérieures SW
● ○ Graves de Vayres
● Haut-Médoc
● – Ch. Cantemerle
● – Ch. Cissac
● – Ch. Hanteillan
● – Ch. La Lagune
● – Ch. Sociando-Mallet
● – Ch. Larose-Trintaudon
● Lalande-de-Pomerol
● – Ch. des Annereaux
● – Ch. de Bertineau
● – Ch. Siaurac

● Listrac
● – Ch. Clarke
● – Ch. Fourcas-Hosten
○ Loupiac SW
● Lussac-St-Emilion
● Margaux
● – Ch. d'Angludet
● – Ch. Giscours
● – Ch. d'Issan
● – Ch. Lascombes
○ – Ch. Margaux
● – Ch. Palmer
● – Ch. Prieuré-Lichine
● – Ch. Rausan-Ségla
● – Ch. du Tertre
● Médoc
● – Ch. Loudenne
● – Ch. Potensac
● Montagne-St-Emilion
● Moulis
● – Ch. Chasse-Spleen
● – Ch. Maucaillou
● – Ch. Poujeaux
● Pauillac
● – Ch. Batailley
● – Ch. Grand-Puy-Lacoste
● – Ch. Haut-Bages-Libéral
● – Ch. Haut-Batailley
● – Ch. Lafite-Rothschild
● – Ch. Latour
● – Ch. Lynch-Bages
● – Ch. Mouton-Rothschild
● – Ch. Pichon-Lalande
● – Ch. Pontet-Canet
● Pomerol
● – Ch. Certan de May
● – Ch. L'Evangile
● – Ch. La Grave-Trigant-
       de-Boisset
● – Ch. Lafleur
● – Ch. Latour-à-Pomerol
● – Ch. Petit-Village
● – Ch. Pétrus
● – Clos René
● – Ch. de Sales
● – Ch. Trotanoy
● – Ch. Vieux-Château-
       Certan
● ○ Premières Côtes de Blaye
● ○ Premières Côtes de
       Bordeaux
● Puisseguin-St-Emilion
○ Ste-Croix-du-Mont SW
● St-Emilion

● – Ch. L'Angelus
● – Ch. L'Arrosée
● – Ch. Ausone
● – Ch. Balestard-la-Tonnelle
● – Ch. Belair
● – Ch. Canon
◐ – Ch. Cheval-Blanc
● – Ch. la Dominique
● – Ch. Figeac
● – Ch. Larmande
● – Ch. Magdelaine
● – Ch. Monbousquet
● – Ch. Pavie
● St-Estèphe
● – Ch. Calon-Ségur
● – Ch. Cos d'Estournel
● – Ch. Haut-Marbuzet
● – Ch. Lafon-Rochet
● – Ch. Meyney
● – Ch. Montrose
● – Ch. de Pez
● St-Georges-St-Emilion
● St-Julien
● – Ch. Beychevelle
● – Ch. Ducru-Beaucaillou
● – Ch. Gruaud-Larose
● – Ch. Lagrange
● – Ch. Léoville-Barton
● – Ch. Léoville-Las-Cases
● – Ch. St-Pierre
● – Ch. Talbot
○ Sauternes SW
○ – Ch. Bastor-Lamontagne
       SW
○ – Ch. de Fargues SW
○ – Ch. Gilette SW
○ – Ch. Guiraud SW
○ – Ch. Lafaurie-Peyraguey
       SW
○ – Ch. Lamothe-Guignard
       SW
○ – Ch. de Malle SW
○ – Ch. Rieussec SW
○ – Ch. St-Amand SW
○ – Ch. Suduiraut SW
○ – Ch. d'Yquem SW

• BURGUNDY •

Côte d'Or
The village appellations are listed
followed by the major Grands
Crus. Grands Crus in Burgundy
are not obliged to specify the
village on the wine label.

● ○ Aloxe-Corton
● ○ – Corton (part of)
○ – Corton-Charlemagne
     (part of)
● ○ Auxey-Duresses
● ○ Beaune
● ○ Blagny
● ○ Chambolle-Musigny
● – Bonnes-Mares
● ○ – Musigny
● ○ Chassagne-Montrachet
● – Batard-Montrachet
     (part of)
○ – Criots-Bâtard-
     Montrachet
○ – Montrachet (part of)
● Chorey-lès-Beaune
● Côte de Beaune-Villages
● ○ Côte de Nuits-Villages
● ○ Fixin
● Flagey-Echézeaux
● – Echézeaux
● – Grands-Echézeaux
● Gevrey-Chambertin
● – Chambertin
● – Chambertin Clos-de-Bèze
● – Chapelle-Chambertin
● – Charmes-Chambertin
● – Griotte-Chambertin
● – Latricières-Chambertin
● – Mazis-Chambertin
● – Ruchottes-Chambertin
● ○ Hautes-Côtes de Beaune
● ○ Hautes-Côtes de Nuits
● ○ Ladoix-Serrigny
● ○ – Corton (part of)
●◐ Marsannay
● ○ Meursault
● Monthélie
● ○ Morey St-Denis
● – Bonnes-Mares
● – Clos des Lambrays
● – Clos de la Roche
● – Clos St-Denis
● – Clos de Tart
● ○ Nuits-St-Georges
● Pernand-Vergelesses
● ○ – Corton (part of)
○ – Corton-Charlemagne
     (part of)
● Pommard
● ○ Puligny-Montrachet
○ – Bâtard-Montrachet
     (part of)

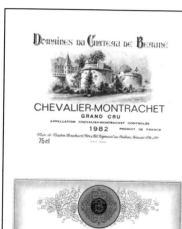

○ – Bienvenues-Bâtard-Montrachet (part of)
○ – Chevalier-Montrachet
○ – Montrachet (part of)
● ○ St-Aubin
● ○ St-Romain
● ○ Santenay
● ○ Savigny-lès-Beaune
● Volnay
● Vosne-Romanée
● – Echézeaux
● – Grands Echézeaux
● – Richebourg
● – La Romanée
● – Romanée-Conti
● – Romanée-St-Vivant
● – La Tâche
● ○ Vougeot
● – Clos de Vougeot

Mâconnais
●◑○ Mâcon
○ Mâcon-Clessé
○ Mâcon-Lugny
○ Mâcon-Prissé
● Mâcon-Supérieur
○ Mâcon-Uchizy
○ Mâcon-Villages
○ Mâcon-Viré
○ Pouilly-Fuissé
○ Pouilly-Loché
○ Pouilly-Vinzelles
○ St-Véran

Côte Chalonnaise
○ Bourgogne Aligoté de Bouzeron
● ○ Givry
● ○ Mercurey
○ Montagny
● ○ Rully

Beaujolais
●◑○ Beaujolais
● – Beaujolais Nouveau
● Beaujolais Supérieur
● Beaujolais-Villages

Beaujolais crus
● Brouilly
● Chénas
● Chiroubles
● Côtes de Brouilly
● Fleurie

● Juliénas
● Morgon
● Moulin-à-Vent
● Regnié
● St-Amour

Chablis
○ Chablis

Grands Crus
○ Blanchots
○ Bougros
○ Les Clos
○ Grenouilles
○ Les Preuses
○ Valmur
○ Vaudésir

Premiers Crus
○ Beauroy
○ – Troesmes
○ Côte de Léchet
○ Fourchaumè
○ – Côte de Fontenay
○ – L'Homme Mort
○ – Vaulorent
○ – Vaupulent
○ Les Fourneaux
○ – Morein
○ – Côte des Près-Girots
○ Mélinots
○ – Les Epinottes
○ – Roncières
○ Mont de Milieu
○ Montée-de-Tonnerre
○ – Chapelot
○ – Pied d'Aloup
○ Montmains
○ – Butteaux
○ – Forêts
○ Vaillons
○ – Beugnons
○ – Châtains
○ – Les Lys
○ – Séchet
○ Vaucoupin
○ Vaudevey
○ Vaulignots
○ Vaupulent
○ Vosgros
○ – Vaugiraut

Basic Burgundy
●●○ Bourgogne

○ Bourgogne Aligoté
●◑○ Bourgogne Grand Ordinaire
●◑ Bourgogne Passe-Tout-Grains
△△ Crémant de Bourgogne

· CHAMPAGNE ·
△△ Champagne
● ○ Coteaux Champenois
◑ Rosé des Riceys

· THE RHONE VALLEY ·

Northern Rhône
○ Château Grillet
○ Condrieu
● Cornas
● Côte-Rôtie
●◑○ Côtes du Rhône
● ○ Crozes-Hermitage
● ○ Hermitage
● ○ St-Joseph
○ △ St-Péray

Southern Rhône
● Beaumes de Venise
● Cairanne
● ○ Châteauneuf-du-Pape
△ Clairette-de-Die (Tradition)
●◑○ Côtes du Rhône
●◑○ Côtes du Rhône-Villages
● Gigondas
●◑○ Lirac
□ Muscat de Beaumes de Venise SW
●◑○ Rasteau
■□ Rasteau SW
◑ Tavel
● Vacqueyras

· LOIRE ·
●◑○ Anjou
○ Anjou SW
○ Bonnezeaux SW
● Bourgueil
◑ Cabernet d'Anjou
● Chinon
○ Coteaux de l'Aubance SW
○ Coteaux du Layon SW
○ Coteaux du Layon-Villages SW
△ Crémant de Loire
○ Jasnières
●◑○ Menetou-Salon
○△ Montlouis

○ Montlouis SW
○ Muscadet
○ Muscadet de Sèvre-et-Maine
○ Muscadet des Coteaux de la Loire
○ Pouilly-Fumé
○ Pouilly-sur-Loire
○ Quarts-de-Chaume SW
○ Quincy
●○ Reuilly
◐ Rosé d'Anjou
◐ Rosé de Loire
● St-Nicolas de Bourgueil
●○○ Sancerre
●○△ Saumur
● Saumur-Champigny
○ Savennières
○ Savennières Coulée-de-Serrant
○ Savennières la Roche-aux-Moines
●○△ Touraine
●○○ Touraine-Amboise
●○○ Touraine-Azay-le-Rideau
●○○ Touraine-Mesland
△ Vouvray
○ Vouvray SW

· ALSACE ·

○ Alsace Chasselas or Gutedel
○ Alsace Edelzwicker (blend of grapes)
○ Alsace Gewürztraminer
○ Alsace Grand Cru
○ Alsace Muscat
● Alsace Pinot Noir
○ Alsace Pinot Blanc or Klevner
○ Alsace Riesling
○ Alsace Sylvaner
○ Alsace Tokay (Pinot Gris)
△ Crémant d'Alsace

· FRENCH COUNTRY WINES ·

●○○ Arbois
●○○ Bandol
■ □ Banyuls SW
●○○ Bellet
●○○ Bergerac
△ Blanquette de Limoux
● Cahors
●○○ Calvi

●◐○ Cassis
○ Château-Chalon
○ Clairette de Bellegarde
○ Clairette du Languedoc
○ Clairette du Languedoc SW
● Collioure
●◐○ Corbières
●◐○ Costières du Gard
●◐○ Coteaux d'Aix-en-Provence
●◐○ Coteaux d'Ajaccio
●◐○ Coteaux des Baux-en-Provence
●◐○ Coteaux du Lyonnais
●◐○ Coteaux du Tricastin
● ○ Côtes de Bergerac
● ○ Côtes de Buzet
● ○ Côtes du Duras
○ Côtes du Duras SW
●◐ Côtes du Frontonnais
●◐△ Côtes du Jura
○ Côtes de Montravel SW
●◐○ Côtes de Provence
●◐○ Côtes du Roussillon
● Côtes du Roussillon-Villages
●◐○ Côtes du Ventoux
○ Crépy
○ l'Etoile
● ○ Faugères
● Fitou
□ Frontignan SW
●◐○ Gaillac
○△ Gaillac SW
●◐○ Irouléguy
○ Jurançon
○ Jurançon SW
● Madiran
■ Maury SW
●◐ Minervois
○ Monbazillac SW
○ Pacherenc du Vic Bilh
●◐○ Palette
●◐○ Patrimonio
● Pécharmant
●◐○ Porto Vecchio
■■□ Rivesaltes SW
● St-Chinian
●◐△ Savoie
○△ Seyssel

VDQS
○△ Bugey
●◐ Châteaumeillant
●◐○ Cheverny

△ Cheverny
●◐○ La Clape
●◐○ Coteaux d'Ancenis
●◐○ Coteaux d'Ancenis SW
●◐○ Coteaux du Giennois
●◐○ Coteaux du Vendômois
●◐○ Coteaux Varois
●◐ Côte Roannaise
●◐○ Côtes d'Auvergne
●◐ Côtes du Forez
●◐○ Côtes du Luberon
● ○ Côtes du Marmandais
●◐○ Côtes du Vivarais
○ Gros Plant du Pays Nantais
●◐○ Haut Poitou
△ Haut Poitou
○ Picpoul de Pinet
○ Rosette SW
●◐○ St-Pourçain-sur-Sioule
○ Sauvignon de St-Bris
●◐○ Vin de l'Orléanais

vin de pays
●◐○ Ardèche
●◐○ Aude
●◐○ Bouches-du-Rhône
●◐○ Charentais
●◐○ Comtes Tolosan
●◐○ Coteaux de l'Ardèche
●◐ Coteaux de Peyriac
●◐○ Côtes de Gascogne
●◐○ Gard
●◐○ Hérault
●◐○ Ile de Beauté
●◐○ Jardin de la France
●◐○ Loir-et-Cher
●◐○ Maine-et-Loire
●◐○ Oc
●◐○ Pyrénées Orientales
●◐○ Sables du Golfe du Lion
●◐○ Uzège
●◐○ Vallée de Paradis
●◐○ Vin de Corse
○ l'Yonne

	red	rosé	white
still	●	◐	○
sparkling	▲	△	△
fortified	■	◨	□

SW = sweet
AC = Appellation Contrôlée
VDQS = Vin Délimité de Qualité Supérieure

· BORDEAUX ·

The grape-picking gets under way at the famous Château Yquem. Huge estates like this dominate wine production in many parts of Bordeaux.

Bordeaux is the finest wine region in the world. Not only for producing great wine, but also for good wine and ordinary wine it is exceptional; for both red and white wines and for sweet and dry it is exceptional. Most fine wines are produced in tiny amounts on privileged pockets of land around the world, but in the Bordeaux areas of Médoc, Pomerol, St-Emilion, Graves and Sauternes there are over a hundred properties which regularly turn out wine of peerless quality in quantities averaging at least 100,000 bottles per year – each! As for straight Bordeaux Rouge, northern Europe's staple red for generations, it is measured in tens of millions of bottles every year.

So, where is this wine wonderland, and why is it so special? Bordeaux is an area in the south-west of France, stretching a good 90 miles (145km) from north to south and over 40 miles (65km) east to west. It spreads itself across the Garonne and Dordogne rivers, which converge just above the city of Bordeaux in a combined estuary called the Gironde.

Bordeaux's reputation as a vineyard has been established for 2,000 years at least – the Romans are known to have taken a fancy to the local wines – but between 1152 and 1453 its wine fame spread right across northern Europe, establishing a supremacy no other red wine has ever matched. The reason is simple (but don't say it too loudly if you're talking to a Frenchman): during this 300-year period Bordeaux was English! It was acquired by the English crown as part of the dowry Eleanor of Aquitaine brought to her marriage with Henry II and was only lost at the end of the 100 Years' War in 1453. Those 300 years were quite long enough to establish the port of Bordeaux as a great trading centre, and the light red wine called *clairet* – hence the British name 'claret' – was one of the region's main export commodities.

· CLIMATE AND SOIL ·

There are several natural advantages which help to account for Bordeaux's greatness. In the first place, the whole region enjoys a particularly temperate climate. The estuary and the Atlantic Gulf Stream provide calming, warming influences, and a protective barrier of pine forests between the vineyards and the sea soaks up many of the rainstorms and salty gales which might otherwise batter the vines.

The soil, too, is important. The Médoc region and the Graves are founded on deep gravel banks over a sand or clay subsoil. Gravel drains wonderfully well and also retains warmth while, being poor in nutrients, it forces the vine to struggle for food and produce fewer grapes, but grapes of a higher quality. For the Cabernet Sauvignon grape, this happens to be perfect terrain, and most of the great Médoc and Graves reds are based on Cabernet.

The gravelly areas produce the best red wine, but, in the Graves stretching south of Bordeaux there is much white wine produced too, especially where the gravel covers a limestone subsoil. In the far south, along the banks of the tiny river Ciron, where gravel covers limestone and chalk, the warm, humid autumns create some of the world's greatest sweet white wines at Sauternes and Barsac.

On the right bank of the Dordogne, around the towns of Libourne and St-Emilion are the wine areas of Pomerol, St-Emilion and Fronsac. Gravel is rare here apart from one special ridge in St-Emilion, but there is clay and limestone, and these, although cooler and damper for the vine roots, are packed with iron and minerals. The Merlot vine, ripening earlier than the Cabernet Sauvignon, thrives in such conditions, and produces exciting reds.

The other areas you can see on the map (right) have soils which are also mostly a mix of clay and limestone. They produce good, but not memorable, reds and whites and, occasionally, rosé and sparkling wine.

· THE GRAPES ·

The brilliance of Bordeaux comes from the leading grape varieties grown and the methods used to make them into wine.

Cabernet Sauvignon is the greatest of the red wine grapes. It ripens late and needs warm, well-drained gravel to thrive. In wet years it can have a rather sharp, green-grassy rawness to it, but when the sun shines, and the rains hold off, and the purple juice squirts from the presses into the waiting vats – then the blackcurrant sweetness hidden beneath the tannic black skins is a revelation. Age it for a year or two in 225-litre oak barrels (called *barriques bordelaises*, or Bordeaux barrels, the world over), and you have the basis for one of

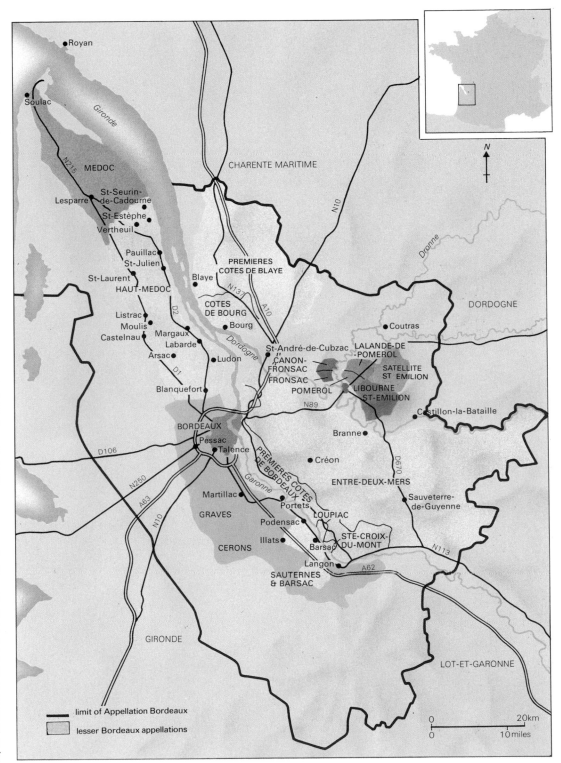

the world of wine's most enthralling flavours. This is the flavour winemakers worldwide try to copy, but few succeed. They don't have the soil or the climate, and they are only just learning that the Cabernet Sauvignon achieves most in Bordeaux when it is blended with another important red wine grape, the softer, juicier Merlot, or with the minor varieties Cabernet Franc (a sort of second cousin Cabernet Sauvignon, lighter and less intense), the Petit Verdot and the Malbec. Also, great Bordeaux red wine needs to age in bottle for a number of years to blend its component parts – often five years, sometimes ten, twenty, or even more for the tannins to soften and the perfume and the fruit to mingle into magic. You need to have the patience of generations for that, and few modern winemakers outside

Left The crypt-like cellar at Lafaurie-Peyraguey. All Bordeaux's greatest wines are matured in oak barrels.

Several famous châteaux have Anglo-Saxon names, reflecting the historical connection between Britain and Bordeaux. Château Palmer (below), was founded by a general who fought alongside Wellington in the Napoleonic Wars.

Bordeaux itself possess such virtues.

Sémillon and **Sauvignon Blanc** are the chief white grapes. Increasingly, Bordeaux winemakers produce good dry white wine from these. The Sauvignon grape, initially from the Loire valley, is the more popular variety, giving a tangy nettle-fresh white wine. But in Bordeaux it is inclined to be earthy by itself and is much better mixed with the heavier more brooding flavours of the Sémillon. If you ferment these two in the traditional way in wooden vats at quite high temperatures – say 25–30°C, you will lose all the Sauvignon freshness without gaining any Sémillon complexity. However, forward-looking properties and co-operatives have installed temperature-controlled stainless-steel vats, where they can ferment at, say, 15–20°C. This takes longer but preserves fruit and freshness, and all good dry Bordeaux whites are now made in this way. In the Graves, they are often then aged in Bordeaux barrels and the results can be superb.

The same grapes, with, perhaps, a little perfumy Muscadelle, are used for sweet wines. They are left on the vine late into the autumn to develop the ugly, but sugar-enriching 'noble rot' fungus (see page 80). Age the wine in those Bordeaux barrels for a year or two, bottle it and leave it for anything from five to twenty-five years and the result is an unbelievable intensity of honey and spice and smoothness.

· THE CHATEAUX ·

If you look along any shelf of Bordeaux wine, after a few bottles just labelled 'claret' or 'Bordeaux' with a merchant's name, you will see that the rest of the wines are virtually all described as 'Château this' or 'Château that'. Now, strictly speaking, in French 'château' means 'castle', like the ornate masterpieces of the Loire valley. Well, there *are* many fine buildings in Bordeaux which call themselves châteaux, but often the 'château' will just be a farmhouse and some outbuildings; sometimes little more than a shack and a shed.

This is because in Bordeaux the concept of a château is tied up with land and not fancy dwelling places. During the 18th century, the legal and political 'aristocracies' of Bordeaux

bought up the small farms of the Médoc in particular, and consolidated them into single units which they, rather grandly, called châteaux. It may have been a little presumptuous but such delusions of grandeur meant that the produce of each of these huge estates, instead of having 50 smallholders' names, was marketable under a single château name. Given that these large estates were also bent on producing quality as well as quantity, the château name became, in effect, a brand name for the owner to promote. The practice of calling your farm a château gradually spread throughout Bordeaux and there are now nearly 4,000 of them.

Technically the wine should also be made at the property, but increasingly co-operatives collect grapes from a number of small growers in lesser areas and plonk a château name on the wine. These will be labelled *mis en bouteille à la propriété*. But all the best wines are now bottled at the château and will say so on the label (*mis en bouteille au château*). A château will try to provide a consistent style of wine, and if everything from planting to bottling is in the château owner's hands, the wine is much more likely to measure up to expectations.

· APPELLATIONS ·

Although Bordeaux has a readily understandable system of *appellations contrôlées*, it is complicated by the numerous 'classifications' which have sprung up in the last 150 years, all of which try to influence our judgement of various properties and the value of their wines, with greater or lesser justification. So let's sort out the *appellations* first. As with the rest of France the AC is only a basic guarantee that the wine originated in the region or locality stated, and is made from the right grapes using the right techniques. The more specific the *appellation*, the better. Even so, Bordeaux has been much less concerned than other regions with giving little plots of particularly good land extra-special ACs, because by the time the *appellation* laws were formulated in 1935, the above-mentioned classifications had been trying to do the same thing for the best part of 100 years, and the 1855 classification of the Médoc and Sauternes, in particular, was very firmly entrenched.

Working from the bottom upwards, Bordeaux is the regional 'catch-all' *appellation* for red, white, rosé, and sparkling wine. Achievement of an extra half a degree of alcohol in the wine allows a wine to be called Bordeaux Supérieur – superior in strength, not necessarily in quality.

Inside this framework, there are large areas – like Médoc, Graves, St-Emilion, Entre-Deux-Mers – each of which has its own AC. Some, like Entre-Deux-Mers, have no subdivisions of significance, but within the major areas, each subdivision is important.

The 1855 classification of the Médoc and Sauternes was based arbitrarily on the prices various properties had fetched for the previous 50 years. This classification had such a dramatic and unexpected effect in cementing a rigid hierarchy of the relative worth of various properties and excluding many others to their considerable financial distress, that other regions jealously sought their own classifications. But it took a long time. Graves achieved an official one in 1953, St-Emilion in 1955, and the 'left-out' properties in the Médoc, dismissively dubbed 'Bourgeois', only began classifying themselves in 1920 and are still unfinished today.

· FOOD AND WINE ·

They do some weird things with wines in Bordeaux. They drink their red wines with fish (lamprey) and with strawberries and they drink their luscious sweet Sauternes as aperitifs – but, oddly enough, it works. A chilled bottle of Sauternes makes a wonderful outdoor appetizer in the heat of the Bordeaux summer. And lampreys, which they stew in red wine, have a tremendous meaty flavour which is accentuated by the dark red wine sauce, and a St-Emilion or Pomerol seems the perfect partner. Claret with strawberries? Yes, you actually pour the claret *over* the strawberries – a little castor sugar, a twist of black pepper – mmmm! I once did it with the dregs of some Château Margaux 1961. Sacrilege! Loved it!

Maybe they do such things because Bordeaux cuisine is not that varied. They do have very good oysters from the nearby Charente, and dry white Graves to go with them. Those wonderful big flat mushrooms called *cèpes* are also much eaten locally, sautéed with shallots and garlic and parsley and accompanied by young red Graves or Médoc. They grill entrecôte over vine twigs – the smoke is fragrant and spicy and beef never tasted better; nor the draught of young Margaux or St-Julien drunk with it.

A study in tranquillity – neat rows of vines slope down to the River Garonne idling by, as the harvest approaches in the beautiful but little known Premières Côtes de Bordeaux.

· THE MEDOC ·

Famous wine areas don't have to be the most fetching landscapes, but it does help if you can find them! The Médoc is *not* terribly fetching, being a gently undulating wedge of land covered in vines and scrub; and, if you were in your car in the city of Bordeaux looking for road signs, you'd never guess it was a mere dozen miles to the north. There aren't any road signs! (Psst. Inside tip – you have to take the Soulac road.) It's astonishing; the most famous area of the world's most famous wine region and no one has thought of putting up a road sign!

In a way, it is typical of this very reserved, superior part of the wine world, where secrecy is often esteemed more than openness, and many of the properties – and their owners – display a distant air. The wines, too, start life cold, harsh and unfriendly, demanding patience and persistence before they reveal their glories. But no red wines consistently achieve such heights as the great Médoc wines.

The Médoc was originally a marsh, and it wasn't until the 17th century that the land was drained and estates were established. But by 1708, the Médoc wines were being sought out; single property names, starting with Margaux, first appeared in 1714 and by 1759 the previously favoured Graves producers were bitterly complaining about England's new love affair with the Médoc.

Amazingly, the love affair continues. From about 25,000 acres (10,100 hectares) of vines, the Médoc *still* produces what is regarded as the epitome of great Bordeaux. It is a combination of soil and grape variety, allied to the enduring strength of the system of good-sized châteaux estates, which has achieved this. All the best wines are grown on the gravel ridges which are most obvious in the leading villages of Margaux, St-Julien, Pauillac and, to a lesser extent, St-Estèphe, and from vineyards planted primarily with Cabernet.

Although the grapes ripen quite late and the yield isn't massive, the wine is of exceptional quality. It starts life very tough and fierce but, with ageing in oak barrel and bottle, it acquires the famous blackcurranty flavour, spicy even, laden with fruit, and the dry but exotic fragrance of cedar. There's no taste like it in the whole world of wine.

· APPELLATIONS ·

The name 'Médoc' covers the entire region north of Bordeaux to Soulac. However, there are two distinct wine areas.

Médoc is the *appellation* for the northern part, between Soulac and St-Seurin-de-Cadourne. It makes lots of good claret but has no famous names.

Haut-Médoc applies to the southern part, stretching down to the gates of Bordeaux, which has all the luminaries.

Margaux, Moulis, Listrac, St-Julien, Pauillac and **St-Estèphe** are the six major villages within the Haut-Médoc *appellation* area which are allowed to use their own name on the label. (Any white or rosé wines can only be called Bordeaux.)

In the Haut-Médoc often more attention is paid to the classification of different properties than to their *appellation*. The 1855 classification is the most famous one, and its pros and cons form the basis of many a wine-buff's argument, but it was never meant to be permanent. It's just that when Napoleon III decided to hold a Paris Exhibition in 1855 to try to eclipse London's Great Exhibition of 1851, he wanted to exhibit some Bordeaux wines. But which ones? A group of brokers worked out a system based on the prices which the various wines traditionally fetched and divided the wines into five categories. Simple as that. It was supposed to be a temporary expedient. Those brokers would be flabbergasted to realize we're still using their classification today.

The 1855 classification covers red Haut-Médoc wines (with one Graves, Château Haut-Brion) and white Sauternes. Although it is still accurate in most cases, it is difficult to see why, because the classification does not

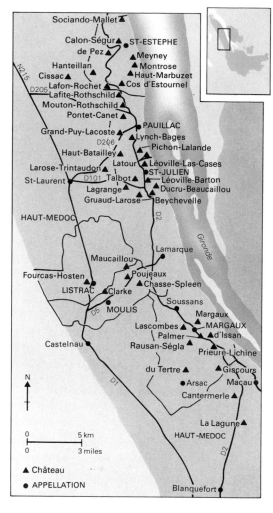

apply to vineyard *land,* only to the name of the château. If I own a First Growth château (the most expensive) and buy some land off a Fifth Growth (the least expensive) that land automatically qualifies to be part of my First Growth wine. A Fifth becomes a First simply because somebody else owns it! Daft.

Even so, most of the best gravelly land was included among these 'Classed Growths'. (The French term is 'Cru Classé'. 'Cru' usually means the produce of a specific piece of land, but in the Haut-Médoc it behaves more like a trade mark which a person owns, rather than an unchangeable definition of a vineyard, as, for instance, in Burgundy's Côte d'Or.)

The Classed Growths can command

· MATURITY CHART ·
1981 CRU CLASSÉ
A lean but well-balanced year

Bottled	Ready	Peak	Fading

0 1 2 3 4 5 6 7 8 9 10 11 12 13 14 15 16 17 18 19 20 Years

Above The cellar at Château Clarke, in Listrac, positively bursting with oak.

Until it was reclaimed in the 17th century, the Médoc was a fly-infested swamp. Drainage ditches, or *jalles,* like this one at Château Mouton-Rothschild – perfectly sited at the bottom of a steep slope – are still a feature of the vineyards (*right*).

considerable premiums in price, with the top First Growths selling for up to ten times the price of good 'non-classified' wines. The general term for the latter is 'Cru Bourgeois', implying something worthy and honest. The best are definitely of Classed Growth quality. There have been many attempts to classify them, but none are conclusive or comprehensive. At the moment the most widely accepted is a 1978 classification of 127 châteaux listed as Cru Grand Bourgeois Exceptionnel (18), Cru Grand Bourgeois (41) and Cru Bourgeois (68), in descending order of importance. However, the classification is decided according to size of property, wine-making technique, and general area, not according to specific

· THE 1855 CLASSIFICATION ·

First Growths (1ers Crus)
Lafite-Rothschild, *Pauillac*; Latour, *Pauillac*; Margaux, *Margaux*; Mouton-Rothschild *Pauillac* (since 1973); (and Haut-Brion, *Graves*)

Second Growths (2ème Crus)
Rausan-Ségla, *Margaux*; Rauzan-Gassies, *Margaux*; Léoville-Las-Cases, *St-Julien*; Léoville-Poyferré, *St-Julien*; Léoville-Barton, *St-Julien*; Durfort-Vivens, *Margaux*; Lascombes, *Margaux*; Gruaud-Larose, *St-Julien*; Brane-Cantenac, *Margaux*; Pichon-Longueville-Baron, *Pauillac*; Pichon-Longueville-Lalande, *Pauillac*; Ducru-Beaucaillou, *St-Julien*; Cos d'Estournel, *St-Estèphe*; Montrose, *St-Estèphe*

Third Growths (3ème Crus)
Giscours, *Margaux*; Kirwan, *Margaux*; d'Issan, *Margaux*; Lagrange, *St-Julien*; Langoa-Barton, *St-Julien*; Malescot-St-Exupéry, *Margaux*; Cantenac-Brown, *Margaux*; Palmer, *Margaux*; La Lagune, *Haut-Médoc*; Desmirail, *Margaux*; Calon-Ségur, *St-Estèphe*; Ferrière, *Margaux*; Marquis d'Alesme-Becker, *Margaux*; Boyd-Cantenac, *Margaux*

Fourth Growths (4ème Crus)
St-Pierre, *St-Julien*; Branaire-Ducru, *St-Julien*; Talbot, *St-Julien*; Duhart-Milon-Rothschild, *Pauillac*; Pouget, *Margaux*; La Tour-Carnet, *Haut-Médoc*; Lafon-Rochet, *St-Estèphe*; Beychevelle, *St-Julien*; Prieuré-Lichine, *Margaux*; Marquis-de-Terme, *Margaux*

Fifth Growths (5ème Crus)
Pontet-Canet, *Pauillac*; Batailley, *Pauillac*; Grand-Puy-Lacoste, *Pauillac*; Grand-Puy-Ducasse, *Pauillac*; Haut-Batailley, *Pauillac*; Lynch-Bages, *Pauillac*; Lynch-Moussas, *Pauillac*; Dauzac, *Margaux*; Mouton-Baronne-Philippe, *Pauillac* (formerly known as Mouton d'Armaihacq); du Tertre, *Margaux*; Haut-Bages-Libéral, *Pauillac*; Pédesclaux, *Pauillac*; Belgrave, *Haut-Médoc*; de Camensac, *Haut-Médoc*; Cos Labory, *St-Estèphe*; Clerc-Milon-Rothschild, *Pauillac*; Croizet-Bages, *Pauillac*; Cantemerle, *Haut-Médoc*

Château Margaux (*right*), is one of the few Médoc Classed Growths to produce a white wine – Le Pavillon Blanc – as well as the claret for which it has long been renowned. Some of the bottles in its cellar (*above*) date back to the 1860s.

vineyard or proven quality of a particular wine (that is, whether it *tastes* better). Also, some leading 'Bourgeois' have refused to take part, and in practice the more committed proprietor produces the best wines and eventually gets the highest price, regardless of rank.

· MARGAUX ·

The road through the grey industrial suburbs of northern Bordeaux is so drab and featureless that it is difficult to believe you are within a 15-minute drive of the villages of Labarde, Cantenac and Margaux, whose wines, all with the *appellation* 'Margaux', are there to remind us that life isn't all warehouses and railway sidings.

Ah, Margaux! Of all the red wines I would most like to find the perfect description for, the great Margauxs top my list. They seem strangely light; they start life a little dry and lean, and often have a period at five to seven years old when they seem hollow and unlikely to make old bones. Then it begins, the first signs of sweetness and richness coil up from the slowly maturing wine. Pauillac is more

impressive, St-Julien more classically consistent, but Margaux has the teasing brilliance which ensnares you and nags at your thoughts, till you open another bottle to try once more to understand and possess its mystery.

Merlot is planted to soften the wine, and Cabernet Franc to cajole a slightly less aggressive attitude from the new wine; but the causes of all this purple prose are the gravel banks and the Cabernet Sauvignon. The gravel is particularly deep here and so long as there is a fair amount of sun, wine of remarkable perfume is produced. In fact, there are islands of gravelly soil in a sea of clay – and two great châteaux – even before we reach the Margaux *appellation*: La Lagune at Ludon, and Cantemerle, hidden deep in a dreamy copse – both excellent Classed Growths, but with only the general Haut-Médoc *appellation*.

The first substantial bank of gravel is at Labarde as the D2 road comes out of the wood past Macau. Over to the left is a wonderful building looking like a Biarritz casino, Château Giscours, which seems to make finer wine every year. After crossing the railway and

heading past some very scrubby vines to right and left, we're in the sleepy little village of Cantenac. Here the second great gravel ridge swells up behind the few houses and extends from Château d'Issan, a moated delight down towards the river, across the chalky pale fields of Prieuré-Lichine, Kirwan and Brane-Cantenac, back into the silent woods near Arsac, where d'Angludet and du Tertre make fine wine.

Towards the town of Margaux, famous names appear on all sides – the multi-turretted Château Palmer, part British-owned, on our right; then across the fields to our left Rausan-Ségla, and finest of all, hidden behind its avenue of trees, the splendour of Château Margaux itself. For once, the quality of the wine is matched by the sheer opulence of the château.

The little town of Margaux is hemmed in on all sides by vineyards and châteaux. It has more than its fair share of properties which have failed to reach their potential in recent years, but as we head away north past Soussans there is one further clutch of fine vineyards, exemplified by Château Lascombes to our left, and by the rising stars of La Gurgue and Labégorce-Zédé to the right.

· MOULIS AND LISTRAC ·

Suddenly the carpet of vines is gone. Scrub returns, and forest and pasture. This is because the gravel has been largely replaced by the heavier clay soil. It is significant that in this area there are no Classed Growths. Even so, to the west, there are two fine gravel ridges at Moulis and Listrac which include some of the Médoc's most attractive vineyards because the pinewoods crowd the gravel and chalk banks at every point, and some of the vineyards have the appearance of forest glades. Moulis wines are slightly softer, especially from the vineyards clustered round the village of Grand Poujeaux, many of which incorporate Poujeaux into their names. The best of these are Poujeaux, Maucaillou and Chasse-Spleen, the last two of which make wine consistently up to Classed Growth standard. Listrac is sterner stuff, with Château Clarke, Fourcas-Hosten and Fourcas-Dupré leading the way.

A few miles further up, near the village of St-Laurent, there are three rather forgotten Classed Growths using the Haut-Médoc *appellation*, and one remarkable creation – Château Larose-Trintaudon, also Haut-Médoc, 20 years ago an overgrown ruin, now the Médoc's largest estate, and, incidentally, the Médoc's biggest-selling wine in America. It's never expensive and always delicious.

· ST-JULIEN ·

There's an old Médoc saying that if you've got pebbles under your feet and you can see the Gironde you'll make fine wine. Seven miles north of Margaux just as the vineyards seem to have petered out completely, the tree-lined road dips towards a little stream, then climbs a bank and veers left to avoid the splendid battlements of Château Beychevelle. Suddenly vines are everywhere. The soil is pale and pebbly, the Gironde glints in the sun to our right, and we're back in the big time with the wines of St-Julien.

There isn't much to St-Julien in terms of volume – it is the smallest of the main Médoc

The famous tower seems stranded among the vines at Château Latour, where the gravelly soil and predominance of Cabernet Sauvignon vines produce Bordeaux's longest-living wine.

communes – but it is sheer concentrated quality, with over 75 per cent of its vineyards belonging to Classed Growths. Beychevelle, to the south, with its neighbour Château Branaire-Ducru produces a wine immediately soft, plummy even, but which develops a lovely, always gentle flavour. The greatest exponent of this style of St-Julien is Château Ducru-Beaucaillou, just north of Beychevelle. Its wine is so soft and rich it sometimes seems coated with honey – remarkable for a dry red wine – but as it ages it gradually begins to reveal the hallmark of great St-Julien, that penetrating, uplifting scent of cedar.

Château Gruaud-Larose, just to our left as the road turns north past Ducru-Beaucaillou is also very fine, but for me the heart of St-Julien lies in this tiny commune's northern vineyards, and in particular Léoville-Barton and Léoville-Las-Cases.

· PAUILLAC ·

You need a local expert to show you where the boundary between St-Julien and Pauillac lies, but you don't need a local expert to see the very real difference in style of wine. Pauillac is the home-base of the Cabernet Sauvignon, its citadel and its greatest glory.

Cantemerle and Giscours are almost neighbours, yet have different ACs. Cantemerle – occupying a gravelly outcrop on otherwise unsuitable land – is merely 'Haut-Médoc'. But Giscours is the first vineyard on the gravel banks which sweep north, and is 'Margaux'.

Left The surprisingly exotic cellar buildings of Cos d'Estournel, the best property in St-Estèphe.

becoming heady with cassis and mint. Although we can't see it, the ridges hide another excellent château, Grand-Puy-Lacoste, just to the west, but otherwise it's best to hurry through the town, and breast the last of the Médoc's great gravel banks where Mouton-Rothschild makes astonishing, rich, cedary wine, strangely perfumed, like celestial pencil sharpenings, and Lafite-Rothschild makes something lighter, appreciated by wealthy connoisseurs, but loved less by we ordinary mortals who work long hours to earn our wine money.

· ST-ESTEPHE ·

There's just one great gravel bank to come, and it stares you in the face as you pass Lafite-Rothschild and the road once more dips and climbs, turning sharp left in front of the remarkable pagoda towers of Cos d'Estournel – remarkable wine too, St-Estèphe's best. Two other Classed Growths, Lafon-Rochet and Cos Labory share these south-facing slopes but not the same quality in wine.

The large area of St-Estèphe has few distinguishing features – large flattish fields, twisting lanes, silent, glum villages as the gravel turns to clay and the magic seeps away from the wine. There are still two more famous châteaux over towards the river – Montrose and Calon-Ségur – and the wines of de Pez, Meyney and Haut-Marbuzet are pretty impressive; but the heavier, cloddy earth does leave its mark on the area's wines. Many of them reflect the clinging dampness of clay

Château Mouton-Rothschild has as much as 85 per cent Cabernet Sauvignon, and elsewhere 70 per cent is commonplace. Ally this to a hefty shoulder of gravel which runs from the St-Julien border, past the town of Pauillac, to the little stream north of Château Lafite-Rothschild which brings the *appellation* abruptly to an end, and you have the recipe for several pretty special wines. And you certainly get them.

Pauillac has three of the Médoc's five First Growths – although Mouton-Rothschild only forced its way to the top in 1973 (the sole change ever admitted in the classification) – and its 18 Classed Growths cover over 72 per cent of the area. We dive straight in at the top because, on leaving St-Julien, the first sight on the right is the round ruined tower which marks the vineyards of Château Latour. Latour is Bordeaux's most imposing, longest-lasting wine, impenetrably tough and dark to begin with yet slowly building to a rich blackcurrant, mint and cedar strength, tremendously arrogant and unbending.

Yet right next door is the great Château

Pichon-Longueville-Lalande, the lushest, most succulent, most absurdly delicious of all Pauillacs. It is interesting to see that some of Pichon's vineyards are actually in St-Julien, and that only 46 per cent of the vines are Cabernet Sauvignon, with the soft, rich Merlot taking an unusually large 34 per cent. But that's no criticism: this is a great wine.

The road goes through several little hamlets heading for Pauillac and just short of the town the land swells on the left, and the sprawling buildings of Lynch-Bages announce another great wine – fat, juicy almost, but with time

Grapes from young vines or from less good parts of a top vineyard are kept separate and the wine sold under a 'second wine' label; but they can have much of the character of 'château' wine. Les Forts de Latour is the second wine of Château Latour, and Réserve de l'Amiral, of Beychevelle.

Top **The pale worn-out soil of the Médoc slips through your fingers leaving a fistful of pebbles. Paradoxically, this unpromising terrain is ideal for great wines, like those of Lafite-Rothschild.**

Above **Grape-pickers at the British-owned Château Loudenne.**

after rain, and most vineyards need much Merlot to add ripeness and body to their wines.

Yet the gravel does surface a few more times: inland at Cissac in the Haut-Médoc *appellation*, where Hanteillan, Cissac and Lamothe-Cissac make impressive wine, at Vertheuil, just to the north, and, with one final challenging fling, at St-Seurin-de-Cadourne. There the last plateau rises down by the river bank, and Bel-Orme-Tronquoy-de-Lalande, and, especially, Sociando-Mallet, produce classic, long-lasting flavours.

· BAS-MEDOC ·

When you finally leave the Haut-Médoc, the new landscape noticeably reflects the changed character of the wines. The swells and billows of gravelly outcrops which characterized the peaks of quality in Pauillac, St-Julien, and the other Haut-Médoc villages, are absent here. The soil has none of the dry crunch of gravel of the Haut-Médoc. So why not turn back, to the grand châteaux of the south?

Why not? Because there *are* some very good wines coerced from this unpromising soil.

· VINTAGES ·

Man has increasing control over the health of the wines he makes, the style, the weight, the strength – but the *heart* of the wine, the flavours which sing, the pleasure you can recall long after the drinking is done, these come from the soil of the vineyard, and the weather conditions throughout the year. It's a 12-month gamble.

The startling, painfully intense flavours of the great 1961 vintage, when every ounce of life in the vine seems to have been distilled into the wine, are due to dreadful weather when the vines flowered in June, causing a drastically reduced crop which gorged itself on the perfect summer and autumn weather.

In 1964, it was a different story: the weather was tremendous right through to October. Less ambitious growers picked early and made good wine. Ambitious growers held on in the hope of making great wine, but on 7 October the heavens opened. For nine days the Médoc was awash, and this 'great vintage' was ruined.

In 1980 and 1982 the same amount of rain fell in October. It poured right through the 1980 harvest, diluting the wine and diseasing its reputation. 1982, on the other hand, is hailed as one of the most exciting vintages ever created. That's because 1982 had a hot June, the vines flowered early and so were harvested early, during September. When the rains came the wine was already made. 1980 had had a rotten June, the vines flowered later, the vintage was therefore late and was walloped by the October rain. Two hot weeks in June made one vintage great, two cold weeks in June reduced the other vintage to an also-ran.

Potensac is a great wine, and Greysac, La Tour-St-Bonnet, La Tour-de-By and Loudenne are all worth seeking out. Also the ordinary everyday red, the staple, thirst-quenching accompaniment to food and friendship, is actually *better* here than in the Haut-Médoc. Labelled 'Médoc' and probably coming from one of the vast co-operatives which dominate the area, this is simple claret at its best. Because of the clay soil, there is more Merlot planted here than Cabernet Sauvignon, and the result is juicy, fruity reds, a little earthy, but with a strong streak of grassy blackcurrant fruit. You don't waste time pontificating about wine like this – you just drink it.

· ST-EMILION AND POMEROL ·

The vineyards strung across the slopes and plateaux of the right bank of the Dordogne river, and centred round the sleepy little port of Libourne, have one great unifying factor, the Merlot grape. Used in Pomerol almost exclusively, it is also the dominant grape in St-Emilion, and the mainstay of neighbouring Lalande-de-Pomerol and Fronsac. It gives a juicy, slightly 'sweet' accessibility to all the wines, regardless of the soil the vines have been grown on. In a blind tasting you can tell which is the best and which is the worst of these rich red wines, but you can't often tell from which of the interlinked areas the particular wine actually hails. On the map, the region looks tiny in comparison with the long-limbed Médoc, but it is intensely cultivated, and regularly produces larger quantities of wine.

· ST-EMILION ·

This is the biggest and most important right bank area. The thick carpet of vines begins just over a mile to the east of Libourne, and sweeps along the plateau threatening to engulf the little Roman town of St-Emilion. Squeezed into a fold in the hillside, with steep narrow streets and thin, tumbling houses, and with every gap in the buildings revealing a new perspective on the vines lapping and gnawing at the boundaries of the town, St-Emilion is Bordeaux's most beautiful, and relaxing, spot. It is completely committed to its wine; its very foundations are eaten away by ancient caves burrowing into the rock, where, even today, much wine is made and stored.

There are three types of vineyard in the *appellation* 'St-Emilion': the *côtes*, the *graves* and the *sables*. The town itself is the axis for the *côtes* or 'slopes' vineyards. These are tightly packed into an area of some 350 acres (140 hectares), following the contours of the steep south-facing slope for only a couple of miles. Most of St-Emilion's greatest wines are made here, where the soil is mixed limestone and clay, and the châteaux perch precariously on the top of the cliffs, or crouch diffidently at the bottom.

The *graves* vineyards (not to be confused with the vineyards of the Graves *appellation* south of the Garonne) are less spectacular –

Many of the vineyards in St-Emilion are situated on the steep slopes which fan out below the town. The wires are in position ready to train the branches of these young vines as they ripen.

flat, undulating fields spreading back across the plateau towards Libourne and Pomerol. In spite of the name there is only one surge of gravel, running through its two greatest vineyards – Figeac and Cheval-Blanc – the rest of the area is sand and clay.

The third area is the *sables* (or 'sands') area down by the river, where there are no famous properties for neighbours to envy.

The relative lack of gravel explains the unimportance of Cabernet Sauvignon in the region – it just won't ripen properly. But the Merlot ripens triumphantly, thriving on the clay and limestone, while the Cabernet Franc grape (here called Bouchet) provides the backbone and relative toughness without which a purely Merlot wine might seem fat and pudgy.

· APPELLATIONS ·

St-Emilion is one overall AC – but there are several satellite *appellations* for surrounding villages which traditionally used to market their wines as St-Emilion. These communes now tack 'St-Emilion' on to their own names. The most important are Lussac-St-Emilion, Montagne-St-Emilion and Puisseguin-St-Emilion. Their wines can be very tasty if a little solid.

Potentially St-Emilion has the best of Bordeaux's classification systems because it is re-assessed every ten years or so, most recently in 1984. All the wines are subject to tasting to confirm or deny their position, and the ranking is based on actual vineyard land.

The eventual objective is that all the wines will be adjudged either of 'Grand Cru Classé' standard (comprising about 90 top properties), or merely 'St-Emilion', but for all vintages up to 1985 we'll still find the older hierarchical system being used.

Premier Grand Cru Classé (First Classed Great Growth) comprises 11 properties. Two of these – Ausone and Cheval-Blanc – are in a 'premier plus' category of their own which is the equivalent of a First Growth in the Médoc. The other nine are between Second and Fifth Growth in quality.

Grand Cru Classé (Great Classed Growth), as it is now, is a group of 63 properties and covers the whole spectrum of quality from memorable to instantly forgettable.

The words 'Grand Cru Classé' are a good deal less reliable in St-Emilion than in the Médoc. However, Figeac is one of the finest wines of all Bordeaux, and Pavie-Decesse an example of a lesser property making very good wine due to a committed proprietor.

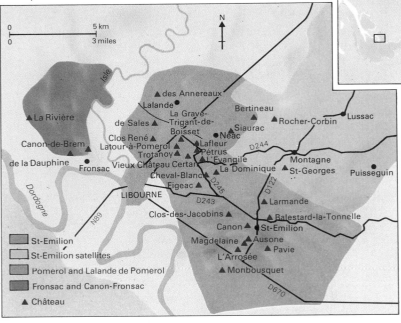

St-Emilion – all ramparts and huddled houses, scrambling alleys and walkways. The vineyards come right to the gates of the town – there is even one inside the boundaries.

Grand Cru (no Classé here) applies to 200 or so châteaux and means almost nothing, despite sounding very grand. The trouble is there are just too many wines involved – and so the idea of a 'Great Growth' becomes completely debased.

Although the re-assessment in 1984 did demote a few châteaux, it's still chaos down there amongst the welter of châteaux claiming Grand Cru status. It'll take another re-assessment or two yet before the ideal that Grand Cru should really mean something becomes a reality.

This emphasizes one arresting feature of the St-Emilion production pattern – the tiny average size of the properties. There are 1,000 different properties in the 12,355 acres (5,000 hectares) of vineyard, and some properties are minute, like Château le Couvent which nestles inside the walls of the town, its 1 acre (0.4 hectares) producing just 1,200 bottles of rather good wine. This also explains the enormous importance of the local co-

operative (the Union de Productions). The co-operative is a great big sprawl of buildings down by the railway. It has 330 members producing 550,000 dozen bottles a year – over 20 per cent of the entire St-Emilion output. The quality is good rather than brilliant, and this is where many of the grandest merchants in Bordeaux and Libourne buy their basic St-Emilion.

· THE WINES ·

This isn't going to be a scenic trip. It's a case of field after field covered with vines, and very few major buildings to get excited about. All the excitement is in the wine itself.

Still, the *côtes* are impressive, and at times they seem almost too steep to allow anyone but a mountaineer to tend the vines. The best properties are arranged along the cliff edge, many having vines at the top and bottom of the slope, and also on the plateau behind. The soil at the top is so thin you can actually see the limestone substratum poking through at the cliff edge. But it isn't for nothing that nine of the eleven top growths are sited here, because they produce a wonderful balance of fruit and toughness, sometimes succulent, juicy and gulpable, with a richness of honey

and raisins and buttery fruit cake, from properties like Canon, Pavie, l'Arrosée and l'Angélus. Sometimes they start slower, tighter, more drawn-in like a Médoc, till a few years ageing coaxes out a smiling nature and your mouth fills with this honeyed richness again. Ausone, Belair, Magdelaine and Curé Bon La Madeleine are wines like this.

Towards Pomerol, we hit the swelling gravel billows of the *graves* section of St-Emilion and its two great châteaux – Cheval-Blanc and Figeac. These are powerful wines, flooding

· VINTAGES ·

Vintages on this side of the river *are* different to the Médoc. The wines are based on the Merlot grape which always ripens earlier than the Médoc's Cabernet Sauvignon so they are picked sooner and will miss any bad autumn weather. In years like 1982 and 1985, wines of stunning richness were made from super-ripe Merlot grapes. However, the Merlot is *much* more susceptible to disease at flowering time in May and June when the size of the harvest is determined. In 1984 a wet June meant that most Merlot vines failed to flower, the crop was tiny and the quality pretty feeble.

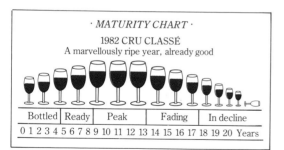

· MATURITY CHART ·
1982 CRU CLASSÉ
A marvellously ripe year, already good

Bottled	Ready	Peak	Fading	In decline

0 1 2 3 4 5 6 7 8 9 10 11 12 13 14 15 16 17 18 19 20 Years

your mouth with rich, ripe fruit, less immediately honeyed and soft than most St-Emilions. However, these two between them use up just about all the gravel, and the rest of the *graves* is actually clay and sand. La Dominique and Corbin do best.

The wines of the *sables* don't have much stuffing, but that's not really the point. They're quite pale, quickly fading to orange, but for a short youthful burst of sweet, honeyed, buttery fruit, they are hard to beat, and it's simple soft flavours like these that got me hooked on St-Emilion, and that I still crave now and then. The classiest example of this is Château Monbousquet.

There have been great improvements in wine-making in St-Emilion recently, with much more careful fermentation, selection and maturing of the wine, and an increasing use of stainless steel for making the wine and new oak barrels for ageing it. This has led to the emergence of several châteaux to the north and east of the town which can now number themselves as among the best in the region, including Balestard-la-Tonnelle, Fonroque, Cadet-Piola, Soutard, Cardinal Villemaurine and Larmande. Since they lack identity as a group, they tend to be just a little bit cheaper than the opposition. However, for the only near-bargains in St-Emilion, it is worth looking to the satellite *appellations* where the wines are often half the price – but only half as good as well! Exceptions are Château St-Georges, Belair-Montaiguillon, Maquin-St-Georges, Roudier, and Vieux-Château-St-André.

· POMEROL ·

You can take a bus to St-Estèphe, stop off for a meal in Margaux en route, and then post a letter at Pauillac post office. Famous wine names all, with villages and towns round which they've developed. But you can't do that with Pomerol. There's no bus stop, no post office, not even a café, and the reason for that is simple – there *isn't* a village of Pomerol! Pomerol is a formless block of fields on the north-east outskirts of Libourne 25 miles (40km) east of Bordeaux, which just happens to produce the greatest red wine in the world, Château Pétrus, a staggeringly rich concentrated wine so full of exciting, unexpected flavours that it's impossible to pair with any food and sometimes seems almost worth its astronomical price.

Forty years ago, no one had ever heard of Pomerol or Pétrus. It must give heart to all the other wine areas of the world which believe that they make great wine, and struggle to persuade someone to listen to them, to know that even 25 years ago, most Pomerols could be bought for the price of their loose change; nowadays you need a written re-assurance from your bank manager even to read the price list. (A bottle of Pétrus could cost you a hundred times as much as plain Bordeaux Rouge from a few miles down the road.)

This tiny wine region measures barely 1,800

The *vendange* in full swing in Pomerol. There is such a worldwide demand for these expensive, luscious wines that every square yard is packed with Merlot and Cabernet Franc vines.

acres (730 hectares) and 650 of those bear vines; the land is too precious to raise a goat or grow cabbages. The châteaux buildings are tiny: except for the smart lick of paint, Château Pétrus' cellars look more like a tractor shed from the outside – and the properties are tiny too – usually between 12½ acres (5 hectares) and 25 acres (10 hectares) in size and rarely producing more than 50,000 bottles of wine.

As with St-Emilion, it is the Merlot grape which provides the key to Pomerol. It is even more extensively planted here, many of the best properties having between 80 and 95 per cent with the balance usually made up by Cabernet Franc. This is because the central swathe of fields, spreading across to the boundary of St-Emilion at Cheval-Blanc, is thick, impenetrable clay – damp and cool enough to squeeze the life out of any stray Cabernet Sauvignon vine, but a positive playground for the Merlot, which produces succulently lush red wines of relentlessly high quality right across the commune.

If this all sounds like the perfect place for a really definitive classification system, we've got another suprise in store. There is *no* classification at all! Everyone accords Pétrus top of the tree status, but the other dozen or more châteaux jostling for position in the pack behind the leader seem more intent upon proving their point by brilliant wine-making than by wasting time and energy on classifications.

Anyway, if the point of most of the classifications is to allow the select few to charge more money, it's not necessary in Pomerol. They're charging quite enough already. Seen overall, these are Bordeaux's most expensive wines, but, just for once, it's nice to be able to say they're worth it.

· THE WINES ·

The taste of good Pomerol really is an experience. With years like 1985, 1983 or 1982, or, looking way back, 1971, 1970 and 1964, it is difficult to believe that these really are dry red wines. They're buttery, honeyed, creamy, plummy – and then you find there's a taste of mint too, and of blackcurrant jam and chocolate. These are the remarkable flavours you'll find in good Pomerol. But there is one more taste, a taste of iron. This provides the backbone without which the flavours might be almost too luscious to take seriously.

Some of the properties in the west like Clos René and de Sales, are on sandier soil, and these are quite absurdly rich and yummy almost as soon as they're made; how anyone ever waits long enough to age them I'll never know. Conversely, there are a few properties like Petit-Village and Beauregard over near St-Emilion, where the lighter soil and a sprinkling of Cabernet Sauvignon makes for a leaner, more Médoc-like style.

But the heart of the matter lies in the scarcely discernible swell of land heading north from the centre of the *appellation*. Here the clay is as thick as plum pudding, with nuggets of iron and minerals occasionally breaking the surface for air. Here are the great flavours which make Pomerols the most accessible, the most openly delicious of great red wines. And here are the properties on whose shoulders their fame has been built. Pétrus is first and finest, followed by Trotanoy, Lafleur, Lafleur-Pétrus, Certan-de-May, Latour-à-Pomerol and La Grave Trigant de Boisset. These are the great names, but the lesser lights like Bon-Pasteur, Bourgneuf-Vayron, Franc-Maillet, and Clos du Clocher have most of the sweetness and much of the weight.

· LALANDE-DE-POMEROL ·

To get something of the flavour of Pomerol without having to pay quite the full whack, Lalande-de-Pomerol is worth a quick look. These wines, neighbours to Pomerol proper just north of Libourne, used to be a steal, having a lovely plummy richness and a price tag which didn't reflect the quality at all. Nowadays the wines are much more expensive, but this 2,160-acre (875-hectare) *appellation*, with more gravel and less clay than Pomerol, produces deep, full-tasting reds, immediately attractive and good for ageing a bit too. Wines to look out for – Siaurac, Annereaux, les Hauts-Tuilleries, Bertineau St-Vincent and Lavaud la Maréchaude.

Winter in a Fronsac vineyard. Whatever the weather the vines have to be pruned; but the snow is welcome because it protects the vine stocks from the frost.

· FRONSAC AND CANON-FRONSAC ·

Everyone has been saying that Fronsac and Canon-Fronsac to the west of Libourne are going to be the next major wine 'discovery' in Bordeaux for so long, that I've given up taking any notice. They should have been discovered years ago, but Fronsac and Canon-Fronsac are still also-rans.

The chief reason is that the organization of the area is virtually non-existent, and there have been none of the programmes of investment and exploitation by merchants which have brought fame and fortune to other areas. With the arrival in Canon-Fronsac of the great Pomerol company of J-P. Moueix, this should change. Canon-Fronsac is an enclave just inside Fronsac, and because of its particularly favourable steep vineyard sites, should make the better wines, but I have seen little evidence of it so far. So I keep on hoping, and in the meantime these are some properties already making good wine: in Canon-Fronsac look out for Canon, Canon de Brem, Toumalin and Vray-Canon-Boyer; and in Fronsac look for la Dauphine, la Rivière, la Valade and Mayne-Vieil.

Above left The solidly traditional label of Pétrus, the world's most expensive red wine, calling itself merely Grand Vin. Lalande-de-Pomerol and Fronsac offer some of the Pomerol flavour for much less money.

· GRAVES ·

As the plane bounces on to the tarmac at Bordeaux's Merignac airport, you should get a warm glow from knowing that you are bang in the middle of one of the historic wine-producing areas of Bordeaux's most traditional region, the Graves. Pity about the airport, the runway, the terminal buildings – all that. We're never going to know Merignac's potential as a wine producer, because our plane has just landed where the vines used to be.

Graves was the first region of Bordeaux to become famous precisely because it encircled the town of Bordeaux, north, west and south. This proximity to Bordeaux was the region's strength around 700 years ago when travel was difficult and dangerous and the Médoc was just an unhealthy swamp. The gravel deposits – the *graves* – gave their name to the excellent light red wine produced there in those days and until the 18th century Bordeaux red wine was virtually synonymous with Graves.

In our century, this reputation has been lost to the Médoc, and many of the formerly good vineyards close to the town are now the back gardens of suburban semis. Although the very top properties managed to retain their prestige – and their vines – Graves came to mean one thing only, nasty, sulphurous white wine of indeterminate sweetness. This was because, although the vineyards round the town were of high quality gravel, the region as a whole stretches much further south for 35 miles, along the left bank of the Garonne river; and from Martillac, a few miles south of Bordeaux, right down to past Langon, almost on the

edge of the Gironde *département*, the soils are increasingly sand and clay. It was easier to get a reasonable crop of white grapes than red, and until the late 1970s there was more white wine made than red, and more white grapes planted.

However, the world has moved on from badly made off-dry white, and the Graves region has responded by a drastic reduction in white wine acreage and consequent increase in red – which now accounts for over twice the acreage of white – and this has all happened in the last ten years. Wine-making techniques have also been modernized and improved here faster and more effectively than any other region of Bordeaux.

It is unusual for an *appellation* to be equally known for red and white wines. Traditionally the reds, based on the Cabernet Sauvignon grape, but backed up by Cabernet Franc, Merlot, and, sometimes, a little Malbec, are made in the gravelly vineyards close to Bordeaux and aged for one to two years in small oak barrels before bottling. The grapes ripen earlier than in the Médoc, being further south; and with a higher percentage of Merlot to soften the Cabernet, the wines rarely have the attack and definition of, say, a great Margaux. However, they do develop a delicious tobacco-cedary scent, and the wines also have the slightly plummy roundness of the Merlot and a definite minerally earthiness. The result is classic claret, somewhere between Pomerol and Médoc in style. Further south, there has been much pioneering work to produce early maturing, substantial reds, and many wines – particularly from leading

merchants like Coste and Mau – simply labelled 'Graves' can be tremendous, juicy mouthfuls. Among the whites, although there *are* still examples of 'headache juice' white Graves around, today's whites are more likely to be too clean and ultra-dry, rather than dirty and sludgy-tasting. Sémillon and the Sauvignon grapes are both used. The Sauvignon adds a little of the green grassy tang it is famous for in the Loire valley, the Sémillon a bit of weight and roundness. Nowadays the wine is normally

Château Haut-Brion was the only red wine outside the Médoc awarded '1st Great Growth' status in 1855. La Tour Martillac produces stubbornly old-fashioned wine of good quality, while Smith-Haut-Lafitte is much keener to update itself; this label is for their fresh, dry white, which strangely is not a Classed Growth wine although their red is.

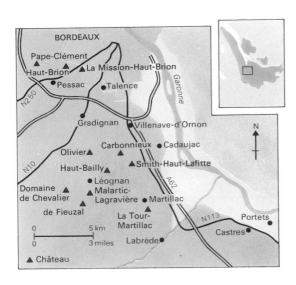

Left **A good winemaker will keep a close watch on the quality of the grapes arriving at the winery. Here Monsieur Ricard surveys his crop of ripe healthy Sauvignon which will be made into a rare and exciting wine – Domaine de Chevalier Blanc.**

fermented very cold, often in stainless steel, at a temperature of 15–20°C. This gives a sharp but fairly full apple-fresh wine.

The best wines, though, from the best châteaux, follow this with six to twelve months' ageing in new oak barrels. These are more expensive but worth it, because they prove Graves to be a great red *and* white area. The wines start wonderfully nutty, round, soft, and as they age they go deep, honeyed and slightly smoky. They can get better for 10 to 20 years – longer than most white burgundies, and they're as good as all but the very best burgundies – and half the price.

· APPELLATIONS ·

The *appellations* in Graves are fairly simple. **Graves** is applied to reds and dry whites. **Graves Supérieures** is supposed simply to mean a white wine with a higher minimum alcohol – 12° instead of 11° – but in practice means a wine veering between slightly sweet to very sweet (in the case of the remarkable Clos St-Georges).

The little sweet-wine district of Cérons, in the southern part of Graves, can also call its dry reds and whites 'Graves'. Pessac and Léognan in the north have recently won the right to add their village name to the label.

The Graves also has its own classification. Its greatest château, Haut-Brion, was deservedly made a First Growth in the 1855 classification – the only non-Médoc red. The rest of the wines had to wait for a century, till 1953 for red wines and 1959 for red and white.

The classification has no subdivisions, and covers a very wide range of quality, though, with the dramatic rise in fine wine prices in the last few years, all these properties are bent on improving their wines. There is also an increasing number of 'non-classified' properties making wine of similar quality.

The Classed Growths are mostly centred round the villages of Pessac and Talence, in the very suburbs of Bordeaux, and Léognan, dispersed in the forest a few miles south. Pessac's pride is the delicately brilliant Château Haut-Brion, and the rather Médoc-like Pape-Clément, while Talence wards off the encroaching housing estates with the more heavy-fisted La Mission-Haut-Brion.

Léognan's top billing is the wonderful, lean and fragrant Domaine de Chevalier, whose red *and* white are world class. Château Fieuzal is the rising star, making richer flavoured exciting reds and whites, while Malartic-Lagravière makes slow-moving reds and whites of high quality, and Haut-Bailly succulent ripe reds.

Martillac used to be regarded as the end of the 'good Graves'; this idea is now out of date, because it is from Martillac south that the enthusiasm, determination and imagination are spreading to the more privileged, but in at least half the cases, more complacent Classed Growth owners in the north. Some of the more exciting properties are Carbonnieux, Chicane, Ferrande, Domaine la Grave, la Louvière, Rahoul, Respide, Roquetaillade-la-Grange, Tourteau-Chollet.

· VINTAGES ·

The Médoc and the Graves usually claim the same vintages as great, because, despite the Graves being further south and picking earlier, these two regions on the south bank of the Gironde have similar weather patterns and the same predominance of Cabernet Sauvignon. However the Graves can be particularly successful in less-than-perfect years, while finding the really blockbuster years like 1982 just a bit too much to bear. 1978, 1979, 1981, 1983 and 1985 were all very good in Graves for reds, and 1983, 1984 and 1985 for whites.

· SAUTERNES AND BARSAC ·

If there is one wine region which has suffered more than any other from the unlawful adoption of its name around the world, it must be Sauternes. In Spain, South Africa, Australia, America and Canada 'Sauternes' has been taken to mean 'anything sweet'. Yet Sauternes is a region which, though small, proud and beleaguered, is as much a geographical fact as London, New York or Rio de Janeiro. And this region, through several quirks of nature, and long historical precedent, struggles to make one of the rarest, most expensive wines in the world – sweet, liquorous, memorable – to which it alone may honestly give the name 'Sauternes'.

The Sauternes region is a little huddle of five villages in the south of the Graves region – Sauternes, Barsac, Preignac, Fargues, and Bommes. The river Ciron trickles through the centre, providing almost the only landmark in a crisscross of country lanes, and shy, nameless vineyards where it is perfectly possible to drive round in circles for hours, totally lost within a few hundred yards of where you're trying to go. Chill and fresh from its source, the Ciron heads for the warmer Garonne, and with the summer days shortening, mists rise slowly off the river, dampening the surrounding vineyards, and filling the air with a humidity which, as the sun climbs in the sky, becomes warm and clammy.

· NOBLE ROT ·

As any gardener will tell you, such a climate is terribly dangerous for the fruit, and so it is. The healthy bloom on the grapes begins to crack, then they shrivel into ill-formed, wizened brownish raisins. The crop looks ruined, wrecked by rot. But just stop and pick one of these horrid, sticky berries, and taste. It will dissolve in your mouth, the skin so ravaged it can hardly contain the flesh, but the sweetness! Instead of being sour and foul, these grapes are intensely sweet, raisined, honeyed – coating your mouth with richness.

What has happened is a rare and exciting natural phenomenon. The rot on these grapes is 'noble rot' (*pourriture noble* in French), related to 'grey rot' – which would indeed reduce the crop to a stagnant, pulpy mush –

You can almost feel the damp autumn mists hanging in the air over the rows of golden vines (*above left*). It is such humid September days that produce the sugar-intensifying 'noble rot' in the grapes (*above*), which is exactly what the Sauternes-maker wants. It will produce great wines which, in some cases, can age almost indefinitely, when the pale green gold of the young wine deepens first to burnished honey and, eventually, to a deep brown old age.

but crucially different. Noble rot feeds only on water, weakening the skin, but leaving the sugar and acidity in the grape untouched. If the grape is ripe when attacked, all that sweetness will be concentrated and intensified, and the richness enhanced by every extra day those fogs rise from the river.

The grape which 'rots' best is the Sémillon, and it provides the thick, gooey richness which is the heart of all good Sauternes. The Sauvignon is less important; it doesn't rot so well, but it does provide a fresh, fruity acidity which is important for balancing the richness, and the Muscadelle is sometimes used in small quantities for its musky, scented sweetness.

Leaving the grapes to 'rot' is a hazardous business, because the weather is by no means always suitable – too much sun will make the grapes too healthy and dry, too much rain, or rain at vintage time, will cause grey rot, or dilute all the concentrated richness. If the noble rot doesn't strike, there is no way you can make truly sweet Sauternes. Some growers first pick grapes and pile in sugar: the result shouldn't be allowed the Sauternes name.

When noble rot does strike, it is rarely all at once, and teams of pickers have to go through the vineyards picking off only single berries, or at least the most affected bunches. Then they have to do it again and again, each time picking off a few more berries. It's a *very* expensive business, and at the end of it all, they'll end up with at most only a quarter as much juice as neighbours who make dry wine.

But this juice should contain perhaps twice as much sugar as juice from a normally ripe grape. In the vat the yeasts begin to convert this nectar with a fair amount of enthusiasm, but the alcohol eventually makes them as drunk as it would us swimming around in a vat of it. At a strength of about 13–14° alcohol they literally give up and drown. The natural grape sugar that remains unconverted is what makes the wine sweet – that, and only that.

· APPELLATIONS ·

The *appellation* which covers all the sweet-wine villages is 'Sauternes', although the village of Barsac can call itself either 'Barsac' or 'Sauternes' and often ends up calling itself both. Because sweet wines have been out of vogue for some time, many proprietors have resorted to making dry white and red under a separate label. Despite Sauternes being an enclave in the Graves region, the name Graves is forbidden to these wines, and they may only be called 'Bordeaux', which doesn't make life any easier for the growers.

The Sauternes classification – like that of the Médoc – was devised in 1855. Yquem has its own 'Great First Growth' status, and there are 11 First Growths and 14 Second Growths.

· THE WINES ·

All of the wines will share the intense glyceriny richness to some extent. The greatest First Growths, like Suduiraut and Rieussec, have a concentrated, silky texture which coats your mouth, as you get to grips with their remarkable sweetness. Yet one of the features of Sauternes sweetness is its lack of any 'grapy' taste. As the wine ages – and good Sauternes needs seven or eight years, and may be best after twenty – the fruit flavours which develop are more likely to be apricot, or peach, or pineapple – not only in their ripe sweetness, but also their fresh, just-off-the-tree acidity.

The use of new oak barrels to age the wine will also affect the flavour. This adds a creamy flavour to the wine, and the vanilla from the wood often combines with the fruit to produce an exotic spiciness and a taste of coconut. If the barrels have been slightly charred on the inside when they were made, the flavour may become a little burnt or 'toasty'. (Think of *crème brulée* – it's *that* kind of smokiness I'm talking about.) And then there's honey. Noble rot's sweetness isn't the sweetness of sugar from a packet: it's honey, as rich and satisfying as when spread on hot toast and butter for a well-earned tea-time by the fire in deep mid-winter.

There are some disappointments in these wines, usually due to a lazy or uncommitted

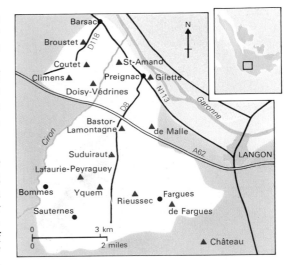

proprietor, but the following make great wine: among the First Growths, Yquem, Lafaurie-Peyraguey, Suduiraut, Coutet, Climens, Guiraud and Rieussec; and the Second Growths, Doisy-Daëne, Doisy-Védrines, d'Arche, Broustet, Nairac, de Malle, Romer-du-Hayot and Lamothe-Guignard.

Because of the enormous expense of making Sauternes, there are few exciting wines from unclassified properties, but the following can be excellent: Fargues, Raymond-Lafon, Bastor-Lamontagne, Cantegril, Chartreuse, Gilette, Guiteronde, Ménota, Piada, Rolland, St-Amand.

· VINTAGES ·

Vintages are *very* important in Sauternes, and they do not necessarily coincide at all with those of the red wine districts to the north and east. After all, what the Médoc, Graves and St-Emilion/Pomerol want are lots of long, dry sunny days to ripen the grapes and keep them healthy. Sauternes doesn't want that: it wants damp, clingingly warm days which will encourage the grapes to develop noble rot. The best recent vintage is 1983 – a classic, packed with brilliant wines. 1981 and especially 1980 were good to very good, and 1986, 1976 and 1975 were excellent. The fine Bordeaux vintages of 1978 and 1979 weren't great shakes here – too dry for too long in the autumn – and the Sauternes of 1982 and 1985 also produced some sweet simple flavours, but not much to shout about.

Gold on the label reflecting golden wine. Château Coutet was designated a 1st Growth in the classification of 1855.

· OTHER WINES OF BORDEAUX ·

The rows of vines cut geometrical patterns across the hillsides of the Côtes de Bourg (*left*). These, and those of Blaye (*right*), are some of Bordeaux's original vineyards, and though now somewhat in eclipse, can produce full meaty reds.

Although it is the famous châteaux like Pétrus, Yquem and Mouton-Rothschild and their ilk which get all the headlines and sell for hundreds of pounds a bottle, they represent at most a couple of per cent of the region's output. They're the gloss, the glitter; but for most producers, Bordeaux is a workaday place. Most growers are faced with a relentless struggle to get a few sous more for their wine, which will make the difference between a new suit or a hand-me-down, a summer holiday at the seaside or a long week-end with the in-laws.

· ENTRE-DEUX-MERS ·

The largest, and the most anonymous, of these areas is Entre-Deux-Mers. 'Between Two Seas', this means, and if you look on the map, you'll notice that the 'two seas' are the river Dordogne coming from the east and the river Garonne from the south-east. Entre-Deux-Mers is the mighty wedge which drives up between them, past Bordeaux and on towards the sea. It's lovely country, the vines sharing the land with all the other bits and bobs of an agricultural society, and the wine, while rarely stunning, can be pretty good. The *appellation* 'Entre-Deux-Mers' applies only to dry whites from the Sémillon, Sauvignon and, to soften things up a bit, the Muscadelle grapes. However, an increasing number of vineyards have switched to red, and although their *appellation* can only be Bordeaux or Bordeaux Supérieur, there's some good stuff to be had.

· PREMIERES COTES DE BORDEAUX ·

Premières Côtes de Bordeaux sounds very grand indeed; the reality is somewhat different. In terms of scenery, this sliver of land running down the right bank of the Garonne is certainly in Bordeaux's first division, but the wines are rather flattered by their *appellation*. Some of the reds have an attractive juicy fruit which is worth a gulp or two, but, though a good château-owner makes all the difference to the end product, these rather rich clay vineyards are never going to set the pulse racing too furiously.

At the south end of the Premières Côtes, however, there are three tiny *appellations* which do, just occasionally, capture a little of the glory of Bordeaux's major names; these are the sweet whites of Cadillac, Loupiac and Ste-Croix-du-Mont. When the autumn weather manages to blend warmth with humidity in just the right proportions, the Sémillon and Sauvignon grapes can get a touch of 'noble rot' and châteaux like Fayau, Loubens and de Ricaud can be luscious and rich. However, since it costs a lot of money to pick noble-rotted grapes, and few proprietors can get a decent price for their wine, most of them have turned to dry wines to keep the wolf from the door.

· CERONS ·

The growers in Cérons have done exactly the same. Cérons is a tiny patch of land immediately north of Barsac, within the Graves area. Its *appellation* is for sweet white wine, and

the Bergerac are the Côtes de Francs and the Côtes de Castillon whose names may appear on the label, although the *appellation* is simple 'Bordeaux Supérieur'. For a long time, Castillon was known simply as the place where the English finally lost control of Bordeaux. More recently some of Bordeaux's most interesting low-priced reds have been appearing from the vineyard slopes round the old town, with much more fruit than usual and sometimes, just sometimes, that elusive hint of blackcurrant. Wines to look out for include Pitray, Moulin Rouge and Parenchère.

· BOURG AND BLAYE ·

The hint of blackcurrant can be quite marked in the two final right bank *appellations*. These are the Premières Côtes de Blaye and the Côtes de Bourg. 'Premières Côtes', as usual, doesn't imply a superior product, because the wines of the Blaye vineyards aren't all that hot. Although they are some of Bordeaux's original vineyards, the wines, primarily red, have a slight jammy sweetness which isn't inspiring in a red wine.

Bourg is better. It is a riverside enclave inside the larger Blaye area, with vineyards tumbling down to the water's edge, and a lovely, river-cooled tranquillity. The wines are almost all red, and a few streaks of gravel in the predominantly clay soil, as well as the occasional use of new oak, gives the good Bourg wines some of that dry blackcurrant fruit and whiff of cedar which makes for very attractive shadows of the wonderful wines just a mile or two across the Gironde in Margaux, St-Julien and the rest.

some of it used to be pretty good. But, once again, nobody wants it any more, and so the growers all end up making dry white and red Graves in considerable quantity, with just a very few continuing the sweet wine tradition.

· DORDOGNE OUTPOSTS ·

On the right bank of the Dordogne the action is mostly red. Tucked between St-Emilion and

The bottle of 1794 Yquem which was sold at Christie's auction house in London in 1986 for £36,000, then a world record for a white wine!

No, not *the* Château Latour in Pauillac, but one of the many lesser wines using La Tour in their names. Tanesse and Tertre du Moulin are typical examples of good modern red and white wines respectively.

· BURGUNDY ·

Unlike the large holdings typical of Bordeaux, wine production in Burgundy is a much more fragmented affair, with many small plots of land owned by a multitude of different growers. These can be rather domestic operations as here, near Beaune. Sometimes the growers will vinify their own crop; or they will sell their grapes to a merchant – the *négociant* – who will vinify and blend the wines of many small producers.

Burgundy is the name of the Grand Duchy which once covered much of eastern France, right up to the North Sea in what is now Belgium. It was famous for all kinds of things – its lavish architecture, its patronage of the arts, its great monastic establishments. But Burgundy had something even more to offer – its inspiring cuisine and its remarkable wines. Standing in the heart of the Saône valley, Dijon, Nuits-St-Georges, Chalon, Mâcon and Lyon were all on the main route through France from Europe's chilly north to the sunbaked Mediterranean. Returning travellers would make a point of slowing their journey, sometimes to snail's pace, in these last outposts of the south, and they would linger long over the sumptuous food and the extraordinary wine. As they headed home to the Netherlands, to the Baltic States and Scandinavia, their last memories would be perfumed by the tantalizing beauty of those wines. And it is on the tales of thousands of such travellers that Burgundy's reputation was built and maintained, long after its political importance had disappeared.

The Côte d'Or, between Dijon and Chagny, has always been the heart and soul of great Burgundy wines, but nowadays we list several other areas under the same heading – Chablis, the Côte Chalonnaise, Mâconnais, and Beaujolais. Most northerly of these is Chablis – just five miles to the east of the *Autoroute du Soleil* at Auxerre. This whole area used to be covered with vines to supply Paris with wine, but the building of the railways, facilitating rapid transport of wine from the more fertile south of France, and the devastation caused by the vine-louse phylloxera, which hit Chablis particularly hard in the 1870s, meant that the vineyards almost became extinct. Only the best, planted in the claustrophobic folds of the Serein valley round the little town of Chablis, and on a couple of wide slopes at St-Bris, Irancy and Coulanges survived.

The Côte d'Or – the 'Golden Slope' – is about 100 miles south and slightly east of Chablis. It comprises a single, east-facing slope of land divided into two parts, the Côte de Nuits in the north and the Côte de Beaune – rising just below Dijon, and fading idly away just west of Chagny. At first it's difficult to believe that such renown can have been gained by this tiny sliver of hillside, stretching for only 30 miles (48km) north to south, and measuring hardly 200 yards (183 metres) in width at its narrow points, and scarcely a mile at its widest. Then you taste the wines – the round, rich exotic reds and the luscious, intense yet totally dry whites, and it begins to make more sense. The reds from the Pinot Noir grape, and the whites from the Chardonnay have flavours so beautiful, so exciting that at their best, no other area in the world can match them.

As the Côte d'Or trails off south of Santenay, the Côte Chalonnaise begins. This is far less defined than the Côte d'Or, because there is no longer a single slope, but numerous ins and outs of hillside, only some of which have the desirable southern or eastern aspect. These parts of the slope have vines, the rest is forest and pasture.

Then there is a gap in the vines, but around Tournus they come back with a vengeance in the area of the Mâconnais. And beyond the southern boundary of the Mâconnais there is Beaujolais, vine-covered wild granite outcrops butting into the flat Saône valley.

· THE GRAPES ·

There are only two important red grapes in Burgundy – the Pinot Noir and the Gamay. They have completely different flavours, and neither likes the other's company much; the

Pinot Noir is wonderful in the Côte d'Or, but the Gamay is pretty crabby; the Gamay is brilliant in Beaujolais, whereas the Pinot Noir is muddy and dull.

Pinot Noir is the aristocrat – but not a well-behaved one. Its greatness is only evident in infuriatingly small quantities, at very few sites, nearly all of which are on the Côte de Nuits or Côte de Beaune. You can't overcrop it or it loses all its personality, it is susceptible to rot, and is one of the most unpredictable of grape varieties – endlessly mutating and changing. Yet when a good vinegrower on a good site is blessed with good weather to mature and gather in his harvest, and the resulting juice is lovingly pressed and transformed into wine by a talented winemaker, then all is forgiven; the soft, red-fruits richness, turning to chocolate, cherries, plums and cream as it matures is one of the most beautiful flavours in wine. Sadly, for every one bottle of red burgundy which approaches the ideal, nine will be cheapskates and imposters.

Gamay has no such pretensions to immortality. Its main purpose in life is to produce purple-fresh, gurgling, bright-eyed Beaujolais. 98 per cent of the Beaujolais region is planted with Gamay, which thrives on the rough granite slopes to produce one of the world's gulpiest reds. Sometimes it tries to get a bit more serious, in the top Beaujolais villages like Moulin-à-Vent, but if it isn't winking behind its solemn exterior there's no point to it.

Chardonnay dominates the whites. This has become the superstar of the wine world, upstaging even Bordeaux's red Cabernet Sauvignon. In a world increasingly keen on quality white wine, Chardonnay combines crisp, fresh flavours with a remarkable ability to be enriched by ageing in oak barrel and in bottle, and an adaptability to almost any soil or climate throughout the world. From the steely, taut attack of good Chablis to the musky apple softness of Mâcon, Chardonnay lives up to its reputation. On the limestone outcrops of the Côte de Beaune, round Aloxe-Corton, Chassagne-Montrachet, Puligny-Montrachet and Meursault, its creamy, buttery flavours, smoky sometimes, honeyed sometimes, make it the most sought after, utterly satisfying variety in the world of white wine.

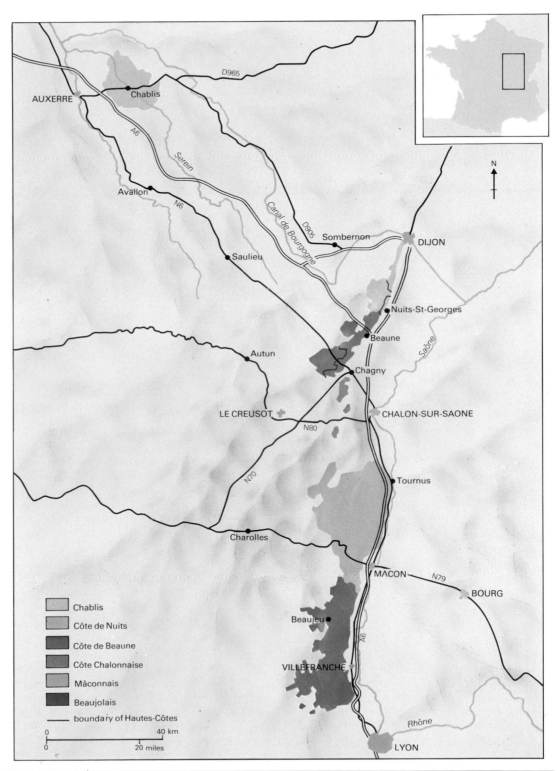

Chablis

Côte de Nuits

Côte de Beaune

Côte Chalonnaise

Mâconnais

Beaujolais

boundary of Hautes-Côtes

Above **Two *vignerons* take their first appreciative sips in the cellars of Bernard Michelot, one of Meursault's leading growers.**

Left **The Côte d'Or is barely 200 yards wide here at its narrowest point, Clos Arlot, south of Nuits-St-Georges.**

Aligoté is the only other white grape of any importance. It's not planted on the best sites, but gives a tangy lemon-sharp wine, not exactly earth-shattering, but welcome enough on a hot summer's day.

· WINE PRODUCTION ·

The organization of wine production and commerce in Burgundy is more complicated than that of any other French wine region. Part of the reason lies in the fragmentation of vineyard land in Burgundy, which resulted from the dismantling of the great estates after the French Revolution of 1789, and was subsequently worsened by the French laws of inheritance. In France, all the offspring must inherit, not just the eldest son. So each successive generation holds less and less land and therefore has less chance of making a living from it. From the broad sweep of a few huge estates, the landscape changed to being a patchwork of private holdings.

But that's not all. Chablis and the Côte d'Or, and to a lesser extent the other areas, traditionally defined and delineated all the different parts of their vineyards according to the minute changes of quality and style which only generations of living off the land can teach you. So different parts of a single field were given different names and each bit was regarded as producing a separate wine. This meant that not only were the winegrowers'

holdings being diminished each generation, but that they might be spread over a dozen different vineyard names.

It isn't possible to build anything but a strictly local trade on tiny amounts of numerous different wines all made in a variety of styles by thousands of individual growers. So, as the fame of these wines spread and repeat orders started to pile in, a merchant class – the *négociants* – developed, particularly in Beaune and Nuits-St-Georges, which would buy barrels of wine from a variety of little growers in the various villages, blend them all together and sell them as Maison So-and-So's Beaune, or Volnay, or whatever. And, in this way, it was the merchants who were responsible for creating a reputation for the wines worldwide. Unfortunately, this led to a quite unforgivable exploitation of many famous wine names by merchants more concerned with profit than the integrity of their wines, and during the 1970s a belief grew that only through buying wines from a single grower could you guarantee authenticity. Luckily the better merchants saw the dangers of their losing all credibility, and they are now once more producing honest and at times exciting wines from individual vineyards.

· APPELLATIONS ·

The *appellation d'origine controlée* system is at its most precise in Burgundy, on paper that is. There is no other region in which it goes into such detail – but by doing so it also reveals one fundamental flaw in the system. The *appellation* guarantees the *origin* of the wine – a specific field in a specific village, planted with the correct grape varieties grown in the right way – but that is *all* it guarantees. It does *not* guarantee *quality*. One might expect that the more specific the vineyard designation, the finer the wine, but you have to remember – a vineyard of, say, 10 acres (4 hectares) may have 20 different owners, some making barely a barrel of wine. Some will bottle their own wine; some will sell in bulk to merchants; the label may say it's all the same wine but it won't taste like it. It might sound like a cop-out, but in Burgundy it is more important to track down a good grower or *négociant*, regardless of the rank of his vineyard holdings, than it is to be a slave to the classifications.

There are five basic levels of *appellation*: general regional, specific regional, village, Premier Cru and Grand Cru.

General regional *appellations* 'Bourgogne' red, white and sometimes pink or sparkling are the most general. They are the catch-all ACs from the Yonne *département* in the north down to Brouilly in the south, and apply to wines which do not qualify for one of the higher ACs – or which have been declassified for commercial reasons. Whites on the whole must be made from Chardonnay or Pinot Blanc grapes and reds from Pinot Noir. The exceptions are Aligoté for whites and the permitted, but unlikely, de-classification of one of the top Beaujolais 'Cru' villages to Bourgogne Rouge, in which case the grape would be Gamay. Bourgogne 'Passe-Tout-Grains' is a blend of Pinot Noir and Gamay and can be good. 'Bourgogne Grand Ordinaire' can contain almost anything and is usually filthy.

Specific regional *appellations* are a sort of halfway house between general regional and single village ACs. 'Chablis' covers all the less good vineyards in Chablis. 'Hautes-Côtes de Nuits' and 'Hautes-Côtes de Beaune' cover the whole range of villages in the hills behind the main slopes of the Côte d'Or and provide quite classy Pinot Noir and Chardonnay. 'Côte de Beaune-Villages' and 'Côte de Nuits-

Villages' can be blends of various villages in those areas. 'Mâcon' and 'Beaujolais' cover the total production in each of their areas; 'Mâcon-Villages' (always a white wine) or 'Beaujolais-Villages' (always red) apply to specific villages, but may be blended.

Village *appellations* apply to the produce of a single village – 'Meursault', 'Pommard', 'Volnay', 'Vougeot', 'Gevrey-Chambertin' and so on – but there is now a welcome move to include vineyard names on the label even if they're not of the top rank. These *lieus dits* (stated place names) – for example, Meursault 'le Cromin' – will be in letters not more than half the size of the village name. In Beaujolais, only the top ten villages may use their village names, and these, too, are increasingly accompanied by a vineyard name.

Premier Cru, meaning 'First Growth' is, confusingly, the group of second best vineyards in Burgundy! Usually, in the Côte d'Or, these are very specific sites which have traditionally produced superior wine. They can be as small as half an acre or as big as five football fields. The village name on the label will be followed by the vineyard name and maybe the phrase 'Premier Cru' between them, as in 'Meursault Premier Cru, le Goutte d'Or'. If several Premier Cru vineyards are blended together, the label will simply state the village name and 'Premier Cru' without a vineyard name, as in 'Meursault Premier Cru'.

Grands Crus (Great Growths) are the tiptop vineyards. This *appellation* only applies in Chablis and the Côte d'Or and, even so, most villages don't have one. Grand Cru wines should reflect that indefinable magic of soil and climate which makes burgundy so rare and desirable. At their best they are outrageously exciting and unforgettable. But, as always in Burgundy, the winemaker's reputation is everything since Grand Cru vineyards are owned both by fine fellows and by frauds, and Grand Cru wines are put together and blended by the seedy merchant and the sincere.

In Chablis the Grands Crus are crowded on to a single bank above the town. In Côte de Nuits they are spread along the middle of the slope between Gevrey-Chambertin and Vosne-Romanée, and, except for a few white vines in Musigny, are all red. The Côte de

· *VINTAGES* ·

There is no such thing as a great vintage in Burgundy – if by 'great' is meant consistently impressive, characterful and exciting wines *across the board*. Because of the tortuous subdivisions of vineyard ownership, and the gamut of joker to genius who may be making the produce of a single parcel of vines into 20 different actual wines, you cannot say 1985, or 1983, or 1978 is a great year for Burgundy as a whole. You *can* say the weather patterns gave the conditions for a fine vintage. But that isn't the same thing at all: the human element enters into wine quality in Burgundy as nowhere else.

However, for the Côte d'Or and Côte Chalonnaise, and assuming you have a good winemaker dealing with good grapes, here are some guidelines: for the reds, 1986 produced *some* good wines, but late summer rains spoiled the chances of a lot of others; 1985 is richly delicious, as fine as any recent year; 1983 is sulky and tough, though *some* wines will be great if you give them time; 1982 is soft, very attractive and underrated; and 1980 is dry, lean, but even more underrated.

The whites are easier. 1986 is a bit special with some abundantly ripe wines to enjoy; 1985 is lovely, ripe, round and tasty; 1984 is rather fresher and more acid, but it's good nippy stuff; 1983 is *supposed* to be great – most of it is heavy, oily and flat. There are a few exciting, lush wines – but not many. Yet the less well thought-of 1982 vintage is full of fresh, gentle classic Chardonnay. It just goes to show – you can't trust generalizations in Burgundy.

Beaune has red and white Grands Crus at Aloxe-Corton, but all the other Grands Crus in the Côte de Beaune are white.

Grand Cru vineyards do not need to use their village name on the label; their renown is reckoned to be greater than that of the mere village. In some cases Grand Cru boundaries straddle two villages (for example, Bonnes Mares is in Chambolle-Musigny *and* Morey-St-Denis). The proliferation of hyphenated village names in Burgundy stems from villages wishing to bask in the reflected glory of their most famous vineyard. Thus the village of Puligny annexed the name of its star vineyard to become Puligny-Montrachet; and Gevrey became Gevrey-Chambertin, and so on.

· COTE D'OR ·

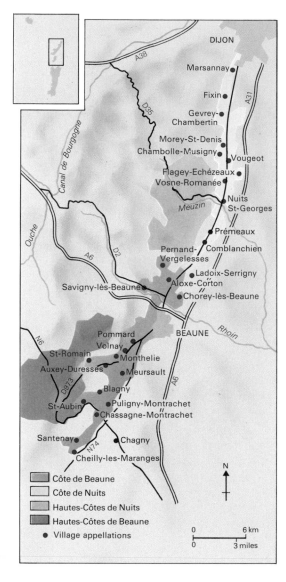

Côte de Beaune
Côte de Nuits
Hautes-Côtes de Nuits
Hautes-Côtes de Beaune
● Village appellations

0   6 km
0   3 miles

It's just a hillside. That's *all* it is. Yet about this particular hillside there has always been something special. The 'Golden Slope', they call it. Is that because of the splendour of the vines all fiery gold at vintage time? Is it because of the liquid gold the soil produces? Sometimes it seems a fancy based on a thousand disappointing pitchers of 'fool's gold'. Whatever the reason, its great wines are gastronomic gold of a rare kind.

There are two very distinct units in the Côte d'Or. Geographically the Côte de Nuits

– taking its name from its chief town Nuits-St-Georges – begins in the suburbs of Dijon, but the wine-producing area starts at Fixin, seven miles (11km) to the south. From here it runs down another 12 miles (19km) to Corgoloin, just south of Nuits-St-Georges. In that 12 miles there are a mere 3,500 acres (1,400 hectares) of vines. At the southern end, the paucity of good vineyard land is most starkly illuminated – to the east, the flat, vineless, Saône basin stretches for 50 miles (80km) to the Jura mountains. To the west, the steep-ranked vines come to an exposed halt a mere few hundred yards from the road. Although the occasional white vine does grow here – usually Pinot Blanc rather than Chardonnay – all the important wine is red. The best sites are east or south-east facing, and are predominantly clay – heavy, rich soil, often mixed with limestone. The strong, slow-maturing flavour of many Côte de Nuits reds seems to reflect the muscular nourishment drawn up through the vines from this ancient alluvial earth.

The Côte de Beaune, running from Aloxe-Corton down to a little huddle of villages west of Santenay, is less claustrophobic; and there is a greater expansiveness about the vineyards. The slopes are gentler, and the area is about double that of the Côte de Nuits, at 7,500 acres (3,000 hectares). Again, we're in primarily red wine country; but good though the reds are, it is the whites, comprising only a quarter of the crop, which have the drinkers of the world on bended knee, gasping for their share. I believe I can say that every year, somewhere in the limestone vineyards of Corton-Charlemagne, Meursault-Charmes or Perri-ères, Montrachet or Chevalier-Montrachet, perfect dry white wine is made.

The *appellation* system of Burgundy described earlier is most detailed in the Côte d'Or. Not only is every patch of vines minutely classified according to its potential quality, but every row inside each field is analysed and judged. In a recent review of the 'classification' of the Côte d'Or vineyards, for instance, in the Epenots vineyards of Pommard, generally regarded as Premier Cru, plots 2 to 8 and 13 to 29 of Les Petits Epenots are accorded the honour, while 9 to 12 are not. Why not? Was it a tiny dip in the land making those plots

more susceptible to spring frost or autumn rot? Did the clay suddenly thicken and spoil the drainage, or was there the merest tilt of land towards the north, which, in this danger-ously cool vineyard area, made the difference between the ripe and unripe grapes?

It is on tiny considerations of this sort that the classification system of Burgundy is founded. In Bordeaux, for example, the mighty Château Lafite-Rothschild shares the same AC as a couple of vines a chap tends in his spare time after running the local petrol station. If they're both in the bounds of the Pauillac commune, they both have the same *appellation* – Pauillac. But in Burgundy, were there a single vineyard of Lafite's size – something almost inconceivable in this patchwork of small holdings – it is extremely unlikely that the whole vineyard would qualify as a Grand Cru; much of it would be Premier Cru or even simple village wine – and would not, by law, be allowed to call itself Château Lafite. The statutory link between classification and *appellation* in Burgundy is a most commendable attempt to promote the individual excellence of the region's wines. Sadly, because of the absence of landowners either big enough or committed enough to quality, it rarely achieves its ends of guaranteeing that the consumer gets what he pays for.

· COTE DE NUITS ·

The flavours for which the Côte de Nuits is famous are uncompromising and memorable. Most of these wines begin life tough, rather bitter, and intense with the chewy, sour-sweet attack of damsons or plums eaten whole and not quite ripe. Great red wines need this kind of tannic cloak, this unfriendly scowl, if they are to keep drinkers at bay long enough to develop beyond that first simple strength of fruit and alcohol. With the Pinot Noir on the Côte de Nuits, this necessary belief in the evolution of flavours is tested to the limit.

That tough-lipped surly start frequently seems to promise little but sore teeth and disillusionment, but the most remarkable transformation takes place, given time – often seven to ten years, sometimes more. The rasping tannin seems to melt into the wine, leaving firstly the flavours of plum, damson

Left A typically Burgundian patchwork of small vineyards at Vosne-Romanée in the Côte de Nuits. This village's 5 Grands Crus and 10 Premiers Crus produce some of the most expensive red wines in the world.

Below The bottle cellars of Bouchard Père et Fils, a leading Beaune *négociant* handling a huge range of wines from Bourgogne Aligoté de Bouzeron to Bonnes-Mares, Chevalier-Montrachet and Montrachet among others.

and cherry in full flight, growing more scented and perfumed by the hour. But this is followed as the wine begins to brown and lighten with the years by a most astonishing sea-change. Those fruit flavours go deeper, sweeter, more cooked, chocolaty, toffee-rich, and they are overlaid by perfume and fragrances, then stenches – yes, I mean it – completely unconnected with any fruit. Rotting cabbage; long-hung pheasant; damply smoking autumn bonfires; the compost of fallen leaves trodden into mush on a forest footpath; the unnerving savoury decay of big country mushrooms sweating in the pan; shoe-leather, worn and worn through. Or, as one of Burgundy's best tasters once put it, with unrestrained enthusiasm – 'undergrowth and wet foxes'! I know what she meant, because great burgundy has to be approached with imagination and time to spare. The wild Pinot Noir is less correct, less wonderfully consistent in its grandeur of fruit and perfume than Bordeaux's Cabernet and Merlot, but this majestic meld of the rich and the rotted, fruit, fragrance and farmyard

is Pinot Noir's and burgundy's alone.

The Côte de Nuits starts mildly enough, rather wearily holding back suburbia's march at Larrey and Chenove. But by Marsannay we are heading towards the real thing, though Marsannay is famous for pleasant rosé rather than red, and Couchey is famous for neither. But breast the swell in the road above Fixin and it all begins.

· THE WINES ·

Fixin doesn't sound pretty, and its wine isn't pretty. It's as though good intentions are still only half translated into good manners and delicate behaviour. Solid, dark reds, needing a long time to age – even the lesser vintages often need ten years – they never really open out and sing, but make up for this by being relentlessly true to pedestrian form and 'worthily' enjoyable.

Gevrey-Chambertin represents the full glory of Burgundy. The most famous Grands Crus, Chambertin Clos de Bèze, Charmes-Chambertin and Griotte, can be everything a

red wine dares to be – weighty, muscular, proud, yet larded with fruit and perfume: somewhere between breathless mayflower, the late summer orchard fragance of cherries or plums, and finally that brilliant compost richness of chocolate and prunes and high, moist game.

Purple prose for these mighty few but, I'm afraid, faint praise for the majority. There is far too much wine being squeezed out of these vineyards, which anyway spread remorselessly across the main road and down towards the

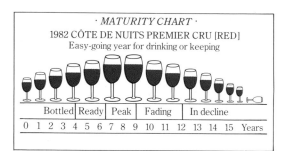

· *MATURITY CHART* ·
1982 CÔTE DE NUITS PREMIER CRU [RED]
Easy-going year for drinking or keeping

Bottled	Ready	Peak	Fading	In decline
0 1 2 3	4 5	6 7 8	9 10 11	12 13 14 15 Years

railway. With very few exceptions good vineyards don't cross the N74 on to the valley flatlands. But Gevrey-Chambertin has decided to exempt itself from this unwritten rule. Overproduced Gevrey will be light, rather raisin-jammy in its sweetness and with just enough tannin to fur your teeth and remind you of what you're missing.

Morey-St-Denis has done a rather unfortunate turnabout in recent years. It used to have a certain recherché fame for the very reason that no one knew about it! In those days there was a good, strong, meaty flavour to the wine, redcurrant fruit and a flicker of dark liquorice

intensity filling out the style. But this village more than most went on an overcropping spree with the Pinot Noir, and the result was many famous wines nearer rosé than red. You *cannot* overcrop the Pinot Noir and expect great results. It is left to good growers like Bryczek, Dujac, Marchand and Ponsot to restore this tarnished reputation.

Chambolle-Musigny, the next village, has a rather different problem. If Pinot Noir doesn't ripen fully, it will make rather frail, lean wine, so you are allowed to add sugar (a process called chaptalization) at fermentation time to increase the alcohol and fatten the wine up a bit. Carefully done this is fine, but any excess sugaring spoils the bouquet and coarsens the texture while merely diluting the taste. Chambolle-Musigny should be the most fragrant of burgundies – floral scents of violets and roses in bloom really do mean something here. But over-sugaring is so rife and most wines so solid and gooey I despair of finding the heart-fluttering scent of roses and taste of cherries I first found in a Chambolle-Musigny Les Amoureuses and haven't forgotten yet.

The two Grands Crus are Musigny and Bonnes-Mares – the latter being marginally more exciting at the moment.

Vougeot, the village, isn't that important, although they make a tiny bit of rather good white wine there. It is the walled vineyard of Clos de Vougeot which is world famous; all 125 acres (50 hectares) are classified Grand Cru, though only perhaps a quarter of the land is good enough to merit it. At its best it is a delicious, almost creamily soft, plummy wine. But the name is just too famous. Too many people want it. Not enough is made. And in Burgundy that leads to overcropping, 'stretching' – and no reduction in price either.

Flagey-Echézeaux always sounds to me more like a bronchitic's sneeze in November than a wine village, and its unpronounceable anonymity is compounded by its being way down in the valley, completely cut off from its vineyards. These are Grands Crus – Echézeaux and Grands-Echézeaux – lovely, fragrant, raspberry-rich wines. Not famous. So not so expensive either.

Vosne-Romaneé *is* famous, and expensive.

Once the summer residence of the Dukes of Burgundy, Fixin, *above*, produces about 19,000 bottles a year of worthy but rarely exciting red wine. Part of the vintage is sold as Côte de Nuits-Villages.

The vineyard name, Clos de Thorey, is the same size as the village name, Nuits-St-Georges, so we know the wine is a 1er Cru. But Griotte-Chambertin, a Grand Cru, is not obliged to state the village name (Gevrey-Chambertin) at all.

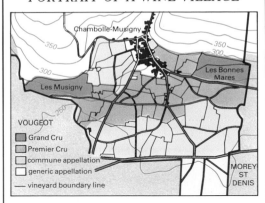

It has a cluster of Grand Cru vineyards – dominated by the estate of Domaine de la Romanée-Conti – which *can*, when they're on form, transport Burgundy on to a new plane of experience. How can you find such flavours and textures as the sensuous creaminess of fresh *foie gras*, the mouthwatering whoosh of smoke and charred beef fat exuded by a mighty roast as it is whipped out of the oven, and the brandied intensity of sweet plums and prunes – all in a dry red wine? But you can – in mature bottles of the great Grands Crus of Richebourg, Romanée-St-Vivant, La Tâche and Romanée-Conti. With Château Pétrus in Bordeaux, they are the world's most expensive red wines. Such flavours eventually go beyond price, and I only hope modern vintages mature as well as their forebears. There are a host of other good wines in Vosne-Romanée in particular, the Premiers Crus of Malconsorts, Beaux Monts and Suchots – often savoury, sometimes burly with tannin, but full of fruit and eagerness to age and boast the joys of great burgundy.

Nuits-St-Georges used to be both the most famous of Burgundy names, and the least reliable. That name obviously did something for the Anglo-Saxon imagination, St George

Let's take a detailed look at one village – Chambolle-Musigny in the Côte de Nuits. Inside its boundaries wine of every quality level is made, from Grand Cru (the best) in the vineyards of Les Musigny and Les Bonnes-Mares, and Premier Cru (from over 20 vineyards including two of the Côte d'Or's best, Les Amoureuses and Les Charmes), right down to Bourgogne Grand Ordinaire (the worst). The classification depends upon the soil and the grapes grown.

Pinot Noir is the quality grape and, on the Côte de Nuits, is usually at its best around the 300-metre contour and on east to south-east facing slopes. The Grands Crus are just below the 300-metre mark, where the elevation to the sun is perfect – steep enough for maximum warmth, not too steep to cultivate. The Premiers Crus are on the slightly flatter slopes with a less distinct east to south-east aspect. The grapes do not ripen here quite so well, the elevation and drainage are not quite so good, but the quality of the wines is still very fine.

At the bottom of the slope the soil is heavier, the drainage and the elevation to the sun less perfect, but the wines are still good enough for the village AC of Chambolle-Musigny. The same is true of vineyards on the 300-metre mark just south of the village, where the slopes are north-facing and the grapes do not ripen fully.

But above these vineyards in the crannies of land approaching 350 metres the ripening is too irregular even to warrant the village AC; as it is below the village, across the main road in the flatlands, where the drainage is too poor, the soil too heavy. If Pinot Noir is used, these wines can be Bourgogne Rouge AC, if mixed with Gamay, the AC is Passe-Tout-Grains or Bourgogne Grand Ordinaire.

'Clos' is the Burgundian term for a walled vineyard. The Clos de Vougeot afloat in an autumnal sea of gold, *left*, was a monastic foundation, but its château is now famed chiefly as the home of the Chevaliers du Tastevin ('Knights of the Tasting Cup') a brilliant public relations organization involving endless razzamatazz. Clos St-Jacques, *left opposite*, is a fine 17-acre Premier Cru in Gevrey-Chambertin.

being the national saint and all that, because the British used to drink an almighty number of bottles with the Nuits-St-Georges label on them.

Things have changed. Nuits-St-Georges is now an increasingly reliable, though expensive burgundy. It doesn't have any Grands Crus, but in the vineyards of Pruliers, Thorey, Vaucrains and Les St-Georges some wine of Grand Cru quality is made, particularly in difficult years like 1983. It usually starts a bit tough, but after a few years there's that wonderful mixture of rich prunes and chocolate, plus the smoky, delicious decay of vegetables and game. Once again, the description sounds frightful and anyway doesn't do the taste justice, but it just shows the tangled web of flavours the Pinot Noir will get caught up in if given the chance.

Prémeaux's vineyards are also included in the Nuits-St-Georges *appellation* and are in fact some of the best, with Clos des Argillières,

Clos Arlot and Clos des Corvées excelling.

Although Nuits-St-Georges is the major town of the Côte de Nuits, it's a quiet, reserved little place, despite having a number of merchants' companies based there. It is the centre for the manufacture of liqueurs and cordials based on such fruits as blackcurrant, and also for the local 'sparkling wine' industry. These use the 'Crémant de Bourgogne' *appellation*, and although people seem to enjoy being rude about them, these champagne-method sparklers are pretty good.

Côte de Nuits-Villages The Côte de Nuits peters out below Prémeaux, with limestone and marble quarries obviously bringing a better return than grape-growing. The villages of Comblanchien, Corgoloin and the Prissey part of Prémeaux used the general *appellation* Côte de Nuits-Villages, which is also used by some of the vineyards in Brochon and Fixin, north of Gevrey-Chambertin. The wines are becoming increasingly good as growers decide to go it alone rather than monotonously sell into the merchants' blending vats.

· COTE DE BEAUNE ·

The Côte de Beaune begins in grand style with the hill of Corton which juts out of the plain just north of Beaune. For some reason it reminds me of a monk's forehead – that must be the ring of trees at the top resembling a tonsure. Three villages lay claim to this marvellous hill and its red and white Grands Crus: Ladoix-Serrigny, Pernand-Vergelesses and Aloxe-Corton.

· THE WINES ·

Ladoix-Serrigny has some small Grand Cru parcels on the northern tip of the hill of Corton, and if it wasn't for that we'd only ever taste the wine in Côte de Beaune-Villages blends, because it is hardly ever bottled under its own name.

Pernand-Vergelesses, at the western extremity of the hill, shares the Corton and Corton-Charlemagne Grands Crus for those vines squeezed under the rim of the forest, but, in this case, we *do* see quite a bit of it as an *appellation* in its own right. The reds usually have a soft, raspberry fruit pastille gentleness to them while the whites are fairly

dry, direct wines, good, but not seductive. There is a little Aligoté here from old vines, and it is the best Aligoté of the Côte d'Or.

Aloxe-Corton, at the base of the best slopes, produces the larger part of the red Grand Cru Corton and the white Grand Cru Corton-Charlemagne, potentially two of Burgundy's greatest wines. Red Corton should have a magically exciting blend of the savoury richness and beef of Vosne-Romanée in the Côte de Nuits and the mellow, perfumed sweetness of Beaune further to the south. Corton-Charlemagne should blast you with rich, impressive buttery strength. But, as so often in Burgundy, a single strip of a single hill is being asked to provide more than it can manage. The red Grand Cru Corton now covers more than a dozen vineyards, not all of Grand Cru quality, and many of the wines are made and blended in a sweet innocuous style. The whites are still good, but rarely pulsating with the sensuous excitement of untold

The finger-chilling task of pruning back the vines and burning the cuttings in winter on the Côte de Nuits.

Traditional wicker harvesting baskets piled high on the shoulders of a vintager at Aloxe-Corton on the Côte de Beaune.

pleasures ripe for plucking that *should* mark out a really great wine.

Savigny-lès-Beaune is another 'forgotten' village – there are several more in the Côte de Beaune – but it does make some very good reds, a little reserved and light to begin with, but softening to a gentle strawberry and redcurrants flavour with a bit of time.

Chorey-lès-Beaune, opposite Savigny, down in the plain, does much the same job of producing light, strawberryish, easy-drinking reds.

Côte de Beaune-Villages Once again Chorey wines often end up as Côte de Beaune-Villages. This is a fairly widespread red wine *appellation* covering 16 villages in the Côte de Beaune (but excluding the most famous ones – Aloxe-Corton, Beaune, Volnay and Pommard). Usually a merchant will blend the wines of several of these villages together. In the days when the lesser villages couldn't sell their wines under their own name, it was a good source of inexpensive red, but now that even the least of the villages is gaining the confidence to sell under its own name, it is mostly only the scrapings at the bottom of the Pinot barrel which will go to market as Côte de Beaune-Villages.

Beaune itself isn't as famous a wine as once it was – which is a good thing in terms of quality. But Beaune the town has never been more renowned. It's the home of the world-famous Hospices de Beaune wine auctions, and as more and more wine-lovers travel to discover the vineyards of the wines they love, all the roads of Burgundy seem to lead to Beaune. With reason. It's a gorgeous town – still walled about by ramparts, the streets still cobbled, and, frequently, pedestrianized, steep sloping roofs glistening with their multi-coloured tiles. And it has life! The streets bustle with visitors and commerce, the cafés and restaurants brim with locals and tourists alike, and beneath it all, a hundred cellars stealthily mature the wines of all of Burgundy.

With all this, it's easy to forget the actual wine, but we shouldn't, because Beaune is some of the cheapest and most reliably enjoyable wine in the Côte d'Or. It's nearly all red, and there's lots of it, with a great many Premier Cru quality vineyards – Grèves, Teurons, Cent Vignes and Chouacheux among

Most of Burgundy's major merchant houses are based in Beaune, clustered like iron filings around the magnet of the famous Hospices de Beaune and its magnificent Hôtel-Dieu (*far left*). The Hospices are charitable institutions whose income comes from bequests of vineyard land. Each year on the third Sunday in November, an auction (*left*) is held to determine the price of wines of the new vintage from Hospices holdings.

numerous others. These are soft reds, full of redcurrant, raspberry and strawberry flavours, the tannins and acids held in balance by the fruit, with a wonderful, strange whisper of something metallic behind a rose-petal perfume to provide the backbone.

Pommard *has* been called the Côte de Beaune's finest village, but it hasn't got any Grands Crus, and doesn't really deserve any, because the quality of the wines rarely matches the reputation. This is largely because the United States had a love affair with Pommard in the same way as the British were passionate for Nuits-St-Georges. Wines unfit for paupers were sold under princely Pommard titles. As with Nuits-St-Georges, things are on the mend, the good guys struggling against the wheeler dealers who still

flock into the village sniffing for a bargain. When Pommard is real, it is strong, meaty stuff, rich with a fat plummy fruit, sturdy rather than sophisticated. Good 'old-fashioned' burgundy.

Volnay should be the exact opposite. It is thought of as producing the Côte d'Or's lightest, most ethereal wine. Well, there's a lot of chalk in Volnay's vineyards, which makes for light, but beautifully cherry-fragrant wines, and the top vineyards sometimes emulate some of Pommard's brawn without trading in the perfumes.

Monthélie is one of the few bargain red wine villages of the Côte, used to selling its wine as Volnay. Most of the little villages around here suffered a similar fate, selling their wines under the more famous names of Beaune or

No vineyard name on this Beaune 1er Cru means it is blended from several 1er Cru vineyards. The unadorned village name, Chassagne-Montrachet, tells us this is the simple village wine, usually a blend of lesser vineyards.

Above The contented Burgundian features of Monsieur Fleurat contemplate a sample of his red Santenay at Château du Passe-Temps. Santenay was a popular spa town and used to be as famous for its water and its casino as it now is for wine.

Left In the Hautes-Côtes, vineyards share the available land with pasture and grain.

Pommard or Volnay. Modern *appellation* laws put a stop to this, and wines like the full, earthy, cherry-chewy reds of Monthélie, quite unlike Volnay in any case, haven't yet built much of a reputation for themselves, which is good news for us.

Auxey-Duresses is in much the same position. With a fair amount of red and white, it used to shelter beneath neighbouring Meursault's broad shoulders. Juicy reds with a rather spicy fruit and nutty whites of some style are easy to make here, and not expensive to buy, but just at the moment this little Cinderella seems to be sulking a little too openly at the white wine ball which is in full swing in Meursault and its sister villages of Puligny and Chassagne.

Meursault is unique, wonderful wine, and there's a bucketful of it to go round. There's a little red, but the vast majority of these soft,

rolling slopes are crowded with Chardonnay vines capable of producing some of the world's most gorgeously attractive dry white wines. Here the combination of easily ripening grapes and grower after grower prepared to age their wine in new oak barrels produces a flavour so soft, so creamy, so full of honey and peaches and cinnamon and nutmeg spice, sometimes seasoned with fruit like orange peel and apples, that it is impossible anyone could dislike good Meursault. Far more Meursault is good than bad, which is a rare cause for rejoicing in one of Burgundy's famous names.

Blagny, wedged into the hills above Meursault, is another little village, whose whites, though a little drier, are usually sold as Meursault rather than Blagny.

Puligny-Montrachet – a featureless crabby village, whose dull streets and drab dwellings

give no hint that they house the growers and harvesters of a white wine more rare, more perfect than any other – is the surprisingly anonymous focus point for Montrachet. Montrachet, and its fellow Grands Crus – Bâtard-Montrachet, Bienvenues Bâtard-Montrachet, Chevalier Montrachet – keep the adjectives and superlatives flowing long after

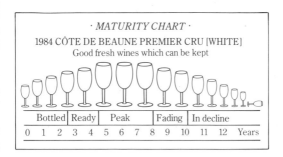

· *MATURITY CHART* ·
1984 CÔTE DE BEAUNE PREMIER CRU [WHITE]
Good fresh wines which can be kept

Bottled	Ready	Peak		Fading	In decline
0 1 2	3 4	5 6 7	8	9 10	11 12 Years

the last glowing mouthful is swallowed. Dry it is, certainly, but only because it contains no sugar, everything else is a richness, a lusciousness, a succulence made of honey and butter, nuts and cream and glyceriny fruit. Yet whereas Meursault might be satisfied with this, Montrachet and its peers have something more – something mineral, something smoky even, coffee bean smoky, crackling wood-fire smoky, incense smoky, all mingling in with perfumes, fruits and an impressive richness of texture. It leaves you marvelling at this brilliant marriage of opposites, and understanding why men will commit dark deeds to get a few bottles of these heavenly wines. Luckily, below the Grands Crus, there are a good range of Premiers Crus of great personality and exciting flavours, in particular, Cailleret, Combettes, Folatières and Referts. And there are straight village wines, but these are very definitely not so memorable.

Chassagne-Montrachet's village wines *are* frequently memorable, and have a lovely, broad, savoury flavour to match the warm buttery core of the wine. Chassagne also has a chunk of Montrachet, and two other Grands Crus – Bâtard and Criots Bâtard – but it is clear that people think of Puligny as the real home of Montrachet, so Chassagne's lesser wines can be fairly cheap and extremely good. That's the whites. Amazingly, Chassagne produces more red than white! It can be fairly chunky and satisfying but is just as prone to have a rather jammy hot plumskins kind of fruit and end up a bit earthy and short.

St-Aubin is hidden away a bit beyond the old Paris road to the west, but makes nice, strawberry-fruited reds and good toasty, biscuity whites.

St-Romain, even further off the beaten track, is home to some fairly solid cherry-stone tasty reds, and fresh flinty whites. The wines aren't much seen, but many of Burgundy's best wooden barrels are made in the village by François Frères.

Santenay will give us one last fling – not a first flush of brilliance, rather a last dance before heading home – with its fairly decent, jam-soft and attractively meaty reds.

And then this precious buttress of east-facing hillside tires, falters and drifts away to

the left, a bit neglected and forlorn – its strength finally spent.

· THE HAUTES-COTES ·

Behind the 'Golden Slope', the valley and forests reclaim much of the land. The relaxing scenery is heavenly and suitably un-winey after the concentrated vineyard vista of the Côte d'Or. However, there are vineyards here dotted about on south-facing slopes and these are the Hautes-Côtes de Nuits to the north and Hautes-Côtes de Beaune to the south. The Pinot does struggle a bit to ripen, but is pleasant, light and slightly strawberryish, except when the vintage is very hot, and it beefs up a bit. Chardonnay is the usual white variety with a little Aligoté. It doesn't achieve the excitement of Côte de Beaune whites but in its fresh way is a pretty decent drink.

Côte de Beaune-Villages, the AC once used by many less well-known villages, is now likely to be a blend of several Côte de Beaune village wines. The Meursault is a 'non-classified' single vineyard wine – denoted by the smaller type used for the vineyard name.

Above Chardonnay vines in Puligny-Montrachet having their foliage thinned before harvesting. These grapes produce some of the finest white wines in the world, notably the magnificent and completely unaffordable Le Montrachet.

· GOOD PRODUCERS ·

Côte de Nuits growers: Magnien, Bryczek, Ponsot, Grivot, Bertagna, Lamarche, Jayer, Michelot; *négociants*: Labouré Roi, Drouhin, Jaffelin, Moillard, Domaine de la Romanée-Conti. **Côte de Beaune** growers: Tollot-Beaut, Chevalier, Bize, Morot, Gaunoux, Mussy, Lafon, de Montille, Domaine de la Pousse d'Or, René Manuel, Pierre Morey, Coche-Dury, Leflaive, Laguiche, Gagnard Delagrange; *négociants* Latour, Jadot, Drouhin, Jaffelin, Moillard.

· COTE CHALONNAISE ·

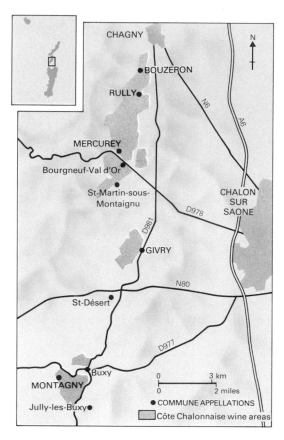

porcelain pot smashed with a baseball bat. The whole area is twists and turns – hummocks, dells and dips, as forest, meadow and vine all fight for their place. So what finally happens is that when there is a suitable chunk of south-to-east-facing hillside, it is planted with vines – usually with forest above and pasture below. Limestone soils, in particular round Montagny and Rully, are planted mostly with white grapes; heavier clay soils – especially those at Mercurey and Givry – are planted primarily with red.

These vineyards are often surprisingly high up – sometimes clearing 1,000 feet (350 metres) – and the local microclimates are cooler and less favourable to grape ripening than the Côte d'Or. So, what with irregular landscapes, high vineyards and uncertain summer and autumn warmth, the wines are light, occasionally sharp, rarely rich, but, from good producers, full of attractive, sometimes unexpected flavours.

· THE GRAPES ·

Pinot Noir is the chief grape occupying two-thirds of the vineyard acreage.
Gamay, although it isn't particularly suited to the cool conditions, has nearly 15 per cent.

Chardonnay, which produces the area's most marketable wine, has only 10 per cent, although new plantations should increase this. **Aligoté**, though not much of a grape in general, comes into its own here, covering almost 10 per cent of the vineyard area.

· APPELLATIONS ·

The difficulty of finding good vineyard sites is demonstrated by the fact that the Côte Chalonnaise is almost as long as the Côte de Beaune, and yet produces little more than a quarter the amount of wine. The *appellation* system reflects this in that there are only five villages important enough to have their own AC, although some of the best Bourgogne Rouge and Bourgogne Blanc is produced in the lesser areas.
Bouzeron, right at the northern tip, is a lovely sleepy little village in a cleft of hills. The road signs are rusty, the windows shuttered and the café in the square wonders if you haven't

Below left **A sociable feel to the harvest at Mercurey, the top village in the Côte Chalonnaise. It produces more wine – mostly red – than Rully, Givry and Montagny put together.**

T he Côte Chalonnaise has always had the reputation, if it has had any reputation at all, of being the half-way house between the Côte d'Or to the north, and the Mâconnais and Beaujolais to the south. This may be justified geographically, because the region is indeed crammed into the hills and valleys between the Côte de Beaune and the Mâconnais. But in terms of style, the wines often have a greater similarity to the wines from Chablis and the Yonne far to the north than to the fat creamy whites of the Mâconnais or the round, plummy reds of the Côte de Beaune.

It's all a question of geography and climate. The Côte Chalonnaise is an extension of the Côte de Beaune, but whereas the latter benefits from a long, low, continuous southeast-facing slope, angling gently to the sun, this begins to skeeter away to the west just past Santenay and what remains to the south is about as predictable and uniform as a

got a home to go to if you're still lingering over your Aligoté as late as 9pm. But the wine deserves its recently acquired AC – Bourgogne Aligoté de Bouzeron. Good growers are able to boast of vines up to 100 years old, and it is only wine from old vines which can achieve the delicious paradox of flavours which makes Aligoté special. It is light green in colour, sometimes with a tiny prickle still in the wine, and it has the clean-living but unctuous smell of buttermilk. Sniff a bit longer, because everything changes when you taste it. The buttermilk disappears, swept aside by a full but curiously neutral lemony freshness and a nip of pepper. It certainly wakes you up if you're dozing, and it should be drunk, for exactly this reason, young and untamed, though a couple of growers do age it a little.

Rully is just over the hill from Bouzeron, but the village seems a full century closer to the present day. This is because Rully has, until recently, been the centre for making sparkling

Below Vineyards near Bouzeron produce the best Aligoté in France which is the white wine traditionally used with Crème de Cassis to make Kir. Its *appellation* was only granted in 1979.

wines, having quite a reputation for its champagne-method Crémant de Bourgogne. Burgundian fizz is getting better and better, and the pale delicate flavour of the Crémant from Rully is particularly refreshing. However, there are decent reds and whites made here too. The reds are rarely full in colour or body, and although the strawberry gentleness of the Pinot Noir is usually there, sometimes I wish it were just a little less ethereal. The whites are also light, but it suits them better, since the dryness usually has a soft edge and they can also have a real come-hither openness – dry, but spicy and herby in a country flowers way. A few growers use oak barrels, but more than just a touch usually unbalances the wine. Many of the vineyards are accorded Premier Cru status, but such definitions are frequently of little relevance in the Côte Chalonnaise.

Mercurey is the most important village, so much so that many locals refer to the Côte Chalonnaise as the *région de Mercurey.* They've got a point. The town of Chalon is an old port on the river Saône to the east, but Mercurey is bang in the middle of the vineyards and produces more wine than all the other villages put together. It's almost entirely red, although there is a little white, which I've usually found to be rather flat-footed and ponderous. The red, however, can be quite special. It is rarely weighty, but makes up for this with an intense strawberry fruitiness, balanced on one side by tannin and earthiness, but finished off with a lingering spicy scent of wood-smoke which I like a lot. They can age, too, which is not generally a Côte Chalonnaise characteristic. As in Rully, there are various Premiers Crus all over the place, but their wine is not noticeably better, it all depends on

the sincerity and talent of the winemaker.

Givry is also mainly a red wine village, with just a tiny dribble of white. Some labels proclaim that Givry was the 'preferred wine' of Henry IV of France. He certainly got about, that king; you can find wines from Champagne to the Pyrenees which he is supposed to have 'preferred'. Anyway, Givry can be really good, sweeter-fruited somehow than Mercurey, a little more cherry-perfumed, rounder and smoother. I've had bottles at five years old that seemed to be everything a straightforward burgundy should be.

Montagny is entirely white (red grapes here qualify only for Bourgogne Rouge). You should take even less notice of 'Premier Cru' in Montagny, because it simply means that the wines have achieved an extra half a degree of alcohol. Pretty pointless and I'm afraid that's also true of some of the Chardonnays here, because they can be raspingly chalk-dry and disappointingly fruitless. However, some growers have recently begun to use a little bit of oak for ageing and the results are a dramatic improvement. Although elsewhere in the Côte Chalonnaise growers and merchants are in control, it is the co-operative at Buxy which is the dominant feature in Montagny, and they can produce some really good stuff.

· *GOOD PRODUCERS* ·

Bouzeron Bouchard Père et Fils, Aubert de Villaine.
Rully Noël-Bouton, Delorme, Cogny, Jadot.
Mercurey Juillot, Faiveley, Rodet, Chandesais.
Givry Thénard, Derain, Domaine de la Renarde.
Montagny Cave de Buxy, Moillard, Latour.

The Mercurey label is unusual because it is a special bottling by the local promotional body, the Confrèrie St-Vincent. Rully is most famous for sparkling wine, but it does have a few estates which bottle their own still wine.

· MACONNAIS ·

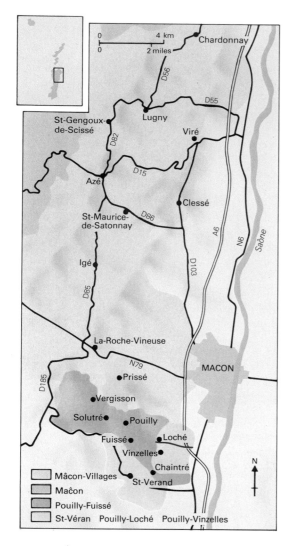

Map legend:
- Mâcon-Villages
- Mâcon
- Pouilly-Fuissé
- St-Véran Pouilly-Loché Pouilly-Vinzelles

Both these wines are 'lookalikes' for Pouilly-Fuissé. St-Véran is a fairly new AC and most of its wine is bottled by merchants, in this case, Georges Duboeuf. Vinzelles is also bottled by a merchant, Protheau from the Côte Chalonnaise.

I t's too easy to dismiss both the Mâconnais and its wine as dull, flat, boring and unworthy of much further investigation. That's not fair to the region or to its wines.

Admittedly, there is only one truly memorable sight in the Mâconnais – and that is the startling rock of Solutré which thrusts like the prow of a dreadnought battleship out above the little villages which produce Pouilly-Fuissé. One could say that this is good planning, because Pouilly-Fuissé, at its best, is the only stupendous wine of the region. But the Mâconnais is much more than that. As you leave the Côte d'Or and the Côte Chalonnaise, a perceptible change takes place. The air feels warmer and less damp, the fogs lift, and under a sky which seems to be gaining that deep, demanding azure of the south with every mile you travel, the houses have changed too. The cramped, grey tiled roofs of the north give way to warm Provençal orange, straight tiles become rounded, steep roofs become flat, and the people who live there build porches and verandahs along their walls to soak up the sun. The Mâconnais is where I always feel that sudden surge of pleasure, knowing I have reached at last the warm climes of the Mediterranean and shed the drab, drear north.

The wine styles have changed too. Although we are still dealing with the same range of grapes as in the rest of Burgundy – white Chardonnay and Aligoté, red Pinot Noir and Gamay, the end results are quite different. The reds are rougher, coarser, lacking the smooth touch and fragrant fruit of the Côte d'Or and Côte Chalonnaise wines, while the whites, even at the most basic level, have something fat, something ripe, grapy, and not quite dry about them – southern characteristics from Burgundy grapes. Indeed the vintage does usually start a good week before the more northerly regions, as the grapes rush to ripeness in the warmth.

· THE GRAPES ·

Red Mâcon was until recently a predominantly red wine area, with more Gamay than Pinot Noir. I've never been very taken with red Mâcon. There's a rawness, a brusque, earthy attack to the wine and rather a lot of acidity. It never has the class of the Pinot Noir wines to the north, and it also fails to capture the joyous burst of fruit which the Gamay achieves in Beaujolais just a few miles to the south. The market obviously reflects this because the Gamay acreage is now down to 25 per cent and Pinot Noir has increased to 7.5 per cent.

White The rest, with the exception of a little Aligoté, is planted with the golden grape – the world's favourite, Chardonnay. I'm not sure they realize how lucky they are in the Mâconnais to have Chardonnay as their main grape occupying two-thirds of the vineyards, because their efforts at marketing this most marketable of wines have been generally dire. The exception, Pouilly-Fuissé, almost suffocates in its own renown, but the rest of the Mâconnais has allowed the name 'Mâcon' to become debased and derided. Mâcon is the biggest producer of white wine in Burgundy, yet it is only now that we are beginning to see a reliably high quality emerging, which makes the best of the juicy, honeyed flavours the grapes can produce.

· APPELLATIONS ·

Mâcon This is the basic AC for reds or rosés from Gamay and white from Chardonnay. (Bourgogne Rouge is the *appellation* for Pinot Noir wine.)

Mâcon Supérieur The same as 'Mâcon' but with one degree more alcohol. Many of the white wines in this group are declassified into Bourgogne Blanc.

Mâcon-Villages is wine from one or more of the 43 best villages in the region. A few red wines use it but it is overwhelmingly a white AC. Among the villages, there is a small group which tacks on the village name – as in Mâcon-Viré, Mâcon-Lugny and so on. These are very slightly more expensive, and worth the price.

St-Véran applies to wine from eight villages surrounding Pouilly-Fuissé. The villagers reckoned that their wine was better than the other Mâcon-Villages, but the Pouilly-Fuissé producers weren't going to share *their* name with anybody. So they plumped for St-Véran. They hoped to get a reputation for being nearly as good as Pouilly-Fuissé, and therefore, presumably, they wanted nearly as good a price for their wine. Well, the wine *is* very good, usually better than all but the best Pouilly-Fuissé – full, soft, buttery, lovely stuff. But the world at large hasn't got the message so the price has remained low. This is bad luck for the growers, but excellent news for us, since St-Véran gives us the chance of drinking lovely wine at a knock-down price.

Pouilly-Vinzelles and **Pouilly-Loché** are made in the villages of Vinzelles and Loché. They are similar to St-Véran, maybe a bit leaner, although rather more expensive, but nothing like as expensive as Pouilly-Fuissé, the tawdry, glitzy superstar of the region.

Pouilly-Fuissé is, without question, *capable* of making the Mâconnais' finest wine. A tiny handful of producers – like Vincent, Noblet, Ferret and Corsin – proud and jealous of their reputations, make wine, dripping with ripe, melon-juicy fruit, and swathed in coils of honey and spice. These growers demand, and get, a price equivalent to good Meursault. However, 98 per cent of the Pouilly-Fuissé production is lumped together and made at the local Chaintré co-operative, and three-quarters at least of that is sold anonymously under a variety of merchants' labels – at horrendous prices. Steer clear. There are few worse bargains than a 'commercial' Pouilly-Fuissé.

· CO-OPERATIVES ·

Interestingly, co-operatives dominate the Mâconnais, producing about 85 per cent of the wine, and, in general, they have had a highly beneficial effect on quality. It all depends on whether the co-operative has a strong or weak director, one who will push through modernization and reform in the teeth of the notoriously conservative wine-growing fraternity, or one who will give in to the petty jealousies and in-fighting of the community. Ideally, a single grower's wine is still best, but the following co-operatives have deservedly high reputations: Lugny-St-Gengoux-de-Scissé, Viré, Prissé, Clessé, Vinzelles and Mancey usually deliver the goods.

Above **Vineyards nestle on the lower slopes of the spectacular outcrop of the rock of Solutré in the Mâconnais. This region is a large producer of mostly easy-going reds and whites between Chalon and Lyon.**

A rainbow forms after summer rains in the vineyards of Fuissé, a village which with Pouilly, Solutré, Vergisson and Chaintré, produces the Mâconnais' most renowned but most over-priced wine, Pouilly-Fuissé.

· VINTAGES ·

Most Mâconnais are for drinking young – up to two years old. Only top Pouilly-Fuissé will mature excitingly.
1986 Vintage of good, but not exceptional wines.
1985 Wonderful, super-ripe, balanced wines.
1983 Excellent wines, mostly now a bit past it.

· GOOD PRODUCERS ·

Duboeuf, Loron, Thévenet, Latour, Corsin, Vincent (both Pouilly-Fuissé and St-Véran), Caves at Viré, Prissé, Lugny-St-Gengoux-de-Scissé.

· BEAUJOLAIS ·

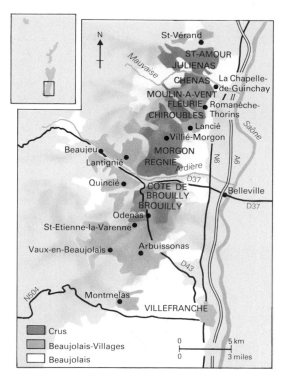

Crus

Beaujolais-Villages

Beaujolais

I can never see a picture of the tumbling hills and dales of the Beaujolais without feeling a tiny smile flicker across my lips, a glint begin to brighten my eyes. If you haven't yet given yourself a few days away from the cares and worries of everyday existence in these dreamy vine-clad valleys and peaks, do it soon, because magic is here – in the people, the land, the life they live – and the wines they make.

The granite hills above Lyon, the last splutter of the Massif Central before it declines into the flat repose of the wide Saône valley, are above all red wine slopes. There is a little rather feeble rosé and some reasonably good but stone-dry white, but Beaujolais to me is red – purple-red, pink-red, foaming, gushing fruit-of-the-vine red. And it comes from only one grape – the Gamay. Elsewhere in France, the Gamay is endlessly derided as a common vulgar grape – doesn't that sound patronizing? Well, those same belittlers of the Gamay would also be the first to dismiss contemptuously what Beaujolais stands for – bright, easy-breezy, gurgling draughts of unpretentious happy-juice. Beaujolais is certainly not a wine

to pontificate about, mark out of a hundred, or lay down for your godchild – it's there to drink, to enjoy – and that's it!

Well, most of the time, that's it, anyway. There are a group of ten villages in the north with particularly good hillside slopes called the 'Crus' or 'Growths'. They make a richer flavoured wine, which may improve with a little age – but even here we're talking about months, not years. The vast majority of Beaujolais should be drunk as soon as you can get your hands on it. And there's no better time to start than in November of each year when Beaujolais Nouveau arrives.

· BEAUJOLAIS NOUVEAU ·

We think of Beaujolais Nouveau (which simply means New Beaujolais, this year's vintage) as a recent phenomenon because of all the razzamatazz of the Beaujolais 'race', lunatics of all shapes and sizes attempting wild, weird feats of derring-do in the annual dash to be the first home with the new wine. But it isn't recent at all. Drinking the first wine of the new vintage has been a time for celebration and partying among winemakers since time immemorial; it's just that the rest of us have only just discovered the fun and games and so, on the third Thursday of November each year, when Nouveau is released, we all have a wild time and a good laugh and end up ever-so-slightly tipsy – just as they did 1,000 years ago. Far from being 'modern', it actually takes us close to the time-honoured traditions of wine – and the fogeys and kill-joys who get so snooty about Nouveau would do well to remember that.

· MAKING BEAUJOLAIS ·

We can drink Beaujolais so early because the Gamay naturally has a simple, bright, almost peachy taste, and it is fermented in a special way to capitalize on this. Instead of being pressed, the grapes are all piled into a vat, stalks and all, and the vat is covered over. The grapes at the bottom get squashed, the juice oozes out, and starts to ferment in the normal way, heating up considerably and giving off carbon dioxide. This warm blanket of gas rises up the vat and envelopes all the uncrushed grapes nearer the top, which then start to

Madame Bloud and *négociant* Georges Duboeuf check how the fermentation is going at Château du Moulin-à-Vent, in Moulin-à-Vent which makes Beaujolais' sturdiest wine.

ferment *inside* their skins – a process called 'carbonic maceration'. It allows the extraction of colour and flavour from inside the skins, but leaves the tannins, which are closer to the surface of the skin, largely untouched. After six or seven days the grapes are splitting and squirting their dark, very fruity, but *very* soft-tasting, low-tannin juice all over the place. It mixes with the tougher juice at the bottom of the vat, and is then drawn off. The remaining grapes are then pressed and, because of the 'carbonic maceration' this juice, too, is full of fruit but *not* tough. This gives the essential burst of fruit which makes young Beaujolais such fun, and *this* is why it is so drinkable, so gluggable, so young.

· APPELLATIONS ·

Beyond 'Nouveau', there are three levels of classification in Beaujolais.

Beaujolais and **Beaujolais Supérieur** are the lowest rank (Supérieur simply means it has a minimum alcohol level one degree higher). This comes mostly from the hordes of little villages in the flatter, sandier vineyards down towards Lyon. It is perfect café wine.

Beaujolais is a magical region of twisting country lanes, rolling hills and vine-clad slopes. Every bend in the road brings fresh pleasures to the eye – and maybe a cellar to try a glass of the gushing, fruity local wine.

More than two-thirds is now made as Nouveau – which is the best use for it.

Beaujolais-Villages is the middle rank, and this wine comes from 38 villages with more granitic soil, mostly in the north of the region. Usually a wine will be a blend from several villages. A good deal of this is also released as Nouveau, and is frequently exceptional, because you really do get that marvellous rush of cherry, peardrops and peaches fruit – all tasting as though the wine has only just finished fermenting – plus a bit more substance. These wines are better to drink throughout the year than most straight Beaujolais. They *will* last longer if you want them to from a good year like 1985 or 1986, but they'll stop tasting like Beaujolais!

The Crus The family similarity of the Gamay flavour is really more important than the differences between the different Crus (the top ten villages in Beaujolais), and it is only from a careful grower or particularly committed *négociant* – like Duboeuf, Ferraud, Loron, Sarrau and Depagneux – that you will find it easy to tell them apart. Even so, there *should* be differences so let's seek them out, going from south to north.

Brouilly is the largest Cru and makes what is often the perfect Beaujolais – full of fresh, peachy flavour, gentle, almost creamy and wonderful when young. It matures quickly and can be delicious at six months old.

Côtes de Brouilly is the knoll of hill-slopes in the centre of Brouilly. The lovely stream of fruit is very much the same as Brouilly's but it *is* a little fuller, fatter even, and doesn't peak quite so soon.

Regnié is a new Cru which isn't, frankly, as good as the others. It makes very good 'Villages' wine, cherryish and bright, but it was lucky to get its promotion in 1984.

Morgon on the other hand, can be really special. The wines begin life in a deeper, more exotic way, redolent of plums and cherries and herbs all twining together, but if you age them

'Tirage de Primeur' means the same as 'Nouveau' – the first wine of the vintage. St-Amour makes a particularly gentle, refreshing red!

they develop a remarkable sumptuous warmth, of chocolate, damsons and cream. In fact, very like old burgundy, but not quite, the extra dimension of delicious decay which Pinot Noir can give is just beyond Gamay's grasp.

Chiroubles matches its name – chirpy, flirtatious wine – springtime innocence. Don't age this: innocence doesn't wear well.

Fleurie All these wonderful names, no wonder this is such a happy, hospitable part of France. Fleurie's wine is juicy, crammed with the scent of flowers and the ripeness of fruit, with apricots, cherry and chocolate filling your mouth.

Moulin-à-Vent isn't cheap either, but is a totally different kind of wine. It hasn't got any of the *joie de vivre* which marks out the rest of Beaujolais, it's tannic and tough when it's young. You have no choice but to wait three, five years, maybe longer, when it will give you a decent impersonation of Côte d'Or burgundy.

Chénas is the least popular of the Crus. Some locals want to disband it, and much of its wine is sold as Bourgogne Rouge, but as a result its rather introspective, plummy wines can be very good value, and do need some age.

Juliénas is a famous area which hasn't quite

got the good-humoured magic of the others. Often, as in 1985, it produces the best wine in the whole region, but although Juliénas does have that lovely cherry and peach fruit it can also have a little more tannin and acid. And, since it isn't popular, it isn't expensive either.

St-Amour Another lovely name and, again, all fruit and perfume. Drink it young, drink it often.

· VINTAGES ·

1986 The basic Beaujolais may be a little light but the top wines are tremendous.

1985 The perfect Beaujolais vintage. From top to bottom the wines are all fruit and fun.

1984 A bit thin, although some Crus have aged quite well.

1983 Very good, surprisingly firm wines some of which are still rather tasty.

· GOOD PRODUCERS ·

Ferraud, Depagneux, Duboeuf, Loron, Sarrau, Dessalle, Thomas la Chevalière, Chanut, Eventail de Producteurs.

· CHABLIS ·

Far left A summer landscape near Milly, looking towards the limestone slopes of Chablis, is densely packed with lush green Chardonnay vines.

Left Spring frosts have always been a hazard in these northern vineyards. Oil-burning stoves are used in some vineyards to warm the freezing night air around vines, though you need about 100 to the acre, and they cost a fortune to run.

Chablis has a problem. Its too easy to pronounce – Shablee – anyone can say that – and everyone does – all over the world. In America, Australia, Argentina, New Zealand, Egypt and for all I know Ecuador and Uruguay. The name Chablis has come to mean any still dry white wine. Or maybe not so dry, medium perhaps. And why not sparkling or 'crackling'? Why not indeed. And while we're about it – why not pink? Sure, anything you want to sell, high volume, low price – call it Chablis and it'll move off the shelves.

Poor old Chablis. Its name, its fame has been wantonly abused across the globe. But, ironically, this has caused a major headache for the region. Chablis is a tiny, isolated valley vineyard area in the Yonne *département* at the northern extremity of Burgundy producing small amounts of high cost, high quality white wine in the teeth of the most difficult weather conditions in France. And from a single grape – the great, long-suffering, all-conquering Chardonnay. And Chablis should *not* be cheap. It is the classic bone-dry white wine, it balances steely, flinty inflexibility with a fruit which unwillingly yet reassuringly soothes the sharp attack of these far-north grapes. Yet how can you sell yourself dear when your name has been so exploited at the rump end of the market? It very nearly destroyed Chablis as a

major force in the wine world during the 1960s, but luckily, a USA-led thirst for Chardonnay wine and improved methods of frost-control and vineyard management have brought Chablis back from the brink to something approaching prosperity today.

True Chablis can *only* come from the Chardonnay grape grown on permitted sites around the town of Chablis in the Serein river valley, situated between Dijon and Paris. In France. But numerous other factors affect the eventual style and quality of the wine.

· SOIL AND CLIMATE ·

First, the soil. Traditionally, the production of Chablis has been limited to vineyards with a basis of Kimmeridgian limestone. All the most famous vineyards have this soil. However, the outlying villages, which for many years produced wine under the scarcely impressive title of 'Petit Chablis' happen to be on a base of Portlandian limestone. Is there a difference? Not to you and me, there isn't, and not to the 'young Turks' of those villages who have now won the right to use the unqualified name 'Chablis' and even, in a couple of cases, 'Premier Cru' for these supposedly inferior wines. In fact, these new additions to the *appellation contrôlée* area produce good, typical Chablis; not Grand Cru quality, but then they never

claimed that it was. Chablis's future prosperity hinges on a proper expansion of vineyards, and a substantial amount of what we now drink is from these very properties.

The second much more crucial factor in Chablis is frost. Because it is so far north, and the river Serein ambles along at the base of the vineyards, pockets of ice-cold air get caught in the valley right into the middle of May. During the 1950s, when Chablis' fortunes were at their lowest ebb, growers risked losing one crop in three owing to late, late spring frosts. The 1960s saw the introduction into the vineyards of stoves and petrol-soaked torches, which would be lit on nights when frost was likely – but they weren't cheap, and those freezing, cloudless spring nights chilled the hapless vineyard workers to the bone. A more important innovation by far has been the installation of water sprinklers. While the temperature remains at or below 0°C, these soak the vines in a fine spray of water which then freezes on to the young buds. Amazingly, this is perfect protection against frost damage, because as the air temperature drops below zero, the continuous formation of ice keeps the vine 'warm' at freezing point! This method, combined with a greater use of weedkillers to reduce the humidity-creating undergrowth between the vines has gone a long way to arresting the frost problem, and ensuring a regular supply of wine on to the market.

· MAKING CHABLIS ·

The wine is made in one of two ways. The great bulk is vinified in stainless steel or cement vats, and then kept inert and neutral before early bottling. This is the best way to catch the zing, the slightly shocking green-fresh acidity which is a crucial component of ordinary Chablis' taste. However, many winemakers believe that to do justice to a wine from the best vineyards – one which will improve for a few years, and end up with a nutty softness and a unique aroma something like warm, wet hay in a summer stable – wooden barrels should be used for ageing. Some of the barrels should be of new oak to impart a vanilla richness, and some of them of old, imparting less flavour but allowing the wine to work slowly with the wood and the air, building the character and complexity you cannot achieve in the neutral environment of a stainless steel tank. As with everything else in Chablis the argument rages fiercely. I'm sitting on the fence. I like the fresh modern style, but for a really special bottle, I'll go for a wine aged in oak.

· APPELLATIONS ·

Petit Chablis is the lowest level. Most of this land has now been absorbed into the full Chablis AC; but the remainder accounts for about five per cent of production, and the wine is usually pretty tart and light.

Chablis is the overall regional *appellation*. It now accounts for about 60 per cent of production, and includes the outlying villages as well as some less good plots of land in the centre. Dry, pale green with a fleck of gold, it should smell very slightly of raw apples just turning from green, but fattened out with a suggestion of bakers' yeast. The taste of Chablis is a paradoxical pleasure – normally a few tantalizing steps away from being as ripe and round as you might like, yet as a consequence it is actually more appetizing.

Premiers Crus are a bit more serious – but not too much so. There are 30 different vineyard sites, but these have been grouped together under 12 different names to simplify selling them. Sometimes a Premier Cru will be a blend of two or more of the 12, in which case the label will say simply 'Chablis Premier Cru', but more often this will be followed by a single vineyard name. The Premier Cru taste moves away from the greenness, and the zing is more likely to be provided by a lean mineral streak of flavour running with an increasingly full style. From winemakers using stainless steel, the fullness may be appley, yeasty, nutty, but from the oak-barrel brigade, a more golden wine emerges with hints of nuts and cream, the mineral hardness mingling with the herbs and vanillas of the oak.

Grands Crus come only from a single sweep of hill directly north of the town of Chablis. 250 acres (102 hectares) are shared by seven Grand Cru plots, and there is a dramatic leap in quality between most Premiers Crus and the Grands Crus. A Grand Cru has weight, an intense penetrating rich personality which almost achieves the sumptuous glories of Corton-Charlemagne or Montrachet. But it doesn't quite. The dry, reserved fruit never quite climbs out of its corsets. It's magnificent, impressive wine, but it's not indulgent. Wine to stop and ponder over, certainly, but wine which will make you swing from the chandeliers in sheer delight? No, hardly ever.

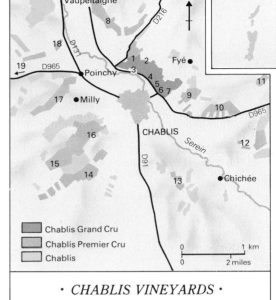

· CHABLIS VINEYARDS ·

Grands Crus Bougros(1), Preuses(2), Vaudésir(3), Grenouilles(4), Valmur(5), Les Clos(6), Blanchots(7).
Premiers Crus Fourchaume(8), Montée de Tonnerre(9), Monts de Milieu(10), Les Fourneaux(11), Vaucoupin(12), Vosgros(13), Montmains(14), Mélinots(15), Vaillons(16), Côte de Léchet(17), Beauroy(18), Vaudevey(19). (*The number after each vineyard name marks its location on the map above.*)

· VINTAGES ·

Because Chablis is very far north and the Chardonnay struggles to ripen here, vintages dramatically affect the style of the wine.
1986 A fair amount of big, ripe wines but with enough acidity to balance the fruit.
1985 Lovely ripe, gentle wines.
1984 Classic steely, tart wines.
1983 Big, rich wines, almost honeyed.

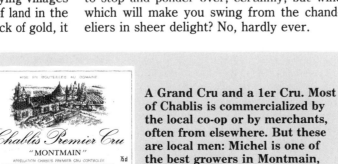

A Grand Cru and a 1er Cru. Most of Chablis is commercialized by the local co-op or by merchants, often from elsewhere. But these are local men: Michel is one of the best growers in Montmain, and Pic is a leading merchant.

· GOOD PRODUCERS ·

Growers Dauvissat, Fèvre, Michel, Raveneau, Vocoret, Testut, Brocard.
Négociants La Chablisienne, Regnard, Simmonet-Febvre, Drouhin.

· BASIC BURGUNDY ·

With Burgundy more than with any other of France's wine regions, the difference between buying good and bad wine lies in the reputation of the man growing the grapes and making the wine, rather than with the choice of the right *appellation*. If this is true for the leading names in the famous villages, it is just as true with the lesser ACs, those also-rans in the race for fame and fortune, because, in many cases, the wine with a basic AC like 'Bourgogne' or 'Passe-Tout-Grains' will be made from land adjoining a better *appellation*, and therefore share some of its characteristics. Alternatively, it may be the product of young vines in good vineyards – these should not be included in the top blend – or it may be excess production from these same plots in high-yielding years like 1982 and 1985. If it is a grower's wine, you can be fairly sure that his reputation and skill will be reflected in the quality of his everyday Bourgogne, red or white.

If it is a merchant's, or *négociant*, wine, it will probably be blended from grapes of a far larger area – perhaps including the Côte d'Or, the Côte Chalonnaise and the Mâconnais – to make tens of thousands of bottles of a single 'brand'. The quality of such simple Bourgognes is often surprisingly good.

However, if you're thinking of buying a cheap burgundy and spy a well-known *négociant's* name on a label with a fancy title – check that the words *appellation contrôlée* are also there, because if not, you may end up with some commercial blend from the far south of France, which has absolutely nothing to do with burgundy wine.

Burgundy, even basic burgundy, is *never* a cheap drink. There just isn't enough of it. In Bordeaux, or in the Côtes du Rhône, the quantity of wine going under the lowest, catch-all *appellation* easily outweighs the classier names. But in Burgundy, the basic ACs frequently make up only 10 per cent of the harvest; the other 90 per cent is produced under the minutely defined communal or vineyard *appellations*.

· THE WINES ·

Bourgogne Grand Ordinaire is the rock-bottom in Burgundy. *Not* very Grand. *Very* Ordinaire. It can be red, white or rosé, and is

made from just about any old grapes on any old scraps of land not fit for cattle or corn. Gamay is the mainstay for the red – and Gamay on poor ground anywhere north of Beaujolais makes pretty unattractive acid stuff. Pinot Noir is obviously allowed, but it's a hopelessly unambitious Pinot Noir which would let itself get caught up in this hotchpotch. And the red César and Tressot, two traditional northern grapes are also allowed in the Yonne area. I have yet to have a single bottle which didn't make me want to wash my mouth out with soap and water. Rosé is hardly seen, except from the village of Orches in the hills above Meursault. The white is, well, less offensive, and is usually based on the Aligoté grape, but to be frank, in any other part of France, with more humility and less renown, these wines would not be thought of as good enough to qualify for an *appellation contrôlée* at all.

Bourgogne Passe-Tout-Grains is reserved for red or rosé wines, but is almost always red. The curious name ('pass all the grapes') just means that you could pile all the available grapes into the vat – you could even mix Gamay with Pinot Noir for once. This was necessary because in the fragmented Burgundian vineyards, growers would often have no more than a few rows of vines in various places, some planted with Gamay, some with Pinot Noir, and not enough of either to fill up a vat with wine. So this somewhat easy-going *appellation* allows them to blend up to two-

thirds Gamay with the rest Pinot Noir. Passe-Tout-Grains is, in effect their own swigging wine. It can often be rather good, full of a bright, perfumy cherry taste which is enjoyable very young, but softer and better after perhaps five years.

Bourgogne Aligoté was a bit of a dead end *appellation* until recently. The Aligoté makes thin, sour stuff unless you really work at it, but as prices for Chardonnay have risen, the Aligoté has become more profitable, and there is now an increasing number of sharp but appetizing wines to be found, mostly in the Yonne, the Hautes-Côtes de Nuits and Hautes-Côtes de Beaune, and the Côte Chalonnaise. The best of all – and one which well deserves its recent promotion – is from Bouzeron, in the Côte Chalonnaise. Another thing – Aligoté really *is* the best wine to mix with Crème de Cassis blackcurrant liqueur to produce the Burgundian aperitif Kir.

Basic burgundies can come from anywhere in the region. Crémant de Bourgogne has traditionally been made from the light Chardonnay wines of the Côte Chalonnaise. This Aligoté comes from the village of St-Bris, better known for its VDQS Sauvignon wine.

Far left Basic burgundies are produced even in the best vineyards. This is Beaune Grèves, one of Burgundy's top vineyards, yet young vines would be used for Bourgogne Rouge, and any stray Gamay grapes on the fringes by the road would have to go into Passe-Tout-Grains.

Left Irancy near Chablis is a red-wine outpost at the very northern tip of Burgundy. The wine is light, but surprisingly good from such a cool area.

Bourgogne Blanc is a relatively straightforward *appellation* in that it is limited to Chardonnay and/or Pinot Blanc grapes, and can come from the entire length of Burgundy. But, as always in Burgundy, there's more to it than that. Much basic Bourgogne Blanc comes from the Mâconnais because this apparently less classy name is sometimes found to sell more easily than simple 'Mâcon'. But the more interesting wines come from further north. There is frequently overproduction in the better vineyards of the Côte Chalonnaise and the Côte d'Or, and Bourgogne Blanc soaks up the excess. The better merchants produce a good, fair-priced Bourgogne Blanc, and if they use a little new oak for ageing, the effect can be quite exciting. Best of all are the growers' wines from villages like Meursault or Puligny-Montrachet. Here wines from less good vineyards just outside the village AC area, or wines not up to *grand vin* quality – because of overproduction or youth of vines – may nonetheless be vinified in the same way as the top wines and offer a rare treat at a fraction of the 'famous name' price. (Look for the words *proprietaire à* and one of the top village names, for example, Meursault.) Up in the Yonne, the village of St-Bris (best known for its Sauvignon) produces particularly good Bourgogne Blanc.

Bourgogne Rouge The majority comes from the Mâconnais and Côte Chalonnaise, where it is usually fresh and fruity, and the Côte d'Or (when a little oak ageing is used, as at the Buxy or Hautes-Côtes co-operatives, a really classy wine can result). The grape in these wines is always Pinot Noir.

In the Yonne, round Chablis, the Pinot can be mixed with the Tressot and César. The result is often very good, light, strawberry-fresh burgundy. The best villages, Epineuil, Irancy and Coulanges-les-Vineuses, may incorporate their name on the label. Confusingly, at the southern end in Beaujolais, the 'Cru' villages may de-classify their wine into Bourgogne Rouge, though only Chénas ever makes much use of this facility. This Bourgogne would therefore be 100 per cent Gamay. As with Bourgogne Blanc, the wines may be excess production or from young vines in good vineyards, though they rarely need the same quality as the whites. But, again, the skills of a good winemaker will shine through in his Bourgogne.

Crémant de Bourgogne isn't that basic at all. It's the *appellation* for sparkling wine made by the champagne method, and this is increasingly the source of the best French fizz outside Champagne, which shouldn't be so surprising, because they are using the same grapes, Pinot Noir and Chardonnay.

· FOOD AND WINE ·

They even cook eggs in wine in Burgundy. *Oeufs en meurette* are eggs poached in a thick reduction of red burgundy, onion, garlic butter and salt pork. It may not look too appealing but it tastes stunning, the broken egg yolk oozing into the murky wine sauce and creating a sensuous blend, gooey egg with strong, penetrating burgundy wine and bacon.

A la bourguignonne as a cookery style has come to mean that the dish is cooked in wine, usually red. There *is* more to it than that – the boundaries of Burgundy range high into the wineless Moruan hills for their fish, game and mushrooms, across the flatlands of the Saône valley to Bresse for France's finest chickens, and south for Charollais beef.

You don't have to drink the same wine as you've used to prepare a dish – but you should drink the same *kind* of wine. I'm not really convinced anyone would ever use Chambertin (an extremely expensive Grand Cru) for Coq au Chambertin but they should use a red burgundy, and should drink a red burgundy with it. I've drunk claret with it, and somehow it didn't quite work, the rather austere Bordeaux wine warring with the fuming flavours of the chicken dish.

The same goes for 'boeuf à la bourguignonne', strong, chunky food demanding a solid Côte de Nuits red, or *jambon persillé*, ham cooked with parsley in white Aligoté, and best accompanied by a fresh, young Bourgogne Blanc. Burgundian fish stew is a grand concoction steeped in red or white wine. Bursting with butter, garlic, cream and bacon and goodness knows what else, it wants the biggest Chardonnay the Mâconnais can muster, or else a slightly cool flagon or two of top Beaujolais from Fleurie or Juliénas. And so it goes on. Food enriched with wine, wine enhanced by food. Big flavours, stomach-proud dishes, and the rounded, fruit-filled character of the region's wines.

· CHAMPAGNE ·

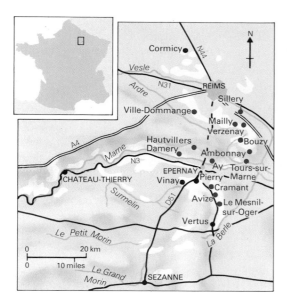

first, this feeble wine does come from very noble grape varieties – the white Chardonnay, and the black Pinot Noir and Pinot Meunier; and second, the skill of the winemakers who turn this unpromising and virtually undrinkable material into a gaudy riot of bubbles and bezazz, frothing, foaming fizz to launch a thousand ships, celebrate a thousand majorities and encourage a million lovers to be brave. And although there has been a worldwide surge of interest in manufacturing sparkling wine of good quality in the last few years, the Champagne region of France still holds on to its supreme position in the world of bubbly.

Yes, Champagne *is* a *region* of France as well as a wine. The wine of Champagne has had undisputed top billing in the world of sparkling wines for more than 250 years, with the result that, in many countries, the name 'champagne' has come to apply to anything which sparkles. This might once have been very flattering to the folk of Champagne, but since the imitations were almost always a grossly insulting debasement of the original product, champagne producers are now working through the courts to try to restrict the term 'champagne' to their own wine, made from authorized grape varieties in the region's authorized vineyards.

· WHERE THE GRAPES GROW ·

True champagne can *only* come from the Champagne region, a generally rather blank, monotonous stretch of prairie land north-east of Paris, which, around the towns of Reims, Epernay and Château Thierry, becomes squeezed and squashed into a series of hills and valleys jutting up from the plain.

This jumble of slopes is divided into four main areas, the Montagne de Reims, Côte des Blancs, Vallée de la Marne and the Aube. Although there is an increasing number of single village wines, champagne has traditionally been a blend of grapes from the various areas, since in this far northern vineyard many of the wines would lack balance by themselves. **The Montagne de Reims** is the furthest north, and, remarkably, most of its best vineyards face north too, and are generally planted with the grape which is most difficult to ripen – the Pinot Noir! The only feasible explanation

Champagne is the northernmost French wine region, and the chalky soil plays a vital role in drainage and reflecting the sun's heat back on to the vines.

seems to be that the valley floor air is warm and, since hot air rises, it is continually drawn up through the vineyards, so warming the vines. The wines from the Montagne are Champagne's deepest and toughest, and always add a firmness to the blends. When they are bottled unblended – known as 'Blanc de Noirs' – as often happens at Bouzy and Mailly, they take years to lose their hard edge. **The Côte des Blancs**, a solid east-facing wall of vines stretching south of Epernay and rising out of some of the flattest, most featureless farmland in France, is planted entirely with white Chardonnay until black grapes reappear at Vertus in the south. These vineyards are the luckiest in the region: even in poor years they produce good quality wine and lots of it. Although the unblended local 'Blanc de Blancs' style is often described as being light and insubstantial, this isn't true at all, and a wonderful combination of yeasty cream and honey becomes apparent in the wine when it is allowed to mature. Even so, this Chardonnay wine is mostly used to impart a lightness and more obvious fruit to blends dominated by Pinot Noir. Below Vertus there is an extension of the Côte des Blancs called the Côte de Sézanne which produces big, soft, tasty wines primarily from Chardonnay grapes. **The Vallée de la Marne** meanders pleasingly from Epernay westwards to Château Thierry.

I f someone wanted to make a champagne look-alike, some of the most potentially successful sites would be in the counties of Kent and Sussex on the hills and slopes just above the English Channel! If that sounds too bizarre for words, the French don't think so: one of the largest champagne companies is already helping a Sussex winemaker to produce some pretty spectacular fizz.

It's the chalk that does it, you see, and the long, cool summers lengthening into an increasingly late autumn. A successful sparkling wine *must* come from fairly acid grapes and should be light and refreshing; chalk gives the lightest, most delicate white wines wherever it occurs in vineyards throughout the world. The South Downs, ending abruptly in those white cliffs which rise and fall along the south coast of England, are part of a seam of chalk running straight across northern France, interrupted only by the English Channel. Around Reims and Epernay, 90 miles (145km) north-east of Paris, the chalk is as much as 650 feet (200 metres) deep. Ally this to a climate which isn't so very different from that of southern England, and you're going to get thin, sharp wine in most years – which is exactly what you want!

If 'thin, sharp wine' sounds light years removed from champagne, indeed it is. But a number of factors explain the transformation:

Both slopes of the Marne valley (*left*) sport vines – south-facing vineyards producing the best wines. The Aube (*above*) is farmland where the vine takes its chances with other crops.

Although Pinot Noir and Chardonnay are planted – with Pinot very strong round Ay – it is the other black grape, the sturdy Pinot Meunier, which is most common here in the damper microclimate and heavier clay soils of the river valley. The Meunier has less character than Pinot Noir or Chardonnay, but it is a crucial component in most champagne blends, because it softens and even enhances the Pinot Noir, making the wine mature more quickly. **The Aube**, well south of the main vineyards, is the fourth area. It is warmer here; the Pinot Noir ripens more easily and so dominates the vineyards. The Aube wines are frequently denigrated as being coarse, and few champagne companies admit to using them in blends. However, there is some delicious, fairly full-flavoured wine to be found, if one's nose is not too high in the air to notice it.

· CLASSIFICATIONS ·

Of all the great French wine areas Champagne is unique in that the bulk of its production is non-vintage. Because the vineyards are so far north and the grapes don't always ripen well, the practice developed in the seventeenth century of blending wines from various different areas so that ripe patches of grapes would compensate for unripe patches of grapes, thus ensuring a reasonably consistent product. This idea developed further when quantities of wine from one vintage were kept back to be blended in with the new wine of the year to provide a more rounded, attractive flavour. Between 80 per cent and 90 per cent of all champagne is now non-vintage. Although the individual villages very definitely have their own personalities, these traits have in the main been submerged in the blends, and in Champagne one is likely to talk of the 'house style' of the producer, rather than the character of the different vineyards, 50 or 60 of which might be blended into a single wine.

Even so, these villages are all classified rigidly according to quality. As in Burgundy there are Grands Crus (Great Growths) and Premiers Crus (First Growths) and ordinary wines. However, in Champagne the entire village is classified, not just its best vineyards. There are 17 Grand Cru villages which are described as rating 100 per cent. There are 41 Premier Cru villages rated 90–99 per cent, and the remaining villages, nearly 200 of them are rated 80 to 89 per cent.

This percentage figure is used to calculate the price per kilo of grapes that a grower may expect at vintage time. A price is set by a committee of growers and merchants for a kilo of top quality grapes. If it is, say, 20 francs a kilo, the grapes from Grand Cru 100 per cent villages will fetch this price, while a lower rated village will get proportionately less – so a 90 per cent village, for example, will get 90 per cent of 20 francs (18 francs) a kilo. It is a pretty basic but effective way of turning proven quality into hard cash. Wines from Grand Cru or Premier Cru villages may be described as such on the label but there is less significance here in such titles than in Burgundy.

· THE CHAMPAGNE TRADE ·

Champagne has always suffered rather from a 'them and us' problem, since it is the entrepreneurial *négociant* houses which have built the fame and fortune of the wine, yet they have never owned much of the land, and so relied heavily on the goodwill of the growers. Even today, the 110 champagne houses own

The chilling brilliance of glistening white frost coats the vines as the winter mists roll off the Côtes des Blancs to the south of Cramant. These vineyards are planted entirely with Chardonnay, and Cramant specializes in Crémant, a champagne made with less pressure behind the cork, and consequently a softer, less effervescent sparkle.

7,400 acres (3,000 hectares), only just over 12 per cent of the land, while the 18,000 growers control the rest. This has been a continual source of tension, and whenever there is a remotely small harvest, prices of the grapes shoot up. The merchant houses *have* to buy, because they don't own enough vineyards, so up goes the price of wine to us, the consumers. Until recently, we then stopped buying, sales slumped, grape prices dropped because the merchants didn't need to buy, wine prices to us dropped, we started drinking again. . .and so it went on. Amazingly, at the moment we're drinking more and more whether the price goes up or not!

There are four main levels of producer:

Négociants-Manipulants are companies which 'merchandize and handle' wine. All the famous names – such as Veuve Clicquot, Perrier-Jouët, Moët and Chandon, Bollinger and so on – are included here, and the companies will buy in grapes or must (unfermented juice) to satisfy their needs, make the wine, and sell it under their label. The letters NM at the bottom of the label indicate a wine from one of these companies.

Récoltants-Manipulants, or 'harvester-handlers', are an increasing number of growers who now make their own wine, having grown tired of suffering the ostentatious wealth and 'superiority' of the companies to whom they previously sold their grapes. They can only blend in 5 per cent of wine from outside their own vineyards, so the wines *may* lack subtlety, but they may make up for that with personality. We are going to see a lot more good growers' champagnes in the next few years (these wines will have the letters RM on the bottom of the label).

Co-opératives Manipulants are the growers' co-operatives in Champagne, who make some excellent wines. They sell under a variety of labels rather then their own names and can be spotted by the letters CM on the bottom of the label.

Marque Auxiliaire is the 'auxiliary brand' for those producers who make wines under any label the ultimate retailer of the wine chooses, including their own name. 'Buyer's Own Brand' they are called, and most 'own-label' champagnes come into this category. The letters MA are on the bottom of the label. You may also see MA on a champagne label, with an imposing title, coats of arms, the lot. This, again, will be an auxiliary brand, either of an independent *négociant-manipulant* who doesn't wish to use his own name or else of one of the few big companies who only deal in this 'own-label' business.

It used to be that the top companies, ten of whom control 50 per cent of the business, dominated the export market where they could make bigger profits, while the growers, selling direct and cutting out the middle-man, dominated the French domestic market. These *Grandes Marques*, or 'great brands' had the advertising and marketing budgets, and fought

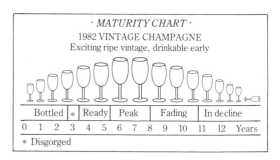

· MATURITY CHART ·
1982 VINTAGE CHAMPAGNE
Exciting ripe vintage, drinkable early

Bottled	*	Ready	Peak		Fading		In decline

0 1 2 3 4 5 6 7 8 9 10 11 12 Years

* Disgorged

hard to establish their brand in people's loyalties. Well, up to a point this worked. Britain and the United States, in particular, became passionate champagne drinkers, but didn't become brand-obsessed. And when the mass market retailers began to offer fine champagnes at cheaper prices under their own labels, drinkers happily switched – and since these own-labels frequently won blind tastings against supposedly classier competitors, consumers had that lovely giddy feeling of getting a de luxe item at a bargain price. This is where the growth in champagne sales has occurred, and, so long as quality stays up, it is likely to continue.

· MAKING CHAMPAGNE ·

So how is this magic sparkling wine created? We've got a series of cool, northerly vineyards, three-quarters of which are planted with black grapes. These black grapes have to be picked and pressed incredibly gently so that the juice, which is white, is not stained by the skins which contain all the colouring matter. Then the juice from each vineyard is fermented separately. So there they are – thousands of different wines sitting around in vats all over Champagne – and not a bubble to be seen, because these wines are all light, slightly sour, completely *still* wines. There are two priorities now. First, make up a blend – or *cuvée* – in the house style of the company concerned. And second, create those bubbles.

· THE CUVEE ·

Samples of the still wines from various areas are brought to a company's headquarters in the January following the vintage, and for the next three months the cellarmaster or chief blender will painstakingly sift through all the

Most *dégorgement* is now done by machine, but traditional skills are displayed here in the Moët cellars in Epernay.

possible permutations of wines available, gradually eliminating unsuitable examples, slowly working towards the proportions and constituents which will perpetuate the house style. I've done it for just a day, and it's exhausting work, trying to differentiate between the scarcely perceptible nuances in wines from neighbouring plots.

April must come as quite a relief. The final blends are assembled, the directors sniff and slurp and spit, making up various blends 'in miniature' in jugs in the tasting room. As the spring sun begins to warm the air, the final decision is taken, the vats are blended together, and we're ready for the great adventure – creating the bubbles in the wine.

· THE CHAMPAGNE METHOD ·

The champagne method – *méthode champenoise* – creates bubbles in a wine by inducing a second fermentation in the bottle. If you add

a solution of sugar and wine and a little yeast – the *liqueur de tirage* – to a bottle of the still wine, slap on a strong cap – usually nowadays a 'crown cap', the same as you find on top of the original glass Coca-Cola bottles – and store it away at 10–12°C, the wine will begin to ferment again. This reaction produces carbon dioxide which, unable to escape, dissolves into the wine. In anything from ten days to three months the second fermentation is complete and the wine will be charged with a positively explosive force equivalent to the pressure of a tyre supporting an enormous freight truck! It should now lie dark and undisturbed for at least a year, but ideally for something like three years, to develop aroma and personality.

Dom Pérignon, a monk who lived at Hautvillers Abbey near Epernay, is the man credited with 'inventing' the champagne method in the seventeenth century. But it wasn't so much that he actually invented anything; it was just that he was highly observant. He noticed that each spring the local wines would begin to effervesce as the fermentation which had been stopped in its tracks by the winter cold was triggered off once more by the warmer weather. He also found that while they fizzed they tasted far better, and that by about June, when the fizz had disappeared because the fermentation was finished, the wine tasted flat and dull again. Capture the fizz, he reasoned, and you could drink bottled magic all year round. He brought in two innovations: the new extra-strength English glass bottles, which could withstand the pressure, and cork stoppers from Spain which were clean and much more effective in conserving this pressure than the nasty oil-soaked rags wrapped round wooden pegs which had been in use till then.

· THE GRANDES MARQUES ·

Ayala, Billecart-Salmon, Bollinger, Canard-Duchêne, Veuve Clicquot, Deutz and Geldermann, Heidsieck Monopole, Charles Heidsieck, Henriot, Krug, Lanson, Laurent Perrier, Massé Pere et Rils, Mercier, Moët and Chandon, Montebello, Mumm, Perrier-Jouët, Joseph Perrier, Piper-Heidsieck, Pol Roger, Pommery and Greno, Prieur, Louis Roederer, Ruinart, Salon, Taittinger.

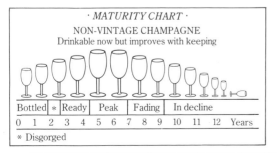

· MATURITY CHART ·
NON-VINTAGE CHAMPAGNE
Drinkable now but improves with keeping

Bottled	*	Ready	Peak	Fading	In decline	
0	1 2	3 4	5 6	7 8 9	10 11 12	Years

* Disgorged

Many champagne houses, like Ruinart (*left*), use subterranean chalk pits excavated by the Romans to mature their wines.

Most of the impressive headquarters of the champagne houses are in Epernay or, like those of Mumm, in Reims.

So, yes, Dom Pérignon does seem to have begun the process of preserving the bubbles, but it wasn't until the nineteenth century when the process of fermentation became more fully understood, and the *liqueur de tirage* could be scientifically employed to produce an exact amount of pressure, that champagne production could be anything other than haphazard.

· THE REMUAGE ·

There was one more vital breakthrough. What about all those dead yeast cells produced by the second fermentation? Won't they be collecting in the bottle? They certainly will. And if you try to filter them out, you'll release the pressure and ruin the fizz? Right again. It took Champagne's most famous widow – *la Veuve Clicquot* – to invent a method of removing the yeast's sludge in 1805. It's called *remuage* – literally, 'removal' – and involves both turning and tapping the bottle regularly, while gradually inverting it so that it ends up standing on its head. In this way the sticky sediment is gradually dislodged from the side of the bottle and slips on to the cap. The widow Clicquot bored holes in her kitchen table to test

this 'turn and tap' theory, but the winemakers soon developed a kind of inverted V-shaped desk full of holes, called a *pupitre*, which has been used ever since.

Remuage is a very labour-intensive affair, since every bottle must be treated a number of times. Legions of beetle-browed men have traditionally roamed the cellars doing this – but, to be honest, it's a dreadfully boring job

and you get terrible arthritis in your wrists. So now, increasingly, the *remuage* is done on enormous mechanical *palettes* of 500 bottles which a computer puts through this 'riddling down' process in double-quick time. Less romantic, but much more efficient – and a lot easier on the wrists.

But even after all this, the sludge is still in the bottle. Not to worry! The sediment is lying on the cap by now. So the bottle is taken and hung upside down with the neck in a bath of freezing brine. This solidifies the sludge. The bottle is turned upright, the crown-cap flicked off and a pellet of icy mush shoots out – a process known as *dégorgement*.

The wine is now clean. And it's totally dry. Most people don't like totally dry wines, whatever they say, so in most cases the last 'act' before ramming in a proper champagne cork and donning the gold foil, is the *dosage*, or *liqueur d'expedition*. The basic champagne may still be harsh and green, even though carbon dioxide does have a softening effect, and this is the chance to ease a little sweetness in. Although 'Brut' is supposed to mean extremely dry, everything's relative, because a Brut wine may contain up to 15g per litre of sweetness, in the form of a cane sugar and wine solution added after the *dégorgement*. That's not a lot, but if you tried one of the totally dry champagnes which occasionally come on the market, I think you'd appreciate the 'relative' dryness of a Brut. The different categories are, in ascending order of sweetness – very dry to totally sweet – Brut, Extra Dry, Sec (dry), Demi-sec, Doux (sweet).

· THE WINES ·

Non-vintage wines The most commonly drunk – and affordable – of champagnes are the non-vintage blends. The objective of these

These labels show four different styles of wine: *far left*, Veuve Clicquot non-vintage, and the vintage-dated de luxe Roederer Cristal; *left*, the rare still red called Coteaux Champenois, and a rosé from Laurent-Perrier.

blends is to keep a uniform house style, since consumers' loyalties in champagne almost always apply to the taste of a particular 'brand' rather than the Cru rating of a particular village. A good house will base its non-vintage style on a single vintage, but will blend in the wine of at least one, and hopefully two or more older vintages. These 'reserve' wines add soft, ripe nutty flavours to the vivacious, exhilarating feeling of the younger wine.

Although the wine *can* be released at only 15 months old, it should mature for two to three years before sale. The famous houses used to be the most reliable, but the small harvests at the end of the 1970s and beginning of the 1980s, allied to increasing worldwide sales, created great pressure on stocks and the release of sharp young wine under famous labels. At the present time, many smaller houses with lesser reputations are offering better non-vintage wines at fairer prices.

Vintage wines A vintage is 'declared' in Champagne when the general consensus is that the quality merits it. So you do not find a vintage dated wine from every year. The feeble 1984, for instance, will all be used for blending – I hope! Vintage wines are made from a selection of the best grapes from a single good year. They are weightier, richer in the mouth, and really shouldn't be drunk before five years old, since they blend their acidity with fruit and gain exciting honeyed, creamy tastes up to 10 or 12 years, while losing only a little of their fizz. But some Blanc de Blancs from, for instance, a soft ripe year like 1982, are delicious at only four years old. Vintage wines are always more expensive, and they certainly have a much fuller, more memorable taste, but they're also less refreshing, so you may prefer the non-vintage.

De Luxe This trend was started by Moët and Chandon in 1921, when they launched Dom Pérignon – the fiendishly expensive one in the funny bottle. Well, there are now lots of other fiendishly expensive little numbers in funny bottles, and few of them are worth the fat wad of folding ones the makers demand, although the empty bottle may be useful as a social climber's candle-holder. But alongside the overpriced show-offs, a few true-blues do stand out – Dom Pérignon, Taittinger Comtes de Champagne, Heidsieck Monopole Diamant Bleu, Laurent-Perrier Grand Siècle, Dom Ruinart, Roederer Cristal and Krug Grande Cuvée are worth the extra.

Some of the best luxury champagnes are described as 'recently disgorged' – 'RD' for short. This means that the wine has been left for much longer on its yeast deposit before being disgorged and corked. This imparts much more depth of flavour. Bollinger RD is the most famous of these.

Rosé Don't let anyone belittle rosé champagne. It's difficult and expensive to make. Most producers mix in a little local red wine at the last moment, but some try to gain a pink colour by macerating the must with the skins for a day or so. Also it's extremely popular. Worldwide demand rises by about 100 per cent a year! Just enjoy it because, properly made, it should have a delicious ripe strawberry taste and a captivating salmon-pink sheen in the glass.

Blanc de Blancs is made only from white Chardonnay grapes. It can be very light and delicate, but from the south, round Vertus, and across to the Côte de Sézanne, the style is big, toasty and creamy.

Crémant, or 'creaming', wines have only about half to two-thirds of the usual pressure, so the wine does feel creamier, a soft foam filling your mouth rather than a whoosh of

· FOOD AND WINE ·

In Champagne the locals mostly drink beer! This may be because the local beers are rather good, or it may be that champagne is a luxury item even in Reims itself, and people just don't swig it down at those prices. I have tried champagne with various local dishes but all the best traditional dishes are curiously unsophisticated to accompany such a civilized drink. *Choucroute*, for instance, is brilliantly done in this region once famous for its cabbages. The town of Troyes is famous for *andouillettes*, sausages made of lamb's stomach which you need a strong stomach yourself to handle. Sainte Ménéhould is regarded as quite a regional gastronomic centre and its fame rests upon its ingenuity with pig's trotters. The fish dishes are better suited to champagne-drinking and *quenelles de brochet* (little sausages of pikemeat, not indigenous, but common here), *pochouse*, a fish stew made with still white wine, or the occasional champagne sauce for firm-fleshed fish like halibut and turbot, can all be washed down enjoyably with the local fizz. Otherwise, the charcuterie, patés and terrines are tremendous, and the cheeses, in particular Brie, Boursault, Chaource and Chaumont are some of France's best, yet champagne doesn't go awfully well with any of them.

· VINTAGES ·

Vintage wines are released much younger than they should be and even non-vintage wines will benefit from a further six months in a cool dark place. With the exception of a delightful forward year like 1982, good vintage wine really needs seven years and would like ten to achieve its full potential. 1983 and 1982 are both excellent vintages. 1981 is good but a little tough, while 1979 is full, soft and nearing its peak. 1978 is concentrated but a little fierce, while 1976 is full, ripe and almost too much of a good thing.

froth getting up your nose.

Still Wines There are a few wines which don't undergo the 'champagne' treatment, and these are called Coteaux Champenois. Red or white, they're usually light and raw – and cry out for bubbles. The Rosé de Riceys, a rare wine from the Aube, is much better, having a full, almost chocolate and raspberry flavour, but it's a pretty steep price for a still rosé!

· THE RHONE VALLEY ·

The Rhône really does deserve the title 'King of the Wine Rivers'. Vines are grown on its banks almost continuously from snow-clad Visp, near the source way up in the Swiss Alps, right down to the sprawling muddy delta of swamps and marshland on the Mediterranean near Marseille. Even the Loire and the Rhine can't match such intense wine activity. And the variety of wines is staggering. The white Visp wines are so pale and feather-like no wine terms are delicate enough to describe them; and the reds and whites of the slopes below Lyon have some of the most intense exotic flavours ever produced from the grape. The estuary flavours of the deep south, however, reflect only the sluggish fatigue of the river-water exhausted by its journey to the sea.

The central stretch of the Rhône valley, spanning some 140 miles (225km) from Lyon down to Avignon, is thought of as the heart of the river, and without doubt all the most memorable wines are made here. Yet the differences in style between the reds and whites of the north, just below Lyon, and the wines of the baking plains around Avignon could not be more marked.

In the north the reds are made from a single grape variety – the Syrah – renowned as one of France's toughest, most uncompromising grapes (although it is sometimes softened by the white Viognier in Côte Rôtie and Marsanne or Roussanne in Hermitage and Crozes-Hermitage). In the south as many as nine different red wine grapes may be blended together, but the predominant variety is the juicy, squashy-edged Grenache – all high alcohol and up-front flavours for quaffing, not keeping.

The whites of the north are rare and remarkable. The Viognier vine – unique to this area – produces tiny amounts of brilliant wine at Condrieu, as expensive as almost any in France, yet not to keep, since its startling fruit is as fleeting as youth and as easy to miss. In complete contrast, a few miles down the road at Hermitage, the Marsanne and Rousanne grapes make whites which often need 20 years to display their daunting, adult breadth of taste. Further south the paradoxes continue. Amid the burly, blood-red wines of the Côte du Rhône pops up one of the world's most delicious sweet Muscats at Beaumes de Venise, while Châteauneuf-du-Pape, whose vineyards are so sun-soaked that you can burn your fingers by touching the stones on the ground in the noonday heat, somehow manages to produce bright, super-fresh aromatic whites which Burgundy, much further north, would be proud of.

· APPELLATIONS ·

The *appellations* for the Rhône Valley go from the sublime to the ridiculous. In the north, you have the minute Château Grillet, a tiny terraced amphitheatre of Viognier vines. This

Left The foothills of the Alps encroach on the vineyards of the southern Rhône valley relieving the arid flatness of the plain. The brilliant orange of the vines near Buis les Baronnies may look gorgeous but it actually shows the vines are not in good health.

Right From the top of the famous hill of Hermitage, looking towards the Rhône flowing majestically southwards.

is the smallest *appellation* in France (excepting a couple of Burgundian Grand Cru vineyard ACs inside the villages of Vosne-Romanée, Puligny-Montrachet and Chassagne-Montrachet). Usually between 5,000 and 10,000 bottles a year are produced. Yet at the other extreme, the Côtes du Rhône *appellation* spreads itself like a blanket across the valley producing over 200 million bottles of red, white and rosé.

Côtes du Rhône is, in fact, the catch-all *appellation* for the whole of this Lyon-Avignon stretch of the Rhône valley, rather as 'Bordeaux' is the generally available *appellation* in Bordeaux for wines which do not aspire to anything more than an acceptable alcoholic degree.

Côtes du Rhône-Villages is another generic AC available to 17 villages in the south for wines of greater depth and character. Otherwise, in north and south, each locality producing superior wines is granted its own particular

appellation as in Condrieu, St-Joseph, Cornas, Hermitage, Châteauneuf-du-Pape, Tavel, Lirac, Gigondas, Rasteau, Beaumes de Venise and so on.

Although some vineyard names are occasionally used on wines, there is no system of Cru Classé or Grand Cru classification as there is in Bordeaux and Burgundy.

· *THE WINE TRADE* ·

Until recently, there is no doubt that the merchants – the *négociants* – held the whip hand in the Rhône. Most of the business involved the buying up and shipping out of vast quantities of fairly alcoholic reds to be bottled by all and sundry in the four corners of the globe. The quality usually ranged from adequate to execrable. But things are now looking up. In the north the merchants are still important with Jaboulet, Chapoutier and Delas holding considerable sway, but almost all the really exciting wine is now coming from the growers themselves, while the co-operatives, at centres such as Tain l'Hermitage and St-Désirat-Champagne are reliable and cheap. In the south the co-operatives have now taken a dominant position, providing good to excellent wine at affordable prices. Beaumes de Venise, Cairanne, Vacqueyras and Chusclan have all made names for themselves. There is still a great deal of *négociant* activity, but little of it is very exciting, while on the other hand more and more growers are plucking up courage to go out on their own, bottle their own wine, make their own reputations and bask in the glowing sense of self-respect that this inevitably brings.

· NORTHERN RHONE ·

You get your first sight of the northern Rhône vineyards where the motorway sweeps across the river below Lyon at Vienne. If you glance right down the valley, you'll notice a near-vertical cliff of rock, which seems to be cross-stitched, as though the patches of pale stony earth were sewn to the rock by mighty threads. It couldn't be a vineyard – it's far too steep, the earth would cascade off the rock in the first rains; and no human being could keep their balance to tend the vines. But it *is* a vineyard. And it's a great vineyard. These

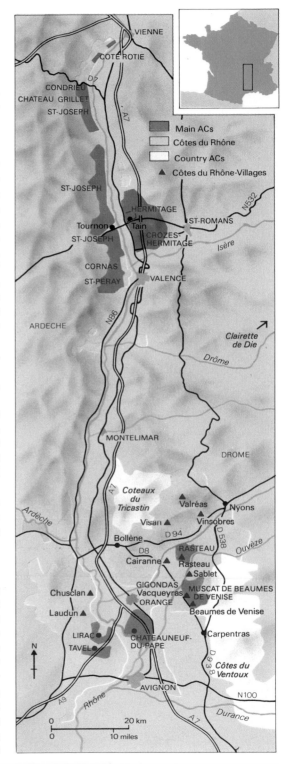

Left A vine-grower in the Côte Rôtie burning the old wood pruned from vines. You need a steady head for this job; these are some of the steepest vineyards in the world.

Below left The entire AC of Château Grillet whose tiny vineyard, the smallest self-contained AC in France, produces delicious but wildly expensive white wine.

are the first cliff-side terraces of the glorious northern Rhône, where men and women struggle to extract great wine from the impossibly steep rockface at the river's edge. **Côte Rôtie**, home of one of France's most delicious but least-known reds, occupies this utterly improbable site. Before I visited it, I'd

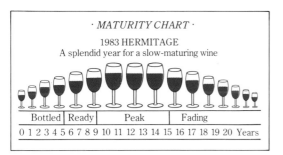

· *MATURITY CHART* ·

1983 HERMITAGE
A splendid year for a slow-maturing wine

Bottled	Ready	Peak	Fading

0 1 2 3 4 5 6 7 8 9 10 11 12 13 14 15 16 17 18 19 20 Years

read all the stuff about precipitous vineyards: remember to take your crampons and mountaineering gear if you're going to do the vintage, don't look down while you're picking the grapes – all that sort of thing – and I'd thought – 'Oh, yeah?' Well, I'm telling you – they weren't exaggerating. As I coaxed my car up the zig-zag track that runs through the vineyard at about one in three I was convinced it would topple over backwards if I stopped. When I got to the top the view was magnificent, so feeling rather shaken I reckoned I'd have a little picnic among the vines. I couldn't do it. It was too steep! I lost both tomatoes and an onion, hurtling down the slope on to some poor unsuspecting pedestrian hundreds of feet below, before I gave up trying to keep my balance, staggered back to the car and sat on the bonnet, still feeling anything but secure.

But the red wine of Côte Rôtie – the 'roasted slope' – can be heavenly. The Syrah grape, frequently softened and soothed by the addition of a little white Viognier, is at its most fragrant here, sweet and lilting from a surprisingly early age, the fruit having the chewy ripeness of damsons in their skins, the perfume like breeze-blown wild raspberries. There are only 250 acres (100 hectares) of true Côte Rôtie (although, sadly, there are moves afoot to extend the area into the flat plateau behind the slope which is far better employed growing fruit trees). So the wine

will always be rare. Fortunately for us, it is usually half the price of a great Bordeaux or burgundy.

Condrieu and **Château Grillet**, two white wine ACs just round the bend in the river below Côte Rôtie, are even rarer. There are only 25 acres (10 hectares) of Condrieu and only 7½ acres (3 hectares) of Château Grillet. Actually the permitted area for Condrieu is much bigger, but the Viognier grape, the only grape allowed for the two ACs, is temperamental and suffers from floral abortion – which sounds awful and means that every time the flowers try to set into fruit, half of them just drop off, and you don't get any grapes. Ally that to absurdly steep slopes again, and it is only the most committed or obsessive growers who keep up the unequal struggle. But what wine Viognier can produce! The fruit is the mellow autumn gold of ripe apricots, the perfume is mayflower blossom and orchard spring-time, and these are spun together into a deep sensuous flavour too ripe to be dry yet too clean and refreshing to be sweet. Rare, expensive wines for days when your head is filled with dreams and your wallet filled with money.

Below Condrieu nature relents a little and the vineyards flatten out. But then, so do the wines – you can't have it both ways.

St-Joseph is the right-bank *appellation* here producing pleasant juicy reds, but it only shows its true breeding further south between Tournon and Mauves where the original slopes once more allow the Syrah to sing. These St-Joseph reds are soft, almost sweet and packed with spicy blackcurrant fruit.

Crozes-Hermitage is the *appellation* for the first vineyards of any note on the left bank. The wines are either red or white. The white can be very good, appley and nutty, soft, but briskly refreshing, while the red is strong, firm Syrah, sometimes rather earthy, peppery, rooty, but even so with a good dollop of smoky raspberry fruit to sweeten things up.

And then, as the river narrows and forces its path between the towns of Tain and Tournon, the great hill of Hermitage rears up on the left bank, one last burst of rocky splendour before the river valley fans out and flattens to the south.

Hermitage a century ago produced a red wine as famous as Château Margaux, and a white as sought-after as Montrachet. Those were the days when grand, roaring flavours were prized more than delicacy and refinement, and the wines of Hermitage bellow and thunder their wares to a world of wine-drinkers. We are only now prepared to listen again.

Marsanne and Roussanne are the white grapes, occupying 30 per cent of the vineyard land, and good examples of white Hermitage are thick with taste, wilfully, arrogantly, throwing together a remarkable array of flavours – pears, apples, peaches, toffee, mint, pine resin, liquorice – they're all there, warring with each other when they're young, yet after 15–20 years patching up their quarrels into an exotic throat-warming blend of nuts and fruit.

Red Hermitage is the Syrah's supreme achievement. When it's young it is so harsh with tannin, tar and dark leathery power that it pummels your gums and fuddles your senses. But leave it for five years at least, preferably ten or twenty, and the brawn is tamed, the hidden flavours parade in a most startling way, the rough hide of youth is now the restful leather of an old armchair, the thick black treacly consistency is now the fragrance of woodsmoke , the acrid beauty of meat seared on the grill, the strange, appetizing perfume of tar spread along the highways. And suddenly, there's fruit! Strawberries and raspberries and plums, then blackcurrants, blackberries, seasoned with mint and liquorice and pine, soothed with cream. Great Hermitage can do all of this. Any Hermitage can suggest at least a part of these pleasures.

Nothing else in the Rhône matches Hermitage at its best, but there are two other small *appellations* just south of Tournon.

Cornas is a rare red from 165 acres (67 hectares) of vineyard. It is *very* tough, and whereas at about ten years old it does shed a lot of its tooth-juddering toughness to show a fairly deep plumskins-and-black-grape sweetness, it doesn't ever achieve the brilliance of Hermitage.

St-Péray is the last of the northern villages. There are only about 120 acres (54 hectares) which produce a somewhat foursquare still

Terraced vineyards at Cornas. In many parts of France terraces in hilly areas have been abandoned: they are impossible to cultivate mechanically and exhausting to work.

La Mouline is the name for a special selection of Côte Rôtie wine from the Côte Blonde. Crozes-Hermitage is not as exciting as Hermitage, but it is much cheaper and can be excellent value.

white and a champagne-method fizz of a pretty solid, humourless temperament. Wagner drank it when he was writing Parsifal, which just about says it all.

· MIDDLE RHONE ·

Although the Rhône wine area is normally divided into north and south, there is one central wine area worth noting. This is Die, way over towards the Alps in the isolated Drôme valley. There are some still wines made with *appellation* Châtillon en Diois, but it is the Clairette de Die sparkling white wine which is memorable. Under the title 'Tradition' a blend of Muscat and Clairette grapes creates a brilliantly grapy wine – soft, dry, but bubbling with fruit and well worth seeking out.

· SOUTHERN RHONE ·

You only have to stand by the chapel on the peak of the hill of Hermitage and look about you to understand the difference between the

· VINTAGES ·

The north and south sections of the valley rely on very different grapes for their best wines. Whereas the vineyards of the north are frequently on perilously steep hillside slopes, much of the southern Rhône is remarkably flat, so the climatic requirements for a great vintage differ. Interestingly, although it is much more difficult to make wine at all in the north, they have had far more spectacular vintages since the stunning year of 1978. 1980 was good, as were 1982 and 1986, and 1983 and 1985 were very good indeed.

In the south, with much more blending together of different grape types, there has been a disheartening lack of balance, with years like 1982 when the Syrah failed and the wines ended up soft and rather lifeless, and 1983 and 1984 when the Grenache failed and the resulting wines were rather tough and tricky. 1985 saw a better balance in the vineyards and consequently impressive wines.

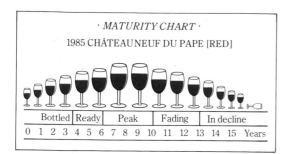

characters of the northern and southern Rhône wines. Below you, dwarfed beneath the precipitous slope, is the town of Tain; to the west and north are the rugged, exhausting cliff faces where terraces of vines produce wines of stark brilliance. Then look to the south. The plains fan out below the hill as far as the eye can see. The Rhône abandons its seaward surge and seems content to snake its way through the fields and villages, as though the hard work has been done and the increasingly torrid sun makes further exertion irksome. So it is with the wines. You don't need to struggle to appreciate the flavours of the southern Rhône as you must with a Hermitage or a Cornas. These are broad, open flavours, rounded, ripened by relentless sun, eased into existence to offer pleasure without pain; thirst-quenching, not thought-provoking.

· THE GRAPES ·

The lack of definition in their flavours is partly owing to the increasingly fierce conditions in which the grapes grow, since overripe grapes rarely give distinctive flavours, and it is partly the result of the basketful of different grape varieties which are permitted in the region. As many as 13 different varieties are permitted for Côtes du Rhône and Châteauneuf-du-Pape is allowed 13 different red and white varieties in its *appellation*. Although this abundance frequently produces rather fuzzy-edged flavours, modern wine-growers, particularly in Châteauneuf-du-Pape, are beginning to realize that this range of permitted grapes gives them enormous scope to experiment.

Grenache Noir is the most important grape throughout the southern Rhône. It ripens quickly to an unnervingly high alcohol level, but gives broad, raspberry-fruited wine, some-

times with a peppery bite, sometimes with a cinnamon and ginger spice, but never with much acid nor much tannin. This is the bright sunny face of the Rhône reds, quick to mature but also quick to fade.

Cinsaut is of the same mind, even softer, less coloured, with even less stamina, and at its best making up the numbers in a young fruity rosé.

With these two occupying a lot of vineyard space, something to give the reds a bit of stuffing is needed, and both Syrah and Mourvèdre do just this.

Syrah is the same tough, tannic heavyweight as in the North, but it never quite develops such exciting nuances down here.

Mourvèdre is an old Mediterranean grape, only a decade ago derided as a peasant leftover, now eulogized for the marvellous mixture of honey, raisin, herbs and deep plummy fruits that its wine can boast of.

Carignan, too, is a beefy grape, but doesn't contribute much except volume, and a tough edge to most Côtes du Rhône.

Other red grapes of some importance are the Counoise, Muscardin, Terret Noir and Vaccarèse, but they are very definitely only bit-part players in most vineyards.

Muscat is really the only white grape of any memorable taste, and that is only used at Beaumes de Venise for sweet wine.

Otherwise Clairette, Roussanne, Marsanne Grenache Blanc, Picpoul and Bourboulenc produce attractive wines in the right hands but none stamp their character on the blends.

· THE WINES ·

Côtes du Rhône Over 80 per cent of southern Rhône wines, from 83,000 acres (33,600 hectares) in a hundred communes, is covered by the Côtes du Rhône *appellation*, and can be red, white or rosé. The regulations are reasonably tight, demanding 11° minimum alcohol, and limiting the yield of the vines to 50 hectolitres per hectare, when they could easily produce far more. There is lots of good wine to be had under simple Côtes du Rhône labels, especially where modern co-operatives have used up-to-date methods to produce bright, fresh reds and whites. However, the leap of quality between Côtes du Rhône and

Côtes du Rhône-Villages is dramatic and well worth the extra cost of the bottle.

Côtes du Rhône-Villages wines can only come from the 17 villages traditionally thought as producing the finest wine. Most of these are strung along the foothills of the Dentelles de Montmirail, to the east of the river, jagged, care-worn teeth of bleached rock, where the scrub and pine can hardly gain a foothold, but which provide billowing ridges of thin stony soil as they subside into the valley floor. The conditions for 'Villages' are strict – the wines must achieve 12.5° alcohol, the vines are allowed to bear only 35 hectolitres per hectare – which is only half what some Burgundy vineyards may produce, and the planting of both Grenache and Carignan is restricted so as to allow finer grapes like Syrah and Mourvèdre more chance to shine through. The reds, from villages like Cairanne, Valréas, Visan, Vacqueyras and Beaumes de Venise are exceptionally full, fruity wines, with a slight earthy, peppery edge, which are delicious young, but age extremely well. The best whites are from Laudun in the flatter land nearer the river, while nearby Chusclan makes the best rosé.

The papal palace in the background surveys the vineyards of Châteauneuf-du-Pape whose unique round pebbles covering the soil preserve heat far into the night.

These wines couldn't be more different. Vacqueyras is a strong dark red, bottled by Jaboulet, a *négociant* in the northern Rhône. Beaumes de Venise is a sweet fortified white from the Muscat grape, bottled by the local co-op.

The villages of Rasteau and Beaumes de Venise also make sweet fortified wines called *vins doux naturels* (natural sweet wines).

Rasteau is based on the black Grenache and ends up a bit like a port which has lost its sense of direction in the fog.

Muscat de Beaumes de Venise uses the Muscat grape to produce a delicious, easy-gulping sweet white full of the flavour of apples and honey and grapes and easily the best of the southern French fortified wines.

Châteauneuf-du-Pape is the best of a group of villages near Orange which have their own *appellation*. This is where AC laws were first formulated in 1923, which shows the esteem in which these big wines, from vineyards so stony you can't see the earth at all, were held. Despite stringent rules however, and the highest minimum alcohol degree in France – 12.5° – the wines got too famous for their own good and Châteauneuf became such a commonplace name that it was easy to dismiss the wine as an overpriced hype. Not long ago there was some truth in this criticism, but the reality now is different. Although much *négociant* Châteauneuf still bears little resemblance to anything very much, Châteauneuf from a good grower can be exciting wine.

The red has a marvellous dusty softness, redolent of high summer heat in a dusty country lane, which is coated with soft raspberry fruit and spice. You can drink them young, but if you wait a few years you may catch glimpses of blackcurrant, chocolate, cinnamon and plums – all wrapped in the warm smoothness of the south.

The white wine is rarer, covering only 3 per cent of the vineyards, but can be absurdly good when young, mixing peaches and licquorice, herbs, lime and nuts in a surprisingly fresh, mouthwatering wine.

Gigondas, near Vacqueyras to the east of Orange, likes to pride itself on being a nearly-Châteauneuf-du-Pape. However, despite some rather good fruity wines from individual growers, most of these reds are fairly thick and jammy, while the rosés are a bit too solid for comfort.

Lirac and **Tavel**, to the west of Orange, are altogether more appetizing. Tavel only makes rosé and it is really rather too expensive, but it certainly does have a good dusty cherry taste even if it's a bit heady to drink much of. Lirac rosé is just as good, but lighter and cheaper, while the red can be really beefy stuff, with loads of fruit and a slight mineral streak. The white is full of fruit when very young although it doesn't really age.

The Mistral-scarred stones of the Dentelles de Montmirail rear up like jagged teeth above the verdant vineyards of Gigondas.

· FOOD AND WINE ·

The Rhône valley itself doesn't have a very distinctive local cuisine, chiefly because it is surrounded by cuisines of great personality and tradition, and seems to act like a suction pad, drawing them into its own repertoire. From the north come a wide variety of Lyonnais favourites, such as *Poulet demi-deuil* – truffled chicken stuffed with sausage and drenched in a cream sauce – or the colourfully described *tablier de sapeau* – 'fireman's apron' – which is a grilled or fried slab of tripe served with tartare sauce, and every conceivable part of the pig turns up somewhere or other. There is also a local emphasis on game because of the forest plateaux to the west. The flavours are strong and the bitter-sweet intensity of the Syrah reds provides a good sparring partner rather than easy refreshment.

As the valley widens out below Valence, vegetables and fruit take over the terrain from the vine, and the chief gastronomic influence is the *gratin*, from the mountainous east – a whole variety of noodles, fish, vegetables and especially potatoes are prepared with various permutations of milk, egg, butter and cheese. Further south still, it becomes obvious that the flavours of Provence are spreading up the valley – the reek of garlic and olive oil is everywhere, peppers, onions, tomatoes and handfuls of hillside herbs impregnate every savoury dish: the casseroles of the north become the *daubes* of the south, and the street stalls are laden with peaches and melons.

This isn't a cuisine for thoughtful drinking, and the new breezy reds and whites of the south are appetizing and refreshing with this kind of food – far more so than the old-style bone-crusher reds can ever have been.

· GOOD PRODUCERS ·

Northern Rhône Guigal, Chave, Desmeure, Barjac, Jasmin, Vidal-Fleury, Coursodon, Clape, de Vallouit, Vernay, GAEC Syrah, Jaboulet.
Southern Rhône Co-operatives like Beaumes de Venise, Cairanne, Tulette and Chusclan. Also Maby, Rabasse-Charavin, Domaine de L'Ameillaud, Domaine de Durban, Domaine du Vieux Télégraphe, Château Rayas, Château de Beaucastel, Château du Grand Moulas, Château des Fines Roches.

· ALSACE ·

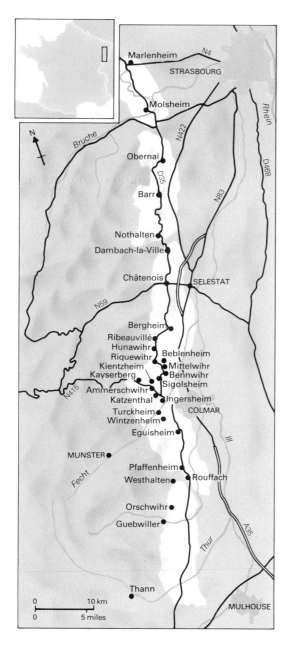

Y ou *must* get off the autoroute to appreciate Alsace. If you restrict your-self to looking out of the window as you tear down the Rhine valley along the French border with Germany, you'll see a lot of hills topped by forest to the west and a flat, wide, dully prosperous valley basin to the east, and maybe not think much of it.

Of course, for the unromantic soul, that *is* Alsace. The flatland produces a fair amount of pretty basic wine and rather more vegetables and fruit. The hills are the first range of the Vosges mountains, which provide a series of east-to-south facing bulges and folds in the valley-side to create very warm microclimates for grape-growing. In the central section of about 70 miles (113km) between Strasbourg and Mulhouse, these are turned into positive suntraps. The Vosges peaks shelter the cast-ern slopes from the damp westerly winds and create an arid rain shadow over the vineyards which roll down from the forest, making this northerly outpost of the vine the second driest area in the whole of France (the driest is around Perpignan in the far south).

That's the bare bones of it. But Alsace is much more than that. North of Ribeauvillé, in Riquewihr, Beblenheim and Kayserberg, you shift back centuries. The gabled houses – criss-cross beams gamely supporting tilting tiled roofs – strain towards their neighbours across narrow streets clogged with people. The chatter of conversation easily drowns out the noise of any cars which may stray up these alleyways, and the smells of wine and meat, pastries and coffee, cheese and chocolate all mingle on the crowded pavements. You are as close as you can be to the wine villages of the distant past. And these are *real* wine villages, not some cheap trickery mocked up for the tourist trade. In many of them virtually the entire population is involved with one or another aspect of wine.

It seems so relaxed, so time-charmed, so spared the rough progress of the outside world. But let us turn briefly from the joys of Riquewihr to Katzenthal or Bennwihr or Mittelwihr. There is calm in these villages also, but it is a cold, blighted calm, and all the buildings are of concrete and plaster. Why? Because some of the worst fighting of World War Two raged through these streets.

But this melancholy remembrance is at the very heart of the character of Alsace. These gorgeous hillsides, thickly clad with vines, represent the natural eastern boundary of France, and every great struggle between France and Germany has seen the vine trampled under the boots of marching men. In 1870 Prussia gained control of Alsace and Germanized its new acquisition, in particular ripping out the decent vines and using these noble vineyards to produce enormous quantit-ies of blending wine to fatten up their thinner brews in the north. France won Alsace back in 1918, but in 1940 the war machine once more crunched through these lovely hills and valleys. Finally, in 1945 Alsace became French again and its war-weary inhabitants started afresh to rebuild their lives and their land.

This see-saw existence has led to a uniquely Franco-German character – in the warm, humorous, but dedicated and industrious people, in the local dialect which seems to switch between German and French yet isn't quite comprehensible as either, in the names of the towns and the doll's-house-proud northern village architecture – and in the choice of grapes and the style of wine they make.

· GRAPES AND WINE STYLES ·

Many of the wines sound Germanic because some of the best grapes have German names

and Alsace was the first French area to do what is commonplace in much of the rest of the wine world – call the wines by the name of the grape which makes them. So we have the Germanic Rieslings, Gewürztraminers and Sylvaners, but in the French corner we have Pinot Blanc, Pinot Gris, Pinot Noir and Muscat – Alsace's split personality again.

As to the character of the wines, they are totally different to Germany's offerings, even though the Vosges mountains of Alsace turn imperceptibly into the Haardt mountains of the Rheinpfalz as you cross the border at Wissembourg and the Rhine ambles on contentedly northwards past both. Germany's Rhine wines have a fundamental fruity sweetness offset by a strong lick of acidity. They are basically light and the flavours often stand out in stark contrast to each other. Alsace's objectives are different. Here the growers look for a big, mouthfilling ripeness in their wines, but they make them completely dry, with all the sugar fermented out. So the flowery sweetness of Germany is translated straight

Alsace is full of delightful villages, miraculously impervious to the modern world, and Riquewihr (left) **is the most famous. The name is a derivation of 'Reichenweier' – rich village – from the time when its prominence as a wine village was already being established. Most of these lovely gabled houses were built before 1640. Eguisheim** (above) **boasts the biggest co-op in Alsace, but also some quiet old streets, in one of which a grower hoses down the wooden grape tubs ready for the next vintage.**

away into a perfume powerful, intense and exotic all at once. These wines often smell sweet, but in the mouth they are marvellously, impressively dry. They are mostly white, but there is a good deal of Pinot Noir in the vineyards which makes anything from a light rosé to a fairly decent red, depending on the heat of the year. And there is a considerable sparkling wine industry making a lot of champagne-method wine under the title Crémant d'Alsace, as well as a fair amount of much better than average tank-fermented (*cuve close*) fizz.

· APPELLATIONS ·

Alsace is the only *appellation* in Alsace. It was gained as late as 1962 and applies to all the wines whatever the grape variety.

Recently, in a bid to move the image of Alsace wines 'up-market', there has been an attempt at a more specific classification. As you might expect, it has followed both a French and a German path.

The French system defines the quality of specific vineyard sites.

Grand Cru Starting with the 1983 vintage, wines from one of 48 traditionally superior vineyards are allowed to call themselves 'Grand Cru' (these words are used on the label together with the vineyard name). There is no doubt that these vineyards can produce remarkably powerful wines, usually requiring several years ageing to show their full flavour, and with three fine vintages in 1983, 1985 and 1986, we should soon start seeing these high-priced beauties on a regular basis.

The German approach to classification is based on the amount of sugar in the ripe grapes, and Alsace has adopted two classifications modelled on this system, rather than on vineyard provenance.

Vendange Tardive means 'late harvest', like the German 'Spätlese'. The grapes have to be fully ripe and reach a minimum alcohol level of 12.9° for Riesling and 14.3° for Pinot Gris and Gewürztraminer. These wines are usually fat and sensuous in their strong fruit flavours – but almost always dry.

Sélection des Grains Nobles means 'selection of superior overripe grapes', and is equivalent to the German Beerenauslese. You

don't see many of these, because the Riesling has to be ripe enough to reach 15.1° of alcohol and Pinot Gris and Gewürztraminer 16.4°, but the wines can be shockingly good, usually retaining some residual sweetness and so intense and exotically perfumed that you wonder whether they should be drunk by the spoonful rather than the glassful. And at the prices they fetch, that's probably all we can afford!

· THE WINE TRADE ·

The wine trade in Alsace is shared between merchants, co-operatives and individual growers. The co-operatives control more than half of the business; and they supply most of the own-label brands which have finally made Alsace wines so popular. In general the quality is good and cost is low. The wines from the merchants will generally be more expensive, but they can have a fuller, rounder personality since a merchant may blend selected wine from all over Alsace. This is the argument used by merchants in Champagne and

· VINTAGES ·

Suddenly great vintages are sprouting like mushrooms after rain in Alsace. 1985 and 1983 are *both* supposed to be the Vintage of the Century! 1986, 1981 and 1979 are good to very good, while even the wet and joyless weather of 1984 failed to stop them making crisp, lean but very refreshing whites. If you judge greatness by the number of tip-top, late-harvested, expensive varieties, then 1976 and 1983 are the finest in recent years. But if greatness means large quantities of brilliantly fruity wines at every price level, wines packed with flavour and excitement at prices we can all afford – then 1985 is the year. And since I believe wine's pleasures should be spread as widely as possible, 1985 is the year for me.

· GOOD PRODUCERS ·
Trimbach, Rolly-Gassmann, Faller, Blanck, Cattin, Kuentz-Bas, Zind-Humbrecht, Hugel, Jos Meyer and various co-operatives, for example, Eguisheim, Beblenheim, Ingersheim and Bennwihr.

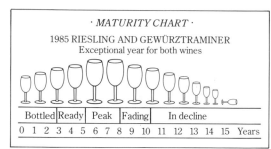

· MATURITY CHART ·

1985 RIESLING AND GEWÜRZTRAMINER
Exceptional year for both wines

Bottled	Ready	Peak	Fading	In decline	
0 1 2	3 4	5 6 7 8	9 10	11 12 13 14 15	Years

Burgundy when they plead superiority over the individual grower. There is some truth in it, because they do have the opportunity to balance blowsy grapes with tart grapes, steel and flint with fruit and honey. Even so, wine is ideally an expression of grapes grown in a single vineyard and, following the trend towards single vineyard wine in the modern wine world, the Alsace growers themselves are becoming increasingly important for their hand-crafted piercingly fragrant wines.

· THE WINES ·

Alsace is very fortunate to have a wide variety of soil types throughout her vineyard slopes, and is unique in France in having so many world class grapes to take advantage of that diversity. Although it is common in countries like Australia, New Zealand and the United States to have a whole array of grapes growing side by side, this is usually because the vineyard areas are too recently planted for the perfect match between grape variety and microclimate to have become evident, and the winemaker may simply not know which variety is most suitable for his vineyard. The silver lining to the black cloud of Alsace's war-wracked history is that in 1945 it was possible to start afresh, with none of the constraints of existing practices and every desire to expunge pain by achieving excellence. A range of great grapes were planted in new vineyards established from scratch and, in white wines at least, Alsace now has a wider variety of wine styles than any other area of France.

Gewürztraminer I place Gewürztraminer above Riesling in my list of Alsatian wines simply because it is so succulently, self-confidently, sometimes outrageously, the most distinctive flavour in Alsace. *Gewürz* means 'spice' in German, and, my goodness, they do

The two faces of autumn in Alsace. On the left the carefully manicured vines around the fortified 14th-century church of Hunawihr soak up the last of the day's sun. On the right the vintage is completed and the leaves are turning gold and crimson in a side valley in the Vosges mountains that provide the rain shadow which makes Alsace, despite its north-eastern situation, one of the driest areas in France.

mean spice. The flavour is all lychees, and mangoes, fresh green grapes, a twist of the black pepper grinder, a slap of Nivea Cold Cream, and a last squirt of scent spray from a Madame's boudoir. OK, that is going it a *bit* strong, but those really *are* the nuances which lurk in fine Gewürztraminer. Nowadays you can also get a lighter, more flowery style which is more refreshing and less palate-blasting but, just occasionally, it is worth trying a Vendange Tardive Gewürztraminer to see what all the fuss is about.

Riesling is the exact opposite of Gewürztraminer. There are no boudoir fragrances here, but instead a steeliness, a streak of arrogant

acidity flashing through the heart of the wine. When it's young it can be rather sharp and appley with the acidity acting like a squeeze of lemon juice, but as it ages the apple becomes rounder, and softer, eventually turning into a pale honey warmth, while the acidity is transformed from the neutral nip of lemon into heady but shocking petrolly fumes, like the forecourt of a busy filling station. Sounds weird? It is! Weird and wonderful! So try it.

Pinot Gris This is also called Tokay d'Alsace because the grape *may* have been brought from Hungary – where Tokay is made – in the sixteenth century. But since the Hungarians say their Tokay grape was brought from

The 'Reserve Personnelle' means the wine is a special selection of better than usual quality. Domaine Weinbach is a single property; the wine is an estate-bottled Riesling from the Grand Cru Schlossberg vineyard in Kayserberg.

· FOOD AND WINE ·

Alsace is a bit too close to a gourmet's paradise for comfort. Or perhaps it's a *gourmand's* paradise, because indulgence and plump bellies are more the marks of the region than the somewhat ascetic pleasures of the new wave in French cooking. But then, Alsace cooking *isn't* entirely French; as with the wine, we are caught between the apron strings of France and Germany.

Choucroute (Sauerkraut as it is known in Germany) is the most famous Alsace dish, but you may find it more easily in Paris or Champagne than you will in Alsace, and it's almost impossible to match it with wine. But there's so much Alsace cuisine that *does* go with wine. The charcuterie here is magnificent; the summit of excitement being fresh *foie gras* or *pâté de foie gras* – created for the first time in Strasbourg around 1780. *Foie gras* needs a big Pinot Gris or even a Gewürztraminer. Then there are the various *pâtés en croute*, the smoked Strasbourg sausages, the tongue and blood *boudin*, numerous salami-type *saucissons* – and quiches! Those Real Men who swear they don't eat quiche can never have been to Alsace for a *tarte à l'oignon*, a *tarte flambée* or a proper *quiche Lorraine*, and a jug of fresh Pinot Blanc.

Then there's the fish. Pike, carp and eels are done to perfection here, often using Riesling in the preparation, and certainly as an accompaniment. Game is brought down from the Vosges, but is more difficult to pair off. One of the rare Pinot Noirs may do – but I would probably throw over tradition and have a big Tokay d'Alsace or a Gewürztraminer.

Alsace, it is obviously not a matter of great consequence! It makes fat, rather smoky wine but, given a year or two to pull itself together, Pinot Gris gets richer and richer, developing a magnificent 'thick' taste like runny honey or burnt toast with raisins!

Muscat Alsace Muscat is one of the most delectable of drinks, because, while most Muscats are rich and sweet and exotic, Alsace Muscat is dry and light, with a heavenly orchard freshness and a scent for once like the bloom in a vine-filled hothouse. Good young Muscat tastes so crunchy and green-grape fresh it's almost as if you had crushed a handful of just-plucked table grapes to your lips.

Pinot Blanc This isn't a grape with a massive personality, but perhaps for that reason it has become a massive success story. It produces light, appley, creamy-soft wines which are low in acid yet wonderfully refreshing. They are the perfect wine-bar whites, and since the grape grows well in the flatter more fertile but less respected plains vineyards, it is always good value.

Sylvaner used to be the 'basic' Alsace grape, along with the unmemorable Chasselas, but this workhorse job has now largely been taken over by Pinot Blanc. The Sylvaners we now see are usually from reasonable vineyard sites and, while they are a little one-dimensional when young – simple, refreshing, fairly acidic – they can age in an unusual earth and honey way, becoming even slightly tomatoey – in the nicest possible sense. Otherwise Sylvaner is used to blend with Chasselas and Pinot Blanc into Edelzwicker – Alsace's basic jug white – or into Crémant d'Alsace – the region's high-quality champagne-method sparkler.

Pinot Noir Alsace really isn't red wine country, but they do have a go with the Pinot Noir. Usually the result is nearer to rosé than red, and pleasant in a light strawberryish way. However, in years like 1983 and 1985 the Pinot Noir can ripen pretty well, and produce fragrant wine with quite a bit of tannin.

· THE LOIRE ·

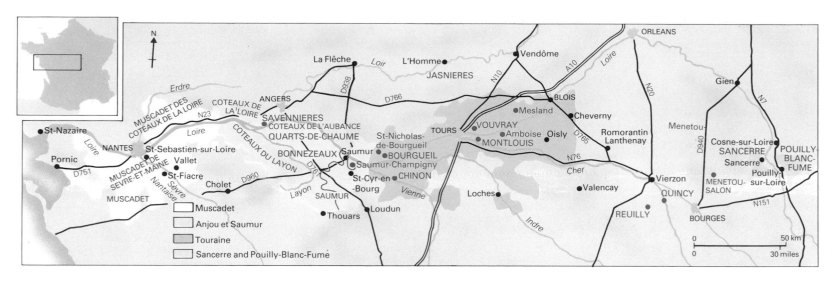

The Loire is a long river, twisting and turning, tumbling and gliding for 620 miles (1,000km) across France from its source in the hills of the Massif Central, only 30 miles (48km) from Valence in the Rhône, and scarcely 100 miles (161km) from the Mediterranean. It travels through the agricultural heart of the country, so you would expect many different wines to be grown along its banks.

Well, there *are* a whole load of wines – about a hundred at the last count – but when you think of it, how many of these wines do you ever come across, let alone actually buy and drink? There's Muscadet, certainly, Anjou – white or rosé – and sparkling Saumur. Vouvray is well-known although few of us seem to drink it anymore and Sauvignon de Touraine is a cheap alternative to Sancerre and Pouilly Blanc Fumé. And that's it! Eight wines!

Now, I'm not saying that there are a hundred different flavours in the Loire wine basket, but there are more than eight. For a start there is some excellent *red* wine made in the Loire. And there is some of France's greatest sweet white wine. However, there is often a strong family resemblance between the wines for two reasons: first, there are only half a dozen major grapes used and in general they are not France's most subtle operators; and second, the Loire *is* very far north for grape-growing especially since it is influenced by Atlantic weather patterns, rather than the more extreme patterns of continental Europe which make Alsace, for instance, so warm in summer despite being further north. This means that a slightly green unripeness can be tasted in many of the wines.

· THE GRAPES ·

Since the grapes are so difficult to ripen, it might have been better to choose varieties with a warm, aromatic personality. Sadly, the Loire is packed with grapes whose chief attributes in cool years can be a quite disturbing aggression and charmlessness.

Chenin Blanc, among the white grapes, is the chief culprit here. It is a late ripener and it is Anjou's sorrow that in more years than not the white grape harvest consists largely of clusters of tough, harsh Chenin which somehow have to be turned into wine. Yet when it *does* ripen, it is an astonishing grape not only making brilliant dry wines, but also being very prone to the sugar-enriching noble rot which allows wonderful sweet wines to be made.

Sauvignon Blanc is the chief grape of Touraine and the Upper Loire and while it can be superbly grapy and tangily refreshing if it's reasonably ripe, it can be raw, over-assertive stuff in cool years.

Muscadet (also known as Melon de Bourgogne) is the white grape which produces Muscadet, and its chief claim to fame is that it is anything but assertive, being one of France's blandest varieties. But then, bland, clean neutrality is what most people are looking for in a Muscadet.

Cabernet Franc is the most important red grape. It doesn't ripen too easily here, but in parts of Anjou and Touraine, it can achieve a piercing, memorable raspberry and blackcurrant flavour, lean but beautiful, the fruit refined to its last decimal point. There is also now some Cabernet Sauvignon being used to add a bit more muscle to the wine.

Gamay is the more common grape, and *can* produce lovely gentle, fresh Beaujolais-type reds in the right hands, and pretty mean stuff in the wrong ones.

Pinot Noir is hardly seen except around Sancerre where, surprisingly, it can produce most aromatic, delicate reds and rosés.

· THE WINE REGIONS ·

The Loire region divides roughly into four areas – Muscadet at the river's mouth, Anjou, Touraine and the Upper Loire. There are no special classifications in any area. The *appellation* system is comprehensive – some might say too comprehensive, with all those different wine names – but this does mean that properties in small areas which have made a special effort to produce extra-quality wine are likely to have their own little AC.

The organization of the regions varies. In Muscadet there is, surprisingly, very little co-operative presence, since there is a multitude of small growers. The merchants occupy the central position, either through long-term contracts with growers, or through owning the land. In Anjou, the merchant houses are the most important, but you can frequently get a better wine from a good co-operative like Brissac or St-Cyr-en-Bourg at Saumur and for the sweet wines you really have to go to a single producer. Touraine is also dominated by merchants, but it is always worth trying to find a wine from a grower, or from a good co-operative like Oisly et Thésée. The Upper Loire, again, is dominated by merchants' blends, but you'll never know what all the fuss is about until you taste a single grower's Sancerre, Pouilly Blanc Fumé or Quincy.

· MUSCADET ·

You could call Muscadet one of France's most successful white wines, simply because it has caught the mood of the times quite brilliantly. It wasn't so much its flavour which did this as its *lack* of flavour.

For several centuries, the Muscadet grape had been quietly making the local sea-food

Left **Flat exposed vineyards in the Pays Nantais at the mouth of the Loire, with a heavy storm threatening the vines.**

quaffer for all the guzzlers of Nantes and Brittany. No one really took much notice of it, but it did slip down very nicely with the mussels, oysters and shrimps. Then along came the 1950s. France was waking up after the War, Paris was beginning to party again and the bistro tables were buzzing with talk of the new wine discovery – Beaujolais Nouveau! It wasn't long before the restaurant and café owners decided they could do very nicely with a young, fresh, light white to go with the laughing purple draughts of Beaujolais, and Muscadet's star rose. They chose Muscadet precisely because it is so neutral and because, contrary to many popular pontifications, good Muscadet is low in acid while remaining very dry. Acid wines need time in the bottle to harmonize: low-acid wines you can drink as soon as the fermentation is finished. It's also low in alcohol; its *appellation* stipulates a *maximum* level of 12.3°.

Ordinary Muscadet is, to be honest, fairly basic stuff, but there is now an effort to upgrade the quality and, naturally, increase the price the producers can ask. Muscadet is divided into three regions:

Muscadet, the simplest AC, is largely from the dull flatlands south and west of Nantes towards the sea. It's chilly and damp down there and usually so is the wine.

Muscadet des Coteaux de la Loire is from the east near Ancenis, on chalky soil, but there are less than 1,000 acres (400 hectares) and

the wine always seems to be a little solid.

Muscadet de Sèvre et Maine is the heartland. This covers almost 20,000 acres (8094 hectares) and contains all the best vineyards, with more clay around Vallet, and sandy soil in the higgledy hills near St-Fiacre. Here domaine-bottled wines can frequently be found.

Muscadet de Sèvre et Maine sur lie is particularly worth looking for. *Sur lie* should mean that the wine has been left after fermentation on its yeast deposits or 'lees', and bottled, without being filtered, directly from the vat or barrel the following spring. There is rather too lax an interpretation of this ruling, but the resulting wine should have just the tiniest prickly pétillance, a slightly peppery apricot fruit and even be ever so slightly honeyed. Note how I qualify each adjective – that's because Muscadet never has a great deal of flavour, but that's no bad thing. With oysters and other seafood I've often chosen Muscadet rather than the more expensive Chablis or Champagne for this very reason – it makes the perfect, unobtrusive partner.

· ANJOU ·

Anjou's vineyards lie almost entirely to the south of the river. It isn't all vines by any means, because Anjou's wide, gently undulating prairie lands are far too useful for grain and vegetable crops. Often the vines look strangely incongruous, isolated amid the corn

The Loire meanders lazily across open Anjou country. Saumur, the chief wine town on the river, is the base for several leading wine companies.

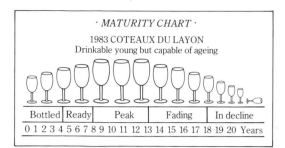

and cabbages. They don't look confident enough to produce great wine, and on the whole they don't.

Anjou's reputation has for so long been based solely on its least impressive wine that we had better look at this straight away.

Anjou Rosé is too often vaguely sweet, stale orange rather than pink, and sulphurous rather than fruity. Yet Anjou Rosé isn't a bad drink. When you get it fresh, from a store with a quick turnover, the colour is a shiny pink and it has a bright rather nuts-and-apple sort of taste – then it can be delicious.

But poor old Anjou Rosé has been pushed into the same 'commodity' cul-de-sac as cheap Liebfraumilch and cheap Soave – as long as the price stays low, many shippers don't care about the quality, so the producer lets the quality slip and slip, the profit margins shrink and shrink until the quality reaches zero. Does Anjou Rosé then bottom out?

Well, it can't go lower, so if it is to sell at all, someone in the region has got to say 'enough is enough', and there are signs that this is happening. The good co-operative cellars, like Brissac, are aware that their members have got great fields full of the Gamay and Groslot grape fit for little else but rosé, and ways *must* be found to sell the wine. Freshness, fruity bright clean flavours – not a lot to ask, and easily within the grasp of a decent producer.

The basic Anjou *appellation* spreads right along the south bank of the Loire from east of Ancenis to west of Saumur. It covers red, white and rosé and though Rosé d'Anjou is the most famous – or infamous – there is much better wine to be had.

Cabernet d'Anjou and **Rosé de Loire**, the one a slightly sweet Cabernet-Franc-based rosé, and the other an attempt at a dry rosé, are better for a start.

But it is the Anjou Rouge and Anjou Blanc which show most signs of improvement.

Anjou Rouge, too, usually from Cabernet Franc, used to be very meagre stuff, but latest vintages have shown a sharp, blackcurrant style which, slightly chilled, makes for excellent summer drinking.

Anjou Blanc, from the Chenin grape, used to be a by-word for harsh acid stuff, but recent examples have been very refreshing with a quite biting fruit but not rasping acidity.

These improvements can be put down directly to modernization and investment at the large wineries in the region, and are very welcome, providing as they do a further source of good cheap French wine – Anjou Blanc is generally the cheapest AC white in France. However, there is more to dry white Anjou wine than this.

Savennières, **Savennières la Roche-aux-Moines** and **Savennières Coulée-de-Serrant** (a single 17-acre vineyard) are venerable dry Chenin whites from the north bank of the river Layon that joins the Loire just west of Angers. Here you will see Grand Cru on the occasional label, but it isn't an official classification, merely an expression of self-esteem. The wine is concentrated, austere to start and slow to reveal its richness.

On the south bank, the Layon valley has one of those rare microclimates where the autumn fogs coil off the river and drift up through the vineyards as the sun heats the air. The clammy humid warmth clings to the Chenin grapes and encourages noble rot to attack them. Noble rot sucks the water from the grapes thus concentrating the sugar to give small amounts of intense and sweet juice. In several parts of the valley, the slopes are as steep as 1 in 4, and, although almost impossibly difficult to work, noble-rotted grapes from these dizzy vineyards produce great sweet wine.

Quarts de Chaume and **Bonnezeaux** are the two best ACs, and together only cover 240 acres (97 hectares). They produce tiny amounts of luscious wine – Quarts de Chaume is only *allowed* to produce 22 hectolitres per hectare. Not quite as sweet as Sauternes, they are very slow to develop and can seem surprisingly dry when young. This is because the Chenin's very high acidity masks the fruit until time softens the wine. At 10–20 years old they have a wonderful gentle richness, all quince and peaches, sometimes apricots, but always kept fresh by the ever-present acidity.

Coteaux du Layon and **Coteaux de l'Aubance** are excellent, less intense sweet wines to drink younger.

Moulin Touchais which only has the simple Anjou AC is made just to the south, and is an amazing sweet wine tasting something like banana split toffee!

Saumur is known primarily for its champagne-method sparkling wine. This is made from Chenin, sometimes mixed with a little Sauvignon, Chardonnay or even Cabernet Franc. The blending does help, because the unripe Chenin grapes which are used can be just too fierce on their own. When properly made by a company like Gratien and Meyer,

Bottle washing? Yes. Not all small winemakers are keen to invest in new bottles every year and these bottles at Vouvray are being given a good going over before re-use.

The best Muscadets are from 'Sèvre et Maine' and 'sur lie'. This wine (*far left*) is particularly tasty as it is produced organically by a single grower. Sauvignon (*left*), the most generally available of Touraine's wines, is similar to Sancerre at half the price.

Langlois-Château, Ackerman or the St-Cyr-en-Bourg co-operative they are refreshing, apple-sharp wines with a good bubble. There is also a little rosé which can be good.

Saumur, however, is not only fizz:

Saumur Blanc can be very pleasant dry white, especially when the Chenin is blended with Chardonnay or Sauvignon.

Saumur Rouge normally uses the Cabernet Franc grape to make lighter, grassy red.

Touraine is the heart of the Loire valley's château country, but Château Luynes is also surrounded by vineyards – surprisingly a relatively rare occurrence in the region.

Saumur-Champigny is the name used by the best group of vineyards making Saumur Rouge. When the vines are old and the wine carefully made, it is as though someone had squeezed essence of blackcurrant into the bottle. Filliatreau produces the best wines.

· TOURAINE ·

While Anjou has always been a pretty four-square agricultural region, with few memorable beauty spots and little sign of excess or indulgence, Touraine has been much more than that. Its meandering rivers, forests full of game, and gardens and orchards full of vegetables and fruit for the table, have made it a playground and holiday haunt for the high and mighty of France for centuries. It is fair to say that the wines of the area are overshadowed by the scenery and the breathtaking fifteenth- and sixteenth-century châteaux which populate the valley, drawing more gasps of appreciation than ever the wines could. I certainly remember the wonders of the châteaux at Amboise, Azay-le-Rideau and Chenonceaux more than the local wines.

Certainly, the wines of Touraine in general have an easy, refreshing quality, marrying well with the local cuisine rather than being memorable in their own right; but there are some high spots, and they start just to the east of Saumur.

Bourgueil and **St Nicolas-de-Bourgueil** and **Chinon** are reds from the Cabernet Franc, and can have a most unforgettable personality – strangely earthy, dry and sharp-edged, yet with a beautiful, almost searing laser-beam of blackcurrant and wild strawberry fruit. They are delicious very young, and last for absolutely ages, more and more resembling good Médoc from Bordeaux as they mature. I'm talking about fine Chinon or Bourgueil from a good grower – like Couly-Dutheil, Caslot-Galbrun or Olek – in a hot year like 1964,

· *VINTAGES* ·

Vintages are very important in the Loire because the sun doesn't shine enthusiastically enough each year. Muscadet can nowadays make a pretty decent fist of things in virtually any weather and the Sauvignon gets to an acceptable state of ripeness most years. But the Chenin is a very late ripener, and the red Cabernet Franc isn't exactly precocious; they need either a warm year or a very hot winemaker.

1986 Reasonably good, but vintage rains spoiled the chances of exceptional quality.

1985 A great year right through. Fine Sancerre and Vouvray, great reds from Chinon and Bourgeuil, wonderful sweet wines from the Layon valley, good Muscadet. Very exciting.

1984 A wet, cool year producing some good, tart Sauvignons and lean but tasty Muscadets, but elsewhere Anjou and Touraine were a bit fierce.

1983 A little too hot for the Sauvignon areas, but Muscadets were good, and the reds of Anjou/ Touraine and the sweet wines were very good indeed and need keeping yet.

The old wines often have a buttermilk softness tempering the rasping acid, and in five to ten years gain an almost honey-and-nuts gentleness, reined in by a green-apple acidity.

Vouvray Demi-Sec (which means somewhere between medium-dry and medium-sweet) is possibly the greatest 'in-between' in the world of wine. These wines have tremendous peachy fruit, they're sometimes smoky, sometimes nutty in a way you could almost chew, and as they age they add in quinces and pears and honey and still hold on to their green-apple-skin acidity for up to 20 years or more. Indeed, one grower is quoted as saying you will only see the sun in a glass of demi-sec after 20 years – and I know what he means.

Vouvray Moelleux (sweet Vouvray) is less often affected by noble rot than Quarts de Chaume. It still has a delicious peach and honey fruit after five to ten years, although to start with it may seem positively dry. Always try to get a single-domaine Vouvray if you can; producers' names to look out for are Huet, Poniatowski, Foreau, Freslier and Château Moncontour.

Montlouis just to the south of Vouvray has always claimed to be an identical twin. Distant cousin, more like, because it's still a Chenin vineyard and it doesn't seem to get as much sun as Vouvray; the wines are therefore leaner and stonier.

Jasnières, north of Vouvray, produces wines so cool and stark that you wonder who on earth would drink them.

Azay-le-Rideau, Amboise and **Mesland** also produce lean Chenin to the west and east of Vouvray, but at least they make a point of some fairly good rosé and red, sometimes from Cabernet Franc, sometimes from Gamay – which can be rather juicy in Touraine. These three villages may tack their own names on to the Touraine AC, as in 'Touraine-Mesland'.

Touraine is the *appellation* which covers most of the rest of the land in the area up to Blois (except for the idiosyncratic VDQS Cheverny, see p129). However, as 'regional'

1976, 1983 and 1985, but there is, sadly, rather more dull stuff about, pleasant enough, but not a patch on the real thing.

Vouvray, a dozen miles up river, is one of the most vexing and tantalizing of Loire wines. In its usual commercial manifestation it is vaguely sweet, and would be innocuous were it not for a bitter peach-kernel acidity, and a mildly meaty whiff of sulphur – and it's cheap. Tasting like that, so it should be.

Yet Vouvray can be *great* wine. Vines have certainly been planted here since the fourth century on the tough chalk and clay plateaux which crowd over the village houses huddled below. The Chenin doesn't exactly thrive on this soil, because, as usual, it needs a really warm vintage to ripen properly and even here in relatively warm Touraine it frequently doesn't get it.

Vouvray Pétillant or **Mousseux** uses up most of the grapes in poor years. This is big, fairly assertive fizz, more expensive than Saumur, but good. In hot years, the good growers can make dry, medium or sweet wines. All of them start life tough, acerbic and high in acidity, but they age wonderfully well.

Pouilly Fumé can be the best of all Loire whites. De Ladoucette is a leading grower in the region, and this is very good stuff. Equally good in a very different way is the rich sweet noble-rot-affected Quarts de Chaume – 1983 was a particularly fine year.

Most of Pouilly's vineyards are set back from the river banks, but just outside the town they do dip down close to the water's edge.

Some of my greatest guzzling sessions have been around Nantes, and further west towards the ocean, where I've devoured every possible form of seafood, but especially the oysters, clams, mussels and prawns, still reeking of the brine and iodine of wave-splashed, weed-strewn rocks, and Muscadet was absolutely brilliant with them.

In fact fish does dominate Loire eating right up to its source in the hills of the Massif Central: eels, freshly grilled over hot coals or in *matelote d'anguilles au vin de Bourgeuil*, a wonderful gooey red-wine stew, sometimes with carp as well; *alose à l'oseille* – shad cooked with the lemon-acid bitterness of sorrel; pike, sometimes in soft, sausage-like *quenelles*, but more often nowadays served in the rather penetrating slightly sour richness of a *beurre blanc:* salmon, occasionally smoked, but best with anchovy butter or *beurre blanc:* and trout, grilled or poached in Vouvray. With all these dishes, the marvellous freshness of the fish benefits from the acid-bright whites Anjou and Touraine offer.

Sauvignon wines are certainly best with fresh-water fish, since they have too much fruit for the iodiny rawness of seafood, yet enough sharpness to complement the fresh river flavour. They also go well with the vegetable dishes: mushrooms – especially *champignons sauvages*, wild mushrooms – play a great part in the cuisine` of Anjou and Touraine. And the sharp, sour Crottin goat cheeses of the Upper Loire make a surprising, but entirely successful partnership with white Sancerre or Pouilly Fumé.

ACs go, this is an extremely good one. Sauvignon de Touraine is a simple gooseberry-fruited, grassy-green white, which often resembles Sancerre – a Sancerre understudy, if you like, at half the price. And there is Chenin, but this is most likely to be made into either Touraine Mousseux or Crémant de la Loire – a supposedly superior but rarely seen sparkler which is also made in Anjou. Rosés are bright and breezy, usually from Gamay or Groslot, while the Cabernet and Gamay make brisk, immediate, sharply fruity quaffing reds. In fact, perfect food wines, all of them, but with enough fruit and none of the toughness which can afflict other Loire wines, particularly from the Chenin – so that they're easy to drink by themselves as well.

· UPPER LOIRE ·

Sancerre and **Pouilly Fumé** have enjoyed the same transformation from unheard-of local café wine to world celebrity as Muscadet at the other end of the Loire. The only differences are that these whites are made from Sauvignon Blanc, a more tangily tasty grape than Muscadet, and the vineyard areas are pretty small – so the limited production sells for a much higher price. As recently as the 1960s no one had heard of Sancerre; then it was discovered by Paris journalists and rapidly became the 'chic' restaurant wine it is today.

These two wines have come to epitomize all that is fresh, sharp, excitingly fruity, yet zingily dry. It's a style which has been copied all over the world by the new wave of winemakers. The flavours which the Sauvignon can achieve when grown on the best chalky limestone slopes are intensely grassy, nettly green even, and can have a gooseberry or asparagus taste, with a whiff of something smoky like the side-walk smell of freshly roasted coffee beans. If anything, the wines of Pouilly are slightly fatter than Sancerre.

Menetou-Salon and **Reuilly** are similar wines in a light, attractive, softer style.

Quincy is often the most unashamedly characterful Sauvignon in the whole region.

Red and rosé wines are also grown in Sancerre and Menetou-Salon, with rosé also in Reuilly – from the Pinot Noir or occasionally Pinot Gris grape. Although the red Sancerre can be a lovely, rather ethereal red, perfumed, cherryish and dreamily light in the mouth, the rosé is rarely anything more than pleasant and since the region makes such delicious whites, which are in such demand, they'd do us all a favour by concentrating more on the whites and less on the pinks.

· FRENCH COUNTRY WINES ·

French Country Wines can sound wonderfully evocative or ever so slightly derogatory, depending on how you look at it. 'Country' – as in clear blue skies, sunshine, green fields and a pub at the end of the leafy lane to quaff local ale and eat hearty rustic fare – unsophisticated maybe, but relaxing, utterly enjoyable. . .and honest. Or 'country' – as in country cousin, country bumpkin – lumpish, short on manners and likely to be parted from his money and his sweetheart by the first smooth-talking city slicker who happens along.

Well, it's a bit of both. France's wines run the gamut from the rustically dreadful to the elegantly sublime. Most of the sublime wines will be fully fledged *appellation contrôlée* with reputations and prices to match. Most of the dire will be lost in the murky depths of the EEC wine lake, although, unfortunately, some pretty dubious stuff may still sport a *vin de pays*, a VDQS or even an AC label.

Far more significantly, some of France's star wines do *not* have famous names and high prices. Maybe they've become unfashionable and becalmed over the centuries, but at one time way back when, they were revered and enthused over much as we now bow and scrape at the altar of red Bordeaux and white Burgundy. Maybe they are little pockets of vineyards producing delicious wines but from the wrong grapes – like the Sauvignon de St-Bris in the Chardonnay territory of Chablis, or Chardonnay itself, struggling to impress in the Chenin fields of Anjou. Maybe their production is tiny, and a grateful local populace laps it all up. Or maybe they are the creations of the Young Turks of the wine world who have headed into the dispirited grape prairies of the far south and set their cap at quality and excellence – defying regulations and tradition in their determination to break new ground and win accolades.

· APPELLATIONS ·

Country wines fall into one of the three categories of French quality control.

Appellation Contrôlée The reason some AC wines are included in the 'country' wine section, rather then under their own regional heading, is because they are usually wines of little more than local fame, often hailing from outside the main wine areas. But there are some absolute beauties lurking there in the backwoods.

Vin Délimité de Qualité Supérieure or VDQS is a rather grand title for this middle rank which is in the process of being phased out. These are partly wines which haven't yet proved that their quality is consistent enough to merit full AC status – though one or two get promoted every year. And partly they are the oddballs inside the major *appellations*, the ones growing the wrong grape in the wrong place. There are some stars here too.

Vin de Pays does, of course, mean 'country wine' in French, but this historic-sounding title was only coined in 1968 as an attempt to encourage producers of the completely anonymous *vins de table* to upgrade quality, regain a bit a self-respect, and increase their earnings. Unfortunately, because of the EEC approach to subsidizing French wine-farmers, it often pays a grower to produce as much rubbish as he possibly can and wait for the government to move in and buy it. Still, the *vin de pays* system is a vital instrument in the move towards less – but better – wine being produced, especially in the far south between Avignon and the Pyrenees.

Throughout the south, the role of the co-operative cellar is crucial, and many *vins de pays* stand or fall by the commitment of the local co-op. Although the *vin de pays* category is primarily concerned with introducing quality controls for existing grape varieties and improved methods of wine-making, it also allows experimentation with non-traditional grape varieties. Consequently, in the Midi many of the best wines are *vins de pays* from grapes like Cabernet Sauvignon, Merlot, Syrah, Sauvignon and Chardonnay, which are outside the *appellation contrôlée* guidelines for the area, but which are showing the way forward for the future. Although a few of these 'innovative' *vins de pays* with noble grape

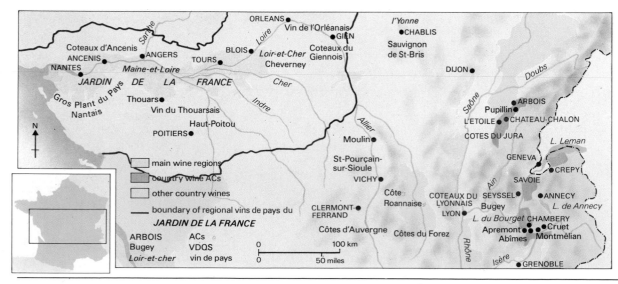

Haut-Poitou is a recently developed vineyard area. Though the quality is good enough for AC, it will need to prove itself for a few years yet, and the Chardonnay grape is still not favoured by the authorities in the Loire.

varieties may repay keeping, in general these wines are best drunk as young as possible.

· THE LOIRE ·

The Loire loops and lingers for such an eternal distance across the heart of France that it looks as though it should be a veritable treasure-house of undiscovered delicacies. But it isn't. Certainly there are lots of different wines being made but, because the Loire, for so many centuries, has been thought of as the garden of France and the holiday haunt of the rich and powerful, most of the local wines have long since been absorbed into the bigger, grander *appellations*.

But there are, in particular, some very tasty VDQS wines; two of the best are way up near the river's source, only a few inebriated bounds from the Beaujolais capital, Lyon. Côtes Roannaises, Côtes d'Auvergne and Côtes du Forez all make light, juicy red gulpers from Gamay, although there are a couple of chaps in the Roannaises who make a deep chocolaty Gamay more akin to a Morgon in full flight.

After this promising start there's a long, albeit scenic, gap. Near Vichy, they make a wine called St-Pourçain-sur-Sioule (VDQS), which is supposed to be effective in taking away the metallic aftertaste of the spa waters, but its curious, smoky flavour isn't so exciting if all you're after is a decent drink. And there are a couple of pretty duff VDQS wines on the arc of the river past Sancerre – the flat and muddy Coteaux du Giennois, and the vinegar-factory-bound Vin de l'Orléanais (though one outfit, Clos de St-Fiacre, makes a lovely sharp Chardonnay they call Auvernat).

· CHATEAU COUNTRY ·

After that the river swoops down into Touraine, passing another relic to the south at Cheverny (VDQS). Cheverny Chardonnay isn't bad, if a bit raw (some of them turn it into very drinkable fizz), but they are also the sole surviving producers of the Romorantin grape. I hope the habit doesn't catch on as the wine is liable to be off-puttingly fierce and dungy.

While we're looking south, way down by Poitiers there is an excellent VDQS – Haut-Poitou. The big modern co-operative seems to have created the region and its reputation

Cheverny is a quiet little-known wine area near Blois with two points of interest. It does have an impressive château, unlike most of the wine villages, and it is the sole producer of a strange raw local wine called Romorantin.

single-handed, and the wines, expecially Chardonnay, Sauvignon and Gamay, are excellent.

On the way back to the Loire, below Angers, you'll find a most unexpected but welcome VDQS – Vin du Thouarsais. There's only 50 acres (20 hectares) left, but Monsieur Gigon doesn't let that – nor the world's ignorance of his existence – stop him from making delicious sharp white Chenin and red Cabernet (which he calls Breton).

We finally get back to the river, and follow the increasingly sluggish flow into Muscadet territory till we get to Ancenis. Ancenis does produce mostly Muscadet – but one man, Monsieur Guindon, isn't satisfied with this and makes Coteaux d'Ancenis (VDQS) from the Malvoisie grape. It's a lovely, gently sweet wine, at once smoky and honeyed. Other

Ancenis, produced from Gamay and Chenin, can be a bit tart.

On through Muscadet, right to the blustery dunes at the Atlantic's edge – but not quite – because there is one more country wine to take in: Gros Plant du Pays Nantais (VDQS). Most of it is grown pretty close to the sea where salt breezes and sharp, unripe grapes make it wincingly abrasive.

· VIN DE PAYS ·

The Vin de Pays du Jardin de la France covers the whole Loire region – what a lovely name – 'Country Wine of the Garden of France'! When the label states Sauvignon or Chardonnay this is well worth buying; other varieties are less consistent. More localized *vins de pays* are Loir et Cher from Touraine, and Maine et Loire in Anjou. Two seaside wines – Loire-Atlantique and Marches de Bretagne – are, with rare exceptions, cuttingly sharp.

· THE NORTH AND EAST ·

At first glance, the east and north-east of France seem to be made up of great names crowding each other for space. Champagne in the far north and Alsace in the east. Then Chablis, Côte d'Or, Mâconnais, Beaujolais... down into the Rhône valley and on to the sea. There doesn't seem to be room for any also-rans.

Well, Alsace is so minutely organized that there really isn't a single country wine there. And in Champagne the profits to be made from the fizzy magic are so large that any fringe areas forced their way into the big-time long ago – even tiny Rosé de Riceys, down near Chablis, charges a fortune for a slug of its weird but fruity dark pink wine. But there are pockets of oddities in Burgundy and in the Rhône, and there are two very major, but rather forgotten, areas in the mountains far away to the east: Jura and Savoie.

· BURGUNDY ·

It doesn't take long to list Burgundy's country wines. Beaujolais has just one understudy in the suburbs of Lyon – the light, fruity Coteaux du Lyonnais (AC). And Sauvignon de St-Bris (VDQS) produces some of the tangiest, tastiest Sauvignon in all France, but it'll probably never

St-Bris is allowed AC Bourgogne for Chardonnay and Aligoté, but only VDQS for Sauvignon, though this produces the best wine! As a Loire grape, Sauvignon is 'foreign' to this region.

Above The manicured vineyards of Savoie occupy the highest parts of the valley, before it sweeps up to the alpine peaks.

Above right A still winter's day, the fruitless vines dusted with snow in the Arbois wine village of Montigny lès Arsures.

get its full *appellation* because the Chardonnay barons of nearby Chablis don't like the idea of a high-class maverick inside their patch. What's more, they have their own Vin de Pays de l'Yonne, which used to be a good source of fresh, bright Chardonnay from young Chablis vines, but they're so keen to exploit Chablis' rather mercurial reputation that they allow even three-year-old vines to make *appellation* wine (there used to be a four-year minimum) – so there isn't too much de l'Yonne on the market now. Just more Chablis.

· SAVOIE ·

If we head down to the Rhône at Lyon, and follow it up towards Switzerland, we pass

Bugey (VDQS) – a few years ago these wines were facing extinction but, in the wonderful way of these things, are now rapidly becoming a cult. The local Chardonnay gives some indication why; the other rather earthy wines do not.

After Bugey, in the various tucks and folds of the Alps, from the shores of Lake Geneva right down to the Isère valley near Grenoble, we catch glimpses of the Savoie *appellation*. I say glimpses, because the vine isn't the most important agricultural product in this dairy and grazing mountain region. Frequently the vines have to claw up the rapidly steepening mountain slopes while corn and vegetables and sleepy Charollais cattle take it easy on the

flatland below. Many of the wines *are* a bit on the light side, and it isn't so fanciful to think you taste something glacier-clean but scarcely intoxicating in the wines. After all these alpine slopes along the Swiss and Italian border harbour many of France's best ski resorts – which is where the majority of the wines are drunk. But there is some charming, almost whimsical, light Pinot Noir in Chautagne north of Aix and in the villages east of Chambéry, such as Chignin and Montmélian.

The best red is from the local Mondeuse grape, again east of Chambéry from villages like Cruet and Montmélian, and this can be tremendous gutsy stuff, full of plums and mulberries – rather like a mountain valley Syrah. You can age it too. The Jacquère grape makes quite a chunky white on south-facing slopes and a wispy one when the vines face north, while Chardonnay is pale from either. Look for the village names Apremont, Abîmes or Chignin. Seyssel is famous for sparkling wine, and it used to be snow-fresh and delicious, but is now rather a thick-headed parody of its old self. Still, the town is lovely with the Rhône rushing through on its eager

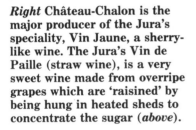

Right Château-Chalon is the major producer of the Jura's speciality, Vin Jaune, a sherry-like wine. The Jura's Vin de Paille (straw wine), is a very sweet wine made from overripe grapes which are 'raisined' by being hung in heated sheds to concentrate the sugar (above).

way south – most wines carry the simple 'Savoie' *appellation*, though better wines also carry a village name.

· THE JURA ·

If the Savoie mountain wines are mostly marked by a high-altitude lightness of touch, the Jura wines are less mountain peak and rather more caveman grotto in style. Jura also mixes its own indigenous and, thankfully, unimitated grape varieties with Pinot Noir and Chardonnay from Burgundy – which is just across the plain to the west. The Trousseau grape is the local red, and pretty sullen and beetle-browed it usually is too. Pinot Noir is altogether more bearable. Poulsard is the local 'semi-red' which makes quite decent rosé. Chardonnay, as so often, comes up trumps, particularly in the area between Puligny and Arbois, with the co-operative at Pupillin being particularly good. Chardonnay is also used to make fine champagne-method sparklers.

And then there's the native Savagnin variety. No wonder we don't see much of these Jura wines, because the Savagnin is lethal: a fierce, farmyardy white, blending oily thickness with a raw volatile acidity and a strong whiff of damp straw. Strangely, it works much better in the Jura's one famous wine – Vin Jaune (yellow wine). Here the Savagnin wine grows a special *flor* yeast on its surface, like *fino* sherry does in Spain; after being kept for anything between a generation and a lifetime, it develops that raging, sour, woody brilliance that only the very best sherries ever get – and only the most devoted sherry freaks ever enjoy. Most of these wines are *appellation* Arbois, Jura or L'Etoile while the Vin Jaune at its best has the AC Château-Chalon.

· THE RHONE ·

There are several fringe areas of the Côtes du Rhône which produce good wines. On the east bank, the most important is the large Coteaux du Tricastin (AC), north of Bollène, which was established virtually from scratch to accommodate French growers returning from Algeria and Morocco after independence. The reds, in particular, are spicy, fruity wines with quite a bit of class – and they're cheap.

Next come the Côtes du Ventoux (AC) vineyards, smothering the southern slopes of Mont

· FOOD AND WINE ·

In Savoie you feel that it is the long calm days of summer which are best catered for as the local mild cheeses, fragrant smoked and air-cured hams, and abundance of freshwater fish have a gentle savouriness to them. Reblochon, the Gruyère-like Beaufort and Tomme de Savoie are creamy and nutty and, despite the lightness of the local wines, both red and white go with these cheeses rather well. The hams and sausages might go better with more gutsy wine, but I think the local Mondeuse is quite gutsy enough. As for the fish they are so fresh and so simply prepared that cool draughts of local Chardonnay or Jacquère wines are absolutely spot on. In the depths of winter when the taverns fill with the fumes of *fondue* and *pommes de terre à la savoyarde* – cooked in meat stock with grated cheese – then the local wines can seem a little insubstantial.

Jura's climate is less immediately charming – being particularly wet and not particularly hot – but then so are its wines! The eating is hearty in these damp, forested hills and valleys. The marvellous local fish are often prepared in rich white or red wine sauces, the smoked meats and sausages like the substantial *Jésu de Morteau* have a real tang to them and, if they're not roasting or casseroling the local pheasant, hare and pigeon, they're turning them into succulent terrines and pâtés. Bresse, down below in the Saône valley, is famous for its *poulet au vin jaune*: chicken cooked in cream and egg yolks, flavoured with local morel mushrooms and the wild, piercing Vin Jaune. The cheeses are a trifle fuller in flavour than in Savoie (for instance Savoie copies Swiss Emmenthal and Jura copies Gruyère). This Gruyère-type is called Comté and is a little saltier than the Swiss version, and the local Bleu de Gex is salty and slightly bitter rather than penetrating. All of which means they calm down the local wines rather than swamp them – and that makes for an eminently satisfying combination.

Ventoux, which stands head and shoulders above the other hills to the east of Orange. Again, the reds are best, having a simple fresh fruit for quick consumption. Côtes du Luberon (VDQS), on south-facing slopes east of Avignon, produces similar wines, but its very fresh whites and rosés are the most impressive.

Various country wines on the west bank of

the Rhône can be equally first-class. The Côtes du Vivarais wines (VDQS) are fresh gulpers, the reds in particular being light and fruity. However the Coteaux de l'Ardèche is positively inspiring. A grouping of co-operatives is showing exactly what the *vin de pays* legislation can achieve. They have imposed cohesion and discipline on this breathtakingly beautiful upland haven of gorges and forests and planted the grapes people *want* – Chardonnay, Sauvignon, Cabernet Sauvignon, Syrah, Gamay – rather than muddle along with their old, unmemorable varieties. They are now producing wines of pinpoint clarity, the fruit proud and unmistakable – at prices low enough for us all to indulge. I wish there were more groups like the *vin de pays* producers of the Ardèche. From slopes on both sides of the river the Vin de Pays du Collines Rhodaniennes is often worth buying since it may be young Syrah from good northern Rhône vineyards.

· PROVENCE ·

I always forgive Provence wines everything – so long as I'm in Provence. There, whether I'm sitting on a bank of wild rosemary and thyme halfway up a mountain side with a hunk of bread, cheese and a mug of rough red, or whether I'm stretched out, glowing pink and unwholesome amongst a thousand other bodies at the edge of the glistening sea, panting in the heat and swigging ice-cold rosé from the bottle. . .whatever I'm doing, the simple wines of Provence are perfect. There are few wines whose appreciation is so tied up with the atmosphere of their homeland, but the swaying pines, the bleached sands, the pale grey crags of rock and the relentless blaze of sun are *part* of Provence wines. There, I love them. Back in the glum urban existence of the north, only the very best still have the talent to amuse.

Provence really begins below Avignon as the Rhône valley flattens out towards Marseille, and the rather sprightly Durance carves a much more stimulating valley of cliff face, tumbled rocks and inhospitable earth away to the east. Immediately we hit upon one of Provence's most recently-established but most exciting regions – Coteaux des Baux (AC). In these parched badlands of rock and scrub good rosés and brilliant reds are made from Grenache, Syrah, and, occasionally, Cabernet

Domaine de Trévallon is the leading property in one of France's up and coming ACs, Coteaux des Baux-en-Provence near Arles. Its vineyards are carved out of the pine forest and rock, virtually in the middle of nowhere.

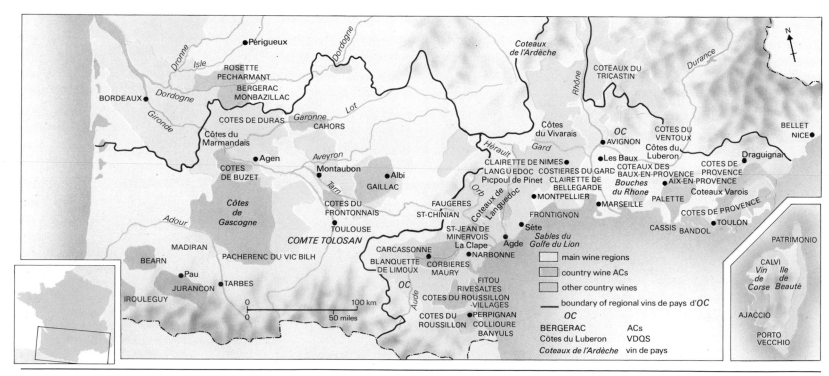

Spring at Les Arcs in the heart of the Côtes de Provence. The tree blossoms and the new foliage on the closely pruned vines sprouts optimistically with the end of winter.

Single estate wines are increasingly common in the Côtes de Provence. Château de Pampelonne is owned by Monsieur de Gasquet-Picard, but bottled by the co-op at the Maîtres Vignerons in St Tropez.

Sauvignon. A wine like Domaine de Trévallon, with its rich cassis and raspberry flavours, from a vineyard hacked out of the rock not much more than a decade ago, is complete vindication of all those brave adventurers who throw up their careers mid-life and decide to devote themselves to wine.

The Coteaux d'Aix-en-Provence (AC) is similarly forward-looking and it does have one particularly famous property – Château Vignelaure – but its wines, though good, just lack the verve to get me really excited. Tucked in the woods by the city of Aix is tiny Palette (AC). People often say you can taste pine and herbs in Provence wines. Well, pine resin I can certainly get in Palette wines and I've never really gone for their rather fierce, dry style.

Coteaux Varois (VDQS) and Côtes de Provence (AC) now take up most of the vineyard land as far east as Nice. Whether the wine is really worth a second glance or not depends entirely upon the commitment of the producer. There *are* good vineyard sites, often on limestone outcrops quite high up in the valleys, surrounded by rock and forest and cooled by the breeze off the bays. The wines here, particularly the reds, may be 'semi-serious', in that they will have some decent fruit and style to offset the tannin and rather empty stoniness which restricts so many Provence reds. These wines will almost certainly have Syrah and

Mourvèdre to give personality to the Carignan, Grenache and Cinsaut which otherwise make up the blend. The rosés, too, can be just a little hard – so chill them right down, shut your eyes and swig them back.

· CASSIS AND BANDOL ·

There are a couple of enclaves of rather superior wine down between Toulon and Marseille: Cassis and Bandol (both AC). Cassis is a little fishing port (unrelated to the blackcurrant liqueur) full of bustling fish restaurants packed with people eating *bouillabaisse* and drinking its white wine. Despite being close to Marseille, Cassis is a lovely exhilarating place, not at all pretentious, and the grandeur of its vineyards, rising up to the imperious jutting cliff a mile or two inland, makes the rather heavy cost of the surprisingly fresh white and fairly fruity rosé a little easier to bear.

Bandol (AC) is a hop-and-a-skip along the coastline towards Toulon. Like Cassis, the town is a fashionable watering-hole, and the wine is expensive. But a good red Bandol – gently spicy with a lovely honey and plum softness and herby edge – is a special wine, largely thanks to the splendid Mourvèdre grape. The rosé is the best on the Mediterranean, but I always jib a little at paying out quite so much for rosé: however good it is, I'm only going to swig it back. The white

· FOOD AND WINE ·

Give me three large bowls. In one I want an *aioli monstre*. This wonder is a thick, creamy mayonnaise seething with garlic and olive oil. I want to be able to smell it 50 paces away, and I expect people to be able to smell me at 50 yards for at least a day after eating it with a selection of fresh raw vegetables, boiled potatoes and sea food.

My next bowl will be a *ratatouille* – aubergines, onions, tomatoes, courgettes, peppers of various colours, and fresh thyme and basil, and then whatever else takes my fancy so long as the whole wonderful aromatic stew is gently, oh so gently, cooked to tenderness in lashings of good Provençal olive oil.

My third bowl shall hold a *bouillabaisse*, a steaming, heady broth of half-a-dozen different fish and shellfish, fresh off the boat, more olive oil and garlic, tomatoes, fennel and bay, but also a spendthrift sprinkling of saffron. And with all of these I shall hardly care what I drink so long as it is local, and preferably chilled.

Of course, this is to simplify Provence's food beyond excuse: what about the aromatic *grillades* of pork and lamb – *au fenouil* or with thyme or sage or rosemary; the wonderful sausages and pâtés – *pâté de sanglier*, wild boar, conjures up another world; the *bourrides* – fish extravagantly drenched in *aioli*; the *pissaladière*, king of pizzas; the fruit – melons and cherries and peaches and grapes from the plains behind the coast; and that simplest of breakfasts – and lunches and dinners – the *pan bagna*, a crusty baguette rubbed with garlic and olive oil and packed with olives, red peppers, tomatoes, anchovies, capers and artichoke hearts.

too, especially if helped by a little Sauvignon, can have an excellent apple and aniseed freshness.

There is one more 'rarity' wine and that is at Bellet (AC) in the hills behind Nice. I've always found it particularly overpriced and particularly unrefreshing. Red, white and rosé, it is modishly popular with the tourists at Nice, but if I'm settling down for a quiet lunch on the waterfront, I'll stick to Rosé de Provence.

Vins de pays are not particularly important here, since the Côtes de Provence AC in particular is fairly lax in its interpretation of what qualifies and what doesn't; in general, anything goes. However, the Bouches du Rhône reds and rosés from the area between Aix and the wild, wind-tossed Camargue marshes aren't bad, and the wines of Mont Caume, near Bandol, can be extremely tasty, especially when, as on the Bunan estate, someone has slipped in a little Cabernet Sauvignon for good measure.

· CORSICA ·

Corsican vineyards are probably the oldest in France, since they were planted by the Greeks and, despite the intervening 3,000 years, the wines still bear more resemblance to their Greek cousins than to the French tradition. In general they are just too heavy and frequently veer towards a rather dangerous sour acidity. The Corsicans take quite a pride in their grape varieties – the red Niellucio and Sciaciarello, and the white Vermentino – and as one of the most vociferous enthusiasts for preserving local personality (and not swamping it with the international stars like Chardonnay and Cabernet), maybe I should try harder to understand the flavours. Well, I have tried harder, and I still think the general standard of wine is lumpish and tired. There are one or two properties who use good oak barrels and modern techniques, but then spoil it all by charging the earth. I hate to say it, but the best results are from international varieties like Syrah, Chardonnay and Cabernet, produced by Sica UVAL and other co-operative groups; these are only allowed the title Vin de Pays de l'Ile de Beauté and Pièves. There are eight *appellations contrôlées*, covering red,

Much *vin de pays* is simply sold anonymously into the blending vats, but there is now a move to promote the individuality of the wines, and many attractive labels like this are helping to get the message across.

white, rosé and fortified *vins doux naturels*, and I shan't give up trying to like them. . .but I'm not there yet.

· THE MIDI ·

Languedoc and Roussillon manage to show off all that is worst about the rump end of French wine-making, and at the same time all that is most optimistic about the Brave New World of 'good wholesome cheap wine for everybody to afford and enjoy'.

Everywhere you look there are vines. Every hillock, every valley-floor seems to be groaning under battalions of stubby, ungainly vines – in winter, black and crabbed like dead hands rising from the earth; in summer, sprawling with untidy foliage like dishevelled revellers.

But these aren't the original vines that the Romans planted when they arrived, thirsty from the trek. Those were in the high, windy hill valleys behind the plains. The phylloxera plague put paid to them in the nineteenth century, and the wine-growers descended into the equally inhospitable but far more productive plains where they've been ever since, spewing out appalling amounts of appalling wine.

That is, until recently. It couldn't go on, this wine lake being fed by an uncaring, unmotivated agricultural community. The *vin de pays* system was brought in specifically to give some sense of purpose and pride to the dispirited populace. At the same time, the original hillside

vineyards were encouraged to up their quality levels – by the carrot of full *appellation contrôlée*. When you think that in 1977 there were only two ACs in the whole of the Midi and there are now twenty, with more coming on stream every year, it must be having an effect.

For red wines, this dramatic improvement has been achieved by the ruthless removal of the Aramon grape which produced oceans of mediocre wine; by the reduction of Carignan vines, which can give good wine but are also prone to overproduce; and by the increased planting of Syrah, Mourvèdre, Cabernet Sauvignon and Merlot to yield wines with fruit and marketable flavour. This has been considerably helped through the adaptation of the 'carbonic maceration' whole-grape fermentation method (see page 100), which produces lovely soft, spicy wine even from the dour, uncommunicative Carignan. Rosés and whites have been improved out of all recognition by modernizing wineries and installing refrigeration systems which allow cool fermentation of the juice even in the heat of a Mediterranean summer.

And they are getting there. Only five years ago a good red or white from the Midi was the exception not the rule. Now it's the other way round. Producers can see the benefit of getting out of the rut, and in this co-operative-dominated region, more and more outfits are deciding that in an area as suited to the vine

Far left **Port Vendres, between Perpignan and the Spanish border, is at the centre of the Collioure (AC) wine-making region, a sort of super-Roussillon red.**

Left **Clermont l'Hérault in the Clairette de Languedoc region, a rare 'white-only' AC which nevertheless sells much of its wine to the vermouth producers.**

as California's Central Valley, where fruit and easy drinkability have long been the watchword, there is *no* reason why the Midi cannot do for European drinkers what the Central Valley has done for Americans.

· LANGUEDOC ·

The Midi starts in the east with the Gard *département*. Gard wines are caught between two stools, not having the life of the Rhône wines just to the north, or the rough charm of the best Hérault and Aude wines to the west. Clairette de Bellegarde (AC) is a fairly dull white, though Costières du Gard (AC) can be a reasonably good, meaty, tarry red. Otherwise the most interesting things are being achieved at the ultra-modern Listel winery out on the sands below the Camargue where a bewildering variety of wines – from most of the classic and local grape varieties – are produced, usually under the *vin de pays* titles Sables du Golfe du Lion or Bouches du Rhône. The Gard's other best *vins de pays* are Uzège and Mont Bouquet.

The Hérault has the most vineyards of any *département* in France and, of them all, most needed to smarten up its act. It now has three ACs, one of which, Faugères, in the hills behind Beziers, makes very good ripe red. Another, St-Chinian, makes a large amount of light, spicy red. There are 13 VDQS, the best of which are the light St-Saturnin red, the fuller St-Georges d'Orques and Coteaux du

Languedoc and the unexpectedly good La Clape white from near Narbonne. However this is really *vin de pays* country, as the authorities attempt to upgrade this ocean of ordinary wine. The name of the producer is more important than the actual locality.

The Aude is another massive producer, but has many more classy hillside sites and is really leaping ahead in quality terms. High in the hills south of Carcassone is Limoux, where a mixture of Mauzac, Clairette and Chardonnay grapes produce sharp, light wine. Most of this is turned into Blanquette de Limoux (AC) sparkling wine by the champagne method, and the result is impressive: the wines have excellent bubbles and a green-apple-skin juicy tang. The Minervois (AC) north-west of Narbonne has transformed itself recently into one of the most reliable suppliers of fresh, spicy reds full of strawberry fruitiness, especially when made by carbonic maceration. Corbières (AC) makes similarly tasty reds, with maybe a little more weight, while Fitou (AC) has deservedly become a chic name for full, brawny reds with a dusty southern feel. There are two VDQS and 21 *vins de pays*, including France's biggest, Coteaux de Peyriac, and the beguilingly named Vallée de Paradis.

· ROUSSILLON ·

The Pyrénées-Orientales *département* is most famous for its dusty, dark, but strawberry-fruited Côtes du Roussillon and Côtes du

· FOOD AND WINE ·

There is a marked shift in food flavours as you move away from Provence towards the Pyrenees. There is an abundance of good fish right round the coastline, and Roussillon is a positive market-garden of early-ripening vegetables and fruit, as well as being thick on the ground with mountain game! What happens to it all in the kitchen is largely influenced by the Catalan onion-tomato-pepper approach to cooking.

Luckily the sturdy Roussillon reds are a perfect match for *perdreau à la catalane* (wild partridge with peppers and oranges), *boules de Picoulat* (meatballs seasoned with garlic and olives), spicy *chorizo* sausage and the like. A little further north, there's the *cassoulet* of Castelnaudary – a gut-stuffing stew of haricot beans, numerous meats, garlic and herbs – and *morue à la Minervoise*, which takes the curse off salt cod by preparing it in red wine with anchovies, olives, garlic and onions.

These are uncompromising flavours and this new generation of Languedoc-Roussillon reds is once again providing the draughts of full blooded flavour they need. And, of course, there's Roquefort blue cheese, the magical mixture of butteriness and mineral bite which comes from the Millau hills to the north. Then there is a whole range of sweet, nutty, honey and chocolate concoctions, including Spanish-style *touron* (marzipan, crystallized fruit and pistachios) – which is lucky, otherwise you'd have to drink the *vins doux naturels* by themselves.

Roussillon-Villages (both AC) which are often some of the best reds in the south, especially when given a little extra ageing in oak barrels. The rosés are also delicious, though the whites are a little blank. Collioure is a tiny AC, terraced among the cliffs on the road to Spain, that produces hefty red.

There are also a number of *vins doux naturels*. These 'naturally sweet wines' are fortified and made in much the same way as port. The base wine, either red Grenache or white Muscat, ferments about half of its sugar. Then a very strong neutral spirit (at least 90°) is added which stuns the yeasts (they can't go on working at alcohol levels of more than about 15°) and raises the alcohol to 21·5°. Banyuls to the south and Maury to the north-west of

Perpignan are the best known reds, primarily from the Grenache grape. The results are rarely very exciting. Rivesaltes also makes red *vin doux naturel*, but is better known for its Muscat de Rivesaltes, a thick, marmalady sweet wine – a bit short on perfume and finesse. Frontignan, Mireval and Lunel in the Hérault near Montpellier, and St-Jean de Minervois in the Aude also make Muscats which do have a good grapy richness but none of the refreshing perfumed fruit of France's best *vin doux naturel*: the Muscat de Beaumes de Venise from the Rhône.

· THE SOUTH-WEST ·

I feel almost embarrassed putting the title 'country wines' on some of these grand old performers from the South-West. Wines like Jurançon, Cahors and Bergerac were doing exciting things when most of Bordeaux was still in baby clothes. But while Bordeaux has gone from strength to strength and is now the most famous wine region in the world, many of the old-timers have slipped into an ill-deserved obscurity from which they are only just beginning to emerge.

Because, grape-wise, there is a fair amount of red Cabernet Sauvignon, Merlot and white Sauvignon, it is possible to think of some of the wines as Bordeaux understudies; indeed, areas like Côtes de Duras, Buzet, and sometimes Bergerac do often end up performing that role – often with considerable distinction. But if we look on the map, the South-West stretches right down to the Pyrenees, north past the Dordogne to the Charente, and east to the Tarn. There is great variation in soils and a considerable difference in climate within these boundaries; consequently, a marvellously colourful ragbag of grape varieties is used to make every possible type of wine – red, white, rosé, still and sparkling, sweet and dry. So let's set out from the high hills of the Tarn, with its sleepy villages and dramatic gorges, and sweep across to the Pyrenees then up to the Dordogne and the Lot.

· *THE TARN AND TOULOUSE* ·

Gaillac (AC) is the local Tarn wine, and in general it is pretty weedy. However, there are a few growers like Cros and Albert who show

Above left Madiran is sometimes called the best red wine of the South-West after Bordeaux.

Above Few places still make Monbazillac in the traditional way from nobly rotted grapes. One problem is the expense of going through the vineyards time and again searching for suitable fruit.

Left Bergerac vineyards at Theynac.

what can be done. They produce an almost painfully peppery dry red which is absolutely delicious and completely unforgettable – once you've got used to it! Even more exciting is the fizz. Made by a variation of the champagne method called *méthode gaillaçoise*, these are so full of apricoty, melony fruit, honey-edged, but strangely tangy too, that it's difficult to believe they're dry. But they are, and you should try them.

It's also difficult to believe that the red Côtes du Frontonnais, from just above Toulouse, are entirely dry because these wines are so incred-ibly *smooth*. Silky smooth, velvet smooth, and absurdly delicious with their strawberry and liquorice fruit. The Negrette is the grape to thank for this, and properties like Flotis, La Palme and Domaine de Baudare produce the best examples.

· *THE PYRENEES* ·

Over by the Bay of Biscay the Pyrenees aren't great wine country: Béarn (AC) produces fairly pallid stuff which isn't a lot of fun even for a holiday picnic in the foothills; and Irouléguy (AC) does a good red which *is* fun in a fresh spicy way.

But the single star is Jurançon (AC). For hundreds of years people have gone batty about Jurançon and draped it with beguiling epithets and fanciful descriptions. Well, I think they were overdoing it a bit, because the dry white is a bit dull, and the rather ordinary co-operative dominates the scene. But there *are* a few independent growers who make a rare, time-revered sweet wine from Petit- and Gros-Manseng grapes which is all honey and nuts and cavalier splashes of ginger, cinnamon and cloves – and a persistent, refreshing acidity. With wine like this from a domaine like Clos Cancaillau, or Clos Uroulat, I can begin to see what all the fuss was about.

Madiran (AC) and Pacherenc du Vic Bilh (AC) – the amazing name translates mundanely as 'posts in a line from the Vic Bilh hills'! – are the main wines from Armagnac-brandy country near Auch. Madiran is often talked about as the South-West's greatest red wine after Bordeaux. Well, it hasn't proved the point yet. It is tannic, heavy, and usually curiously leaden-footed and indistinct in flavour. Properties like Château Montas, which uses new oak barrels to enrich the wine, are the best examples. Pacherenc is rarely seen but has a most memorable taste of pear-skins, quite unlike any other French white wine. Nearby Côtes de St-Mont (VDQS) makes some extremely good, tangy-sharp reds and whites.

· THE GARONNE AND DORDOGNE ·

The Côtes de Duras and the Côtes de Buzet (both AC) along with Côtes du Marmandais (VDQS) lie on either side of the Garonne south-east of Bordeaux's Graves region. They grow the Bordeaux grapes, in particular Cabernet Franc and Sauvignon, and make pretty decent low-priced claret look-alikes. Bergerac (AC) on the Dordogne is a little more adventurous. The overall title Bergerac actually includes 11 separate *appellations*, but they don't have the variety that this might suggest. There is a marvellous, but tiny AC called Pécharmant which does produce delicious, long-lasting reds from Cabernet and Merlot. Look for Château de Tiregand, and Domaine du Haut Pécharmant. Monbazillac (AC), too, can produce exceptional wine – this time sweet white from Sauvignon and Sémillon, but, with the exception of the occasional winner like Château Treuil-de-Nailhac, most Monbazillac is mild and sweetish rather than thought-provoking.

There are several AC for semi-sweet wines of no great personality – Rosette, Côtes de Montravel and Côtes de Bergerac Moelleux being the most important – but the best of the rest in Bergerac are dry. Modern estates like Château la Jaubertie, and Château Courts-Les-Mûts as well as the highly organized central co-operative, can produce delicious, sharp, blackcurranty reds, green-grass tangy whites and full-throated rosés.

· THE LOT VALLEY ·

Away to the east, in some of France's most unspoilt countryside, is the Lot valley with its burly red wine, Cahors (AC), made from the Auxerrois grape mixed with Merlot and Tannat. Well, at its *best* it is burly, managing to be tough and severe as well as brimming with open-armed fruit at the same time. There is some light plummy wine now made, but really good Cahors has a steamily exotic plum-and-prune-and-tobacco richness tempered by tannin and an unflagging appley acidity which makes it one of the most exciting of all the South-West's great originals.

There are only two *vins de pays* of any great importance, and both are used to soak up the excess production of wine in the brandy regions. Charentais is in the Cognac area, and both red and white can be good, sharp refreshing wines. Côtes de Gascogne, in Armagnac, is more exciting and produces excellent dry, but extremely fruity, whites as well as some pretty snappy sharp-tasting reds.

· FOOD AND WINE ·

The South-West is rich in self-indulgent dishes, above all in the black truffle country of the Lot and the *foie gras* homeland of Périgord. These are often served together in a display of self-confident extravagance which makes me clutch nervously at my cheque-book. But so long as someone else is paying, the combination of *foie gras* and *truffes* and a glass or two of chilled sweet Jurançon or Monbazillac is one of the great gastronomic experiences. I have to admit, though, that *my* experiences are usually slightly less rarefied.

We're in one of the best areas here for all the other goose and duck dishes, and the strong reds of Cahors or Madiran are just what's needed for the diet-destroying *rillettes d'oie* or *confit de canard*. There is also loads of game about, and *salamis de palombe* (pigeon casserole) and *civet de lièvre* (hare stew) – padded out with the aggressive savoury depth of the local *cèpes* (mushrooms) and a liberal dose of red wine – again call for the direct flavours of the region's reds. *Jambon de Bayonne* is uncooked ham at its best, but tricky to match with wine; on the other hand, the fish and poultry from the long forested seaboard of the Landes are well-matched by the fresh young whites of Bergerac, Duras and Côtes de Gascogne. And as for Toulouse – well, I've had their garlic-heavy *cassoulet*, I've washed it down with Côtes du Frontonnais, and although I wasn't much good for anything else for the rest of the day, it was a magical combination.

The South-West is full of remarkable tasting reds which are increasingly being sold under their estate name. The rare Château Flotis from Côtes du Frontonnais is the leading exponent of this deliciously plummy local wine of Toulouse. Cahors is the major wine of the Lot region, and despite being made a little lighter for modern tastes is still an impressive long-lasting red.

· GERMANY ·

Give the Germans a problem and you can be sure they will solve it. The particular problem which concerned their winemakers was that most of the suitable sites for growing vines were so far north that the grapes couldn't ripen properly, and their acid juice could only manage acid, sour wine. The solutions were several. To find grape varieties which didn't need so much sun, and if they didn't exist to invent them. To discover the warmest microclimates for vineyards – which in many cases proved to be in virtually uncultivable river valleys, so steep a mountain goat would get vertigo. And somehow to preserve what sweetness there was in the grapes as a weapon against the acidity. This they did by devising a system where the wine is fermented out to acid dryness, and then supplemented with some pure, unfermented grape juice – *Süssreserve* or 'sweet reserve' – to give the grapy slightly fruit-sweet style which has become the hallmark of German wines.

Well, this ingenuity has certainly succeeded in making the wines well known, but unfortunately it is infamy rather than renown which dogs Germany's reputation. This is largely due to a single wine – Liebfraumilch. This one name has become synonymous with German wine all over the world, and its overriding characteristic is that it is gentle, fruity, easy to gulp down, and totally unchallenging. Unfortunately, the entire spectrum of German wines *apart* from Liebfraumilch has been overshadowed by the phenomenal success of this marketing man's dream but serious winemaker's nightmare.

The fact that Liebfraumilch is always seen as easy and reliable is a major source of distress for the winemakers of Germany's classic regions, because for them grape-growing is extremely difficult on inhospitable terrain and with a climate which is anything but reliable. Also, the fact that Liebfraumilch has swept the world by waving the banner of cheap, cheerful German wine has meant that few people are prepared to pay for what can be some of the masterpieces in the world of wine, and which have been produced against all the odds at the climatic limits of wine production for 2,000 years.

· GRAPES AND WINE STYLES ·

The great sensations of German wine exist precisely *because* the grapes are difficult to ripen. The key is the blend of acidity with fruit, especially when it is the Riesling grape. The acidity of the Riesling is piercing, steely, apple-skin sharp and with the tang of limes, depending on where it is grown. The flavour to balance this acidity can be that of Granny Smith apples, fresh with morning dew but picked a week too early to be quite sweet; or ripe Cox's Orange Pippins, their flesh going honeyed with crunchy sweetness as the wasps buzz and burrow into the day's windfalls; or it can be peaches and apricots, melon and mangoes piled in tropical confusion in a heap of musky richness. Somewhere among these different flavours the acidity and the fruit will meet and combine in a wine which can be light as a whisper or painfully intense.

Germany is above all a white wine country, producing 88 per cent white wine and only 12 per cent red. The Riesling is unquestionably the great grape of German white wines. The other traditionally important white grapes are Sylvaner, Ruländer (Pinot Gris) and Gewürztraminer. The traditional reds are Spätburgunder (Pinot Noir) and Portugieser. However in *quantitative* terms the majority of vineyards are planted with 'crossings' invented during the past century in the search for grapes which would ripen early, be reliable in poor weather and produce large amounts of sugar-rich juice. Their inventors would have liked these crossings to taste like Riesling, but none of them does, and the usual flavours veer between flowery and cloyingly exotic. But they do ripen in enormous quantities and they are the reason why Germany, the European wineland with the most difficult northerly climate, can, paradoxically, produce so much easy-drinking, affordable wine.

The Müller-Thurgau, invented in 1882, is now the most widely planted grape in Germany, and is the basis for most cheap wine. The Scheurebe and the Kerner are the two most important crossings for quality, while Bacchus, Morio-Muskat, Ehrenfelser, Huxelrebe and a host of other names crowd the vineyards, especially of the south, with their heady, perfumed grapes.

· REGIONAL CLASSIFICATIONS ·

Anbaugebiete are the 11 large wine regions of Germany, all with their own distinctive styles. From north to south, they are Ahr, Mittelrhein, Mosel-Saar-Ruwer, Rheingau, Nahe, Rheinhessen, Franken, Hessische Bergstrasse, Rheinpfalz, Württemberg and Baden.
Bereiche are 34 very broad groupings of villages within these Gebiete. Inside each Bereich are the single villages (Gemeinde).
Grosslagen – or 'group sites' – of which there are 152, are groups of vineyards from several villages within the same Bereich which, supposedly, enable a wine of a generally similar style to be offered in larger quantities.
Einzellagen – or 'single sites' – are the individual vineyards. Historically there were 25,000 named vineyards, but in the 1970s these were lumped together to produce a mere 2,600! In theory, the more specific the classification the better the wine, so the wine of an Einzellage should be superior to that of a Grosslage, but in practice it is impossible to tell which is which from the label.

· QUALITY CLASSIFICATIONS ·

In France, such a classification by origin of the wine would be considered enough. But since ripeness is more at a premium in Germany than in warmer France, the actual *quality* classification is worked out on ripeness of grapes. The only criterion for whether the vineyard is good or bad is that the grapes should ripen better in the better vineyards. The 'Oechsle' measure of ripeness is used. Expressed in 'degrees', it measures the number of grams by which a litre of grape juice is heavier than a litre of water (a litre of water is 1,000 grams). Since the extra weight will be basically sugar, the heavier the weight of the must (grape juice), the riper the grapes, and the higher the potential alcohol. It is this rating which, each year, determines the quality level of wines from every vineyard in Germany.

Deutscher Tafelwein is the lowest quality level and requires only 44° Oechsle, yielding about 5° potential alcohol. It will be unfermentable without a hefty addition of sugar to the juice, and undrinkable without a big dose of Süssreserve.

Landwein is the supposed equivalent of the French *vin de pays*. The grapes should be a little riper and the wine a little drier than Tafelwein.

Qualitätswein bestimmter Anbaugebiete (QbA) is quality wine from a specific region, that is, from a Gebiet. These must have a 57–60° Oechsle level, yielding up to 7·5° potential alcohol. The Mosel, Ahr and Mittelrhein are allowed slightly lower ripeness levels than the other regions. Since this is still pretty feeble, sugar is added at fermentation. Although the label must display a geographical provenance, and may even show a single vineyard name, the grading is no real guarantee of 'quality' because the ripeness level is just too low.

Qualitätswein mit Prädikat (QmP) is quality wine with special attributes. The chief special attribute is that the grapes ripened fully and that *no* sugar may be added at fermentation although Süssreserve may be added afterwards. *This* is where really special German quality begins. Within this category there are further special ratings as follows:

Kabinett, meaning approximately 'grower's reserve'. The minimum Oechsle is 70–73° giving up to 9·5° potential alcohol. These are light delicate wines, veering from bone dry to slightly sweet.

Spätlese, 'late-picked'. The minimum Oechsle is 76–85° giving up to 11·4° potential alcohol. This is fairly ripe and it shows in the extra depth of flavour. There are some dry Spätlesen without Süssreserve added, but most are quite full and juicy.

Auslese, meaning 'specially selected', has a minimum Oechsle of 83–95° giving up to 13° potential alcohol. These are totally ripe wines, and are often rich and concentrated in flavour. There are a very few dry ones, but usually they are sweet and if the vineyards have been touched by noble rot they will be positively honeyed.

Beerenauslese, made from selected single overripe berries. Minimum Oechsle 110–128°. Potential alcohol up to 16°. Those berries will be very overripe, and may be shrivelled by noble rot. The wine will always be very sweet, but if it is from the Riesling it will keep a limy acidity to match the grapy intensity of fruit.

Trockenbeerenauslese, made from 'shrivelled single overripe berries'. Minimum Oechsle 150°. Potential alcohol 21·5°. These are incredibly rare and expensive. The yield from these noble-rot-affected grapes is miniscule, and the flavour astonishing. The *actual* alcohol will usually only be about 5·5° – all the rest of the sugar remains unfermented, making this most northerly of wines probably the sweetest in the world.

Eiswein is an extra category of wines which does literally mean 'ice wine'. Grapes of at least Beerenauslese ripeness are picked some time in the winter, usually between November and January – though it *can* be later! Frosts freeze the water in the grapes leaving a sludgy concentrate of sugar and acids, and the resulting flavour is so intense and startling it can actually hurt.

Above A mechanized harvester combs some of the flatter vineyards just north of Geisenheim in the Rheingau. In the background is the imposing convent of St Hildegard which gives its name to Klosterberg (convent hill), the Rüdesheim vineyard below.

Left The Mosel vineyards are steep and slaty, and the midsummer task of tying back the vine branches can be extremely arduous.

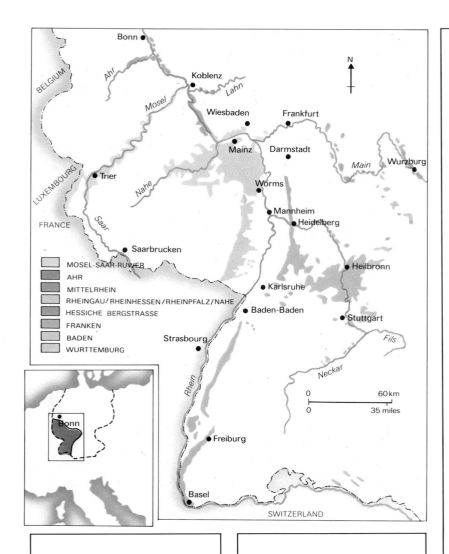

• SELECTED WINES •

In Germany most wines are described either by a Bereich name (for example, Bereich Bernkastel), or by a village name followed by a Grosslage or Einzellage vineyard name (for example, Graacher Himmelreich) – see page 138 for an explanation of these terms. Also, a very few famous wines identify themselves solely by the vineyard name (for example, Scharzhofberg), and these are known as Ortsteil.

• MOSEL-SAAR-RUWER •

○ Bereich Bernkastel
○ Bereich Moseltor
○ Bereich Obermosel
○ Bereich Saar-Ruwer
○ Bereich Zell

○ Avelsbacher
○ – Römerlay (G)
○ – Altenberg (E)
○ Ayler
○ – Scharzberg (G)
○ – Kupp (E)
○ Bernkasteler

○ – Badstube (G)
○ – Kurfürstlay (G)
○ – Bratenhöfchen (E)
○ – Doktor (E)
○ Bernkastel-Kues
○ – Kurfürstlay (G)
○ – Kardinalsberg (E)
○ Brauneberger
○ – Kurfürstlay (G)
○ – Juffer (E)
○ Eitelsbacher
○ – Römerlay (G)
○ – Karthauserhof (E)
○ Erdener
○ – Schwarzlay (G)
○ – Treppchen (E)
○ Graacher
○ – Münzlay (G)
○ – Himmelreich (E)
○ Kaseler
○ – Römerlay (G)
○ – Nies'chen (E)
○ Kanzemer
○ – Scharzberg (G)
○ – Altenberg (E)
○ Klüsserather
○ – St Michael (G)
○ – Bruderschaft (E)
○ Kröver
○ – Nacktarsch (G)
○ Leiwener
○ – St Michael (G)
○ – Laurentiuslay (E)
○ Maximin Grünhauser (O)
○ – Abstberg (E)
○ – Herrenberg (E)
○ Oberemmeler
○ – Scharzberg (G)
○ – Hütte (E)
○ Ockfener
○ – Scharzberg (G)
○ – Bockstein (E)
○ Piesporter
○ – Michelsberg (G)
○ – Goldtröpchen (E)
○ Saarburger
○ – Scharzberg (G)
○ – Antoniusbrunnen (E)
○ Scharzhofberg (O)
○ Serriger
○ – Scharzberg (G)
○ – Kupp (E)
○ Traben-Trarbacher
○ – Schwarzlay (G)

○ Trierer
○ – Römerlay (G)
○ Trittenheimer
○ – Michelsberg (G)
○ – Apotheke (E)
○ Urziger
○ – Schwarzlay (G)
○ – Würzgarten (E)
○ Waldracher
○ – Römerlay (G)
○ – Hubertsberg (E)
○ Wehlener
○ – Sonnenuhr (E)
○ Wiltinger
○ – Scharzberg (G)
○ – Braunfels (E)
○ Wintricher
○ – Kurfürstlay (G)
○ – Ohligsberg (E)
○ Zeller
○ – Schwarze Katz (G)
○ Zeltinger
○ – Münzlay (G)
○ – Sonnenuhr (E)

• RHEINGAU •

○ Bereich Johannisberg

● Assmanshausener
● – Steil (G)
● – Höllenberg (E)
○ Eltviller
○ – Steinmächer (G)
○ – Sonnenberg (E)
○ Erbacher
○ – Deutelsberg (G)
○ – Marcobrunn (E)
○ Geisenheimer
○ – Burgweg (G)
○ – Erntebringer (G)
○ – Kläuserweg (E)
○ Hallgartener
○ – Mehrhölzchen (G)
○ – Schönhell (E)
○ Hattenheimer
○ – Deutelsberg (G)
○ – in Nussbrunnen (E)
○ – Schützenhaus (E)
○ Hochheimer
○ – Daubhaus (G)
○ – Königin Victoria Berg (E)
○ Johannisberger
○ – Erntebringer (G)
○ – Hölle (E)

- Kiedricher
- – Heiligenstock (G)
- – Sandgrub (E)
- Oestricher
- – Gottesthal (G)
- – Lenchen (E)
- Rauenthaler
- – Steinmächer (G)
- – Baiken (E)
- – Wülfen (E)
- Rüdesheimer
- – Burgweg (G)
- – Berg Roseneck (E)
- – Berg Rottland (E)
- Schloss Vollrads (O)
- Steinberger (O)
- Winkeler
- – Honigberg (G)
- – Jesuitengarten (E)

· NAHE ·

- Bereich Kreuznach
- Bereich Schloss Böckelheim

- Dorsheimer
- – Schlosskapelle (G)
- – Goldloch (E)
- Kreuznacher
- – Kronenberg (G)
- – Brückes (E)
- Langenlonsheimer
- – Sonnenborn (G)
- – Rothenberg (E)
- Niederhauser
- – Burgweg (G)
- – Hermannshöhle (E)
- Norheimer
- – Burgweg (G)
- Rüdesheimer
- – Rosengarten (G)
- Schlossböckelheimer
- – Burgweg (G)
- – Felsenberg (E)
- – Kupfergrube (E)
- Traiser
- – Burgweg (G)
- – Rotenfels (E)
- Winzenheimer
- – Kronenberg (G)
- – Berg (E)

· RHEINHESSEN ·

- Bereich Bingen
- Bereich Nierstein

- Bereich Wonnegau

- Binger
- – St Rochuskapelle (G)
- Bodenheimer
- – St Alban (G)
- – Silberberg (E)
- Mainzer
- – Domherr (G)
- Nackenheimer
- – Gutes Domtal (G)
- – Rothenberg (E)
- Niersteiner
- – Auflangen (G)
- – Gutes Domtal (G)
- – Spiegelberg (G)
- – Hölle (E)
- – Orbel (E)
- Oppenheimer
- – Güldenmorgen (G)
- – Kreuz (E)
- Wormser
- – Liebfraumorgen (G)

· RHEINPFALZ ·

- Bereich Südliche Weinstrasse
- Bereich Mittelhardt/Deutsche Weinstrasse

- Deidesheimer
- – Hofstück (G)
- – Mariengarten (G)
- – Herrgottsacker (E)
- ● Dürkheimer
- – Feuerberg (G)
- – Hochmesse (G)
- Forster
- – Mariengarten (G)
- – Schnepfenflug (G)
- – Jesuitengarten (E)
- – Ungeheuer (E)
- Kallstadter
- – Kobnert (G)
- – Saumagen (E)
- Neustadter
- – Meerspinne (G)
- – Pfaffengrund (G)
- Ruppertsberger
- – Hofstück (G)
- – Reiterpfad (E)
- Ungsteiner
- – Honigsäckel (G)

- – Herrenberg (E)
- Wachenheimer
- – Mariengarten (G)
- – Gerümpel (E)

· FRANCONIA (FRANKEN) ·

- Bereich Maindreieck
- Bereich Mainviereck
- Bereich Steigerwald

- Escherndorfer
- – Kirchberg (G)
- – Lump (E)
- Iphofener
- – Burgweg (G)
- – Julius-Echter-Berg (E)
- Randersacker
- – Ewig Leben (G)
- Würzburger
- – Stein (E)

· BADEN ·

- ● Bereich Badische Bergstrasse/Kraichgau
- ● Bereich Badisches Frankenland
- ● Bereich Bayerische Bodensee
- ● Bereich Bodensee
- ● Bereich Breisgau
- ● Bereich Kaiserstuhl-Tuniberg
- ● Bereich Markgräflerland
- ● Bereich Ortenau

· WURTTEMBERG ·

- ● Bereich Kocher-Jagst-Tauber
- ● Bereich Remstal-Stuttgart
- ● Bereich Württembergisch Unterland

· HESSISCHE BERGSTRASSE ·

- Bereich Starkenburg
- Bereich Umstadt

- Bensheimer
- – Wolfsmagen (G)
- Heppenheimer
- – Schlossberg (G)

· MITTELRHEIN ·

- Bereich Bacharach
- Bereich Rheinburgengau

- Bereich Siebengebirge

- Bacharacher
- – Schloss Stahlek (G)
- Bopparder
- – Gedeonseck (G)
- – Hamm (E)
- Oberweseler
- – Schloss Schönburg (G)

· AHR ·

- ● Bereich Walporzheim/Ahrtal

- ● Ahrweiler
- – Klosterberg (G)
- – Rosenthal (E)

· OTHER WINES ·

- △ Deutsche Sekt
- Deutsche Tafelwein
- Liebfraumilch

	red	white
still	●	○
sparkling		△

G = Grosslage
E = Einzellage
O = Ortsteil

· MOSEL-SAAR-RUWER ·

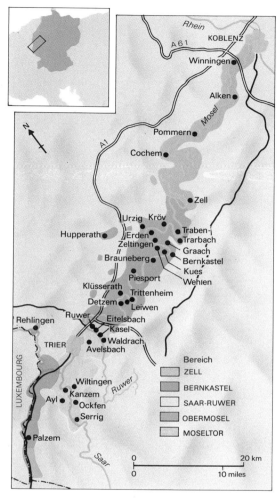

For sheer, heart-stopping beauty you can't beat the Mosel valley: the river is so tranquil as it twists and loops between Luxembourg and Koblenz, the 130-odd villages dotted along both banks are so picture-book pretty, and the vines tumble down the towering slopes rearing almost vertically above you on both sides of the river. And if you clamber breathlessly up the slate scree to the top and survey the majesty of the valley swooping away on both sides, the vineyards glistening in green and gold, don't look down, unless you have a very good head for heights, because you'll wonder how you ever managed the climb, and how you'll ever get down again without slipping on to the roofs of the village houses far below. It is a surprise to see *anything* growing on

such precipitous slopes – let alone this carpet of vines unwinding like a bandage along the hillside. Although the vines grow on both sides of the river, in all the best areas the river has carved an amphitheatre facing south, as it has twisted and turned to find a way through the rock, and because the Mosel is so far north, it is really only on these slopes that the grapes fully ripen.

· THE GRAPES ·

Riesling is the grape with which every good vineyard should be planted. The combination of good winemaker, good slaty vineyard site and Riesling grape is *thrilling*. There is *no* other wine area in the world that can produce something almost water-pale in colour and light as a breeze in texture, yet which pierces and tingles and soothes in flavour all at the same time. And its taste is apples, especially the moment that your teeth crunch through the crisp skin and the first spurt of slightly acid juice squirts on to your tongue.

Then it's slate or steel. I mean it. I admit, I haven't wandered round licking the roofs on

people's houses and the saucepans in their kitchens – but think of slate and steel, what emotional response do they bring out? They're cold, they're hard, they're clean, and steel glistens and gleams like the Arctic sun. Translate that to taste – the leanness, the streak of acidity cutting along the side of the fruit, and the presence of something mildly mineral, like well-washed gravel.

And also there's honey to help the balance. In cool years, you may not get much more than the steel and green apples – in 1984 there was even a sensation of grapefruit! But when the grapes ripen, and the wines are left for a year or two to calm down and put on their party clothes, a tiny splash of honey begins to soften the edges of acidity, gradually spreading through the whole flavour, the dawn-gold colour matching the subtle semi-sweetness of the wine. For wines so light, the slaty soil and the high level of tartaric acid makes Mosel wines age incredibly well – providing they are from the Riesling grape.

Riesling is what makes Mosel wine great, and it used to be that the label on the best

Left Thurant castle at Alken near Koblenz presides over a typically steep Mosel slope, with the tiny parcels of land belonging to each grower clearly defined.

wines never stated Riesling – it was taken for granted that no other grape would be used. There had always been some Elbling grown on the flatter bits of land, especially down towards the Luxembourg border, and its fairly neutral wine was used as a local quaffer, but otherwise it was almost all Riesling. That was before the inexorable march of the Müller-Thurgau grape. **Müller-Thurgau**, invented only a century ago as a Riesling look-alike which ripened earlier and gave more juice, has spread like wildfire through Germany, and has supplanted Riesling in many areas. Nowhere is this more true than in the Mosel, where Riesling now holds on to little more than 50 per cent of the acreage. The Müller-Thurgau does *not* produce exciting wine here, adding an uncharacteristic raisiny fruit and a rather sharp flowering-currant nip to the pure tones of the Riesling, and I'm afraid that if the label does not state 'Riesling' you're probably getting a fair whack of Müller-Thurgau blended in.

However, I can understand the Mosel growers searching desperately for a way to make an easier living off the more amenable Müller-Thurgau. This is *fierce* land to cultivate, and incredibly expensive both in effort and money, because it is virtually impossible to mechanize the best slopes. It used to be even more difficult to stay profitable, because so much space was taken up with stone retaining walls to support the narrow terraces on which the vines grew. There is now a move throughout Germany to rearrange these steep hillside vineyards with vines running up the slopes instead of across thus dispensing with the need for terraces. Although the very steepest Mosel slopes are probably impossible to improve, 72 per cent of the rest of the land has been modernized. The results are already plain to see as productivity rises year by year. If it is Müller-Thurgau which is giving all the extra, this isn't, of course, necessarily a good thing; but the frosts of years like 1985 which savaged the Müller-Thurgau, left the hardier Riesling unscathed and allowed the Mosel to produce nearly 60

A view of Bernkastel and the Mosel river from among some of the most valuable vines in the world – those of the Bernkasteler Doktor vineyard.

per cent more than the national average – mostly from Riesling. As growers replant their frost-slaughtered vines I hope they learn the lesson that quality pays, reject the Müller-Thurgau and return to the Riesling.

· THE WINE TRADE ·

Such an individual wine style is always likely to produce individualistic winemakers, and the Mosel is full of them. Some of the best vineyards are the original monastic or municipal vineyard holdings established hundreds of years ago. It isn't uncommon to see on a label that a winery was established in the 15th or 16th century and that it has a name with an ecclesiastical ring to it still – like the impressive Bischöfliche Priesterseminar! The major individual proprietors have often been there just as long. The Thanisch family, for instance, have owned their section of the Bernkasteler Doktor vineyards for 13 generations.

There are important merchants of widely varying quality. Some have taken the lead in callously exploiting the region's reputation with cheap Müller-Thurgau wines of depressing quality, but the best, like Deinhard of Koblenz, are among the foremost quality producers in Germany. Predictably the presence of co-operatives isn't that strong in an area of such individuality, but the co-operatives *do* process about 20 per cent of the crop, and the biggest – the Zentralkellerei or 'Central Cellars' at Bernkastel – is not only one of the few reliable producers of cheap Mosel, but is becoming increasingly impressive with the more expensive wines.

· THE BEREICHS ·

There are five *Bereiche*, or 'designated districts' in the Mosel-Saar-Ruwer region: Moseltor, Obermosel, Saar-Ruwer, Bernkastel and Zell. Together they produce around 13 per cent of all German wine and it is all white. Moseltor, right down on the French border 107 miles (172km) away from Koblenz, is of little importance. It has no well known villages and little Riesling wine. Obermosel is also far south, running up the east side of the river, and facing Luxembourg which has the west side. Again, there is not a single famous village here. Although the wine can be pleasant, there

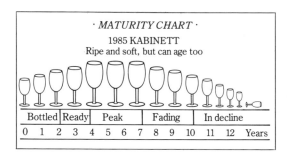

isn't much Riesling and even the Elbling wine is often made into sparkling wine – *Sekt*.

· BEREICH SAAR-RUWER ·

Just before Trier, we enter the Saar-Ruwer district and we're in the big time. In fact, 'big' is the last thing these wines are, because they must rate as some of the world's lightest and most fragrant. The Saar is a tributary river just to the south-west of Trier, while the Ruwer is hardly more than a rill to the east, and although the town of Trier does have some nice apple-fresh wines, all the best vineyards of the Bereich are in these two tiny valleys.

The Saar has some of the most characterful wines in Germany, primarily, I suspect, because many of its best vineyards are owned either by a series of redoubtable old families, by ancient charitable and ecclesiastical foundations in Trier or indeed by the government, which in Germany is one of the best vineyard owners of the lot. It is cold here, the spring comes late and the autumn often sinks into a dank, early winter before the Riesling grapes have had time to ripen. In those years, most of the production is used for Sekt. But when the sun rises in the sky, and continues long into October to ripen and enrich the grapes, then the wines can achieve a scarcely credible mixture of sharpness and fruit and perfume.

All the best vineyards are on a very hard slate here, and this slaty, steely character dominates the wines. If you do want to get to grips with this characteristic, a Kabinett wine from a decent grower in Ayl, Serrig, Ockfen or Saarburg will epitomize it. The Grosslage name for Saar wines is Wiltinger Scharzberg, and usually these are disappointingly soft.

The Ruwer is absolutely tiny, but does boast two world-class vineyards – Maximin Grunhaü-

Left The Mosel seems hardly more than a stream here as the tumbling cascade of rock at Urzig forces the river into one of its many wide loops. The slaty soil and precipitous south-facing terraces give Urzig's wine a strong spicy character (the terraces are actually called Würzgarten – 'spice garden').

Right This Mosel grower doesn't look too happy about his antiquated pump, but this concentrated clutter of barrels and well-worn equipment is typical of many small outfits away from the more famous villages.

ser and Karthaüserhofberg – which have all the steel of the Saar's best as well as a more perfumed intensity. Again, the best vineyards are owned by church foundations, the state (at Avelsbach), and old families. It is rare to see a 'merchant's' Ruwer wine, because there isn't enough of it to go round, and anyway, you'll only get Ruwer style from the top estates.

· BEREICH BERNKASTEL ·

The heart of the Mosel is the Bereich Bernkastel. But since Bernkastel itself is a single village and the 'Bereich' covers absolutely everything from the first really steep Mosel site at Schweich right up to the boundaries of the vineyards of Zell, one could be excused for asking whether this fair title wasn't a mite misleading. The answer, of course, is 'yes'. It *should* be called something like 'Bereich Mittelmosel' so that you could tell where it came from, but didn't think you were getting a wine from the actual village. You get exactly the same problem with Bereich Johannisberg in the Rheingau and Bereich Nierstein in

Eiswein is a rarity, but the Richter estate manages to make some almost every year, usually from the Mülheimer Helenerkloster vineyard. Scharzhofberg is one of a few top vineyards which do not need a village name on the label.

Rheinhessen – great for the growers in less famous villages, not fair for the growers in the actual village or for us the confused consumers. Look for Bereich on the label. If it's there, as in 'Bereich Bernkastel' you're getting a wine from the vague locality, not from a single village.

This Bereich seems naturally to divide itself between two great serpentine coils of the river. The first has Piesport as its centre, and is at its best between Klüsserath, which produces fresh, appley wines, and Brauneberg, which produces the most beguilingly honeyed wines on the river. Piesport too, has soft honey as its keynote, and it and Brauneberg each possess the most perfect south-facing arc of vines. If you go into these vineyards during high summer and compare the temperature with that of the riverside below, the difference is dramatic. The steeply angled slope, and the reflection of heat off the water and the slate mean that you can take your shirt off among the best vines and bask, just as the vines do; while down below you might find yourself wishing you'd brought a jacket.

Piesport *can* produce delicious, fragrant, honeyed wines, the gentlest on the river yet still marked by crisp acidity – but it seldom does. The reason is simply that the name is too popular and Piesporter Goldtröpfchen ('little golden drops', gorgeous name!) – its best vineyard – and Piesporter Michelsberg – the massive Grosslage name for Piesport and the surrounding villages – have been stretched to breaking point; few Piesport wines now really match the light soft style which made the village famous. That style is more available in Brauneberg, with an added hint of steel in the best vineyards, but you'll have to pay more. From these difficult vineyards, that's precisely as it should be if the quality is there.

The second loop in the river is centred on the village of Bernkastel which has, in the Doktor vineyard, Germany's most famous and most expensive wine. Bernkastel's wines are less gentle than Brauneberg's and the acidity often asserts itself in the most delicious green apple-skin way, while the honey and even something slightly grapy and flowery make good Bernkastel a very special drink.

Bernkastel also offers one of the great sights of the Mosel – the long swathe of vines, running up past Graach, Wehlen and Zeltingen to the bend in the river past Urzig. These are softer wines again, with the Wehlen wines in particular capable of honeyed grapiness – but *still*

These are incredibly important in the Mosel because, so long as the grower is attempting to make an honest, un-industrialized product, his finished wine should act as a mirror to the year. Cold years can only give acid wines, yet years like 1977, 1980 and 1984 produced classic dry Rieslings which, with a few years' bottle age, have all the 'steel' you could wish for. Very hot years like 1976 produced large quantities of rather rich, peachy Auslese and Beerenauslese wines quite unnervingly different from the norm. However, years of balance like 1985 and 1983, and to a lesser extent 1986, 1981 and 1979, have produced large amounts of lovely Kabinett and Spätlese wines, the two quality categories which allow the thrilling harmony of acid and honey, fruit and steel to shine through best.

· GOOD PRODUCERS ·

J.J.Prüm, Lauerburg, Thanisch, Loosen, Deinhard, Friedrich-Wilhelm-Gymnasium, Schubert, Bischöfliche Priesterseminar, Staats Weinbaudomäne, Müller, Richter, Höhe Domkirche, Zentralkellerei Bernkastel.

balanced by the streak of acidity. The river then continues to coil and uncoil itself past the good vineyards of Traben-Trarbach and Kröv and on to Zell, but its wine glories are over.

· BEREICH ZELL ·

The people of the Bereich Zell wouldn't agree with that, of course, and Zell, Cochem and, in particular, Winningen right up on the outskirts of Koblenz do make some good wine. But it lacks the flair, the balance. At Winningen the wine is nicely steely, but short on fruit. At Zell it's gently fruity, but short on steel. And this lack of confidence in the product shows because on the export market little wine appears with a village name, although the Bereich Zell title can herald rather a better product than Bereich Bernkastel, since none of the best Bereich Bernkastel vineyards would allow their wines into a regional blend, and quite a few of the Bereich Zell ones do.

· THE RHINE VALLEY ·

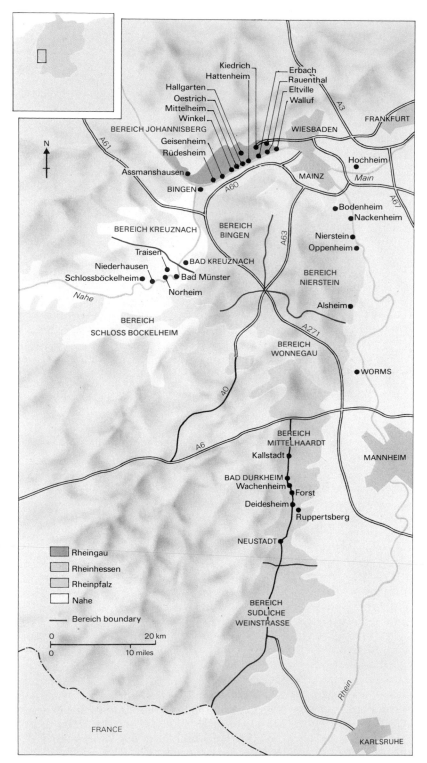

The Rhine is a major industrial river, carrying a heavy traffic of barges and river boats, but this can't dim the splendour of the valley with its steep slopes, vines and castles. This is the view from the Rüdesheimer Berg, past the Gutenfels castle to the quaintly named Mäuseturm (Mouse Tower).

The Rhine shapes the entire German wine-growing culture. It is the lifeblood of every single wine region. As it forms the northern border of Switzerland, and runs through Lake Constance, it drains the southern Baden vineyards of Bereich Bodensee. At Basel it finally deserts Switzerland and flows north through a wide, fertile basin, with Baden's main vineyards crowding the eastern bank. Past Karlsruhe, both banks begin to fill with vines, the Rheinpfalz and Rheinhessen to the west, the northern Baden and Hessische Bergstrasse to the right, until Mannheim, where the River Neckar, along whose banks Württemberg's vineyards flourish, joins the northern Rhine.

At Mainz the river Main pours its waters into the main flow, nearly 50 miles (80km) west of its own Franconian vineyards, then the Rhine meets the mass of the Taunus mountains and sweeps west, bounded by the south-facing Rheingau vineyards. Finally, at Bingen where the Nahe joins the flood, it forces a gap through the hills and sets off north past the Mittelrhein to Koblenz, where the Mosel joins. And as the river surges up to Bonn, even the tiny Ahr river trickles its offering into the mighty Rhine.

· THE WINE REGIONS ·

All of Germany's vineyards owe their existence to the Rhine. But there are four great regions more intimately bound to it than the others, the Rheingau, Nahe, Rheinhessen and the Rheinpfalz.

The Rheingau is generally thought of as producing the greatest of all German wines, and this reputation is built upon the marvellous balance of its flavours, acidity rarely dominating sweetness, perfume rarely being outgunned by the stark, slaty fragrance which seems to rise straight from the cool earth of these northern vineyards.

Nahe is a fairly large, flattish region flanking Rheinhessen's western boundary south of Bingen. This area produces a bewildering array of wines from almost any German grape you care to mention. But between Schlossböckelheim and Bad Kreuznach for a precious five miles only, the river battles to find a way north through a sheer rock cliff face. Its efforts have created some of the most perfect south-facing vineyard sites in Germany.

Rheinhessen is a vast area, comprising 165 villages set back from the river in pleasant, undulating, unmemorable farmland. The wine is equally unmemorable, except for a few miles between Worms and Mainz, where the villages of Oppenheim, Nierstein, Nackenheim and Bodenheim produce some of Germany's most delicious wines.

The Rheinpfalz, to the south, is similarly vast and is mostly gently sloping farmland pumping out oceans of full, soft, undistinctive wines. Again, there is a small central section, encompassing eight villages between Ruppertsberg to the south, and Kallstadt to the north, which can bring a fiery, spicy richness to their wine which is uniquely exciting.

· THE GRAPES ·

In the Rheingau the Riesling is the dominant grape, occupying 79 per cent of vineyard land, and all the best sites are planted with it. As always there is a Müller-Thurgau presence, but at 7 per cent it is far more restrained than usual. Of more interest is the 5 per cent of Pinot Noir, primarily for the surprisingly famous red of Assmannshausen; also, because the Wine Institute at Geisenheim, one of the world's great research centres, is always inventing new varieties, a number of these are present in small quantities. There's even some Chardonnay on an island in the middle of the river!

The best vineyards of the Nahe also have Riesling, which covers 21 per cent of the land, but the Müller-Thurgau at 28 per cent is planted widely in the duller, more northerly vineyards. Silvaner, for once, can make really good wine here and has 15 per cent.

Rheinhessen can muster only 6 per cent Riesling, compared with over 25 per cent Müller-Thurgau, but the biggest 'grouping' is of a bunch of six new crossings which account for almost 35 per cent of the plantings. These are Bacchus, Faberrebe, Huxelrebe, Kerner, Morio-Muskat and Scheurebe. Rheinhessen's reputation for rather flowery, perfumy wines is sustained in fairly unsubtle tones by this little crew.

Riesling does better in Rheinpfalz with about 14 per cent, because there are more big, old estates determined to maintain traditional values. Müller-Thurgau, naturally, heads the list at 24 per cent, but again the 'new' varieties as a group have almost 30 per cent and we are grateful for the presence of both Ruländer and Gewürztraminer to add a good slug of traditional flavour to the new exotics.

· THE RHEINGAU ·

In France's greatest wine regions of Bordeaux and Burgundy, it is possible to predict fairly accurately where the finest vineyards will be. In Bordeaux's Médoc they will correspond to the gravel ridges running through the region. In Burgundy's Côte d'Or they will be in a thin band halfway up the slope where the limestone and marl are best balanced and the aspect to the sun most suitable. In the Rheingau, despite the whole of this 20-mile stretch of south- to south-east-facing slope between Wiesbaden and Rüdesheim being smothered with vines to the exclusion of all else, there is no predictability about where the greatest vineyards will be, and no firm explanations as to why they are where they are. In the village of Erbach, the world-famous Marcobrunn vineyard is virtually in the river, yet despite this unpromising position it constitutes a well-drained, perfectly angled suntrap. At the opposite end of the scale the great Rüdesheimer Berg vineyards climb up a bare exposed outcrop of hill and look as though they would be far too wind-swept and weather-beaten to produce quality.

In the end it is all to do with just how much sun each plot of land can grab. The Rheingau is not particularly wet, but the Riesling grape needs all the help it can get to ripen here. Shelter from wind, a good angle to the sun and the dual influence of the river in its moderating effect on extremes of temperature and the way that it acts as a reflector of the sun's warmth straight on to the vines, all combine to achieve ripeness. In at least half the years, only the very best placed vineyards get to a reasonably ripe crop, and it is only in fine years like 1985, 1983 and 1976 that most of the crop can be classified as QmP (the top category).

· THE WINES ·

The Rheingau wines which grab the headlines are the ultra-sweet Beerenauslesen and above, wines which sell for enormous amounts of money and are quite astonishing, mixing so much beeswaxy, honeyed, grapy succulence with a streak of acidity – part lime, part blood orange, and sometimes with the bittersweet zest of both. They age for ever – and one of these days I hope to own one.

However, for me the genius of the Rheingau is expressed lower down at Kabinett and Spät-lese level, because the richness of the great creations can mask the more simple beauty of how these slopes express themselves through their wine. With a good Kabinett, the fruit is grapy, gently so, with a delicious distant promise of raisins and honey, and the flicker of acidity is more juicy blood orange and less piercing lime. What adds the Rheingau dimen-sion is a cold steel taste of the mineral soil, matched by a smoky warmth as subtle as it is delicious. There are an increasing number of Rheingaus now made as 'Trocken' dry wines, and given a few years' age they can also be quite good.

All the best Rheingau wines come from individual growers. About 400 bottle their own wine, and they are worth seeking out. There are some fair co-operatives, particularly at Hallgarten, but the very special taste of Rhein-gau is best achieved through one man's vision,

Left Looking across the Rehbach vineyard to the town of Nierstein on the banks of the Rhine. Although the name of Nierstein is generally associated with simple cheap wine, the best vineyards, like Rehbach, make very fine sought-after wine.

Right Many of the best German vineyards are owned by ecclesiastical foundations. This blue nun is doing the vintage in the Rheingau vineyard of Rüdesheimer Klosterberg. Until 1987 she wouldn't have been able to drink Blue Nun because it was only sold on the export market.

not blended with that of his neighbours.

The Rheingau vineyards actually begin at Hochheim 15 miles (24km) east of the Rhine on the River Main. The old-fashioned English term for Rhine wine – 'hock' – came from here, and Queen Victoria was particularly partial to a drop. The best vineyard, Königin Victoria Berg, is named after her. The wines have a rousing earthiness and flashing orange acidity.

Just west of Wiesbaden, the main stretch starts high up at Walluf and Martinsthal, with the big time commencing in a riot of spicy perfume at Rauenthal whose wines are very expensive but absolutely gorgeous. Nearer the

river, both Eltville and Erbach harbour great vineyards, with Eltville being marked out by its being headquarters of the Staatliche Wein-baudomäne (State Wine Domaine) – unlike the equivalent in most countries, State Domaines are always good in Germany. Erbach has the Rheingau's deepest, most sultry, brooding wine – the Marcobrunn.

High on the slopes Kiedrich and Hallgarten produce high quality wines with the accent on fruit, while close to the river, Hattenheim and Oestrich produce rather rich honeyed wines; but the Steinberg vineyard above the town of Hattenheim is the quintessence of slate and

In the Rheinpfalz, co-operatives are important. 'Winzerverein' denotes a co-op and Ruppertsberg is one of many good examples. The Rheingau is more the domain of individual growers, unlikely to plant anything but Riesling on the best sites.

grapes and honey Rheingau. The 12th-century Kloster Eberbach abbey above Hattenheim is the home of the German Wine Academy.

Steinberg is like a Grand Cru in Burgundy – it does not have to use its village name – and the best vineyards of the next two villages, Schloss Vollrads of Winkel and Schloss Johannisberg of Johannisberg, share the same distinction. Johannisberg is nonetheless the best known of the villages, and the 'Bereich' for the whole Rheingau is 'Bereich Johannisberg' which, interestingly, can often be reasonably good. Geisenheim is better known

for its Wine Institute than any particular vineyards, but Rüdesheim has the great, block-busting Berg vineyard, all ripeness and up-front flavours, as its most famous site. The Rhine uses the Berg vineyard as a pivot to turn north again, past the red Pinot Noir vineyards of Assmannshausen and the Riesling vineyards of Lorch, where the Rheingau ends and the Mittelrhein takes up the refrain.

· NAHE ·

The Nahe wine region touches the Rheingau and Rheinhessen and reaches out towards the Mosel, and there is no doubt that the best wines have something of all three regions. They have a bit of the floweriness of Rheinhessen, and a little of the light tongue-tingling fresh acidity of the Mosel, but above all they have the grape and honey fruit of the Rheingau, and a little of the slate and smoke too. This makes the top wines some of the loveliest in Germany, because the perfume of the fruit is more open, more orchard-scented than in the Rheingau, yet the acidity and slate are always there to keep the flowers and perfumes in place and add a mineral sheen to the fruit. However this only applies to the central vineyards of Bad Kreuznach, Traisen, Norheim, Niederhausen and Schlossböckelheim whose wines can also add a steamy passionate spice to the fruit in the top quality categories. Elsewhere, much merely adequate soft wine is made, usually seen under the Bereich Schloss Böckelheim or Rüdesheimer Rosengarten label.

The Nahe, which amounts to 4·6 per cent of Germany's vineyard acreage, differs from other wine regions in that as much as 40 per cent is sold straight to the consumer from the

A good vintage for the Rhine is reckoned to be one when not only do the grapes fully ripen, but they also succumb to noble rot which adds extra honeyed sweetness to the wines. This is commonplace in the Rheinpfalz and in Rheinhessen to the south, with examples being produced in 1986, 1985, 1983, 1981, and 1976, but is much rarer in the Rheingau and Nahe, where 1985 and 1983 produced ripe, clean-tasting wine, but only 1976 produced much noble rot. In poorer years like 1984 and 1981, the wines will have much more acidity and less body, but may also have a strong, rather sharp fruit flavour which can be very refreshing.

· GOOD PRODUCERS ·

The Rheingau Ress, Staatsweingut Eltville, Deinhard, Schloss Reinhartshausen, Aschrott, Krayer, Diefenhardt, Nägler, Weil, Simmern, Schloss Vollrads.
Nahe Staatsweinbaudomäne Niederhausen, August Anheuser, Crusius.
Rheinhessen Senfter, Balbach, Villa Sachsen, Hermann Franz Schmitt, Gustav Adolf Schmitt.
The Rheinpfalz Buhl, Bürklin-Wolf, Bassermann-Jordan, Weinkellerei Niederkirchen, Weinkellerei Bad Durkheim.

farm. This is at least partly because there are more decent-sized holdings in the Nahe, making it worth a grower's while to make and bottle his own wine. The co-operatives which do exist are quite good, but much wine bottled by the big merchants in the area is pleasant rather than exciting. The Nahe's classification of QmP category is also special. Up to Kabinett the Mosel and the Nahe follow the same ripeness requirement, but for Spätlese and Auslese, the Nahe requirement is 2° Oechsle more, while for Beerenauslese it is 10° Oechsle more.

· RHEINHESSEN ·

Rheinhessen – with 24·7 per cent of Germany's vineyard acreage, the largest single area – is a curious blend of world fame and complete anonymity. Although it has 165 wine villages, scarcely half a dozen have a fame of any sort, and even the most renowned – Nierstein – is famous largely because of the abuse of its reputation.

Nierstein is on a thin strip of angled valley bank sloping down to the Rhine called the Rheinfront. It has some wonderful sites which produce delectable Riesling wine, soft, but intense and fragrant, sweet grapes and spring flowers mingling into a giddy loveliness. It also has one rather poor and fairly small vineyard of 84 acres (34 hectares) on the worst slopes called Gutes Domtal. This name has caught on, so much so that 15 neighbouring villages have lobbied and bargained and gained the right to use the name Niersteiner Gutes Domtal for their own wine. This is abuse of the Grosslage (group vineyard site) principle at its worst, and poor old Nierstein has even had to give its name to the Bereich covering all the vineyards in the east of Hesse. Altogether the name of Nierstein is attached to a third of all the wines of the Rheinhessen, almost all of them unmemorable, while the true growers of Nierstein struggle to maintain their high reputation, and smart at the debasement of their proud name.

Of course most of the other villages don't bother to promote themselves, because the vast majority of their wine is mopped up by the cheap and cheerful Liebfraumilch. Since most villages grow light flowery Müller-Thurgau or soft, slightly flat Silvaner, they are probably best suited to contributing a reasonable standard of freshness in enormous quantities to Germany's most successful wine. (Abroad, that is; the Germans hardly drink it.) The vineyards that grow the more aromatic 'new crossings', which are not allowed in Liebfraumilch, can put their wine into a Bereich blend with equal success.

Because of the preponderance of blending wine being produced, the big merchant houses buying wine for their brands hold a dominant position in the area, and 70 per cent is sold in bulk straight to the merchants for blending. The co-operatives are mostly pretty good, but since their prime purpose is to provide anonymous blending wine, to a price, they're never going to get that well known. To taste the greatness of Rheinhessen, you must go to a grower.

The villages worth seeking out are mostly on the Rhinefront. Oppenheim is particularly good for Silvaner, the slight earthy local style suiting the broad strokes of Silvaner fruit. Nierstein on form is as scented and fragrant as any wine in Germany. Nackenheim and Bodenheim aren't quite so good but in the same mould. Then at the north, looking out across to Johannisberg in the Rheingau is Ingelheim, which makes some tasty red, and at the junction of the Nahe and the Rhine stands Bingen, best known as a business town, but with one superb hill rising steeply by the Nahe which produces steely, coal-smoky Rieslings touched with honey which are true originals and very exciting.

· THE RHEINPFALZ ·

The Rheinpfalz has its eyes very firmly set on its own well-being because the area is highly mechanized, much less fragmented, with an extremely efficient and motivated co-operative movement, and, in any case, its incredibly fertile soil regularly produces the most wine of any German region. Just as French Alsace, which is directly to the south, enjoys warmth

and dryness due to the Vosges rain shadow, so these same mountains, here called the Haardt mountains, do the same protective job for the Rheinpfalz. The vines are mostly on gentle east-facing slopes some way from the river, and the rest of the land is eagerly taken up by agriculture.

This isn't visually arresting land like most of Germany's vineyards, and I always find a sense of slightly smug, small-town well-being about these smart little villages and their obviously contented and well-fed inhabitants. There is something of this, too, in much of the wine. There's a round-cheeked, rather warm, self-satisfied fruit to the wines as though life

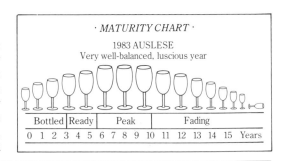

· MATURITY CHART ·

1983 AUSLESE
Very well-balanced, luscious year

Bottled	Ready	Peak	Fading

0 1 2 3 4 5 6 7 8 9 10 11 12 13 14 15 Years

Left Intricate carved designs are traditional on these huge ageing barrels at the Kurfürstenhof cellars in Nierstein.

Far left The vintage is supposed to be a time of sunny days and happy smiling faces, the grapes bursting with ripeness on the vine. In Germany, however, it is more likely to be damp and cold, as here in the 1986 vintage in the Rhine valley.

· LIEBFRAUMILCH ·

Blue Nun, the most successful Liebfraumilch brand, alone exports over 20 million bottles a year. People want it, people like it and because people like it, 60 per cent of Germany's wine exports are of Liebfraumilch. In the booming British wine market almost one bottle in six of wine drunk is Liebfraumilch. In the United States, when a leading wine importer set out to find the red wine which the populace would most like to drink, he found it was – Liebfraumilch dyed red with a dash of cochineal!

So no one can deny its popularity, and the name – it means 'Our Lady's Milk' – is an absolute master-stroke. Originally the wine did come from the Liebfrauenstift vineyard beside a church in Worms (Rheinhessen). But now it comes from all over the vast areas of Rheinhessen or the Rheinpfalz and, theoretically, Nahe and the Rheingau. It is supposed to be predominantly Riesling, Silvaner, Kerner or Müller-Thurgau, although in practice it is generally a Müller-Thurgau dominated wine. Other than that, the official definition is vague in the extreme. It is a Qualitätswein – but since 95 per cent of German wine somehow is included in this category, that's not difficult. It must have at least 18 grams of residual sugar to give it a light grapiness, and it should be 'mild' and 'of a pleasant character'. And that's it!

Because it has done so much to draw people into the world of wine-drinking, Liebfraumilch actually deserves more praise than it gets. Its real problem is that the market for Liebfraumilch has become *too* competitive, as brands and own-labels slug it out in an endless downward spiral of prices. The best thing that could happen is an *increase* in prices with a consequent improvement in quality. That would be good for us the consumers, and good for the reputation of what is, after all, a very pleasant drink. The best Liebfraumilch often comes from generally less good years, because many fine vineyards then sell their good, but unripe, wine to the blenders, adding a classy nip of acidity to the final product.

Although co-operatives and merchants market much of the wine in the Nahe, there are some good estates in the central part of the valley who concentrate on Riesling and bottle their own wine. These are two outstanding examples.

was really a bit too easy in the vineyards to inject the flash of acidity which would snap your eyes open and make you sit up. And that fruit can quickly go exotic if the wine is left to age, mangoes and apricots and lychees all popping up in an ordinary bottle of Rheinpfalz white – lovely in a good wine, a bit overpowering in an ordinary one. A large amount of Liebfraumilch comes from the Rheinpfalz, and it is usually a little fuller and spicier than the Rheinhessen version.

This overview is fair to the Südliche Weinstrasse Bereich, which is co-operative-dominated country, whose main objective is producing large amounts of decent wine efficiently. But just above Neustadt, where the Bereich Mittelhaardt begins, the level of ambition changes dramatically. Suddenly we

find Riesling planted in the best sites, perceptibly steeper than further south. The co-operatives are smaller, and still very good, but the growers' signs sprout proudly by the side of the road, and in the vineyards round Deidesheim, Forst, Wachenheim and Bad Dürkheim, great wine is made.

Even the Riesling regularly ripens in the Rheinpfalz. In less hot years, the resemblance to, say, a Rheingau Kabinett is uncanny. But in hot years (the majority here) the Riesling takes on an oriental role, filling the wine with peach, apricot, lychee and mango flavour, yet still maintaining that sharp reminder of good-mannered acidity. It can be a bit of a shock to find such musky spice in a Kabinett wine, but in an Auslese or Beerenauslese it couldn't be more enjoyable. Indeed even the 'Trocken'

style Rieslings can be fairly good here because of the ripeness of the fruit. The Scheurebe also excels itself in these villages, and can bring out an explosion of aggressive pepper and grapefruit power, spitting spice and fire, while even the Müller-Thurgau seems prepared to let its hair down a bit.

· OTHER GERMAN WINES ·

The Kaisterstuhl, an enormous outcrop of volcanic rock (its name means 'Emperor's seat'), gives some of Baden's best Ruländer and Spätburgunder. These futuristic looking slopes have indeed been reconstructed to increase productivity and allow mechanical cultivation and harvesting.

This section covers the wine regions which are in general less well known internationally, although most of them contain wines of considerable local renown. We also take a look at German sparkling wine, and another special category which crosses several regional boundaries and which must be among the greatest glories of German wine – the magnificent, intensely sweet wines made from noble-rot-affected grapes, often ripened and gathered under conditions which defy belief. These are available in tiny quantities, sometimes only a few hundred bottles, but the struggle to bring them into being has often created a memorable intensity of flavour matched by no other wines in the world.

· FRANKEN ·

Franken, or Franconia, is unique in Germany. First, it has been using funny dumpy little flasks of green glass called 'Bocksbeutels' to bottle the wine since long before Mateus Rosé was a gleam in its inventor's eye. And second, it has always specialized in dry, unaromatic wines, when most of Germany has turned more and more to perfumy, fruity, slightly sweet wine styles.

Franconia is a good 50 miles (80km) away from the Rheingau on the River Main. It certainly doesn't seem like a wine area when you visit, despite some of its beautiful towns – like Würzburg – having vineyards within their walls. There are few concentrated stretches of vineyard land; forest, rock and pasture occupy much of the landscape. Even so, in all there are 11,540 acres (4,670 hectares), representing five per cent of Germany's vineyards. Apart from the traditionally German vine-covered, south-facing river valley slopes, most of the other vineyards are scattered in small pockets haphazardly across the region, wherever there

is a particularly warm cranny or the risk of frost is low. Frost, however, is a terrible problem in Franconia, where harsh winters are commonplace and the summer is short, and it can cause wildly fluctuating yields. In 1985 appalling frosts reduced the yield to 13 hectolitres per hectare.

These full, earthy, alcoholic Franconian wines used to be made almost entirely from the Silvaner grape. Although Silvaner is often regarded a bit sniffily as an inferior grape type, it really depends where you grow it. The Gamay, for example, is also thought of as pretty mediocre, but in Beaujolais it produces brilliant wine – so it is with the Silvaner in Franconia. The Silvaner has something honeyed and earthy with a vegetal overtone which is more tomatoes than cabbage. And it does go splendidly with food. It needs to if it's to stand a chance against one of the favourite local pastimes – beer-drinking. Franconia is in the north-west tip of Bavaria, Germany's foremost beer-brewing state, and on my first visit to the regional capital, Würzburg, I admit I drank beer, straight out of the barrel.

Unfortunately, Silvaner is no longer the main grape variety. As in most other parts of the country, the easy-pleasing Müller-Thurgau is now the chief grape. But at least here it leaves its light flowery style at home and manages to make a fairly broad, mouth-filling wine similar to Silvaner, but with a tiny whiff of grapiness too. There isn't much Riesling because it rarely ripens here, though in a hot year like 1976 Franconian Riesling can be a sensation.

We don't see much Franconian wine abroad, and it is always expensive. To be honest, there is so much choice from the other countries of the world which find producing dry white wines easy that there is rarely a reason to choose Franconian. If you are in the region, however, the villages of Escherndorf, Iphofen, Randersacker and the regional capital Würzburg produce the best wine.

The majority of wine is made by co-operatives who are very good here, especially at Randersacker, but the best wines come, as so often in Germany, from the ancient ecclesiastical foundations of Juliusspital and Bürgerspital and the state-owned Staatliche Hofkeller, all at Würzburg.

· BADEN ·

Baden produces a lot of wine and it is dominated by a huge single producer. The wine-making areas are situated mostly along the east bank of the Rhine, looking across to France's Alsace vineyards in the west. These vineyards are on the slopes of the foothills of the Black Forest, and run for 80 miles (129km)

from Baden-Baden down to Basel in Switzerland. There are a few vineyards north of Baden-Baden, and there are some pleasant summer resort wines made along the north banks of the Bodensee (the German name for Lake Constance).

The huge producer is the ZBW co-operative (Zentralkellerei Badischer Winzergenossenschaft) at Breisach, which is the largest in Europe and produces 90 per cent of Baden's wine output. Since Baden has 16 per cent of Germany's vineyards, covering 36,700 acres (14,851 hectares) and producing nearly *25 per cent* of German wine, that's coming it pretty strong, and it's no surprise to learn that the co-operative produces between 400 and 500 *different* wines every year! What *is* a surprise is that the quality is good, and makes up for the relative lack of top private growers in the region.

What is also encouraging is that in this area of mass production, the traditional grapes are still holding out well against the new crossings. This is largely because Baden doesn't need their early-ripening abilities, since the area is the warmest in Germany, but it is also because, along with Franconia, Baden has always been primarily involved with producing tasty, dryish wines for drinking with food. The rich soil and warm climate mean that the wines easily reach a satisfactory alcohol level, although they lack acidity. This suits the Ruländer (Pinot Gris) grape perfectly, allowing its raisin and honey fruit full rein even in the prevailing Trocken (dry) style. The fat spice of the Gewürztraminer blossoms blowsily, and the lean features of the Riesling are softened by honey. Even the Müller-Thurgau and the notoriously neutral Gutedel take on a sunny southern flavour, and the Spätburgunder (Pinot Noir) gets a little

flesh on its bones and colour in its cheeks for once. Baden's reputation is for good, full-flavoured quaffing wines. But think of this: over the last 20 years – and especially over the last 5 – the plantings of the great Riesling grape are up by 97 per cent. Some people down there know that Germany's future lies with quality, and they don't intend to miss out.

· WURTTEMBERG ·

Württemberg has two things in common with the Mosel far to the north. First, the river Neckar and its numerous tiny tributaries runs a similarly convoluted, tortuous course, particularly in the best vineyard district between Heilbronn and Stuttgart. This provides a thousand small, steep, south-facing slopes to capture all the warmth of the summer sun. Second, Riesling is the major grape!

For vineyards so far south this is a great

· FOOD AND WINE ·

I am often accused by those whose gastronomic interests never seem to descend below the heights of *nouvelle cuisine* fantasy, of being far too interested in smoked meats, sausages, thick stews and soups and rough and ready cheeses. Well, this is probably because when *I* go to a wine area, I try to eat what the locals eat.

If ever there were a country where the good solid basics of long tradition are far better than trendy innovations it is Germany. But it must be said that most Germans will still drink beer with their meals rather than wine. Even so, simple Rhine wines are extremely good unobtrusive partners for most food – be it smoked trout, Bismarck herring, a Sauerbraten of beef topside pot roast, marinated in red wine and vinegar with dried fruit and nuts, or a great chunk of Schweinhaxe – pork hocks pickled and served in a rich strong brown sauce with potatoes and sauerkraut. . .I haven't mentioned sausage once, have I? But the finer German wines can easily be overwhelmed by any but the lightest of meats – fresh river trout will be fine with a Mosel Kabinett, eels boiled in white wine and covered in a thick sauce of herbs, onions and sour cream will kill it stone dead! And with those sausages and hams and. . .I'd go for the fatter spicier wines of the Rheinpfalz or Baden – especially from the Scheurebe, Ruländer or even Gewürztraminer grapes.

Franken wines are in general full and dry. It is the only area of Germany where the Silvaner often makes the best wine. Weissherbst is a Baden speciality – a rosé from a single grape variety, Spätburgunder.

surprise, since sightings of Württemberg Rieslings are extremely rare, and the region's reputation is built on rather pallid, vaguely red wines from the Trollinger grape tasting of coal smoke and strawberries.

Yet it is easily explained. Although the area under production is quite large – 23,660 acres (9,575 hectares) representing 10·3 per cent of the German total – over half the growers own less than a quarter of a hectare, and over 80 per cent of the wine is made at the co-operatives for quick local consumption. Many of those south-facing folds in the river bank can only squeeze in a few hectares of vines. When you add to that the presence of the heavily industrialized and famously thirsty city of Stuttgart and the traditionally hearty approach to food and drink of the Schwabian locals, there was never going to be much left over for export, and there isn't. Drink it enthusiastically when you visit the region, but don't seek it out too enthusiastically elsewhere, because it isn't cheap and the best stuff stays at home anyway.

· HESSISCHE BERGSTRASSE ·

Bensheim in this tiny side-valley vineyard region east of Worms is the hottest town in Germany. Arriving there you notice first the fruit trees and the balmy Mediterranean warmth rather than the vines, which isn't that surprising – they represent only 0·39 per cent of Germany's total, and amount to 890 acres (360 hectares), spread out over 48 miles (77km) down towards Heidelberg. The Riesling is the main grape, and although 90 per cent of the wine is made at co-operatives, the Bensheim Rieslings made by the local Staatdomäne are full of soft peachy taste and are ever so slightly smoky. But there's so little made you'd be *very* lucky to find any outside the area.

· MITTELRHEIN ·

If you want fairy-tale castles, near vertical sheets of vineyard rising out of the tumbling river water, with picturesque gabled villages snuggling into the foot of the rockface, and the distant strains of the Lorelei maidens humming away in the depths of your imagination – then *this* is the place for you. But you'll have to

remember that it's also the place for several million other like-minded tourists, all flocking in for the romance of the Rhine gorges, and the siren song of the Lorelei will get drowned in the clamour.

Even so, this stretch of the Rhine valley between Bingen and Koblenz is intensely beautiful. The wines are not so much beautiful as impressively strong tasting, racy, slaty with a good rough fruit and a sting of acidity. They are nearly all Riesling and their character reflects these steep, barely workable slopes. With 1,814 acres (734 hectares) they represent only 0·8 per cent of Germany's vineyards, and with so many tourists filling so many Weinstube, there is rarely any left to sell outside the region. If you visit, the best wines are generally from Boppard, Bacharach and Oberwesel.

· AHR ·

Hardly any Ahr wine is exported, partly because the white wine is pretty light and insubstantial even by northern German standards, and partly because most of the wine is, in fact, red. It is difficult to believe that the Ahr, Germany's most remote northern wine area, is thought of as the best place for reds, but it is!

The Germans seem to like this extremely pale, very slightly cherry-tasting red, usually from the Spätburgunder grape, but I admit, I wouldn't cross the road for it. Yet I *would* drink it in the Ahr valley, because this lovely side valley of the Rhine, just south of Bonn is extremely attractive, and I suppose what they would call *gemütlich* (which means roughly genial and welcoming). Most of the wine is made by co-operatives, but there is also a

Staatsweingut (state winery) at Kloster Marienthal which makes good wine.

· SEKT ·

The Germans drink an enormous amount of their own sparkling wine which they call *Sekt*. I'm not sure how they do it, because the general standard is absolutely hopeless. The usual base wine has always been thought to consist of the tart, green juice of grapes, often Riesling, which failed to ripen, so the very least the wine should be is tangy and refreshing. However, until very recently there have frequently been far more dull, dirty southern European dregs of a vintage in the product than true German wine. Not only will the

Ahr wines are mostly light reds and seem insubstantial to palates brought up on fuller reds from warmer countries. Hessische Bergstrasse further south ripens its grapes more easily. Kerner is a new variety with some Riesling features.

Far left One of Germany's great rarities is Eiswein. Overripe grapes are left on the vine until a hard frost freezes the water in the juice. The vintagers then have to pick the grapes in the icy hours of first light and the sugary sludge is separated from the ice by very gentle pressing. It's no fun to make and very expensive to buy, but absolutely delicious.

Left Bacharach is one of a string of lovely gabled resort towns along the Mittelrhein, all with a tame castle or two and their steep vineyards, which produce good racy Riesling wine, descending often right into the town.

· SWEET WINES ·

If there is a League Against Cruelty to Grape-Pickers, the largest membership must be in the Rhine and Mosel valleys in Germany. Here Germany's great, rare, sweet wines are made, and for the poor pickers, who probably ambled out in sunny October to pick the grapes for ordinary wines, it may well be into chilly November before the grapes for Auslese, the first sweet-wine category, are ready.

That's just the start. To pick the berries for the rare Beerenauslese and Trockenbeerenauslese wines, not only will they have to tramp up into the vines in the teeth of winter, but they will pick mostly shrivelled, brown berries, covered with fungus. This horrid coating is noble rot, which feeds on the water in the grapes and leaves the sugar intact.

And there's more torture yet. Eiswein can only be made from frozen berries, so as the frosts begin to bite, the picker waits gloomily for the phone call. It may come on Advent Sunday, or Christmas Eve, or New Year's Day or Valentine's Day – but when it comes it will shrill through the chill silent hours between midnight and dawn, as the grower finally gets the savage frost he needs to freeze all the water in the grapes but leave the sugar more concentrated than ever.

In the Rheingau and Mosel and, usually, the Nahe, the grape will be the Riesling. In the Rheinhessen and the Rheinpfalz, it is often Riesling, but Scheurebe and Silvaner can also be stunningly good, as the Silvaner can be in Franconia. Further south all kinds of grapes may be used.

In the Mosel and Rheingau, the conditions of warm sun and mist which cause noble rot and make Beerenauslese and Trockenbeerenauslese possible will only occur, and the grapes will only be ripe enough, perhaps two years in ten. In the Rheinhessen, the Rheinpfalz and further south, the conditions are more frequent. Yet it is the piercing acidity of the grapes from further north which makes for the most astonishing mixture of gooey richness and mouthwatering freshness so that you feel as though you are drinking the very essence of ripe fruit.

Great vintage years are very rare, but when they do come the wines will fill out and mature for as much as 50 years, and they positively demand 10. The rarity of suitable vintages is shown by the fact that the most recent star vintages are 1976, 1959, 1945 and 1921!

resulting brew be devoid of fruit and acidity, it will also require heavy dosings of sulphur to stop it turning to vinegar.

Since 1986 things have improved. All wine labelled Deutscher Sekt must be from 100 per cent German grapes. However there will not suddenly be a flood of brilliant, clean Riesling sparklers, since most of these German grapes will be Elbling and Müller-Thurgau. Also the vast majority of Deutscher Sekt is made by the closed tank method. This means that the second fermentation, which creates the bubbles, takes place in a sealed tank under pressure – a process which is inferior to the champagne method during which the second fermentation takes place in the bottle.

There are a few 'estate' wines, particularly in the Mosel-Saar-Ruwer, but the best chance of getting a decent drink is first, *never* to buy one of the rock-bottom cheapo brands, and second, try to find a wine labelled 'Riesling'. The best ones I've found are Deinhard Lila Imperial, Deinhard Mosel, Fürst von Metternich, and Schloss Reinhartshausen.

· ITALY ·

Italy has been making wine for 35 centuries, yet after all this time it remains the biggest puzzle in the world of wine. There is hardly an inch of land which could not ripen grapes of some sort, and wines are made from her mountainous north, right down the long limb which is her mainland, to Sicily and, further still, to the tiny island of Pantelleria which almost touches the African shores off Tunisia.

From this gigantic vineyard, which the Greeks called Oenotria, 'the land of wine', comes more than one fifth of the world's entire output. Italy produces more than all the non-European nations put together, and her exports account for nearly two-fifths of *all* wine exports from any and every country in the world.

These are daunting figures, and I should now be able to follow this by reciting a joyous listing of great wines which have been a credit to Italy over the centuries. But I can't. Barolo and Barbaresco are famous and expensive wines. Chianti is famous or infamous depending how you look at it. But what then? Lambrusco tops the bill – but how many people think of it as wine at all? Soave, Bardolino and Valpolicella? Not exactly renowned for the memorable quality of their offerings. Frascati, Verdicchio, certainly Orvieto – I'm running out of names. Marsala? Possibly. Lacryma Christi? Est! Est!! Est!!!? No, surely not – two joke labels rather than decent drinks. Ah, Asti Spumanti. Yes, an excellent wine, but one which is continually and ignorantly derided by those who set themselves up as wine experts. And if I were then asked to name famous properties, famous single vineyards, which I could easily do in France or Germany, I could come up with only a few names.

The sad fact about Italy is that almost all of the wines it has been sending round the world have been the most basic imaginable. France and Germany import enormous quantities of Italian wine to blend into numerous anonymous concoctions of their own. The United States takes shiploads of wine, but these are almost entirely made up of Lambrusco, Soave, Frascati and nameless blends from the South. Britain, too, takes a lot of wine, but it is Chianti, Soave, Valpolicella and the rest of the crew which dominate sales, often because their price is so low.

This is a totally misleading picture. Italy has more exciting, original and undiscovered flavours than any other wine nation. Whereas France has created a series of classic flavours against which equivalent wines from other countries can be measured, Italy's classic flavours are without imitations or emulators, and indeed are largely unknown. We cannot say we know what a Chianti, Barolo, Soave or Lambrusco should even taste like, because there are rarely two winemakers who *agree* on precisely what a particular wine's flavour should be.

France has made a certain conformity of style into a virtue – but you know the Italians, and so do I; conformity is *not* one of their strong points. But imagination *is*, originality *is*, and fierce pride *is*. These are the virtues which make Italian wine an astonishing treasure house, full of flavours which may seem harsh, or bizarre, or uncomfortably extreme besides France's more sophisticated styles. However it is these, and not the blandly acceptable factory-produced half-dozen famous names we should seek out, because if we don't, we're missing out on an artistry and originality which is all too rare in the modern world.

This very individuality makes it extremely difficult to say exactly how many Italian wines there are. Burton Anderson, the world authority on Italian wine, says if there are 1,605,785 registered vineyards in Italy, then there are 1,605,785 individual wines. He has a point, because the maverick and freelance approach of the winemakers usually outweighs the dictates of law! Basically, Italy is still a land of small holdings. Where these growers all bring their produce to a local co-operative, as in much of the South, or where they are contracted to large commercial producers, as is often the case in Tuscany and the Veneto, obviously their grapes will merge into whatever house style is being looked for. Where they make their own wine anything goes! There are a number of large private estates, particularly in Tuscany and parts of the North-West and North-East, and it is frequently from these producers that the most exciting results are emerging.

· CLASSIFICATIONS ·

These flavours may be within or outside the framework of the appellation of origin laws, here called the *Denominazione di Origine Controllata*, which is called DOC for short. This covers about 220 different zones, but new ones are still being created every year. These 220 zones produce over 500 distinct wines, and yet DOC covers only 10–12 per cent of the Italian wine output.

The objectives of DOC are basically the same as for the French *appellation controlée* system, but so far they have been less successful in guaranteeing at least a reasonable level of quality and authenticity, partly because the system was only introduced in 1963 and has been far too susceptible to political interference concerned with defending tradition, good or bad, rather than quality.

Denominazione di Origine Controllata e Garantita (DOCG) is the top tier. This is a new 'super' DOC for the top wines – six so far, more to come. Rules on grape types, yields and wine-making methods are more stringent, but results so far don't show the sudden leap in quality everyone hoped for.

Denominazione di Origine Controllata (DOC) is the usual appellation of origin. In concept it is fine, but frequently the grapes which are allowed are merely a zone's commonest rather than a zone's best. For instance there are numerous white DOCs based on the mediocre Trebbiano simply because farmers find it so easy to grow, not because the wine is exciting. However, DOC has imposed a shape on Italian wine which was lacking, and it is slowly improving quality as well.

Vino Tipico is rather similar to France's VDQS or *vin de pays* category, in that it is used for non-DOC wines which nonetheless do have a locally recognized individuality and quality level. The regulations are looser than for DOC.

Vino da Tavola con Indicazione Geografica, means everyday table wine with regional origin stated. Usually it is wine simply, say, red or white of such and such a village – as in Rosso di Bellagio, a pleasant country wine from near Lake Como, but it may sometimes state a grape variety too. Controls here are even looser!

Vino da Tavola, supposedly the most basic of descriptions, meaning simply everyday table wine, is where, apart from fundamental health requirements, there are no controls at all, and though this is the bottom quality rating, many of Italy's top wines are only *vino da tavola*! This is because fine winemakers are well aware that DOC laws frequently hinder originality and innovation, and therefore they renounce the right to DOC, so that they may pursue the goal of quality in whatever way they choose. In Tuscany especially, many of Italy's greatest wines now come into this category, selling for high prices on their own reputation rather than that of any DOC. Sassicaia is thought by many to be Italy's finest red and it doesn't have any DOC, but it does have a stratospheric price tag.

Italy is a land of immense geographical contrasts. When you visit Alto Adige in the North-East (*above left*) with its fairytale castles, alpine peaks and a population whose language is German, it is difficult to believe you *are* in Italy. Tuscany (*left*), is more typically Italian. Here it's in its green mood, the fields raked with rows of cypresses, the gentle slopes plaited with vines and dotted with olive trees. In the far south the vines are trained in bushy clumps, as in Marsala (*above*), Sicily, so that the dense foliage will protect the fruit from the summer sun.

	red	rosé	white
still	●	◐	○
sparkling	▲		△
fortified	■		□

DOC = Denominazione di Origine Controllata

DOCG = Denominazione di Origine Controllata e Garantita

SW = sweet   AM = amber

· SELECTED WINES ·

All wines are DOC unless otherwise indicated. However, in some parts of Italy controls are somewhat haphazard, so do not be surprised if you find some DOC wine names on non-DOC wines. For instance Barbera is grown all over Italy; sometimes it is DOC, sometimes not.

· NORTH-EAST ·

Alto Adige
- ● Bozner Leiten (Colli di Bolzano)
- ● ○ Etschtaler (Valdadige)
- ○ Goldenmuskateller (Moscato Giallo)
- ● Kalterersee (Lago di Caldaro)
- ◐ Rosenmuskateller
- ● St Magdalener (Santa Maddalena)

- ●◐○ Südtiroler (Alto Adige)
- ●◐○ Südtiroler (Alto Adige) SW
- ○ Terlaner (Terlano)

A large number of different 'varietal' – single-grape-type – wines are also allowed DOC in Trentino and Alto Adige.

Trentino
- ●◐ Casteller
- ● Marzemino di Isera
- ●◐ Teroldego Rotaliano
- ● ○ Sorni

Friuli–Venezia Giulia
- ●◐○ Aquileia
- ● ○ Carso
- ● ○ Colli Goriziano
- ● ○ Colli Orientali
- ● – Picolit SW
- ●◐○ Grave del Friuli
- ● ○ Isonzo
- ● ○ Latisana
  vino da tavola
- ○ Picolit SW

Veneto
- ●◐ Bardolino
- ○ Bianco di Custoza
- ● ○ Breganze
- ● ○ Colli Berici
- ● ○ Piave
- ○ Prosecco di Conegliano-Valdobbiadene
- ● Raboso
- ○ – Gambellara
- △ – Recioto di Gambellara SW
- ○ Soave
- ○ Tocai di Lison
- ● Valpolicella
- ● ○ – Recioto della Valpolicella Amarone
  vino da tavola
- ● Campo Fiorin
- ○ Masianco
- △ Torcolato
- ● Venegazzù della Casa

· NORTH-WEST ·

Piedmont
- △ Asti Spumante SW
- ● Barbaresco (DOCG)

- Barbera d'Alba
- Barbera d'Asti
- Barbera del Monferrato
- ▲ Barbera del Monferrato
- Barolo (DOCG)
- Boca
- ▲ Brachetto d'Acqui SW
- Bramaterra
- Carema
- ○ Cortese di Gavi (or Gavi)
- Dolcetto d'Acqui
- Dolcetto d'Alba
- Dolcetto d'Asti
- Dolcetto delle Langhe Monregalesi
- Dolcetto di Diano d'Alba
- Dolcetto di Dogliani
- Dolcetto di Ovada
- ○ Erbaluce di Caluso
- ○ Erbaluce di Caluso Passito AM/SW
- Fara
- Freisa d'Asti
- ▲ Freisa d'Asti SW
- Gattinara
- ○ Gavi di Gavi
- Ghemme
- Grignolino d'Asti
- △ Moscato d'Asti SW
- Nebbiolo d'Alba
  vino da tavola
- ○ Arneis dei Roeri
- ○ Chardonnay
- Spanna

Lombardy (Lombardia)
- ●◑○ Franciacorta
- △ Franciacorta
- ○ Lugana
- ●◑○ Oltrepò Pavese
- Oltrepò Pavese Bonarda
- ▲ Oltrepò Pavese Sangue di Giuda
- △ Oltrepò Pavese Pinot Spumante
- ●◑ Rivera del Garda Bresciano
- ● ○ Valcalepio
- Valtellina
- Valtellina Superiore

Liguria
- ○ Cinqueterre
- Rossese di Dolceacqua (or Dolceacqua)

vino da tavola
- ○ Picato di Albenga

Valle d'Aosta
- Donnaz
- Enfer d'Arvier
  vino da tavola
- ○ Blanc de Morgex

· CENTRAL ·

Tuscany (Toscana)
- ○ Bianco Vergine della Valdichiana
- Brunello di Montalcino (DOCG)
- ●◑ Carmignano
- Chianti (DOCG)
- ● ○ Elba
- ● ○ Montecarlo
- Morellino di Scansano
- △ Moscadello di Montalcino SW
- ● ○ Pomino
- Rosso di Montalcino
- ○ Vernaccia di San Gimignano
- Vino Nobile di Montepulciano (DOCG)
  vino da tavola
- Ca' del Pozzo
- Ghiae della Furba
- Sammarco
- Sassicaia
- Tignanello
- Vinattieri
- ● ○ Vin Santo AM/SW

Umbria
- ●◑○ Colli Altotiberini
- ● ○ Colli del Trasimeno
- ●◑○ Colli Perugini
- Montefalco
- ○ Orvieto
- ● ○ Torgiano
  vino da tavola
- Cabernet Sauvignon di Miralduolo
- ○ Chardonnay di Miralduolo San Giorgio
- ○ Solleone AM
- ○ Vin Santo AM/SW

The Marches (Marche)
- Rosso Cònero
- Rosso Piceno

- ○△ Verdicchio dei Castelli di Jesi
- ○ Verdicchio di Matelica

Emilia-Romagna
- ○ Albana di Romagna (DOCG)
- △ Albana di Romagna SW
- ● ○ Colli Bolognesi
- ● ○ Colli di Parma
- ▲ △ Colli di Parma
- ●▲ Colli di Piacentini
- ▲ Lambrusco di Sorbara
- ▲ Lambrusco Gasparossa di Castelvetro
- ▲ Lambrusco Salaminodi Santa Croce
- Sangiovese di Romagna
- ○ Trebbiano di Romagna
  vino da tavola
- ●◑○ Lambrusco

Abruzzi (Abruzzo)
- ●◑ Montepulciano d'Abruzzo
- ○ Trebbiano d'Abruzzo

Latium (Lazio)
- ●◑○ Aprilia
- ● ○ Cerveteri
- ○ Est! Est!! Est!!! di Montefiascone
- ○ Frascati
- ○ Marino
- ● ○ Velletri

· SOUTH ·

Molise
- ●◑○ Biferno
- ●◑○ Pentro

Campania
- ○ Fiano di Avellino
- ○ Greco di Tufo
- ●◑○ Lacryma Christi del Vesuvio (or Vesuvio)
- Taurasi
  vino da tavola
- ○ Aspino

Basilicata
- Aglianico del Vulture

Calabria
- ●◑○ Cirò
- ○ Greco di Bianco SW

- Pollino
  vino da tavola
- ○ Squillace

Apulia (Puglia)
- ●◑ Brindisi
- ●◑○ Castel del Monte
- ○ Moscato di Trani SW
- Primitivo di Manduria
- Rosso di Cerignola
- ●◑ Squinzano
  vino da tavola
- Il Falcone
- ○ Five Roses

Sardinia (Sardegna)
- ●◑ Cannonau di Sardegna
- ●◑ Cannonau di Sardegna SW
- ●◑ Carignano del Sulcis
- ○ Malvasia di Bosa AM/SW
- ○ Nuragus di Cagliari
- ○ Vermentino di Gallura
- ○ Vernaccia di Oristano AM
  vino da tavola
- ■ Anghelu Ruju SW
- Carmonan
- ○ Vermentino

Sicily (Sicilia)
- ○ Alcamo
- Cerasuolo di Vittoria
- ●◑○ Etna
- ○ Malvasia delle Lipari AM/SW
- ○ Marsala AM/SW
- △○ Moscato di Pantelleria
- ○ Moscato di Pantelleria AM/SW
- □ – Passito di Pantelleria AM/SW
  vino da tavola
- ● ○ Corvo
- △ Corvo Spumante
- ● ○ Libecchio
- ○ Rapitalà
- ●◑○ Regaleali

· NORTH-EAST ITALY ·

These vines, overlooking Lago di Caldaro in Alto Adige, are trained high on pergolas which improves yields and prevents overripening. The reds and whites produced on these valley side slopes are some of the most immediately attractive in Italy.

The north-east of Italy is by far the most difficult to put into a straitjacket of generalizations – and that's why I'm so keen on it. It is a positive jumble of different identities and different nationalistic pressures which only seems truly Italian around the central town of Verona. Alto Adige, a breathtaking mountain region to the north of Verona, is practically Austrian; Venice to the east has always had a slightly exotic tinge, and the Friuli region up by Trieste is heavily influenced by its Slavic neighbours – after all Trieste became Yugoslavian for a few years after World War Two.

Inside this patchwork of influences are wildly differing styles of wine and food. The cooking styles of Alto Adige and Friuli owe little to mainstream Italy, and the wines, too, are totally different from those found elsewhere. Venice itself is surrounded by flat vineyard land full of grapes not found at all further south; Verona on the other hand is at the core of an over-exploited trio of DOCs – Soave, Valpolicella and Bardolino – which seem to epitomize Italy's cheap and sometimes not so cheerful wine image abroad.

Of all the Italian regions, the North-East was the first to modernize its approach. This is partly because of the different nationalities which populate the region, who, despite being pre-occupied with their own local problems, are less prey to the political interference which hampers creativity further south. And that also explains why, along with some fascinating indigenous grape varieties, the French and German classics have been grown here for well over a century – Pinot Bianco, Chardonnay, Riesling, Cabernet Franc, Cabernet Sauvignon, and Pinot Noir can be seen as 'traditional' varieties, rather than the carpetbaggers they may resemble elsewhere. But gratifyingly, they do not swamp wines made from genuine local varieties like Tocai Friulano, Verduzzo, Lagrein and Refosco.

The enormous variety of wines and styles is further helped by the presence of some of Italy's most innovative winemakers and wine institutions. In Alto Adige, Herbert Tiefenbrunner and Alois Lageder; in Trentino, Pojer and Sandri, and Istituto San Michele all' Adige; in Veneto, the Conegliano Wine School and the Venegazzù Estate; in Friuli, Jermann, Plozner, and EnoFriulia; all these are shaping a future which the rest of Italy would do well to follow.

· ALTO ADIGE ·

Establishing an identity for this high mountain-valley paradise isn't exactly easy because even the inhabitants don't know what to call it. The Italian-speakers call it Alto Adige, since it is the Adige river which runs between the dizzy mountain slopes towards the Adriatic. The German-speaking majority, however, call it the Südtirol since the South Tyrolean Alps form the northern section towards Austria; and neither side will willingly give in to the other.

We'll call it Alto Adige simply because that's what the Italian government calls it, but in fact this long fringe of land reaching high into the Alps above Trento only became Italian

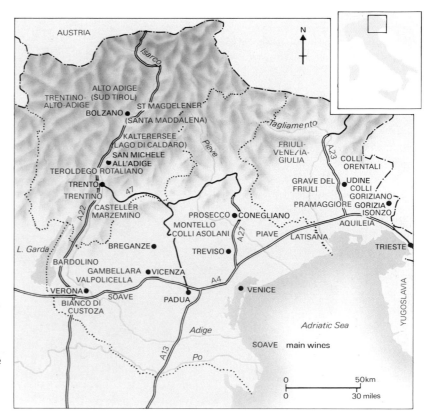

These Sylvaner grapes are growing on the sides of the Eisack Valley at heights well over 2,000 feet. On the far side the landscape is more typically alpine, the pasture land dotted with little farmhouses and the towering mountain peaks behind.

when it was traded to Italy as the spoils of victory after World War One. Before that it had been part of Austria since 1363, and the majority of the inhabitants would be more than happy for this state of affairs to return.

As it is, it means that we have to cope with wine labels which can list grape variety, village of production and name of DOC in either Italian or German, and even, occasionally, French! However, it's worth the effort to try to find our way around, because this is one of Europe's most fascinating wine areas.

Until recently we saw relatively little of Alto Adige wines because there was an enormous market for them in Austria, Switzerland and Germany. A light red wine from the Vernatsch, or Schiava, grape was shipped north to these markets in enormous quantities at a very low price, and the quality was feeble to say the least. However, in the early 1980s, this market began to disintegrate, which was the best thing that could have happened to the region, since the winemakers had to pull themselves up by

their own bootstraps and the only way forward was through quality.

· GRAPES AND WINE STYLES ·

About 80 per cent of Alto Adige vineyards are planted with red grapes and 20 per cent with white. Altogether 84 per cent of the wines are DOC – which is the highest proportion of any region in Italy – and as grapes like Chardonnay, which has only just been accepted for DOC, increase, so the percentage will rise. It is the growers who undoubtedly make the best wines here, but they do not only use their own grapes and since certain microclimates are traditionally best for certain grapes, good growers supplement their own grapes with special batches bought from these localities. There are also various large commercial companies, but the extensive co-operative system produces the more interesting wines, with most co-ops having one or two specialities.

Vernatsch (Schiava) dominates the red plantings, accounting for two-thirds of the vine-

yards. When properly made, either as Kalter-ersee (Lago di Caldaro in Italian) or St Magdalener (Santa Maddalena), it can be a delicious summer red, having almost no tannin or acidity, and with a surprisingly tasty mix of strawberry yoghurt and woodsmoke!

Lagrein not only makes one of Europe's best strawberry-fresh rosés (Lagrein Kretzer), but also produces deep chewy reds (Lagrein Dunkel), which have a tarry roughness matched by plums and chocolate richness, quite unexpected in a high mountain valley.

Cabernet Franc and **Cabernet Sauvignon** can be very good, though there is usually more of the earthy Franc style and less of the ripe blackcurrant of Sauvignon.

Pinot Noir (Pinot Nero), although usually rather light and sometimes vinified as a fragrant rosé, can nonetheless be brilliantly fruity in a plums and cherries way at least half reminiscent of good burgundy.

The white wines, however, are the ones which created the most waves here because

Alto Adige is one of the most memorable of all vineyard areas, with the snow-covered peaks providing a spectacular backdrop to the vines. These are the vineyards of Santa Maddalena which makes good quality light reds.

they are so unlike traditional Italian whites. It is interesting to note how many producers further south are now trying to achieve the glacier-sharp fruit and purity of flavour which marks out the best from Alto Adige.

Chardonnay from the region is reckoned to be the finest in Italy, always retaining a sharp edge despite a beautiful honey-flecked gentle richness too. Although the tradition for white wines is not to use small oak barrels, first attempts by Tiefenbrunner and Lageder among others have been great successes.

Weissburgunder (Pinot Bianco) is widely grown and often just as good as Chardonnay.

Gewürztraminer may well have originated in the local village of Tramin, and although the wines seem a little flat when they're young, with two or three years ageing they achieve a fragrant fruity spice not so startling as that of an Alsace Gewürztraminer, but maybe a little easier to drink for that very reason.

Müller-Thurgau and **Sylvaner** can both produce lovely, sharp, nettles and green-grapes kinds of wines when they're grown high enough up in the mountains.

Rheinriesling (Riesling Renano) can be as steely and fresh as a Mosel Kabinett – but with more strength and weight.

Muscat (Moscato) is the final group. When the wines are made dry, they are the only other Muscats in Europe to achieve the same crunchy green-grape delicacy of Alsace. However, when they are sweet they are overpoweringly perfumed, bursting with flavour.

Rosenmuskateller is a very rare grape. Made sweet or dry, it is without parallel anywhere, blending grapiness with the heady perfume of roses in bloom and the oriental tang of fresh-brewed Darjeeling tea. And if that doesn't make you want to try Alto Adige wines, nothing will.

· TRENTINO ·

Whereas Alto Adige is dominated by German-speaking Tyrolean winemakers, Trentino is

truly Italian, looking south to the Mediterranean, rather than north to Austria. It has also, after a promising start a decade ago, been left behind by its Germanic neighbour to the north as far as quality wine production is concerned. The two reasons are first, the domination of the area by the Cavit co-operative group which controls almost 75 per cent of the area's production and, despite its producing some good wines, this does inhibit individuality. Second, that a good deal of its white grapes go straight into the production of sparkling wines which rarely mention the region on their labels. Ferrari and Equipe Five are extremely good Pinot Bianco and Chardonnay champagne-method fizzes, though they do cost an arm and a leg, while the ubiquitous Cavit makes excellent and affordable Chardonnay Spumante.

This difference between the two areas is most obvious as you drive south through Alto Adige. The flat valley floor is covered in apple trees; the difficult, treacherous plateau and slopes up the side of the mountains are festooned with vines. At the very border, as Alto Adige becomes Trentino, the valley floor

Alto Adige Chardonnay, acknowledged to be among the finest in Italy, was only granted DOC status in 1985. Pinot Grigio is the Italian equivalent of the French Pinot Gris. In Italy it is usually made light and neutral, but in the hilly Collio region of Friuli it is often fuller and more exciting.

there is Recioto della Valpolicella Amarone, one of the greatest, but most unusual red wines in the world. The ripest Valpolicella grapes are picked, then hung indoors to dry and shrivel. Then the wine is fermented painfully slowly to about 16·5° alcohol making it just about the strongest natural wine possible. The result is memorable – bitter, certainly (*amaro* means bitter), but blended in with grapeskins, plums, chocolate, smoke, sometimes even the savouriness of grilled meat, and all bound in with a sweet-sour acidity. Reciotos can also be made fully sweet (not Amarone) when they resemble a brilliant untamed vintage port.

There are an increasing number of superior *vini da tavola* in the region. These are made by good producers who are tired of having to bow to the DOC laws and wish to improve upon the grape blends, as with Masi's Masianco which is made in Soave but includes Sauvignon. There is also a group of producers who make Valpolicella and then pass the finished wine back over the lees of a Recioto or Amarone for a slight refermentation which gives some of the disturbing sweet-sour beauty of an Amarone to a straight table wine. Masi's

Campo Fiorin and Tedeschi's Capitel San Rocco are the most famous versions.

Other wines Soave has two look-alikes in Bianco di Custoza and Gambellara which are usually far better than Soave itself. Breganze has some rather good peppy whites, some deliciously blackcurranty reds and a wine called Torcolato from Maculan which is so creamy and honeyed *and* sweet it could almost be a dessert Chardonnay. In the Montello hills is the Venegazzú estate which produces challenging smoky Cabernet-based blends and rather lean Chardonnay and fizz, while nearby the Prosecco grape gives strangely gentle but refreshing sparkling wine at Conegliano. Most of the rest of the region is concerned with producing quaffing wine for Venice and its neighbours. The two main regions for this are Piave and Pramaggiore, and much of the produce is light unmemorable Cabernet, Merlot and Pinot Bianco. However, the knowing locals drink Raboso, a tremendous, gutsy rough-house red, Verduzzo, a nutty, low-acid ultra-soft white, or Tocai, which is sharp yet also nutty, and now and then ever so slightly spicy.

· FOOD AND WINE ·

Rice and peas sounds more Caribbean than Italian, but this is, amazingly, one of the most famous Venetian dishes – delicious simplicity itself from a city renowned for its complicated, decadent brilliance. Rice, beans and the rib-sticking *polenta* made from maize flour are the base for a large variety of dishes, and the easy-drinking reds and whites – Raboso, Cabernet, Verduzzo and Bianco di Custoza – are ideal accompaniments for dishes which really do need some washing down.

Friuli, too, uses beans, rice and *polenta* rather than pasta as her staples and the mixture of alpine and Italian cuisine is best seen in the goulashes, the *paparot*, a thick cream and spinach soup, the even thicker *jota*, a type of Italian cassoulet with pork, beans, cornmeal and turnips, and the fish soups of the coast below Trieste. In all of them you can't decide which influence is strongest, so it is lucky that the region has some of Italy's most adaptable 'food' wines, in the Merlots, Cabernets, Pinot Grigios, Tocais and Verduzzos from the west and north of Trieste.

Up in Alto Adige, there's little doubt that the influence is Austrian even to the extent of serving the excellent local asparagus in a biting sauce of vinegar and chopped eggs. But the basic diet consists of dumplings and pastas filled with spinach and meat and nutmeg, smoked pork – *speck* – and *sauerkraut* and sausages. With these the light reds of Kalterersee and St Magdalener go surprisingly well, and the fine-flavoured but light Chardonnays, Rieslings and Sylvaners are equally at home. I can't think of a better way of seeing in spring than hiking up to a mountain *gasthaus* and sitting in the chill, bright sunlight, eating *speck* and gulping St Magdalener as the drone of Bozen's industry drifts up from way below.

· GOOD PRODUCERS ·

Alto Adige Lageder, Tiefenbrunner, Höfstatter, Walch, Niedermayr, St Michael-Eppan co-op.
Trentino Barone de Cles, Conti Martini, Pojer and Sandri, Istituto San Michele all'Adige, Bollini.
Veneto Guerrieri-Rizzardi, Anselmi, Masi, Tedeschi, Zenato, Santa Sofia, Quintarelli, Maculan, Venegazzù.
Friuli EnoFriulia, Jermann, Plozner, Capelletti, Collavini, Ca' Bolani, Schiopetto.

· NORTH-WEST ITALY ·

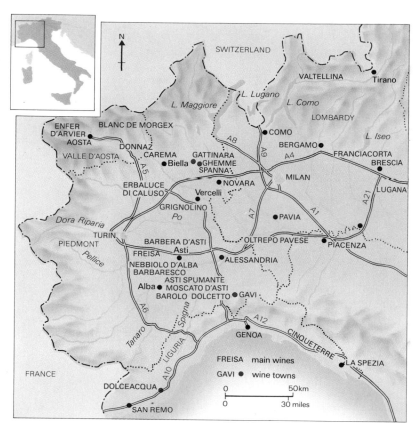

The north-west of Italy was always described to me in history lessons as the 'serious' part of Italy. Here people worked hard, made money, and occasionally raised armies which won battles. A sort of Prussia-on-the-Po. I was always a little unnerved by these ultra-efficient Lombards and Piedmontese, and harboured a sneaking regard for what was portrayed as the feckless, corrupt but wonderfully colourful life of the Neapolitans and Sicilians to the south of Rome.

If we just took Piedmont and its most famous red wines, Barolo and Barbaresco, as our examples then this grim-faced seriousness could be seen to be typical of the region's whole attitude to life. But we'd be missing the half of it. More than half. In Piedmont alone, Barolo's haughty self-esteem is punctured not only by Dolcetto, one of the most laughingly delicious of all reds, but also by a wine, far *more* famous than Barolo, which is the complete antithesis of seriousness – Asti Spumante, and

its miraculous tasty stablemate Moscato Naturale d'Asti. Lombardy, also, is famous not for beetle-browed reds but for some of Italy's best sparkling wines, and the table wines it *does* have are easy and delicious. As for Liguria – well, there's hardly room to plant vines on this sliver of Riviera land. Valle d'Aosta does not sound Italian, and to be honest, its wines don't taste Italian; since the pistes are excellent, not much of its minute production gets past the après-ski crowd.

· PIEDMONT ·

You want to approach Piedmont (in Italian, Piemonte) from the south. As you climb into the high Apennines above the Mediterranean, the roads become tortuous and pitted with use, the forest-covered mountain slopes only barely disguising the jagged rawness of the rock face as it careers down to the valley floor. But you keep on climbing, and all of a sudden, the effort eases, the slopes drop back from the roadside

The vineyards of Barolo are situated on a series of hills and slopes in a small area just to the south-west of Alba. These vineyards at Serralunga d'Alba produce some of the sternest wines.

and the billowing waves of high plateau vineyard take the place of rock and pine.

From Diano d'Alba – where they make succulent soft Dolcetto – you can see into the heart of Piedmont. To the right are the gentle hills of Asti, coated with Muscat vines; ahead, as the road snakes down towards the plain, are the slopes of Alba with their Barbera vines and the more distinctive, steeper parcels of land which grow Nebbiolo to make Barbaresco; and way below to the left is a plain interrupted by eruptions of rock shaped like Indian tepees. This is Barolo, and the finest Nebbiolo vines clamber up the sides of these cones of rock topped by villages whose names – La Morra, Serralunga d'Alba, Barolo itself – should be as familiar as the villages of Burgundy's Côte d'Or or Bordeaux's Médoc.

This is the heart of the region but there is much more to discover, and each time I get to Piedmont or taste a range of the wines, it is the unsung minor wines which I find most exciting. The revival of the delicious white Arneis grape, and the tart and tangy pale red Grignolino, as well as the froth and fun of Freisa and Brachetto, vaguely red and vaguely sparkling – all these excite me. Moscato Naturale from Asti – whipped into bottle before they can be fizzed up for Asti Spumante – leaves me stunned at how delicious Muscat can be. The Cortese grape makes big, serious, rather Burgundian whites at Gavi as a foil to the hefty Nebbiolo reds. Way to the north near Lake Maggiore they make sumptuous reds which can rival Barolo for power and surpass it for pleasure.

The offical classification system is very important here, and Piedmont, with 35 different zones, has more demarcated wines than any other region. It also has two of only six DOCG wines in all Italy – Barolo and Barbaresco. However, there is much activity in the non-DOC camp. A marvellous old traditional wine like Arneis dei Roeri does not have the DOC, much of the region's Barbera, Brachetto, Dolcetto, and Grignolino is not DOC and nor, for that matter, is some of the best Moscato d'Asti. Spanna, the commonest Nebbiolo wine from the far north, is never DOC. Finally, we are now seeing French interlopers – Cabernet Sauvignon and Chardonnay – in the Piedmontese heartland of Barbaresco. The wines made from these grapes do not qualify for DOC and it's extremely unlikely they ever will, despite their undoubted quality.

Since almost all the major wines are based on a single grape, we will look at the most important of the wide range of Piedmont wines from the viewpoint of their major grape variety.

· THE RED WINES ·

Nebbiolo
This tough, late-ripening, surly grape bestrides Piedmont, and was until recently completely unprepared to offer so much as a nod in the direction of modern taste. Simple economic necessity, however, is now forcing a re-think, and the brilliant black cherry and plums fruit, which always lurked behind the savage tannin, is sneaking to the fore. Nebbiolo is the grape responsible for two of Italy's greatest reds – Barolo and Barbaresco.

Barolo (DOCG) is the most revered red in Italy. It is also one of the most difficult to love, but maybe that's all part of the game – you have to suffer the brusque tannins and sour acidity of many poorly made Barolos so that when you do find a great one, you're absurdly grateful and appreciative. Barolo is a far more complicated taste than, say, the great Cabernet-based character of the top Médocs, but there is also far more nuance.

You start with tannin, sometimes so throat-clutching as to leave a patina coating your palate as bitter as day-old cold tea. There is also an acidity which can often have the sourness of half-fermented grapes. The fruit flavours which go with this are very wide-ranging: plums, greengages, blackberries can all be there, as well as prunes, raisins, chocolate and liquorice, and to add to this melting pot of tastes there may also be tobacco, pine, herbs and tar. Great wines should be able to shock and bewilder you with their cavalcade of unexpected fruits and perfumes – and Barolo at its best does *just* that.

Straight Barolo is released at three years old; Riserva at four years old; Riserva Speciale at five years old. Traditionally the majority of this time would be spent in big, old barrels – but modern winemakers prefer to preserve fruit by less time in barrel and more time in bottle. Light Barolos can be delicious at five years old, top wines need 10 years, but rarely the 20 or more some people seem determined to give them.

Barbaresco (DOCG) Almost always a little gentler than Barolo but, for that reason, often easier to enjoy. The tannin is still a major problem, though acidity is rarely so marked, and although the dark, shadowy richness of prunes and raisins steeped in brandy does linger in the background, the fruit can be easier – more damson skins, raspberries and redcurrants, liquorice, mint and chocolate, although there is often a slight dusty dryness cooling down the brightness of the flavours.

Basic Barbaresco is released at two years old, Riserva at three and Riserva Speciale at four. **Nebbiolo d'Alba (DOC)** and **Nebbiolo delle Langhe (DOC)** show both the richness and the toughness of the Nebbiolo grape at an earlier, more approachable stage.

Carema (DOC) in the far north makes a light, but intense Nebbiolo wine.

Gattinara (DOC) and **Ghemme (DOC)** at their best are softer styles, with a juicy plum fruit and a slight bitterness making them very enjoyable.

Spanna (vino da tavola), from a great producer like Vallana, has a marvellous, gentle brown-sugar-and-raisins richness rare in a red table wine, although the Nebbiolo is often mixed up with all kinds of grapes like Montepulciano, Aglianico, Bonarda and goodness knows what else.

Barbera
This is the most widely planted grape with over 52 per cent of the entire Piedmont acreage, and three DOCs.

Barbera d'Alba (DOC), **Barbera d'Asti (DOC)** and **Barbera del Monferrato (DOC)** are excellent food wines, especially when young, because the acidity is high, there's usually a whiff of tobacco and resin, yet there's also a strong, rather brown-sugary fruit and some sour-raisins bite.

· VINTAGES ·

Vintages are of great importance in Piedmont, of some importance in Lombardy, and of very little importance in Liguria and Valle d'Aosta where the wines are almost all intended for current consumption locally. Lombardy will produce decent quality in most vintages, and, because of her quick-drinking reds and heavy commitment to sparkling wine production, full ripeness isn't of overriding importance. However, Piedmont really does need the sun for its reds, and especially for the late-ripening Nebbiolo. Luckily there have been tremendous years recently, 1985 and 1982 – rich, intense, amazingly strong wines with the potential to be outstanding and classic from the best producers. 1986 and 1983, while less overwhelmingly exciting, are nonetheless great years, a little lighter, but none the worse for that.

Dolcetto

Dolcetto can be incredibly good. There are seven DOCs, the best being Ovada, Diano d'Alba and Alba. Almost every example you taste seems different, but when it's young, it should be bursting with plummy fruit, honey and cream, and even angelica and cinnamon spice.

· THE WHITE WINES ·

Moscato

People who look down their noses at Asti Spumante might like to know that the Moscato grapes which go to make the wine are the most expensive grapes in Italy, being difficult to grow and meagre of yield.

Asti Spumante (DOC) is, after champagne, the most popular and sought after sparkling wine in the world. Put a bottle in the fridge for a couple of hours, then crack it open and simply wallow in the wonderful, surging fruit, the blend of apples and juicy, crunchy, green grape brightness which, allied to a very low alcohol level – often only 7.5 per cent – and a good rush of bubbles makes it utterly beguiling and refreshing.

Moscato Naturale d' Asti (DOC and vino da tavola), on the other hand, is the *most* addictive, gorgeously indulgent flavour in all of Italian wine . This is the fresh, half-fermented Moscato wine bottled with just a tiny prickle rather than a full fizz. It is *heaven* – so grapy, so apple fresh, cigar-spicy and honeyed too, it's hard to believe it's wine at all – and, at 5 per cent alcohol, it only just is!

Cortese

Gavi (DOC) in south-east Piedmont is where the Cortese grape excels. The wine is very dry and at its best has a stony, lemony streak of acidity but a big, fresh apples and liquorice fruit to match. It's best young, but since it really is a bit pricey the temptation is to age it, and the results are reasonably good, something like a mature, ripe Chablis.

Erbaluce di Caluso (DOC) is a similar wine to Gavi, very dry, but with a soft, creamy apple flavour. And it's half the price, so maybe we should drink this until the present fashion for Gavi fades.

Arneis dei Roeri

A few years ago it would have been almost impossible to include this grape, because there was hardly a vine left. Now it's back in action, making a brilliantly original, fairly dry white vino da tavola with the same name, packed with the flavour of apples, peaches and liquorice, and finishing with the astonishing bitter-perfumed tang of fresh hops! It's wonderful young, and with a little age becomes strangely like a top quality Chardonnay from Mâcon.

· LOMBARDY ·

If Piedmont seems to be the proud upholder of tradition and unmistakable 'personality' in north-west Italian wine, Lombardy must come as a bit of disappointment, because the last thing Lombardy seems to have is definable, historical character traits in her wine. With the huge industrial city of Milan as the focal point, and with the largest most cosmopolitan population of any Italian province, perhaps they are all too busy with money and careers and sophisticated living to realize they've got some first-rate wines on their doorstep.

It is weird, though. You can roam the streets of Milan, looking for bottles of Barbera and

Above Precipitous slopes at Manarola, Liguria. Until recently parts of the Cinqueterre vineyards could only be reached by boat.

Bonarda – the two commonest black grapes in Lombardy – and be offered wine from virtually every other province except Lombardy. Instead of locally produced *spumante*, you are assailed with fizz from Trentino, Piedmont – even France. But there are good local wines, so let's try to find them.

Oltrepò Pavese (DOC and vino da tavola) is the largest of Lombardy's wine zones – the name means 'across the Po from Pavia'. It includes red, white, rosé and sparkling wines – yet only 17 per cent of this 130 million bottles per year production is DOC. Many of the wines have fanciful names – like Buttafuoco which means 'sparks like fire', and is, in fact, a surprisingly good, dark, slightly fizzy red, and Sangue di Giuda, meaning 'Judas' blood', which is a frothy red – which only goes to show that, despite being Lombardy's most important zone, the basic name of Oltrepò Pavese is ineffectual; indeed, local producers themselves dismiss it as sounding cheap. However, the Barbera can be excellent, acid yet grapy at the

This Dolcetto is a good quality wine from a single defined area (Bussia), and is in a numbered bottle. The other label is interesting: Bricco Rocche is a single vineyard name, but it has been registered by Ceretto as a brand and has been used here on a wine from the Brunate vineyard, not even a neighbour.

same time, with its habitual hint of resin, and the Bonarda is one of Italy's most easily gluggable reds, mixing cherries and plums and liquorice with the tiniest of sparkles and an attractive bitter finish. The Oltrepò Pavese whites, along with the pale but tasty red Pinot Nero, usually end up as sparkling wine, though generally without any indication on the label that the grapes are from Oltrepò Pavese.

Valtellina (DOC) is made near the Swiss border from the Nebbiolo grape and the production is actually higher than that of Barolo, but, excepting the occasional quite tasty Superiore from the best sites, and the even rarer Sfursat bittersweet red from semi-dried grapes, Valtellina reds are hard and uninspiring.

Franciacorta Rosso (DOC) and **Valcalepio (DOC)** are better bets for attractive reds. In Franciacorta Nebbiolo is blended with Cabernet Sauvignon and Merlot to produce a grassy blackcurranty appetizing wine, and Valcalepio is the only Italian DOC permitting the Bordeaux mixture of Cabernet Sauvignon and Merlot.

Lugana (DOC) is the best of those whites which don't get processed for the fizz. It comes from a superior clone of the generally dull Trebbiano grape, and makes full, soft, nutty wine on the south-western shore of Lake Garda opposite Bardolino.

· LIGURIA ·

I have a good friend from Liguria. He is passionate about his homeland and I ask him to bring me back something from this thin crooked finger of coastline and towering mountains. So far he hasn't managed a single bottle because the tiny local producers always say their bottles are far too precious to their faith-ful Genovese customers to be wasted on a mere Englishman!

Ligurian vineyards are squashed into little patches of terrace where the unrelenting mountain slopes ease off for a few yards, so this scarcity means all the good stuff stays at home. There are, astonishingly, more than a hundred grape varieties, though only two DOCs.

Cinqueterre (DOC) is the most famous, and it used to make a great show of the fact that you could only reach its vineyards on their cliff-face terraces by boat. But don't buy it, its fame outstripped its quality long ago.

Rossese di Dolceacqua (DOC) is a red which, in its curiously heavy but perfumed way, I have found enjoyable enough to take my mind, momentarily, off the *pasta al pesto* steaming away in front of me.

Pigato (vino da tavola) and **Vermentino (vino da tavola)** are the most common whites, though I've found them so bruised and acetic as to need the *capponada* of local fish I was generally wolfing down at the time.

· VALLE D'AOSTA ·

The Valle d'Aosta doesn't make a great job of producing wine, but, my goodness they can toss it back. Although its production is the lowest of any Italian province, these mountain folk make sure it isn't wasted by registering the highest average per capita wine consumption in Italy! This would explain why you only come across about one Aosta wine a year outside the region itself. When you think that it's pretty cool up there at best, and vineyard land is negligible, they don't do too badly.

Blanc de Morgex (vino da tavola) and **Blanc de la Salle (vino da tavola)** are the sort of breath-catching acid whites you down in draughts on the spot, but would be mad to export.

Malvoisie de Nus (vino da tavola) and **Vin du Conseil (vino da tavola)**, from the nuts and apples-tasting Petite Arvine grape of Switzerland, might better stand the journey.

Donnaz (DOC), a red from Nebbiolo of all things, is surprisingly good.

Enfer d'Arvier (DOC), from the Petite Rouge grape, is like a strange, glacier-cool Syrah in a sharp, raspberryish way.

· FOOD AND WINE ·

I always seem to visit Piedmont at the wrong time of the year, because I'm normally touring about in August and September, while Piedmont wines and Piedmont food seem to match best as co-mates in comfort against the onset of winter cold. On the other hand, I seem to hit Aosta in the thick of winter to find wines and food far more suited to springtime and summer.

Well, that is a bit of a generalization, because *risotto alla milanese* – rice cooked in chicken broth and flavoured with saffron and Parmesan cheese and served with Osso Buco – has always tasted wonderful in winter, especially if it's helped down by the strong plummy fruit of a Bonarda or the tangy herbiness of a Barbera. And the pasta filled with pumpkin paste and nutmeg which I devoured in a little town just south of Lake Garda went marvellously with the full, nutty softness of the local Lugana. And in Aosta, though I'd rather be sitting out in the mountain pastures in July, picnicking on *bresaola* (wind-dried beef sliced wafer-thin) and the local cheese, I must admit a few bowls of *zuppa valpellinentze* – a soup full of cheese and ham and vegetables – washed down with Donnaz has done me pretty well after I've shaken the snow from my boots.

But Piedmont food is rarely picnic fare. The famous *bagna cauda* – a lethal sort of garlic and anchovy-dominated oil fondue in which you dip raw vegetables – or the cheese fondue – here called a *fonduta* and sometimes topped with shaved white truffles – are marvellous winter restoratives eaten with great draughts of Dolcetto or Freisa. *Bollito misto* is a boiled meats' hotchpotch served with a green garlicky sauce which is just made for a big rich Spanna. When you've gorged yourself on all this, you have two choices – either a long cooling drink of Asti Spumante, or the quiet 'meditation' provided by old rare Barolo or Barbaresco.

· GOOD PRODUCERS ·

Piedmont Gaja, Ceretto, Conterno, Bruno Giacosa, Produttori del Barbaresco, Pio Cesare, Franco-Fiorina, Ratti, Vietti, Poggio, Alfredo Roagna, Luciano Sandrone, Vallana.
Lombardy Ca' del Bosco, Berlucchi, Monte Rossa, Montorfano, Longhi-De Carli.

· MATURITY CHART ·
1982 BAROLO RISERVA
A big fruity year, but vintages vary widely

Bottled	Ready	Peak	Fading

0 1 2 3 4 5 6 7 8 9 10 11 12 13 14 15 16 17 18 19 20 Years

· CENTRAL ITALY ·

Everything seems so tranquil here at Pieve di Panzano in the heart of Chianti Classico, the traditional home of Italy's most famous red wine. This scene is repeated time and again in Tuscany – the vines, the olives, the cypress trees, a sprinkling of spring flowers, and the farmhouse with the hills rolling away into the distance.

To combine these widely differing wine regions, stretching from the Marches on the borders of Veneto down to Latium south of Rome, is not entirely arbitrary. There is a thread connecting them. The north of Italy is packed with DOC wines and is the home of freshly aromatic whites and well-defined reds based either on local grapes or imports from France and Germany. The south is the land of very few DOCs, overripe grapes and bland, heavy flavours dominating the handful of individual creations. Between these is the colourful, characterful centre of Italy where we gradually lose the aromatic, orchard-fresh styles of the north but still hold on to a wealth of individuality. Indeed for red wines, the centre, and in particular Tuscany,

already has some of the most exciting wines in Italy, and in future years will without question take the lead in the production of high quality reds, and possibly even of some barrel-aged styles of white.

· TUSCANY ·

Lovers of Tuscany talk of Michelangelo and Botticelli, of the effortless rise and fall of the Tuscan hills, the columns of cypress trees stalking the horizon, the silver-green clumps of olives splattered across the valley sides, and of course the wines, for this is the region of Chianti, of Brunello di Montalcino, and of Vino Nobile di Montepulciano, three of Italy's most celebrated reds.

The heart of Tuscany's wine regions, indeed

the heart of Tuscany, is the hauntingly beautiful hinterland of twisting, dipping hill valleys between Florence and Siena. These are the Chianti hills, and the site of the Classico region of Chianti. The name Chianti has been used to describe the wines of the district since the thirteenth century, but the area of production is now very much wider. Although at one time much of the wine was white, nowadays the name Chianti applies only to reds.

While Classico is the best, most traditional, area with a profusion of excellent vineyard sites, there are now six other areas. Chianti Rufina is just east of Florence on the Sieve river, while Colli Fiorentini (*colli* means 'hills' in Italian) is south and east of the city and the rivers Arno and Pesa. Both these can make excellent wine. Chianti Montalbano is west of Florence, but is better known for its enclave of Carmignano (DOC), while Colli Aretini to the south-east and Colline Pisane in the flatter land near Pisa make adequate light wine. The final zone is Colli Senesi a wide arc from the west to the south-east of Siena. This is the largest zone, and produces wine varying from the barely adequate to the exceptional.

The Consortium of Chianti Classico, the first consortium of growers formed in Italy to protect their wine's interests, marks the bottles with a black rooster. The other Chianti regions, grouped under the title Chianti Putto, use a faintly bucolic cherub as their symbol.

To the south and east are Brunello di Montalcino (DOCG) and Vino Nobile di Montepulciano (DOCG), two strong, intense red wines when they're made properly, and two overpriced shams when they aren't. And to the west of Chianti Classico, round San Gimignano, hilltop town of towers and turrets, is Tuscany's leading white – Vernaccia di San Gimignano.

· THE GRAPES ·

Sangiovese is the grape used for almost all the red DOC wines of Tuscany. It is blended with other varieties in Chianti and Vino Nobile di Montepulciano, but is the sole ingredient of Brunello di Montalcino. Sangiovese comes under various names, but all the finest wines are from old strains of Sangiovese Toscano. This is increasingly called Sangioveto to distinguish it from the Sangiovese di Romagna

Above San Gimignano is an old hill town bristling with Renaissance towers. It is also the centre for one of Tuscany's best white wines, Vernaccia di San Gimignano, made from the Vernaccia grape (*left*).

1   Chianti Classico
2   Chianti Colli Aretini
3   Chianti Colli Fiorentini
4   Chianti Colli Senesi
5   Chianti Colline Pisane
6   Chianti Montalbano
7   Chianti Rufina

0   40km
0   30 miles

MONTECARLO   main wines
ORRVIETO ●   wine towns

grape – a higher-yielding, lower quality version of Sangiovese from Emilia-Romagna, much planted in Chianti during the 1970s when quantity was thought to be more important than quality. The reverse is now true. There is too much poor Chianti and not enough good, and those vineyards planted with Sangioveto are always going to produce better, tastier wine. The Brunello grape in Brunello di Montalcino and the tasty-sounding Prugnolo Gentile in Vino Nobile di Montepulciano are basically similar to Sangioveto.

Cabernet Sauvignon and **Cabernet Franc** are the most important of other red grapes in Tuscany. Although they are feared by traditionalists as being the vanguard of an invasion of French ideas and styles, in fact they've been around in varying amounts since the nineteenth century. They are brilliantly suited to Tuscany. The flavours are deep and complex but also marvellously fresh and blackcurrant-juicy and capable of the mysterious cedary scent which makes the greatest Pauillacs from Bordeaux almost worth the price they ask. One wine – Sassicaia (*vino da tavola*), a 100 per cent Cabernet Sauvignon from Bolgheri on the coast is just about as

perfect an example of Cabernet Sauvignon as you can find; it *is* wildly expensive, but other examples of Cabernet, or, ideally, Cabernet-Sangiovese blends of which Antinori's Tignanello is the best known, are *not* expensive for wines of such quality.

Canaiolo, a component part of Chianti of diminishing importance, is the only other widely planted red grape.

Trebbiano is the leading white grape – not because it's the best – it isn't, it's the worst – but because there's so much of it. It is a neutral-tasting, high-yielding nonentity

through most of Italy. Disgracefully, it had come to constitute up to 30 per cent of the acreage in many parts of Chianti, and had to be blended into the red wine *by law*, with the consequent disintegration of whatever quality might have been lurking there. The DOCG regulations have now reduced the minimum white grape content in Chianti Classico to a mere 2 per cent, so at least good winemakers are not *forced* to compromise their standards simply because farmers had planted far too much Trebbiano over the years. Its chief characteristic is high acidity, and some new

Tuscan whites like the Galestros are now showing this somewhat one-dimensional personality to good effect.

Malvasia is also planted in the Chianti zone and elsewhere. Again it doesn't have much to offer a Chianti blend, and is rarely used for this purpose, but it does have a good, soft, nutty, even smoky character as a white wine, though it quickly fades and must be drunk young. Both these varieties are used to make the sweet, rather oxidized, dessert wine Vin Santo, though the Umbrian Grechetto grape is better suited.

Other white grapes Vernaccia is important for Vernaccia di San Gimignano. Elsewhere there are increasing amounts of Chardonnay as the 'new wave' winemakers, experimenting with small barrels and Cabernet Sauvignon for their reds, look to the world's superstar white grape for their white-wine forays. And there are varying amounts of Pinot Grigio, Pinot Bianco, Sauvignon, Sémillon and Roussanne – all of these figuring, amazingly, in Montecarlo, an impressive DOC from near Lucca. And in the south, at Montalcino, the American Villa Banfi company, who have invested a staggering $100 million in creating a space-age winery and a 700-hectare rising to 1,000-hectare vineyard, have planted half of it not with Sangioveto, but with Muscat – the Moscadello Toscano which they say is traditional to the region and which is now making a distinctly untraditional slightly fizzy sweet white!

There are three DOCGs and 21 DOCs – some pretty obscure – and a host of *vini da tavola* – often high quality wines choosing not to conform to DOC regulations. Tuscany has led the way for Italian experiments with the kind of wine-making methods which Bordeaux has used to propel herself to the top of the wine-making tree, and which California and Australia have also used to tremendous effect. These centre round the employment of small new French oak barrels to age the wine (the Bordeaux barrel is 225 litres, much smaller than the traditional Italian one, which is anyway more likely to be made of chestnut or Slovenian oak and pride itself on its antiquity). Wines can draw out richness and complexity from the vanillins and tannins present in the new wood of the small barrels, whereas the more traditionally Italian big, old barrels have nothing left to offer; excessive use of them merely serves to oxidize the wine and destroy its fruit.

· THE RED WINES ·

Chianti (DOCG) is the most important red wine in Italy in terms of volume, accounting for 16 per cent of the national DOC total with its average annual production of 170 million bottles. Since the application of DOCG rules in 1984 it is improving its image, helped by good to great vintages in 1982, 1983, 1985 and 1986. Sangiovese (Sangioveto) is the chief grape, comprising up to 90 per cent of the blend, Canaiolo is limited to 5 per cent, and white grapes to 2 per cent (slightly more of these are allowed in non-Classico wines). A maximum of 10 per cent of 'other' grapes are allowed. This enables growers to use the high quality and fashionable Cabernet Sauvignon – 10 per cent of Cabernet can make a dramatic difference to the wine.

Two sorts of wine are made. Ordinary Chianti may be released as early as 1 March following the harvest. Riserva may not be released until it is three years old. The Riservas are largely from the Classico and Rufina areas, though the Colli Senesi also produce some good examples. They *can* be tremendous, having a most arresting sweet-sour chewiness, and a rather fundamental grape-skin toughness, which can develop flavours of pepper and tobacco and tea leaves filled out with fruit which is occasionally reminiscent of blackcurrants or cherries, but more usually closer to prunes and raisins. Since the acidity always stays high, this can be delicious, but if the wine is aged too long in big old barrels it will lose its colour and fruit and you'll be left with a tart, orange-coloured mixture of acidity, peppery bite and tomatoes. The 'new wave' in Tuscany is now making this problem less common – thank goodness! Most Riservas are ready at four years, and don't want more than eight years. Some don't even survive four.

Basic Chianti is closer to the original style formulated by Baron Ricasoli in the nineteenth century, and is the norm in the lesser Chianti areas. Here the wine is made light, sharply fruity, and raspingly refreshing to be drunk young. This effect can be highlighted by the use of the *governo* technique – whereby a little concentrated grape must or, occasionally, dried grapes is added back to the finished

Vino Nobile di Montepulciano can be one of Italy's most impressive reds, and ageing in these large old wooden barrels is a crucial part of the maturing process; but if it is overdone, the wine can often end up dried out and fruitless.

wine, causing a slight re-fermentation. This creates more glycerine, but also a rather appetizing sourness and a very slight prickle on the tongue.

Brunello di Montalcino (DOCG), from some producers like Biondi-Santi Italy's most expensive red, is 100 per cent Sangioveto. It *should* have a deep dark colour, starting out intensely plummy and tannic, and maturing over 5–10 years into a marvellously individual flavour, your palate being assaulted by the pepper, acidity and tannin, yet soothed by an almost viscous richness of prunes and liquorice, meaty savouriness and bitter black chocolate. Few Brunello wines ever approach this ideal since excessive ageing in old wood is the norm here – they are supposed to spend at least 3½ years in the barrel – so it's often better to go for the DOC Rosso di Montalcino, which is the name used for the young reds – this can be superb, punchy stuff at 2–4 years old. Brunello cannot be released before four years, Riserva before five years.

Vino Nobile di Montepulciano (DOCG) This was once described as 'the king of wines'. Well, it isn't. Ever. But it *can* be good. The grapes are the same as for Chianti – although Cabernet doesn't usually put in an appearance – so the style is similar too, but at its best the slightly heavy sweet-sour raisiny quality is superseded by a creamy oak softness, a good bash of acidity, and then a delicious fruit mixing blackcurrant and cedar with an exhilarating dry sandalwood spice. As with Brunello, over-ageing in barrel is a major problem. The wine may be released at two years, Riserva at three years and Riserva Speciale at four years.

Single-estate Chianti Classico is increasingly being offered instead of monotonous blends. Villa Antinori is owned by the Marchesi Antinori, the leading figure in updating Chianti's image.

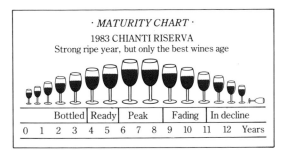

· *MATURITY CHART* ·
1983 CHIANTI RISERVA
Strong ripe year, but only the best wines age

Bottled	Ready	Peak	Fading	In decline
0 1 2	3	4 5 6 7 8	9 10	11 12 Years

Carmignano (DOC) A little area within the Chianti Montalbano zone, which produces a very good, slightly blackcurranty but patently Tuscan red from the Chianti mix of grapes with 6–10 per cent Cabernet Sauvignon. There is also a little rosé and Vin Santo.

Vini da Tavola There is a 'super-league' of *vini da tavola* in Tuscany. They do not qualify for DOC because, in general, they are reds aged in small oak barrels – which is not the local tradition – and often contain anything from 10–100 per cent Cabernet Sauvignon or Cabernet Franc. Sassicaia from near Bolgheri on the Tyrrhenian coast is a brilliant 100 per cent Cabernet, but most of the other Cabernet-only wines seem a little too tough although there is plenty of fruit behind them. Of these Sammarco, made on the Rampolla Chianti estate, is the most successful, having a gorgeous rich blackcurrant fruit tempered by a grassy freshness and some cedary spice. Otherwise the Cabernet-Sangiovese blends are best. Most famous is Antinori's Tignanello, followed by Ca' del Pazzo from Tenuta Caparzo in Montalcino, Grifi from Avignonesi in Montalcino, Cetinaia from San Polo in Rosso and Vigorello from San Felice. Wines like Coltassala from Volpaia, I Sodi from Castellare, Sangioveto di Coltibuono and Vinattieri Rosso, based on Sangioveto, are equally exciting, and can be delicious and bursting with class at only four years old. Up in them thar hills they're even doing the unthinkable and blending Nebbiolo with Sangioveto. And it works, creating an entirely new experience in Italian taste.

· *THE WHITE WINES* ·

Vernaccia di San Gimignano (DOC) It 'kisses, licks, bites, thrusts and stings'. Well,

it did, because that's Michelangelo's description of Vernaccia, but my experiences haven't been half so exciting. Even so, when it's on form, it can be delicious, blending a peppery edge with a surprisingly nutty fruit and a lick of honey. There's the 'lick', anyway.

Montecarlo (DOC) can be a cracker, as fat and succulent as lanolin and sharply acidic too. Good stuff.

Pomino (DOC) Sharp, dry, neutral but pleasantly full-bodied white from Chardonnay, Pinot Bianco and Trebbiano. Given oak treatment it can go way over the top and is often positively difficult to drink.

Bianco Vergine della Valdichiana (DOC) from the Chiana valley is a very attractive appley white when drunk really young.

Moscadello di Montalcino (DOC) We're going to be seeing a lot more of this courtesy of Villa Banfi, but so far, although there's lots of grapy fruit, it doesn't have the magic of good Moscato from Piedmont.

Galestro (vino da tavola) This is the chief grouping of lemon-sharp, sometimes slightly prickly whites which are being made to use up the excess Trebbiano and Malvasia now that their use in red wine has been restriced. At their best they are tangy and refreshing. Galestro has a *maximum* alcohol level of 10·5° to try to keep it that way. Some top estates go their own way with considerable success. Villa Antinori Bianco adds Chardonnay; Rampolla's Trebianco uses Gewürztraminer.

Chardonnay (vino da tavola) An increasing number of producers are having a go, usually ageing the wine in small new French oak barrels to give it creaminess and richness. The wines so far have been surprisingly tough for whites, and the oak and fruit aren't yet marrying perfectly. But as the vineyards mature, there are sure to be exciting wines.

Vin Santo (vino da tavola) The name, meaning 'holy wine', derives from the fact that Vin Santo was traditionally racked off its lees during Holy Week, when atmospheric pressure was reckoned to be most suitable due to the phase of the moon. It is a strong wine made sweet, semi-sweet or dry from semi-dried Trebbiano and Malvasia grapes. Avignonesi makes a fiendishly expensive but reliably luscious example; but other exciting examples are few and far between. For my money the next best is made by Adanti in Umbria.

· ABRUZZI ·

Abruzzi, a largely mountainous province due east of Rome, has always been sufficiently poor to be included in 'the South', but enormous sums of government money have been poured in recently and the province is gradually moving away from its earlier 'poverty-line' image. The inhabitants must be helped by the presence of at least one of Abruzzi's two DOCs – Montepulciano d' Abruzzo.

Montepulciano d'Abruzzo (DOC) is a thoroughly enjoyable and reliable red – always full of a strong plummy fruit matched by a chewiness and a slightly citrous acidity. The Montepulciano is a first-class grape wherever it grows (confusingly, it does *not* grow in the Tuscan town of Montepulciano).

Trebbiano d'Abruzzo (DOC) on the other hand is not so memorable. The Trebbiano is always a lesser grape, although these winemakers do use a superior clone of the basic variety to produce an adequate nutty dry white.

· LATIUM ·

I really would rather spend my time talking about the gorgeous vine-clad Alban hills above Rome where the Pope lives when it gets too hot in the Vatican, and where the steep rock-faces have little towns clinging like limpets to their sides, than talk about the local wines, since, unless you have a local guide well-versed in the hostelries of the hills, you're going to find it jolly difficult to sample the stuff. I spent a pretty dispiriting hour or two recently wandering around the admittedly delightful streets of Frascati looking for a decent glass of wine of that name. The first three places I tried had none at all, and the others charged me handsomely for the privilege of a pretty inferior snifter.

Frascati (DOC), is the chief Latium white, and is based on the Malvasia and Trebbiano grapes – as always, the less Trebbiano the better. It does have a most original flavour, which, absolutely fresh and unflustered by travelling, or even, ideally, by bottling, is a

Left The Marches are better known for beautiful beaches than fine wines. But in the rolling hills of the hinterland the famous light dry white Verdicchio is made as well as soft reds like Rosso Piceno and Rosso Cònero.

mix of apples and nuts, with a weird and wonderful soft butteriness veering between sour cream and toffee! There are now a few examples leaving the area which are true to this style. Drunk as young as possible, they can still be pleasantly unnerving.

Marino (DOC) and **Montecompatri (DOC)**, neighbours to Frascati, are very similar, with the Marino being a fuller wine and the Montecompatri pleasantly apple-fresh.

Other wines Latium's flat sprawl is largely reflected in its lesser wines. Exceptions are the grapy, dusty reds of Velletri, the good juicy Aprilia Merlots from Santarelli (they even make a reasonable white Trebbiano) and the sturdy Cerveteri reds. There is one other famous, nay, infamous white north of Rome past Viterbo called Est! Est!! Est!!! This seems to mean,'It is! It is!! It is!!!' –' the best', I suppose – and shows that at one time these wines were capable of sending people into raptures. Not any more; most producers are keener on making sure the label will attract the passing tourist trade than trying to achieve the warm, rounded almonds and angelica flavour the wine is capable of.

· THE MARCHES ·

The Italian view of the Marches is slightly different to ours. We tell them knowingly that

Frascati is the commonest Latium wine, and most of the wines are made by the local co-ops. Superiore simply means the wine has a minimum of 12 per cent alcohol. Most of Latium's wines are white, and the majority are grown in the hills to the south-east, but Cerveteri is a pleasant red grown in the flat area north of Rome.

Away from the plains of Emilia-Romagna the Colli Bolognese give a wide variety of good vineyard sites where increasingly interesting wines are being made.

In Tuscany in particular, although it's perfectly possible to say which years had the right weather conditions to produce delicious wine, it's much less easy to say that a particular year's wine is *good*. The reason is that, more than in most areas, the varying methods of making the wine can crucially affect the quality of the end product. Unfortunately, several obviously detrimental practices – like excessive wood ageing in Brunello di Montalcino, and the permitted use not only of white grapes, but also of musts from completely different parts of Italy in various parts of Chianti (*not* Classico), are still enshrined in DOC and DOCG law. Since the Sangiovese grape is not a variety with enough weight to suffer dilution gladly or enough fruit to survive, two, three, four or even more years in a fusty old barrel, the following notes are *only* generalizations. All the white wines should be drunk within two years, and most of the reds, excepting top examples of DOCG, within four.

1986 is very good to superb for reds which are medium-weight, with lots of fruit and balance. The increasingly modern approach to wine-making with use of stainless steel, controlled fermentation temperatures, and reduced ageing in big old barrels, will make them more consistent too. Whites are very good for quick drinking.

1985 is brilliant for reds – dark, intense concentrated wines of great potential. Again, modern winemaking will allow the proportion of good wines to be high. Whites were often just too ripe and top-heavy.

1984 is pretty feeble for reds, although the whites had a delicious sharp fruit unusual in the area. Now fading.

1983 A very hot, drought-affected vintage. Some blockbusters, but only when the tannin doesn't swamp the fruit. Whites now tired.

1982 Excellent – perfect ripening conditions led to a wonderful harvest of ripe grapes.

the best, the most famous, and the only decent wine in the region is Verdicchio. They rejoin, 'Which Verdicchio?' Having put us in our place about that, they will then suggest that we try a glass or two of Rosso Piceno next time we're in town, because *that* is the largest DOC of the region, and in some people's minds the *best* wine made there too.

Of course, it would rather depend on why you were in the Marches in the first place, because this long hilly knuckle of sea-board running down Italy's east coast below Emilia is a province with two totally different faces. Many people come to fry themselves in the sun on the beaches which seem to stretch almost unhindered along the province's entire length. A few hours of self-inflicted basting doesn't build up much of a thirst for a serious red. But if you head off into the Apennines and explore the lovely mountain scenery which runs from Urbino in the north to Ascoli Piceno in the south, and beyond, that will put you in the mood for Rosso Piceno or its brother red Rosso Cònero.

Rosso Piceno (DOC), from a mix of 60 per cent Sangiovese and 40 per cent Montepulciano grapes, is a fairly strong red, quite biting in the herby, sharp way the Sangiovese has,

but fattened out in a pretty blunt way by the Montepulciano. There is sometimes a slight prickle to the wine, because the *governo* system of inducing a slight, refreshing re-fermentation may still be used here.

Rosso Cònero (DOC) is the more exciting wine because it is at least 85 per cent, if not 100 per cent, Montepulciano. Suddenly you're mixing herbs with a rather blatant plums and raisin fruit and sharpening that up with a citrous, resiny edge as well. One or two people like Mecvini are even using small oak barrels, to good effect.

Verdicchio (DOC and vino da tavola) is, even so, the province's most famous wine to us foreigners, and especially Verdicchio dei Castelli di Jesi (DOC) which is the second most popular DOC in the United States after Soave, probably due to its green amphora bottle which isn't original at all – it was invented in the 1950s as a sales gimmick! The Verdicchio grape is usually mixed with Trebbiano and Malvasia and the result is at the very least one of the cleanest, frankest dry whites in Italy – a genuinely good 'sea-food' wine. When you're lucky, it can have a splendid smoky apples fruit with a touch of honey. Verdicchio di Matelica (DOC) is rarer, but less exploited

and with a fuller, fruitier flavour. And there's even sparkling Verdicchio which is very much in the Italian mainstream of clear, dry wines, a little neutral, but refreshing.

· EMILIA-ROMAGNA ·

Emilia-Romagna is a botch-up of a province because there are eight different, very definable, regions in this extensive, primarily flat chunk of Italy stretching from the Adriatic to past Piacenza along the southern banks of the River Po. This explains why, if you compile a list of all the province's wines, they run into hundreds – although there certainly aren't 100 recognizable wine types, and only about 6 per cent of this vinous tide is DOC; it's just that every style is repeated at least eight times! This goes for wines from the Trebbiano and Sangiovese grapes and, above all, for that much maligned but unique creation – Lambrusco.

It is fitting that the city of Bologna, the provincial capital of Emilia-Romagna, should be called, with a mixture of admiration and envy, the 'belly' of Italy, because Emilia-Romagna does its capital proud – producing astonishing amounts of gulping wine for their gargantuan meals. This one Italian province will usually produce more wine than the *entire* national output of such important wine nations as West Germany, Portugal and Yugoslavia.

The chief reason is that Emilia-Romagna, unusually in a country as mountainous as Italy, has enormous tracts of flat, valley-floor land, and, equally unusually in a country where vines normally occupy the hillier parts so that the plains can grow food, the plains are swamped with vines. Most vines pump out Lambrusco, red, white or rosé, sweet (*amabile*) or dry (*secco*), DOC or non-DOC, according to the market demand.

Lambrusco (DOC and vino da tavola) The name refers also to a *grape*, with rather a high acidity and a sharply refreshing raw raspberry fruit. DOC Lambrusco is made from this grape

or one of its subvarieties like Grasparossa, and the strong, almost fermentation-vat acid fruit is the chief reason why this mildly fizzy, low-alcohol wine is so refreshing. Cheaper Lambruscos are also made in the region without DOC but they are usually too sweet, and lack the crucial acidity, as well being less fizzy and in screw-top bottles – the Superiore DOC cannot have a screw-top to the bottle. These are pale imitations of what can be a really good drink. Lambrusco, most of it non-DOC, is a phenomenal success in the United States, holding around half of all the imports of Italian wine, and this is chiefly due to the efforts of Riunite, the massive co-operative conglomerate (almost half of Emilia-Romagna's output is controlled by co-operatives).

Albana di Romagna (DOCG) is made in the Apennines just to the south where there is a far wider variety of flavours and styles. This pleasant but hardly distinguished wine achieved notoriety when it became, quite undeservedly, the first white DOCG. Politics, not quality, we have to thank for that.

Other wines Elsewhere Trebbiano and Sangiovese dominate proceedings and are fine if they're drunk in the first juicy flush of youth. They don't age. There is also a certain amount of Chardonnay (vino da tavola), Sauvignon (DOC), Cabernet and Merlot (vino da tavola and DOC), which don't age either, but which are absolutely delicious for a year or so. And over in the Colli Piacentini (DOC), on the Piedmont-Lombardy border, there are the big, dark, grapy wines from Barbera and Bonarda, with Bonarda in particular being liquoricey and

soft, and Gutturnio (DOC), a Barbera/Bonarda blend, mixing the liquorice with good acidity and a raspberry freshness.

· UMBRIA ·

Umbria is a heady mixture of wine styles. It is the home of Orvieto, one of the most famous of all Italian wines, which has been made for over 2,000 years and which had its heyday as the deep golden draught which kept the Renaissance artists' spirits up if their inspiration showed signs of flagging. It is also the home of Dr Lungarotti, one of Italy's most indefatigable self-publicists but also a brilliant 'creator' and innovator, whose range of reds and whites from his vineyards at Torgiano outside Perugia can be thrillingly different to what we have come to expect of Italy. *And* it is the home of some of the great, unsung, 'artisanal' originals, in particular from the Grechetto and Sagrantino grapes, wines neither dry nor sweet, neither fruity nor austere, but unashamedly delicious.

Orvieto (DOC) hails from the town of the same name perched on a huge rocky outcrop which you come across suddenly as you drive up the Rome-Florence *autostrada*, but which you only fully appreciate if you approach it on the back road from Montefiascone. The rocks are so steep and angular they resemble Gothic arches with the houses rising sheer and precarious from the cliff face. Present-day Orvieto is rarely better than typically modern, over-clean dry white, but the potential is there, both for dry wines and semi-sweet. Ideally the wine should be really *golden*, with Grechetto and Malvasia grapes edging out the Trebbiano. Both dry (*secco*) and semi-sweet (*abboccato*) should be full, nutty and smoky, with a touch of honey and even some peachy orchard freshness. Bigi's and Barbi's single vineyard wines from the central Classico area are the best examples.

Grechetto (vino da tavola) by itself has a full, slightly liquoricy, apple and greengage freshness, and it can also have a smoky perfume – but it isn't DOC.

Sagrantino (DOC and vino da tavola), especially in Montefalco where it is DOC, is splendid, rip-roaring stuff, plummy, strawberryish, raisiny and tobaccoey all in turns. I once

LUNGAROTTI

Cabernet Sauvignon DI MIRALDUOLO
1979

VINO DA TAVOLA DELL'UMBRIA
PRODOTTO E IMBOTTIGLIATO DALLE
CANTINE LUNGAROTTI S.p.A. - TORGIANO - ITALIA

e 75 cl   12% vol

PRODOTTO IN ITALIA

CASTELLO di LUZZANO

GUTTURNIO
DEI COLLI PIACENTINI
vino a denominazione di origine controllata

Imbottigliato all'origine dalla
"Azienda Agricola Luzzano" Ziano P.no (Italia)
M. G. FUGAZZA

lt. 0.750 ℮   PRODUCE OF ITALY   12 % vol.

Single-estate wines are not common in Emilia-Romagna, but in the hills above Bologna and Piacenza quality-conscious producers are beginning to bottle their own. Gutturnio is a traditional wine made of Barbera. The Cabernet is from the Miralduolo vineyard inside the Torgiano DOC, but made solely from Cabernet rather than the Sangiovese-based blend the DOC requires.

The lovely town of Orvieto on its outcrop of rock turning golden in the evening sun. Orvieto's best wine is golden too, full of soft, nutty flavours and very slightly sweet.

noted it down as a 'rash' wine, meaning, I suppose, one would be rash to essay more than a little at a time. Sometimes it is made sweet, and the damson and plum and chocolate richness, balanced by acid and tannin, is really exciting and *very* 'rash' indeed.

Torgiano (DOC) comes from the flat Tiber valley south of Perugia. Torgiano is a one-horse town, with Dr Lungarotti virtually owning the DOC, and the following wines are all his. The best wines without doubt are the special Riservas although the ultra-fresh white Torre di Giano is almost 'Alto Adige' in its crisp youthful fruit. The Lungarotti red Rubesco Torgiano is round and mellow but always tastes to me as though it never quite finished fermenting. However the Rubesco Riserva Monticchio is a different story. Based on Sangiovese, Canaiolo, Montepulciano and Ciliegiolo (a form of Sangiovese) and aged in newish barrels, it is oaky and smooth like creamed coconut but there is loads of soft, almost sweet fruit to back it up.

San Giorgio (vino da tavola), using Cabernet Sauvignon, Canaiolo and Sangiovese grapes, is also a very good wine, gently black-currant and drinkable quite young.

Cabernet Sauvignon di Miralduolo is 100 per cent Cabernet, and a pure, blackcurranty red which needs 7–10 years to soften and bloom. The Miralduolo vineyard – the nearest thing to a decent hill-site in the DOC – also produces an exceptional oaked Chardonnay.

Just to show that nothing is too daunting for Dr Lungarotti he produces a 'sherry' called Solleone which, I have to say, is absolutely delicious and would put many of Spain's originals to shame.

· GOOD PRODUCERS ·

Tuscany Antinori, Badia a Coltibuono, Rampolla, Volpaia, San Polo in Rosso, Fonterutoli, San Felice, Amorosa, Capezzana (Chianti); Frigeni (Vernaccia di San Gimignano); Biondi-Santi, Altesino, Il Poggione, Col d'Orcia, Caparzo (Montalcino); Avignonesi, Poliziano (Nobile).
Abruzzi Pepe, Mezzanotte, Casal Thaulero.
Latium Colli di Catone, Gotto d'Oro.
Marches Colonnara, Garofoli.
Emilia-Romagna Vallania, Luzzana, Paradiso.
Umbria Lungarotti, Adanti, Bigi, Barbi.

· FOOD AND WINE ·

Some people don't know how lucky they are. The Umbrians pride themselves on their unsophisticated cuisine and yet they are Italy's leading producers of one of the all-time expensive indulgences – truffles. The Umbrians are canny, though; they sell them rather than eat them, just keeping back the odd batch for simple dishes like *spaghetti alla norcina*, where the pasta is served with a cream sauce and topped with shaved truffles, or the *crostini alla norcina* – little croutons covered in an anchovy, garlic, olive oil and black truffle sauce. The best Orvieto or Grechetto I could find is what I'd drink with these.

I've always found Roman food difficult to match with wine, since the flavours all pile on top of each other, and that's probably why the glugging whites of Frascati and Marino are drunk perfectly happily with just about anything. But Tuscany is very much a wine and food land, especially since the local reds positively demand food much of the time. Tuscans are called 'bean eaters' and certainly the local beans are good, whether they're the tiny early-season broad beans known as *fave* and eaten raw in their pods, or *fagioli all' uccelletto* haricots with tomatoes, garlic, oil and herbs. Youngest, gutsiest Sangiovese red or new Chianti is what I'd drink with them. This would also go pretty well with *pappa di Pomodoro* – bread soaked in wine vinegar, squeezed out, mashed with tomato, basil and local olive oil then served with even more olive oil trickled over it.

To accompany the expensive reds, I'd plump for the local Valdichiana beef, which, charcoal-grilled *alla Fiorentina* is served yet again with beans but tastes far more exciting than that sounds. And every year when I leave Tuscany, my last act is to pop into the local market at Cortona and take away a hunk of the tangiest, most piercingly delicious *pecorino* cheese, so tasty that it softens the stern flavours of mature Riserva Chianti or Brunello di Montalcino.

In Emilia-Romagna, I easily slip into a gourmandizing role. Every sort of pasta with every sort of filling I down, hot *piadine* – dishes of unleavened bread looking like Indian nan, but here stuffed with cheese or ham – and those cheeses – Parmesan is a local cheese – and the hams; all these I guzzle – and with most of them I want draughts of bubbly, purple red Lambrusco, preferably dry, but definitely young.

· SOUTHERN ITALY ·

Vineyards near Alcamo, in the western part of Sicily where they produce quantities of soft dry white wine.

The time is coming for the wines of southern Italy. After generations of anonymity, when the only names we knew were Marsala from Sicily and Lacryma Christi from Naples – well, that's where they were supposed to come from – and when the only flavour we knew from the south was the tough, thick jammy fruit which seemed to turn up in cheap wine of all colours and from all countries – and which usually originated in the chock-full vineyards of Apulia in Italy's heel, whatever the label said – things are changing.

They have to, because as domestic wine consumption drops in volume terms, but increases in quality terms, only those who aim for quality will survive. The south of Italy is one of Europe's earliest vineyard sites, and many of the strange grape varieties down there have been producing their fruit since the Greeks first arrived. There is the possibility of great, exciting wine to be made, dramatically different from what we are used to at present. To achieve this, two things will have to be done: one is to persuade the producers to put in the effort and commitment which fine wine requires; the other will be for *us* to be brave and step off our well-trodden paths for a taste of something unique which can trace its ancestry back thousands of years. I'm optimistic, but I'm not sure either side is quite ready yet.

· MOLISE ·

The only thing Molise has ever had in its favour is that it is wet. To find somewhere in the south where they curse the rain is virtually unheard of anyway, but this rain is probably Molise's single source of wealth – it is now being conserved in vast lakes which will supply crucial irrigation to other regions further south. Since Molise is virtually 100 per cent hills and mountains, it doesn't need much of the water itself. I suppose they could use the water to dilute the wine because, until recently, Molise had *no* wines thought worthy of DOC. There are now two – each one for red, white and rosé – Biferno di Campobasso and Pentro di Isernia, but the quality still isn't up to much.

· CAMPANIA ·

This absurdly beautiful region round the Bay of Naples and beneath Mount Vesuvius with its crumbly volcanic soil is wonderfully suited to the vine. Indeed most of the wines the Romans and Greeks waxed wet-eyed and lyrical about came from Campania – the site of the fabled Falernum vineyards is only an hour's drive north of Naples. Yet most Campanian wines are hopeless – even in a café in Naples they're not terribly inviting.

Lacryma Christi (vino da tavola) Less than one per cent of the Campania's considerable production is DOC, and although the authorities have tried to get the Lacryma Christi growers to submit to DOC regulations, they still haven't signed on the dotted line – since the name has become so debased, who cares about quality anyway?

There are a few bright spots.

Vesuvio (DOC) now encompasses some Lacryma Christi vineyards, and although the wine can be red, it is often best as a fairly sweet white. Inland, round the town of Avellino, Mastroberardino, one of Italy's more self-confident and renowned winemakers, produces several fascinating wines.

Taurasi (DOC), a red from Aglianico grapes, is no fun when it's young, but given at least five years age and preferably ten, it develops a chocolate and liquorice richness, thrown into disarray by high acidity, herbs and a 'Mr Universe' beefy texture which is nothing if not impressive.

Greco di Tufo (DOC), a peppery, liquoricy white, is easier to deal with.

Fiano di Avellino (DOC) isn't, tasting like apple skins steeped in well-used stable straw. They say you have to try it at least seven times to appreciate it. I'm well past that, yet no nearer.

· BASILICATA ·

It can't be a lot of fun living in Basilicata. It's very rugged, it's barren, it's windswept, it's *cold* – amazingly the capital Potenza is frequently cooler than Bolzano, Italy's most northerly city just a few miles away from Austria. The bad luck seems further compounded by its tiny wine production – only Valle d'Aosta produces less as a province. This fairly miserable state of affairs is somewhat alleviated by one famous wine – Aglianico del Vulture. It's a red wine grown from the late-ripening Aglianico grape way up on the cool, uninviting slopes of Mount Vulture, but in the hands of the best grower, Fratelli d'Angelo, it can sometimes achieve an amazing flavour: chocolate richness, the bitter-sweet bite of almonds and the perfume of green peppercorns, with a dusty southern starkness too and a streak of acidity which in less good producers' hands can get out of control, but with him stops just the right side of dangerous.

· CALABRIA ·

Calabria is an absolutely gorgeous place, with hardly a square mile of dull, flat land, and instead an exhilarating succession of craggy mountains and swooping hillsides ending abruptly in cliff-edges which drop down to tiny bays and warm arcs of bleached sea-side sand. But that means there isn't a great deal of wine, and most of what there is is gulped down pretty sharpish by the locals. Cirò (DOC) is the most famous wine, but the only one that's really grabbed me is the Greco di Bianco (DOC), or Greco di Gerace, which is a challenging mixture of straw from the stable and a rich, sweet, orange peel fruit. Certainly *not* for the timid, but good.

· APULIA ·

Apulia is the 'heel' of Italy, and probably has as bad a reputation as any of Italy's wine regions. This is really because the grape grows easily and naturally here, and many of the vines ripen as early as August, so that the temptation to slip them off to the cooler north of Italy, but also France and Germany, to 'beef up' their less full-blooded brews has been difficult to resist. But recently Apulia has been attempting to improve the quality, which is long overdue. It was the global downturn in consumption of basic everyday wines in favour of something better which thankfully forced their hands.

There are 20 DOCs, but these cover only two per cent of the province's wines, and as so often in Italy, the DOCs aren't necessarily the best wines. There are a fair number of 'new-style' whites and rosés, crystal-clear, dry, straight as a die – and there *is* Chardonnay, Sauvignon Blanc and Pinot Blanc in the vineyards. So far these are all clinically correct, yet without real style; they are a big improvement, nonetheless.

The reds are more exciting because Apulia already possesses two good grapes: Negroamaro which means 'bitter black' and, mixed with Malvasia Nera as in the Patriglione of Brindisi, can have an intense bitter chocolate and pine resin taste, and Primitivo, a burly early-

Rincione is a table wine without a DOC, but from a specific area – in this case Calatafimi in western Sicily.

ripening grape which may well be the same as California's Zinfandel. These are the archetypal hefty blending reds, but can be exciting mouthfuls by themselves, though rarely as good as the juicy DOC red based on Montepulciano – Castel del Monte.

· SARDINIA ·

What Sardinia has most in its favour is the presence of one of Italy's most forward-looking companies – Sella and Mosca – in the northwest of the island. They have completely transformed the image of the island's wines, and, if you're after old-style hill-bandit flavours, then I'm afraid they, and a couple of very modern co-operatives, have rather messed things up for you – because the general level of taste is bland and easy-going. If you're looking for more personality, then go for the dry but amazingly strong, sherry-like Vernaccia (DOC), the less exciting, but rather more adaptable dry white Torbato (*vino da tavola*), and the potentially outstanding Cannonau (DOC and *vino da tavola*) which when made red and sweet, as in the Sella and Mosca Anghelu Ruju (*vino da tavola*) is an impressive rich and plummy dessert wine. The best known Sardinian DOCs are the white Nuragus and Vermentino – usually light, dry and pleasingly forgettable. Non-DOC versions can be better.

· SICILY ·

Sicily is unrecognizable from the hide-bound, tradition-steeped island of closed doors and dark secrets that it was 20 years ago. Then the wines were thick, hot-tasting and torpor-inducing – which may explain why Sicilians

drink less wine than other Italians. It's all change now. Production has more than doubled – some years more is produced than in *any* other Italian region – and it is chiefly light, fresh, simple wines of remarkably good quality. There is a white DOC Alcamo, and Etna is a DOC for all colours, but all the best wines are sold as vino da tavola. The whites are usually quite substantial but remarkably fresh – there is a little acid Sauvignon on the island – and the reds have a deep old-fashioned plums and chocolate style, without the harsh pressed grape-skins taste of many other southern reds. Names to look for are Settesoli, Regaleali, Libecchio, Rapitalà and Corvo Colomba Platino.

However, the most wonderful Sicilian products are the fortified wines.

Marsala (DOC), a long-forgotten name (except by people who make *zabaglione*), is undergoing a revival. There is a distinctive smoky, even slightly acid tang in the wine which itself veers between nutty dry and syrup sweet. **Moscato di Pantelleria (DOC)**, a deep, dark, gooey Muscat wine from a tiny island within a giant's spit of Africa, is impressive. **Malvasia delle Lipari (DOC)**, a lovely raisins, brown sugar and peaches sweet wine from islands just north-west of Messina, is just occasionally available and must be snapped up.

· FOOD AND WINE ·

Naples sets the tone for food and wine in the south – simple ingredients, fresh from the fields or from the sea, seasoned with herbs and eaten in a rush with draughts of nameless local wine. The *pizza napoletana* – so simple it is merely crust, tomato, oregano and basil, no cheese – is the most famous dish, one of the most famous in the world; and throughout the south dishes are more likely to be based on dough and pasta livened up with vegetables and herbs, than on meat. There is a certain amount of lamb and goat, especially in Sardinia, but wherever the coastline is close, fish and seafood are far more important. It sometimes seems as though the only indulgence in the south, especially Calabria and Sicily, is the dessert, with the riotous party of chocolate and fruit flavours of the *cassata alla siciliana* featuring as one of the most over-indulgent cakes of all time.

· SPAIN ·

Spain must be proud to have exclusive rights to the world's most widely-planted grape. It's called Airén. Well, no, I hadn't heard of it until a few years ago either, and, until I made a determined foray into the arid plains of La Mancha south of Madrid, I wasn't even sure I'd tasted it. But I had, hundreds of times. It's just that it was too shy to put its name on the label. Every bottle of Spanish 'Chablis' or Spanish 'Sauternes' I'd had would have been Airén. Every bottle of brand-name Spanish dry/medium/sweet white was the same. But I couldn't tell you what it tasted like. Well, could you? 'Spanish white' is usually the cheapest white on the shelf. We don't buy it for the taste; we buy it because we want the cheapest possible drinkable wine.

That, in a nutshell, has been the problem facing Spanish wines: a gross excess of uninspiring grape varieties, and an image firmly rooted in the bargain basement. It may come as another surprise to learn that it isn't France, or Italy, or Germany – the countries hogging the most room on the wine shop shelves – which have the world's biggest acreage of grapes, but Spain. Yes, Spain has a staggering 3,953,545 acres (1,600,000 hectares) of vines, as against France's 2,718,000 acres (1,100,000 hectares) and Italy's 2,804,546 (1,135,000). Poor old Germany only has 237,721 (96,200)! In the world top 20 for grape varieties, Spain has five almost exclusively – the Airén, Macabeo (France has a bit of this) and Xarel-lo whites, and the Monastrell and Bobal reds – as well as the lion's share of the world's most widely-planted red, Garnacha Tinta (again France has most of the rest), and over half the Garnacha Blanca.

Why, if these varieties are so prolific, are they so anonymous? They're not good enough, that's why. Except for Garnacha (the French Grenache) hardly anyone has bothered to export these vines. As for the great international varieties like Cabernet Sauvignon, Chardonnay and Riesling, the amounts as yet planted in Spain are so tiny that they don't rate a percentage point in the global total.

It is as though the Pyrenees provide a highly effective two-way obstacle between Spain and the rest of Europe. Very little wine is imported *into* Spain, while the country's own vineyards have primarily concerned themselves with supplying large amounts of basic wine to an uncritical, but overwhelmingly wine-drinking, population. However, as the affluence of northern Europe slowly seeps south, and the advent of EEC membership forces open the psychological and geographical barriers Spain has existed behind for centuries, a dramatic change has come about. Wine is suddenly seen as an 'old-timers' preference; beer, spirits and soft drinks appear more 'chic'. The result is a drastically declining internal consumption and little prospect of alternative export markets at anything above subsistence prices.

Certainly the lack of interesting grape varieties is a problem, but at least excessive yield is not. Despite its enormous acreage, Spain's average crop produces only 23 hectolitres per hectare as against France's 60 hectolitres per hectare and Germany's 90 hectolitres per hectare or more, while Italy easily outstrips all these countries in total production. This is because Spain is an extremely dry country – except for the vinously unimportant coast below the Bay of Biscay where it seems never to stop raining – and vines are usually only planted on land which isn't fertile enough to grow other crops. Since irrigation is banned and vineyard practices are still pretty archaic, the crop remains small, the quality poor, and the income pitiful.

Things *must* change, and, thank goodness, they are, but it's a struggle. The Spanish *denominación de origen* system is a case in point.

The round white windmills were once the only distinguishing feature of La Mancha in Central Spain. Nowadays more utilitarian wind pumps are a commoner sight, but this line of targets for Don Quixote still stalks the ridge of low hills near Consuegra.

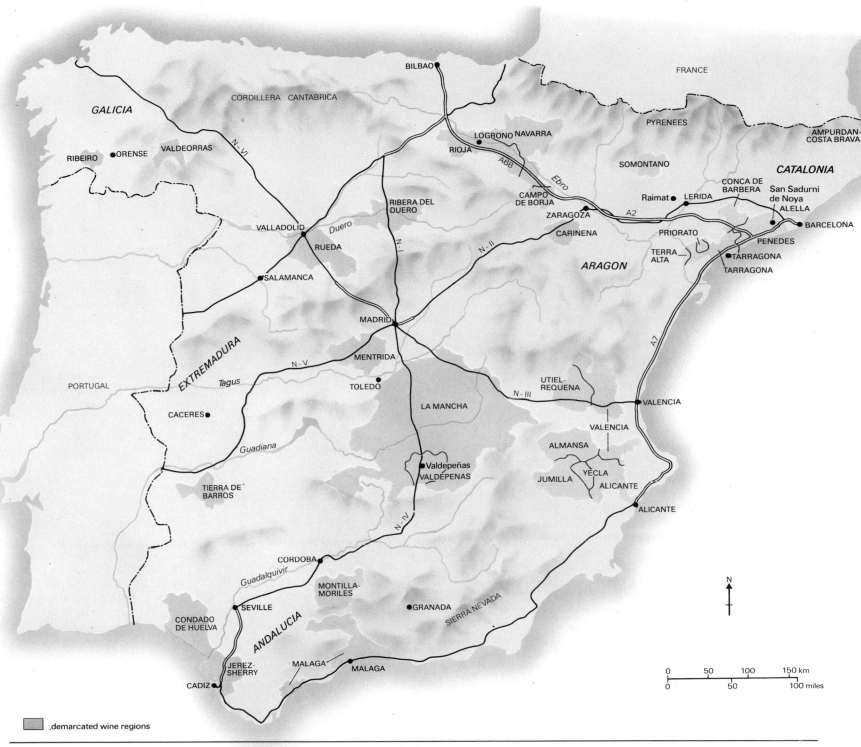

GALICIA

CORDILLERA CANTABRICA

BILBAO

FRANCE

PYRENEES

AMPURDAN-
COSTA BRAVA

RIBEIRO ●ORENSE VALDEORRAS

N-VI

LOGRONO NAVARRA

RIOJA

A68

SOMONTANO

CATALONIA

RIBERA DEL
DUERO

Ebro

CAMPO
DE BORJA

CONCA DE
BARBERA

San Sadurní
de Noya

Raimat ● LERIDA

ALELLA

VALLADOLID

Duero

ZARAGOZA

A2

BARCELONA

RUEDA

CARINENA

PRIORATO

PENEDES

●SALAMANCA

ARAGON

TERRA
ALTA

●Tarragona

TARRAGONA

MADRID

EXTREMADURA

MENTRIDA

N-I

N-II

A7

N-V

Tagus

PORTUGAL

TOLEDO

LA MANCHA

UTIEL-
REQUENA

N-III

VALENCIA

CACERES ●

VALENCIA

Guadiana

ALMANSA

TIERRA DE
BARROS

Valdepeñas
VALDEPENAS

JUMILLA

YECLA

ALICANTE

N-IV

ALICANTE

CORDOBA

Guadalquivir

MONTILLA-
MORILES

SEVILLE

GRANADA

SIERRA NEVADA

CONDADO
DE HUELVA

ANDALUCIA

JEREZ-
SHERRY

MALAGA

MALAGA

CADIZ

N

0   50   100   150 km
0   50   100 miles

demarcated wine regions

Like the French *appellation contrôlée* system it attempts to guarantee the geographical origin of the wines, the grape varieties used, the permitted yields and so on. It covers over half of Spain's vineyards, yet there are only 31 DOs (as they are called) in total. The vast central region of La Mancha has almost 25 per cent of the national total acreage yet just four DOs: La Mancha (much smaller than the geographical area), Valdepeñas, Mentrida and Almansa. So, unfortunately, most of the DOs mean very little and give scant idea of style or even quality.

In fact, in Spain itself, there are only three wines which are regarded as 'quality' across the board, and in plush restaurants from the Costa Brava to Cádiz you'll find them featured, while the local wines are served anonymously in carafe. These are Cava (*méthode champenoise* sparkling wine), Rioja, the DO traditionally and rightly seen as Spain's most significant red wine, and now producing good whites as well. And then there's Torres. Torres isn't a place, and it isn't a DO – it's a man, or rather two men. The father is one of Spain's best salesmen, and the son is one of the world's greatest winemakers. They don't believe in DO but from their redoubt in Penedés they produce Spain's finest range of red, white and rosé wines.

Although Torres leads the way, it is interesting that many of the most exciting wines now emerging from elsewhere in Spain are following the same path – intelligent selection of native and imported grape varieties, up-to-the-minute wine-making techniques, and also a brusque dismissal of DO restraints which inhibit experimentation and limit wine-growing to traditional grape varieties vinified traditionally in traditional areas.

As in Italy and in southern France, the laudable attempts to create some order out of chaos which fired the whole movement for appellations of origin have created straitjackets for innovative forward-looking winemakers, since they enshrine tradition rather than encourage experimentation. And it is interesting to note that many of Spain's most expensive wines are those disdaining DO and sporting a simple 'table wine' label. This message of quality at a price is now getting through to many of the vineyard areas, especially in northern Spain. They are starting to invest in equipment and expertise, re-planting vineyards with better varieties and employing highly-trained winemakers. The colossus of La Mancha, the red enclave of Valdepeñas, the entire Catalonian pot-pourri of wine styles and personalities. . .*are* all changing, and the Spain of ten years' time will be very different from the Spain of today.

· CLASSIFICATION ·

Vintages are of great importance in Spain, especially in the north where, in the high Rioja valley, Navarra and the Penedés Superior,

	red	rosé	white
still	●	◐	○
sparkling			△
fortified			□

RA = *rancio*
(see A-Z of Wines and Wine Terms)
SW = sweet
DO = Denominación de Origen

Stark lines of olive trees stretching across the rain-starved landscape of Andalucía (*left*), a shepherd leading his flock homewards past ruined ramparts in Old Castile (*far left*) – images of Spain where the relentless sun and a stubbornly traditional view of life are still dominant influences on the vineyards and their wines.

lack of sun may well cause red grapes not to ripen, but bring white grapes to a perfect peak of freshness. Hot years are likely to overripen white varieties but create marvellous concentration in reds. In the south the general rule is the cooler the better, but drought is more common than flood. Red wines are called *tinto* (dark red) or *clarete* (light red). Pinks are *rosado* and whites are *blanco*.

Many Spanish red wines are marked *reserva* or *gran reserva*. In general this is a worthwhile quality mark and will show the wine has undergone certain legal minimum ageing requirements.
Reserva wines have three years ageing of which one year at least must be in cask.
Gran Reserva means five years ageing with a minimum of two years in cask.

Whites and rosés also use these terms but the minimums are shorter (two and four years respectively). Except for the occasional white Rioja or Penedés, however, they are not to be sought out since almost all the best Spanish whites nowadays are made to be drunk as young as possible.

You may occasionally see 3° año, 5° año or such like on a label. This is a traditional way of saying the wine was bottled in the 3rd year after the harvest, the 5th year after, and so on. With EEC membership, this terminology will be phased out.

· SELECTED WINES ·

· NORTH-EAST ·

DO
●◐○ Alella
●◐○ Ampurdán-Costa Brava
△ Cava
●◐○ Conca de Barberá
●◐○ Penedés
●○□ Priorato RA
Tarragona
●◐○ – (Tarragona Campo) Ribera de Ebro SW
● □ – Falset RA
●◐○ Terra Alta
○ Terra Alta SW

vino de mesa
●◐○ Raimat
△ Raimat
●◐○ Torres

· SOUTH ·

DO
○□ Condado de Huelva
□ Jerez – Sherry (Dry)
□ – Fino
□ – Manzanilla
□ – Palo Cortado
□ Jerez – Sherry (Medium)
□ – Amontillado
□ – Oloroso
□ Jerez – Sherry SW
□ – Cream
○ Málaga SW
○□ Montilla-Moriles SW

· NORTH-WEST ·

DO
● ○ Ribeiro
● ○ Valdeorras

vino de mesa
○ Albariño
●◐○ Valle de Monterrey

· NORTH ·

DO
●◐ Campo de Borja
●◐○ Cariñena RA
●◐○ Navarra
●◐ Ribera del Duero
●◐○ Rioja
○ Rioja SW

Rueda
○ – Rueda Superior
○ – Rueda
□ – Dorado Rueda
□ – Pálido Rueda
●◐○ Somontano

vino de mesa
●◐○ El Bierzo
● Cebreros
● Cigales
● ○ Marqués de Griñon
● Toro
● Vega Sicilia

CENTRE AND WEST ·

DO
●◐ Almansa
●◐○ La Mancha
○ La Mancha SW
●◐ Méntrida
● ○ Tierra de Barros
●◐○ Valdepeñas

vino de mesa
●◐○ Vinos de Madrid
●◐○ Manchuela

· SOUTH-EAST ·

DO
●◐ Alicante
Jumilla
●◐ – Jumilla Monastrell
●◐○ – Jumilla
○ – Jumilla SW
●◐ Utiel-Requena
Valencia
○ – Alto Turia
● ○ – Clariano
●○□ – Valentino SW
Yecla
● – Campo Arriba
●◐○ – Yecla

· RIOJA ·

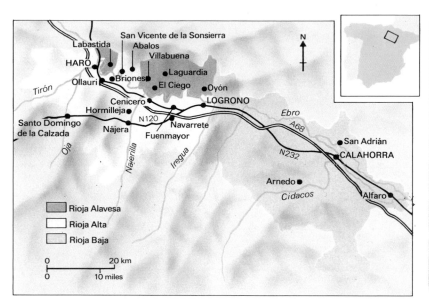

There can't be many wines whose first sip I remember so clearly, but my first sip – no, my first sniff – of Rioja I can remember as though it were yesterday. I'd never thought that a red wine could smell so sweet, so creamy. I'd never guessed that a red wine could taste so gentle, so rich in vanilla and butter-toffee flavours and with a lingering strawberry perfume. All this, and so affordable! And I remember gushing out enthusiasm for my new-found treasure to two rather venerable members of the wine trade. I remember, too, the sting of rebuke as they smiled indulgently, dismissed Rioja as a 'simplistic flavour' and returned to discussing the latest vintage in Bordeaux.

There wasn't a latest vintage in Bordeaux to discuss when Rioja started making wine. The Rioja vineyards are generally reckoned to pre-date even the Romans who, a mere 2,000 years ago, set Bordeaux on the road to fame and fortune. And what grape did Bordeaux use to create its unique style of wine over the centuries? The Cabernet Sauvignon. Interesting. Some historians reckon that there was Cabernet Sauvignon thriving in Rioja long before then, and that Roman soldiers found it in Rioja and introduced it to Bordeaux. Many people have dubbed Rioja the 'Bordeaux understudy' because of its remarkable quality and low price. Maybe they should be more histori-

cally accurate, and dub Bordeaux the 'Rioja understudy'!

Well, that's a little fanciful, because Bordeaux did grasp its chance with both hands and go on, through generations of inspired wines, to claim the title of the world's greatest wine area, whereas Rioja, after its flying start, faded from the race. Until scarcely a dozen years ago it was content to enjoy the purely domestic glory of being regarded, throughout Spain, as producer of the finest Spanish wines; indeed (with few exceptions like the wayward genius of Vega Sicilia from Valladolid) as the *only* producer of fine Spanish wines, a sad comment on the rest of Spain's production. And although things nationally are at last changing for the better, Rioja will continue to dominate wine lists throughout Spain for many years to come.

· THE WINE REGIONS ·

So let's look a little more closely. The Rioja area spreads some 80 miles (130km) along the river Ebro's banks in a high mountain valley in northern Spain which runs east-south-east from the Cordillera Cantábrica down towards Zaragoza and on to the Mediterranean. It gets its name from the little Rio Oja which joins the main flow of the Ebro at Haro – one of the region's main towns. Although Rioja's fame is built on red wine, good white and rosé are also

Above Although Rioja takes its name from the tiny Rio Oja, the river Ebro is the region's main artery. Here, in the Rioja Alavesa – near the Embalse de Cortijo – vines are trained in the traditional bushy style. Rioja shares the Ebro with neighbouring DO Navarra (*right*) which makes similar style wines, but less distinguished; reds predominate.

produced. The Rioja DO divides into three sub-regions – the Rioja Alta, Rioja Alavesa and Rioja Baja. Each gives very different characteristics to the wines, and most Riojas are a blend of wines from two or more of these regions. **Rioja Alta** is right at the north-western end of the valley, up to altitudes of 1,575 feet (480 metres), where the mountains crowd in on the town of Haro and the River Ebro relaxes a little after its battle through the Cantabrian gorges. Haro is a lovely, quiet, rather idiosyncratic town, with no real centre but substantial outskirts – *bodega* buildings of wild eccentricity dating from a super-confident late nineteenth century. (*Bodega* is the Spanish term for a cellar and is often applied to a wine company as a whole.) In general the Alta vineyards – on a soil mix of alluvial silts, and iron- and lime-rich clays – lie south of the Ebro, stretching eastwards to Logroño, the actual wine capital (although Haro with 13 out of the region's 20 *bodegas* is much more wine-orientated).

Covering 40,000 acres (16,000 hectares), the Alta vineyards produce wines which have a strong, firm style, and the reds normally age well.

Rioja Alavesa, just 20,000 acres (8,000 hectares) of chalky clay, swoops down from the foothills of the Cordillera Cantábrica to the Ebro's north bank. As in the Rioja Alta, the climate comes under the joint influence of mountains and ocean, giving warm, wet springs, short, hot summers and mild autumns. The Alavesa wines are the softest, most lightly coloured of Riojas and the reds are rarely seen unblended but, from a company like Bodegas Alavesas, they are delicious young yet age surprisingly well. This small area has 12 *bodega*s, mostly of good quality.

Rioja Baja, which starts literally at the gate of Logroño and continues right to Rioja's eastern boundary, is lower – going down to 1,000 feet (300 metres) – flatter, and hotter. Within reach of Mediterranean sunshine, the wines are rougher, heavier, and higher in alcohol – around 13° as against 10–11° elsewhere in Rioja. Although much in demand for adding colour and brawn to lighter wines, they don't have a particularly exciting character.

· THE GRAPES ·

There are seven grapes allowed in the Rioja DO, four black and three white; sometimes a little white is blended with the red.

Tempranillo is by far the most important for quality with 40 per cent of plantings. This grape turns up elsewhere in Spain under names like Cencibel (La Mancha) and Ull de Llebre (Catalonia), but is at its best in Rioja Alta and Alavesa where the relatively cool ripening conditions produce a wine which is often fairly light in colour, but which has a lovely gentle strawberry and raspberry fruit. In hot years, however, this very quick-ripening variety (*temprano* means 'early' in Spanish) yields deep, dark spicy wine which will require years of ageing before it smooths and softens. Although it can be fairly tannic, Tempranillo has a low acidity and so almost always needs to be blended with more acid or more sturdy varieties. Its surprising resistance to oxidation, however, makes up for low acidity.

Garnacha Tinta also accounts for about 40 per cent of the vineyard, concentrated mostly in hot Rioja Baja. Here it produces strong, rather coarse, peppery wine which, if not blended with Rioja Alta or Alavesa fruit, is thick, jammy and uninteresting. Yet many of Rioja's finest reds, like Bodegas Rioja Alta's marvellous Viña Ardanza, have a high proportion of Garnacha. There is also a fair amount of Garnacha grown along the little Rio Najerilla near Nájera in the Rioja Alta which produces stunning raspberry and pepper flavours in one of Europe's best rosés.

Graciano used to be much planted and much prized for its strong fragrant blackberryish fruit, its dark colour and its ability to age. There's very little of it left, though, because its yield is low and farmers prefer the easier pickings with Tempranillo. All inquiries about Graciano in Rioja are met by shifting of feet or attempts to change the subject.

Mazuelo, on the other hand, still thrives, which is a pity, because this is merely the Cariñena, here giving tannin, a rough-and-tumble fruit and not much else.

If you think you detect blackcurrant in some older Riojas and find yourself saying – 'Cabernet Sauvignon? Surely not' – have the courage of your tastebuds! There *is* still Cabernet planted although the DO laws don't allow it; after all, it was traditional for a couple of thousand years and many old vineyards have some left. Marqués de Riscal have around 25 acres (15 hectares) remaining and even as recently as 1970 over half the grapes in their top *reserva* wines could have been Cabernet Sauvignon.

Viura, (elsewhere Macabeo), is easily the dominant white variety, with more than 10 per cent of the vineyard acreage. It is absolutely spot-on for the new-style, razor-sharp, grapefruit-tart, high-tech wines which Rioja has latched on to, but it is not a particularly exciting grape unless vinified very cold in stainless steel. In fact, it is yet another of the endless array of Mediterranean white grapes whose very neutrality seems to be their chief virtue. It is to Rioja's credit – in particular, the firms of Faustino, Montecillo and Marqués de Cáceres – that cool fermentation methods were developed which at least draw out a very sharp, snappy fruit for drinking young.

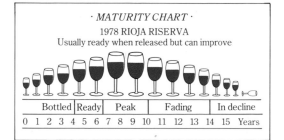

· MATURITY CHART ·
1978 RIOJA RISERVA
Usually ready when released but can improve

Bottled	Ready	Peak	Fading	In decline

0 1 2 3 4 5 6 7 8 9 10 11 12 13 14 15 Years

The delicious vanilla smoothness of red Rioja is inextricably linked to the use of American oak barrels for ageing; even basic *garantía de origen* wines may spend a few months in wood. These barrels, at Bodegas Muga in the Rioja Alta, are being steam-cleaned.

Malvasía used to be Rioja's great white grape, but now occupies less than five per cent of the vineyard. It gives fat, nutty, musky wine, fragrant in an indulgent honeyed way. Nearly all the great wood-aged white Riojas – which so closely resembled fine white Burgundy – will have been at least 50 per cent Malvasía, but it isn't suitable for the ultra-modern wine styles: it is quite weighty and oxidizes quickly, and sadly fewer and fewer *bodegas* now use it for those rich, buttery whites which can still be one of Rioja's great glories.

Garnacha Blanca is the least important white variety, since the wine is rather heavy and alcoholic but quickly fades. It *does* respond well to modern methods, but Riojan winemakers prefer the more amenable Viura.

· MAKING RIOJA ·

The great majority of Rioja wine is red and all the best examples are made by *bodegas*. There are very few single estate Riojas because the practice of blending different wines from all three areas, and the need to carry substantial stocks for ageing, has given financially powerful trading companies virtual control, especially on the export market.

There are two methods used for vinification. Traditionally the grape bunches are piled into great open stone troughs or *lagares* where a

Beaujolais-type fermentation of whole, uncrushed berries takes place and produces delicious, fruity 'Nouveau-style' wine. One or two wineries, like Faustino, have adapted this method to produce an extremely good Rioja 'Nouveau' from Tempranillo which is bursting with spice and fruit and is absolutely delicious.

The other method, common to most wine areas around the world, is now the most widespread: grapes are crushed and stems removed prior to fermentation. This method is relatively recent in Rioja, as is the use of Bordeaux-size oak barrels of 50 gallons (225 litres). When phylloxera devastated the French vineyards in the late nineteenth century, Bordeaux merchants flocked over the Pyrenees and set up wine-making operations in phylloxera-free Rioja, imposing their own techniques on the locals. Phylloxera arrived in Rioja in 1901 and the French merchants all hopped back north over the mountains, but left their know-how behind. Ever since, the very essence of Rioja has depended on the length of ageing in American oak barrels. All the warm vanilla softness, and the gradual lightening of the Tempranillo strawberry fruit which make Rioja absurdly delicious and very similar to mature Côte de Beaune of ten years age – and at a fraction the cost – are due to maturation in new and newish oak barrels. Though there has been a sensible reaction to over-ageing in barrel recently, all the best Riojas still taste of oak.

· QUALITY RATINGS ·

There are four different levels of ageing, which can be checked on a bottle's back label.

Garantía de Origen covers the simplest wines; young reds with little or no cask ageing and, often, not much personality either.

Vino de Crianza means the wine has spent at least one year in barrel and some months in bottle. Not released before its third year, it can be an attractive light red with a pleasant taste of oak.

Gran Reserva is the top quality level for Rioja, and indicates that this Marqués de Villamagna is a very special wine aged in cask and bottle for at least 5 years before release. The white CUNE label, unusually, specifies the grape variety, Viura. But in practice almost all white Rioja is from this grape.

Reserva wines are matured for at least three years of which at least one must be in barrel. At five or six years old, these can be the most delicious Riojas – soft, incredibly easy to drink, and excellent value for money.

Gran Reserva is the top category. The wine must be aged at least three years in barrel and two in bottle – or, confusingly, vice versa. At 8–12 years old these wines can add blackcurrant , and blackberry richness and spice-rack perfume to the gentle Rioja flavours, but don't age them too long – few nowadays stand up to more than a dozen years before fading.

White and rosé wines Similar ageing regulations exist for white wines although the minimum ageing periods are shorter. *Crianzas* can be released after six months in cask, *reservas* after two years' ageing (six months in cask) and *gran reservas* after four years' ageing (a minimum of six months in cask). However, the vast majority are released merely sporting the simple *garantía de origen*. Best examples of this style are Marqués de Cáceres and Montecillo, and these should be drunk as young as possible. The old tradition of long maturation in oak – producing painfully intense, gradually oxidizing, nutty, golden *reservas* – is followed only by a few companies like López de Heredia, Monte Real and Marqués de Murrieta. The best balanced whites are the lightly-oaked *crianza* wines of Muga and Olarra.

Some wonderful *rosado* is made by companies like Marques de Cáceres and Montecillo, but hardly anyone seems to drink it. What a pity. Drunk young it is a revelation of fruit and spice and almost spritzy freshness.

· RIOJA'S NEIGHBOURS ·

Aragón, to the east, is not a particularly distinguished wine area. It has three DOs – the relatively brutal mouthfuls of Cariñena and Campo de Borja and the surprisingly light and refreshing Somontano.

Navarra (DO) is directly to the north and east of Rioja and has for years produced cheaper, lighter, less interesting versions of Rioja – red, white and rosé. In fact, because of the low price, the wines can be fair value but since Garnacha Tinta is the main grape, the Rioja resemblance is quite basic – unless the vanilla taste of oak helps out, as at Chivite, Villafranca and Vinicola Navarra. There is one famous estate, Señorio de Sarría, but more regularly enjoyable wines come from the merchants or co-operative groupings named above.

Rioja's neighbours to the south-west are famous, one for a single enduring unclassifiable masterpiece, the other for being the centre of some of Spain's most exciting innovations.

Ribera del Duero (DO) has, in Vega Sicilia, the masterpiece, albeit a flawed one. It has long been Spain's most expensive wine, and is based on Cabernet Sauvignon, Merlot and Malbec grapes, though blended with some Spanish varieties – Tinta Aragonés which is a vaguely Garnacha, vaguely Tempranillo grape, and the white Albillo. The wines are aged for ten years or more in small oak barrels and are often not offered for sale before the 16th year. The result is a wine which makes you catch your breath with shock because the deep inky depths contain tannin and volatile acidity and you have to make several attempts to find its greatness. But it is there – a turbulent whirlpool of chocolate and moist sugar and sweet-sour overripe plums.

Rueda (DO) further west, south of Valladolid, is changing from being the home of dour, oxidized sherry-type wine to being the base for some of Spain's most modern creations. The Marqués de Riscal company, of Rioja origin, makes an ultra-modern dry white from the local Verdejo grape, and a very good, softly oak-aged version called Reserva Limousin. Marqués de Griñon is another local whizz-kid firm, noted for its fresh, bright white, and what is quite simply one of the finest Cabernet Sauvignons in Spain. Professor Peynaud and Alexis Lichine of Bordeaux are involved – and it shows. The habit is spreading too. Toro, just to the west, is also using French know-how to tame its heady reds.

Galicia is the far north-western tip of Spain. In a hot but wet climate, most of the wines resemble the *vinho verdes* of Portugal and are rarely exported. There are two DOs: Ribeiro – its whites pale, fresh and slightly sparkling – and Valdeorras, with smoky reds and astringent whites. Sometimes you may find a bottle from the local Treixadura or Albariño grapes – these spicy, grapefruit-sharp whites are the best in the region.

· FOOD AND WINE ·

You know that you're a good few miles from the sea in Rioja because dish after dish is characterized by the quantity of vegetables packed into it, and the incredible time it must have taken to cook them. This kind of virtually solid stew or *cocido*, full of chickpeas and potatoes, artichoke hearts and all kinds of other vegetable as well as whatever meat and sausage is available, seems to crop up every time you sit down to table. It isn't that much of a trial, though – in winter you actually start to look forward to it quite unreasonably because the vanilla tastes of the red *reserva* wines make a perfect match.

In fact the whole north Spanish cuisine is well suited to the gentle, oaky flavours of Navarra and Rioja, as well as the more intense fruit of Ribera del Duero and Rueda. *Chorizo* sausage is so spicy and chillied it must have a tasty red, as must *morcilla* blood sausage, the smoked hams, slivers of which appear in the bars at the drop of a foreign accent, and the exciting mountain roasts of sucking pig and baby lamb.

If you're wondering when the whites get drunk, all you need do is try the *truchas a la montañesa* – mountain trout cooked with wine or herbs – or the deep fried, spitting hot *anguillas* – mountain stream eels. I'd start with ice-cold white to chill its heat, but as the dish cooled and my thirst declined – you know, I'd switch to red.

· VINTAGES ·

For white and rosé wines, it is always best to buy the youngest vintage possible, unless the wine is a wood-aged *reserva*. Red wines have had a run of good vintages with 1986, 1985, 1983, 1982 and 1981 all doing well. Although a simple *garantía de origen* red may be fine in a less good year, go for a good year for *reservas* as the wines have more fruit and staying power.

· RIOJA PRODUCERS ·

The general standard is very high. Here are some of the best: Rioja Alta, López de Heredia, López Agos, Marqués de Cáceres, El Coto, CUNE, Domecq, Berberana, Montecillo, Murrieta, Bujanda, Alavesas, Muga, Olarra, Beronia, Faustino.

· CATALONIA ·

For many people Catalonia, in the north-east just below the Pyrenees, is holiday land. And I must say I adored what was my first experience of Spain there, on the Costa Brava. There was only one thing wrong – the wine was pretty dire. Well, OK, that *was* a fair few years ago, and on my last visit it became increasingly obvious that this is no longer the case. The awful wines of the region are gone, replaced by fruity, breezy whites from Alella and Penedés, light fresh reds from Ampurdán, stronger and classier reds from Penedés and of course the sparkling Cava wines – from Penedés again.

From that little list it's pretty obvious that Penedés is more than slightly important. Although there are eight DOs in Catalonia (including Cava which belongs to the whole region), Penedés completely dominates wine-making in this part of Spain and provides not only the widest variety of wine-styles, but also the most innovative leadership in wine – for the whole of Spain. There is probably no single influence on Spanish wines more important than Miguel Torres, the brilliant winemaker at Penedés' top winery, Viñedos Torres. His pioneering of ultra-modern methods, both in the vineyard and in the *bodega*, combined with his respect for tradition, has brought him inter-national acclaim.

· PENEDES ·

The Penedés DO, between Barcelona and Tarragona, comprises about 62,000 acres (25,000 hectares) of vineyard, spreading from the sun-baked seaside to the high, cool hinter-land.

Bajo Penedés, along the coast, is pretty sauna-like in summer and is best at producing sweet wines – or else quite beefy reds.

Medio Penedés, the traditional quality area, centres round Vilafranca del Penedés, about 650 feet (200 metres) above sea level. It's still fairly hot but the vineyards are mostly planted with white grapes – especially Xarel-lo and Macabeo – because Spain's Cava sparkling wine industry is also based here, at San Sadurní de Noya. The reds are better balanced than in the Bajo and there is increasing evidence of grapes like Cabernet Sauvignon, Merlot and Pinot Noir alongside the traditional Ull de

Torres, the top Catalonian table-wine company, does not use the DO system but relies on its own brand names, in this case Gran Coronas.

Left A traditional vintage scene at San Pedro de Ribes in the Bajo Penedés. Here, picking begins in early September.

Llebre (Tempranillo), Monastrell (Mourvèdre) and Garnacha Tinta.

Penedés Superior is the highland section, mountainous and wild, ranging up to 2,600 feet (800 metres). Here the grapes may not ripen till November, but if they are French varieties like Chenin or Chardonnay, they will have a startling intensity of fruit unlike any others in Spain. The Parellada is the main native grape, and a variety of imports like Chardonnay, Gewürztraminer, Riesling, Muscat d'Alsace and Chenin also produce racy perfumed wines of exceptionally high quality. Wines like Torres 'Waltraud' Riesling or the Torres 'Esmeralda' blend of Muscat and Gewürztraminer are literally revolutionizing Penedés whites. It is this tremendous differ-ence in growing conditions across a mere 25-mile (40km) stretch of land that makes enthusiasts call Penedés 'Spain's Napa Valley'.

· WINE STYLES ·

The general quality of Penedés reds and whites is still 'solid' rather than 'exciting' because there are few estate wines, and most merchants own very little land. Many of them buy in new wine and blend it, or buy grapes from co-operatives and growers on contract, but have little control over the actual quality of fruit, and have had little luck in trying to persuade farmers to plant better varieties such as Chardonnay and Cabernet Sauvignon. The total of such 'imported' grape varieties only amounts to five per cent, with Cabernet Sauvignon making up more than half of that.

There is definitely a need for leavening with better grape varieties, because the local whites have little fruit or bouquet by them-selves – even the much-vaunted Parellada is in fact dull, peppery stuff unless vinified very cool and fresh, as Torres does with his Viña Sol. Then it has a delicious citrous zing to it for about a year, but quickly fades after that. Blending with Chardonnay or Sauvignon makes an enormous difference.

The reds too are mostly a little clumsy and peppery, but some new oak-barrel ageing, and the addition of a French varietal with marked fruit like Pinot Noir, Cabernet Sauvignon or Merlot has a most beneficial effect, and lifts the flavours up to Rioja's level of quality. With devoted personal attention – such as León

Traditional and modern methods co-exist in Catalonia. Unlike the vintagers in San Pedro de Ribes (*opposite*) Torres' workers are using the very latest harvesting machinery.

· CAVA ·

Cava – the *méthode champenoise* sparkling wine with its own DO – is the other Penedés creation which should be world-class. The champagne method of creating the sparkle by re-fermentation in bottle is adhered to strictly, and there is a satisfying variation in the characters of the wine companies, which range from small businesses – fermenting in wood and doing the *remuage* and *dégorgement* by hand – to Codorniú, leader in sparkling wine technology (to whom even the Champenois bow, and maybe they should), and the biggest sparkling wine concern in the world; even the giant Moët & Chandon has to be content with second place.

However, at the highest level, the wines don't rival champagne. Their bubble is less persistent, their flavour is softer, more peppery, less refreshing, and they lack the 'something special' which makes champagne-drinking such a blithely diverting indulgence. One problem is the grape varieties. Parellada, Xarel-lo and Macabeo don't have enough fruit and although they may have an adequate ripeness level and attractive acidity as early as August, it is rarely possible to persuade co-operatives and growers to harvest them in this heretically 'under-ripe' state. The gradual introduction of Chardonnay, Chenin and Sauvignon will eventually produce far finer results. Right now, it is best to enjoy Cava for what it is – the cheapest champagne-method sparkler around – and as such, chilled right down, a very fair fizz. Decent producers are Codorniú, Freixenet, Mascaró, Jean Perico, Segura Viudas, Castellblanch and Marqués de Monistrol.

gives to his pure Cabernet Sauvignon and Chardonnay, and Torres to his virtually 100 per cent Cabernet Sauvignon Gran Coronas Black Label – the results can be world-class. The 1970 Black Label proved this when it beat a variety of French stars including Château Latour 1970 and Château La Mission Haut-Brion 1961 in a celebrated 'Gault-Millau' Wine Olympics in Paris in 1979. When the event was repeated in 1986, Torres took third and fifth places with his 1981 Black Label and his new Chardonnay against glittering opposition.

Torres and León are the leading quality producers, but Masia Bach and René Barbier can also produce good wine, and we are beginning to see the emergence of high-quality newcomers like Can Rafols dels Caus.

Vintages are remarkably consistent and almost all years are good for red. However things can get too hot for whites. 1985, for instance, was too hot except in the highest parts of Penedés Superior, while the cool 1984 was ideal for whites.

· OTHER WINES ·

The most important development in Catalonia outside Penedés is at Lérida, in the parched wastelands between Barcelona and Zaragoza. Here the Raimat winery, owned by the Raventos family of Codorniú fame, rises from the scrub. Raimat is now producing low-priced, super quality reds and whites and excellent sparkling wine. Its Cabernet is superb, its Chardonnay very good, and a more traditional Cabernet-Tempranillo blend also delicious.

Back on the coast, Ampurdán-Costa Brava (DO) – hugging the French frontier – specializes in fresh *rosados*; towards Barcelona, the little Alella (DO) mostly produces rather unexciting wine – but one company, Marqués de Alella, makes up for this with some delicious off-dry white, full of the flavours of nuts and apricots.

Things get heavier south of Barcelona and Penedés, although Conca de Barberá (DO)

looks promising for French varieties. Tarragona (DO) has some fairly decent full-flavoured red, white and rosé, but the rich dessert wines, raisiny and strong, are the best and much of the world's communion wine is, in fact, from Tarragona. To the south are the hefty reds of Terra Alta (DO), and in the hills inland from Tarragona lies Priorato (DO). This is renowned as the darkest wine in Spain. I think I'd agree: one of the toughest, too, even in its natural state. When it is allowed to oxidize and decay and is then proudly labelled *rancio* and sold to a – presumably appreciative – public, I head back north to Penedés, where tradition is respected, but not at the cost of one's teeth.

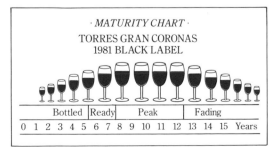

· MATURITY CHART ·
TORRES GRAN CORONAS
1981 BLACK LABEL

Bottled	Ready	Peak	Fading
0 1 2 3 4 5	6 7 8 9 10 11 12	13 14 15 Years

· CENTRAL SPAIN ·

Central Spain typically produces blending wines but, led by firms like Felix Solis, is moving towards higher quality. The oak ageing this wine has received is still uncommon.

Left La Mancha – in summer, dry, dusty and searingly hot – produces a vast quantity of bulk wine: mostly white from Spain's workhorse grape, the Airén.

It's the flatness that first strikes you, and the monotony: the bleak, scorched-brown landscape, with its cross-hatching of stubby vines, its huddled clumps of stunted olives, and its dusty sweeps of grain stretching away like an artist's exercise in perspective. Then it's the heat: searingly insistent in this high, waterless plain at the centre of which is La Mancha. You can see why Don Quixote went a bit barmy out in these wide open spaces—scudding white clouds in the burning sky, quite disturbingly flat prairie, and then the shimmering mirage of a windmill – or is it a giant – on the far horizon. Yes, I'd have had a tilt at that if I were him.

· THE WINE REGIONS ·

La Mancha, in many wine-drinkers' minds, epitomizes Spanish wine: one vast vineyard of over a million acres, it's the source of all those dirt-cheap, thick-fisted reds, whites and rosés that for many of us served as our introduction to wine-drinking. At their best, they were heavy, satisfying wines – strong on flavour, short on subtlety. At their worst, they were concoctions of the direst order. It's difficult to believe that such wines were ever regulated – and most of them aren't: the La Mancha DO covers only 300,000 acres (120,000 hectares) and produces just 400 million bottles of wine annually (around 25 per cent of the region's total)! Even so, this DO is never going to climb very far up the quality ladder while it relies on the white Airén grape for its wine. Over 90 per cent of its vineyards are Airén, the world's most widely planted grape – and a serious contender for the title of dullest grape too. To make the reds, the Airén is mixed with Cencibel (Tempranillo).

Modern techniques of cold fermentation are now bringing about some improvements, but to visit one of the enormous co-operatives which dominate the region, to look at the *tinajas* (fermenting jars) bubbling away and smell the stale fruitlessness of the wine hanging in the air is to step back into another age.

Apart from its namesake, Big Daddy La Mancha features three other DOs.

Valdepeñas (DO), an enclave to the south, is capable of producing some fairly classy reds.

The firm Felix Solis, and in particular the outstanding Señorio de los Llanos, are even bringing oak barrel ageing back into fashion for their reds with some stunning results and a taste veering between coconut cream and toffee!

Almansa and **Mentrida (both DO)** aren't so exciting, but they do produce a fair amount of wine that disappears into the black hole of the blending vats.

Tierra de Barros (DO) is on La Mancha's periphery and, in the south-east, there is a clutch of another five DOs.

Valencia (DO), over on the coast between Alicante and Valencia, is no slouch at sweet Muscat and extremely good at dry rosé.

Utiel-Requena, Alicante, Yecla and **Jumilla (all DO)** can make some of the solidest reds yet known to man. Solid, yes; memorable, as yet, no – and again the ravenous appetite of the world's blenders finds good use for them.

Co-operatives completely dominate winemaking in these central *denominaciones* while Valencia's output is in the hands of several

Parched, cracked earth and irregularly-planted, straggly bushes characterize this vineyard near Valencia. The arid climate and out-dated methods – in both viticulture and vinification – account for Spain's yield per acre being the lowest of any European wine country.

gigantic blending and shipping companies. Wine which is not sold direct by a co-operative will be sold to a merchant for blending and retailing under whatever title he chooses. Estate-bottled wines are almost unheard of here, though there are signs of a 'quality first' mentality emerging in Valdepeñas. In general if the director of a co-operative or merchant house is forward-looking, a reasonable quality of wine at a very low price can be achieved. But it can be a struggle to persuade introverted rural communities to change their ways and make the effort to please in a world which is increasingly discriminating about what it chooses to drink. One visit to a typical co-operative, its jumbled old sheds full of concrete tanks greasy with age, and the air heavy with volatile vinegary smells, will show you how far there is still to go.

· GRAPES AND WINE STYLES ·

Airén dominates central Spain; indeed it dominates all Spain, and the world too! So when you ask me what the world's most popular grape tastes of, I should be able to manage something slightly better than – 'Um, er, not a lot, really'. But I can't! Airén is sensationally neutral and its chief claim to fame is that it produces prodigious amounts of alcohol, thus making up the bulk of any cheap blended Spanish white. If it's an old-fashioned white it will taste flat, vaguely muddy, with a slight flavour of hard-tack biscuit being about as close to fruit as it gets. This single grape, vinified traditionally, has probably been the biggest obstacle to improving Spain's wine image. However, there are modern winemakers, in La Mancha particularly, who are discovering that this ineffectual dull variety can be turned to good effect, and that you *can* find fruit in its flavour if you use high-tech, low temperature fermentation methods.

Red grapes are less homogeneous in this central area.

Garnacha Tinta – which is the world's *second* most-planted grape! – is widespread, particularly in Valencia and neighbouring DOs.

Bobal and **Monastrell**, two other Top 20 varieties, are also popular, though not permitted in La Mancha and Valdepeñas DOs. All three are inclined to the strong, pepper and grape-skin jam style which makes it extremely difficult to tell one from another – not that you'd really want to in any case.

Cencibel – another name for Tempranillo – is a more subtle operator. As one of Spain's best red varieties, it gives the special quality to Rioja reds. It is fairly delicate up there in the north, but here, further south, it ripens enthusiastically to make a rich, deep flavoury wine with a lot of tannin, which is almost always reduced into numerous light reds by adding up to 90 per cent Airén!

With the advent of EEC membership and the possibility that the Strasbourg commissioners won't look kindly on wines which are blends of red and white, an increasing number of 100 per cent Cencibel reds are being made which have a deep colour and a yeast softness tempering a plumskin-and-pepper fruit. There's even a little Cabernet Sauvignon being planted in experimental patches out of sight of the authorities which, on recent tasting, really add style to the Cencibel.

The reds of the east are very hefty in general, but Valencia rosé can be delicious, especially since the wine is often drawn off the top of the vats of fermenting red so as to achieve a heavier red. For us the best result of this 'bleeding' process is a good fruity rosé which, chilled down, goes extremely well with Valencia's great speciality *paella*. The local Muscats are best with the abundance of fresh fruit along the Mediterranean shores, even better with *turrón*, Alicante's nut-and-honey nougat.

La Mancha whites are traditionally drunk old and un-chilled and any dish going would be welcome to drown out the taste. Yet the modern whites can have quite a sharp lemon or lime acidity, and a fruit a bit like peaches and anise. It's good quaffing white, though the acidity has a habit of running slightly sour if the wine is kept too long.

It is red La Mancha which is Madrid's favourite drink. Throughout the city this soft, vaguely strawberry-tasting mixture of red and white grapes is the carafe-wine in the *tapas* bars – the standard accompaniment to squid, *tortilla*, chicken livers, grilled peppers, olives, spicy *chorizo* sausage or whatever else the bar owners put out.

· SHERRY ·

You wouldn't think that sherry has a lot in common with champagne – but it has. Two factors in particular link these obviously dissimilar drinks. First, chalk: wherever chalk crops up in Europe, and wherever there is enough sun to ripen white grapes, the result is vineyards of special quality. In the far north of France, chalk produces the most refreshing, exhilarating wine in the world: champagne. Well, the last outcrop of chalk in Europe, before the continent is swallowed by the billowing Atlantic ocean, occurs just north of Cádiz, in the south-western tip of Spain. Here, despite blistering heat, the blindingly white chalk vineyards of Jerez manage to yield grapes which give a light, delicate juice that will one day be put into bottle and sold as 'sherry'.

But, as with champagne, that day is a long way off, because the second crucial similarity is that both champage and sherry are 'creations': the base wine must be manipulated and changed over a number of years for its unique character to become evident. The still wine of Champagne, lacking sun, would be thin, sour stuff if the bubbles weren't put into it. Likewise, the ordinary wine of Jerez, wearied by excess of sun, tastes flat and dull if drunk young as table wine. But put it through the sherry-making process and that flabby local wine is transformed into one of the most memorable tastes in the world.

Going back 500 years, that taste was as thick and sweet as treacle. The 2,900 barrels which Sir Francis Drake removed from Cádiz in 1587 while he was 'singeing the King of Spain's beard' would have been coarse and rich. The 'sack' which warmed Falstaff's blood and stoked the fires of his wit was heady, sweet and intoxicating. Sack was the general name for the many wines of this type being created in the south of Europe – in Spain, the Canary Islands, Italy and Greece – usually enriched and fortified by the addition of Moscatel *arrope* (a syrupy concentrate produced by boiling down a sweet wine to only 20 per cent of its volume). Drake's raid brought Jerez Sack to the fore in England; with time Jerez became anglicized to sherry, the name 'sack' was dropped altogether and the wine became just sherry.

Throughout the seventeenth century, sherry remained popular in Britain, despite strained Anglo-Spanish relations, but in the eighteenth and nineteenth centuries, things really took off, and a flood of Scottish, Irish and English merchants headed south to make their fortunes in the sun. Most of today's great sherry houses are descended from these adventurers, with names like Harvey, Croft, Williams and Humbert – and even the wonderfully-titled Rafael O'Neale – testifying to the fact.

Though, initially, their trade was in these sweet wines, they realized the need to expand their range. In particular, they sought to make sherry a more sophisticated drink, as against mere tavern fodder, and so during the mid-nineteenth century the sherry styles we know today – dry, medium and sweet – evolved.

· CLIMATE AND SOIL ·

It all starts in those vineyards on the Atlantic seaboard of Andalucía. The Guadalquivir river runs down from Seville through the parched countryside, reaching the sea at Sanlúcar de Barrameda. From Sanlúcar, down the coast to Puerto de Santa María and inland to the main town of Jerez de la Frontera, in an arc of

about 20 miles (32km), lie the finest vineyards. These are chalk soils, called *albariza*, and luckily they constitute 85 per cent of vineyard land. Chalk's ability to produce light-bodied wine is the key, along with its capacity for moisture retention – vitally important in an area which gets 295 days of sun a year, but only 22 inches (560mm) of rain. There are two other types of soil allowed under the Denominación de Origen regulations, though neither is encouraged. *Barro* is a brown clay which yields fairly hefty thick wine; and *arena* is sand, which produces some Moscatel, but is actually better at producing grain and tomatoes.

· THE GRAPES ·

Palomino, which when grown elsewhere is a dull white variety, is by far the most important grape and it is the very neutrality of the juice which is so highly prized. Attempts have been made to find other suitable varieties, but growers always revert to the Palomino, because it produces large amounts of fairly bland juice – the perfect raw material for the sherrymaker to work on.

Pedro Ximénez is another significant grape, though increasingly less so since it is more prone to disease. Primarily a sweet sherry grape, its main job is to provide sweetening for blends of sherry. For this reason it is usually allowed to overripen on the vine, and then laid on mats or under tunnels of polythene to raisin in the sun. The raisined grapes are then pressed and, in general, fortified immediately to provide a dark rich 'wine', which the sherrymakers call PX. By itself it produces one of the most remarkable intensely sweet flavours in wine, reminiscent of some kind of celestial Christmas cake. Used in small amounts, it adds enormously to the complexity and flavour of a great many medium and sweet sherries.

Moscatel also occurs in sherry. It isn't much

Left Jerez de la Frontera is the town in southern Spain from which 'sherry' takes its name, and most of the leading sherry shippers – like Gonzalez Byass – have their headquarters here.

planted, but its strong grapy taste can often be discerned in cheap sweet sherries to little good effect.

· MAKING SHERRY ·

Picking, which begins in early September, is still done by hand, although mechanical harvesting is gradually encroaching and some vineyards have now been trained higher with machines in mind. Traditional treading, done in special nailed boots, has been replaced by modern presses which gently, delicately squeeze out the juice without lacerating skins or crushing pips and stalks. Fermentation happens in the normal way although in the heat it can be a bit violent. To combat this it usually takes place in water-cooled stainless steel tanks, but sometimes in earthenware or concrete *tinajas* – like giant Ali-Baba jars.

The wines are then put into 110-gallon (500-litre) barrels called 'butts', which are left four-fifths full. This exposure to air during maturation is unique to sherry and the key to its magic ingredient: *flor. Flor* is a thick, creamy layer of yeast that quickly develops on the surface of the lighter, more delicate wines. *Flor* protects the wine against oxygen and gradually impregnates it with a highly distinctive pungent flavour over a period of four to five years in barrel (this used to be entirely haphazard, but can now be induced through the degree of pressure on the grapes at pressing and careful use of selected yeasts in fermentation).

The heavier wines are less likely to grow *flor*, so they are fortified with grape spirit and also left in barrel, four-fifths full, but in this case the intention is that they should oxidize slowly. Such a practice would be anathema to most winemakers whose object is to avoid oxidation, but it is what gives *oloroso* sherries their special flavour. These, too, are left in barrel for at least five years to gain character.

· THE SOLERA SYSTEM ·

You may have noticed that sherry never has a vintage date. This is because the market has been developed by commercial brand names not by individual growers and winemakers, thus making consistency of product more important than vintage date. So a system of blending has been developed called the *solera* system. This is how it works.

A sherrymaker selects certain butts of a similar style and 'lays them down' in the company's cellars to begin a *solera*. In succeeding years, wines resembling this first selection are also put aside, and laid in tiers above the previous year's butts. So gradually a pile of barrels is built up, with the youngest at the top.

When the bottom barrels (the oldest) are ready for use, they are partially drawn off – only partially, never more than a third – and topped up or 'refreshed' with wine from the barrels above *them*, and so on to the youngest wine at the top. What happens is one of those magical mysteries the scientists can't fully explain. As near as dammit, the younger wine in each transfer acquires the personality of the older wine, so you can develop a never-ending flow of similar wines taking on the characteristics of their older brothers, and the wine drawn from the bottom barrel will, in effect, be the same year in year out. That's why you don't see a vintage date on sherry. You may see a *solera* date, like 'solera 1842', but that simply means the *solera* for that wine was laid down in 1842 – pretty impressive, but not *quite* the same as 'vintage 1842' would be!

The greatest *soleras* do contain a lot of *very* old wine and are only drawn off in small quantities to improve blends. Whereas a commercial *fino solera* might only have wine averaging four to five years old, a great *oloroso solera* could average nearer 20–30 years of age. When the wine from each solera is drawn

The Palomino grape is traditionally picked early to make a light wine for conversion into sherry. However, it is increasingly being used for sweet sherries, and these bunches are overripening and beginning to wrinkle on the vine.

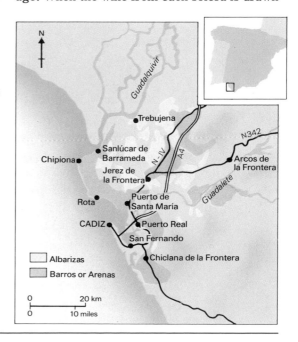

Left The vast cellars of the sherry companies are called 'cathedrals'; this new Gonzalez Byass plant holds 60,000 butts, stored in tiers for the *solera* system with the oldest wines at the bottom. The chalk markings show the *solera*'s name and the number of butts in each tier. *Far left* This worker has sunk his long crook-handled cup, called a *venencia*, through the *flor* into the cask and drawn up a sample of bitingly dry *fino*.

Left Barbadillo are the biggest producers of the ultra-dry Manzanilla style of sherry in Sanlucar de la Barrameda. *Far left* An 'almacenista' or unblended sherry from a single butt.

off, it is normally blended with other *soleras*, then further fortified with a little high-strength spirit, and bottled. A *fino* should be drunk as quickly as possible, but a fine *oloroso* can go on improving in bottle for years.

· SHERRY STYLES ·

Sherry styles fall into three main categories: dry, medium and sweet.

Dry The chief type of dry sherry is *fino*, with a sub-category of *manzanilla* for *finos* from the fishing-port of Sanlúcar de Barrameda. *Finos* are *flor* wines and it is the yeast layer, preventing oxidation, which gives them their straw colour and unusual taste. They should be very pale and *very* dry. Many modern so-called *finos* have been softened and slightly sweetened as merchants think consumers can't take the real thing. In which case they should drink

something else, I should have thought, because *fino* has a biting dryness, almost a baker's yeast sourness, and a wonderful, unnerving perfume which is as cold as raw steel, and as insidious as the dank smell of floorboards at the top of a disused staircase! A *manzanilla* may often be lighter than a straight *fino* and can have an appetizing, salty tang.

There is an in-between category: wines which started out life as *finos* but have changed personality as they matured, or else gone on ageing in barrel after they would normally have been bottled. *Palo cortado* is the most exciting of these in-between styles, having the zesty tang of a *fino* twinned with rich demerara sugar nuttiness – yet despite the concentration of flavour this exquisite sherry style is almost always dry. *Manzanilla pasada* is a *manzanilla* which is allowed to go on ageing in barrel

past the usual four- to five-year span.

Medium Medium sherries are created in two ways. They can be based on *oloroso* wines. These are wines which did *not* grow the *flor* yeast after fermentation (or grew very little of it), and so are fortified with high-strength spirit up to 18° and left in barrels four-fifths full to react with the air – in effect to oxidize. Slowly a remarkable deep nutty flavour develops, sometimes with a raisin flavour too, sometimes best Muscovado brown sugar, sometimes the toffee richness of buttered brazils and butterscotch – all this and a fairly piercing acidity, and yet the wine is basically still *dry*. This category of *oloroso* is usually sweetened for sale. The best 'medium' sherries are those true *olorosos*, only slightly sweetened, which *feel* sweet because of their richness, yet taste totally dry. *Oloroso seco* (dry *oloroso*) is a rare label worth looking for.

Medium sherries can also be created from *finos* by fortifying the *fino* up to $16 \cdot 5°$ which means that any *flor* present will die. The wine then ages in barrel and a rich, nutty flavour develops. This style is the true *amontillado* style (meaning 'in the style of Montilla', a town near Córdoba) and it can be delicious, though most modern *amontillados* are spoiled by too much sweetening.

Sweet These should be *oloroso* sherries, well aged, then sweetened up with Pedro Ximénez wine. Usually they're anything but, and nowadays are often simply young *finos* sweetened with Moscatel. In the case of Pale Creams they are usually poor *finos* sweetened by an artificial mixture of glucose and laevulose – two sugars present in grapes.

Normal sweet sherries are sold under the names 'Brown' or 'Cream', and occasionally there is a fairly sweet style called *amoroso*. Good examples of all of these should improve

• FOOD AND WINE •

Poor old sherry seems stuck with the idea that you don't eat anything with it, when nothing could be further from the truth. To get the best out of dry sherry, you need the wine chilled right down, the atmosphere ever so slightly seedy and the conversation quite nice – and a table groaning with plate after plate of *tapas*, the sharpness of olives in brine, the smoky fragrance of roast almonds, *chorizo* sausage – chewy and spicy hot – anchovies, grilled red pepper, squid or mushrooms, kidneys, mussels and *tortillas*; they're all there in little trays, and the pungent, biting flavour of good dry sherry is totally at home. The sweeter wines *are* sweet enough for puddings, but I'd drink them as I worked my way contemplatively through a plateful of nuts, *membrillo* – quince jelly – with mild Manchego cheese, and those dry, powdery *polvorones* sweetmeats. After that I'd be ready for a very substantial snooze.

Above **The intensely red soil provides a striking backdrop to the golden leaves of Pedro Ximénez vines in these Montilla vineyards. The wine they produce is similar to sherry, and is made in much the same way except that the fermentation takes place in huge earthernware *tinajas* (*right*).**

with age after bottling, and be marked by a real sensation of alcoholic strength, a fairly high acidity, and a richness of raisins and currants and treacle and plums – mother's home-made fruitcake in liquid form.

• MONTILLA-MORILES AND MALAGA •

These are two other areas of Spain making similar wines to sherry.

Montilla-Moriles is north-east of Jerez, to the south of the city of Córdoba. Until recently Montilla wines were freely used in Jerez by their winemakers. The Pedro Ximénez grape is used almost exclusively and the range of wines parallels sherry going from very dry to very sweet. However, *montillas* rarely need fortification, since the very hot ripening season produces grapes of at least 16° potential alcohol. On the other hand *flor* does appear for *fino* styles, and the *solera* system is used to age the wines. The name 'Montilla' is more common than Montilla-Moriles, and the wines are generally labelled dry, medium or cream.

Fino sometimes appears on labels, but *amontillado* – despite being geographically correct – is rarely used. The wines are generally softer and less assertive than sherry, and slightly lower in alcohol – but they're lower in price too, and make a very good cheaper alternative to sherry.

Málaga is on the Mediterranean coast, and is chiefly notorious for being the place where the dreaded vine louse phylloxera first attacked Spain in 1876. Its wine used to be known as 'Mountain' and in the eighteenth century export sales far exceeded those of sherry. But by the end of the nineteenth century the area was in ruins, thanks to phylloxera, and it has only recently shown any real sign of revival.

• SHERRY PRODUCERS •

The sherry trade is dominated by large merchant houses and one never sees a grower's name on the label. Producers either buy grapes on contract from the growers or from the co-operatives who control about 20 per cent of the vineyards. There is also a small group of people called *almacenistas*. Traditionally 'amateurs' – doctors, lawyers, businessmen – they buy up butts of special sherries and age them, unblended. These are eagerly sought after by quality-conscious companies and are also occasionally released in their wonderful, undiluted form, usually through the company of Lustau. Among producers in general Lustau, Barbadillo, Hidalgo, Domecq, Garvey, Don Zoilo, Gonzalez Byass and Osborne are some of the most reliable names.

In fact the chief use of the vineyards today is to provide table grapes. However, the wines they make are well worth drinking. Mostly they are sweet to very sweet and have a delicious smokiness adding interest to the fairly strong raisin or chocolate taste of the fruit.

Well-matured examples can be found and they're worth a search, because the *solera* system is also used here for ageing.

· PORTUGAL ·

P ortugal has the rare distinction of being famous for the wines its own inhabitants drink least of – the traditional fortified wines of port and madeira (yes, despite being an island way out in the Atlantic, Madeira *is* part of Portugal), and the decidedly untraditional Mateus Rosé.

It's difficult to believe that Mateus Rosé, one of the most famous wines in the world (along with Lancers' Rosé from the United States, and its host of imitators), didn't *exist* before 1942. It was invented by a Mr Guedes, and it now sells a million bottles a week – but the Portuguese don't drink it. A Portuguese wine-drinker knocking back rosé? No chance. Red, white or nothing is their rule at home. There wasn't an awful lot of chance that they'd knock back port or madeira either until recently; these wines were invented for the export market by the British, and it's only in the last few years that anything more exacting than an occasional white or tawny port has passed the native lips.

But although not very keen on the wines *we* like best, the Portuguese are some of the most determined wine producers and wine drinkers in the world. They are sixth in terms of production and second in per capita consumption – which makes them unique among the historical wine-drinking nations (all the others are currently suffering a serious slide in wine consumption). Largely this is caused by Portugal's extreme isolation from the rest of Europe – even from Spain – and by its innate conservatism and relative poverty. Since Portugal is a poor country with a weak currency, there is rarely any money to spend on importing such luxuries as other countries' alcoholic beverages! So the trends away from wine-drinking which other Mediterranean countries are experiencing can't affect Portugal because the alternatives are, quite simply, not available.

Instead the drinkers go for their own produce with a vengeance, consuming over three-quarters of their annual wine output every year themselves. This also explains why we get so few chances to discover the hidden treasures – and the hidden horrors – of Portuguese wines: they never leave the country.

But it definitely is worth making an effort to experiment with Portuguese wines – apart from the pleasant but hardly memorable well-known brands – because some of the flavours lurking there, down below the Bay of Biscay, are quite unlike any others in the world of wine. And Portuguese traditions, allied to the slow acceptance of its best table wines by the rest of the world, mean that Portugal's reds – often 10–15 years old – offer some of the best mature red wine bargains it is possible to find.

· THE WINE REGIONS ·

The country divides into three main regions – with Madeira off in the ocean making a fourth.

The northern section starts on the very first yard of Portuguese soil, on the banks of the Minho river which flows along the border with Spain's Galicia. This climatically chaotic region – a baking morning always seems to be followed by a lunchtime drenching and vice versa

– positively crawls with vegetation and is the home of *vinho verde*. The vines are frequently trained up trees, on top of walls, over hedges and along trellises above rows of vegetables. Partly this is because most of the grapes are grown by smallholders who need to make as much use as possible of their land, and partly because in such a wet climate rot would be rife if the vines were trained low. The high training also means fewer ripe grapes at vintage – and the mark of *vinho verde*, red or white, should be its shocking, rasping flare of acidity as the liquid hits your tongue. This wine is the staple wine of the Portuguese and accounts for 25 per cent of the national total.

The other important area of the north is the Douro Valley. This is famous for its port, but in fact only about 40 per cent of the valley's wine is made into port; the remainder is sold as Douro table wine and can be extremely good. Just to the north, in the wild hills towards Vila Real, is the home of Mateus Rosé – but demand has now so exceeded supply that the grapes come from all over Portugal.

The central section between Oporto and Lisbon is best known for Dão, traditionally Portugal's leading red wine. There is white Dão too, and both can be excellent. But there is a new area on the coast, Bairrada – only demarcated in 1979 – which is already showing signs of outstripping its venerable neighbour. Below Bairrada are the large areas of the Estremadura and Ribatejo which have always been dismissed as jug wine regions. This is largely because their names never appeared on the labels – nor did Bairrada's – but much fine wine was and is made, providing the class for many companies' top-of-the-range

Above Most of the corks used to seal wine bottles come from Portugal where there are about 2½ million acres of cork forests. Corks are made from the bark of the tree – a kind of oak (*quercus suber*) – which is stripped when it is at least 20 years old, and thereafter at 9-year intervals.

Left Port is Portugal's most famous wine, but is drunk much more outside Portugal than in it. Even so, it's been a lucrative export commodity for generations, and everybody, young and old, helps during the vintage in the Douro Valley.

Left many of northern Portugal's best vineyards are way up in the mountain valleys towards the Spanish border. The land is steep, rugged and difficult to work, and, as here in the Douro Valley, most of the vineyards are strung across the hill-side terraces.

Right The home of Mateus Rosé! These vineyards in Vila Real, just north of the Douro Valley, are where it all began, and still produce excellent light red and rosé wine, but Mateus now draws on grapes from the plains vineyards further south to meet the enormous demand.

brands. There are also now some single estates, which is a new and welcome move in Portugal.

The south has four much-revered wine regions grouped round Lisbon – but they are of waning significance. Carcavelos has virtually disappeared under the sprawl of Estoril, Colares somehow holds out against the Atlantic on its beach vineyards west of Sintra, and Bucelas – while surviving a little more obviously – isn't making wine of any great character. However Setúbal, just south of Lisbon, does produce a famous and impressive Muscat.

The Arrábida peninsula is also beginning to produce some of the most exciting table wines in Portugal, especially around Palmela and Azeitão where the giant Fonseca company has its headquarters.

There is some fairly interesting – but fairly unobtainable – red away to the east in the Alentejo, and the Algarve has its own demarcated region – though why it should need one when the quality of the wine is so dull (and tourists drink it all anyway) I can't imagine.

· CLASSIFICATIONS ·

The Portuguese system of controlled appellation of origin is similar to the French one – covering geographical authenticity, permitted grape types, yields and so on. Although formulated in 1908, attempts at protection of individual wines had begun as early as 1113!

There are now 11 demarcated regions (*regiãos demarcadas*) – the port region, Douro, Madeira, Vinho Verde, Dão, Bairrada, Bucelas, Colares, Carcavelos, Setúbal and Algarve. All these are marked by a seal – the *selo de origem* – over the cork. There are 27 other regions which are allowed to use their name on the label, but which have not yet been guaranteed *região demarcada* status. Most of these are in the co-operative-dominated area of Estremadura, Ribatejo and Alentejo.

· WINE STYLES ·

There are basically two styles to Portuguese table wine: *vinho verde* and *vinho maduro*.

Vinho verde means 'green wine' – but that's not to suggest it is the deep eye-catching green of a snooker table's baize. Far from it. Although most of what we know as *vinho verde* is pale yellow, with a tiny prickle in it, the majority is actually red! *Verde* here means 'young, immature' – to be drunk as soon as the wine is in bottle, or even sooner if you're in the area.

Vinho maduro means 'mature wine', and the Portuguese are likely to go to town on the ageing. It is quite common for a straightforward red or white to have had five years ageing – usually in cement tanks or big old wooden barrels – before it is released for sale. More special wines may be easily available with 10 to 15 years behind them. This

can result in some spectacular bottles – stern, proud, difficult to love at first with their tough, tight style – but it can also result in tired, dead, fruitless wines with nothing but an ancient birth certificate to boast about. Finding out which is which is a priority – because prices are so good it would be a crying shame to miss out on some of Europe's best wine bargains.

• SELECTED WINES •

• NORTH •

RD
- ● ○ Douro
- ■ □ Port
- ■ – Vintage
- ■ – Single Quinta
- ■ – Crusting
- ■ – Late Bottled Vintage
- ■ – Tawny
- ■ – Ruby
- □ – Sweet white
- □ – Dry white

Vinho verde
- ● ○ – Amarante
- ● ○ – Basto
- ● ○ – Braga
- ● ○ – Lima
- ● ○ – Monção
- ● ○ – Penafiel

vinho de mesa
- ●◐○ Alijo
- ● ○ Lafoes
- ●○△ Lamego
- ● ○ Meda
- ●○△ Pinhel
- ●◐○ Sabrosa
- ●△ Vila Real

• CENTRE •

RD
- ●○△ Bairrada
- ● ○ Dão

vinho de mesa
- ● ○ Cartaxo
- ●△ Palmela
- ●◐○ Torres Vedras

• SOUTH •

RD
- ● ○ Algarve
- ○ Bucelas
- ■ Carcavelos
- ● ○ Colares
- ■ □ Setúbal

vinho de mesa
- ● Borba
- ● Reguengos
- ○ Vidigueira

• MADEIRA •

RD
- ■ □ Madeira
- □ – Malmsey
- □ – Bual
- □ – Verdelho
- □ – Sercial

	red	rosé	white
still	●	◐	○
sparkling		△	△
fortified	■		□

RD = Região Demarcada

· TABLE WINES ·

Individuality is the greatest asset Portuguese wines possess. They have styles and flavours which no other country approaches, and they are produced from grapes not found anywhere else in the mainstream of wine-making. Because tradition has ruled for so long in Portugal and conservatism has consistently defeated innovation in the vineyard and winery, we still don't know just how good these grape varieties can be. But the occasional sighting of a ripe Bairrada from the Baga grape, a carefully matured Dão from the Touriga Nacional, a bramble-and-blackberry-fragrant Periquita from Azeitão or a startling, sharply perfumed pepper-and-peaches *vinho verde* from the Loureiro and Trajadura grapes are enough to convince me that the *potential* in Portugal to provide an entirely new generation of exciting, different table wine flavours is bettered only by Italy.

However, the way that vine-growing and wine-making is at present organized doesn't make it easy. Single properties – in all other countries the springboard from which character and excellence take off – are almost totally absent. The whole country is heavily dominated by its 113 co-operatives. In an important area like Dão there is only *one* independent estate, and the major companies have to make 'special' arrangements with a particular co-operative to try to ensure a supply of reasonable grapes. The co-operative movement has none of the drive that good directors often instil in it in other countries. One reason must be that the director of a co-operative may not, by law, be paid! So I don't see many bright sparks seeing *that* as much of a career to follow.

· CLASSIFICATIONS ·

Another problem is the official attitude to appellation of origin. Portugal, in fact, demarcated its vineyards a good quarter of a century before France did but the demarcations were very general and fairly uncritical of wine-making techniques. Vinho Verde, for instance, is a demarcated area of over 2 million acres (810,000 hectares) – although only 62,000 acres (25,000 hectares) at present grow grapes.

Traditionally vines are trained high in Portugal. The trellises once used are now increasingly being replaced by the *cruzeta* system of concrete poles and wires (*left*). The vines leave plenty of room underneath for other crops, like these cabbages (*above*), but harvesting on the tall ladders needed to reach the fruit can be precarious.

Consequently, what quality-conscious merchant houses do is to blend grapes from wherever they want and call the wines by brand names. Their *reservas*, and in particular *garrafeiras* (*garrafeira* means 'a merchant's specially matured selection' – his best wine), without any geographical or grape indication at all, are often Portugal's finest wines!

Still, European Economic Community membership is changing attitudes, and there is already a move to give regional and varietal identity to the wines, which, much as I love some of those old *garrafeiras*, can only be a good thing.

· THE WINES ·

Vinho verde, from the north, at least goes under its own name, although it can be processed anywhere in Portugal. However, all the best wines are made and bottled in the Minho region. Seventy per cent of the production is red and although I'm a great fan, I'm probably the only extant non-Portuguese enthusiast because red *vinho verde* is fierce stuff. It is deep purple and has a passionate raw smell both harsh and spicy-plummy at the same time, like an untamed Italian Dolcetto. The taste really is a shock because it is so dry, but there is a tremendous depth of flavour which gradually softens – if you can hold it in your mouth that long. Its great virtue is that *no* food is too savage for it – which makes it a *perfect* match for the oily Bacalhão salt cod dishes.

White *vinho verde* is less of a trial, but should be almost water-white with the slightest tint of canary yellow. It should taste of peaches, pepper and apricots – rich spicy tastes in a lashingly dry wine. This, with a little sparkle left over from the malolactic fermentation – or, more usually, pumped back in just before bottling – is a magical summer wine. Most export versions are sweetened, but their low alcohol and lemony tang still make them refreshing drinking.

Douro wines are newcomers to the export market, but have immense potential. The reds are more exciting than the whites and really manage to bring some of the sweet intensity of port to a table wine. Roriz, Touriga Nacional and Touriga Francesa are the most important grapes, and the wines can have the medicinal depth of port together with a gentle liquorice and raspberry fruit and a perfume like unripe tobacco. Fascinating stuff. The Tras os Montes area near Vila Real is better known for rosé but produces a beautifully gulpable red wine tasting of candy spice and fruit pastilles.

Bairrada shot on to the international scene in the early 1980s with wines made from the Baga grape which seemed determined to out-Cabernet Cabernet, they were so brimming with blackcurrant and eucalyptus fruit. Sadly the first flush has subsided a little, but this scrubby, placid lowland area of vines, wheat and meadows has the ability to produce great wine and, having received acclaim once, let's hope it now has the appetite to look for it again.

Dão, too, hidden high in the hills and only reached by mountain valley roads which twist up the forest-choked river gorges at snail's pace, has the potential to make great wine. The reds are supposed to be velvet-smooth and full of glycerine but are more likely to be tough, fairly tannic, and not over-endowed with fruit after all that ageing they undergo before they are bottled – and yet, despite all that, rather impressive in their vaguely resiny, raisiny way. The wine has a gentle strawberry fruit when young, and the few classics I've tasted have developed, after 15–20 years, a wonderful plummy fruit with undertones of herbs and leather and tannin. One 1966 from

São João was like an inspired blend of Barolo and Pomerol with a touch of Grange Hermitage thrown in for good measure!

The reality, I'm afraid, is usually more mundane, but Dão does make a very good all-purpose food red; in a local tavern, eating kid fresh off the spit or milk-fed lamb straight from the oven, I'll scarcely notice any rough edges. About three per cent of Dão is white – dry, stony, sometimes nutty, rarely exciting.

Of Lisbon's rarities, Carcavelos is actually rather a good nutty fortified wine and Colares a staggeringly unfriendly blackstrap bruiser which seduces you with its perfume, then wallops you with tannic ferocity. I suppose it *has* to improve with age, but I've never had one older than I am – and that wasn't enough! Bucelas I've found rather fruitless and oily and generally unexciting.

Setúbal *is* more exciting – partly because of its Moscatel, a surprisingly unperfumed, rather spirity, fortified wine which certainly improves with age for 20–30 years but is never actually mouthwatering – the usual Portuguese problem of lack of fruit.

The majority of Daõ wine is red, but some reasonable white is produced. The Grão Vasco brand is owned by the Guedes family who also own Mateus Rosé. Vinho Verde is the very dry light wine of northern Portugal. Again, most of it is actually red, but this is white (branco).

However the surrounding region is full of interesting wines. To Lisbon's north Torres Vedras and Arruda provide gutsy mouthfuls at a very affordable price. To the south, of particular importance are Fonseca's various *garrafeiras* and *reservas*, such as Camarate and Periquita (used here as a brand name rather than a varietal). The fascinating innovations being instigated by Fonseca may yet shake Portugal's very foundations. Two farms, the Quinta do Anfora and Quinta do Bacalhoa, are using small barrels to age their wines – almost unheard of in Portugal! And they are producing wines full of fruit and a tannin which is tough but not astringent. The Bacalhoa is a Cabernet wine and has lovely blackcurrant fruit while yet retaining a wind-swept, piny Atlantic coast bite. These wines are made by Peter Bright, an iconoclastic Australian, and at Palmela he makes a Muscat – light, fragrant and fruit-sweet rather than luscious – for João Pires which is so delicious I can't help but return to my original thought: Portugal has the raw materials, but needs another hundred Peter Brights to make it all happen!

The Ramisco of Colares is one of the rarest wine grapes in the world. It has never had to be grafted against the lethal vine louse phylloxera because the vines grow in windswept sandy pockets along the Atlantic shore, and phylloxera cannot survive in sand.

· GOOD PRODUCERS ·

Dão and Bairrada São João, Grão Vasco, Cantanhede, Caves Velhas.
Vinho Verde co-operatives: Ponte de Barca, Ponte de Lima, Moncão, Verco-ope, Solar de Bourcas, Palacio de Brejoeira; Vinho Verde is also made by all the producers listed for other wines.
Other wines Fonseca, Carvalho, Ribeiro & Ferreira, Borges & Irmão, da Silva and Aliança.

· PORT ·

We've got the French to thank for port. Not that the Portuguese will take too kindly to this point of view, but it's true! Hostile Anglo-French relations, triggered by the War of Spanish Succession in 1702, cut off supplies of Britain's favourite wine, claret, and a replacement was needed in double quick time. Responding to the situation, British wine merchants – encouraged by recent trade agreements with Portugal like the Methuen Treaty of 1703 – sought to create a new 'claret' in the Douro valley, inland from Oporto.

Although they failed to produce anything remotely resembling Bordeaux red, by throwing in a bucket or two of brandy to keep the wine healthy for the long voyage home, they *did* lay the foundations for an entirely new category of great wine: fortified wine. This is wine with brandy added either after (most sherries) or during fermentation.

In time, the merchants realized that when they added brandy half-way through fermentation, the wine tasted sweeter and far better, and by the mid-nineteenth century it was universal practice. They also realized that some areas of the Douro valley were clearly superior: the further they pushed up to Pinhão and beyond – where the slopes are as sheer as ski runs and the earth arid and unyielding – the more remarkable the wine.

· THE VINEYARDS ·

There are actually 600,000 acres (240,000 hectares) of permitted land, but only 60,000 (24,000) are planted with vines – simply because the wild country cannot be tamed. And although some shippers are now buying up vineyards, the smallholding run by a family to cover their needs and little else is still the norm in the Douro valley; as a result, these 60,000 acres are divided into 80,000 vineyards.

The vineyards are mostly on terraces, supported by painstakingly constructed drystone walls, and so narrow that they cannot be worked mechanically. But now, even in the best areas round Pinhão, as replanting occurs the mini-terraces are bulldozed away and wider, more manageable stretches of vineyard

Now there is a good road snaking through the wild mountainous region of the Upper Douro. But once wine boats had to brave the swirling waters and shoot the rapids of the 'golden' river to take their precious cargo of wines downstream to the port merchants and shippers in Oporto.

are cut from the hills. In some less precipitous vineyards, terraces are being abandoned altogether, and the vines are in rows running up the hills as they would be elsewhere in Europe.

· CLASSIFICATIONS ·

A considerable amount of Douro wine is sold as red or white *vinho de mesa* (table wine). However, the best wine is usually reserved for port, but the government, through the Instituto do Vinho do Porto, controls the amount which may be made into port wine each year, and the price for grapes. This is where classification becomes important. All the vineyards are classified A to F, according to geographical position, microclimate, soil composition, altitude, gradient, level of production, and also age of vines, quality of grape varieties and even vineyard maintenance!

Technically a superstar vineyard could get 1,680 points, but anything over 1,200 is classified as A and allowed to make 600 litres of port per 1,000 vines. Class F means you've scraped together 400 points or less and are only allowed to make 260 litres per 1,000 vines. The rest has to go for table wine – at a much lower price.

There are 48 authorized grape varieties for port, although only about eight red and eight white are in common usage. Of these the most important are the red varieties Tinta Roriz, Tinta Francisca, Touriga Nacional and Touriga Francesa.

· MAKING PORT ·

Once picked, grapes are brought in to a central farm or *quinta*. Traditionally, they were piled into wide concrete troughs called *lagares*. Then, as soon as the men returned from the vineyards, they had a quick tea break, washed their feet – and all jumped into the *lagar* to spend the rest of night treading tons of grapes.

Some *quintas* still use this method, but most now use 'autovinificators' – like giant coffee percolators – where the juice is constantly forced upwards into a tank by the carbon dioxide from fermentation and then flows down onto the cap of grape skins and pulp. This process is repeated perhaps 150 times over a 36-hour period, during which time maximum colour and flavour are extracted and the alcoholic level reaches about 6°. Then the juice is run off, and the brandy – here called *aguardente* (translating approximately as 'firewater' and, at 77°, nearly twice the strength of whisky) – is added; usually 29 gallons (110 litres) to 116 gallons (440 litres) of wine.

After resting for a few months, this blend is either put into barrels at the *quinta* or else transported to Vila Nova de Gaia, the town opposite Oporto across the river Douro where port-shippers have their 'lodges' – their cellars and offices. Until 1986 all port *had*, by law, to be shipped through Vila Nova de Gaia. This

Quinta do Noval's Nacional Vintage is particularly prized because it comes from a tiny patch of ungrafted vines not affected by phylloxera. The Taylor's is a tawny port. All wines with a statement of age but no vintage date are likely to be aged primarily in barrel, and are therefore gentler to taste than a vintage wine of equivalent age.

· VINTAGES ·

The best vintages are 'declared' by shippers and these wines usually take a long time to mature. Best recent declarations are 1983, 1977, 1970, 1966 and 1963. 1982 is good but not spectacular, 1980 better, and underrated, 1975 generally uninspiring and ready to drink now – far too soon really. However, since you may have to wait 15–20 years for these to mature, the 'off-vintage' wines are often far better value, and the pleasure hardly any less. 1978, 1976, 1974 and 1968 all produced excellent Single Quinta wines.

restriction has now been lifted and may result in a proliferation of unfamiliar port names.

· PORT STYLES ·

The wines are classified and aged according to their quality, and market requirements. There are various alternatives.

Vintage port is the most exciting, glorious, exhilarating experience port has to offer. The best wines from the best sites in the best years are kept apart. A shipper will let the wine develop through two winters before he decides if he will 'declare a vintage' from this special selection. (Not all shippers declare, even in excellent years.) The chosen few are then blended and aged in oak 'pipes', barrels of 139 gallons (630 litres), for two years. This means the wine, at bottling, is still tough, fiery, uncompromisingly savage, rich and heady – all at once. It will generally need between 15 and 25 years in bottle to soften the passionate mix of headstrong flavours into something sweet, perfumed, with the most delicious blend of blackberry, blackcurrant, cherry and damson fruits, a tobacco or herby spice, something peppery, and at its heart something medicinal, mineral, animal, still growling with the memory of the uncivilized hill valley ledges whence it came.

Single Quinta wines are from the best farms, but in 'non-declared' years. They are usually bottled at about two years, but not sold until they are ready for drinking – around ten years old or more. Much cheaper than 'vintage' port, they nevertheless have all the characteristics, although less intensely, and generally represent a very good buy.

Crusted ports are also an excellent buy. They can either be from one vintage or else be a blend of high quality wine from two or three vintages, bottled at between three to four years. Like single *quinta* wines, these offer vintage-style at a much lower price and are at their best between two and six years after bottling; the date of bottling appears on the label. Crusted refers to the deposit the wine throws in bottle, though it won't be quite so heavy as that of a vintage port.

Late Bottled Vintage ports were, traditionally, high quality wines from good but not 'declared' years, bottled after four years. This meant they had softened, and lost some colour and fire, but still needed a few years in bottle to blossom. There still are a few good examples around – Warre and Smith Woodhouse are two – which are delicious at six to twelve years old. They are marked by having driven corks rather than ordinary stoppers. However, most LBVs – as they are called – are now bottled at nearer six years after heavy filtering. They are sweet, light, do *not* have any real 'vintage' character, and do *not* improve in bottle. Vintage Character wines are similar, but without out vintage date.

· GOOD PRODUCERS ·

Taylor, Graham, Warre, Dow, Fonseca, Smith Woodhouse, Cockburn, Quinta do Noval, Churchill, Santos Junior, Calem, Ferreira.

Tawny wines have done all their maturing in wood. They range from quite a full tawny brown tinged with red, to the palest of tawny golds. They are soft, subtle-flavoured ports – with a sweetness akin to moist brown sugar and raisins. They can be drunk chilled and tend to be at their best between 10 and 20 years; age is normally marked on the label, though some labels merely say 'Fine Old Tawny' or something similar – usually for wines less than ten years old.

Ruby ports are the bread-and-butter, most basic wines: a blend of the lesser wines in a shipper's lodge, bottled after about three years. Although they *can* age in bottle, that isn't the point: ruby ports should be drunk for their simple grape-skin sweetness and for the spirity 'throat-warming' qualities of youth.

White port is popular in Portugal but, sweet or dry, these wines tend to be fairly fat and heavy-flavoured, with something of the grapy sweetness of half-fermented wine still present. Dry whites will say 'dry' on the label and are much the better – though since the Portuguese themselves often drink white ports with tonic water or lemonade they're not exactly held in awe. However you drink them, ice cold is the temperature they need to be.

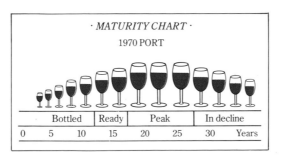

· MATURITY CHART ·
1970 PORT

Bottled	Ready	Peak	In decline
0 5 10	15	20 25	30 Years

· MADEIRA ·

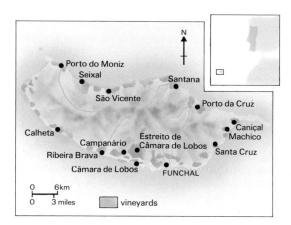

Left **The vines in the foreground will only produce table wine. True madeira will come from the terraces below the chapel on the right and scrambling up the steep cliff face behind. Some terraces here are so precipitous that they cannot be reached by road.**

Right **Winter pruning gets under way high above the Atlantic waves.**

Often called 'The Pearl of the Atlantic', Madeira hasn't always made such a favourable impression: when the first Portuguese explorers got to nearby Porto Santos in 1418, all they could see of the island of Madeira, off to the south-west, was a turbulent pile of dark clouds. The intrepid seamen decided that these were 'vapours rising from the mouth of Hell'; but they thought the earth was flat too, so they scuttled back to the Algarve for fear of falling off the edge!

Well, Madeira is still a majestic outpost of sheer cliff face and jagged rock 400 miles (644km) off the coast of Morocco, but its name has now become inextricably linked with leisure and pleasure. The leisure fame is due to its equable climate which, throughout the winter, lures northern European sun-lovers away from the ice and snow at home. Madeira's 'pleasure' reputation is more far-reaching, since it is the home of one of the world's finest, yet least known wines.

Madeira is one of the three classic fortified wines, the others being port and sherry. The island itself is rocky and precipitous, and was so thick with forest when the Portuguese did begin to settle it, soon after that first abortive attempt, that their leader – called 'Zarco the blue-eyed' – had them set fire to the island to clear spaces for houses and agriculture. They made a thorough job of it; the blaze lasted for seven years! Although Madeira is now a bit short of trees, the resulting wood ash created a unique soil for the vines combining with the volcanic soil to give high acidity – crucial for ageing the wines – and the strange, smoky tang that marks all madeiras, sweet or dry. The other factors creating this taste are the unusual grape varieties and the even more unusual method of maturing the wine.

· GRAPES AND WINE STYLES ·

Traditionally madeira is labelled according to its four main grape varieties. All of them are white, and each is vinified separately to produce a distinctive style.

Sercial produces the driest wine and may be related to the German Riesling. With its light gold colour, steely acidity and dramatic savoury 'attack', it sometimes bears a fleeting resemblance to a wayward Alsace Riesling. This is the most 'shocking' of madeira flavours, and not only needs a good ten years to be remotely ready, but can last for a century, by which time it is so intense it is positively painful.

Verdelho may be related to the Pedro Ximénez, the sweet sherry grape, and here gives the softest of the four wine types. But 'soft' is a relative term with madeira, since the wine is still pungent and smoky, although with a fair amount of medium sweet fruitiness.

Bual, or Boal, grape has so far defied any attempts to link it with mainland European grape varieties and gives rich brown wine, but with ever-present madeira acidity. This is the most common madeira style.

Malmsey, the original and best, is probably the Greek Malvasia grape which was the first type planted in Madeira (at the instigation of Henry the Navigator) more than 500 years ago. This dark brown wine is startingly sweet, yet its almost caramel richness is intertwined with a smoky perfume and a refreshing nip of acidity which is unexpected in such a luscious wine, and which makes it less cloying than port.

Sercial is a wonderful aperitif wine, more original than Fino sherry, more appetizing than dry port. Verdelho can also be drunk as an aperitif and was the type which would traditionally be drunk mid-morning with madeira cake a century ago. Bual and Malmsey are for drinking by themselves.

Although these four grapes are the famous names they occupy only about 10 per cent of the vineyard area. A fifth type, the red Negra Mole, has more acreage than all the others combined, and, until Portugal joined the European Economic Community in 1986, many wines would be made from the adaptable Negra Mole, whatever they said on the label. Nowadays a wine must be at least 85 per cent constituted from the grape named on the label, but cheaper madeiras, without a grape name, will probably be Negra Mole.

· MAKING MADEIRA ·

The initial 'creation' of madeira is, ideally, similar to that of port and the level of sweetness

are poured into barrels (or, in the case of cheap wines, concrete vats), and placed in hothouses or *estufas* where they are gently baked at about 45°–50°C for up to six months. Some especially prized barrels are placed in a room next to the *estufa*, so that they are only gently warmed. This process – the key to madeira's greatness – is the result of a happy accident. In 1665 a British law forbade the export of European wines to British colonies except by British ships using British ports. Well, Madeira is closer to Africa than Europe, and the Americans and West Indians, not taking at all kindly to being ordered about from London, began shipping their wine – in their own boats – direct from Madeira. The long sea voyage in the baking hold was found, to everyone's amazement, to improve the wine dramatically.

So the shippers went one further. They began supplying wine to ships en route for the East Indies as ballast, on the understanding that it would be kept in the hottest part of the hold – and returned undrunk, of course. The result was wonderful smoky wine, and soon there were holds full of madeira zigzagging backwards and forwards across the equator, and returning home transformed. Nowadays this nautical roasting is no longer possible, what with air travel and containerization, so it is achieved more economically but less romantically in the *estufas*. This cooking process not only gives the wine its remarkable smoky taste and gold-to-brown colour, but also is largely responsible for its limitless longevity; in effect, the wine undergoes a kind of 'semi-pasteurization'.

Madeira is almost always sold without a vintage since, as with sherry, the *solera* system (see page 195) is used to blend the finished wine. Each madeira company has batches of good madeira wines laid down as the foundation for a blend, and every year these are 'refreshed' with younger wine of a similar type, which then, luckily, takes on the character of the older wine, rather than simply diluting the style. You may find some wines sold with a *solera* date. These are likely to be tremendously good, tangy mouthfuls and worth the fairly high price.

A 'vintage' madeira from a single year is one of the wine world's greatest rarities. They don't usually announce a 'vintage' until the wine is 30 years old; there was a great fuss in the mid 1980s when they announced 1954 and 1956! A 1956 madeira will not be approaching its peak till something like 2020, and will probably improve for at least another 50 years after that. I've tasted madeiras back to 1808 and they've just got more and more astonishing!

· CLASSIFICATIONS ·

However – back to the real world – madeiras are now classified at three levels. Reserve, for blends whose youngest component is at least five years old. Special Reserve is for blends with a minimum of ten years age, and Extra Reserve for wines of at least 15 years age. Descriptions like 'over 10-years-old' may also be seen on the labels. These wines should have a grape name on them. If there is only a description such as 'Finest', 'Selected', 'Choice'. with a description of the relative sweetness of the wine, then the wine will be a blend based on Negra Mole.

The name 'Rainwater' is occasionally seen. This is a light Verdelho style which became very popular in the United States, seemingly after some barrels had been diluted with rainwater whilst awaiting shipment. Instead of sending the weaker brew back, the Americans loved it, and this designation can still sometimes be found.

Although madeira has rather lost its place in the drinks cabinet there are at last signs of a revival, based on quality, so do give it another chance. The wines are of tremendous quality and quite striking individuality, and the world of wine can't afford to lose one of its great originals.

is fixed by the addition of extremely strong grape alcohol – usually at least 95 per cent by volume. This firewater is added to the fermenting wine, and, not surprisingly, stuns the yeasts into premature retirement so that no more fermentation can take place. According to how sweet you want the end product, this is done early or late in the fermentation, either when there is still a great deal of unconverted sugar left in the juice – as for rich Malmsey – or when almost all the sugar has been converted to alcohol – as for dry Sercial. However, there is an increasing move to create the lesser Buals and Malmseys by fermenting the wine dry, and then adding a sweetening 'mistella'of grape juice fortified with strong spirit – as in the making of sweet sherries.

Then comes the fascinating bit. The wines

Most madeiras are labelled according to their grape variety. Here we have Malmsey – the sweetest style – and Boal, the alternative spelling for Bual – the second sweetest style.

· UNITED STATES ·

What I love about the United States is that the time-honoured description – Land of Opportunity – still holds good. And nowhere is it more obvious than in the world of wine. Whereas in Europe it may take generations of struggle for a winemaker to gain full acceptance from his peers, in America it can happen overnight. One day you can be a greenhorn, with a wine-making manual in one hand and a bunch of grapes in the other; the next, you can be hailed as a sensation. It means *everyone* has a chance, and it means that people are prepared to 'have a go', untrammelled by tradition and elitism. And it *doesn't* always involve throwing money around. Many of the most exciting developments are miles away from the 'aristocracy' of California's Napa Valley, on smallholdings in California's Lake County and Anderson Valley, in Washington and Oregon, and in Maryland, Connecticut and Long Island. If you look at the list of gold medal winners in major US wine competitions, half of them didn't exist a decade ago, and some don't even produce enough wine to supply their local market town. Yet the 'Land of Opportunity' tag doesn't just apply to the new high-fliers. America has recently led the way in providing the 'opportunity' for mass-market consumption – enjoyable wine at affordable prices, and, as a result, cheap wine worldwide owes an amazing debt to the US and its winemakers, and their revolutionizing of wine-making techniques.

Twenty years ago, as now, most of the world's vineyards were concentrated in the hot flatlands of France, Italy, Spain, Argentina – and California. The wine they made veered between adequate and appalling. California did better than most: having suffered along with the rest of the country the humiliation of Prohibition when everyone reacted to repression by turning to hard liquor and 'kicks at any cost', it pumped out an enormous quantity of the strong, sweet fortified wines which seemed to be about all that the scarred palates of the 1940s and 1950s could cope with. The rest of the world's *vin ordinaire* prairies just plodded on producing tasteless, oxidized rubbish for an audience which had never known anything better.

Well, thank goodness for the sixties, and thank goodness for America. In this most liberal and uninhibited of eras, Americans turned against the heavy, sweet gut-blasters in a big way. The Central Valley of California, providing more than four bottles out of every five that Americans drank, was faced with chaos and bankruptcy. So in true American style, the local university – the University of California at Davis, at the northern end of Central Valley – set out to save the situation. What started as a purely domestic exercise, catapulted California into the front-line of international wine-making.

· NEW DEVELOPMENTS ·

Davis scientists discovered that the very same heat that ripened grapes in the vineyard was the chief agent of disaster in the winery. Hot cellar conditions and hot fermentation temperatures could turn decent grapes into vinegar since bacterial action becomes uncontrollable at a temperature of 30°C or more. Also, any fruit or aroma the grapes might have had was literally 'boiled off' during fermentation. So they worked out

methods of cooling the grapes and cooling the fermentation. They picked at dawn; they picked at night; they developed machines which, in a couple of hours, could harvest as much as a team of pickers in a day; and they developed 'refrigeration'.

Refrigeration is probably the single greatest advance in wine-making. By air-conditioning the wineries, and fermenting the wines in tanks – preferably of stainless steel – fitted with cooling devices, the winemaker gained *control* for the first time.

· VINE SPECIES ·

America's earlier gift to the wine world wasn't quite so welcome. It was phylloxera. This aphid is endemic along the eastern seaboard. Although the native *labrusca* species of vine on the East Coast can tolerate phylloxera, the *vinifera* species, from which *all* good wine grapes derive, can't. One stray shipment of vine cuttings, via the Botanical Gardens at Kew in London, set phylloxera on a path of destruction which devastated Europe's vineyards. Happily the country which caused this plague also brought its salvation. *Vinifera* vines, grafted on to American rootstocks can survive phylloxera, and today

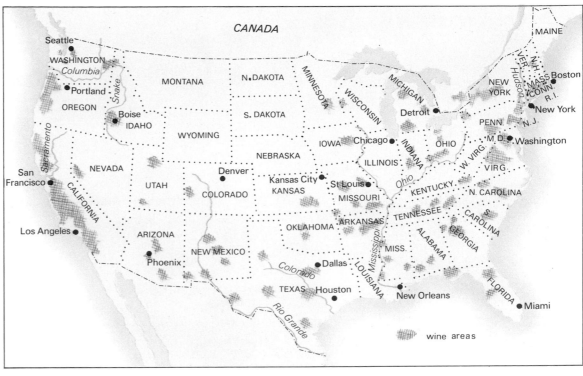

The Sonoma Valley (*above*) is where modern American wine-making began in the 1850s, yet it is the Napa Valley (*left*) which has powered Californian wines to prominence during the 1970s and 1980s.

almost all the world's wines are grown from *vinifera* vines courtesy of American rootstocks.

This also explains why America has such a varied wine culture. On the East Coast early settlers tried to use imported vines. These all died, so they had to use the native *labrusca* varieties and after a generation or two probably got used to its strange sickly scent. From the Atlantic, right into the Mid West, *labruscas* predominate and almost all wine companies base their business on these vines. It is only since the 1970s that more than a handful of wineries even considered *vinifera*. In the deep south – hot, humid and exhausting as it is – they don't even try. There, the local *rotundifolia* variety with its enormous, loosely bunched berries is the only vine type which doesn't rot in such a climate. The wine it makes is certainly memorable – memorable enough for most outsiders not to order it twice.

· CURRENT TRENDS ·

Until the 1970s the American wine industry was purely domestic, only concerned with local markets or, in the case of California, the national market. It looked inwards, not outwards. However, a few wineries were aware of what was happening elsewhere – particularly in France – and wondering if they could do the same. They needed a leader and, in 1966, they got one. When Robert Mondavi set up his winery at Oakville in California's Napa Valley he proved himself to be a brilliant winemaker, showman and born publicist all in one. He realized that,

with the remarkable growing conditions of California as yet hardly tested, the future lay in stretching the state's capabilities as a producer of great wine. He was also canny enough to take as models the famous red and white wines of Bordeaux and Burgundy in France.

There were some mighty tasting battles in the seventies and eighties, and California won most of them; the rest were frequently won by wineries from Washington and Oregon which followed California into the fine wine arena during the 1970s. Indeed there was a time when California seemed solely concerned with saying, 'Anything you can do I can do better'. Maybe they can – if it boils down to concentrated flavours from superripe grapes which blast the opposition off the table. But California has done all that now and has gained the confidence to sit back and work out what it does *best*. And it's perfectly clear that within the confines of the state there are fine vineyards to suit every possible style of wine. By adding in Washington and Oregon you create a kind of 'European Economic Community on the Pacific' – conditions similar to the best of Germany, France, Spain, Italy. . . all ready to be exploited.

With the will to succeed and the means to do it, all the New World lacks is the patience of the few hundred years it took Europe to find out what *it* did best. But with modern insights into how to grow vines and make wine, you can now do as much experimenting in a year as you could do, just a century ago, in a generation. The world hasn't seen the best of America's wines yet, but it won't be long before it does.

· CALIFORNIA ·

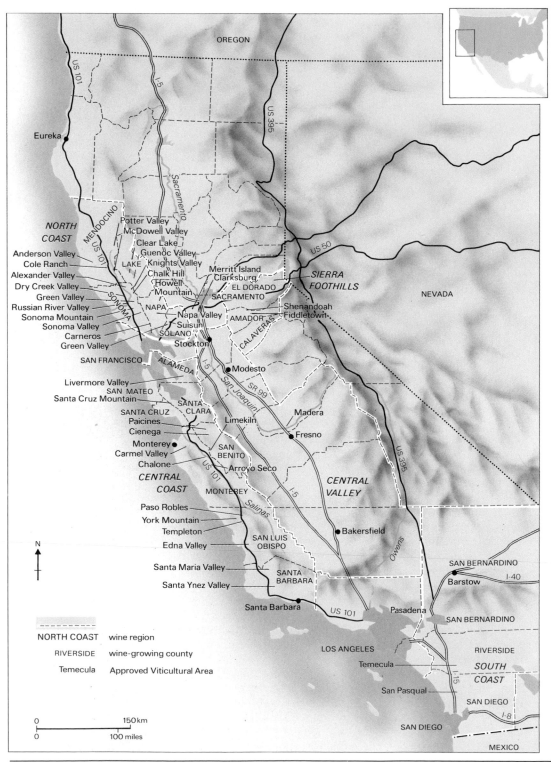

NORTH COAST wine region
RIVERSIDE wine-growing county
Temecula Approved Viticultural Area

California's potential as a fine wine producer has never been in doubt since missionaries first planted vines there, around San Diego, in 1767. But it needed the right kind of market to prove the point. The heady days of the nineteenth century were marked by the crazy, thirsty expansion of the Gold Rush, and by the flood of immigrants from the eastern states and from Europe – all bringing with them preconceived ideas of what wine should taste like and how it should be made. You won't get a German, a Hungarian, an Italian and a Frenchman to agree now on how wine should taste, and you didn't then. But you could get them to agree that wine must be made and so, until Prohibition, California produced the riotous mishmash of wine styles its population demanded – and never thought to seek wider markets.

Prohibition stunned wine industries throughout the United States and few survived. But California hung on aided by its strength in the dessert grape market, and by some fairly sharp practice in the sale of communion wine (which was still allowed) and of grape juice – which usually carried a stern warning that the addition of yeast to this pure, wholesome beverage would have the unfortunate effect of causing it to ferment. Sales of yeast boomed. California survived.

But by the time Prohibition was repealed in 1933, serious damage had been done. Good wine varieties had been uprooted in favour of high-yield eating grapes – indeed it wasn't until 1974 that wine grapes once more accounted for more than half the grapes grown; wine-making equipment had been abandoned, skills forgotten, and, crucially, a whole generation of Americans had no experience of wine as one of life's pleasures.

So the easily-irrigated Central Valley, inland from the coastal ranges, set to making what the market seemed to want after years of palate-numbing cocktails and bootleg whisky – and that was big, sticky fortified wines. A few outposts of excellence around San Francisco Bay, largely in the Napa and Sonoma Valleys, went back to high-grade grapes and top-quality wine-making – but demand was discouragingly low.

The 1960s changed all that. In the new

cosmopolitan climate wine emerged as a sophisticated social drink, ideal for entertaining, and a natural adjunct to food. The necessary market finally existed and California grasped its chance in both hands. Between 1970 and 1985 the acreage of wine grapes more than trebled. More importantly, the acreage of the top varieties like Chardonnay, Cabernet Sauvignon, Riesling and Pinot Noir increased eightfold. California now has twice as much Cabernet Sauvignon as the Médoc in Bordeaux – its traditional home. There is five times more Chardonnay in California than in Burgundy's Côte d'Or. And during those 15 years wineries increased fourfold.

California – a single American state – is now the sixth biggest producer in the world. It completely dominates the US wine scene, and, in global terms, it has arguably done more for wine over the last 20 years than any other producing area. During the sixties and seventies, California led the world in wine-making technology – thanks to the University of California's wine school at Davis.

· WINE TECHNOLOGY ·

In general the Davis oenologists – wine scientists – worked on two fronts. First, they examined Europe's achievements and tried to emulate them. They had mixed success, but the work they did on barrel-ageing, yeast selection, fermentation control, and other related subjects taught the whole world – including Europe – that great wine-making wasn't some mystical exclusive skill but could be learnt. Second, they revolutionized the handling of bulk wines. The vineyards of the world's hot countries have, for generations, been turning out lakes of spoilt, oxidized, pleasureless wine. In its own grape-bowl, the Central Valley, California showed that – with vineyard mechanization, scientific selection of grape varieties' best clones, night-picking, scrupulously clean wineries and cool fermentation – good, fruity, enjoyably fresh wine could be produced from any vineyard in the world.

· CLIMATE AND GEOGRAPHY ·

California's wine-growing areas are moulded by two major geographical features. The first

Jekel Vineyards at Greenfield in the Arroyo Seco AVA was one of the leaders of the move to find cool-climate conditions south of San Francisco. Arroyo Seco is in the Salinas Valley in Monterey County, and though Jekel is highly successful many grapegrowers have actually found conditions *too* cool due to the funnel of sea air which races up the valley each day from the Pacific.

is the Pacific ocean. Contrary to expectations, its inshore waters are surprisingly cold. Yet California is far south, on a similar latitude to Spain and North Africa. The sun beats down day after day, heating the air to sauna level. But if you stand on San Francisco's Golden Gate Bridge around noon you will see a remarkable phenomenon: on the horizon appears a sea-mist, which becomes a bank of fog sliding into the Bay as if drawn by some unseen force.

That is exactly what is happening. On every hot day, in all the mountain valleys leading off San Francisco Bay (in particular the Sonoma and Napa Valleys), the air warms and rises, creating a vacuum which sucks in cool air off the Pacific – and with it the fog, formed off-shore by the morning sun. In most European wine areas the idea of regular fog would be regarded with horror. But California has a relentlessly hot climate. Without some way of cooling the grapes it would be impossible to prolong the ripening period and produce fine wine.

So all California's fine wine areas – with a couple of exceptions where high altitude does the cooling job equally well – are situated where a break in the Coast Range or a river valley heading seawards creates a funnel for this cold air blanket. And amazingly, the further south you go, the more ferocious it can be. The northernmost vineyards of Mendocino County are considerably warmer than those of the Salinas Valley, 100 miles (160km) south of San Francisco, where the funnel effect is as strong as a winter gale and grapes must often be left till November to ripen. Another 100 miles south, in the San Luis Obispo Valley – and even further down towards Los Angeles in the Santa Maria Valley – conditions can be more like the north of France, with grapes hardly ripening at all as they struggle to get at some of the over-efficient brilliant sunshine through the shielding fog blanket.

The second natural feature is the mountain chain known as the Coast Range. Where there is no gap to create a cool air funnel, the valleys behind the mountains boil. Although a blistering, arid climate makes fine wine production impossible (but port and sherry styles may do well), with irrigation, it does allow you to produce a stupendous amount of grapes – which ripen very quickly and which, because of the dry air, are virtually free of the rots that bedevil a damper vineyard. The San Joaquin Valley – colloquially known as the Central Valley – fits this description of a super-efficient bulk grape producer perfectly. It runs for over 400 miles (640km) from well north of San Francisco almost down to Los Angeles; but it is the southern section, from Sacramento to Bakersfield – over 200 miles (320km) long and between 50 and 100 miles (80–160km) wide – which provides the brawn for Californian grape production. Over 80 per cent of the State's wine grapes grow in this one region and, as cheaper brands are often made from table and raisin grapes as well, over 90 per cent of the state's wine has its origins in this rich earth.

· RED WINES ·

Most grape varieties of any importance have been tried in California, and a number of new varieties have also been developed with considerable success. But some grape types have shot to prominence.

Cabernet Sauvignon is by far the most spectacular. As the leading Bordeaux grape, it was the one chosen by winemakers most eager to copy Bordeaux classics. Although Cabernet

Sauvignon rarely produces wines exactly in the Bordeaux mould, it has developed a rich, exciting style of its own, intense, strong, black-curranty, fairly tannic, and making up for its slight lack of complexity with tremendous, satisfying fruit and flavour.

Pinot Noir is not such a success story. The problem is that everyone has attempted to follow the Burgundian model, but no one, even in Burgundy, is sure what that model ought to be. The result has been vintage after vintage of adequate but insubstantial Pinot Noirs which, even when they do have the weight, lack the excitement and romance which make great burgundy great. Since the 1983 vintage more good wines have begun to appear, particularly from grapes grown in the cool Carneros area on San Francisco Bay – and if perserverance, investment and dedication will do it, then California will get there. However, while the Cabernet Sauvignon is a strapping, confident grape which doesn't mind being pushed about, Pinot Noir is a sulky primadonna which you can't bully, only wheedle, cajole and bribe. Perhaps fittingly, much Pinot Noir is now successfully turned into sparkling wine – the primadonna's delight.

Zinfandel, on the other hand, is a wonderful, bright-faced, easy-going grape which will make almost anything: some of the world's best port-type sweet wines, blockbusting reds or fresh fruity ones, even absurdly delicious rosé known, disarmingly, as blush wine. This is usually called White Zinfandel and generally has a stunning un-winey flavour of peaches and cream, grapes and fragrant tobacco. Zinfandel is probably in origin the bulk-wine producer Primitivo, from southern Italy, but it has achieved fame and fortune as California's very own variety. Its wine is marked by a pepperiness and a exhilarating black-berry and raspberry fruit. It's going out of fashion, which is very sad, because it's a great original.

Merlot is increasingly planted to soften the Cabernet Sauvignon, but also makes a lovely, rich, soft red wine in its own right.

Petite Sirah, originally the Duriff from France and not, confusingly, the great Rhône Syrah, makes good, tough, rather raisiny, tarry wines.

There are also various Italian and Portuguese varieties, as well as some new Davis 'crossings' like Ruby Cabernet and Carnelian

Above One of wine-making's muckiest tasks is taking place at Dry Creek Winery in Sonoma's Russian River – removing all pulp of skins, pips and stalks from the tanks at the end of fermentation.

The use of new oak barrels to age both red and white wines was pioneered by Hanzell winery in the 1950s. However the Mondavi winery (*above left*) was the first to embrace the technique wholeheartedly. This view of Mondavi's cellar shows French oak barrels being filled from enormous American wood vats, and in the background stands a row of German-style oval casks!

grapes which give fairly good wines in the Central Valley.

· WHITE WINES ·

Chardonnay is the star here, but by no means a star without personality problems. Growing the vine is the easy bit – it thrives in all but the hottest parts of the state. However it is the style of wine which still vexes producers. They set out to copy the white burgundy model, but the California fruit is too ripe to achieve the delicate power of the best Côte d'Or whites. They also bought new oak barrels to mature the wine which gave it an enormous toasty vanilla richness – but back in Burgundy hardly any producers were wealthy enough to use *all* new oak, they'd resort to some older barrels, with *far* less personality. For the Californians, it was really a case of thinking that money and commitment would bring forth a string of Montrachets. Well, it didn't, but it did produce some impressive rich, creamy Chardonnays with a wild and wonderful blend of fruit flavours – lychee, mango, peach, fig, melon. The style has now lightened a little as more cool vineyard sites come into production and less emphasis is placed on alcohol levels and new oak barrels; the 1984, 1985 and 1986 vintages have produced the best, most balanced Californian Chardonnays yet, and I'm sure there are better to come.

Sauvignon Blanc makes big wines here, which sometimes lack personality. Again, new plantings in cooler areas are producing far better results and there is now some delicious grassy, gooseberryish Sauvignon on the market. Robert Mondavi made the grape popular in the 1960s when he labelled a Sauvignon 'Fumé Blanc' (smoky white), reminiscent of Pouilly Blanc Fumé, the top Loire Sauvignon. It *can* have a slightly smoky flavour, and was an instant success. Nowadays, wines labelled Sauvignon are usually very dry and fresh; wines labelled Fumé Blanc may have a little oak richness, or may be mixed with less assertive Sémillon.

Riesling is here known as Johannisberg Riesling or White Riesling. In most of California the dry wine it makes is a little heavy and dull, but the late-harvest, noble rot-affected wines are tremendous, wonderfully grapy and honeyed and as soft and sweet as sultanas – yet with intense fruit and edge.

Gewürztraminer is grown, but rarely manages the blend of fresh fruit and spice which makes it exciting in the Pacific North-West.

Chenin Blanc and **Colombard** have been used as workhorse grapes for a long time, because they retain acidity in hot climates. Usually made as semi-dry gulpers, recent releases have shown they can do much better in a full, but sharp and dry style. These two grapes account for two-thirds of California's white wine crop, yet rarely appear on the label!

There is a wide variety of other grapes, mostly grown for blends, but Pinot Blanc has a slightly more important role to play as the base for many sparkling wines.

· WINE STYLES ·

California is now predominantly a table wine producer. However, this is a fairly recent development, mirroring the worldwide growth in consumption of light table wine and the fading away of the heavy 'dessert', high-strength fortified wine market. In the early 1960s over half the production was of fortified wine. Now it is less than five per cent; table wines make up about 80 per cent of the total with sparkling wines taking up the rest. In the 1980s, Wine Coolers – mixes of wine, fruit juice and carbonated water – have soaked up a lot of excess grape production in the Central Valley.

Many of California's cheap wines are sold either with a simple brand name or else with a completely spurious generic title like Chablis – which means absolutely nothing since Chablis, France's classic bone-dry white Chardonnay from one small area in northern

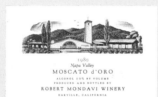

Heitz wines are some of Napa's biggest reds. 'Produced and bottled' in the Cellars means that vinification and maturation took place there – a quality pointer. Robert Mondavi was the Napa Valley champion who, during the 60s and 70s, persuaded the world of the worth of Californian wines.

Burgundy, when translated on to a cheap Californian wine can be sweet or dry, white, pink, sparkling, probably fortified too for all I know. So the Californians developed the idea of naming their best wines by grape variety: varietal labelling as in 'Chardonnay', 'Pinot Noir' and so on.

In Europe this is seldom necessary in classic areas, because the grape types allowed are already rigidly defined and enforced, and their use is taken for granted: for example, Pinot Noir is always used for Nuits-St-Georges and Sauvignon Blanc for Sancerre. However, since California's wine industry is still experimenting with what grows best where, you can't necessarily identify a wine type simply from where it grows. Much more accurate is to say what grape it is from, and so varietal labelling took hold in the 1960s. Of course, since grape varieties' flavours are so different, it makes excellent sense, and the system is now used all over the world in areas where a certain grape variety is not a foregone conclusion – or where there aren't too many in use to fit on the label.

Reserve, as a definition of wine style, does carry some weight in California. A variety of 'reserve-like' terms may be used – Private Reserve, Proprietor's Selection and so forth. Usually the wine is a selection of particularly good batches, maybe from named vineyards and will probably have more new wood ageing. All of this gives a bigger, longer-lived style – but also a higher price tag. Vineyard names are increasingly seen on labels and are also generally a sign of quality.

· REGIONAL CLASSIFICATION ·

The most far-reaching analysis of California's different areas and the kind of wines they are likely to produce, is the Davis temperature scale which classifies regions from One to Five on the basis of what are called 'degree days'. This system measures the amount of time the temperature stays above 50°F – the tempera-

Right **Two mighty rigs filled with just picked grapes from Santa Clara valley head south to Paul Masson's giant winery at Soledad. It is common practice for grapes to be trucked considerable distances to wineries in California.**

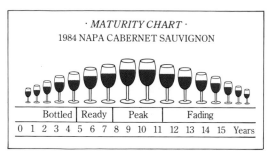

· *MATURITY CHART* ·
1984 NAPA CABERNET SAUVIGNON

Bottled	Ready	Peak	Fading

0 1 2 3 4 5 6 7 8 9 10 11 12 13 14 15 Years

ture which activates the vine's ripening cycle – between 1 April and 31 October, approximately the growing season for a grape harvest. So if a region had a week at a mean temperature of 60°F there would be seven days when the mean temperature was 10°F over 50°F – which would earn 70 'degree days'. If each day between 1 April and 31 October is monitored in this way, the resulting 'degree-day summation' will categorize an area as cool, medium or hot. It's really very simple, because *I* understand it, and for me to understand anything numerical, it *has* to be simple.

The grades for the five 'regions' are:

Region I 2,500 degree days or less. Very cool for California and best suited to white grapes, though Pinot Noir thrives; similar to northern European vineyards.

Region II 2,501 to 3,000 degree days. More like Bordeaux and generally good for red and white.

Region III 3,001 to 3,500 degree days. Pretty hot, similar to France's Rhône valley and, in the same way, best for big reds and fat whites.

Region IV 3,501 to 4,000 degree days. *Very* hot and really only suitable for dessert and fortified wines.

Region V 4,001 plus degree days. Frankly you can't make very exciting wine at this kind of North African temperature, but port varieties are successful.

· APPROVED AREAS ·

I shall refer to this 'degree day' system – despite the fact that it is an oversimplification, with little microclimates occuring all over the place – because it is a useful general guide. But one could say the same about Europe's

classifications based on geographical provenance. It does reveal, however, what was one of the fundamental differences of opinion between California and Europe. California said only climate mattered, Europe said nonsense, soil and geology are more important. Clearly they are *both* of vital importance, and it is worth noting that the Californians are now becoming much more interested in geology and geography as is shown by the establishment of their AVA system: Approved Viticultural Area – in effect, an Appellation of Origin.

So far AVA regulations are fairly rudimentary and do little more than define a geographical area, with the requirement that any wine sold under a particular AVA contains 85 per cent of wine from the named area and 75 per cent of wine from whatever grape variety is specified, if any. This is hardly very demanding, but the appellation concept is very new to California, where traditionally a winemaker bought his grapes or wine wherever he felt they suited his needs. Remembering that suitability of sites and, most important, suitability of grape varieties to different sites and soils, took hundreds of years to establish in Europe, it is perhaps best to see the AVA – so far – as simply providing some useful guidelines rather than anything more conclusive. Some areas are already showing particular suitability for particular grape varieties: Carneros, at the bottom of the Napa and Sonoma Valleys, is producing California's best Pinot Noir; the Edna Valley in San Luis Obispo is especially good for Sauvignon Blanc; but it will be another generation or two before all this is decisively sorted out.

There are now more than 40 AVAs. Some are single property appellations, some are subdivisions of bigger areas – there are nine subdivisions so far in the Sonoma County appellation – but the main ones are the County appellations, such as Napa County, 95 per cent of which is the famous Napa Valley, and five regional AVAs. Of these, North Coast (above San Francisco) and Central Coast (between San Francisco and San Luis Obispo) are the most interesting, Central Valley is the most

important for volume, and Sierra Foothills and South Coast are as yet of minor importance.

· NORTH COAST ·

This region covers all the finest vineyards to the north of San Francisco Bay, and two counties in particular are of enormous importance: Napa and Sonoma.

Napa County runs the length of the Napa Valley from Carneros on the Bay up to the warm springs spa of Calistoga in the north, and includes small areas of the Chiles and Pope Valleys to the east, Howell Mountain to the north, and hilltop eyries in the Mayacamas mountains to the east. There are about 25,000 acres (10,118 hectares) of vines, two-thirds planted with classic French varieties as well as with decent amounts of Johannisberg Riesling and Zinfandel. The styles of wine change dramatically as you move up the valley.

Carneros, at the bottom, is classified Region I cooled by the cold Bay breezes and fogs. It doesn't seem like a world-famous vineyard area at all, because the landscape is gently undulating grass hillocks obviously designed for grazing. Well, Carneros means 'sheep' and there were pastures here till some canny grape-growers realized the conditions mirrored France's Burgundy. There was a rush to buy up and plant Carneros land, but the vines still look strangely out of place, stitched on to their little slopes like gawky patterns on a grass-green quilt. But there is no doubting the potential of the wine. Pinot Noir from Carneros is cool, restrained, yet beautifully scented with the cherries and strawberries of burgundy.

Chardonnay is also cool, quietly building its character over the years into a marvellously refined wine, and Sauvignon is beautifully fresh and grassy. Wineries from all over the North Coast region buy Carneros grapes, and though many vineyards are still young Carneros is sure to go from strength to strength.

North of the small town of Napa, the flat valley floor is crammed with vines and, on

1982
SONOMA MOUNTAIN
CABERNET SAUVIGNON
TABLE WINE GROWN, PRODUCED AND BOTTLED BY LAUREL GLEN VINEYARD
GLEN ELLEN, CA BW 5010

Bandiera
Fumé Blanc 1983
Sauvignon Blanc
Mendocino County

Produced & Bottled by Bandiera Winery, Cloverdale, CA
BW3998, ALC. 11% VOL.

Laurel Glen in the Sonoma Mountains aims to make Bordeaux-style reds to the highest standard possible. First releases show they're getting there. The Bandiera is made from Sauvignon Blanc grapes but labelled Fumé Blanc, implying a fuller than usual style with possibly a little oak treatment.

both sides, slopes gradually climb up towards the trees and the tumbled rocks of the mountains. Through Oakville to St Helena, the climate gradually warms up to Region II, and many of the greatest names in American wine are here; Mondavi, Stag's Leap, Caymus, Domaine Chandon, Clos du Val, Heitz and Beaulieu. And here, along a stretch of magic dirt called the Rutherford Bench – running up the west side of the valley from Oakville to Rutherford – most of California's greatest Cabernet Sauvignons have originated. The wines of this 'Pauillac of the West' – tannic and difficult to tackle when they're young – are bursting with blackcurrant, mint, maybe eucalyptus, maybe cedar flavours. Although the Rutherford Bench is primarily Cabernet county, the whole range of grapes is grown in the central Napa giving good, strong flavoured wines.

The top end round Calistoga is hot, Region III – but also prone to spring frost. Although it makes good Zinfandel, the best wineries such as Cuvaison and Sterling predominantly use cooler Napa grapes from the south, or else like Schramsberg and Diamond Creek are up in the chillier mountains.

Sonoma County is very diffuse, covering nine different AVAs, as well as taking in some Carneros land in the south. It, too, has some exciting hidden mountain vineyards like Laurel Glen, Kistler and Carmenet, who are achieving great things with their dry, fragrant reds. However, Sonoma doesn't have the concentrated valley-floor carpet of vines which distinguishes the Napa. Furthermore Napa fame was built on long-established wineries, some pre-Prohibition, whereas most of Sonoma's finest wineries are relative newcomers, still making their reputation. Until the 1970s Sonoma wine was generally sold for blending, but in the last 20 years, vineyard land has trebled and plantations of Cabernet Sauvignon, Pinot Noir, Sauvignon and Chardonnay have risen fifteenfold.

If anything, Sonoma wines are softer and juicier, more easily approachable than Napa wines, and they are usually cheaper. However, this is a generalization, since some of America's densest and most expensive reds, like Jordan, come from Sonoma, as well as some of

Concannon Chardonnay from the Livermore Valley is designated 'California', showing that the grapes may have originated anywhere in the state. Although using the 'Central Coast' AVA, Sanford is based in the Santa Ynez Valley. As a young winery (founded 1982), it won't necessarily be able to buy all the local grapes it needs.

its most famous whites, like Chateau St-Jean.

Sonoma Valley itself runs up through a mixture of farmland, commuter towns and vineyards to Santa Rosa. From here, north to Cloverdale, lies the most concentrated group of Sonoma AVAs, and what used to be primarily a bulk wine supplier is now full of different personalities. Green Valley, to the west, is one of California's coolest regions with one of its best wineries – Iron Horse; while Chalk Hill to the east contains many important wineries such as Rodney Strong, and sparkling wine-maker Piper Sonoma. Knight's Valley, on the way to Calistoga in the Napa, is excellent for Cabernet.

However the three main Sonoma AVAs are Russian River, Dry Creek and Alexander Valley. Russian River was originally known for

bulk wine and sparkling wine – Korbel has its operation here – but Sonoma-Cutrer and Mark West are now blazing a trail of quality white wine for others to follow. The Dry Creek AVA, to the north-west of the town of Healdsburg, first became noticed for its excellent Sauvignon Blanc; Dry Creek Winery has continued with good Chenin and Chardonnay too, while Preston has supplemented its Sauvignon with Zinfandel. Alexander Valley, north of Healdsburg, seems able to grow almost any grape, and at any price level: Jordan's Cabernet Sauvignon and Chardonnay are excellent but appallingly expensive, while Clos du Bois' Chardonnay, Cabernet and Merlot are marvellously good and some of the best value in California.

Mendocino is the last important vineyard area in the North Coast region. Centred round Ukiah, 120 miles (193km) north of San Francisco, it features a range of AVAs – from the catch-all Mendocino to the single property Cole Ranch. Most of Mendocino is surprisingly warm, well into Region III because the Coast

California has led the way in wine-making developments of the last 20 years. More recently attention has turned to the vines themselves – in 'grafting-over' one vine type can actually be grafted on to the mature rootstock of a different type. Unfashionable varieties can be replaced by fashionable ones with the loss of only one harvest as against 3–4 if the vineyards were to be replanted. This experiment at Callaway Vineyard in Temecula has resulted in Chenin Blanc and Zinfandel growing on the same vine!

Range is hardly broken here, so big Cabernets and briary Zinfandels are common. Fetzer and Parducci lead the way in making a wide range of balanced, tasty and very well-priced reds and whites. The area also produces some of the best blush wine – like Bel Arbres' White Zinfandel – in the USA. In contrast to the rest of Mendocino, little Anderson Valley – between Ukiah and the Pacific – is extremely cool. The Louis Roederer Champagne House thinks it can produce first-class sparkling wine from Anderson grapes; Scharffenberger Cellars already does. In neighbouring Lake County the Kendall Jackson winery can make stunning whites.

· CENTRAL COAST ·

This region takes in the area from San Francisco Bay right down to San Luis Obispo.

Alameda County contains the Livermore Valley, which, along with the Napa, was California's original quality wine area; now it is so pressed by urban development that activity has largely moved away south. Only Wente and Concannon are still of much importance there.

Santa Cruz County only has 100 acres (40 hectares) of vineyards, but some of California's top wineries are perched in the mountains between San Jose and the sea. They have made their reputations on grapes bought from other areas: Ridge, for example, makes world famous Zinfandels and Cabernet Sauvignons from grapes grown in the Napa (York Creek), Sonoma (Geyserville), and San Luis Obispo (Paso Robles), as well as in the Santa Cruz Mountains (Monte Bello).

Santa Clara County, primarily known as headquarters of the giant Almadén operation, is also losing ground to urban sprawl – to such an extent that Almadén now has most of its vineyards well to the south, at Cienega and Paicines in the San Benito mountains, (where Calera also makes exceptional Pinot Noir).

Monterey County, centred on the Salinas Valley, has seen dramatic expansion – from less than 2,000 acres (809 hectares) of vineyards in 1969 to around 33,000 (13,355 hectares) – and now constitutes the most important Central Coast region. The vineyards are the most up-to-date in California, wide-spaced for machine picking, fitted for drip irrigation – and cool. So cool, in fact, that early plantings in the upper Salinas Valley have been grubbed up because the grapes just wouldn't ripen and the winds were too wild. The best vineyards are now in the Arroyo Seco AVA. The best quality wines come from Chalone, a single-property AVA 2,000 feet (610 metres) up and committed to 'recreating' Burgundy; Jekel, a more conventional producer in the heart of Arroyo Seco; and from Paul Masson and the Monterey Vineyard whose middle-of-the-range reds and whites are excellent value.

San Luis Obispo County has also increased in size phenomenally, from only a few hundred up to around 6,000 acres (2,428 hectares) of vineyards in less than 20 years. Again the cooling breeze is prominent, especially in Edna Valley AVA where the Chardonnay ripens very slowly into the autumn. Paso Robles AVA is warmer, but still cooled by altitude, so that Zinfandel and Cabernet have real intensity.

Santa Barbara County, to the south, includes Santa Maria Valley AVA – if anything, too cool – and Santa Ynez Valley AVA which is a little warmer and, despite a slightly green edge to some of the wines, does well with Sauvignon, Chardonnay, Pinot Noir and even Cabernet Sauvignon. Zaca Mesa, Firestone and Sanford are the leading wineries.

· CENTRAL VALLEY ·

This vast area, distinguished by the size of its wineries, is unrelentingly hot. Yet the biggest winery in the world – E & J Gallo at Modesto – is quite happy with that, and pumps out almost 176 million gallons (800 million litres) of very passable wine each year. Altogether five Central Valley companies control 72 per cent of California's output and the general standard is 'good commercial'.

· SIERRA FOOTHILLS ·

This is old Gold Rush Country, north-east of San Francisco and centred on Amador County. Its Zinfandels can be the spiciest, strongest-tasting and most memorable in all California.

· SOUTHERN COAST ·

There are only two areas, the rapidly shrinking, city-threatened San Bernadino and the rapidly growing Riverside. South of Los Angeles, in Temecula AVA, one would expect all fortified wines and bloated reds, but no – a gap in the mountains called the Rainbow Gap sucks up cool ocean air, and Callaway, the leading producer, has become famous as a *white*-wine-only winery!

· VINTAGES ·

Trying to do a vintage chart for California is as major and complex a task as trying to do one for all of Europe, since the variation in climatic conditions is absolutely dramatic – from the virtual desert of Central Valley to the foggy chill of Santa Maria Valley. Napa conditions are often held to be typical, but that is like saying Bordeaux represents all Europe. Patently this isn't so. However, to generalize, 1986 and 1985 have both been highly successful and 1984 was cool and first rate; 1983 wasn't quite so exciting, with some rather dilute reds, but good whites; 1982 was very attractive for simple, straight-up flavours; 1981 was a little unbalanced with many reds turning out a bit fierce, though the whites were gutsy; 1980 was an excellent balanced vintage – the reds are now approaching their peak. There is still a lot of argument as to whether older vintages keep well: so far only the best properties show signs of doing so.

· GOOD PRODUCERS ·

Napa Mondavi, Trefethen, Clos du Val, Stag's Leap Wine Cellars, Heitz, Domaine Chandon (sparkling), Schramsberg (sparkling), Acacia, Caymus, Cuvaison, Diamond Creek, Far Niente, Mayacamas, Monticello, Phelps, Schug, Saintsbury, Sterling.

Sonoma Clos du Bois, Laurel Glen, Sam Sebastiani, Chateau St-Jean, Iron Horse, Jordan, Kenwood, Matanzas Creek, Sonoma-Cutrer, Kistler, Simi.

Mendocino Fetzer, Scharffenberger.

Lake County Kendall-Jackson.

Santa Cruz and Santa Clara Ridge, Mount Eden Vineyards, David Bruce, Felton-Empire.

Alameda Concannon, Wente.

Monterey Chalone, Jekel, Calera, Monterey Vineyard.

Santa Barbara Firestone, Sanford, Zaca Mesa.

San Luis Obispo and Temecula Edna Valley, Callaway.

· PACIFIC NORTH-WEST ·

In 1966, when David Lett planted Pinot Noir at Eyrie Vineyards, there was not a single winery producing *vinifera* wines in the north-western states of Oregon, Washington and Idaho. Twenty years later the Pacific North-West, as this grouping is now called, is the USA's number two wine region. Oregon has led the way in terms of headline-grabbing achievements, winning countless medals and tasting competitions against the best that France and California have to offer and, in particular, making a speciality of the world's most temperamental red wine grape – Pinot Noir.

Washington hasn't worried so much about winning medals, but has turned a semi-desert area centred on the Yakima and Columbia rivers into a massive irrigated vineyard producing large amounts of exceptional wine at a fair price.

And even Idaho, which until recently I'd only associated with topnotch potatoes for baking round the campfire, has now begun to produce some startlingly good Chardonnays and Rieslings.

· OREGON ·

Although Oregon began making wine as long ago as the 1820s, Prohibition effectively wiped out those efforts and it wasn't till the late 1960s that a revival began. It started when some of the wine pioneers of California realized that their hot, even climate would never produce the light, fragrant styles of Germany, the Loire valley and especially Burgundy; Oregon with its cool growing season and 40-plus inches of rain a year became a focal point. Others realized that they'd never be able to afford to buy into the burgeoning Napa and Sonoma wine scenes. But from the very start Oregon has been a wine community of smallholders – there are only two properties, Knudsen Erath and Tualatin, over 50 acres (20 hectares), and while this does mean, as in that other famous region of smallholdings – Burgundy – that inconsistency is a problem, it also means that there are an increasing number of devotedly hand-crafted wines being produced. The pioneers started in the relatively warm Umpqua Valley 180 miles (290km) south of Portland, but then centred their efforts on the Willa-

mette Valley just to the west and south of Portland.

Pinot Noir was then, and is now, the grape everyone wanted to tame, and results show that growers like Knudsen Erath, Bethel Heights, Yamhill Valley and above all Rex Hill are getting there. In 1979 a 1975 Eyrie Pinot Noir came second to a 1959 Chambolle-Musigny in a blind tasting competition in Paris – and it beat a Chambertin 1961! Obviously on the right lines. In 1985 Oregon went one better. Or rather three better. Ten Oregon 1983 Pinot Noirs were set against seven Burgundian 1983s and took the first three places! Such tastings are never conclusive, but they do show that Oregon's claim to be America's answer to Burgundy has some substance. In hot years like 1983 and 1985 Oregon Pinot Noir has more character and fragrance – but also more power and intensity than California's offerings. In cooler years like 1984 it can seem a bit too delicate for its own good. Pinot Noir dislikes easy growing conditions and mass production methods, and the Oregon vineyards, on a similar latitude to Bordeaux, and largely cultivated by bands of

committed enthusiasts in numerous small hilly sites may well indeed be the 'Promised Land'. If wines like the Rex Hill 1983s, or the Knudsen Erath, Bethel Heights and Yamhill Valley 1985s are anything to go by, Pinot Noir has found a second home at last.

Chardonnay, as so often, seems to work well, here often achieving a cool crisp character rather similar to a lightly wooded Chablis, but too often its lighter style is surprisingly marred by slightly sloppy wine-making. Both Riesling and Gewürztraminer are excellent, lighter and sharper than Californian versions, but with a delicious grapy spice. They're even making something of a speciality of Pinot Gris; and first efforts at sparkling wine also look promising. There is a little Cabernet and Merlot in the Umpqua Valley, but such wines would usually be made with grapes bought from Washington.

This practice of trucking grapes inter-state is allowed, but it *must* be stated clearly on the label since Oregon has the strictest labelling requirements in the USA. There are legally four delimited areas which must be stated on the label – the southerly Rogue River region,

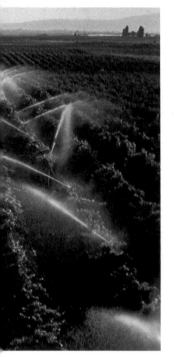

Far left The Pacific North-West is a fascinating mixture of 'homesteading' vineyards – in Oregon, small in size and frequently cleared from the surrounding forest – and the brash, confident, high-tech operations in the Yakima Valley in Washington State (**left**), where irrigation and mechanization have created high quality vineyards in near-desert conditions.

the Umpqua Valley, the Willamette Valley, and the new plantings in the east on the Columbia River. Each wine must contain at least 90 per cent of the grape variety stated (except Cabernet Sauvignon, which can be 75 per cent, blended in with 25 per cent of its traditional Bordeaux partners Merlot and Cabernet Franc). California, by comparison only requires 75 per cent across the board. Ninety-five per cent of the wine must be the vintage stated, and none of the 'generic' names still popular in California – like Chablis, Sauternes and the like, are allowed.

· WASHINGTON ·

While Oregon began on a strictly individualistic path and is only now moving into mass production, Washington's strength was built on the ability to produce large amounts of fresh, agreeable wine at a low price with more marked acidity and fruit than the bulk wines of California. The Yakima and Columbia Valleys are in an almost total rain shadow on the east side of the Cascade Mountains. With annual rainfall of only 6–8 inches the wild dry moonscape of semi-desert land has been

transformed into an enormous irrigated vineyard, capable of producing yields five times as high as Oregon. The days are very hot, but the nights, affected by the mountains and the desert are extremely cool. Also the days are long – in June, for instance, Washington averages 17·4 hours of daylight per 24 hours against California's 15·8. All this makes for a rare combination of very ripe grapes rich in sugar from the daytime sun balanced by high acidity from the cold nights.

The conditions could have simply created a fruitbowl turning out massive quantities of jug wine at an ultra-low price. Luckily Washington decided high quality affordable wine was where the future lay. As glut and a fall in demand hit the jug wine producers of California, they have been proved triumphantly right. They produce beautifully fragrant Riesling and Gewürztraminer, ripe, soft Chardonnay, excitingly typical grassy Sauvignon and honey-rich but tangy Sémillon. Reds, too, are exciting. The Cabernets are full of an almost Australian blackcurrant and mint fruit but dark and tannic enough for long ageing, and the Merlot is softer but equally impressive.

With approaching 15,000 acres (6,000 hectares) now planted to *vinifera* grapes, Washington is second only to California in acreage, and there are another 12,000 acres (4,850 hectares) earmarked for expansion if the demand for Washington wines stays healthy. To this end the most important of the 50-plus wineries still keep their headquarters at Seattle, where their customers are, and where they can benefit from a tourist trade. At vintage time some of these wineries have to truck the grapes from their distant vine-

yards at night, to avoid them oxidizing in the daytime heat, but an increasing amount of wine is now made in wineries constructed in the vineyards, and only taken to Seattle as a finished product.

One interesting phenomenon has been the recent establishment of various small vineyards and wineries in the damp, green, rather English countryside round Seattle. You'd never get such varieties as Chardonnay or Cabernet to ripen here, so the customers have to acclimatize themselves to wines very much in the 'English' tradition and made from such grapes as Siegerrebe and Müller-Thurgau which they wouldn't even have heard of in California!

· IDAHO ·

Idaho has been encouraged by the growth of the Washington wine industry, and has begun to develop its own, particularly on the high land above the Snake River Valley near Caldwell. The Sainte-Chapelle winery is the leader here, and first releases of Chardonnay, Riesling and a marvellous Pinot Noir sparkling wine show that there's another star rising in the west.

American labels are keen to inform the consumer. Eyrie Vineyards can boast a bit as well, since its Pinot Noir has outperformed top French Burgundies in blind tastings in France. Rex Hill is another of the new breed of Oregon wineries, concentrating on small amounts of high quality classic wines.

· OTHER WINES OF THE USA ·

It says a lot for California's dominance of the US wine scene that the state with the second highest production – New York – only manages seven per cent of the total. Of that, little would be familiar – still less, palatable – to an ordinary wine drinker brought up on Californian or European wines, since most are made either from *vitis labrusca* or from hybrid crossings of *vinifera* and species like *labrusca*, both of which are banned in quality vineyards throughout Europe and California.

Yet, except for the Dakotas, Nebraska, Wyoming, Louisiana and Alaska, (someone reported vines in Maine so, astonished, I count them in!) it looks as though all the other states do produce some kind of wine from some kind of grapes. Because of this you *could* say that America grows a greater variety of wines than anywhere else in the world. Which other country can make dry white wines equivalent to the greatest white burgundies, dry reds which rival the best of Bordeaux, sweet whites which emulate the great Rhine Beerenauslesen and sparkling wines as good as those of Cham-

Grape-growing is only possible in up-state New York because of the moderating influence of the Finger Lakes. Even so the climate is pretty extreme, and most grape varieties can't stand the winter cold there, which is why New York is the only major wine area of the world whose wine industry is based on the rugged, cold-resistant *vitis labrusca*. *Labrusca* wines are a distinctly acquired taste.

pagne? And then continue with a parade of names and flavours like sparkling Catawba, Maréchal Foch Reserve, and Scuppernong – all historic, all individual? Scuppernong. Now there's a grape for you – the Scuppernong grows its enormous grapes in loose clusters more like cherries than normal grapes. The flavour of its wine – a speciality of the southern states – is like a cross between cherryade, grape jelly and Euthymol toothpaste. Well, you mustn't damn it if you haven't tried it. Some people love it: a Scuppernong, Virginia Dare, was America's Number One brand for years before Prohibition (although the label said it

was made of Tokay grapes). Unique, it certainly is.

So, it's very important not to impose a *vinifera*-based snootiness on what is obviously a tradition of some considerable importance. Many of these wine areas were established in the last century by European settlers who used the experience of generations to do the best they could with the curious-tasting local raw material. And although California does produce over 80 per cent of the nation's wine, out of the 1,100 or so wineries in America, more than 500 are outside California.

· THE GRAPES ·

The East Coast is the most active area, and New York State its hub. New York is fascinating because it bases its wine industry on three grape species: *vitis labrusca* (an American native regarded, almost universally outside the United States, as unsuitable for wine-making – although Canada, Brazil and one or two central African countries do what they can with it), hybrid crossings between American *labrusca* and European *vinifera*, and *vitis vinifera* itself – the true wine grape.

Labrusca, indigenous to East-Coast America, has two crucial strengths. It can cohabit with phylloxera, the vine louse which eats European *vinifera* for breakfast and which is naturally present in the East-Coast soil. And it can survive the intensely cold winters. Its weaknesses are its taste – a pretty fundamental minus – and the fact that its grapes are usually low in sugar and high in acid. That taste! It's a strange, insidious, slightly nauseous, sweet perfume that wine people call 'foxy'. I've never been close enough to a fox to check out what perfume it was wearing, but this weird pungent sweetness (actually an ester called methyl anthranilate, but that doesn't leave me any wiser than 'foxy') pervades all wines made from *labrusca* grapes.

Labrusca grapes totally dominate New York plantings – though over half of them are used for jelly and juice in which the weird perfume is unexpectedly attractive – but it is the hybrids and *viniferas* which catch the attention. They were given a great boost in 1976 when the Farm Winery Bill allowed farmers to bypass usual retail channels and sell their wine at their own gate. Suddenly wine could be tourism too, and all the types of 'enthusiastic amateurs' who transformed the California wine scene in the 1960s began to open small wineries in New York. More than 50 wineries have been established since 1976, almost all of these growing hybrid and *vinifera* grapes.

The hybrids, which have unfamiliar names like Baco Noir, Maréchal Foch, Seyval Blanc and Vidal Blanc, were introduced in the 1930s by Philip Wayne at Boordy Vineyards, Maryland, in an attempt to find phylloxera- and frost-resistant vines which would provide decent drinks. They are mostly a bit dull, but they *aren't* foxy and represent a crucial half-way house between *labrusca* and table wine.

Vinifera, on the other hand, *can* be a sensation. It was a Rumanian and a Frenchman, Constantin Frank and Charles Fournié who, against everyone's advice, began planting *vinifera* (grafted on to *labrusca* rootstock to beat phylloxera). In the 1960s they began producing small amounts of remarkable wine: Frank's 1961 Vinifera Cellars Trockenbeerenauslese was launched at $45 a bottle and found its way to the White House high table. Since 1976 there have been a series of new wineries making up for lost time, though the local Vine Experimental Station at Geneva, NY, still classifies *viniferas* as 'marginal'.

· NEW YORK STATE ·

Lake Erie, in the north-west of the state, is planted with Concord *labrusca* almost entirely, but estates like Woodbury and Schloss Doepken show *vinifera* can work.

Finger Lakes, also in the north-west, are long thin lakes running north-south, and have been the centre of New York wine-making for over a century. Most of the wines are *labruscas* of every shade, consistency and sweetness, but since 1976, emphasis is being placed more on hybrids and *vinifera*. The big companies, with the exception of Gold Seal who make a speciality of Chardonnay and Riesling, are primarily *labrusca*-makers only dipping their toes in the *vinifera* pond. But small enterprises, like Heron Hill, Wagner, Wiemer, Vinifera Cellars, and Glenora, are making a series of relatively light but very successful Chardonnays, Rieslings and Gewürztraminers, as well as some slightly less inspiring reds, mostly Pinot Noirs.

Hudson River is the original New York State wine area, but has only recently become involved in the New Wave, though there are now more than 20 wineries. Best known is Benmarl – producing good Seyval Blanc and Chardonnay – and West Park, who obviously understand Chardonnay, because theirs is delicate, toasty soft and beautifully balanced like a light-weight Meursault.

Long Island, however, is where the action is. This is New York's newest area, and was first planted by Hargrave as recently as 1973 – at Cutchogue on the North Fork. This was originally potato farmland, but the temperate climate is absolutely ideal for vines. Hargrave has now been followed by a string of others – Pindar, Lenz, Ressler, Bridgehampton (on the South Fork) – making a total of towards 1,000 acres (405 hectares) of vines. The Chardonnays are crisp, excitingly intense, softened a little with oak, and are set to be some of America's finest whites. Sauvignon, too, is brilliantly sharp and grassy, and, though Pinot Noir and Cabernet Sauvignon are still a little too green, as the vineyards mature these will

also be exciting. On the East Coast, *this* is the place to watch.

· OTHER WINE REGIONS ·

Things are happening in other states, too.

Connecticut's Crosswoods Winery makes beautiful Chardonnays which sell without effort at about $15 a bottle.

Virginia, back in 1619, was the first area to try planting *vinifera*, and it's now nearly 200 years since Thomas Jefferson finally realized *he'd* never make *vinifera* grow in this phylloxera-infested soil. Yet today there are over 60 wineries hard at it, with hybrids and *viniferas* and Meredyth and Rapidan have made quite a splash with whites.

Maryland, next door, does best with Cabernet Sauvignon – as Byrd and Mowbray show.

Pennsylvania, where America's first commercial winery was established in 1793, is getting it right with reds *and* whites; Naylor makes good Riesling and Allegro does well with Cabernet Sauvignon and Chardonnay.

Texas, too, has decided to have a go. Of course! America just wouldn't be America if Texas didn't. And when Texas has a go – look out California! 'Wine – the next *big* thing from Texas' is the Department of Agriculture's slogan. So far the best areas are in the Dallas-Fort Worth area, the Hill country north-west of Austin, the High Plains area near Lubbock and the north-east border with Oklahoma. The wines are amazingly good for an industry hardly away from nanny's apron strings. And look at these figures. In 1982, Texas made around 300,000 bottles, in 1984, a million bottles, and in 1985, one and a half million bottles. Texans boast they'll be Number Two to California in quantity and quality within a decade. That's very modest of the Texans. I thought they were only content with being Number One!

This Gewürztraminer is made by Great Western Winery, but the specially selected grapes are from a single vineyard, Laursen Farm – a sign that quality is becoming increasingly important in New York State. The 'champagne' label does a good job of looking French but only wine from France's Champagne region is true champagne.

· AUSTRALIA ·

Australia has set the world of wine on fire more than once. During the 19th century, Australian wines rapidly built a reputation for quality, so much so that in the 1873 Vienna Exhibition a 'Hermitage' wine from Bendigo in Central Victoria was judged best of its type by an international jury. When it became clear that the wine wasn't French, the French jurors resigned in protest saying the wine was so good it *had* to be French! Then, as if that wasn't enough, Australians marched straight into the lions' den when they attended the 1882 Great Bordeaux Exhibition and Victoria carried off the trophy as most successful exhibitor from 'the rest of the world'. Exhibitions were deadly serious in those days and an award of this sort was a major achievement.

After that, however, the phylloxera scourge and a loss of interest in good table wine on the home market meant the disappearance of most exciting wines for the best part of a century. The fierce, tarry reds and heavy, soggy whites which then became the normal table tipple of Australia were of little interest to outsiders. But Australia, like California, woke up to the rest of the world in the 1960s, and the results since then have been just as dramatic. Australia now has the highest per capita consumption of table wine in the English-speaking world – over 26 bottles a year. In 1960 the figure was less than 3 bottles.

There has been a most fundamental change in wine-making philosophy. Whereas previously most of the effort went into ripening the grapes as quickly and efficiently as possible under the scorching southern sun, now the emphasis has shifted. Winemakers began to search out the coolest parts of the landscape. We always think of Australia as being one long frolic in the sun, but in fact, round the coastal strip, and particularly in Southern Victoria and South Australia, (and Tasmania, of course) there are regions which actually get less warmth than areas like Bordeaux and Burgundy in France, and the great Coonawarra region of South Australia is nearer Champagne in temperature – and that's cool!

· THE GRAPES ·

The realization that cool vineyards can produce the greatest wines has seen a change in the type of grapes planted. Previously it was all the hot country grape types which completely dominated the reds, and a mixture of dull Mediterranean varieties, aromatics like Rhine Riesling (the Australian name for German Riesling), Muscat and Gewürztraminer, and a bit of Sémillon which made up the whites. While Shiraz (the French Syrah) remains important for reds, the Cabernets, Merlot, Malbec and Pinot Noir are the grapes the new cool climate regions are now concentrating on. Sauvignon and Chardonnay – virtually unheard of a decade ago – now head the list of good quality white plantings, though Sémillon and Rhine Riesling are also surviving because of their innate qualities, which new wine-making techniques are bringing out.

· NEW DEVELOPMENTS ·

Because so much of Australia's original vineyard land *is* hot, winemakers there were in the forefront of developing refrigeration and temperature control techniques, the understanding of yeast behaviour and refined filtration systems. The ability to preserve some fruit freshness in the wine by cool-

Arid, sun-baked meadow land thirstily grazed by the sheep; unlikely, gawky gum trees sticking up above the horizon into the pale, hot sky, and vines, looking prim and green pressed against this tough, dry background – but this is the contrast upon which all Australian vineyards are founded.

fermentation, however hot the vineyard it came from, and then leave some sugar quite safely in the wine, owing to very precise filtering, allowed the creation of fruity, slightly sweet whites, and this style swept Australia, finally providing a wine style which would wean Australians off beer and fortified wines. It is still far and away the biggest sector of Australian wine and may account for as much as 60 per cent of the domestic market.

The vineyards are of several kinds. There arc thc rc-plantings of the regions which made Australia famous a century ago – like the Yarra Valley, Bendigo and Geelong in Victoria. There are the wholesale developments by large companies, who have developed the Coonawarra, and Padthaway/Keppoch areas of South Australia and Drumborg in Victoria single-handed. And there are the totally new developments, usually by individuals who might be farmers, scientists, lawyers or doctors (there are loads of these last two) who just wanted to get back to the land and justify the belief that perhaps they, too, could make great wine. They've approached the task by investing in good vines, keeping yields low, consulting

expert winemakers, and not skimping on good equipment or high quality new oak barrels.

More often than not the wines are a sensation. Although many start out with a French model in mind, the flavours they produce from Cabernet Sauvignon, Shiraz, Chardonnay and Rhine Riesling are unique in today's world of wine. They are once again winning competitions whenever they are entered. And while you might have expected young Australian winemakers to troop over to Europe to learn how the past masters did things, one of the most heartening things for the brotherhood of wine is that you can go into an Australian winery at vintage time and find the sons and daughters of some of France's and Germany's greatest winemakers in there with their sleeves rolled up, learning the time-honoured skills from the brilliant newcomers of Down Under.

· THE LABELS ·

Australian labels can be extremely helpful to the initiated, and fairly bewildering to the newcomer. Nowadays most Australian wines are labelled according to grape variety, but traditionally words like 'Burgundy' or 'Chablis' were used to describe a type of wine regardless of grape. These 'generics' could then be subdivided by having 'Bin' numbers – a favourite Australian way of identifying a particular batch of wine kept separate from the others. Since there are around 500 Australian wineries, some of them producing two or three dozen different types, the whole thing could be impossibly confusing! What would somebody's 'Bin 255 Burgundy' mean to you? Not a lot if you hadn't done your homework. Also, just because the label gave the address of the winery, it didn't mean you had any idea where the wine actually came from. Trucking wine from one state to another is still perfectly acceptable in Australia, and many top wineries still do it. One of New South Wales' top wineries is proud of the quality of wine it blends in from Coonawarra in South Australia. The majority of South Australian wines are blended for extra balance – the winner of the Best Young Red Wine trophy in 1980 was a blend of Barossa, Southern Vales and Coonawarra fruit, hundreds of miles apart. One of the best

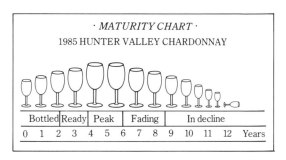

· *MATURITY CHART* ·
1985 HUNTER VALLEY CHARDONNAY

Bottled	Ready	Peak	Fading	In decline	
0 1	2 3	4 5 6	7 8	9 10 11 12	Years

Sauvignon wines released in 1985 was a blend of Australian and New Zealand wine!

· CLASSIFICATIONS ·

With this kind of tradition it is easy to understand that attempts to produce an 'appellation system' have met with limited success, though almost all the top wines are now labelled according to grape variety and will state their provenance.

The first attempts at devising appellation regulations were in the little regions of Mudgee in New South Wales, Margaret River in Western Australia and in Tasmania. These seem to work well, but they are for small isolated regions in whose interest it is to promote their own identity.

Victoria, however, is now trying out a statewide 'authentication' scheme involving seven regions, divided into 21 subregions. It has had the sense not to be too dogmatic – restrictive appellation systems in Italy and Portugal are the bane of imaginative winemakers – and so it may work. Eighty per cent is the magic figure. An Authenticated Victorian Wine must be 80 per cent Victorian grapes, and at least 80 per cent of a blend must be made in Victorian wineries. Stated varietals and 'regional' specifications must also be valid for at least 80 per cent of the wine and the vintage for 95 per cent. That all seems fair enough; it makes one wonder what was happening before really!

Victoria was probably the least 'blend orientated' of the main states, so it is uncertain whether either South Australia or New South Wales will want to submit even to these controls. Also, there's the endless problem of what you're actually trying to do. Many of Australia's greatest wines have been blends of wine from all over the place, because there is a noble tradition of blending in the industry. But then many of its worst wines will also be statewide, nationwide blending jobs. It really all comes down to saying, 'Blending is fine – but don't try to pretend on the label you haven't done it'. If that's what the legislation wants to achieve, I'm all for that.

Hunter Valley in New South Wales has taken a rather different line. They have started an 'Accreditation' scheme for wines which are wholly from the Hunter Valley. They are submitted for blind tasting, and wines which are regarded as particularly good – and typical of the region – can be accredited at two levels. The 'Classic' crest is awarded to wines judged as being 'the pinnacle of wine quality ... representing the ultimate standard that can be expected from the grape variety and vintage'. These are often special stocks held back for release when mature and usually available in strictly limited quantities. The 'Benchmark' crest is awarded to younger wines, not yet mature, but which the judges feel could achieve 'Classic' status – there may be as many as

5,000 cases of these available. If, I repeat, *if* this can be made to work efficiently and impartially, this 'Accreditation' could prove a useful guideline for the consumer.

The other way a consumer can judge Australian wine quality is to read the list of medals it has won at the Australian Wine Shows. These are major events and a trophy is a major achievement. A gold medal should ensure you a *very* good wine, a silver or bronze something well worth drinking. Look on the label for the wine's show track record.

· NEW SOUTH WALES ·

Not so long ago, New South Wales, with its boast of being the 'Premier State', could have expected to take up the greatest amount of space in any chapter on Australian wine, because its Hunter Valley was reckoned to be Australia's top quality wine region. Well, the Hunter is still New South Wales's top area, but it can no longer lay undisputed claim to being Australia's best, and, in a time of tremendous change and progress, the Hunter has

found it more difficult to adapt than most other regions.

To a great extent this is because the Hunter is the furthest north of any of Australia's great regions, and can be almost subtropical at times. James Halliday, Australia's leading wine scholar, says of this inland river valley 125 miles north of Sydney, 'In modern wine-making terms you could never professionally allow anyone to plant here'. The growing season is far too hot and humid, you get a drought in the spring when you need rain and a downpour in the autumn when it's the last thing you want, hail is always threatening and frequently arriving – and until recently you also had the pollution of nearby Newcastle's smelters to contend with. At least cloud cover appears over the mountains every afternoon like clockwork during summer to cool down the vineyards or else you just couldn't grow grapes at all.

The Hunter is in two parts – the original, lower Hunter Valley, near Cessnock, and the newly established irrigated Upper Hunter round Muswellbrook.

Lower Hunter Valley is full of history and many famous wines have been produced. Historically these have been based on Shiraz (here called Hermitage) and Sémillon (here called Hunter Riesling: they were an idiosyncratic lot these Hunter old-timers, and their descendants still are). The old Hermitage wines start out tarry, chunky, leathery, stinking of the soil, but with ten years' ageing can achieve an amazing mellow softness. The Sémillons start out lean, but become rich and oily and almost unnervingly powerful with 10–15 years' age, as in old Lindeman, McWilliams and Tyrrell wines.

The modern Hunter Valley owes its fame much more to Cabernet Sauvignon and Chardonnay. Lake's Folly with Cabernet and Tyrrells with Chardonnay gave the valley new life and revived faith in its potential. Tyrrells (whose Pinot Noir is also one of Australia's best) and Rothbury (excellent modern Shiraz) have, with smaller high-class operations like Lake's Folly, Evans Family, Peterson and Sutherland, put the Hunter valley back on the map in the 1980s.

Upper Hunter Valley was developed to provide reasonable quality wines in quantity

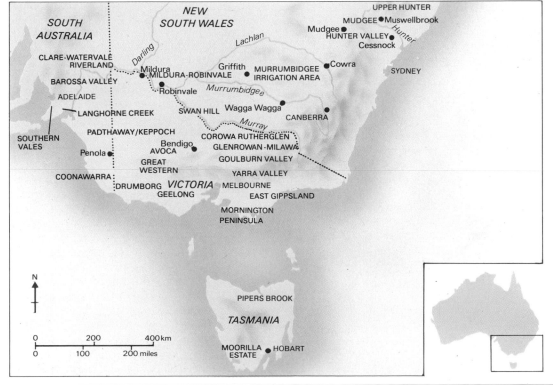

A surprisingly green vineyard scene in the Hunter Valley just north of Sydney, where the vines are continually stressed by heat and lack of water, yet manage to produce some of Australia's most individual reds and whites.

Mudgee was one of the first regions to instigate an appellation system along French lines. Federal law only requires a wine to be 80% from the region specified, but certified Mudgee Appellation wines must be 100% from Mudgee. 'Boutique wineries' (small-scale operations often run by gifted amateurs) are now commonplace in Australia, but the great original is Lake's Folly established in the Hunter Valley in 1963, by Sydney surgeon Max Lake.

during the boom years of the 1960s and 1970s. Penfolds started it, but the banner is now held aloft by Rosemount who have made a remarkable success of their estate near Denman; their Chardonnays, in particular, have set new standards worldwide for affordable super-quality dry white wine.

There are three other special areas in New South Wales.

Mudgee is important for applying an 'appellation of origin' system ahead of the rest of Australia. Its wines are good without being inspiring.

Cowra is a source of good Chardonnay for several major wineries.

Murrumbidgee Irrigation Area (MIA) is New South Wales's grape basket, producing a large amount of cheap decent wine with McWilliams the most important company, while De Bortoli have shown that not only can fine table wines be produced in the irrigated outback, but that intensely sweet Sauternes-type wines of remarkable quality are also possible – and in quantity too.

· VICTORIA ·

Victoria was the only state to be devastated by phylloxera (South Australia and most of New South Wales are still phylloxera-free). The vine aphid destroyed what was Australia's leading wine region in the 1880s and 1890s with distressing thoroughness. Although a few wineries like Brown Brothers, Best's, Seppelt, Chateau Tahbilk, and the Muscat-makers of the North-East survived, all the other traditions of quality were lost.

In the 1960s enthusiasts began replanting the nineteenth-century vineyard areas. And since the slate had been wiped clean, the exciting blend of modern knowhow and old-fashioned commitment to quality could be brought to bear immediately. As a result Victoria is again producing the most exciting, original range of wines in Australia. It is only the third biggest producer, but it is expanding vineyards faster than any other state and the majority of new plantings have only one thing in mind – quality.

Altogether there are 12 major wine districts now in Victoria, and each district has several definable subdivisions. Some of these, like East

Gippsland, are so new and so isolated, that many locals have not tasted the wines. Other fine vineyards, like Seppelt's Drumborg way down in the cool south, or the startlingly good and totally original Delatite in the Mansfield Hills belong to no 'official' area (both of these are banded together in Central and Southern Victoria) – but the unique quality of their wine flavours means others are sure to follow. Victoria does have irrigated areas like Mildura on the Murray (where Mildara in particular produces good table wines and some of the finest 'sherry-type' wines in the world) but its great strength is the variety of cool climate locations scattered across the state.

The South Along with Drumborg and East Gippsland, there is the infant Mornington Peninsula area, and some of Victoria's most exciting wines are being made near Geelong, south of Melbourne, and in the Yarra Valley north-east of Melbourne. These are two of the original Victorian wine areas killed off by phylloxera, lack of interest and urban development. Well, they're fighting back in the best possible way – with quality. The blackcurranty, cedary beauty of the Cabernet Sauvignons and the delicate balanced depths of the Chardonnays already rank them among the best in Australia, and therefore the world. They also do great things with Shiraz, Rhine Riesling (Seville Estate's Trockenbeerenauslese sweet Rhine Riesling is very special) and even Pinot Noir. Wineries to look for are Hickinbotham, Idyll and Prince Albert in Geelong, and Yarra Yering, Lillydale, Seville Estate, and St Huberts Coldstream Hills (among others) in the Yarra Valley.

Central Victoria has a swathe of fine vineyard areas. Great Western makes good sparkling wine (Seppelt's new Salinger is outstanding) and marvellous Shiraz (look for Best's, Mount Langhi-Ghiran and Cathcart Ridge). The Pyrenees also make good sparkling wine (Chateau Remy) as well as some fine Sauvignon and outstanding Cabernet and Shiraz for ageing (Taltarni, Warrenmang, Redbank). Bendigo is a large area with potentially Victoria's best sparkling wine (Yellowglen) to the south, but reds in general predominate with Balgownie, Mount Ida and Chateau Le Amon leading the pack. The Goul-

Above **Bailey's of Bundarra in north-east Victoria, where world-class fortified Muscats and Tokays bake gently to a rich, brown brilliance.**

burn Valley provides the microclimate for many of Victoria's pace-setters, Tahbilk and Mitchelton in the central Goulburn, and the remarkable Tisdall in the north, whose creamy Chardonnays and delicate minty Cabernets age beautifully but are too absurdly delicious when young to hang on to.

North-East Brown Brothers at Milawa are one of the few survivors of the original nineteenth-century companies. They are a table wine specialist in a fortified wine area, and blend tradition with modernity as well as anyone in Australia. They make an enormous range of wines varying from good to excellent, and are heavily involved in the nearby King River Valley in finding cool high-altitude vineyards, even in this hot-spot corner of the state. Their Koombahla Cabernet is a good example. Finally, in Glenrowan and Rutherglen, you have the 'stickies' from Baileys, Morris, Chambers,

Above **Rugged individualists like Mick Morris make Liqueur Muscats in the Rutherglen area of north-east Victoria which equal the finest in the world.**

Stanton and Killeen and All Saints. These fortified Liqueur Muscats are sweet, so luscious they seem to be bursting with richness of raisins and honey and the exotic heady scent of clusters of hot-house table grapes in mid summer. Australia does many wines as well as the rest of the world. For Liqueur Muscats, North-East Victoria has few rivals in sight.

· SOUTH AUSTRALIA ·

South Australia's vineyards spread from Clare Valley and the massive irrigated Riverland on the Murray River north of Adelaide, right down to the southern tip of the State where the isolated Coonawarra suddenly appears on the famous slash of red earth, out of nowhere. In between are the major areas of the Barossa just north of Adelaide – which at one time, through its Barossa Riesling, seemed almost synonymous with Australian white wine – and

the Southern Vales just to the south of Adelaide, as well as the Adelaide Hills perched above Adelaide, Langhorne Creek at the mouth of the Murray River and Padthaway/Keppoch down towards Coonawarra.

South Australia does produce enormous amounts of wine, rarely less than 60 per cent of the national output and usually nearly three times as much as second placed New South Wales. Indeed the Riverland area alone produces more than all of New South Wales.

Riverland, an endless vista of fruit trees and vines stretching along the route of the Murray River, is almost unnervingly verdant through irrigation, while to both sides away from the sprinklers near-desert crouches at bay. More than any other single region it is the reason for the endless supply of good cheap wine on to the Australian market – often in the form of bag-in-box, which is the Aussies' favourite way of purchasing light whites. This is because the Riverland is a supremely efficient grower and processor of grapes using the ultimate in modern equipment. Most of the wine grape varieties are grown here, but the bulk of the crop is made up of Shiraz and, in particular, enormous amounts of Muscat, which doubles as a table grape if there is the demand.

Clare Valley is best known for its soft though very individual Rhine Rieslings, and more recently soft but beautifully balanced Chardonnays from producers such as Enterprise, Mitchell's Jeffrey Grosset and Jim Barry. Other producers, such as Pike and Mount Horrocks, make remarkable Sauvignon and Sémillon. Reds are less exciting, except from makers like Grosset.

Barossa Valley is finding that its big, super-

ripe styles of reds and whites don't meet the modern taste and is having to adapt its wine-making philosophy accordingly. Modern companies like Hill-Smith and Orlando have been most successful, and Orlando are past masters at mixing high quality with low price. The most exciting Barossa wines in the future will come from the high, cool vineyards of East Barossa Ranges in Pewsey Vale, Eden Valley and Springton.

Adelaide Hills is the most exciting recent development in South Australia and it is spear-headed by Australia's most lionized young winemaker – Brian Croser. At Petaluma in the foggy highlands above the city, he is producing Pinot Noir and Chardonnay of such crisp, dry

elegance that his aim to make the finest sparkling wine in Australia (he has Bollinger as a partner) looks sure to be realized.

Southern Vales used to be known for big, hefty reds, but things are changing here too and an increasing amount of finely balanced Cabernet and Shiraz from growers like Pirramimma, Coriole and Geoff Merrill is now supplementing the old blockbusters. The big companies like Hardy's are also swinging successfully to fresh modern styles.

Padthaway/Keppoch in the far south is providing fresh, bouncy Sauvignon, Chardonnay and Rhine Riesling as well as good Sémillon and Pinot Noir.

Coonawarra, in splendid southern isolation, continues, despite some plantings of whites, to excel at producing plummy, juicy Shiraz and unique Cabernet Sauvignon tasting of mulberry, blackcurrant and stewed plums. That may not sound appetizing, but it's this blend of flavours from companies like Wynns

This arid hill-top is the home of the Steingarten vineyard where the vines actually fail to ripen as often as not. Altitude is the reason; and those tiny plots of Rhine Riesling vines produce one of Australia's steeliest dry whites.

way in brouhaha, but that's OK because the wines really are exciting and the Chardonnay can be world-class.

Margaret River, where Leeuwin is situated, is a newly developed, cool climate region with a string of fine properties making great Cabernet and Chardonnay, very good Pinot Noir, Shiraz, Sémillon and Sauvignon, and even the occasional delicious oddity like Zinfandel. It was only 'pioneered' in 1967 and hasn't looked back. Wineries like Leeuwin Estate, Moss Wood, Cullens Willyabrup, Cape Mentelle and Redbrook lead the way.

Great Southern (or Mount Barker) is an ultra-cool area further south. This is still in the formative stage, but first signs are that the whites do have a thrilling, crisp style which in time could equal Australia's best. Plantaganet Vineyard, Redmond and Chateau Barker are the highest profile estates, but a lot of the wine is trucked north to the blisteringly hot Swan Valley just inland from Perth.

Swan Valley is the original wine area in Western Australia, but with temperatures in the hundreds for weeks at a time, it was virtually impossible to meet modern lighter-style market demands successfully, which is why the light, sharp Mount Barker wine is hauled north to blend. Gentler conditions, cooled by sea breezes, are now being exploited by Houghton at Moondah Brook to the north, while Evans and Tate do best in the Swan heartland.

South-West Coastal Plain is another area just below Perth which is a highly unlikely assortment of vineyards on grey sand! Peel Estate and Capel Vale show surprisingly good results so far.

· TASMANIA ·

Although there were vines in Tasmania in the nineteenth century, the most lasting effect they had was to provide the vine-cuttings from which both the Victorian and the South Australian wine industries sprang! It wasn't until the

'Bin' numbers are a uniquely Australian method of identifying separate batches of wine. Bin 28 is the name of a Shiraz grown in the Kalimna vineyard at Moppa. Pewsey Vale, maker of some of Australia's finest Rhine Rieslings, was established in 1847, but it fell into disuse until the 1960s when winemakers began searching out cool sites where grapes would ripen more slowly.

and Petaluma which has led this part of South Australia to be called the 'Médoc of Australia'!

And then there's Grange Hermitage. Only 'invented' in 1952 by Penfolds winemaker Max Schubert, the grapes used to come from Magill in the Adelaide suburbs, but are now largely from Kalimna and Coonawarra. This wine is so piled with flavours of spice and chocolate and rich plummy blackcurrant, the most patriotic Frenchman couldn't fail to be impressed. Most of the Magill vineyard is now a housing development, but I've had a foretaste of Magill Shiraz from the remaining part of the vineyards

and it's so good I reckon Grange may have found itself a younger brother.

· WESTERN AUSTRALIA ·

There is absolutely no doubt that Western Australia is making some amazing wines, and in its new super-confident style it is letting everybody know. But then Western Australia is a very long way from anywhere, and since the best wine areas are some of the most isolated in Australia, they have to shout pretty loud to let anyone know they're there. Leeuwin Estate, in the Margaret River region, and its quality-fanatical owner Denis Horgan lead the

Pinot Noir has not yet been notably successful in Australia, but Leeuwin Estate's winery in Margaret River has produced many good examples.

In Swan Valley Evans & Tate produce classy wine by using oak barrel ageing.

1970s that anyone took much notice of the wines themselves, which is when I had my first taste – a Moorilla Estate Cabernet, marvellous stuff – followed in the early 80s by my discovery of steely dry, eucalyptus-scented reds and whites from Heemskerk. Tantalizing experiences; lone, lovely bottles from these two wineries and the almost unobtainable Pipers Brook Vineyard were followed by long periods when I literally could not find a bottle at any price. Yet Tasmania is a state which has been described as having the most 'European' (that is, temperate and cool) of all Australian wine regions, as long ago as 1972! Plantings are still tiny – 330 acres (130 hectares) in 1986 – but I do believe the word is getting through, because people are now experimenting with these cool, 'European' conditions in almost every part of the state.

By far the most important areas are in the north; Piper's Brook and the Tamar Valley between them have nearly 70 per cent of the vineyards. The Derwent Valley in the far south has less than seven per cent of the vineyards but these include Moorilla Estate with its piercingly cassis-flavoured Cabernet Sauvignons, so the quality is there. It seems unlikely that

Tasmania will ever be a volume producer, though vineyard acreage is increasing by about 25 per cent per annum at the moment, and Heemskerk and Louis Roederer are having a go at a 'champagne' sparkling wine, but those sharp, fruity, thirst-quenching tastes are too memorable for them to be overlooked – if they ever grow enough wine down there to gain more than strictly local acclaim.

· OTHER AREAS ·

Queensland is a state, mention of which is likely to provoke a few guffaws in wine terms since it has a distinctly macho 'ice-cold amber nectar' image. But they've had a wine industry since the 1860s, and during the 1970s one particular area near the New South Wales border, called the 'Granite Belt', gained some notoriety. Especially round the town of Stanthorpe, south to Ballandean, the altitude is up to 900 metres and despite loads of sun, it doesn't get that hot – well, it gets about as hot as the Rhône Valley in France, but that's cool for Australia! The result is that we're already seeing some splendid, tough, peppery Shiraz and some deep, brooding Cabernet Sauvignon as well as the first signs of exciting

· VINTAGES ·

In France and Germany the chief objective is to get as much sun as possible, but in Australia a good vintage is usually marked by a lack of sun, since normal weather conditions consist of sun relentlessly beating down for months on end. Ripeness is never a problem; overripeness often is. Consequently cooler years are highly prized, and cool microclimates are avidly sought after by would-be makers of high-class wines.

1987 Yet another cool and even rather rainy summer has produced a crop of delicious, balanced reds and whites.

1986 A cool ripening period has produced an outstanding crop of reds and whites, with higher acidities than usual and striking fruit flavours. The whites are already lovely, the reds are prime candidates for laying down.

1985 An enormous harvest of generally good to very good quality with all except the top red already very good to drink.

1984 An outstanding cool year. The reds in particular have an elegance and 'European' dryness not often found in Australia.

1983 A combination of severe drought, freak floods and rot in the Coonawarra area produced patchy results and, by Australian standards, many of the wines are disappointing.

1982 Very hot, but in general a good year particularly for superripe reds.

1981 A drought year, producing good quality but rather chunky reds.

1980 Excellent. Similar to 1984 in the structure of the wines. The reds are now at their best.

Chardonnay, from Robinson's Family, and Sémillon from Rumbalara. There is also quite a trend to produce fresh 'nouveau' style reds, which makes sense if your market is going to be thirsty locals, but the overriding character I have found in red and whites so far is a definite, though not off-putting, hardness – as though the granite was asserting itself in the wines. And why not?

There is, incredibly, a wine property in the desert of the Northern Territories. Chateau Hornsby is at Alice Springs, last outpost of civilization for 1,000 miles, and even that's being polite! It is tempting to say it's all a joke, but you wouldn't find me setting up a vineyard about three days' drive from the nearest decent restaurant unless I meant business.

· NEW ZEALAND ·

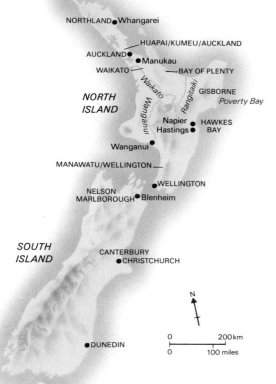

New Zealand is a wine country becoming famous at breakneck speed. Vineyards have been established since the first settlers arrived and were sufficiently successful by 1840 for a visiting Frenchman, Dumont d'Urville, to say of the local wine, 'I was given a light white wine, very sparkling, and delicious to taste, which I enjoyed very much'. That's high praise from a Frenchman. But things didn't go quite as swimmingly as they did in Australia. New Zealand vintners didn't scoop armfuls of medals at the international exhibitions in Europe, and there was trouble at home too – from the temperance societies. In Australia they were often positively helpful to those trying to set up wineries, since they wanted to cut down on the consumption of spirits; but in New Zealand, from the 1860s onwards, they campaigned vociferously for a complete prohibition of alcohol.

They didn't quite achieve this, but they created an atmosphere in society where every

attempt to further the development of the wine industry was an uphill struggle, and for most of this century, New Zealand wine was largely dismissed as inferior even by New Zealanders themselves. In the 1960s, having been persuaded that conditions in the vineyards were similar to those in Germany, many growers struggling to find a way forward had opted to make German-style wines, but their model was the cheap wine of the Rhine, made from a Müller-Thurgau base, rather than the glorious Riesling. A New Zealand style of low alcohol, fruity light white based on Müller-Thurgau (or Riesling-Sylvaner as they called it) developed, which was very nice – better than most Liebfraumilch – but New Zealand was capable of far greater things than that and the 1970s provided the spur that was needed.

The same winds of change that were sweeping across America and Australia were fanning ambitions in New Zealand too. Everyone in Australia and California was talking about the

The North Island vineyards of New Zealand are just as prone to the diseases of wet, cold weather as their northern counterparts in France and Germany. Here the Cooks vineyards are protected against vintage-time rot by mechanical spraying.

need for a cool temperate climate to make great wine, and they were going to all kinds of lengths to create 'cool' vineyards in their own hot countries. New Zealand didn't have to try.

The vine had been established primarily in the steamy humid area of the North Island round Auckland, where Yugoslav immigrants congregated to work in the gum forests, and they demanded their local supply of wine. It wasn't up to much and was nicknamed 'Daily Plonk' by the rest of New Zealand. But elsewhere there were conditions as good as any in the world. The country lies between the 34th and 48th parallels – the same span as

Cabernet Sauvignon doesn't ripen easily here, but Cooks' Te Kauwhata wines have achieved a reasonable rather lean but refreshing style. Montana pioneered plantings in the South Island and their vineyards at Marlborough near Blenheim are now white wines of world class.

from North Africa to the Rhône in Europe – so it is a bit silly to say the conditions most resemble Germany where it is an endless struggle to ripen grapes at all. It would be more accurate to say that the conditions resemble those of the best years in Germany, good to excellent years in Champagne and the Loire, and average to good years in Bordeaux and Burgundy. Even this is far too simplistic, but it does give some impression of New Zealand having a cool climate, but a very flexible one.

· WHITE WINES ·

There is no doubt at all that the country's present fame is based on white wines, and this is likely to continue. New Zealand has already achieved great things with her Chardonnay, Sémillon and Sauvignon.

Chardonnays here are far lighter than those of Australia and California, and usually have a freshness and a crispness more reminiscent of Chablis. But the flavour is quite different – much more piercing in fruit, and with far more richness added from ageing in new French oak barrels.

Sémillons can have the lanolin fatness of Australia or the lean, green sharpness of Bordeaux, but they are often given a little French oak treatment and blended with Sauvignon, and the result is as near a fine Classed Growth Graves as you could wish – and at a much lower price.

Sauvignon Blanc is the wine which has made the greatest splash. It seems to embody everything green in flavour – grass, nettles, asparagus, gooseberry – all these tastes which occasionally surface in Sauvignon elsewhere come piling out of a New Zealand Sauvignon.

Indeed the latest releases have cut back a little on the startling splat of flavours, and with this extra restraint, and with a tiny bit of wood ageing, New Zealand Sauvignon Blanc can lay claim to being the finest in the world. Gewürztraminer, too, although not riding high on the 'dry-white' bandwagon at the moment, is nonetheless spicy, and dry in a style which only the best Alsace growers ever achieve.

· RED WINES ·

Reds are more of a problem. Red wine vines need to be much older than white wine vines to give really good wine, and most good red vineyards in New Zealand are still too young. The most popular grape traditionally is the South African Pinotage but it gives a rather pale, dusty wine here. The Pinot Noir *will* work, and once or twice has already been sensational (St Helena in the South Island is already delivering the goods). Cabernet Franc and Cabernet Sauvignon now and then bring forth deep, exciting styles, but are usually light, grassy, yet fruity too and so are very pleasant, easy drinking.

· THE WINE REGIONS ·

Northland at the top of the North Island is a minor grapegrower, but the areas of Kumeu, Huapai, Waimaku and Henderson, just to the north and west of Auckland, are some of New Zealand's finest. Initially dominated by reds with Nobilo and Corbans the most important producers, there has recently been a rush of new blood into the area, and most of them have excelled in whites. Sometimes the outperformers have been old companies revitalized, like Collard Bros, Selaks, Babich and Delegats, sometimes they're completely new,

like Matua Valley and Coopers Creek, but the results, in Sémillon, Chardonnay, Sauvignon, Gewürztraminer and even Müller-Thurgau are excellent.

The remaining vineyards of the North Island are divided into three bays. Bay of Plenty/Waikato is most famous for the Te Kauwhata Viticultural Research Station and also for the presence of Cooks who did more than any other company to promote the image of New Zealand wines in the late 1970s and 1980s. Their Chardonnays and Cabernet releases are always some of New Zealand's best. Recently Morton Estate has enhanced the area's reputation with fine Chardonnay and Sauvignon.

Poverty Bay, in particular the Gisborne plains, contains about one third of all New Zealand's vines, and since the practice of blending wines from various areas is as established in New Zealand as it is in Australia, most Gisborne fruit is processed elsewhere. Nobilo's finest wine of recent years, for instance, is their Dixon Chardonnay 1985 – made out of grapes from Hexton Hill in Gisborne. Collards, Selaks and Delegats make some of their best wines from Gisborne grapes. It is very much a white wine region, and the outstanding local winery is Matawhero whose Gewürztraminer in particular is world-class.

The third bay is Hawkes Bay. This is one of the original wine areas, and is outstanding for both white and red. Wineries like Te Mata are producing some of New Zealand's best Cabernet Sauvignon, and Mission, Vidal, and Eskdale are producing delicious, crisp whites.

The South Island was little regarded till the 1970s as a wine area, but in the last decade the Marlborough region has emerged as one of New Zealand's most important regions. This is largely the wholesale vine-planting by Montana whose ultra-fresh white wine styles epitomize the brighter, easy-drinking flavours New Zealand is so good at. Although Montana completely dominate Marlborough, new wineries are following their lead, and Hunter and Te Whare Ra are typical of the new small-scale arrivals. And it's happening further south too, at Canterbury and Central Otago. That St Helena Pinot Noir which rocked the wine world – that was from Canterbury!

Wine-making in England goes back a *very* long time. And for a *very* long time, as far as we can tell, it was highly successful. It's just that a 400-year hiccup interrupted the development pattern, and only in the last decade have things got going again.

In the beginning, the Romans *probably* brought the vine to England – the spread of viticulture in Europe can mostly be attributed to them. But whoever it was, by William the Conqueror's time there were – according to Domesday Book – at least 40 vineyards. Vines and wines flourished for the next century, but in 1152 Henry II married Eleanor of Aquitaine, and things were never *quite* the same again. After all, the capital of Aquitaine is Bordeaux and until France regained Aquitaine in 1453, the English carried on a love affair with the red 'claret' wines of Bordeaux.

The vineyards survived this infidelity – especially where they were attached to monasteries – but they did not survive the latter's Dissolution in 1536; England's vines were then ripped up and replaced with other crops. And that's pretty well how things remained until after World War Two.

The first stirrings came in 1952 with the establishment of Hambledon Vineyard in Hampshire (very suitable – cricket started there as well). It seemed like a false dawn: when the English Vineyards Association was formed in 1967 there were barely a dozen members, and rather fewer acres of vines! But the universal surge of interest in wine during the 1970s provided a spur and there are now nearer 90 vineyards and 1,000 acres (404 hectares) of vines.

A glance at the location of vineyards in the Middle Ages reveals that the most popular areas today were popular then, with the exception of Sussex. Modern vineyards in the Thames Valley, Kent, Hampshire, Somerset, Hereford, Essex and Suffolk are just part of an age-old pattern.

· CLIMATE ·

Medieval maps also show that vineyards used to extend further north, which implies that the weather was better then than now; and it's true, northern Europe did have warmer summers in the Middle Ages. But the endless jokes about terrible British weather do make it difficult for vineyard owners to persuade the public to take them seriously. Well, the facts don't entirely bear out this scepticism. Certainly you can't plant warm-country red varieties like Cabernet Sauvignon and Syrah and expect them to ripen and, to be honest, England really is a white wine country. But it can be a *good* white wine country, if the right grapes are planted and the wines vinified in the most suitable manner.

Sun (not enough) and rain (too much) are the usual British moans – with justification. Measuring the temperature needed to ripen grapes by the degree days system (see California), 1,000 degree days is generally reckoned as the bare minimum. Even in relatively warm southern England the average is only 762, and in the frequently blustery conditions, any warm air collecting between the vines is quickly blown away; in the west, the rain-bearing westerlies, and in the east those icy blasts straight from Siberia, can crucially lower the temperature in a vineyard unprotected by seclusion or a proper windbreak.

As for rain, well it takes a lot of skill to ripen healthy, disease-free vines with more than 30 inches (760mm) of rain a year. Some of the relatively warm areas in the west get as much as 100 inches (2,540mm) a year. East Anglia may be cooler, but at least the average rainfall is nearer 20 inches (500mm). (On the plus side, there's not a spring frost problem in England as the vines bud so late anyway.)

Decent English wine is made possible in these conditions largely because of the Germans. Their scientists have spent decades inventing new grape variety crossings which

The quiet beauty of a small Kent village and its surrounding downland is given a more European look by Lamberhurst's vineyards spreading over what used to be meadow. The plastic netting round the rootstocks of the young vines show that the rabbits welcome this new source of nibbles.

Chalkhill's label shows the blue butterfly typical of chalky downland. Like most good English wines it also specifies the grape – Bacchus, an aromatic German variety. The Magdalen Rivaner in 1985 won a Wine Challenge against all-European competition.

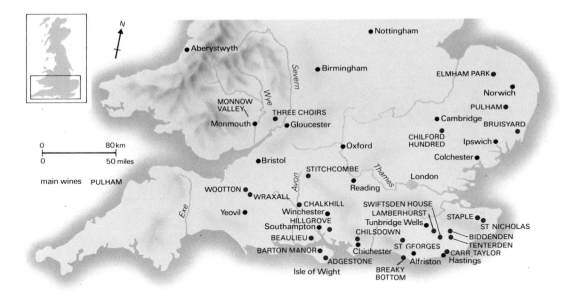

Map labels: N; Aberystwyth; Nottingham; Birmingham; ELMHAM PARK; Severn; Wye; MONNOW VALLEY; Norwich; PULHAM; THREE CHOIRS; Cambridge; BRUISYARD; Monmouth; Gloucester; CHILFORD HUNDRED; Ipswich; Oxford; Colchester; Bristol; STITCHCOMBE; Thames; London; Avon; Reading; WOOTTON; WRAXALL; SWIFTSDEN HOUSE; Exe; CHALKHILL; LAMBERHURST; STAPLE; Yeovil; Winchester; Tunbridge Wells; ST NICHOLAS; HILLGROVE; CHILSDOWN; Southampton; BIDDENDEN; BEAULIEU; ST GEORGES; TENTERDEN; BARTON MANOR; Chichester; CARR TAYLOR; Alfriston; Hastings; ADGESTONE; Isle of Wight; BREAKY BOTTOM

0 — 80 km / 0 — 50 miles

main wines   PULHAM

will ripen ultra-early. By the beginning of September, in vineyard areas like Baden and the Rheinpfalz, these grapes are already bulging with sugar – and, to be frank, little else, because they've ripened far too fast to develop an interesting personality. Translated to the much cooler vineyards of England, these early varieties ripen very slowly and, as the winter begins to close in – late October, early November – they will just be ripe enough to make wine. And instead of the burnt-out dull tastes of much cheap, overripe southern German wine, all the essential acids and perfumes are only just coming to the fore when the grapes are finally picked. Take a simple analogy: a cool-climate English Cox's Orange Pippin and a hot-climate French Golden Delicious. Which has the better flavour, the crisp appetizing acidity, the orchard-fresh fruity sweetness? It's always the Cox – and in the same way, grape varieties which struggle to ripen at the limit of their capabilities always produce the most exciting flavours.

· WINE STYLES ·

The German influence explains why most English wines have names like Müller-Thurgau, Schönburger, Huxelrebe, Reichensteiner, Ortega and Siegerrebe (although a few also boast the French early-ripening crossing, Seyval Blanc). These are the only sensible grapes to plant. Their flavours depend on how they are made. English winemakers will always have to chaptalize – add sugar – during fermentation to raise the alcohol content, since even these grapes will never make enough sugar by themselves. But once the wine has fermented out, they can either leave it bone dry or give it sweetness and fruit by the German trick of adding back Süssreserve – unfermented grape juice.

Winemakers are fiercely divided on the use of Süssreserve. Some won't add any at all – among them highly individualistic wineries like Breaky Bottom in Sussex and Chilford Hundred in Cambridge. In this case, the wines often take five years or more to mature. They will always be intensely dry, but can be absolutely delicious. The other school feels Süssreserve is crucial, imparting a lovely fragrance and fruit to the high-acid wine. Wines made in this way by wineries like Biddenden in Kent and Pulham in Norfolk can be wonderful to drink at only a year old and in *no way* inferior to the rather more purist wines of the 'dry' school. They will also age reasonably – for three to four years – and it is simply a question of personal choice which is better.

There are a few large concerns in English wine-making (the best known of these are Carr Taylor near Hastings, Lamberhurst near Tunbridge Wells and Three Choirs at Newent,

· VINTAGES ·

There has been a string of fair to good vintages. The gentleman who pronounced 1983 the best English vintage for 2,000 years was not forthcoming about how he'd done his research into the other 1,999, but 1983 *was* good – and 1984 was better, after a good summer for once. Both 1985 and 1986 had poor summers but very good autumns: late harvests gave reduced amounts of some of the best English wine yet. Well, since World War Two, anyway.

· GOOD PRODUCERS ·

Kent/Sussex Some of the softest, ripest styles, with vines like Gutenborner and Schönburger giving quite big, musky wines. *Kent*: Biddenden, Lamberhurst, St Nicholas, Staple, Tenterden. *Sussex*: Breaky Bottom, Carr Taylor, Chilsdown, Ditchling, St George's, Swiftsden House.
Isle of Wight/Hampshire A lot of dry wines, but reasonably aromatic too. Adgestone, Hillgrove, Barton Manor, Beaulieu.
West Country Strong, sharp, very individual styles. Chalkhill, Stert, Stitchcombe, Wootton, Wraxall.
East Anglia Many of the driest, least aromatic styles, with some exceptions like Pulham. *Norfolk*: Elmham Park, Pulham. *Suffolk*: Bruisyard St Peter, Cavendish Manor, Highwayman's.

Gloucestershire) but the best wines come mostly from small estates – minute in European and American terms, since many are five acres or less. Here, actual wine-making is often done on a contract basis – particularly by Kit Lindlar and Lamberhurst in Kent, Carr Taylor in Sussex, and Mark Thompson and Colin Gillespie in the West Country. If you like a wine, ask who made it, so that you can build up some experience of whose style you prefer.

The best way, indeed the *only* way, to find some of these wines is to visit the vineyard or a local centre such as the English Wine Centre in Alfriston, Sussex. There are in fact a couple of wineries in Wales – Monnow Valley is very good – and in the Channel Islands; in wine-making terms, both areas rank as 'English'. So far, there is no classification system but the English Vineyards Association (EVA) does award a gold seal to guarantee quality.

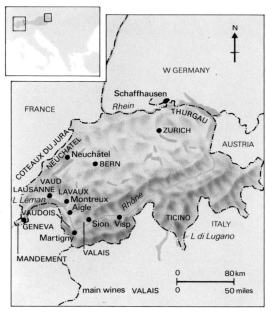

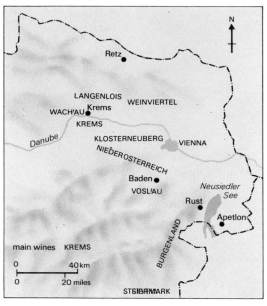

O ther Wine-making Regions should not be taken to mean that there is little of interest in the countries whose wines are described in the following pages. Several of them are major producers but their wines, for one reason or another, do not at present make much impact on the international market. Others are countries still young in the practice of making wines and whose reputation may be dramatically increased in a decade or two's time. And others have an output quite simply too small to warrant more than a few lines' coverage. If you see major producers like Austria, Yugoslavia and Hungary in these pages and wonder why they do not have sections to themselves, I make no apologies. While the rest of the world of wine has moved ahead at a tremendous rate, these have stagnated or even gone into reverse. Either they fail to achieve more exciting levels of wine-making or their best wines are not available to us, and there is so much else that is *good* to cover.

· AUSTRIA ·

I freely admit, I would *like* to give more space and more approval to Austrian wines. I have had some delicious wines in Austria, text-book examples of how to make fragrant, fruity and dry wines from such grape varieties as Müller-Thurgau, Rhine Riesling and even Welsch Riesling (another name for the Laski or Olasz Riesling; a dull grape and *not* real Riesling). I have had marvellously brisk, frisky jug wine – *Heurigenwein*, it is called – only a month or two old and full of the gaiety and laughter of a new vintage, and I have had deep, brooding, sultry-sweet beauties from the noble-rot infected vineyards of Rust and Apetlon. But when I have looked for such wines outside Austria I have almost always been disappointed. With the exception of a few remarkable sweet wines, it has seemed to me that the winemakers were often less than careful with the products they aimed at the export market. The diethylene glycol scandal of a couple of years ago reinforced this opinion,

and gave Austria's wine a worldwide fame which had so far eluded it – infamy would be a better description, since exports of Austrian wine virtually dried up in the aftermath.

Even so, with a new extra-strict Wine Law in place, and a bitter, impassioned reaction against the wrongdoers from the Austrian winemakers who *did* care, the future of Austria's wines looks a good deal brighter than the slightly murky recent past.

Austria is placed between west and east Europe, and its wines reflect this. Although many of the grapes are Germanic, and although the 'quality' system is a tighter version of the German one, based on ripeness levels in the grapes, yet it also uses grapes totally unfamiliar to Western palates and the bulk of the wine has always followed the line of spicy, tangy, dry whites and surprisingly strong-tasting reds which used to be the hallmark of Hungary, just to the east. Indeed the 'national' grape, the Grüner Veltliner, is a classic half-way house, since it can have the sharp attack of a young German Riesling yet this is swamped by a peppery fire which makes you wonder if someone really did shake the pepper pot into the vat.

All of the 150,000 acres (60,700 hectares) of vineyards are in the east of the country, and are divided up into 14 areas under four regional headings – Niederösterreich, Wien, Steiermark and Burgenland. By far the most important and varied region is Niederösterreich (Lower Austria) which is a fairly arbitrary division covering 87,000 acres (35,200 hectares). It is in three parts. The most interesting is along the Donau (Danube) valley where Krems, Langenlois and Wachau produce most of Austria's best dry whites

Saint Laurent is a red grape virtually exclusive to Austria. The wine is slightly sweet in a scented way. Luxembourg's appellation system is strict, delineating vineyard, grape and ripeness level – Grand Premier Cru is the ripest.

from Rhine Riesling, Grüner Veltliner and Müller-Thurgau. Often grown on terraces way above the river, they can blend perfume and steely dryness superbly.

The second section is the Weinviertel or 'wine quarter' which stretches north of Vienna to the Czech border and produces loads of light, attractive white Grüner Veltliner. Falkenstein is the commonest name. North towards Czechoslovakia, the Retz area is promising for reds. The third part is the Südbahn – literally 'southern railway' – which follows the railway track down south of Vienna to Gumpoldskirchen, Baden and Bad Vöslau. Big, musky dryish whites from grapes like Zierfandler and Rotgipfler are produced, and some surprisingly good reds from the more familiar Merlot and Cabernet Sauvignon as well as more rustic reds from the St-Laurent and the Blauer Portugieser.

The city of Vienna (Wien) is a wine area of 2,000 acres (8,094 hectares) in its own right. All the hills on the edge of the capital, in particular to the north and north-west, have vineyards, and each village has its wine cellars and taverns, where the Viennese spend carefree evenings with music and laughter and the gleaming, frothy-fresh local Heurigenwein.

Down by the Yugoslav border is Styria (Steiermark). The best wines are the Ruländer and Gewürztraminer which can be fairly broad and spicy, but don't often leave the region.

However, the Burgenland produces an enormous amount of intensely sweet wine which can be found all over the world – though the Austrians themselves don't drink very much of it. The vineyards are clustered round the Neusiedler See, an astonishing lake which is 20 miles long but only just over 3 feet deep! It's a hot, dry area and every autumn without fail, mists rise off this sheet of warm water and cause noble rot by the bucketful. The wines, from Welsch Riesling, Neuburger, Gewürztraminer, Muskat-Ottonel and others, do not have the thrilling blend of limy acidity, raisin fruit and honeyed lusciousness of the best German Beerenauslesen, but at about a quarter the price, they are excellent introductions to the top flights of sweet wine. They are labelled Auslese, Beerenauslese,

Ausbruch and Trockenbeerenauslese in ascending order of sweetness.

The best Austrian producer easily available on the export market is Siegendorf. Other good wines are produced by Klosterneuberg, Schlumberger, Lenz Moser and the Krems co-operative.

· LUXEMBOURG ·

The Mosel runs through Luxembourg before it reaches Germany, and provides some fairly good riverside vineyard sites. The Rivaner (Müller-Thurgau) occupies 50 per cent of the acreage, while Elbling, Riesling and Auxerrois are also common. *All* the wines are feather-light, and none of them age well, but the Elbling can be refreshing and tart, and the Rivaner and Auxerrois give pale wispy wine with enough fruit to enjoy. Pinot Gris – giving a gentle, nuts and honey wine, and Gewürztraminer, here giving a wine as fleeting as a shadow but discernibly spicy in that passing moment, are rare but successful. There is a lot of 'Luxembourgeois' sparkling wine sold. Most of it is made from

cheap imported Italian wine and should therefore be avoided.

· SWITZERLAND ·

It won't come as much of a surprise to learn that Switzerland has the highest vineyards in Europe (at Visperterminen in the Valais grapes still grow at 3,700 feet) or that it has some of the most beautiful – in the Vaud where the vineyards tumble down to the edge of Lake Geneva, or in the Valais where the vines cling to the mountain slopes high above the valley of the fledgling river Rhône. But it may be a bit of a shock to learn that Switzerland, a country packed full of enthusiastic wine drinkers whose annual consumption is already around 66 bottles a head, is suffering from a wine surplus, and has begun imposing restrictions on imports to try to contain the crisis!

The thing is that, as you would expect, the Swiss are highly efficient at wine production. Having increased their vineyard acreage by 13 per cent during the last decade to about 32,000 acres (13,000 hectares), and having become expert at coaxing the last drop from

The mountains are never far away from the vineyards in Switzerland but the Valais region nonetheless is a veritable suntrap as the south-south-east facing slopes bask in a rain shadow which makes irrigation obligatory most years. These vineyards at Salgesch are in the driest part of all Switzerland, and show the fragmented pattern of many Swiss vineyards with the owners frequently tending small plots as a money-spinning hobby rather than a full-time job.

their vines – the vineyards have traditionally produced twice as much as France's acre for acre and are now *averaging* over 100 hectolitres per hectare – they are now suffering from too much of a good thing. And, on the whole, Swiss wine *is* a good thing. It may seem impossibly expensive outside its home territory, but it can be at the least frothy, mountain-fresh and gluggable, and at the best, remarkably deep, fascinating and rich.

· THE WINE REGIONS ·

Swiss wine regions are divided by language. The Italian-speaking Ticino cantons in the south produce a fair amount of gentle juicy red from the Merlot grape. The German cantons to the north all produce a little wine, mostly light Pinot Noir (Blauburgunder) though the wine of Graubünden has a bit more stuffing.

However, all the best wine is made in the French-speaking cantons. Neuchâtel makes pleasant light Pinot Noir red and some fizz. Geneva makes pale white Perlan from the Chasselas grape and equally light Gamay. And then there are Vaud and Valais.

Vaud is the long slope, much of it vine-covered, which runs up the whole northern arc of lake Geneva, right round and past Montreux and into the Rhône valley.

The wine is mostly Chasselas – here called Dorin – and if you drink it really young – still slightly spritzy, incredibly pale to behold, feel and taste, it can be delicious, though its only discernible characteristic, apart from its excessive lightness, is a very slight hint of lemon and pepper.

The Valais is just as spectacular, and is a solid south-facing slope centred on the town of Sion. It gets surprisingly hot here, and they actually need to irrigate, but the results can be exceptional. Dôle, a Pinot Noir-Gamay blend, is the top red, the light cherry fruit of the Pinot being given quite a peppery kick by the Gamay.

But it is the whites which are the real stars. Chasselas (called Fendant this time!) is fatter here, creamier, less likely to have the refreshing prickle on the tongue, but young and cold it can still be delicious. Sylvaner, here called Johannisberg, can do great things and achieve an unbelievable honeyed, yet 'savoury', almost salty richness. Riesling, Muscat, Marsanne (called Ermitage) and Pinot Gris (called Malvoisie) can also be excellent, and there are some weird and wonderful ancient grape varieties like Amigne, Petite Arvine and Humagne. The first two are thick, heavy, nutty whites and marvellous to keep the cold out. Humagne is one of those tough, almost sour mouthfuls of grape tannin and cochineal which makes you wonder how it survived – but, as you wash away the taste with a draught of Fendant, you can secretly be glad that it did.

Most Swiss wine is made by large companies, but it is always worth trying to find a single estate wine, since there is an unmistakeable leap in quality. Some top names are Domaine du Mont d'Or, Vuignier and Caves de Riondaz in Valais, and Testuz, Dubois, Badoux and Isoz in Vaud. The wines will be dry unless labelled *légèrement doux* (lightly sweet) or *avec sucre résiduel* (with residual sugar).

· SOVIET UNION ·

The USSR has the second largest vineyard acreage in the world after Spain. Why then, do we not see any of its wines? Because the government has made a long-term policy decision that people should be persuaded to drink wine instead of vodka, and so the whole lot is drunk at home. There's still not enough though – the USSR imports about 900 million bottles of wine a year as well!

I just wish I knew where they drank it. On my visits to Russia, I have only been able to get sweet, heavy reds, and the pretty unrefreshing Champanski which you eventually start to drink out of sheer boredom. As for the famous reds of the south – the rivals to Château Lafite which are supposedly being produced in Crimea – I think you had to know someone pretty high up in the hierarchy to get a sniff of those – and I didn't.

· HUNGARY ·

Little is nowadays seen of Hungary's fine wine tradition, which is as long and as proud as any in Europe. With challenging titles like Badacsonyi Szürkebarát, Badacsonyi Kéknyelü and Debrői Hárslevelü glowering at you from the label you have a right to expect a fiery mouthful of Magyar magic. You won't get it. These great wines – normally the first part of the title is the place name and the second is the grape variety – are now pale, embarrassed shadows of the proud barbarians which used to shock and excite my palate when I first encountered them. In particular, the wines of Mount Badacsony on Lake Balaton are now an enduring disappointment.

Most Hungarian wine nowadays exported comes in four types. Light, often sweetened red, usually from Sopron on the Austrian border and using the Kadarka or Kékfrankos grape; light, off-dry whites which use the Olasz Riesling (alias Welsch or Laski Riesling, not related to German Riesling). This style is at its least impressive from Hungary. Then there is Bull's Blood, which used to be a fine red – Hungarian-bottled under the title Egri Bikavér, it was excitingly different from the reds of Western Europe, and it aged superbly. I *still* have some 1964 and 1967. Now it is just another red, and a tough one at that.

Most of Bulgaria's wines are from well-known international grape varieties, but Mavrud is an indigenous type making burly wine at Assenovgrad in the south. Tokaji is the local spelling of Tokay, Hungary's most famous wine. Aszú Essencia means it is made from sticky, syrupy grapes infected by noble rot.

Finally, Tokay is *still* a great wine, though not a particularly popular taste. It comes from the fearsomely named Bodrog river, where noble rot conditions regularly occur. Three grapes – Yellow Muscat, Hárslevelü, and in particular Furmint are picked late and noble-rotted. Some is then vinified dry as Szamorodni ('as it comes') – a rather harsh and oxidized style. The rest goes to make a wine of varying degrees of sweetness. A syrupy paste or *aszú* is made of the noble-rotted grapes, and then *puttonyos* (35-litre hods-ful) of this mush are added to 140 litres of ordinary wine. The usual strength is 3 *puttonyos* – which means 105 litres of ultra-sweet *aszú* will have been added to 140 litres of wine. This will then ferment very slowly, and may also develop a 'flor-like' fungus while it is being aged in small, un-bunged barrels. You should buy the highest *puttonyos* you can afford – they go up to six – because the deep, treacly-brown sweetness, shocked into life by the knife-edge sharpness of an almost sour acidity, is quite an experience.

There are two even rarer Tokays – Tokay Aszú Essencia, where the wine is made entirely from *aszú* paste – and Tokay Essencia – which is made only from the glutinous golden drops which ooze from the slab as the noble-rotted grapes are waiting to be pounded into paste. This is the stuff they say used to

revive Czars and Emperors on their deathbeds, and on the rare occasions it turns up at auction, the price it fetches implies that someone ill and rich obviously believes in its reputation.

· BULGARIA ·

Bulgaria has almost no long-standing wine-making traditions – and yet it is making by far the most impressive wines in Eastern Europe. This is because it set out to please the market, and in Bulgaria that means the export market. Bulgaria started a wine industry virtually from scratch after World War Two, and the reason was simple: the need to earn foreign currency. From a standing start, it is now the fifth biggest exporter in the world, exporting 85 per cent of its total output.

The country seems to divide fairly naturally into red and white grape areas. The north and south grow red grapes and the east grows white. The grapes themselves are a mix of Eastern European varieties and the classics of France and Germany, but all the best wines so far are from French varieties. The Cabernet Sauvignon and Merlot can be brilliantly simple and impressive – an all-at-once splash of blackcurrant fruit, and a lick of honey too for the Merlot. The local Mavrud is similar in a smoky way. The best regions are Sukhindol (or Suhindol), Lositza and Svishtov in the

Lake Balaton is the home of Hungary's most individual grape varieties: Furmint, Kéknyelü and Szürkebarát wines have great potential excitement which rarely survives poor handling and bottling.

north, and Sakar, Orjahoviza and Assenovgrad in the south.

The whites have been slower to impress, because there was too much dull Rkatsiteli planted – the Russians like it, dosed up with Muscat, but no one else did. However, Chardonnay, Sauvignon, Riesling and Traminer are making better wines every year. Han Krum and Varna are the most interesting areas.

The great thing in Bulgaria's favour is the superb quality/price ratio, which has not been disturbed even as the prices have crept upwards, because quality has improved too. There are now 14 Controliran Regions (that is, regions subject to proper appellation of origin regulations) and since 1985 there has been a new category of 'Reserve' for superior wine given special oak barrel ageing. First signs are very promising – so long as they don't overdo the barrel-age.

· ROMANIA ·

I would like to have more to say about Romania because the potential for fine wine is

If asked to state where this vineyard was, I would say – oh, deep in English downland. Well, England is where most of its produce is drunk, certainly, but the terraces in the background give it away: these are the Lutomer vineyards in the north of Yugoslavia, the home of one of the world's most famous wines – Lutomer Riesling.

considerable – a hundred years ago Moldavian wine was ultra-chic in Paris bistros. Not any more. The vast majority of wine exported is from the ubiquitously boring Laski Riesling – usually from Banat – disturbingly sweet Pinot Noir, and lifeless Cabernet – from Banat, Dealul Mare or Moldavia. They could do *much* better if only they'd follow Bulgaria's market-conscious lead, and anyone who has tasted the strong musky wine of Cotnari, the Furmint or Pinot Gris of Transylvania, or the honeyed, spicy Traminer and Pinot Gris from Murfatlar, would surely agree.

· YUGOSLAVIA ·

Yugoslavia has about 300 traditional grape varieties. But with the exception of the occasional bottle of Vranać which surfaces, you'll have to go and snoop around in Yugoslavia itself to get a taste of them, because if ever a country has become identified with a single grape variety, it is Yugoslavia

with its Lutomer Laski Riesling.

I have to admit that Lutomer Riesling (as it is usually called) has done a brilliant job, and has probably, in its innocuous, vaguely un-dry, vaguely fruity-ish, vaguely inoffensive way, introduced more people to wine-drinking than any other single product. But poor old Yugoslavia's entire wine identity has been daubed with this single wine's bright and breezy logo. Actually, Yugoslavia is the country *least* likely to produce such mass-market weaklings, because its reputation 'before-Lutomer' was for strong, hairy-chested stuff, with those 300 traditional grape varieties not mincing words when it came to flavours.

Don't expect to be able to pronounce all these – but have you ever thought of ordering Grk? (Yes, that's the right spelling: supply your own vowels.) Or Zilavka, Plovdina, Prokupać, or Dingać? Well, these are some of the glories of Yugoslavia. If you're holidaying there, just get hold of the wine list or menu and point – and expect fierce bandit flavours. But you won't find them on the export market. You *will* find a little Sauvignon, and Traminer, which can be good, and you *will* find a bit of Cabernet, Merlot and Pinot Noir, which are usually rather tough and jammy. But the nearest you'll get to the real taste of Yugoslavia is Vranać, a burly two-fisted red which ends up surprisingly gentle, and is occasionally found outside its homeland.

· GREECE ·

It's a depressing comment on Greece when I say that the Greek wine which consistently gives me the most pleasure is retsina – which many people hate so much they wouldn't classify it as wine at all! But it's true. Greece, whose wines were once famous and sought-after throughout the civilized world, nowadays produces very little attractive wine – a full 37·5 per cent of production is made into retsina by adding pine resin during fermentation. Although Greece is now a member of the European Economic Community and has initiated a system of *appellation contrôlée* for 25 different regions, the general effect has been slight, and exports of wine have actually declined.

Still, there are a few brighter spots. The Peloponnese has Nemea – which *used* to be a tremendous flavoury red, though recent offerings have all been from the dull co-operative. Mavrodaphne, however, is still alive and kicking in the far south, a rich blackberry-sweet dessert wine of real individuality.

The only other mainland area producing much excitement is Macedonia whose Naoussa is the most reliable red *appellation* in Greece, and can occasionally be a full, tannic sort of swarthy Bordeaux in style. The Tsantali company is playing around successfully with Cabernet here, which compounds this impression. Château Carras in the Halkidiki Peninsula is doing the same with occasional success. Otherwise I can only recommend island wines, and the best of these is undoubtedly Samos – dry or sweet. It makes excellent syrupy, grapy sweet Muscat, one of the best in southern Europe.

· EASTERN MEDITERRANEAN ·

The Eastern Mediterranean has one established star, and one rising star. Neither of them are in Turkey. Although Turkey has the fifth largest vineyard acreage in the world, only three per cent of the grapes are used for wine. At every opportunity, I try the Buzbag,

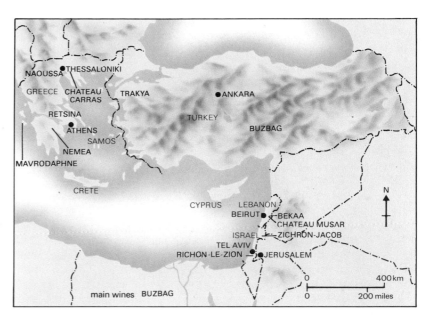

Far left The Greek island of Samos where the Muscat grape produces good dry table wines and excellent syrupy dessert whites. The southern part of Greece has the majority of the vineyards, but most of the interesting developments are taking place in the north. The monks on Mount Athos (*left*) in Macedonia are harvesting recently planted Cabernet Sauvignon which is turned into good quality reds.

the Hosbag and the Trakya and what have you – tough, oily, resinous wines. I wonder why I come back for more. Nor are these stars in Cyprus. Although the wine tradition here is ancient, and its rich, raisiny Commandaria was once a wine at the top of the quality tree, most of its modern reputation has been made on sherry look-alikes. The table wines, hindered by a lack of decent grape types, are dull, and the promising moves to exploit what look to be hopeful conditions in the Troodos mountains for varieties like Cabernet and Syrah, are painfully slow.

No; the established star is in Lebanon. Serge Hochar is a very brave man who continues to make Château Musar wine under the impossible conditions of civil war from his vineyards in the Bekaá Valley – the heart of the conflict. He trained in Bordeaux, and clearly has a Médoc château as his model, although the red wine's flavour is truly Levantine in that its rich musky Casbah perfume has a strong resiny hint – just maybe of cedar! Made of Cabernet Sauvignon, Syrah and Cinsaut, the best years can age as long as a good Bordeaux. There is also a white but it isn't in the same class.

The rising star is in Israel. Although there have been modern vineyards in Israel since the 1880s, mostly on the hot coastal strip, the standard of wine has never been exciting. In 1967 the decision was taken to plant vines on the Golan Heights at altitudes of up to 3,000 feet (10,000 metres). The first unblended releases were in 1986, and the Gamla Cabernet Sauvignon and the Yarden Sauvignon Blanc are outstandingly good and fresh, clean, excitingly typical of their grape varieties. And they *are* kosher.

· NORTH AFRICA ·

In the 1950s the trio of Tunisia, Algeria and Morocco accounted for two-thirds of the entire international wine trade! This was because, although they made a great deal of wine, their populations were basically Muslim, so virtually the entire production was exported – mostly to

France, where it was used to provide welcome body and flavour in a large number of France's most famous wines. Since the wines in those days were extremely tasty and packed with a rather over-rich fruit, they probably did more good than harm.

However, when the French left in the 1960s, the principal market disappeared, and with little domestic demand, things have gone into steady decline. Tunisia's wines are dull and tired before they even reach the market. Algeria has some reasonable reds from Mascara, but little else, despite having a VDQS quality control system based on that of France. Morocco, helped by the cool Atlantic influence, does best. It has an *appellation contrôlée* system and has managed to continue to turn

Far left One of Yugoslavia's most characterful reds from the Vranać grape. There is an official '*appellation d'origine contrôlée*-type system here – the red letters mean red wine from Montenegro. Château Carras in Macedonia has Bordeaux's famous Professor Peynaud as its consultant

out the plummy, soupy, but very enjoyable reds from Meknès – under the names Tarik and Chante Bled – and Sidi Larbi, which made its reputation in the 1950s.

· SOUTH AFRICA ·

South Africa was probably the first of the 'New World' wine nations to make an impact on the international market. And did it with its most basic wines, the cool, dry, beautifully balanced whites which were turned out in gigantic quantities by the KWV – the all-embracing wine co-operative which dominates the Cape wine industry. The grape they used was the Chenin Blanc, usually rather tart and mean in France, or bland and flabby in California, but here perfectly balanced, its gentle, positively creamy fruit sharpened up with carefully controlled, mouthwatering acidity. It was the perfect easy-drinking white, and everyone waited eagerly for the next move.

It never came. California began to blast the world with its mouthfilling super-ripe Chardonnays and Cabernet Sauvignons. Australia picked up the baton and joined California at the front with a whole range of world-beating reds and whites. New Zealand, which could barely tell Chardonnay from champagne when South African Chenin first wowed wine-drinkers, swept past on the backs of some truly stupendous white wines.

It's sad, because some observers reckon that South Africa has some of the most perfect vineyard sites in the world, capable of producing every sort of wine, from the lightest most fragrant reds and whites on the last tip of land south of Cape Town, to big, brawny reds or intensely luscious fortified wines in the increasingly warm areas north and east of Cape Town. Making the best use of them is altogether another matter.

You'll notice a special label on the top of most bottles of South African wine. This is the seal of the *appellation* system and each colour on it signifies a particular control. There are three 'Wine of Origin' regions, divided up into nine 'districts' and there are also another seven sub-districts outside the three main regions. A blue band signifies that the wine comes from one of these 'Regions of Origin'. A red band is the vintage band, and means that the wine is at least 75 per cent the vintage stated. A green band shows that the wine contains at least 75 per cent of the grape varieties named. If these colours are printed on a gold background, the wine has been tested and adjudged 'superior'. These regulations sound pretty lax, but they are an enormous improvement on what went before.

The most important region is the 'Coastal Region' which includes the districts of Constantia, Durbanville, Stellenbosch and Swartland. Although Constantia is known for its historic dessert wine, the region, stretching south of Cape Town is actually very cool and ideal for elegant table wines. Stellenbosch, to the east, is as yet South Africa's best red wine district. The Boberg region is hotter, and contains Paarl and Tulbagh, which produce sherry-type wines and good whites. The Breede River region further east is primarily a dessert wine and fortified wine area.

Although the export trade was built on 'sherry-type' wines, many of them very good, table wines have long since taken over as the most interesting products. Reds are mostly from Cabernet Sauvignon, Cinsaut and Pinotage (a cross between Cinsaut and Pinot Noir), because these were the only grapes available. Most South African reds have a slight smokiness, even top quality Cabernets from estates like Vriesenhof, Meerlust, Kanonkop and Blaauwklippen, and Pinotage tastes positively smouldering, the smoke combining in unique style with a rich raspberry and marshmallow fruit. Pinot Noir isn't much of a feature yet – but Hamilton Russell's from Heaven and Earth Valley is one of the best outside Burgundy.

Although there are occasionally sightings of Chardonnay (or Auxerrois as it sometimes turns out to be), Sauvignon Blanc and Riesling (here called Weisser- or Rhine Riesling) from estates like de Wetshof and le Bonheur, the vast majority of white wines are based on the Chenin or Steen grape. Usually these are light, crisp and clean, and are often at their best from the bulk producers – KWV with their gently honeyed Chenin and Bergkelder with their tangy, Sauvignon-sharp Fleur du Cap Chenin. However, it can come at any level of sweetness, and Nederburg's Edelkeur is great sweet wine.

· CENTRAL AND SOUTH AMERICA ·

America's first wines were made in the early 1500s in Mexico, and the skills were then gradually filtered up the Pacific coast to California. Well, since then Mexico has languished while California has excelled. Its per capita wine consumption is hardly greater than that of Muslim Morocco and most plantings produce distilling wine. However, there are some increasingly good wines being made in Baja California, by companies like Santo Tomás and Domecq, and in the centre of Mexico around Zacatecas and Aguascalientes by companies like Maria Orsini, whose Cabernet Sauvignon and Ruby Cabernet show remarkable blackcurrant promise.

On the South American continent, Peru has begun to make some surprisingly good wines in Ica, just south of Lima (Tacama Vineyards lead the way), and Brazil and Uruguay make large amounts of wine (Brazil calls a lot of its Vinho Verde) but, despite recent efforts by European companies like Domecq and Moët et Chandon, and advice from the University of

Far left This is the same Miguel Torres who makes outstanding wine in northern Spain. In a short time he has revolutionized Chile's white wines by introducing stainless steel, cold fermentation and new oak barrels. Omar Khayyam (*left*) is a good Indian sparkler.

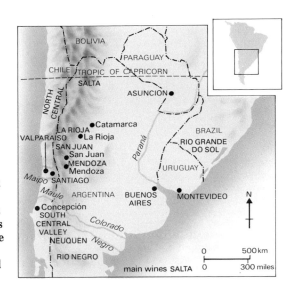

Argentina's Mendoza region produces 70% of all Argentina's wine (and over 50% of South America's), but they wouldn't be there at all if it wasn't for the melting snows from the Andes in the background which irrigate the region all year round.

California, I'm still waiting to be convinced.

Argentina on the other hand is *very* important as a producer and also as a consumer. Its acreage is the fifth largest in the world but, with its per capita consumption the fourth largest, it means that little of it leaves the country. However, especially from Mendoza – a vast, previously desert region irrigated by the Andes' melting snow – the reds, usually from Malbec, Cabernet Sauvignon or Syrah, have a rich, rather overripe juicy flavour, though the whites – from Chardonnay and Sémillon if possible – are just a little hefty.

Chile has already made great wines and is going to make a lot more in the future. So far it has almost all been red, and most of it has been from the Cabernet Sauvignon grape, but there are increasing signs that Chardonnay, Sauvignon Blanc and Sémillon are capable of very special things too.

In the nineteenth century luck was certainly running Chile's way, because they chose to start a fine wine industry in 1851, and imported all their cuttings from Europe – just before the twin scourges of oidium (mildew) and phylloxera (the lethal vine aphid) struck. Consequently they have disease-free vineyards, and the combination of the Pacific Ocean, the Andes and arid desert to the north has kept phylloxera out.

Although there are six wine regions, most of them are either too hot (in the north) or too cold (in the south), but the Central Valley Zone has a wide variety of growing conditions. Traditionally, the Maipo Valley has produced the best reds, and it is Maipo Cabernet Sauvignon which has created Chile's reputation. It positively reeks of blackcurrants, and the fruit is stoked up with a coal-fire smokiness which is unique and delicious. This type is most easily seen in Cousiño Macul and Marqués de Casa Concha. Santa Rita make a more European, oakier style (it was top Cabernet in the 1986 Gault and Millau Olympiad), while further south, Los Vascos' Cabernet is bright and juicy, while Torres' Cabernet is lean and beautifully balanced for ageing.

Torres' strength, however, in the cool Maule region near Curico in the south, is in white wine. Most traditional Chilean whites are rather fat and oily. They grow a lot of Sémillon which at least reacts reasonably well to this style, but Torres is showing the way forward with crisp Chardonnay, steely Riesling, pale, fragrant Gewürztraminer, and sharply grassy Sauvignon, which, both with and without oak, are memorable wines.

· CANADA ·

No-one could accuse Canada of having a perfect grape-growing climate – long arctic winters alternating with short, exhaustingly hot summers. But make wine it does. Most of it is unmemorable *labrusca* wine – the strange, sickly-perfumed wine which is also the stock-in-trade of much of the north-east of the United States. However, in the Niagara area, good Gamay and Chardonnay are made (especially by Château Charmes) while in British Columbia, the Okanagan Valley, which has always looked to be good grape-growing land, is beginning to produce decent stuff.

· ASIA ·

The most exciting Oriental discovery recently has been Indian champagne! Well, that's how they describe this sparkling wine called Cuvée Omar Khayyam made in conjunction with a 'real' champagne winemaker, in the hills above Bombay. The wine is extremely good – and so it should be because the price is about the same as a minor champagne.

Japan doesn't have the climate for vines, which is perhaps why its only exciting offering so far has been a Sauternes look-alike.

China, though, is dabbling in wine. There are several joint ventures under way, and the Cabernet and Muscat from Shandong province between Shanghai and Beijing aren't too bad. Remy Martin help produce the softly perfumed Muscat Dynasty from Tianjin, but wine in any case isn't particularly suited to most Chinese food, and doesn't seem to attract much response from the Chinese themselves.

· A–Z OF WINES AND WINE TERMS ·

A cross-reference in small capitals indicates that a substantial entry on the subject appears in the main text; the page number given refers to the beginning of the appropriate chapter. For example: Chianti ITALY/CENTRAL (170) *means that the chapter on Central Italy, beginning on page 170, includes more information on Chianti than is covered by the A–Z.*

Abboccato Italian for 'semi-sweet'.
Abruzzi ITALY/CENTRAL (170) Important wine region on the Adriatic coast east of Rome.
AC See *Appellation d'Origine Contrôlée*.
Acetic acid Occurs naturally in wine, but in excess gives a sharp, vinegary taste.
Achaia Clauss Greece's largest wine firm, based at Patras.
Acid Naturally present in grapes and essential to wine, providing the refreshing tang in white wines, and the appetizing 'grip' in red wines. Principal wine acids are acetic, carbonic, citric, malic, tannic and tartaric.
Adega Portuguese for 'cellar' or 'winery'.
Adelaide Hills AUSTRALIA (220) New cool-climate wine area in South Australia; high-quality sparkling wines.
Aftertaste ENJOYING WINE (42) Flavour left in the mouth (and nose) after a wine has been swallowed or spat out; can be pleasant or unpleasant, and is a crucial factor in determining the likely development of young wines.
Aglianico Quality Italian red grape, which originated in ancient Greece. Now mainly grown in Basilicata and Campania.
Aglianico del Vulture ITALY/SOUTH (178) Red wine from Basilicata.
Ahr GERMANY/OTHER WINES (152) Small wine region off the Rhine south of Bonn, which surprisingly, given its northern position, specializes in red wine.
Ain-Bessem-Bouira Algerian wine area south-east of Algiers; quality reds, whites and rosés.
Airén SPAIN/CENTRAL (190) (or Lairén) Low quality white grape predominant in La Mancha.
Alameda County USA/CALIFORNIA (208) Prestigious wine area in the Central Coast division across the Bay from San Francisco. One AVA: Livermore Valley.
Albana ITALY/CENTRAL (170) Italian white grape grown in the Romagna hills since the Middle Ages. Its best-known wine is Albana di Romagna.
Albariño Wine area near Pontevedra in Galicia, Spain; noted for dry, delicate whites (from grape of the same name)

which generally have a slight prickle. See also *Alvarinho*.
Albariza Chalk vineyards in the Jerez area of Spain.
Alcohol Ethyl alcohol, naturally formed during fermentation when yeasts act on the sugar content of grapes.
Alcoholic content The alcoholic strength of wine, usually expressed as a percentage of the total volume.
Alcoholic fermentation FROM GRAPES TO WINE (22) Biochemical process whereby yeasts, natural or added, convert the grape sugars into alcohol and carbon dioxide; normally stops either when all the sugar has been converted or when the alcohol level reaches about 15%.
Alella SPAIN/CATALONIA (188) Tiny DO bordering Barcelona; its fruity wines, predominantly white, have at least one year's ageing in oak and one in bottle.
Alfold The Great Plain in Hungary; major vineyard area for everyday wines.
Algarve Demarcated region in the extreme south of Portugal, producing unremarkable high-acid reds and whites.
Alicante SPAIN/CENTRAL (190) South-eastern DO, spreading inland from the port of Alicante; predominantly planted in Monastrell vines, producing robust reds and rosés.
Aligoté FRANCE/BURGUNDY/COTE CHALONNAISE (96) White grape with high acidity. A permitted variety in Burgundy; also popular in Eastern Europe.
Alijo Wine area in the upper Douro, Portugal, making all-purpose reds, whites and rosés.
Alken GERMANY/MOSEL (142) Wine village of some importance near Koblenz.
Almacenista SPAIN/SHERRY (192) An old, unblended sherry; usually dry, dark-coloured and of high quality.
Almansa SPAIN/CENTRAL (190) Upland DO between Valencia and La Mancha which produces strong, ruby-coloured reds from Monastrell and Garnacha Tintorea.
Aloxe-Corton FRANCE/BURGUNDY/COTE D'OR (88) Leading Côte de Beaune village, with Grand Cru vineyards for red and white.
Alsace FRANCE/ALSACE (118) North-eastern French wine region specializing in varietal wines from German and French grape varieties. AC Alsace covers the whole region.
Alto Adige (Südtirol) ITALY/N-E (160) Northern half of Trentino-Alto Adige region, producing many of Italy's best whites and very individual reds and rosés.

Bilingual (Italian-German).
Alvarinho A white *vinho verde* grape from the Minho region of Portugal; also grown, across the border, in Galicia (Albariño).
Amabile Italian for 'medium sweet'; sweeter than *abboccato*.
Amador County USA/CALIFORNIA (208) Expanding wine region in the Sierra Foothills division; Zinfandel predominates. Two AVAs: Fiddletown and Shenandoah.
Amarante Sub-region of the *vinho verde* RD in north Portugal, making quite strong, full wines.
Amaro Italian for 'bitter'.
Amontillado SPAIN/SHERRY (192) Technically, a matured *fino* sherry; but now generally used to describe a medium sherry.
Amoroso SPAIN/SHERRY (192) Type of sherry. Sweeter and paler than an *oloroso*.
Ampurdán-Costa Brava SPAIN/CATALONIA (188) Small DO in the extreme north-east; produces a range of wines but is best-known for its rosés and young reds.
Amtliche Prüfungsnummer (AP Nr) Official control number appearing on the label of a German quality wine.
Anbaugebiet GERMANY (138) Term for 'wine-region'.
Anjou FRANCE/LOIRE (122) Large wine region in the Loire valley; most famous, or infamous, for its rosé. Increasingly good for cheap dry whites, as well as some excellent reds and two sweet wines, Quarts de Chaume and Bonnezeaux.
Annata Italian for 'vintage date'.
AOC See *Appellation d'Origine Contrôlée*.
Appellation d'Origine Contrôlée FRANCE (58) Legal designation, guaranteeing a wine's origin (geographical) and production methods. Abbreviated as AC or AOC.
Approved Viticultural Area USA/CALIFORNIA (208) Appellation system introduced in the 1980s and still in infancy. AVA status requires that 85% of grapes in a wine come from a specified region, delimited by soil and climate.
Aprilia ITALY/CENTRAL (170) Region within Latium, producing adequate-to-good wines of all colours.
Apulia ITALY/SOUTH (178) Italy's heel, mostly known for its blending wine; an increasing number of individual wines are now appearing.
Aquileia ITALY/N-E (160) Large zone in Friuli-Venezia-Giulia producing fruity reds and whites.

Arinto Portuguese white grape traditional to Bucelas.
Arneis dei Roeri ITALY/N-W (166) Ancient white grape, traditional to Piedmont where it produces a rare but delicious dry wine.
Arruda Wine area north of Lisbon, producing good everyday reds and whites.
Arvine White grape from the Valais, Switzerland; makes rich dessert wines.
Asenovgrad Major wine area in the south of Bulgaria; makes full-bodied reds from Mavrud.
Assemblage Final cask-to-cask blending of fine wines in Bordeaux and Champagne.
Assmanshausen Village on western end of the Rheingau, Germany; best-known for red wine from Spätburgunder.
Asti Spumante ITALY/N-W (166) Sweetish sparkling Muscat wine from Piedmont. The epitome of fresh, fizzy grapiness.
Aszú HUNGARY (234) Approximate translation from Hungarian is 'syrupy', referring to grapes affected by 'noble rot'; applies to the sweetest Tokay.
Aszú Essencia HUNGARY (234) Rare Tokay, second only to Tokay Essencia, made entirely from Aszú berries (as opposed to a mix of shrivelled and non-shrivelled grapes).
Attica Region round Athens, Greece, and home of retsina.
Ausbruch AUSTRIA (233) Term for very sweet wines from Burgenland.
Auslese GERMANY (138) Term for 'selected', referring to a QmP wine made from selected bunches of fully-ripe grapes; normally sweet.
Auxerrois See *Malbec*.
Auxey-Duresses FRANCE/BURGUNDY/COTE D'OR (88) Lesser village in Côte de Beaune producing good reds and whites.
AVA See *Approved Viticultural Area*.
Avelsbacher Small zone on outskirts of Trier, Germany, producing light but piercingly fruity Riesling wine.
Ayl Leading German wine village in the Saar with excellent steely Riesling.

Babic Yugoslavian red grape, producing good everyday wine.
Bacchus White grape bred from a Silvaner/Riesling cross and Müller-Thurgau; popular in Germany for blending. Also found in the UK.
Back-blending New Zealand term for adding unfermented grape juice to wine for sweetening.
Badacsony HUNGARY (234) Mountain near Lake Balaton; its vineyards produce dry and sweet whites.

Baden GERMANY/OTHER WINES (152) Major wine area spreading from Franconia to the Bodensee, but concentrated in the Rhine valley; produces large amounts of soft, fruity whites and reds.

Bairrada PORTUGAL/TABLE WINES (200) Demarcated region, just south of Oporto, producing rich, fruity reds and some whites; also champagne-method sparkling whites.

Baja California CENTRAL AMERICA (238) Arid region in Mexico now producing above-average reds and whites from Cabernet Sauvignon and Sauvignon Blanc.

Barbaresco ITALY/N-W (166) Leading DOCG in Piedmont. Can make surprisingly delicate or dark, intense reds from the Nebbiolo grape.

Barbera ITALY/N-W (166) Popular red grape; native to Piedmont but now planted countrywide. Makes dry, high-acid fruity wines. Also used in California, Australia and South America.

Barbera d'Alba ITALY/N-W (166) Strong, biting red from Piedmont.

Barbera d'Asti ITALY/N-W (166) Full, fruity red from Piedmont.

Barbera del Monferrato ITALY/N-W (166) Light, sharp, herby red from Piedmont near Alessandria.

Bardolino ITALY/N-E (160) Very light, cherryish red with a bitter finish, from Lake Garda in Veneto.

Barolo ITALY/N-W (166) The country's most daunting, yet potentially most exciting red; DOCG. From south of Alba in Piedmont.

Barossa Valley AUSTRALIA (220) Major wine area in South Australia, making a range of quality reds and whites.

Barrel ageing Time spent maturing in wood, normally oak; the wine takes on flavours from the wood.

Barrique French barrel, holding 225 litres.

Barsac FRANCE/BORDEAUX/SAUTERNES (80) One of Bordeaux's two great sweet wine areas. Barsac is an enclave in the Sauternes AC and can use either AC.

Basilicata ITALY/SOUTH (178) Isolated mountain region with one famous wine, Aglianico del Vulture.

Basto Sub-region of the *vinho verde* RD in north Portugal, making very light astringent wines, mostly reds.

Baumé Hydrometric scale which measures the sugar content of grape juice from its density; this indicates alcoholic content.

Bay of Plenty NEW ZEALAND (228) Major wine area on the North Island; noted for its fine whites but also some reds.

Beaujolais FRANCE/BURGUNDY/BEAUJOLAIS (100) Major wine area to the south of Burgundy. Its red wine, from the Gamay grape, is best known as Beaujolais Nouveau, but fine wines, worth ageing, come from 10 Cru villages.

Beaujolais Nouveau FRANCE/BURGUNDY/BEAUJOLAIS (100) Beaujolais wine released very young, during the November following the vintage.

Beaujolais-Villages FRANCE/BURGUNDY/BEAUJOLAIS (100) An AC group of 38 villages producing wine of more character than straight Beaujolais, yet not entitled to use their own name.

Beaune FRANCE/BURGUNDY/COTE D'OR (100) Major wine town and vineyard zone making very reliable reds and good, though rare, whites.

Beerenauslese GERMANY (138) Term for 'berry selection', referring to very sweet QmP wine made from overripe nobly-rotted grapes, individually picked.

Bendigo AUSTRALIA (220) Major wine area in central Victoria with many small vineyards producing top-quality wines, especially sparkling and reds.

Bentonite MODERN WINEMAKER (26) Clay-like substance used as a fining agent to clarify wine.

Bereich GERMANY (138) Term for a district within a wine region or *Anbaugebiet*.

Bereich Bernkastel GERMANY/MOSEL (142) Wine district embracing all the best middle Mosel villages.

Bereich Bingen GERMANY/RHINE (146) Rheinhessen wine district covering the area bordering the Nahe and Rheingau districts.

Bereich Johannisberg GERMANY/RHINE (146) Wine district covering the whole of the Rheingau.

Bereich Kaiserstuhl-Tuniberg (152) A Baden wine district producing good, spicy whites and reds.

Bereich Kreuznach GERMANY/RHINE (146) Wine district covering the villages in the lower Nahe between Bingen and Kreuznach.

Bereich Mittelhardt/Deutsche Weinstrasse Wine district in northern Rheinpfalz, Germany, including all the best villages.

Bereich Moseltor GERMANY/MOSEL (142) Tiny Mosel wine district on the border with Luxembourg and France.

Bereich Nierstein GERMANY/RHINE (146) The best-known Rheinhessen wine district, covering villages in the north and east of the region.

Bereich Obermosel GERMANY/MOSEL (142) Mosel wine district covering most of the vineyards on the slopes opposite Luxembourg.

Bereich Saar-Ruwer GERMANY/MOSEL (142) Wine district centred on Trier and embracing the Saar and Ruwer rivers.

Bereich Schloss Böckelheim GERMANY/RHINE (146) Wine district covering the best villages in the central Nahe as well as numerous scattered vineyards in the upper Nahe.

Bereich Südliche Weinstrasse GERMANY/RHINE (146) Southern Rheinpfalz wine district producing enormous amounts of fruity, reasonably priced wines.

Bereich Zell GERMANY/MOSEL (142) Wine district covering the area between Zell and Koblenz. Mostly pleasant, soft wines.

Bergerac FRANCE/COUNTRY WINES (128) Area east of Bordeaux producing wide range of red, rosé and dry, medium and sweet whites.

Bernkastel GERMANY/MOSEL (142) Leading Mosel village, home of world-famous Doktor vineyard which produces wines of remarkable steely brightness combined with deep, ripe fruit.

Bianco Italian for 'white'.

Bianco di Custoza ITALY/N-E (160) Good, fresh, bouncy, Soave-style white from Lake Garda, Veneto.

Biferno ITALY/SOUTH (178) One of Molise's two DOCs. All colours, rough and ready but adequate.

Bikavér HUNGARY (234) Traditional full-bodied red wine from the Eger district; sold abroad as 'Bull's Blood'.

Bin number AUSTRALIA (220) System of numbering batches of wine for identification purposes.

Bingen GERMANY/RHINE (146) Rheinhessen town facing the Rheingau. Some very exciting Rieslings – dry and elegant.

Black rot Fungus, thriving in hot humid conditions, which infects vine and fruit; causes small, hard berries.

Blagny FRANCE/BURGUNDY/COTE D'OR (88) Village above Puligny and Meursault making good red and white wines.

Blanc French for 'white'.

Blanc de blancs White wine (especially champagne) made only from white grapes.

Blanc de Morgex ITALY/N-W (166) Light, sharp, tongue-tingling white from mountains of Valle d'Aosta.

Blanc de noirs White wine (especially champagne) made from red grapes.

Blanco Spanish for 'white'.

Blanquette de Limoux FRANCE/COUNTRY WINES (128) Good champagne-method sparkling wine from the Aude valley.

Blatina Yugoslav red grape, grown in the Mostar area; makes agreeable table wines.

Blauburgunder German and Italian (Alto Adige) name for Pinot Noir.

Blauer Portugieser Basic red grape in Germany and Austria. Also widely planted in Hungary and Yugoslavia.

Blaufränkisch Austrian name for Gamay.

Blending Mixing together wines of different origin, styles or age, often to balance out acidity, weight, etc.

Blush wine Pink wine, usually sweetish and extremely fruity, initially from red Zinfandel grapes, now also from Cabernet, Merlot etc.

Bobal SPAIN/CENTRAL (190) Important Spanish red grape; dominant variety in the Utiel-Requena DO.

Boberg South African wine region, including Tulbagh and Paarl, specializing in fortified wines.

Bodega Spanish for 'cellar' or 'winery'; also 'wine shop'.

Bolgheri ITALY/CENTRAL (170) Minor Tuscan DOC for rosé and white on Tyrrhenian Sea, but famous as home of Sassicaia, world-class non-DOC Cabernet Sauvignon.

Bonarda Italian red grape producing good fruity wines around the Lombardy-Piedmont border.

Bonnezeaux FRANCE/LOIRE (122) Small Anjou AC producing delicious, under-rated sweet wines from the Chenin grape.

Borba Portuguese wine area in the Alto Alentejo, mostly making robust reds.

Bordeaux FRANCE/BORDEAUX (64) France's most important wine region, famous for reds and sweet whites; also good dry whites, rosés and sparkling wine.

Bordeaux mixture Copper sulphate, slaked lime and water; sprayed on to vines

throughout the growing season to prevent downy mildew.

Bordeaux Supérieur FRANCE/BORDEAUX/OTHER WINES (82) AC for red, white and rosé covering the same general area as AC Bordeaux, but with higher minimum alcoholic strength and lower yields in vineyards.

Botrytis cinerea FROM GRAPES TO WINE (22) Fungus, prevalent in cold, wet weather, which attacks grapes; particularly harmful to red grapes. But on healthy white grapes, in warm, humid conditions, it can become 'noble rot'. Noble rot shrivels the fruit and so concentrates the sugars to produce quality sweet wines like Sauternes.

Bottle-ageing MODERN WINEMAKER (26) Continuing maturation in the bottle, especially applicable to fine wines.

Bottling MODERN WINEMAKER (26) According to wine type, bottling takes place either months, or years, after the vintage; the process is now usually automated, especially for jug wines. Sterilized equipment is essential.

Bourgogne FRANCE/BURGUNDY (84) French name for Burgundy, a major wine area centred on the Saône valley in eastern France; produces world-famous reds from Pinot Noir and Gamay and whites from Chardonnay. The Bourgogne AC is a catch-all appellation covering wines which do not qualify for one of the higher classifications.

Bourgogne Aligoté FRANCE/BURGUNDY/COTE CHALONNAISE (96) White wine from the Aligoté grape.

Bourgogne Passe-Tout-Grains FRANCE/BURGUNDY/BASIC (104) Red wine made from a maximum of 2/3 Gamay and 1/3 Pinot Noir. Underrated, but can be delicious.

Bourgueil FRANCE/LOIRE (122) Leading Touraine AC producing sharp, fruity and surprisingly long-lasting red wines from the Cabernet Franc.

Bouvier Austrian white grape, grown mostly for blending. In Yugoslavia makes the sweet wine, Tiger's Milk.

Bracchetto ITALY/N-W (166) Red grape, planted mainly in Piedmont where it makes a sweetish, strawberry-coloured *frizzante* wine.

Braga Sub-region of the *vinho verde* RD; produces both reds and whites.

Branco Portuguese for 'white'.

Brauneberg GERMANY/MOSEL (142) Village with one great vineyard, Juffer.

Breganze ITALY/N-E (160) Increasingly well-regarded Veneto DOC north of Vicenza, producing dry white and reds.

Brindisi ITALY/SOUTH (178) Good southern Apulian reds and rosés based on the Negromaro grape.

British wine Wine made in the UK from imported, dehydrated must; it is reconstituted with water and then fermented.

Brix A scale, used in the USA and Australia, to measure sugar levels in grape juice.

Brouilly FRANCE/BURGUNDY/BEAUJOLAIS (100) Beaujolais cru producing large amounts of light, fruity red.

Brunello ITALY/CENTRAL (170) Tuscan red grape, known for its highly-prized wine, Brunello di Montalcino.

Brunello di Montalcino ITALY/CENTRAL (170) Expensive, renowned Tuscan red.

Brut French for 'unsweetened', used mostly of sparkling wines; drier than 'extra dry'.

Bual PORTUGAL/MADEIRA (204) Portuguese white grape used to make the second-sweetest madeira (after Malmsey); authorized on the mainland for white port. Also called Boal.

Bucelas Tiny demarcated region just north of Lisbon, Portugal, producing a dry white wine.

Bugey FRANCE/COUNTRY WINES (128) Little known but tasty VDQS from Savoie; dry, still and sparkling whites.

Bull's Blood HUNGARY (234) See *Bikavér*.

Burgenland AUSTRIA (232) Wine area on the Hungarian border, producing table reds and whites but most noted for its 'noble rot' sweet wines.

Buzbag Dark, strong red wine from Anatolia, in the south of Turkey.

Cabernet Franc GRAPE VARIETIES (18) French red grape, widely planted in Bordeaux, the Loire and north-east Italy.

Cabernet Sauvignon GRAPE VARIETIES (18) Classic red grape, synonymous with Bordeaux, but making great wines worldwide.

Cadillac FRANCE/BORDEAUX/OTHER WINES (82) Small AC known for good sweet whites.

Cahors FRANCE/COUNTRY WINES (128) Ancient south-western region making strong, individual reds capable of ageing.

Calabria ITALY/SOUTH (178) Mountainous, remote region – Italy's toe – producing some interesting wines of possibly Roman descent.

Calveras County Small wine area in the Sierra Foothills division of California, USA; planted in Zinfandel and Sauvignon Blanc.

Campania ITALY/SOUTH (178) The area round Naples with potential for great wine, but lacks organization.

Campo de Borja Recent DO in Aragón, Spain; planted in white Macabeo and red Garnacha, making reds and rosés; much used in blending.

Campo Fiorin ITALY/N-E (160) Unusual, fascinating Veneto *vino da tavola* made by leaving a Valpolicella wine on the pressings of a Valpolicella Recioto.

Cannonau ITALY/SOUTH (178) The Sardinian name for the Grenache grape.

Canon-Fronsac FRANCE/BORDEAUX/ST-EMILION (74) The central part of Fronsac to the west of Libourne, with good vineyard sites.

Cantina Italian for 'cellar' or 'winery'.

Cap FROM GRAPES TO WINE (22) Layer of skins and pips which rises to the top of the vat during red wine fermentation.

Capsule In bottled wines, the metal or plastic top fitted over the cork.

Carbonic maceration FRANCE/BURGUNDY/BEAUJOLAIS (100) Wine-making method where grapes are fermented whole in a closed vat; produces light, fruity red wine for early drinking. Now widely used in warm areas to preserve the fruity flavours, it is an adaptation of the traditional Beaujolais fermentation method.

Carcavelos Tiny demarcated region, west of Lisbon, Portugal; its fortified nutty wines range from medium-dry to sweet.

Carema ITALY/N-W (166) North Piedmont DOC: a light, but penetrating red wine made from Nebbiolo.

Carignan Commonest red grape grown in France, especially in southern *départements*. Also widely planted in California (as Carignane) and South America. Used for jug wines, mostly blended to lessen its natural astringency.

Cariñena Windswept DO, south of Zaragoza, Spain, producing dry, high-alcohol everyday reds and rosés; also dry whites, called *pajarillas*, and sweet wines.

Carmignano ITALY/CENTRAL (170) Small Tuscan DOC chiefly noted for its permitted use of Cabernet Sauvignon in a blend with Sangiovese, to make a smooth, elegant wine.

Carso ITALY/N-E (160) Small Friuli DOC near Trieste on the Yugoslav border, producing dry red and white.

Cartaxo Wine area, bordering the Tagus in the Ribatejo, Portugal; makes full-bodied reds and fruity white, both high-alcohol.

Carthage Tunisian wine area in the hills around Tunis, producing adequate reds.

Cask Wooden (oak) barrel used for ageing and storing wine; sizes, and names, vary with the wine area.

Cassis FRANCE/COUNTRY WINES (128) Small Provençal wine region producing the French Riviera's best whites, also good rosés and reds. Not to be confused with the blackcurrant liqueur Crème de Cassis.

Castel del Monte ITALY/SOUTH (178) Excellent plummy Apulian red as well as some white and rosé.

Casteller ITALY/N-E (160) Light refreshing red from Trentino.

Catalonia SPAIN/CATALONIA (188) Important north-eastern province with a wide range of wine styles.

Cava SPAIN/CATALONIA (188) Champagne-method sparkling wine; 90% of production comes from the Penedés region, centred on the town of San Sadurní de Noya. The remainder is made elsewhere in Catalonia and in the Rioja.

Cave French for 'cellar'.

Cebreros Wine district in the Gredos mountains west of Madrid, Spain. Mostly planted in Garnacha and Aragonés and white Albillo, making vigorous reds and *claretes*.

Cencibel SPAIN/CENTRAL (190) Valdepeñas name for Tempranillo grape.

Central Valley USA/CALIFORNIA (208) Major inland wine area, along the Sacramento and San Joaquin valleys, producing 80% of all California's wine. Three AVAs: Madera, Clarksburg and Merritt Island.

Centrifuge FROM GRAPES TO WINE (22) Machine for filtering wine by means of centrifugal force (rapid spinning).

Cepa Spanish for 'grape variety'.

Cépage French for 'grape variety'.

Cérons FRANCE/BORDEAUX/OTHER WINES (82) Small enclave in Graves district of Bordeaux, AC for sweet wines.

Cerveteri ITALY/CENTRAL (170) Pleasant reds and whites from north-west of Rome.

Chablais Wine area at the eastern end of Lake Geneva in the Vaud, Switzerland; makes notable Dorin (Chasselas) whites.

Chablis FRANCE/BURGUNDY/CHABLIS

(102) White wine region producing very dry, high class Chardonnay.

Chai Bordeaux term for the building in which wine is stored before bottling.

Chambolle-Musigny FRANCE/BURGUNDY/COTE D'OR (88) Côte de Nuits villages capable of producing the most aromatic, perfumed of Pinot Noirs.

Chambrer To bring a wine to room temperature, ready for drinking; usually applied to reds.

Champagne FRANCE/CHAMPAGNE (106) Northern wine region, centred on Reims, and the *only* place which makes true champagne sparkling wine.

Champagne method FRANCE/CHAMPAGNE (106) Traditional process of making sparkling wine by inducing a second fermentation in the bottle.

Champanski Sweet red sparkling wine, properly called Tsimlanskoye; mostly produced in the north of the Soviet Union. Also general term for white sparkling wine in USSR.

Chaptalization MODERN WINEMAKER (26) Legal addition of sugar during fermentation to raise a wine's alcoholic strength. More necessary in cool climates where lack of sun produces insufficient natural sugar in the grape; mostly illegal in hot lands.

Chardonnay GRAPE VARIETIES (18) Classic white grape, traditional to Burgundy, but also making great wines in California and Australia and good wines almost anywhere warm enough to ripen it. One of the main champagne grapes.

Chassagne-Montrachet FRANCE/BURGUNDY/COTE D'OR (88) The lesser-known of the two Côte de Beaune villages which share the great Le Montrachet vineyard in Burgundy. Good whites and a lot of fair red.

Chasselas Historic white grape, possibly the oldest wine grape still in cultivation. Most important in Switzerland (as Dorin or Fendant), making a soft dry wine. Also grown for eating.

Château FRANCE/BORDEAUX (64) A French wine-producing estate, big or small; particularly common in Bordeaux.

Château Grillet FRANCE/RHONE (112) Tiny one-vineyard AC producing high-class, high-price white wine from Viognier grapes.

Châteauneuf-du-Pape FRANCE/RHONE (112) Large, famous AC in southern Rhône producing much excellent red and a little outstanding white.

Chelois French-American hybrid red grape; planted in the eastern USA.

Chénas FRANCE/BURGUNDY/BEAUJOLAIS (100) Small but good and sturdy Beaujolais cru.

Chenin Blanc GRAPE VARIETIES (18) Classic white grape of the Loire; also important in South Africa and California.

Cheverny FRANCE/LOIRE (122) VDQS for both red and white, making good Chardonnay and fizz, fair Pinot Noir and Romorantin.

Chianti ITALY/CENTRAL (170) Italy's most famous wine, and the largest DOCG zone, split into seven subdivisions headed by Chianti Classico.

Chianti Classico ITALY/CENTRAL (170) The most famous and finest of the seven Chianti zones in Tuscany.

Chinon FRANCE/LOIRE (122) Good-to-excellent red wine from Cabernet Franc.

Chiroubles FRANCE/BURGUNDY/BEAUJOLAIS (100) Beaujolais cru producing light, juicy wine for early drinking.

Chorey-lès-Beaune FRANCE/BURGUNDY/COTE D'OR (88) Little-known Côte de Beaune village with several very good growers.

Cigales Historic wine district in Valladolid province, Spain, celebrated since medieval times for its *claretes*, light red wines, made by mixing red Garnacha and white Palomino, Verdejo and Albillo.

Cinqueterre ITALY/N-W (166) Cliff-vineyard Ligurian white wine of much historical and romantic importance, but little modern day pleasure.

Cinsaut (Sometimes spelled Cinsault.) Common red grape in southern France. Mostly blended with other Midi varieties, like Grenache and Carignan, for basic *vin de table*.

Cirò ITALY/SOUTH (178) Historic Calabrian red, white and rosé of fair quality.

Clairette Basic white grape, once abundant in southern France but now less popular. Low on acid, and mostly blended into ordinary *vin de table*.

Clairette de Die FRANCE/RHONE (112) Sparkling wine from small Rhône AC.

Claret English name for red Bordeaux.

Clarete Spanish/Portuguese for 'light red'.

Clare Valley AUSTRALIA (220) Small wine area in South Australia noted for its quality whites, especially its Rieslings and Sauvignons, as well as soft, attractive reds.

Classed growth See *cru classé*.

Classic crest AUSTRALIA (220) Top category of accreditation scheme pioneered in Hunter Valley; denotes a high-quality wine.

Classico Italian term for wines from a specific zone within a DOC, usually the original one; usually superior quality.

Climat Specifically delimited vineyard, often very small, in Burgundy.

Clos French term for a vineyard that is (or was) enclosed by a wall; mostly associated with Burgundy.

Coastal Region SOUTH AFRICA (238) Most important designated wine region, located in Cape Province.

Colares Small demarcated region at Portugal's westernmost point; its vines, often planted in sand, survived phylloxera. Makes classic, full, deep reds, very tough, yet also exotically aromatic!

Collio Goriziano ITALY/N-E (160) Friuli wine area on Yugoslav border above Gorizia sometimes simply called Collio; dry whites and reds.

Colli Orientali ITALY/N-E (160) Good Friuli wine area, predominantly white, on Yugoslav border north of Collio Goriziano.

Collioure FRANCE/COUNTRY WINES (128) AC in Pyrénées Orientales making strong, dark reds.

Colombard USA/CALIFORNIA (208) Important white grape in California where it is used for varietal wines and for blends; high-acid and fragrant. Also planted in south-west France and in South Africa.

Columbia Basin Irrigated wine region centred on the Columbia river east of the Cascade Mountains, USA; expanding in both Washington and Oregon. Classic European varietals predominate.

Commandaria Ancient liqueur-like dessert wine, very sweet, from Cyprus; made from raisined red and white grapes in the Troodos foothills.

Conca de Barberá New DO, bordering Penedés, Spain, making everyday wines, mostly whites.

Concord American *labrusca* red grape associated with New York State; also planted in Brazil. Concord wine is, in the *labrusca* tradition, 'foxy' and sweetish.

Condado de Huelva Spanish DO in Andalucía, producing young everyday whites and two fortified wines: Condado Pálido and Condado Viejo.

Condrieu FRANCE/RHONE (112) Beautiful white wine from Viognier in very short supply.

Constantia South African wine district in the Coastal Region, noted for historic Muscat dessert wine.

Coonawarra AUSTRALIA (220) Important wine area in South Australia, famous for fine reds – mostly Shiraz and Cabernet Sauvignon. Also quality Riesling and Chardonnay.

Co-operative Winery run collectively by a group of growers; common for jug wine (plonk) production, but increasingly important for affordable varietals.

Corbières FRANCE/COUNTRY WINES (128) Important AC for red, white and rosé in mountainous south of France below Carcassonne and Narbonne.

Cork IDENTIFYING WINES (36) Bottle-plug, invented in the 18th century; made from bark of the cork oak.

Corkage Charge made by restaurant for allowing customers to bring in and drink their own wine.

Corked SERVING WINE (46) Wine spoilt by a defective cork. The mouldy, stale smell is unmistakeable once you've suffered it.

Cornas FRANCE/RHONE (112) AC making small amounts of hefty red.

Cortese ITALY/N-W (166) Good Italian white grape grown in south-east Piedmont and used for the top-quality Gavi.

Corvina ITALY/N-E (160) Italian red grape; major ingredient of Valpolicella.

Corvo ITALY/SOUTH (178) Successful Sicilian brand name wine.

Costières du Gard FRANCE/COUNTRY WINES (128) Enormous southern VDQS producing reasonable reds, whites and rosés.

Cot See *Malbec*.

Côte French for 'hillside'; incorporated into the name of many wine areas.

Coteaux Champenois FRANCE/CHAMPAGNE (106) Still wine, red or white, from the Champagne region.

Coteaux de l'Ardèche FRANCE/COUNTRY WINES (128) Large *vin de pays* to the west of the Rhône, producing some excellent varietal reds, whites and rosés.

Coteaux de Mascara Designated area of Algeria, south-east of Oran, producing full-fruited reds and soft whites.

Coteaux des Baux-en-Provence FRANCE/COUNTRY WINES (128) Outstanding new southern AC, best for reds but also good for rosé and white.

Coteaux de Tlemcan Designated area

on the Moroccan border of Algeria, making above-average table wines.

Coteaux du Layon FRANCE/LOIRE (122) Good sweet wine AC with one or two exceptional villages.

Coteaux du Zaccar Designated area in the hills west of Algeria, making basic reds and whites.

Côte Chalonnaise FRANCE/BURGUNDY/COTE CHALONNAISE (96) Small area south of Côte d'Or with good, if light, reds and whites.

Côte de Beaune FRANCE/BURGUNDY/COTE D'OR (88) Southern part of the Côte d'Or producing much excellent red, and some excellent-to-great white.

Côte de Beaune-Villages FRANCE/BURGUNDY/COTE D'OR (88) Red wine AC of dwindling importance used by some lesser Côte de Beaune villages.

Côte de Nuits FRANCE/BURGUNDY/COTE D'OR (88) The northern part of the Côte d'Or, containing many of Burgundy's greatest red wine villages.

Côte de Nuits-Villages FRANCE/BURGUNDY/COTE D'OR (88) Small AC for red and dry white, covering five lesser wines in the Côte de Nuits.

Côte d'Or FRANCE/BURGUNDY/COTE D'OR (88) The centre of Burgundy's finest wine-growing region, stretching from Dijon to Santenay.

Côte Roannaise FRANCE/COUNTRY WINES (128) Area in the upper reaches of the Loire making fresh rosés and light reds from the Gamay.

Côte-Rôtie FRANCE/RHONE (112) Fine red wine from small AC of precipitous vineyards in northern Rhône using Syrah and a little Viognier.

Côtes de Brouilly FRANCE/BURGUNDY/BEAUJOLAIS (100) Good Beaujolais cru making fine, fruity wines.

Côtes de Buzet FRANCE/COUNTRY WINES (128) Good AC making similar wines to Bordeaux from the same grapes.

Côtes de Gascogne FRANCE/COUNTRY WINES (128) *Vin de pays* using the excess wine from Armagnac production to tremendous effect especially in delicious dry whites.

Côtes de Provence FRANCE/COUNTRY WINES (128) Large southern AC for red, white and rosé of varying quality, but at its best extremely good.

Côtes du Duras FRANCE/COUNTRY WINES (128) AC just to the east of Bordeaux making good reds, but

particularly bright, snappy whites from Sauvignon.

Côtes du Frontonnais FRANCE/COUNTRY WINES (128) Local AC of Toulouse making marvellously soft, juicy reds and some rosé.

Côtes du Jura FRANCE/COUNTRY WINES (128) General AC for red, white and rosé from the southern Jura.

Côtes du Luberon FRANCE/COUNTRY WINES (128) Wild, hilly region in the south producing cheap and decent red, white and rosé VDQS.

Côtes du Rhône FRANCE/RHONE (112) Large general AC for red, white and rosé – the heart of the Rhône valley.

Côtes du Rhône-Villages FRANCE/RHONE (112) AC for red, white and rosé from the best villages inside the Côtes du Rhône area.

Côtes du Roussillon FRANCE/COUNTRY WINES (128) Large AC just north of the Pyrenees. Good reds, fair rosés, adequate whites.

Côtes du Ventoux FRANCE/COUNTRY WINES (128) Good 'mini-Côtes du Rhône' AC for red, white and rosé.

Cotnari Traditional Romanian dessert wine, delicate and sweet; made in Moldavia.

Coulure Vine disease causing flowers to drop prematurely.

Cowra AUSTRALIA (220) Vineyard area in New South Wales supplying grapes to wineries in other districts; also some wine production of its own.

Cream SPAIN/SHERRY (192) Style of sweet sherry made by sweetening aged *olorosos* or *amontillados*.

Crémant French sparkling wine made by the champagne method (but with fewer bubbles) in Champagne.

Crémant d'Alsace FRANCE/ALSACE (118) Champagne-method sparkling wine.

Crémant de Bourgogne FRANCE/BURGUNDY/BASIC (104) Burgundy's champagne-method sparkler which ranges from good to outstanding.

Crémant de Loire FRANCE/LOIRE (122) Champagne-method Anjou AC often less aggressively fizzy due to lower atmospheric pressure in the wine.

Crete Greek island with four designated red-wine areas: Archanes, Daphnes, Peza and Sitia. Wines tend to be dark, heavy and, often, sweet.

Criadera Spanish term describing the series of butts from which (sherry) wine is taken to replenish a *solera*.

Criado y embotellado por . . . Spanish for 'grown and bottled by . . .'

Crianza SPAIN/RIOJA (184) Spanish term for wines with at least two years ageing, one in oak; 'sin crianza' means unaged.

Criolla Basic red grape of Argentina, making pretty ordinary table wine.

Crozes-Hermitage FRANCE/RHONE (112) AC surrounding Hermitage producing good affordable reds and whites.

Cru French term literally meaning 'growth' but used to designate a single vineyard (normally with some additional quality reference).

Cru bourgeois FRANCE/BORDEAUX/MEDOC (68) In the Médoc classification, the quality level below *cru classé*; divided into *cru grand bourgeois exceptionnel*, *cru grand bourgeois* and *cru bourgeois*.

Cru classé FRANCE/BORDEAUX/MEDOC (68) French term literally meaning 'classed growth'; indicates that a vineyard has been included in the top-quality rating system of its region. The most famous system is the 1855 classification for Médoc, in which *cru classé* (with five sub-divisions) is the top category.

Crust Heavy sediment cast off by vintage ports in the bottle.

Crusted port PORTUGAL/PORT (202) Vintage-style port, blended from several vintages, bottled after three years and aged in the bottle – where it forms a 'crust' sediment.

Cuve close French for 'closed vat', referring to the method of making sparkling wine in which the second fermentation takes place in closed tanks.

Cuvée Contents of a *cuve* or vat; also term for a given quantity of blended wine.

Dahra Algerian wine area, east of Oran, Algeria, making strong, fruity reds and interesting rosés.

Dalmatia Middle coastal region of Yugoslavia, producing a range of wines on the mainland and on the offshore islands.

Dão PORTUGAL/TABLE WINES (200) Mountainous demarcated region, centred on the river Dão, producing good all-purpose reds and whites.

Dealul Mare Major Romanian wine area in the south-east Carpathian foothills; produces rather ordinary reds from Cabernet Sauvignon, Merlot, Pinot Noir and the local Feteasca Neagra.

Débourbage Allowing white-wine must to stand, settle and have its solid matter drawn off before fermentation.

Debrö Hungarian wine town, known for its sweet Harslevelü, in the Mátraalya.

Decant SERVING WINE (46) Separate a bottled wine from its sediment by carefully pouring it into another, clean container.

Dégorgement FRANCE/CHAMPAGNE (106) Stage in champagne-making when sediment is removed from the bottle.

Delatite AUSTRALIA (220) Cool-climate vineyard in the Mansfield hills, central Victoria; noted for its elegant whites and startlingly intense, though soft, reds.

Delaware American hybrid pink grape making delicate, spicy wine. Grown in the eastern US, Brazil and Japan.

Demi-sec French term, literally 'half-dry' but often meaning quite sweet, especially for sparkling wines.

Denominación de Origen (DO) SPAIN (180) Equivalent of the French AC.

Denominazione di Origine Controllata (DOC) ITALY (156) Equivalent of the French AC.

Denominazione di Origine Controllata e Garantita (DOCG) ITALY (156) Category for quality wines, above DOC.

Deutscher Sekt GERMAN/OTHER WINES (152) Sparkling wine made from German grapes.

Deutscher Tafelwein GERMANY (138) Term for table wine made wholly from German grapes, rather than a blend of EEC grapes.

Diano d'Alba ITALY/N-W (166) Leading Dolcetto community in Piedmont, near Alba; its wine is among the best.

Dimiat Bulgarian local white grape, widely planted.

Dingac Rustic, sweetish Yugoslav red wine from the Plavać grape.

DO See *Denominación de Origen.*

DOC See *Denominazione di Origine Contrallata.*

Doce Portuguese for 'sweet'.

DOCG See Denominazione de Origine Controllata e Garantita.

Dolce Italian for 'sweet'.

Dolcetto ITALY/N-W (166) Marvellous, rustically over-powering red grape from Piedmont, producing dark, fruity wines.

Dolcetto d'Alba ITALY/N-W (166) Round, grapy, almost raw-fruit-juice red wine to drink young.

Dolcetto di Ovada ITALY/N-W (166) Remarkable mouthfilling yet soft red

wine for drinking young.

Dôle Swiss Gamay-Pinot Noir red wine from the Valais. Light and fruity with a icy tang.
et soft red
wine in Burgundy.

Donnaz ITALY/N-W (166) Light, tasty Nebbiolo DOC in Valle d'Aosta.

Dosage FRANCE/CHAMPAGNE (106) Topping up champagne bottles after *dégorgement* with a mixture of sugar and wine; means of regulating the final sweetness.

Douro PORTUGAL/TABLE WINES (200) Demarcated region centred on the upper Douro valley; produces dry whites and fruity reds.

Doux French for 'sweet'.

Downy mildew Common vine fungus which destroys leaves and shrivels fruit; controlled by spraying with Bordeaux mixture. Also called *peronospera*.

Dragaşani Established vineyard area in southern Romania.

Drumborg AUSTRALIA (220) Cool-climate vineyard area in southern Victoria supplying grapes, predominantly white, to Great Western wineries.

Dulce Spanish for 'sweet'.

Dürkheim GERMANY/RHINE (146) Important Rheinpfalz wine zone centred on Bad Dürkheim.

East Gippsland AUSTRALIA (220) Remote wine area in southern Victoria, replanted in the 1970s; makes a range of quality whites and reds.

Edelfäule German for 'noble rot'.

Edes Hungarian for 'sweet'.

Eger Major wine area in the north of Hungary, noted for its full Bikavér reds and delicate Leanyka whites.

Egrappage French for 'destemming', the removal of stalks prior to fermentation.

Egrappoir-fouloir French term for machine which both destems and crushes grapes before fermentation.

Ehrenfelser German white grape, a Riesling/Silvaner crossing. Riesling-like but lacking in acidity, yet it ripens earlier and more easily.

Einzellage GERMANY (138) German term for an individual vineyard.

Eiswein GERMANY (138) Very sweet wine made in winter from grapes harvested while still frozen; Germany, Austria and, most recently, Canada.

Elaborado y añejado por ... Spanish for 'made and aged by . . .'

El Bierzo Spanish wine area in León province bordering Galicia. Makes fruity reds and whites with quality potential.

Elbling Early-ripening white grape grown in the Mosel and Luxembourg; makes rather thin, sharp wine.

El Dorado County Minor wine region in the Sierra Foothills division of California; Zinfandel predominates. One AVA of the same name.

Elevage French term covering all the wine-making processes between fermentation and bottling.

Eltville Important Rheingau wine village and home of the outstanding Staatsweingut, the German State Domain, a major wine producer.

Embotellado de origen Spanish for 'estate-bottled'.

Emerald Riesling White grape, developed in California from a Riesling/Muscadelle cross. Produces a German-style fruity, aromatic wine.

Emilia-Romagna ITALY/CENTRAL (170) Central Italian region producing enormous amounts of easy, thirst-quenching wines, epitomized by the major product – Lambrusco.

Enfer d'Arvier ITALY/N-W (166) One of Valle d'Aosta's two DOCs, a sharp, rasping red.

Engarrafado na origem Portuguese for 'estate-bottled'.

English Vineyards Association Represents and promotes viticulture and wine-making in the UK. Its gold seal, awarded annually to selected wines, encourages quality.

Enology See *Oenology*.

Entre-Deux-Mers FRANCE/BORDEAUX/OTHER WINES (82) Large wine zone, best known for straightforward dry whites. Also produces red wine sold as Bordeaux.

Erbach Rheingau village with many good vineyards and one superb one, Marcobrunn.

Erbaluce di Caluso ITALY/N-W (166) Pleasant white and interesting amber sweet wine from Piedmont.

Ermitage Name for the Marsanne grape in the Swiss Valais, where it makes a rich wine.

Erzeugerabfüllung German for 'estate-bottled'.

Escherndorf Important Franconian wine village. Lump is the best vineyard.

Espalier Basic training system for vines, using parallel wires.

Espumante Portuguese for 'sparkling'.

Espumoso Spanish for 'sparkling'.

Essencia HUNGARY (234) Super-sweet concentrated Aszú juice used for top-quality Tokay; very low in alcohol, very concentrated in flavour.

Estate-bottled Wine bottled on the premises where it has been made.

Est! Est!! Est!!! ITALY/CENTRAL (170) Silly name for, until recently, a silly wine from the Latium town of Montefiascone. Latest sightings suggest better wine is on the way.

Estufa PORTUGAL/MADEIRA (204) Literally 'stove', refers to the special hothouses where madeira is made.

EVA See *English Vineyards Association*.

Faber White grape, developed in Germany from Pinot Blanc and Müller-Thurgau; popular in Rheinhessen and the Nahe. Riesling-type characteristics.

Falkenstein AUSTRIA (232) Eastern section of the Weinviertel wine region.

Faros Smooth yet robust Yugoslav red made from the Plavać grape on Hvar island.

Fehér Hungarian for 'white'.

Fermentation See *Alcoholic fermentation* and *Malolactic fermentation*.

Feteasca Widely-planted Romanian grape: *neagra*, red and *alba*, white.

Filtration FROM GRAPES TO WINE (32) Method of removing impurities from wine, especially white, before bottling; also, juice for white wine is often filtered after pressing.

Finger Lakes USA/OTHER WINES (218) Traditional wine region, on lake-side slopes, in upper New York State. *Labrusca* varietals predominate; but some French hybrids and *vinifera*.

Fining MODERN WINEMAKER (26) Method of clarifying wine by adding a coagulant to the surface; as the substance drops it collects impurities.

Fino SPAIN/SHERRY (192) Pale, dry sherry.

Fitou FRANCE/COUNTRY WINES (128) Small, increasingly popular AC zone for red wine in the Midi, France.

Fixin FRANCE/BURGUNDY/COTE D'OR (88) Côte de Nuits village near Gevrey-Chambertin. Good wine, not great.

Flagey-Echézeaux FRANCE/BURGUNDY/COTE D'OR (88) Village with two of the Côte de Nuits' least-known Grands Crus: Echézeaux and Grand Echézeaux.

Fleurie FRANCE/BURGUNDY/BEAUJOLAIS (100) The most popular, the most expensive and, frequently, the most delicious of the Beaujolais cru wines.

Flor SPAIN/SHERRY (192) Special yeast which develops on dry sherries (and some other wines) in barrel; prevents oxidation and creates a unique taste.

Focsani Major Romanian wine region east of the Carpathians, producing everyday reds and whites. Main centres are Cotesti, Odobesti and Nicoresti.

Forst GERMANY/RHINE (146) Important Rheinpfalz village producing rich, spicy wines.

Fortified wine FROM GRAPES TO WINE (22) High-strength wine, made by adding extra alcohol, e.g. sherry.

Franciacorta ITALY/N-W (166) Good red and still or sparkling white from Lombardy.

Franken GERMANY/OTHER WINES (152) Region on the Main river specializing in full-bodied but dry wines.

Frascati ITALY/CENTRAL (170) Famous Roman white. Can be delicious in a strange, soft-sour way.

Free-run wine FROM GRAPES TO WINE (22) Newly-fermented wine drawn off from the grape residue before pressing.

Freisa ITALY/N-W (166) Piedmont red grape, often made into slightly sparkling light red wine, with a unique sweet-sour taste.

Friuli-Venezia-Giulia ITALY/N-E (160) Region bordering Yugoslavia with potential for juicy, modern wines.

Frizzante Italian for 'semi-sparkling'.

Fronsac FRANCE/BORDEAUX/ST-EMILION (74) A 'coming' red wine area, just west of Libourne, and using the traditional Cabernet-Merlot blend.

Fumé Blanc Fashionable pseudonym for Sauvignon Blanc. Sometimes applied to Sémillon/Sauvignon Blanc blends.

Furmint Distinctive Hungarian white grape, traditional to the Tokay region and its wines. Also grown in the USSR and elsewhere in Eastern Europe.

Gaglioppo Red grape from southern Italy; makes tannic, high-alcohol wines.

Gaillac FRANCE/COUNTRY WINES (128) Important south-west French region, *too* dominated by the co-operative movement, but capable of remarkable peppery reds and sensuously spicy sparklers.

Galestro ITALY/CENTRAL (170) New-wave, light, low alcohol whites from

the Trebbiano grape in Tuscany.

Gamay FRANCE/BURGUNDY/BEAUJOLAIS (100) The Beaujolais grape, making lively, light, fruity red wines. Also grown in the Loire and in Switzerland.

Gamay Beaujolais Californian red grape; clone of Pinot Noir, not Gamay.

Gambellara ITALY/N-E (160) Veneto zone east of Soave, making similar pallid white wines.

Garganega Italian white grape from the Veneto.

Garnacha See *Grenache*.

Garrafeira Portuguese term for a merchant's 'special reserve' wine – aged and usually superior quality.

Gattinara ITALY/N-W (166) Good, raisiny, chocolaty reds based on Nebbiolo, from northern Piedmont.

Gavi ITALY/N-W (166) Area of south-east Piedmont producing very dry, nutty whites from Cortese grape.

Geelong AUSTRALIA (220) Traditional wine area in southern Victoria; recently re-planted and now producing top-quality whites and reds.

Geisenheim GERMANY/RHINE (146) Good Rheingau village and home of Germany's leading viticultural school.

Generic Term describing a wine either by type (e.g. sparkling) or by region (e.g. Bordeaux) – as opposed to varietal.

Gevrey-Chambertin FRANCE/BURGUNDY/COTE D'OR (88) Leading Côte de Nuits village for some of Burgundy's longest-lived reds.

Gewürztraminer GRAPE VARIETIES (18) Major white grape variety known for its pungent spiciness. Best in Alsace but also successful in Italy, Germany, Austria, New Zealand, Australia and cool vineyard areas in the USA.

Ghemme ITALY/N-W (166) Good Nebbiolo-based red from Piedmont.

Gigondas FRANCE/RHONE (112) Near neighbour of Châteauneuf-du-Pape, producing strong, chewy reds.

Gisborne NEW ZEALAND (228) Quality white-wine area adjacent to Poverty Bay on the North Island.

Givry FRANCE/BURGUNDY/COTE CHALONNAISE (96) Historic village, producing full, tasty Pinot Noir reds and some good whites.

Glycerol Important chemical component of wine, produced during fermentation; thick, colourless and sweet.

Gobelet Training system in which each vine is tied to a separate stake. Used in the Mosel and Rhône.

Goron Swiss red wine from Valais, of inferior quality to Dôle.

Goulburn Valley AUSTRALIA (220) Wine area in central Victoria, mostly producing high quality wines.

Governo ITALY/CENTRAL (170) In Chianti, traditional practice of adding raisined grapes to the fermented wine to soften it and start a slight refermentation, which leaves a refreshing, acidic prickle in the wine.

Graach GERMANY/MOSEL (142) Important village next to Bernkastel producing full, soft wines.

Graciano High quality Spanish red grape, formerly important in Rioja.

Grafting GROWING GRAPES (14) Since phylloxera, the only sure method of propagating grape vines; involves growing a cutting (scion) of *vitis vinifera* in a notch on phylloxera-resistant *vitis riparia* stock. Also, by grafting one vine variety on to another, less popular varieties can be converted to more desirable ones.

Grand cru French term meaning 'top quality'; most specific in Burgundy, but also used in Alsace, Champagne and Bordeaux.

Gran reserva SPAIN (180) Top category of Spanish wines which requires minimum ageing (cask and bottle) of five years for reds, four for whites.

Grasâ Indigenous Romanian white grape, widely planted in the east; major ingredient of Cotnari.

Grave del Friuli ITALY/N-E (160) Extensive region in Friuli-Venezia-Giulia concentrating on juicy, gulpable reds.

Graves FRANCE/BORDEAUX/GRAVES (78) Important wine area, around Bordeaux, capable of great reds and dry whites.

Graves de Vayres Delimited section of Entre-Deux-Mers in Bordeaux.

Graves Supérieures AC usually applicable to reasonably sweet white wines from Graves area.

Gray Riesling White grape widely planted in California where it makes a neutral, medium-dry wine.

Great Western AUSTRALIA (220) Small, but prestigious, wine area in central Victoria; famous for its champagne-method sparkling wine.

Greco White grape, grown in southern Italy; mostly used for blending.

Greco di Bianco ITALY/SOUTH (178) Rare but good sweet white from Calabria.

Greco di Tufo ITALY/SOUTH (178) The leading dry white from Mastroberardino,

Campania's most important winemaker.

Grenache Basic red grape, common in Spain (as Garnacha), southern France, California and Australia. Usually blended, to add fruit and alcohol; also makes varietal rosés.

Grey rot Vine disease caused by *botrytis* (as opposed to noble rot).

Grignolino Red grape from Piedmont, where it makes a strange but enticing wine – dry, acid and herby.

Grk Yugoslav white grape, grown on the island of Korcula; makes a dry, light wine and a heavier sherry-type.

Grombalia Tunisian wine area producing reasonable reds and rosés.

Gros Plant See *Folle Blanche*.

Gros Plant du Pays Nantais FRANCE/COUNTRY WINES (128) Raw white from the mouth of the Loire. Frightening on its own, but pretty good with sea food.

Grosslage GERMANY (138) In Germany, a group of vineyards from the same area, producing wines of similar character and quality.

Grüner Veltliner Leading white grape of Austria, where it produces fruity, high-acid wines. Also grown over the Czech, Yugoslav and Hungarian borders.

Gumpoldskirchen Austrian town south of Vienna, famous for its heady, spicy white wines.

Gutes Domtal GERMANY/RHINE (146) Vast Grosslage centred on Nierstein, but embracing 15 villages; the Nierstein name is normally employed.

Gutsverwaltung German for 'winery administration'.

Guyot Training system in which vines are tied to two parallel wires; the lower one for fruiting canes, the upper one for leafy young shoots. Popular in Bordeaux and Burgundy.

Halbtrocken German for 'medium dry'.

Hallgarten Good Rheingau village high above the river; fine, fruity Rieslings.

Hárslevelü Aromatic white grape, virtually exclusive to Hungary where it is used in the production of Tokay.

Hattenheim GERMANY/RHINE (146) Good Rheingau village producing rich Riesling. Also site of Steinberg, one of Germany's greatest vineyards.

Hautes-Côtes de Beaune FRANCE/BURGUNDY/COTE D'OR (88) Hilly vineyard area just west of Burgundy's Côte de Beaune.

Hautes-Côtes de Nuits FRANCE/BURGUNDY/COTE D'OR (88) Hilly

vineyard area west of the Côte de Nuits.

Haut-Médoc FRANCE/BORDEAUX/MEDOC (68) The most important section of Bordeaux for red wines. It contains the great wine communes of Margaux, St-Julien, Pauillac and St-Estèphe as well as being an AC in its own right.

Haut-Poitou FRANCE/COUNTRY WINES (128) Remote VDQS area south of the Loire producing excellent Sauvignon, Chardonnay and good Cabernet.

Hawkes Bay NEW ZEALAND (228) Traditional wine area on the North Island, exceptional for whites.

Hectare Metric measure of area equal to 10,000 square metres (2·471 acres).

Hectolitre Metric measure of liquid equal to 100 litres (22 imperial gallons).

Henderson New vineyard area on New Zealand's North Island.

Hermitage AUSTRALIA (220) Hunter Valley name for Shiraz (Syrah) grape.

Hermitage FRANCE/RHONE (112) Top AC in northern Rhône for long-lived reds and whites.

Hessische Bergstrasse GERMANY/OTHER WINES (152) Germany's smallest wine area producing some pretty good Riesling in diminutive quantities.

Heurige Austrian term for 'new wine'; also the tavern where it is drunk.

Hochheim GERMANY/RHINE (146) Important Rheingau village on the river Main, separated from the rest of the region.

Hock English name for any German wine made along the Rhine, derived from the village of Hochheim.

Hogshead Cask; its capacity varies from country to country, but 225 litres is the commonest measurement.

Huapai NEW ZEALAND (228) Traditional vineyard area on the North Island, especially successful for reds.

Hudson River Valley USA/OTHER WINES (218) Oldest wine region in New York State. *Labrusca* varieties are being replaced by European classics.

Humagne Ancient grape of the Valais, Switzerland; its reds are tough and tannic; the whites, strong and full.

Hunter Valley AUSTRALIA (220) Important wine area, some 125 miles north of Sydney. Famous for its Hermitage reds and Sémillon whites; also noted for its Cabernet Sauvignon, Pinot Noir and Chardonnay.

Huxelrebe Modern white grape, with a hint of Muscat, from Germany. Popular in Rheinhessen, Rheinpfalz and the UK.

Hybrid Grape variety bred from an American vine species and a European *vitis vinifera*; contrary to a crossing, which is bred from two *vinifera* varieties.

Imbottigliato dal produttore all'origine Italian for 'estate-bottled'.
Iphofen GERMANY/OTHER WINES (152) Village in Franconia producing big, tasty, usually dry whites.
Isinglass Common fining agent; a form of gelatine obtained from fish.
Isonzo ITALY/N-E (160) Friuli-Venezia-Giulia zone best known for Cabernet and Merlot reds.

Jardin de la France FRANCE/COUNTRY WINES (128) All-embracing *vin de pays* covering the whole Loire valley.
Jasnières FRANCE/LOIRE (122) Small zone in Touraine producing ultra-dry Chenin whites which often take 5–10 years to soften and blossom.
Jerez-Xeres-Sherry SPAIN/SHERRY (192) DO in Andalucía famous for its fortified wines, matured in the *solera* system. The three basic styles are *fino*, *amontillado* and *oloroso*.
Johannisberg GERMANY/RHINE (146) Famous Rheingau village producing top-quality Rieslings.
Juliénas FRANCE/BURGUNDY/BEAUJOLAIS (100) Cru village producing big, fruity wines with potential for ageing.
Jumilla SPAIN/CENTRAL (190) Mountainous DO in the south-east. Typical wines are Jumilla, a strong purple-red blend of Garnacha and Monastrell for drinking young; and Jumilla-Monastrell, a rich, robust high-alcohol red with potential for ageing.
Jurançon FRANCE/COUNTRY WINES (128) Ancient wine region in the far south-west of France best at producing rare and highly individual sweet wine.

Kabinett GERMANY (138) The lightest category of German QmP wines; relatively dry and low alcohol.
Kadarka Leading Hungarian red grape, widely planted; also important, as Gamza, in Bulgaria. At its best, produces a tannic, spicy wine.
Kalteresee (Lago di Caldaro) ITALY/N-E (160) Lake in the Alto Adige, giving its name to a popular light Vernatsch red of low acidity.
Karlovo Bulgarian town noted for its aromatic Misket.
Karthäuserhofberg GERMANY/MOSEL (142) Superb single vineyard estate at Eitelsbach in the Ruwer valley.
Kasel Good village in Ruwer valley, Germany; light, fragrant Rieslings.
Kékfrankos Central European grape variety, similar to Gamay. Known as Blau Frankisch in Austria.
Kéknyelü Ancient white Hungarian grape, traditional to Badacsony; makes spicy, high-alcohol wine.
Keller German for 'cellar'.
Kern Modern crossing of Trollinger and Riesling grapes; makes good, rather than great, whites in a slightly Muscaty style.
Kiedrich Small but high-quality Rheingau village.
Klevner Swiss name for Pinot Noir. In Alsace, a Pinot Blanc-Auxerrois blend.
Kloster Eberbach GERMANY/RHINE (146) Twelfth-century Cistercian abbey above Hattenheim in the Rheingau. Now centre of the German Wine Academy.
Krems Town and district in the Austrian Niederösterreich, making dry whites.
Kröv Decent Mosel village famous for its indecent wine Nacktarsch, which translates as 'bare bottom'.
Kumeu Vineyard area on the North Island of New Zealand.

Lacryma Christi del Vesuvio ITALY/SOUTH (178) Famous Neapolitan wine; all colours, variable quality.
Ladoix-Serrigny FRANCE/BURGUNDY/COTE D'OR (88) Little-known Côte de Beaune village, which possesses a small part of the famous Corton Grand Cru.
Lafoes Portuguese wine area in the Beira Alta; full-bodied reds and fresh astringent whites.
Lagar Spanish and Portuguese term for traditional stone trough in which grapes were crushed underfoot.
Lage German term for a vineyard that has been officially recorded in the vineyard register.
Lagrein ITALY/N-E (160) Red grape producing powerful reds and delicate rosés in Trentino-Alto Adige.
Lake County USA/CALIFORNIA (208) Small upland wine area in the North Coast division. Two AVAs: Clear Lake, Guenoc Valley.
Lake Eyrie US lake-shore wine region shared by New York and Ohio states. Important pre-Prohibition, and newly re-developed in the 1970s.
Lalande de Pomerol FRANCE/BORDEAUX/ST-EMILION (74) Satellite AC of Pomerol producing similar though less exciting red wines.
Lambrusco ITALY/CENTRAL (170) Lightly fizzy Emilia-Romagna wine, red, rosé or white, sweet or dry; low alcohol.
Lamego Portuguese wine area in the central Douro; makes dry white and champagne-method sparkling wines.
Landwein GERMANY (138) Classification just above Tafelwein; equivalent to French *vin de pays*.
Languedoc FRANCE/COUNTRY WINES (128) Swathe of vineyards centred on Gard, Hérault and Aude *départements*, making enormous amounts of very basic stuff, but an increasing proportion of cheap interesting wines as well.
Laski Riesling Yugoslav name for Welsch Riesling.
Late-bottled vintage PORTUGAL/PORT (202) Type of port; made from a single vintage and bottled when mature (after 4–6 years in wood).
Latisana ITALY/N-E (160) Friuli-Venezia-Giulia zone producing good reds and whites.
Latium ITALY/CENTRAL (170) Large region round Rome; mostly white wines.
Leányka Important Hungarian white grape, aromatic but low in acidity. Also leading white grape in Romania.
Lees Coarse sediment thrown by a wine in cask and left behind after racking.
Liebfraumilch GERMANY/RHINE (146) All-embracing term for basic, soft, undemanding whites from the Rhine.
Liguria ITALY/N-W (166) The Italian Riviera region; produces interesting wines, mostly whites.
Lima Sub-region of Portugal's *vinho verde* RD, best known for its astringent but refreshing reds.
Lirac FRANCE/RHONE (112) Southern AC, north-west of Avignon, making excellent reds and rosés as well as good, quick-maturing whites.
Listrac FRANCE/BORDEAUX/MEDOC (68) Village in Haut-Médoc with own AC, making good, slightly tough reds.
Litre Metric liquid measure, equal to 0·22 gallons (imperial).
Lombardy ITALY/N-W (166) Important wine region around Milan; produces some of Italy's best sparklers and most easily-enjoyable reds and whites.
Long Island USA/OTHER WINES (218) Newest wine district in New York State, next to New York City.
Loupiac FRANCE/BORDEAUX/OTHER WINES (82) AC in Premières Côtes de Bordeaux making good sweet whites.
Loureiro Important white grape in the *vinho verde* region of Portugal; also common in Galicia, Spain.
Lower Great Southern AUSTRALIA (220) New isolated wine area in Western Australia; promising whites.
Lugana ITALY/N-W (166) Gentle, fruity dry white from Lombardy.
Lussac-St-Emilion FRANCE/BORDEAUX/ST-EMILION (74) Satellite region of St-Emilion, producing sturdy though quick-maturing reds.
Lutomer YUGOSLAVIA (236) Major wine area in the north-east, famous for its Laski Riesling – unpretentious but internationally popular.
Lyre Trellis system for training vines used in Bordeaux.

Macabeo SPAIN/RIOJA (184) Spanish white grape, producing fresh, sharply fruity wine; now taking over in Rioja (as Viura) from the more interesting but heavier Malvasía.
Macération carbonique See *Carbonic maceration*.
Mâcon FRANCE/BURGUNDY/MACONNAIS (98) Major wine area in southern Burgundy; famous for white wine, particularly Pouilly Fuissé, but also producing reasonable reds.
Mâcon Supérieur FRANCE/BURGUNDY/MACONNAIS (98) AC covering red or white from anywhere in the Mâconnais, but with higher minimum alcohol than straight Mâcon.
Mâcon-Villages FRANCE/BURGUNDY/MACONNAIS (98) White wine from the better Mâcon villages. The best may add on their own name.
Madeira PORTUGAL/MADEIRA (204) Atlantic island famous for its fortified aperitif and dessert wines: from dry to sweet, they are Sercial, Verdelho, Bual and Malmsey.
Maderization Browning of white wines caused by age or poor storage.
Madiran FRANCE/COUNTRY WINES (128) Sturdy, slow maturing red from the south-west, based on the Tannet grape.
Maipo SOUTH AMERICA (238) Major wine district in Chile centred on the Maipo river south of Santiago; irrigated.
Málaga SPAIN/SHERRY (192) Andalucian DO producing sweet dessert wines.
Malbec Red grape, rich in tannin and flavour, from south-west France; major ingredient of Cahors wine, where it is

known as Cot or Auxerrois. Also found in South America and South Australia.

Malic acid Sharp green-apple acid, contained in grapes, which converts into soft lactic acid during the secondary or malolactic fermentation.

Malolactic fermentation FROM GRAPES TO WINE (22) Secondary fermentation whereby harsh malic acid converts into mild lactic acid and carbon dioxide; occurs after the alcoholic fermentation. It improves red wines, softening them and reducing their acidity, but is often prevented in whites to preserve a fresh taste. Top white wines, however, will frequently undergo malolactic fermentation in order to create a deeper, more complex flavour.

Malvasia SPAIN/RIOJA (184) Historic white grape variety, with low acidity but lots of rather unctuous flavour. Formerly important in Rioja. In Italy, often mixed with Trebbiano for dry whites, or made into rich dessert wines. Also found in Greece, Portugal, Eastern Europe and California.

Malvasia di Bosa Sardinia's leading Malvasia dessert wine.

Malvoisie Valais name for Pinot Gris grape; used for sweet dessert wines.

Malvoisie de Nus ITALY/N-W (166) A rare dessert wine from Valle d'Aosta.

La Mancha SPAIN/CENTRAL (190) Historic wine region (and DO) on the high central plateau south of Madrid; ranks as the world's largest demarcated vineyard.

Manchuela Newly-created Spanish DO on the eastern edge of La Mancha plateau.

Mandement Swiss wine area immediately west of Geneva; light Gamay reds and pale whites from Perlan (Chasselas).

Manzanilla SPAIN/SHERRY (192) Very dry, pale sherry – with a hint of salt – from Sanlúcar de Barrameda on the coast near Jerez.

Marc FROM GRAPES TO WINE (22) Mush of skins, stalks and pips left behind after grapes have been pressed; also, the spirit distilled from this residue.

The Marches ITALY/CENTRAL (170) Large wine region below Venice.

Marcobrunn GERMANY/RHINE (146) Great Rheingau vineyard between Erbach and Hattenheim; produces brilliant wine on the marshy riverbank soil.

Maréchal Foch Hybrid red grape; cold-resistant and so grown in Canada and the north-eastern US.

Margaret River AUSTRALIA (220) New

cool-climate wine region in Western Australia; fine reds and whites.

Margaux FRANCE/BORDEAUX/MEDOC (68) Large red-wine AC in the Haut-Médoc, centred on the village of Margaux but including vineyards in nearby Soussans, Issan, Cantenac, Labarde and Arsac. At their best, Margaux wines are the most gloriously-scented in Bordeaux.

Marlborough NEW ZEALAND (228) Dominant wine area of the South Island, developed in the 1970s and mostly producing quality fresh whites.

Marsala ITALY/SOUTH (178) Famous dessert wine from Sicily. Undergoing much-deserved revival.

Marsannay Burgundy village in the Côte de Nuits, best known for rosé from Pinot Noir.

Marsanne Solid French grape, making bulky whites of impressive girth and beguiling perfume; widely planted in the northern Rhône. Also found in Australia.

Marzemino di Isera ITALY/N-E (160) Fresh, grapy, grassy red from Trentino.

Mavro Greek for 'black', meaning 'dark red wine'.

Mavrodaphne Indigenous Greek red grape, grown in the northern Peloponnese and on the island of Cephalonia; its celebrated wine is dark, sweet and aromatic.

Mavron Basic red grape of Cyprus; produces most of the island's everyday wine – robust and tannic.

Mavroudi Greek red wine, dark and rich, from Delphi and Corinth.

Mavrud Bulgarian red grape, common in the south; makes a dark, smooth wine, often ranked as the country's best.

Maximin-Grünhauser GERMANY/MOSEL (142) Great Ruwer vineyard.

Mazuelo Synonym for the *Carignan* grape in Rioja, Spain.

Meda Portuguese wine area in the northern Beira Alta; makes full, fruity Douro-like wines.

Médéa Algerian designated area in the highlands south of Algiers; adequate reds, whites and rosés.

Médoc FRANCE/BORDEAUX/MEDOC (68) General name for the whole vineyard area north of Bordeaux on the left bank of the Gironde. As an AC, Médoc applies only to the less-distinguished, northern section.

Meknes-Fez Important Moroccan wine area producing smooth, dark reds.

Melnik Bulgarian red grape, especially important in the south-west; its wine is dark and tannic, high in alcohol and aroma, and repays wood-ageing.

Melon de Bourgogne (Muscadet) FRANCE/LOIRE (122) French white grape almost exclusive to the lower Loire where it makes a very dry, light wine. Also planted in California under the misleading name of Pinot Blanc.

Mendocino County USA/CALIFORNIA (208) California's northernmost wine area in the North Coast division; rugged and mountainous. Five AVAs: Mendocino (covering the whole county), Anderson Valley, Cole Ranch, Potter Valley and McDowell Valley.

Mendoza Province in the Andean foothills of Argentina with over two-thirds of the country's vineyards, all irrigated.

Menetou-Salon FRANCE/LOIRE (122) Small AC near Sancerre, making good white Sauvignon as well as rosé and reds from Pinot Noir.

Mentrida Central Spanish DO lying south-west of Madrid; strong, thick reds and fruity rosés.

Mercurey FRANCE/BURGUNDY/COTE CHALONNAISE (96) Important wine village, best known for good quality reds from Pinot Noir.

Merlot GRAPE VARIETIES (18) Classic red grape, traditionally Bordeaux's second variety after Cabernet Sauvignon (with which it is normally blended). Also successful in Italy, Eastern Europe, Australia, New Zealand and in California and Washington, USA.

Méthode champenoise See *champagne method.*

Meunier French red grape; important champagne ingredient. Elsewhere, notably in the Loire, Yugoslavia and Australia, makes a light-red table wine.

Meursault FRANCE/BURGUNDY/COTE D'OR (88) Leading Côte de Beaune village producing marvellously rounded, almost luscious, dry whites – and some red, normally sold as Blagny or Volnay.

Mildew See *downy mildew* and *oidium.*

Mildura Irrigated wine area on the Murray river in northern Victoria; makes reds and whites for bulk sale to wineries outside the district.

Millésime French for 'vintage date'.

Minervois FRANCE/COUNTRY WINES (128) Superior area of Languedoc-Roussillon producing spicy, fruity reds.

Mise en bouteille French for 'bottled'.

Mission Californian red grape, probably descended from the first *vinifera* vine planted in North America.

Mistella Unfermented grape juice fortified with grape alcohol, added as a sweetener to sherry and madeira.

Mittelrhein GERMANY/OTHER WINES (152) A small and diminishing Rhine wine area north of the Rheingau area. Good Riesling from usually stunning vineyards.

Moelleux French for 'mellow and soft'; used of a sweet wine.

Moldavia North-eastern province of Romania producing everyday whites from local varieties; could do better.

Molise ITALY/SOUTH (178) Italy's least-known wine region, with two DOCs; average reds, whites and rosés.

Monastrell Common Spanish red grape, producing dry, light-coloured wines capable of ageing.

Monbazillac FRANCE/COUNTRY WINES (128) AC in the south-west, capable of excellent sweet white wines.

Monção Sub-region of Portugal's *vinho verde* RD producing some of its best wines, especially whites.

Montagne-St-Emilion FRANCE/BORDEAUX/ST-EMILION (74) Satellite region of St-Emilion, producing good, gently fruity reds.

Montagny FRANCE/BURGUNDY/COTE CHALONNAISE (96) Whites-only AC in the Côte Chalonnaise. Wines can be lean, but improve with oak-ageing

Montecarlo ITALY/CENTRAL (170) Tasty full-bodied Tuscan white which includes grapes like Sémillon, Sauvignon and Roussanne. Now in red, too.

Montepulciano d'Abruzzo ITALY/CENTRAL (170) Good, beefy red from the Adriatic coast.

Monterey County USA/CALIFORNIA (208) Recently-developed wine area in the Central Coast division. Four AVAs: Monterey, Carmel Valley, Arroyo Seco and Chalone.

Monthélie FRANCE/BURGUNDY/COTE D'OR (88) Lesser-known Côte de Beaune village capable of soft, plummy reds.

Montilla-Moriles SPAIN/SHERRY (192) Inland DO in Andalucía noted for sherry-style high-strength wines and for dessert wine made from raisined grapes.

Montlouis FRANCE/LOIRE (122) Loire AC overshadowed by its neighbour Vouvray; produces similar Chenin Blanc wine.

Morey St-Denis FRANCE/BURGUNDY/COTE D'OR (88) Important, but little-known Côte de Nuits

village containing several Grands Crus.

Morgon FRANCE/BURGUNDY/BEAUJOLAIS (100) Major Cru making big, soft juicy red which ages well.

Mornington Peninsula Newly-established Australian cool-climate wine area south of Melbourne, Victoria, with potential for top-quality production.

Moscato Italian *Muscat* grape.

Moscato di Pantelleria ITALY/SOUTH (178) Muscat wines, light or dessert, grown on a small island almost within sight of Africa.

Moscato Naturale d'Asti ITALY/N-W (166) Heavenly mixture of grapy freshness and slight fizz; Muscat wine in its natural state before being turned into fully fizzy Asti Spumante.

Mosel GERMANY/MOSEL (142) Major wine area, centred on the river of the same name, and producing brilliantly-balanced racy Rieslings.

Mosto Italian, Portuguese and Spanish for 'must'.

Moulin-à-Vent FRANCE/BURGUNDY/BEAUJOLAIS (100) Cru making Beaujolais' heaviest wines, capable of ageing.

Moulis FRANCE/BORDEAUX/MEDOC (68) Haut-Médoc village with own AC making good but rarely spectacular reds.

Mourvèdre Red grape, primarily used for blending; widely planted in southern France. Also found in Australia and California (as Mataro).

Mousseux French for 'sparkling'.

Mudgee AUSTRALIA (220) Isolated NSW wine region, with own appellation, making full reds and whites.

Müller-Thurgau GERMANY/MOSEL (142) Major German white grape, making soft, scented young wines. A Riesling/Silvaner cross, it is the leading variety in Germany and the UK; also important in Eastern Europe and New Zealand.

Murfatlar Modern Romanian vineyard area bordering the Black Sea, noted for sweet whites; now also dry whites and reds.

Murrumbidgee AUSTRALIA (220) Large irrigated wine area in NSW, producing good everyday wine and some astonishing sweet Sauternes styles.

Muscadelle Bordeaux white grape, scented and sweet; minor ingredient in Sauternes. More important in Australia for rich, strong dessert wines.

Muscadet For grape, see *Melon de Bourgogne*.

Muscadet FRANCE/LOIRE (122) Simple, dry white wine from the lower Loire; increasingly popular.

Muscadet de Sèvre-et-Maine FRANCE/LOIRE (122) Central, and best, section of Muscadet region, capable of producing distinctly superior wines, especially when bottled 'sur lie' – i.e. straight off the lees.

Muscat GRAPE VARIETIES (18) Generic name grouping over 200 grape varieties; mostly used for sweet dessert wines, often fortified.

Muscat de Beaumes de Venise FRANCE/RHONE (112) Fortified sweet white wine from the Côtes du Rhône village of Beaumes de Venise.

Muscat Ottonel White grape, with Muscat connections. Planted in Alsace, but most common in Austria, Hungary, Romania and Czechoslovakia.

Must Grape juice or crushed grapes before fermentation.

Must weight Sugar content of ripe grapes; an important factor in deciding when to harvest.

Nackenheim Small, but excellent neighbour to Nierstein in Rheinhessen.

Naoussa Full, tannic, dry red wine, made from the Xynomavro grape in Macedonia, Greece.

Napa County USA/CALIFORNIA (208) Well-established wine region in the North Coast division with over 100 wineries. Three AVAs: Napa Valley (covering the whole county), Carneros and Howell Mountain.

Napa Gamay See *Valdiguié*.

Navarra SPAIN/RIOJA (184) Major DO extending from the Ebro to the Pyrenees. Red varieties predominate, producing rich, robust wood-aged wines. Also some rosés and whites.

Nebbiolo GRAPE VARIETIES (18) Major Italian red grape grown in the north of the country, especially Piedmont where it is used for Barolo, Barbaresco and other top quality wines.

Nebbiolo d'Alba ITALY/N-W (166) Soft, fruity DOC red from Piedmont; based on the Nebbiolo grape.

Nebbiolo delle Langhe ITALY/N-W (166) Second-tier title for Barolo and Barbaresco wines not sold under their DOCG title. As a tasty, muscular red for drinking quite young, can be very good.

Négociant FRANCE/BURGUNDY (84) Merchant or shipper who buys in wine from growers and prepares it for sale by maturing, blending, then bottling it.

Negra Mole PORTUGAL/MADEIRA (204) Workhorse red grape of Madeira; widely used in the island's fortified wines. Also important on the Algarve.

Nemea Above average Greek red table wine made from the Agiorgitiko grape in the eastern Peloponnese; also known as Blood of Hercules.

Neusiedler See AUSTRIA (232) Large shallow lake on the Hungarian border; its autumn mists foster 'noble rot'.

Niagara American *labrusca* white grape, bred from a Concord/Cassady crossing; sweet and very 'foxy'. Grown in the eastern USA and Brazil.

Niagara Canada's principal wine region, producing *labrusca* wines and, increasingly, hybrid and *vinifera* ones.

Niederhausen GERMANY/RHINE (146) Small Nahe village producing some excellent wines.

Niederösterreich AUSTRIA (232) Major wine region, located in the north-east; top-quality dry whites.

Nierstein GERMANY/RHINE (146) Fine wine village in Rheinhessen identified with superb Riesling. But because the mediocre Grosslage Gutes Domtal and also the regional Bereich use the Nierstein name, few examples of this top-quality wine are seen abroad.

Noble rot See *Botrytis cinera*.

Northland Minor wine area on New Zealand's North Island.

Nostrano Everyday Swiss red wine from the Ticino region.

Nuits-St-Georges FRANCE/BURGUNDY/COTE D'OR (88) Major Côte de Nuits wine town, at one time the most abused of all French wine names, but now a major source of high quality burgundy.

Nuragus di Cagliari ITALY/SOUTH (178) Famous Sardinian white but usually a little neutral.

Oak MODERN WINEMAKER (26) Preferred wood for wine casks; imparts important flavours during ageing.

Oechsle GERMANY (138) Scale for measuring the sugar content of grape juice.

Oeil de perdrix Literally 'partridge's eye'; French term describing *vin gris*.

Oenologist Wine scientist or technician.

Oenology Science of wine and wine-making.

Oidium Common fungus disease attacking vine leaves, shoots and tendrils; also called powdery mildew.

Okanagan Valley Main wine area of British Columbia, Canada, producing agreeable whites from Gewürztraminer, Riesling and Chardonnay.

Olasz Riesling Hungarian synonym for the Welsch Riesling grape (now, by law, called Rizling).

Oloroso SPAIN/SHERRY (192) A sherry style, full, rich, aged and dry; often sweetened for the market as Cream.

Oltrepò Pavese ITALY/N-W (166) Large wine region in Lombardy producing many exciting reds, whites and sparklers.

Opol Agreeable Yugoslav light red made in Dalmatia from the Plavać grape.

Oppenheim GERMANY/RHINE (146) Good Rheinhessen village producing fine, slightly earthy wines.

Orjahoviza Southern Bulgarian wine zone, best for Cabernet Sauvignon and Merlot reds.

Ortega German white grape making full, flowery wines often used for blending.

Orvieto ITALY/CENTRAL (170) Famous Umbrian white, dry or semi-sweet; now re-asserting itself after long decline.

Oudjda-Taza Wine area in the north-east of Morocco; known for rosé and Muscat de Berkane.

Oxidation Decay in a wine caused by over-exposure to air. Slight oxidation, such as occurs through barrel wood, is part of the ageing process and can enhance flavour.

Paarl South Africa's wine capital, north-east of Cape Town. Specializes in sherry- and port-style wines, also full reds and whites.

Pacherenc du Vic Bilh FRANCE/COUNTRY WINES (128) Obscure AC in Armagnac. Its pear-flavoured white can be remarkable.

Padthaway/Keppoch AUSTRALIA (220) Major new vineyard area in South Australia; good whites.

País Leading red grape in Chile, producing basic table wine.

Pale Cream SPAIN/SHERRY (192) Popular sherry style, made by sweetening *fino*.

Palmela Portuguese wine area south of Lisbon, producing fruity reds and sparkling rosés.

Palo cortado SPAIN/SHERRY (192) Quite rare dry sherry style, similar to *oloroso* but less heavy, with a tangy flavour.

Palomino SPAIN/SHERRY (192) Major Spanish white grape grown in the Jerez

area; also used for sherry-style wines in South Africa and Australia.

Pamid Widely planted Bulgarian red grape, making very ordinary jug wines.

Passito Italian term for strong, sweet wine made from part-raisined grapes.

Pasteurization MODERN WINEMAKER (26) Sterilization by heating. Cheaper wines are often pasteurized before bottling to guard against decay; unsuitable for fine wines as it prevents ageing in bottle.

Pauillac FRANCE/BORDEAUX/MEDOC (68) Bordeaux's greatest wine village, boasting three First Growths; deep, slow-maturing reds.

Pécharmant FRANCE/COUNTRY WINES (128) Small, but high quality AC in the south-west, making delicious Cabernet-based reds capable of ageing.

Pedro Ximénez SPAIN/SHERRY (192) Spanish white grape, producing a neutral, high-alcohol wine. Its traditional role as a sherry grape is diminishing but still dominant in Montilla-Moriles. It is grown widely in southern Spain, Argentina, Australia and New Zealand for blending.

Peloponnese Southern peninsula of mainland Greece containing half the country's vineyards.

Pelure d'oignon French term, literally 'onion skin', used to describe the slightly tawny orange tint in some wines, especially when they are beginning to age.

Peñafiel Sub-region of Portugal's *vinho verde* RD producing medium-quality wines.

Penedés SPAIN/CATALONIA (188) Important DO lying between Barcelona and Tarragona, producing quality wines – in particular rich, brooding reds and fruity fresh whites.

Pentro Little-known southern Italian DOC in little-known Molise.

Perla Light, semi-sweet and blended white, from Tîrnave, Romania.

Perlan Swiss name in Mandement (Geneva) for the Chasselas grape; undistinguished pale, dry wine.

Perlwein German term for semi-sparkling wine.

Pernand-Vergelesses FRANCE/BURGUNDY/COTE D'OR (88) Neighbour to Aloxe-Corton in Côte de Beaune, and possessing part of the Grands Crus Corton and Corton-Charlemagne.

Peronospera See *downy mildew*.

Pétillant French for 'semi-sparkling'.

Phylloxera STORY OF WINE (12) The vine aphid *phylloxera vastatrix* devastated vineyards in the late 1800s. Since then, the vulnerable European *vitis vinifera* has been grafted on to resistant American rootstocks.

Piedmont ITALY/N-W (166) The north-west's leading wine area with 35 DOC zones.

Piesport GERMANY/MOSEL (142) Major Mosel village with one excellent vineyard – Goldtröpfchen; but known for its Grosslage Michelsberg.

Pigato ITALY/N-W (166) White grape, native to Liguria, producing rare and very individual wines.

Pinhel Wine area in the upper Douro, Portugal, making some reds but mostly whites and champagne-method sparklers.

Pinotage Quality South African red grape bred from Pinot Noir x Cinsaut. Some plantings in California, New Zealand and Zimbabwe.

Pinot Blanc ALSACE (118) Major white grape used for quality blending and some varietal production; makes soft, low-acid wines which can be quite exciting. Plantings in Alsace, southern Germany (called Weissburgunder), northern Italy (often for sparkling wine), Eastern Europe, Chile and California.

Pinot Grigio See *Pinot Gris*.

Pinot Gris FRANCE/ALSACE (118) Major white grape, producing full spicy wines. Significant in Alsace (called Tokay), Switzerland and Eastern Europe; small acreage in Germany (called Ruländer), and in Oregon, USA.

Pinot Noir GRAPE VARIETIES (18) Classic red grape, the only grape allowed for the great Côte d'Or burgundy and crucial to champagne (juice only, which is white). Also important in Germany (as Spätburgunder), northern Italy, Eastern Europe and, increasingly, in Oregon, USA.

Piper's Brook Important wine area in Tasmania, producing quality reds and whites.

Plavać Mali Yugoslav native red grape, common on the Dalmatian coast and islands; its wines are sweet and heavy.

Plovdina Ancient Yugoslav red grape; generally blended with Prokupac to make a lightish, everyday wine.

Podere Italian 'farm' or 'estate'.

Pomace Alternative term for *marc*.

Pomerol FRANCE/BORDEAUX/ST-EMILION (74) Small but very high quality area of Bordeaux, producing big, exotically rich, red wines based on the Merlot. Contains Bordeaux's most expensive red – Château Pétrus.

Pommard FRANCE/BURGUNDY/COTE D'OR (88) Important Côte de Beaune village producing big, meaty reds.

Port PORTUGAL/PORT (202) Heavy, strong fortified wine from the Upper Douro. Main styles are vintage, single quinta, crusted, late-bottled vintage, tawny, ruby; also aperitif-type white.

Portugieser See *Blauer Portugieser*.

Postup Yugoslav red wine, heavy and sweetish; made in Dalmatia.

Pouilly-Fuissé FRANCE/BURGUNDY/MACONNAIS (98) Potentially excellent, but always expensive Chardonnay white from the southern Mâconnais.

Pouilly-Fumé FRANCE/LOIRE (122) The best Sauvignon-based wine in the Loire valley and the inspiration behind Fumé Blanc – as many new-world Sauvignons now style themselves.

Pourriture noble French for 'noble rot'; see *botrytis cinerea*.

Poverty Bay NEW ZEALAND (228) Important wine area on the North Island; includes the Gisborne plains and noted for its quality whites.

Premier cru FRANCE/BORDEAUX/MEDOC (68) Top category of the *cru classé* system in Bordeaux; second category (after *grand cru*) in Burgundy. Also used elsewhere in France.

Premières Côtes de Blaye FRANCE/BORDEAUX/OTHER WINES (82) Not particularly inspiring red and white wine district opposite the Haut-Médoc on the Gironde's right bank.

Premières Côtes de Bordeaux FRANCE/BORDEAUX/OTHER WINES (82) The south-western flank of Entre-Deux-Mers, facing the Graves across the Garonne; mostly simple reds and sweet whites.

Press wine FROM GRAPES TO WINE (22) Red wine extracted from its grape residue by pressing, after the free-run wine has been drawn off; usually bitter and tannic, it is often blended in with the free-run wine to provide backbone.

Primeur French term for 'early wine', especially Beaujolais; applied to wine of the most recent vintage.

Priorato SPAIN/CATALONIA (188) Inland DO known since the Middle Ages for its rich, robust reds; also produces *rancio*, maderized sweet wine often drunk as an aperitif.

Prohibition 18th Amendment to the US Constitution, passed in 1920, banning alcoholic beverages; ruined most wineries, but some survived making grape juice, communion and medicinal wines. Repealed in 1933.

Prokupać Leading Yugoslav red grape; its strong, dark wine is generally used for blending, but can make a reasonably attractive rosé.

Prosecco ITALY/N-E (160) Local white grape, making a lovely soft almond wine in the Veneto.

Prosek Yugoslav dessert wine from Dalmatia; nutty, very sweet and strong.

Prüfungsnummer See *Amtliche Prüfungsnummer*.

Pruning GROWING THE GRAPES (14) Trimming vines to control quantity and quality of fruit; takes place annually in winter.

Puget Sound New US cool-climate wine region centred on Seattle, Washington. German-style, or even English-style wines are most successful.

Puisseguin-St-Emilion FRANCE/BORDEAUX/ST-EMILION (74) Satellite region of St-Emilion; some good, conservative reds.

Puligny-Montrachet FRANCE/BURGUNDY/COTE D'OR (88) Côte de Beaune village, arguably the greatest white wine village in the world! Home of Montrachet and other Grand Cru and Premier Cru white burgundies.

Punt IDENTIFYING WINES (36) Indentation in the base of a bottle, designed to trap sediment.

Pupitre Rack used for holding bottles of sparkling wine upside down so that sediment can collect on the cork ready for *dégorgement*.

Puttonyos HUNGARY (234) Measure of sweetness for Tokay.

Pyrenees AUSTRALIA (220) Wine region in central Victoria producing good sparklers and quality reds and whites.

QbA GERMANY (138) Qualitätswein bestimmter Anbaugebiete; German quality designation for wines made in a specified region and from authorized grapes; between Tafelwein and QmP.

QmP GERMANY (138) Qualitätswein mit Prädikat; top German quality designation for wine made in defined areas and, importantly, from grapes not requiring any additional sugar to achieve correct alcohol level. Comprises five categories: Kabinett, Spätlese, Auslese,

Beerenauslese, Trockenbeerenauslese.

Quarts de Chaume FRANCE/LOIRE (122) Small area in the Layon valley which makes good noble-rotted sweet whites.

Quincy FRANCE/LOIRE (122) Small AC in upper Loire producing strong, grassy Sauvignon whites.

Quinta Portuguese for 'estate'.

Rabat-Casablanca Moroccan coastal area producing soft reds and *vin gris*.

Raboso Excellent, burly, unsophisticated Italian red wine from Veneto.

Racking MODERN WINEMAKER (26) Gradual clarification of a quality wine as part of the maturation process. The wine is transferred from one barrel to another, leaving the lees behind.

Radgonska Ranina Sweet white wine from north-east Yugoslavia; also known as Tiger's Milk.

Raimat SPAIN/CATALONIA (188) Medieval estate in Lérida province, recently replanted and now making exciting wines.

Raisined Made of grapes left in the sun to dry out, thus concentrating sweetness. Traditional in Jerez for sweet sherries.

Ramisco PORTUGAL/TABLE WINES (200) Red grape exclusive to Colares, near Lisbon, where it makes heavy, perfumed reds which take ages to soften and mature.

Rancio Maderized or oxidized white wine, popular in Catalonia, Spain. Rancios are deep amber, high in alcohol and sherry-like; the best, aged in *soleras*, resemble *olorosos*. Also found in Languedoc-Roussillon, from a red- or white-wine base.

Rapitalà ITALY/SOUTH (178) High quality non-DOC white from Sicily.

Rasteau FRANCE/RHONE (112) One of the 17 Côtes du Rhône-Villages; also produces a fortified Vin Doux Naturel from the Grenache grape.

Rauenthal GERMANY/RHINE (146) One of the Rheingau's top villages, famous for fine, spicy – and expensive – Rieslings.

Recioto della Valpolicella ITALY/N-E (160) Remarkable Veneto red from semi-dried grapes, either sweet or, as Amarone, sort of sweet-sour.

RD See *Região demarcado*.

Récolte French for 'crop' or 'vintage'.

Refosco ITALY/N-E (160) Good, smoky, country red wine in Friuli-Venezia-Giulia.

Regaleali ITALY/SOUTH (178) Important non-DOC Sicilian table wines.

Região demarcado Portuguese for 'demarcated wine region', abbreviated as RD.

Regnié FRANCE/BURGUNDY/BEAUJOLAIS (100) The newest Cru. Good wines but not as consistent as other Crus, and in less successful years really no better than Beaujolais-Villages.

Reichensteiner White grape developed from French, Italian and German crossings; makes unremarkable, neutral wines. Grown in Germany (Rheinhessen), but more useful in England.

Remuage FRANCE/CHAMPAGNE (106) Process in champagne-making whereby the bottles, stored upside down, are twisted each day so that the sediment falls from the sides and collects on the cork ready for *dégorgement*.

Reserva Second-line quality category for Spanish wine; requires minimum ageing (cask and bottle) of three years for reds, two years for whites.

Retsina GREECE (236) Traditional resinated wine; chiefly made from the native Savatiano grape with Aleppo pine resin added.

Retz Austrian wine area, north-west of Vienna towards the Czech border; some reds but mostly whites.

Reuilly FRANCE/LOIRE (122) Small Upper Loire AC making good Sauvignon and some lovely rosé.

Rheingau GERMANY/RHINE (146) South-east-facing vineyard area west of Wiesbaden, producing many of Germany's greatest Rieslings.

Rheinriesling (Riesling Renano) ITALY/N-E (160) Synonym for Riesling, successfully grown in various parts of northern Italy.

Rhine Riesling Australian name for the Riesling grape.

Rhône FRANCE/RHONE (122) Major wine area, centred on the river of the same name; focal point for most of southern France's finest wines, like Hermitage and Châteauneuf-du-Pape.

Ribeiro SPAIN/RIOJA (184) Galician DO producing young light reds and whites, often with a slight sparkle similar to Portugal's *vinho verde*.

Ribera del Duero SPAIN/RIOJA (184) Straggling DO along the Duero river in Old Castile, producing fresh, orange-coloured rosés and ruby-rich velvety reds. The legendary Vega Sicilia is made inside the DO.

Riesling GRAPE VARIETIES (18) Classic German white grape producing top quality wines; fresh, fragrant and fruity.

Planted worldwide but most successful in Alsace, California, Oregon and Australia. Also called Rhine Riesling, Rheinriesling, Johannisberg Riesling and White Riesling.

Rioja SPAIN/RIOJA (184) Prestigious DO centred on the Ebro valley. Its celebrated reds, soft and smooth, are oak-aged blends of Tempranillo, Graciano, Mazuelo and Garnacha. Traditional whites are aged in oak, and deep and buttery. Modern whites, from Viura and Malvasía, are fruity and fresh.

Riserva Italian term applied to DOC or DOCG wines that have been aged for a specified period, depending on the wine.

Rivaner Luxembourg name for Müller-Thurgau, a term also used occasionally in England.

Riverland AUSTRALIA (220) Vast irrigated wine area along the Murray river in South Australia. Major producer of everyday wines.

Riverside County Developing wine region in the Californian South Coast division. One AVA: Temecula (also known as Rancho California).

Rivesaltes FRANCE/COUNTRY WINES (128) Important Roussillon village with its own AC for sweet Vin Doux Naturel.

Rkatsiteli World's second most-planted white grape, making vaguely aromatic wines of fairly basic quality. Very important in the USSR and Bulgaria.

Rogue River Developing warm-climate wine area in southern Oregon, USA.

Rootstock Rooting stump on to which a new vine is grafted.

Rosado Spanish/Portuguese for 'rosé'.

Rosato Italian for 'rosé'.

Rosé d'Anjou See *Anjou*.

Rosé de Riceys FRANCE/CHAMPAGNE (106) Rare, expensive but very tasty Pinot Noir rosé from the southern border of Champagne and Chablis.

Rosenmuskateller ITALY/N-E (160) Rare Alto Adige grape; its wine, sweet or dry, tastes of rose petals and fresh-brewed tea!

Rossese di Dolceacqua ITALY/N-W (166) Liguria's leading red wine.

Rosso Italian for 'red'.

Rosso Cònero ITALY/CENTRAL (170) Good, strong-tasting Marches wine from Montepulciano and Sangiovese grapes.

Rosso di Montalcino ITALY/CENTRAL (170) DOC for wines from Montalcino not aged long enough to qualify as Brunello.

Rosso Piceno ITALY/CENTRAL (170) Marches red, usually good in slightly rustic way.

Rouge French for 'red'.

Roussanne French white grape from the northern Rhône where it makes lively delicate wines mostly for blending with Marsanne. Adds inestimably to white Hermitage and, further south, to white Châteauneuf-du-Pape.

Ruby Youngest style of port; very sweet, red, and fiery.

Rüdesheim GERMANY/RHINE (146) Leading Rheingau village with particularly fine strong-flavoured Rieslings from the Berg vineyard.

Rueda SPAIN/RIOJA (184) Small DO in southern Valladolid with a long tradition of fortified dry wines: Pálido (oak-aged for 3 years) and Dorado (for 2 years).

Ruländer German and Austrian name for Pinot Gris grape.

Rully FRANCE/BURGUNDY/COTE CHALONNAISE (96) Village traditionally known as the centre of the Burgundian sparkling wine industry, but now also as a source of good, light reds and whites.

Ruppertsberg Rheinpfalz village producing strong-flavoured whites.

Rust Famous Austrian wine town noted for its sweet, noble-rotted whites.

Rutherglen AUSTRALIA (220) Original wine area in north-east Victoria, best known for its fortified wines, but now developing lighter reds and whites.

Ruzića Yugoslavian term for 'rosé'; traditionally made from Prokupac and deep-coloured.

Saarburg Lovely historic town at the centre of the Saar wine area in Germany producing very good Rieslings.

Sabrosa Portuguese wine area in the upper Douro making reds, rosés and some whites.

St-Amour FRANCE/BURGUNDY/BEAUJOLAIS (100) The most northerly Cru producing fairly fine but juicy reds.

St-Aubin FRANCE/BURGUNDY/COTE D'OR (88) A Côte de Beaune village rather hidden behind Chassagne-Montrachet, and consequently always a bargain for its attractive reds and whites.

St-Emilion FRANCE/BORDEAUX/ST-EMILION (74) Famous hill-town giving its name to the major wine region on the right bank of the Dordogne. Produces a wide range of reds, based on the Merlot, usually marked by their immediate softness and drinkability, though many can age well.

St-Estèphe FRANCE/BORDEAUX/MEDOC

(68) The northernmost of the Haut-Médoc's major villages, on fairly heavy clay-dominated soil; produces strong, impressive reds usually lacking a little of the perfume of the other top villages but none of their longevity.

St-Georges-St-Emilion Probably the best of the St-Emilion satellites.

St-Joseph FRANCE/RHONE (112) Red and white AC covering a west-bank zone north and south of Hermitage. The red, from Syrah, can have a delicious cassis and strawberry fruit, much softer than most northern Rhônes.

St-Julien FRANCE/BORDEAUX/MEDOC (68) The smallest of the Haut-Médoc's major villages, but full of properties which make inspiring wine.

St-Magdalener (Santa Maddalena) ITALY/N-E (160) Light, easy, fresh red from Bolzano in Alto Adige.

St-Péray FRANCE/RHONE (112) Northern Rhône AC, making fairly heavy whites and sparklers – more popular in the 19th century than now.

St-Romain FRANCE/BURGUNDY/COTE D'OR (88) Little-known Côte de Beaune village in the hills behind Auxey-Duresses; its wines are usually a bit rustic.

St-Véran FRANCE/BURGUNDY/MACONNAIS (98) The AC which surrounds Pouilly-Fuissé and makes similar round, soft Chardonnay whites – much more reasonably priced.

Ste-Croix-du-Mont FRANCE/BORDEAUX/OTHER WINES (82) Little known but good AC in the Premières Côtes de Bordeaux for sweet white wines.

St-Laurent Red grape, now virtually exclusive to Austria.

St-Laurent FRANCE/BORDEAUX/MEDOC (68) Rather obscure Haut-Médoc village which nonetheless contains three classed growths; Belgrave, de Camensac and La Tour-Carnet.

Salvagnin Swiss red wine, made in Vaud from Gamay and Pinot Noir.

Sammarco ITALY/CENTRAL (170) One of the most successful Cabernet table wines now being made in Tuscany.

Samos GREECE (236) Aegean island famous for its light-amber Muscat.

San Benito County Wine area in the Central Coast division of California. Three AVAs: Cienega, Limekiln and Paicines.

San Bernardino County Historic wine area in California's South Coast division.

Sancerre FRANCE/LOIRE (122) Village producing the archetypal sharply fruity French white, from the Sauvignon grape. The AC also includes red and rosé.

San Diego County Minor Californian wine area. One AVA: San Pasqual.

Sangiovese ITALY/CENTRAL (170) Important red grape, grown mainly in central Italy; principal ingredient of Chianti.

Sangiovese di Romagna ITALY/CENTRAL (170) Good quaffing red from Emilia-Romagna.

San Juan Province in the Andean foothills of Argentina, north of Mendoza, with the country's second largest acreage of vines.

San Luis Obispo County USA/CALIFORNIA (208) Major wine region in the Central Coast division. Four AVAs: Edna Valley, Paso Robles, Templeton and York Mountain.

Santa Barbara County USA/CALIFORNIA (208) New cool-climate wine region in the Central Coast division. Two AVAs: Santa Maria Valley and Santa Ynez Valley.

Santa Clara County USA/CALIFORNIA (208) Small wine region in the Central Coast division, now threatened by urbanization. One AVA: Santa Cruz Mountain.

Santa Cruz County USA/CALIFORNIA (208) Very small wine area in the Central Coast division; its wineries mostly buy in grapes from elsewhere in California.

Santenay FRANCE/BURGUNDY/COTE D'OR (88) The southernmost village of any importance in the Côte de Beaune. It *can* make tasty reds and fair whites, but too often these lack excitement.

Sardinia ITALY/SOUTH (178) Italy's largest island, with some unique wine flavours but too often neutralized by over-industrial wine-making.

Sassicaia ITALY/CENTRAL (170) A world-class Cabernet Sauvignon *vino da tavola* from Bolgheri, in Tuscany.

Saumur FRANCE/LOIRE (122) Major wine centre in Anjou, most famous for its sparkling wine; but also makes good whites, and, with Saumur-Champigny, one of the Loire's best reds.

Sauternes FRANCE/BORDEAUX/SAUTERNES (80) Great sweet-wine region, producing extravagantly rich whites from its top properties (in good years) and increasing amounts of excellent wine further down the scale.

Sauvignon Blanc GRAPE VARIETIES (18) Major French white grape grown in south-west France and the Loire; its wines are fresh, acidic and aromatic. Successful in north-east Italy, New Zealand, Australia and California. Also called Blanc Fumé or Fumé Blanc.

Sauvignon de St-Bris A good source of Sauvignon from the edge of the Chablis area of northern Burgundy.

Savagnin French white grape, exclusive to the Jura where it makes the traditional sherry-like *vin jaune*, as well as some fairly rustic dry whites.

Savatiano Most widely-planted white grape in Greece.

Savennières FRANCE/LOIRE (122) Small, highly-prized white AC area in Anjou; makes stunning wines from the Chenin Blanc which take years to soften.

Savigny-lès-Beaune FRANCE/BURGUNDY/COTE D'OR (88) Underrated village off the main slope of the Côte de Beaune producing good, strawberryized reds and some white.

Schafiser Light Chasselas wine from the Bierlersee region of Switzerland.

Scharzhofberg Outstanding single vineyard at Wiltingen on the Saar. Intense, piercing flavour from Riesling grapes.

Schaumwein German term for sparkling wine.

Scheurebe German white grape bred from a Riesling/Silvaner; produces a strong flavoured, slightly grapefruity wine which can become rich and fiery from late-picked grapes.

Schiava ITALY/N-E (160) Red grape, common in Trentino-Alto Adige and (as Trollinger) in the Württemburg area of Germany. Can produce the softest of all red wines, with negligible tannin and acidity and a smoky-strawberries flavour.

Schlossböckelheim GERMANY/RHINE (146) Important Nahe wine village with several excellent sites.

Schloss Johannisberg GERMANY/RHINE (146) Historic single estate in Rheingau producing very expensive Riesling wines.

Schloss Vollrads GERMANY/RHINE (146) Famous Rheingau estate planted almost exclusively with Riesling.

Schönburger Modern pink grape, yielding white wine. Some plantings in Germany, more successful in England.

Scuppernong American white grape of *vitis rotundifolia* species (grapes grow singly).

Sec French for 'dry'.

Secco Italian for 'dry'.

Seco Spanish/Portuguese for 'dry'.

Second wine Wine from a designated vineyard but sold separately from the main production for a variety of technical reasons. Pavillon Rouge, for example, is the second wine of Château Margaux in Bordeaux.

Sediment Residue thrown by a wine, particularly red, as it ages in bottle; largely consists of tannin, pigments and tartrates.

Seibel Range of red and white hybrid grapes often used in further hybridization.

Sekt GERMANY/OTHER WINES (152) German term for quality sparkling wine.

Sémillon GRAPE VARIETIES (18) Classic French white grape, traditional to Bordeaux.

Sercial PORTUGAL/MADEIRA (204) White grape used to make the driest style of madeira; used for quality table wine production on the mainland, especially in Dão and Bairrada.

Serriger Important village for top quality Riesling in the Saar, Germany.

Setúbal PORTUGAL/TABLE WINES (200) Small demarcated region on the peninsula south of Lisbon; known for its Moscatel dessert wines.

Seyval Blanc Hardy white hybrid grape; popular in England.

Shandong ASIA (240) Peninsula midway between Shanghai and Beijing, China, with some modern vineyards experimenting in reds and whites.

Sherry See *Jerez*.

Shiraz See *Syrah*.

Sicily ITALY/SOUTH (178) Island at southern tip of Italy, frequently the country's largest single producer; mostly blending wine.

Sidi Larbi See *Rabat-Casablanca*.

Siklos Southern wine area of Hungary noted for its white wines.

Silvaner Major white grape, significant in Germany, Switzerland (called Johannisberger), French Alsace and the South Tyrol.

Sin crianza Spanish term for 'new' or 'unaged' wine.

Soave ITALY/N-E (160) Famous Veneto white wine, deliciously refreshing when good.

Solano County Small inland wine area in California's North Coast division. Two AVAs: Green Valley, Suisun Valley.

Solera SPAIN/SHERRY (192) Spanish and Portuguese system in which barrels of older wine are topped up with younger wines of a similar style to ensure

continuity.

Sommelier French for 'wine waiter'.

Somontano New Spanish DO, north of Zaragoza; produces light reds, rosés and whites with a long-lasting flavour.

Sonoma County USA/CALIFORNIA (208) Major wine area in the North Coast division. Nine AVAs: Alexander Valley, Carneros, Chalk Hill, Dry Creek Valley, Knights Valley, Russian River Valley, Green Valley, Sonoma Valley, Sonoma Mountain.

Sopron Wine area in western Hungary, producing light, fruity reds from the Kekfrankos grape.

Southern Vales AUSTRALIA (220) Major wine area in South Australia; known for its reds and fortified wines.

South-West Coastal Plain AUSTRALIA (220) New wine area below Perth in Western Australia. Already some fine reds and whites.

Spanna ITALY/N-W (166) Blanket term for non-DOC Nebbiolo-based reds in northern Piedmont.

Sparkling wine FROM GRAPES TO WINE (22) Wine which undergoes a second fermentation either in bottle (champagne method) or in a closed vat (*cuve close*); carbon dioxide, released during fermentation, is trapped and so remains in the wine as effervescence. Cheap sparkling wine is also made by injecting carbon dioxide into bottles.

Spätburgunder The German name for the Pinot Noir grape. In general Spätburgunder wines are light, vaguely strawberryish and sometimes markedly sweet.

Spätlese German term for 'late-harvested' wine, usually slightly sweet; the QmP category above Kabinett.

Spritzig German term for wine with a slight sparkle.

Spumante Italian for 'sparkling'.

Staatliche Weinbaudomäne Estates owned by the German Federal State. Frequently produce some of the finest wines of their region. Also involved in training winemakers and in research.

Steiermark Area in south-east Austria producing good, spicy whites.

Steinberg GERMANY/RHINE (146) Famous single vineyard at Hattenheim. At their best, Steinbergers are some of Germany's finest Rieslings.

Stellenbosch SOUTH AFRICA (238) Important wine district in the Cape Coastal Region.

Still wine Non-sparkling (most table wines).

Styria See *Steiermark*.

Südbahn Austrian wine area south of Vienna; pungent whites and smooth reds.

Sugar Naturally present in grapes; transformed, by the action of yeasts during fermentation, into alcohol and carbon dioxide (and by-products such as glycerol and acetaldehyde).

Suhindol North-central wine region of Bulgaria producing elegant reds from Cabernet, Gamza and Pamid.

Sulphur Widely used in vinification: as a disinfectant for barrels and other equipment; as an anti-oxidant with freshly picked grapes; and during fermentation (sulphur dioxide) added to must to delay or arrest fermentation.

Sur lie French for 'on the lees', meaning wine that has been bottled direct from the cask/fermentation vat to gain extra flavour from the lees; common with quality Muscadet.

Süssreserve German term for the unfermented grape juice sometimes added to wine to boost sweetness.

Swan Valley AUSTRALIA (220) Historic wine area in Western Australia. Hot climate favours dessert and heavy-style wines.

Swartland South African wine district round Malmesbury in the Cape Coastal Region.

Sylvaner See *Silvaner*.

Syrah GRAPE VARIETIES (18) Classic French red grape. Used for all northern Rhône reds as well as in blends further south. Important in Australia (called Shiraz) and also doing well in California.

Szamorodni Hungarian term meaning 'as it comes'; used to describe dry Tokay, made without Aszú grapes.

Száraz Hungarian for 'dry'.

Szürkebarát Hungarian name for Pinot Gris.

Tafelwein GERMANY (138) German for 'table wine'; often blended with other EEC wines unless prefixed by Deutscher.

Tamar Valley Major Tasmanian wine area producing good reds and whites.

Tamîioasa Romanian white grape, making pungent, sweet wines.

Tannic High in tannin.

Tannin ENJOYING WINE (42) Harsh, bitter element in red wine. Derived from grape skins and stems, and from oak barrels; softens with ageing and essential for long-term development in reds.

Tarragona SPAIN/CATALONIA (188)

Coastal DO centred on Tarragona. The area is sub-divided into Falset, specializing in vigorous reds and *rancios*, and Tarragona Campo (Ribera de Ebro) which produces lighter wines.

Tartaric acid Most important acid naturally present in grapes (and wine); can be added during fermentation to correct low acidity in certain wine-producing regions only.

Tartrates Crystal sediment sometimes occuring in bottle or cask, produced by the wine's tartaric acid and sometimes by calcium; completely harmless and tasteless.

Taurasi ITALY/SOUTH (178) Hefty, renowned red from Campania, sometimes matures marvellously, sometimes not.

Tavel FRANCE/RHONE (112) Traditionally, a major producer of 'serious' rosé wine.

Tawny PORTUGAL/PORT (202) Port, aged for many years in cask (as opposed to bottle); orange-brown in colour and soft in flavour.

Tempranillo SPAIN/RIOJA (184) Major Spanish red grape; its dark, relatively low-alcohol wines form the major part of the Rioja blend. Known as Cencibel, it is the dominant red variety of Valdepeñas and La Mancha. Also important in Argentina and, as Tinta Roriz, in Portugal for port.

Tendone Italian system of training vines high to create cool ripening conditions and increase yield.

Teroldego Rotaliano ITALY/N-E (160) Local grape variety producing good but slightly bitter red of same name in Trentino.

Terra Alta SPAIN/CATALONIA (188) Recently-created DO, west of Tarragona, producing strong, full-bodied wines.

Ticino Italian-speaking region in the south of Switzerland; red wines predominate.

Tierra de Barros SPAIN/CENTRAL (190) Newly-created DO in Badajoz province near the Portuguese border. Bulk of output is a basic dry white, mostly used for blending; also a pungent, purple red from the village of Salvatierra de Barros.

Tiger's Milk See *Radgonska Ranina*.

Tignanello ITALY/CENTRAL (170) Trail-blazing blend of Sangioveto and Cabernet Sauvignon aged in small oak barrels; from Tuscany.

Tinta Roriz See *Tempranillo*.

Tinto Spanish/Portuguese for 'red' (wine only).

Tokay HUNGARY (234) Traditional, strong, usually sweet wine incorporating noble-rotted Furmint, Hárslevelü and Yellow Muscat grapes.

Torcolato ITALY/N-E (160) Brilliant sweet white wine from semi-dried grapes from the Breganze area in Veneto.

Torgiano ITALY/CENTRAL (170) Important Umbrian DOC.

Torres Vedras Portuguese wine area in Estremadura producing very dry whites and reds and some rosé.

Touraine FRANCE/LOIRE (122) Large area including such famous names as Vouvray; under the Touraine AC produces very good Sauvignon and Cabernet.

Touriga Francesa Portuguese red grape, important in port production.

Touriga Nacional High-quality Portuguese red grape, rich in aroma and fruit; prized for port production.

Training Growing vine up stakes, along wires, etc. Methods vary from region to region according to soil, climate, vine type and land availability.

Trakya Lightish red and white wines from Thrace in Turkey.

Transylvania Central province in Romania. It includes the major wine district of Tîrnave, noted for its sweet whites.

Trebbiano ITALY/CENTRAL (170) Workhorse white grape; mostly produces acidic, featureless wines for blending, especially in central Italy.

Trebbiano d'Abruzzo ITALY/CENTRAL (170) Above-average dry Trebbiano white from the Abruzzi.

Trebbiano di Romagna Pleasant light, fresh white from Emilia-Romagna in central Italy; to be drunk young.

Trentino ITALY/N-E (160) Southern part of Trentino-Alto Adige province, producing large amounts of average to very good table wines and sparklers.

Trittenheim Good wine village in Mosel, Germany, producing light fruity wines.

Trocken German for 'dry'.

Trockenbeerenauslese GERMANY (138) Sweetest category of German QmP wines; made from late-harvested 'noble rot' grapes, individually selected.

Trollinger See *Schiava*.

Tualatin Valley Expanding wine area west of Portland, Oregon, USA.

Tulbagh South African wine district noted for its dry whites, dessert wines, 'ports' and 'sherries'.

Tuscany ITALY/CENTRAL (170) One of

Italy's most important wine regions, not only for major DOCs like Chianti and Brunello di Montalcino, but also for pioneering work in 'new wave' reds.

Ugni Blanc French name for Trebbiano grape.

Ullage IDENTIFYING WINES (36) Small air-space left at the top of a bottle or cask. Excessive ullage causes oxidation in a wine.

Umbria ITALY/CENTRAL (170) Tuscany's neighbour; inconsistent, but capable of marvellous things.

Umpqua Valley Major wine area in southern Oregon, USA.

Upper Hunter AUSTRALIA (220) Irrigated extension of the Hunter Valley in NSW established in the 1960s. Important for Chardonnays and other dry whites.

Utiel-Requena SPAIN/CENTRAL (190) Inland DO bordering La Mancha; produces dark, high-acid wines.

Vacqueyras FRANCE/RHONE (112) One of the leading villages in the Côtes du Rhône-Villages AC; especially good for reds.

Valais SWITZERLAND (233) Major wine area, centred on Sion, in the Rhône valley. Fendant (Chasselas) predominates, but many grape varieties profit from this alpine suntrap.

Valcalepio ITALY/N-W (166) Good red and fair white from Lombardy, between Bergamo and Lake Iseo.

Valdeorras Hilly DO in Galicia, Spain, making fresh low-alcohol wines for everyday drinking.

Valdepeñas SPAIN/CENTRAL (190) Important DO on the central plateau of La Mancha. White Airén accounts for 85% of plantings. The wines, mostly white, are light and young.

Valencia SPAIN/CENTRAL (190) Major DO which divides into: Alto Turia, producing dry whites; Clariano, specializing in full-bodied reds; and Valentino, making liqueur and semi-sweet wine.

Valle d'Aosta ITALY/N-W (166) A mountainous region producing small amounts of very drinkable light wines.

Valle de Monterrey Spanish wine area near the Portuguese border; makes the strongest wine in Galicia, mostly red.

Valpolicella ITALY/N-E (160) One of Italy's most famous names; regarded as the Veneto's leading red, but its quality rarely justifies this reputation. Special

bottlings and Recioto *can* be exciting.

Valtellina ITALY/N-W (166) The biggest DOC zone for Nebbiolo wine, but not the best, since these Lombardy wines rarely have enough fruit to combat the toughness.

Varietal Wine made from, and named after, a single grape variety.

Varna Bulgarian wine region, making Chardonnay and Traminer whites.

Vat Large container in which wine is fermented or stored; traditionally made of wood but now, increasingly, of glass-lined concrete or stainless steel.

Vaud SWITZERLAND (233) Major wine region on the north shore of Lake Geneva; mostly planted in Dorin (Chasselas) to produce young, lively whites.

VDQS See *Vin délimité de qualité supérieur.*

Vega Sicilia SPAIN/RIOJA (184) Prestigious winery in Valladolid province known worldwide for its very expensive, top quality red wines – high alcohol, fragrant, fruity, deep-coloured and usually matured for 10 years in oak and 2 in bottle.

Velho Portuguese for 'aged', of red wine.

Vendange French for 'grape harvest' or 'vintage'.

Vendange tardive FRANCE/ALSACE (118) French for 'late harvest'; in Alsace, same as the German Spätlese.

Vendemmia Italian for 'grape harvest' or 'vintage'.

Vendimia Spanish for 'grape harvest' or 'vintage'.

Venegazzú della Casa ITALY/N-E (160) Good non-DOC red made in the Veneto.

Venencia Long-handled, small-cupped scoop for taking sherry samples from a butt without disturbing the *flor*.

Veneto ITALY/N-E (160) Vast region based on Venice, producing large amounts of ordinary *and* DOC wines. Famous names include Valpolicella, Soave and Bardolino.

Verdelho PORTUGAL/MADEIRA (204) White grape used to make medium-dry madeira; on the mainland, authorized for Douro wines and white port. Successful in Australia.

Verdicchio ITALY/CENTRAL (170) White grape grown in the Marches area.

Verdicchio dei Castelli di Jesi ITALY/CENTRAL (170) The largest Verdicchio region, specializing in dry whites, but also producing some sparkling and a little sweet.

Verduzzo Traditional Italian grape

producing soft, nutty, dry whites and remarkably complex sweet whites.

Vermentino Italian white grape producing full-flavoured wines in Corsica, Sardinia and Liguria.

Vernaccia ITALY/CENTRAL (170) White grape grown in Tuscany and Sardinia; its wine can be vigorous and pungent.

Vernaccia di San Gimignano ITALY/CENTRAL (170) Regarded as the leading Tuscan white wine, from the Vernaccia grape.

Vernatsch See *Schiava.*

Vesuvio ITALY/SOUTH (178) Wines from the slopes of Vesuvius. Superior quality is called Lacryma Christi del Vesuvio.

Vidigueira Portuguese wine area in the centre of the Alentejo; mainly whites.

Vienna The Austrian capital city also ranks as a wine area with surrounding 'suburban' hillside vineyards.

Vigne French for 'vine'.

Vigneron French for 'wine-grower'.

Vignoble French for 'vineyard'.

Vilány Town in southern Hungary noted for its Kékfrankos reds.

Vila Real Portuguese wine area in the upper Douro; main centre for sparkling rosés; also makes fruity reds.

Vin de goutte See *free-run wine.*

Vin délimité de qualité supérieure (VDQS) FRANCE (58) Second rank of French quality control for wines, between *appellation contrôlée* and *vin de pays*; likely to be phased out.

Vin de pays FRANCE (58) French 'country wine'; the third and bottom category in the official classification of French wines, but harbours some first-class wines which don't follow local AC regulations.

Vin de presse See *press wine.*

Vin de table FRANCE (58) Basic French table wine.

Vin doux naturel FRANCE/COUNTRY WINES (128) French term describing a sweet wine fortified with grape spirit. Most of these wines come from the Midi.

Vin gris 'Grey' wine (really pale pink), made by lightly pressing red grapes and drawing off the juice before fermentation.

Vinho de consumo Portuguese for 'ordinary wine'.

Vinho maduro Portuguese term for a matured table wine as opposed to *vinho verde.*

Vinho verde PORTUGAL/TABLE WINES (200) Large demarcated region in the north-west. Its reds and whites are often made from barely-ripe grapes and

undergo a special secondary fermentation; they are fresh, young and have a slight sparkle.

Vinification Wine-making.

Vin Jaune FRANCE/COUNTRY WINES (128) Sherry-like 'yellow' wine made in the French Jura.

Vino da pasto Italian term for ordinary mealtime wine.

Vino da tavola ITALY (156) The most basic description of table wine in Italy, yet including many great wines which do not conform to local DOC regulations.

Vino de mesa Spanish for 'table wine'.

Vino Nobile di Montepulciano ITALY/CENTRAL (170) Leading Tuscan DOCG red based on the Prugnolo Gentile variant of Sangiovese.

Vinos de Madrid Spanish vineyard area immediately south and west of the capital producing a range of everyday wines for immediate drinking.

Vino tipico ITALY (156) Term for wines below DOC rank, yet with definable local characteristics similar to French *vin de pays.*

Vin Santo ITALY/CENTRAL (170) Historic but extremely variable sweet white wine from Tuscany and Umbria.

Vintage The year's grape harvest; also the date and character of the wine produced from that harvest.

Viognier FRANCE/RHONE (112) Rare French white grape; produces exclusive soft, scented wines in the northern Rhône at Ch. Grillet and Condrieu.

Virginia Dare Best-selling US wine before and after Prohibition. Originally made in North Carolina, it was named after the first child born of English parents in America.

Viticulture Vine-growing and vineyard management.

Vitis Latin botanical name for the vine family.

Vitis labrusca GRAPE VARIETIES (18) American vine species, still used for making wine in the eastern States, but more suited to juice and jelly manufacture.

Vitis riparia American vine species, phylloxera-resistant and therefore used for rootstocks.

Vitis rotundifolia Vine species, with grapes growing in clusters not bunches, native to the Gulf of Mexico.

Vitis vinifera GRAPE VARIETIES (18) Vine species, native to Europe and Central Asia, from which almost all the world's wine is made.

Volnay FRANCE/BURGUNDY/COTE D'OR

(88) Côte de Beaune village, traditionally producing the lightest of Burgundy's reds, though they can age well.

Vörös Hungarian for 'red'.

Vosne-Romanée
FRANCE/BURGUNDY/COTE D'OR (88) Leading Côte de Nuits village for savoury, intense, long-lasting reds. Domaine de la Romanée-Conti is the most famous estate.

Vougeot FRANCE/BURGUNDY/COTE D'OR (88) Côte de Nuits village which includes the famous Clos de Vougeot. Simple Vougeot wine can be attractive and gentle.

Vouvray FRANCE/LOIRE (122) Important AC for sparkling white; also dry, medium and sweet wines.

Vranać YUGOSLAVIA (236) Native red grape, used to make a dark, burly wine in Montenegro and Macedonia.

Wachau District bordering the Danube in Niederösterreich, producing some of Austria's finest white wines.

Waimaku NEW ZEALAND (228) New vineyard area on the North Island.

Wehlen Leading German wine village in the Mosel, especially famous for its tip-top Sonnenuhr ('sundial') vineyard.

Weinbaugebiet German term indicating a specific table wine area.

Weingut German term for a wine estate which grows all its own grapes.

Weinkellerei German for 'winery'.

Weinviertel Large Austrian wine region, between Vienna and the Czech border; mostly produces young spicy whites.

Weissburgunder See *Pinot Blanc*.

Welsch Riesling Major white grape popular in north-east Italy, Austria and Eastern Europe.

Willamette Valley USA/PACIFIC N-W (216) Main wine area of Oregon, between Portland and Salem.

Winzergenossenschaft German for a wine-growers' co-operative.

Wood ageing See *barrel-ageing*.

Württemberg GERMANY/OTHER WINES (152) Large south German wine region,

best known for reds but also produces some very good Riesling.

Würzburg Franken's leading wine town capable of stunningly dry yet rich whites.

Xarel-lo Spanish white grape, exclusive to Catalonia; much of its sturdy acidic wine is blended into sparkling Cava.

Xynisteri Native white grape of Cyprus; used for neutral table wines and, more successfully, the very sweet dessert wine, Commandaria.

Yakima Valley USA/PACIFIC N-W (216) Principal wine region of Washington State; its semi-desert vineyards depend on irrigation.

Yarra Valley AUSTRALIA (220) Historic wine area in Victoria, recently replanted and now producing fine reds and whites.

Yeast Single-cell organism which, in the wine process, causes grape juice to ferment. Although yeasts occur naturally on the grapes, many winemakers prefer to use yeast cultures.

Yecla SPAIN/CENTRAL (190) Arid DO, west of Alicante, mostly producing full, smoothish reds; its sub-zone, Campo Arriba, specializes in dark, dry high-alcohol reds.

Yield Amount of fruit, and ultimately wine, produced from an acre/hectare of vines. Varies according to soil, climate, grape variety and vine density.

Zell See *Bereich Zell*.

Zierfandler White late-harvest grape popular in Austria and Hungary, producing a full, heady wine.

Zilavka Rare white grape, traditional to the Mostar area in Bosnia, Yugoslavia. Zilavka Mostar, a rich nutty blend, is one of the country's prestige wines.

Zinfandel USA/CALIFORNIA (208) California's native red grape probably related to Southern Italy's Primitivo; widely planted throughout the State and used for a range of wine types and styles including white, blush, sparkling, light red and blockbusting red.

· INDEX ·

· ACKNOWLEDGEMENTS ·

Photographs supplied by John Wyand *5 left*, Michael Newton *5 right*, J. Alain/Explorer *6 left*, Patrick Eagar *6 right*, Mike Busselle *8*, Anthony Blake *9*, Colin Maher/Fotobank *10 left*, Patrick Eagar *10 right*, Bridgeman Art Library *12 left*, Michael Holford *12 right*, Bridgeman Art Library *13*, Tony Stone Photo Library *14*, QED *16 left*, Roy/Explorer *16 right*, Tony Stone Photo Library *17 left*, Wines of Spain *17 right*, Patrick Eagar *18*, Moët & Chandon *19 top*, Wines of Spain *19 centre*, Jon Wyand/QED *19 below*, Moët & Chandon *20 top left*, Jon Wyand *20 centre*, Pamla Toler/Impact Photos *20 right*, *21 left*, Smith Collection *21 top centre*, Mike Busselle *23 top right*, QED *24 top*, Michael Freeman/QED *24 below*, Martin Sookias/Sookias & Bertaut *25 top*, Food and Wine from France *25 below*, Mike Busselle *26*, Jon Wyand *27 below left*, Wines of Spain *27 top*, Michel Guillard/Scope *27 below right*, Wines of Spain *28 left*, Pamla Toler/Impact Photos *28 right*, Michael Newton *36/37*, Rommy Jacques/Colorific! *42 left*, Michael Newton *43*, Topham Picture Library *44 below*, Michael Newton *46/47*, Mike Busselle *59 top*, Tony Stone Photo Library *59 below left*, Veiller/Explorer *59 below right*, Michel Guillard/Scope *64*, *66 top*, Mike Busselle *66 below*, F. Jalain/Explorer *67*, Michel Guillard/Scope *69 top*, Colin Maher/QED *69 below*, Michel Guillard/Scope *70 left*, Mike Busselle *70 right*, *71*, Patrick Eagar *72*, Michael Holford *73 top*, J. Allan Cash Photo Library *73 below*, *74*, *75*, Anthony Blake *76*, Roy/Explorer *77*, Michel Guillard/Scope *78/79*, *80 left*, *80 top right*, *80 below right*, J. Alain/Explorer *82*, Mike Busselle *83 left*, Christies London *83 right*, Michael Holford *84*, Patrick Eagar *86 left*, Michel Guillard/Scope *86 right*, *89 top*, Maison Bouchard Père et Fils *89 below*, J. Guillard/Scope *90 left*, F. Jalain/Explorer *90 right*, Berthoule/Explorer *91*, J. Guillard/Scope *92 left*, Jon Wyand *92 right*, Patrick Eagar *93*, Mike Busselle *94 left*, J. Guillard/Scope *94 right*, Jon Wyand *95*, F. Jakain/Explorer *96 left*, Mike Busselle *97*, *99*, Anthony Blake *100*, Marco Polo *101*, Mike Busselle *102 left*, F. Jalain/Explorer *102 right*, Maison Bouchard Père et Fils *104*, Mike Busselle *104/5*, Champagne Bureau *106*, Explorer *107 left*, Mike Busselle *107 right*, Danrigan/Explorer *108*, Moët et Chandon *109*, Colin Maher/QED *110 top*, Champagne Mumm *110 below*, F. Jalain/Explorer *112*, *113*, J. Guillard/Scope *114 top*, Comité Interprofessionel Vins des Côtes-du-Rhône *114 below*, Sudres/Scope *115*, Comité Interprofessionel Vins des Côtes-du-Rhône *116*, *117*, John Wyand *118*, Mike Busselle *119*, J. Guillard/Scope *120*, Mike Busselle *121*, J. Guillard/Scope *122*, Tony Stone Photo Library *123*, Patrick Eagar *124*, Mike Busselle *125*, *126*, Anthony Blake *127*, J. Guillard/Scope *129*, Mike Busselle *130 left*, Scope *130 right*, Explorer *131 left*, Mike Busselle *131 right*, *132*, *133*, *134/135*, *136*, Reiser/Bilderberg *139*, Tony Stone Photo Library *142*, Reiser/Bilderberg *143*, Jon Wyand *144*, Stief Pictures *145*, Reiser/Bilderberg *146*, Jon Wyand *148*, Reiser/Bilderberg *149*, *150*, Jon Wyand *151*, Giebeler/Timmermann *152*, German Wine Infomation Bureau *154*, Michael Holford *155*, Tony Stone Photo Library *157 top left*, Zefa *157 top right*, Jan Traylen/Patrick Eagar *157 below*, Tony Stone Photo Library *160*, Tom O'Toole *161*, *162*, Jon Wyand/QED *164*, John Sims *165*, *166*, Zefa *168*, Jan Traylen/Patrick Eagar *170*, John Sims *171*, Anthony Blake *172*, John Sims *174*, Zefa *175*, Tony Stone Photo Library *177*, Picturepoint *178*, Mike Busselle *180*, *182/183*, Anthony Blake *184*, Explorer *185*, Anthony Blake *186*, Eigeland/Susan Griggs *188*, *189*, Mike Busselle *190*, Wines of Spain *191*, Picturepoint *192*, Michael Holford *193*, Anthony Blake *194 left*, Tony Stone Photo Library *194 right*, Mike Busselle *195 top*, Alvear SA *195 centre*, Robert Joseph *197 top*, Loirat/Explorer *197 below*, Robert Joseph *198*, Zefa *199*, Robert Joseph *200*, Patrick Eagar *201*, Loirat/Explorer *202*, Zefa *204*, Martini & Rossi *205*, Image Bank *206*, *207*, Jon Wyand *209*, *210*, *211*, QED *212*, Jon Wyand *213*, Michael Freeman/QED *214*, Bob Thompson *216*, Vernon East *217*, Image Bank *218*, Michael Freeman/QED *220*, Patrick Eagar *223*, *224*, Jean Paul Ferraroi/QED *225*, Patrick Eagar *226*, *227*, *228*, *230*, Zefa *233*, Counsel PR *235*, Teltscher *236 left*, Patrick Eagar *236 right*, Greek Wine Information Bureau *237*, Zefa *239*.

Illustrations by Peter Byatt *cover*, Joe Robinson , Jane Strother *7*, *48*, *49*, *50*, *51*, *52*, *53*, Joe Robinson *11*, Mike McInnerney *14/15*, David Mallott *22/23*, Joe Robinson *29*, Mike McInnerney *30*, *31*, *32*, *33*, *34*, *35*, Joe Robinson *44/45*, *57*, *240–257*.
Maps by Eugene Fleury except for *47*, *60*, *140*, *158*, *207*, *220* by Paul Cooper.